ExamMatrix™
CPA Review Textbook

BEC

BUSINESS ENVIRONMENT & CONCEPTS

SECTIONS 5000–5500

YEAR 2008/2009

Matrix Learning Systems – ExamMatrix CPA Review Production Staff
Director of Accounting/Editorial: Pearl Zeiler, MBA
Coordinating Editor: James O'Leary
Desktop Publishing: Kimberli Mullen

Software Development Group:
Vice President of IT: Delmur Mayhak, Jr.
Testing Supervisor: Randy Morrow, MS
Graphic Artist: Barry Schapiro

Printer: Corley Printing, Earth City, Missouri

Preface

Congratulations on purchasing the ExamMatrix CPA Review. This powerful course is a complete system for success. It will teach you what you need to know, validate your readiness, and allow you to face the CPA Exams with confidence. It will guide you efficiently through your studies and help you achieve what thousands of other ExamMatrix accounting students and professionals before you have achieved—passing scores on the CPA Examination.

We use the power of your computer and our software to do the following:

- Provide you with your own personal instructor, who guides your customized study program.

- Prepare you for what to expect on the examination so there is no guesswork about what you need to know to pass.

- Coach you on ways to be physically, emotionally, and intellectually ready for the examination.

- Provide full printed text of examination preparation materials for you to study.

- Simulate the examination for you, drilling you with thousands of questions, weighted in accordance with the most current examination outlines.

- Give you instant help and guidance on every question, every step of the way, referring you back to the printed study materials when you need remedial help.

- Provide you with an Editorial Support Line to answer any questions that may arise while studying—call 877-272-7277.

- Provide a Pass Update or Pass Refund guarantee.

- Validate your readiness to pass each part of your examination.

You will pass with confidence.

The ExamMatrix CPA Review system components will help you reach that goal. The software portion of the ExamMatrix CPA Review is composed of the following:

- A database of over 3,900 categorized objective questions with immediate feedback to teach and review the points covered in the CPA testing process generated by the published weights from the AICPA Content Specification Outlines.

- Simulation format questions are contained in the following exam sections:

  Audit and Attestation

  Financial Accounting and Reporting

  Regulation

- The ExamMatrix CPA Review textbooks, which accompany your software, utilize a unique cross-referencing system to sections and paragraphs. The software targets your weak areas and, through the cross-referencing system, guides you directly to the section in the textbook that covers that material. Each Review textbook contains the following:

- Concise reviews of authoritative pronouncements needed to pass the CPA Examination in easy-to-understand paragraph form
- Learning aids such as charts, tables, and flowcharts to aid in remembering concepts and procedures

The Review textbooks are categorized as follows:

Section 2000	Financial Accounting & Reporting (FAR)
Section 3000	Auditing & Attestation (AUD)
Section 4000	Regulation (REG)
Section 5000	Business Environment and Concepts (BEC)

Our software and our CPA Review textbooks reflect all legislative changes and are in accordance with the AICPA Content Specification Outlines.

Thinking about achieving an additional designation? Matrix Learning Systems carries reviews for the following exams:

- Certified Management Accountant
- Certified Internal Auditor
- Certified Information Systems Auditor
- Chartered Financial Analyst
- Certified Business Manager
- Certified Associate Business Manager
- Enrolled Agent
- Certified Information Systems Security Professional
- Certified Information Security Manager

ExamMatrix will be at your side throughout your professional career, meeting your educational needs every step of the way.

Acknowledgments

The ExamMatrix CPA Review was developed and written by a team of professionals who are experts in the fields of accounting, business law, and computer science, and are also experienced teachers in CPA Review programs and continuing professional education courses.

ExamMatrix expresses its sincere appreciation to the many individual candidates, as well as accounting instructors, who took time to write to us about previous editions. The improvements in this edition are attributable to all of these individuals. Of course, any deficiencies are the responsibilities of the editors and authors. We very much appreciate and solicit your comments and suggestions about this year's edition.

The editors and authors are also indebted to the American Institute of Certified Public Accountants, the Financial Accounting Standards Board, and the Governmental Accounting Standards Board for permission to quote from their pronouncements. In addition, the AICPA granted us permission to use material from previous Uniform CPA Examination Questions and Answers. AICPA codification numbers are used throughout the Auditing portion of the Review to indicate the source of materials.

We recognize the work and dedication of our team of software designers and developers. Their vision has made this the best product possible. They contributed countless hours to deliver this package and are each fully dedicated to helping you pass the exam. Our thanks go out to the many individuals who have made contributions to both the software and textbook portions of the CPA Review. We extend our gratitude to our team of software testers who ensure that you receive only the highest quality product. Finally, we express appreciation to the editorial teams who have devoted their time to review this product. They have provided invaluable aid in the writing and production of the ExamMatrix CPA Review.

Good luck on the exam!

Matrix Learning Systems

ExamMatrix CPA Review Textbook Authors

Raymond J. Clay, Jr., DBA, CPA, is the author of the ExamMatrix CPA Review Textbook: Auditing & Attestation. He holds the Internal Audit Professorship in Accounting at the University of North Texas. Prior to joining the University of North Texas, he served as Director of Professional Development at Union Pacific Corporation. Dr. Clay has held faculty positions in accounting at Indiana State University and Texas Tech University. He received his bachelor's and master's degrees from Northern Illinois University and his doctorate from the University of Kentucky. He has held significant committee appointments with professional organizations, including serving as a member of the AICPA Accounting and Review Services Committee for seven years. Dr. Clay is the author of 4 books, 10 continuing professional education courses, and numerous articles appearing in professional journals.

Ennis M. Hawkins, DBA, CPA, CMA, CIA, is a coauthor of the ExamMatrix CPA Review Textbook: Business Environment & Concepts and questions relative to this topic. He is currently a Professor of Accounting at Sam Houston State University in Huntsville, Texas. His teaching and research interests include environmental and cost accounting. Dr. Hawkins has served as the Program Co-Chairman and Vice President of the Southwest Region American Accounting Association. He is also a member of the AICPA, the IMA, and the IIA.

David G. Jaeger, JD, MST, MBA, is the author of the ExamMatrix CPA Review Textbook: Regulation. He is also the coauthor of the ExamMatrix CPA Review Textbook: Business Environment & Concepts. He is currently Associate Professor of Accounting and Taxation at the University of North Florida. He has taught numerous courses in taxation and business law at the undergraduate, MBA, Executive MBA, and Master of Accountancy levels, as well as in continuing education courses. His research has been published in such journals as *The Tax Advisor, TAXES, Tax Notes,* the *Journal of Accountancy,* and *Research in Accounting Regulation.* His work has also been cited by the U.S. Tax Court and several U.S. Federal Courts of Appeal.

M. Herschel Mann, PhD, CPA, is the coauthor of the ExamMatrix CPA Review Textbook: Financial Accounting & Reporting and questions relative to this topic. Dr. Mann is the KPMG Professor of Accounting at Texas Tech University. Dr. Mann has had professional experience with the public accounting firm of Grant Thornton & Co. He received his BBA degree from the University of Arkansas (Monticello) and his MA and PhD from the University of Alabama. Prior to joining Texas Tech, Dr. Mann held faculty positions at the University of North Texas and the University of Alabama. He has conducted CPE courses for the AICPA and the IMA as well as for several state societies, public accounting firms, and publicly held companies.

Craig D. Shoulders, PhD, is a coauthor of the ExamMatrix CPA Review Textbook: Financial Accounting & Reporting. He joined the faculty at the University of North Carolina at Pembroke in 2004 after serving over 20 years on the accounting faculty at Virginia Tech. Dr. Shoulders has received the Cornelius E. Tierney/Ernst & Young Research Award from the Association of Government Accountants and has been recognized twice by the AICPA as an Outstanding Discussion Leader. He has recently completed a major research study on the financial reporting entity for the Governmental Accounting Standards Board and coauthors a Prentice Hall textbook on state and local government accounting as well as several continuing education courses on governmental accounting and financial reporting. Dr. Shoulders received his bachelor's degree from Campbellsville University, his master's degree from the University of Missouri-Columbia, and his PhD from Texas Tech University.

Jill Hazelbauer-Von der Ohe, MBA, CPA, CMA, CFM, CVA, is a coauthor of the ExamMatrix CPA Review Textbook: Business Environment Concepts and questions relative to this topic. She has her MBA from Rockford College and is currently a professor at Keller University, where she teaches accounting. She also has coauthored CPE courses with Robert Von der Ohe. In addition to a CPA, she holds CMA and CFM certifications, having received the Gold Award for the CFM exam during the 1997-98 winter exam cycle. She also holds a CVA (Certified Valuation Analyst) through NACVA, a professional organization that focuses on the valuation of closely held business for tax, estate, and other purposes. She has worked on accounting projects in Uganda and Poland.

Robert Von der Ohe, PhD, is a coauthor of the ExamMatrix CPA Review Textbook: Business Environment Concepts and questions relative to this topic. He earned his PhD in Economics from the University of Tennessee and currently holds the von Mises Chair in Economics at Rockford College in Rockford, Illinois, where he teaches economics and finance. He served 11 years as Chief Economist for the Credit Union National Association and has significant international consulting experience in the design and implementation of financial systems, working primarily in Latin America. He has undertaken numerous valuation projects, focusing on valuation of financial institutions and business entities.

Matrix Learning Systems

ExamMatrix CPA Review Question Database Contributors

William V. Allen, Jr., CPA, is currently a Principal in Making Auditors Proficient, Inc. (MAP). MAP provides training, technical assistance, peer reviews, and other services to local CPA firms throughout the United States and Canada. Their specialty and what gives them a unique approach to the various services, including peer reviews, is their proficiency in audit effectiveness and efficiency using a risk-based approach. He is also a recognized expert in Single Audits (Government and Nonprofit). He was the Audit Partner for the City of Los Angeles audit from 1985 to 1991. He was a Partner in a local firm in northern California with responsibility for over 50 small- and medium-sized audit engagements. He is also a contributing editor to the *Single Audit Information Service* published by Thompson Publishing Group.

Paul N. Brown, CPA, is the Director of Technical Services for the Florida Institute of CPAs (FICPA). One of his main duties is to serve as the technical reviewer in Florida for the AICPA Peer Review Program, which administers approximately 600 reviews annually in Florida. Paul has previously been an instructor for the AICPA Advanced Reviewers Training Course and writes and instructs his own course in Florida on peer review called Peer Review Forum for Reviewers, for which he has received several outstanding discussion leader and author awards. He has also served on the AICPA's Technical Reviewers Advisory Task Force to the Peer Review Board and serves as staff liaison to various committees of the Florida Institute of CPAs. Prior to joining the FICPA, Paul was an audit manager with a regional firm in Florida. He holds a BS degree in accounting and finance from Florida State University.

Anthony P. Curatola, PhD, is the Joseph F. Ford Professor of Accounting at Drexel University. He holds a BS in Accounting and an MBA in Finance from Drexel University, an MA in Accounting from the Wharton Graduate School of the University of Pennsylvania, and a PhD in Accounting from Texas A&M University. Dr. Curatola joined the faculty of Louisiana State University in 1981 and returned to Drexel University in 1989 by accepting the appointment to the Joseph F. Ford Professor of Accounting Chair. Dr. Curatola's findings have appeared in media such as *Forbes,* the *Washington Post, Money* magazine, the *Wall Street Journal,* and the *New York Times,* to name a few. Currently he serves on the Foundation of Academic Research. Most recently, he was awarded the R. Lee Brummet Award in Academic Excellence from the IMA.

Donna Hogan, CPA, CFP, is a shareholder in Hogan & Co., CPA, PC, in Fort Collins, Colorado, where she focuses on the areas of taxation and financial planning. She also often advises individuals who are starting businesses (on tax and other issues). She received her bachelor's degree in accountancy from New Mexico State University and was a partner in charge of the tax department at an Albuquerque firm.

Alice A. Ketchand, PhD, CPA, is currently an Associate Professor of Accounting at Sam Houston State University. Her teaching and research interests include professional ethics, behavioral issues, and governmental and not-for-profit accounting. She received her PhD from the University of Houston in 1994 and is a member of the American Accounting Association, the AICPA, and the Texas Society of CPAs.

Taylor S. Klett, CPA, JD, is of counsel for the firm of Havins & O'Dea, PC. He is currently an Assistant Professor at Sam Houston State University and was an administrator and on the adjunct faculty there. He is a CPA in Texas and a member of the Texas Bar. He graduated from the University of Texas and attended law school at the University of Houston Law Center (JD, with honors).

Tabitha McCormick, CPA, CFE, is the owner of Cornerstone Accounting in Millville, Pennsylvania. Cornerstone Accounting concentrates on training small business owners and financial employees to keep accurate accounting records, create efficient and effective policies and procedures, and institute strong internal controls. Cornerstone also assists businesses with implementing accounting software packages. She is a Certified QuickBooks® and QuickBooks Point of Sale® ProAdvisor and enjoys teaching QuickBooks classes for Bloomsburg University's Magee Center and other training institutions. Tabitha is also the author of two CPE courses on Identity Theft for MicroMash. She is a member of the Pennsylvania Institute of Certified Public Accountants (PICPA) and the Association of Certified Fraud Examiners (ACFE).

Paul Pierson is Director of Technical Services for the Illinois CPA Society. In this capacity, he oversees the administration of the AICPA Peer Review Program for approximately 1,300 CPA firms in Illinois. Paul has served as a discussion leader at the AICPA's Annual Peer Review Conference and its Advanced Reviewer Training Course, and is editor for the Society's peer review newsletter. He is also responsible for monitoring the continuing professional education and licensing rules in the state and responding to member inquiries regarding those matters. He currently serves on the Technical Reviewers' Advisory Task Force of the AICPA, having previously served a three-year term, and is the staff liaison for the Illinois CPA Society's Peer Review Report Acceptance and Governmental Accounting Executive Committees. Paul graduated from Illinois State University with a BS in accounting and was an audit manager with a large, local CPA firm in East Peoria, Illinois, prior to joining the Society.

Cheryl L. Prachyl, PhD, is an Adjunct Assistant Professor of Accounting at the University of Texas at Arlington. She is a CPA licensed in the state of Texas. Dr. Prachyl holds a BBA Marketing and MS Accounting from Texas A&M University. She holds a PhD in Accounting with a minor in Information Systems from the University of Texas at Arlington. In addition to her teaching experience, Dr. Prachyl has worked for NCR Corporation and Bosque County Bank and as an accounting systems consultant for numerous small businesses.

Darlene A. Pulliam, PhD, CPA, joined the faculty of West Texas A&M in 1997. A native of eastern New Mexico, Dr. Pulliam received a BS in Mathematics in 1976 and an MBA in 1978 from Eastern New Mexico University and joined the accounting firm of Peat Marwick and Mitchell and Co. (now KPMG) in Albuquerque. After five years in public accounting, she completed her PhD at the University of North Texas and joined the faculty of the University of Tulsa in 1987. During her 10 years in Tulsa, she taught primarily in the University of Tulsa's Master of Taxation program. Her publications include many articles appearing in *Tax Advisor*; the *Journal of Accountancy; Practical Tax Strategies; Oil, Gas and Energy Quarterly*; and the *Journal of Forensic Accounting* as an author or coauthor.

Marianne Rexer, PhD, CPA, is currently an Associate Professor of Accounting at Wilkes University. She has also taught at Drexel University and Johnson & Wales University. She received her PhD in Accounting at Drexel in 1997, her MS in Taxation at Bryant College in 1989, and her BS in Accounting from Wilkes University in 1985. Dr. Rexer has worked at a national CPA firm. She is a member of the American Accounting Association, the AICPA, the AICPA Audit Division, and the Pennsylvania Institute of CPAs.

Bob Thomas, PhD, is an Assistant Professor of Accounting at West Texas A&M University. Thomas holds a PhD from Texas Tech University (2006) and a BBA from Midwestern State University (2003), both with specializations in Management Information Systems and Accounting. Dr. Thomas' current teaching areas include auditing, governmental accounting, nonprofit accounting, accounting principles, and accounting information systems. His current research interests include assessment/improvement of information system success, accounting information systems, knowledge management, petroleum accounting, and social capital. Dr. Thomas has published in *Information & Management* and *Oil, Gas & Energy Quarterly*. He is a member of the Association for Information Systems, the Institute of Management Accountants, and the Texas Society of Certified Public Accountants.

This page intentionally left blank.

Table of Contents

Business Environment & Concepts

This page intentionally left blank.

Section 5000
Overview of the Business Environment and Concepts Examination

5010 The Business Environment and Concepts Section of the CPA Examination

5011 Purpose of the Business Environment and Concepts Examination

5011.01 The Business Environment and Concepts section tests a candidate's knowledge of general business environment and business concepts that candidates need to know in order to understand the underlying business reasons for and accounting implications of transactions, and the skills needed to apply that knowledge in performing financial statement audit and attestation engagements and other functions normally performed by CPAs that affect the public interest.

5011.02 The scope of the content covered in the Business Environment and Concepts section includes knowledge of:

a. business structure;

b. economic concepts essential to obtaining an understanding of an entity's operations, business, and industry;

c. financial management;

d. information technology (IT) implications in the business environment; and

e. planning and measurement.

These concepts are tested in the context of entry-level CPA practice.

5011.03 The Business Environment and Concepts section contains three testlets. Each testlet is comprised of 24 to 30 multiple-choice questions. Testlets are groups of questions that are constructed to appear together. Each testlet within a section of the examination will contain the same number of questions. Approximately 80% of the questions in each testlet will count toward your score. Approximately 20% of the questions in each testlet are included for pretesting purposes only. Pretest questions are *not* used in computing your score and are used to develop future examinations.

5011.04 Material eligible to be tested includes federal laws in the window beginning six months after their *effective* date and uniform acts in the window beginning one year after their adoption by a simple majority of the jurisdictions.

5011.05 References for the Business Environment and Concepts section include AICPA Audit Risk Alerts and current textbooks on business law, managerial accounting, management, finance, economics, accounting and management information systems, and budgeting and measurement. Business periodicals provide background material that is helpful in gaining an understanding of business environment and concepts.

5110   Partnerships, Joint Ventures, and Other Unincorporated Associations

5111   Partnerships

5111.01   A *partnership* is a voluntary legal relationship created by two or more persons to carry on as co-owners of a business for profit. If the profit motive is lacking, it is an unincorporated association.

5111.02   Partnerships are governed by the Uniform Partnership Act (UPA) or the Revised Uniform Partnership Act (RUPA). Generally, if the partners do not specifically address particular matters in the partnership agreement, the applicable Act provision will apply.

5112   Classifications

5112.01   **Trading** (or commercial): Buying and selling or leasing property. A partner in a trading partnership has a great deal of implied authority to act for the partnership.

5112.02   **Nontrading:** Rendering a service; practicing a profession (e.g., CPA, physician, or lawyer). A partner in a nontrading partnership has less implied authority than a partner in a trading partnership.

5113   Legal Entity

5113.01   A partnership is not a legal entity (legal existence separate from the persons associated together to create it) for the purpose of insulating the partners from personal liability.

5113.02   It is a legal entity for the purpose of owning property or employing persons to transact business on the partnership's behalf.

5114   Creation of a Partnership

5114.01   No formalities are required; it is a voluntary contractual relationship. A partnership can be created by express agreement or through an implied agreement. A partnership can also generally be created either orally or in writing.

5114.02   Intent governs. It can be by express words (oral or written) or implied by the actions of the parties.

5114.03   **Tests of Existence**

    a.   The sharing of net profits and losses creates a rebuttable presumption that a partnership exists. This presumption can be overcome by showing that profits are being shared for another reason. The following are examples:

        (1)   Repayment of a debt owed to the other party by way of the transfer of a portion of the profits

        (2)   Wages or rent owed to another party being paid as a portion of the profits

        (3)   Annuity to a deceased partner's spouse (Thus the spouse is *not* a partner simply because the spouse is receiving an annuity payment based on profits.)

        (4)   Interest on a loan owed to another party being paid as a portion of the profits

        (5)   Consideration for the sale of goods being paid from the profits

    b.   Co-ownership of property—this does not of itself establish that a partnership exists but is a factor courts look at in determining if the relationship between the parties is a partnership.

    c.   Joint control and management is another factor considered. Courts often view delegating management responsibilities or giving up control as an exercise of joint control.

5115   Effect of Holding Out to Be a Partner

5115.01   **Partnership by estoppel.** This doctrine is used to hold a person liable as a partner to a third party when they either hold themselves out as a partner or consent to the holding out of themselves as a partner. Partnership by estoppel does not actually make a person a partner, but it creates the same legal effect of being a partner. A partnership can only be created by the voluntary agreement between the persons. Therefore a partner by estoppel receives no rights of a true partner (i.e., right to manage, right to profits).

5116   Types of Partners

5116.01   **General.** Has a right to manage the partnership business. Has unlimited personal liability to the creditors of the partnership for partnership debts.

5116.02   **Limited.** Merely an investor in a partnership whose liability is limited to the possible loss of their capital contribution. This limited liability rests upon the fact that the partner does not participate in management of the partnership.

5116.03   **Nominal (ostensible)/partner by estoppel:** A person who is not in fact a partner but holds himself out as a partner or allows others to hold him out as a partner. In some instances, he may be liable as a partner to third persons who rely on this holding out.

Example: Brian tells Erin that Kevin is his partner during contract negotiations. Kevin is present at the time and does nothing to indicate that this is untrue. Kevin also tells Erin, "We will be sure to do a first-rate job if you enter this contract." If Erin enters the agreement with Brian, Kevin is liable on the agreement as a partner by estoppel.

5117 Partnership Agreement

5117.01 A partnership agreement is also sometimes referred to as *articles of partnership* and *articles of co-partnerships*.

5117.02 A formal written agreement creating the partnership relationship is not required, but it is a good idea to prevent disputes between or among the partners.

5117.03 Generally, a partnership agreement can be oral. If any part of the partnership agreement falls under the statute of frauds, however, a writing is needed as a practical matter to make the agreement enforceable.

Example: Caitlin and Jennifer enter a partnership agreement and specify that the duration of the partnership will last for a period of more than one year (i.e., for two years). For the agreement to be enforceable, a writing is required under the statute of frauds.

5117.04 The UPA fills in the rules regarding the relationship between or among the partners unless the agreement specifies a different rule. Thus, the UPA operates as a gap filler.

5118 Who Can and Cannot Be a Partner

5118.01 **Minor.** May become a partner, but can disaffirm the partnership contract. Partnership creditors have a preference on partnership assets before a minor gets their capital contribution returned. Partnership creditors may not get personal assets of a minor partner if the minor partner disaffirms.

5118.02 **Insane person.** A judicially declared insane person cannot make a contract—any effort is void. If a person becomes insane after making a contract, the other partner may get dissolution due to the insanity by way of a court order.

5118.03 **Corporation.** The UPA allows a corporation to become a partner, but the general corporation laws of some of the states do not allow a corporation to become a partner.

5119 Partnership Property

5119.01 **Partnership capital.** Money and property contributed by partners for permanent use by the partnership is called partnership capital.

5119.02 **Tenancy in partnership.** Tenancy in partnership is the term given to the ownership by partners of the partnership's property. All partners have equal rights to use partnership property for partnership purposes.

A partner has no transferable rights in specific partnership property.

5119.03 **Partnership property.** Partnership capital plus retained profits constitute partnership property.

5119.04 **Real property.** A partnership may acquire real property in the name of the partnership. The partnership is a legal entity for this purpose.

5120   Authority of a Partner

5120.01   Authority of a partner is merely an extension of agency law.

5120.02   Agency law applies to partnerships in the following manner:

a.   Each partner is an agent for the partnership. The partnership is the principal.

b.   A partnership is liable for the actions of a partner if the partner either:

    (1)   has actual authority or

    (2)   is acting within the apparent scope of the partnership activity and the third party does not know the actual authority of the party.

c.   If the partnership is not liable on a contract, then the individual partner making the contract is liable.

d.   A partner is personally liable for the torts the partner commits.

e.   A partnership is liable for the torts of a partner if the partner was acting within the scope of the partnership business when the tort occurred.

f.   A partner is personally responsible for their crimes.

g.   A partnership is not liable for a partner's crimes unless the other partners actually participated in the crimes.

h.   If a partner enters a contract without authority, the partnership may recover damages from the wrongdoing partner if the partnership is held liable to a third party.

5120.03   **Types of authority**

a.   **Actual**

    (1)   Also called *real authority.*

    (2)   May be expressed or implied authority.

b.   **Apparent**

    (1)   Sometimes called *ostensible* or *customary authority.*

    (2)   When a partnership restricts a partner's actual authority, the partner may still have apparent authority to act. This occurs because a third party can reasonably believe that the partner, who is an agent for the partnership, can perform acts necessary to carry out the partnership business.

    Example: Erin, Brian, Kevin, and Caitlin are partners and agree that only Kevin can enter contracts to purchase inventory for the partnership. If third parties are not notified of this restriction, Erin, Brian, and Caitlin will have apparent authority to purchase inventory.

    (3)   Different types of firms have different authority.

        (a)   **Trading partnership:** Much customary authority

        (b)   **Nontrading partnership:** Little customary authority (A nontrading partnership does not normally engage in activities such as borrowing money. There is, therefore, no apparent or customary authority to borrow money. A trading partnership would regularly do this to finance inventory, etc.)

(4) Typical customary or apparent authority examples include the following:

    (a) Entering into usual contracts for that type of business

    (b) Sales in the ordinary course of business

    (c) Purchasing goods in the scope of business

    (d) Loans for a trading partnership

    (e) Insuring property of the partnership

    (f) Employing persons for the partnership

c. Certain actions are completely unauthorized and no partner can bind the partnership by these acts. They require the unanimous consent of all partners. Examples include the following:

    (1) A decision to go out of business

    (2) Suretyship (guaranty)—cannot promise to pay somebody else's debts or obligations

    (3) A decision to arbitrate a dispute between the partnership and a third party

    (4) Confess judgment—this is equivalent to pleading guilty in advance

    (5) Assignment for the benefit of creditors

    (6) Make a personal obligation for the partnership to pay

5121 Partner's Individual Liability

5121.01 Every partner is the agent of the partnership for the purpose of its business. The partnership is bound by all transactions negotiated by a partner if such transactions are within the usual course of partnership business.

5121.02 **Tort.** If the wrongful act is committed within the scope of and in the course of partnership business, the partners and the partnership will be jointly and severally liable. *Severally* means individually.

5121.03 **Crimes.** Only the partner who commits a crime is liable unless the other partners participate.

5121.04 **Contracts.** Partners are jointly (all together at the same time) liable for contracts made by a partner within the scope of the real or apparent authority of a partnership. If the contract is made in the partner's personal name, the other partners are liable as undisclosed principals.

5122 Withdrawal of a Partner

5122.01 Existing creditors are entitled to actual notice of a partner withdrawing. If there is no notice, the withdrawing partner could still be liable to a creditor of the partnership for partnership debts that happened after the withdrawal.

5122.02 Creditors who have not dealt with the partnership previously are entitled only to constructive notice (i.e., in a newspaper).

5123　Admission of a New Partner

5123.01　New partners are liable for all partnership obligations that arise after they are admitted.

5123.02　New partners are liable for all partnership obligations that arose before admission, but only to the extent of their share of the partnerships' assets. The new partner's individual assets are not available to satisfy these claims.

5124　Ordinary Business Matters

5124.01　In deciding ordinary business matters, a majority vote of the partners prevails as long as it does not violate any special provisions in the partnership agreement.

5124.02　A tie vote leaves the matter as it was, since this is viewed as a deadlock.

5125　Extraordinary Matters

5125.01　Unanimous agreement of all partners is necessary to make a change involving an extraordinary matter. A majority vote is not sufficient. The decision to go out of business or to change the nature of the partnership business would be examples of extraordinary matters requiring unanimous agreement of all the partners.

5126　Rights of Partners

5126.01　**Right to share in profits.** Partners share equally in profit regardless of the amount of capital contributions or the amount of time spent in the partnership business. The partnership agreement may specify that profits are shared differently.

5126.02　**Right to return of capital.** When a partnership is being dissolved, each partner has the right to obtain the return of their capital contribution before the partnership profit or loss is calculated. This occurs after partnership creditors are paid.

5126.03　**Right to participate in management.** There is equal right to participation in management among partners unless they agree otherwise. This is true regardless of the amount of capital contributed or the amount of services rendered to the partnership.

5126.04　**Right to information and inspection of the books.** Any partner has the right to demand to see the books and accounts of record at any point in time.

5126.05　**Right to an accounting.** This is the right of a partner to come into court to force other partners to give an accounting of the partnership activities.

5126.06　**Rights in specific partnership property.** Individual partners do not own any part of any specific partnership property. Unless agreed otherwise, the UPA states that each partner has an equal right to possess partnership property for partnership purposes. The right to possess and control partnership property cannot be transferred to a third party.

5126.07　**Right to compensation.** Unless agreed otherwise, a partner is not entitled to any salary for services provided to the partnership. After a partnership is dissolved, however, a partner who is in charge of winding up the affairs of the partnership is entitled to reasonable compensation for those services.

5126.08 **Right to reimbursement.** A partner that incurs reasonable expenses in carrying out partnership business has a right to reimbursement from the partnership.

Example: Dave, a partner, attempts to deliver goods to Brian on behalf of the partnership. Brian breaches the contract by refusing to accept the goods. Dave pays storage expenses for the goods and incurs costs to ship them to another buyer. If Dave pays these expenses, he can generally get reimbursed by the partnership.

5127 Duties of Partners

5127.01 **Fiduciary.** This means trust and confidence, loyalty and good faith to the firm, obedience to the partnership agreement, exercise of reasonable care in doing partnership business, providing needed information to the partnership, and providing an accounting of partnership matters.

5127.02 **Duty to share in losses.** Division of losses is done in the same percentage as sharing of the profits unless agreed otherwise in the partnership agreement.

5128 Assignment or Transfer of Partnership Interest

5128.01 A partner may assign or transfer all or part of her interest in the partnership to someone else.

    a. This does not dissolve the partnership. The assignor is still a partner.

    b. Consent of the other partners is not required for a valid assignment or transfer.

    c. The assignee does not automatically become a partner nor does the assignee have any of the rights of a partner. If the other partners agree, the assignee could become a partner.

    d. The assignee obtains only the right to the assignor's share of partnership profits and what the assignor would receive if the partnership is dissolved.

5128.02 As long as the assigning partner performs their required duties, the other partners are not adversely affected by the assignment.

5129 Ending a Partnership

5129.01 **Dissolution.** This is the point in time when the object of all or any of the partners changes from continuing the organization in its current form to discontinuing it.

5129.02 **Winding up.** Settling partnership affairs after dissolution. No new business can be carried on during the winding-up period. This is the span of time between dissolution and termination.

5129.03 **Termination.** End of the winding-up period.

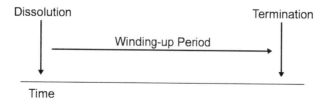

5130 Causes of Dissolution

5130.01 **Without violation of the partnership agreement**

    a. The agreed time limit of the partnership ends.

    b. The agreed partnership purpose has been completed.

    c. A partner quits a partnership that has no stated duration. This type of partnership is called a partnership at will. The withdrawing partner has no liability to the other partners since they may withdraw at any time.

    d. A mutual agreement of all partners may terminate the partnership.

5130.02 **In violation of agreement.** Any partner may dissolve a partnership at any time, but that partner may be liable for damages. The partner has the power, but may not have the right, to dissolve the partnership.

    Example: Caitlin and Erin form a partnership and agree that the partnership will have a duration of five years. After one year a dispute arises and Caitlin withdraws, causing a dissolution of the partnership. Caitlin had the power to dissolve the partnership, but not the legal right; therefore, she could be held liable for damages by Erin.

5130.03 **By operation of law** (done without agreement of the partners)

    a. The business becomes illegal. This automatically terminates the partnership.

    b. Bankruptcy of the partnership or an individual partner. Must be by adjudication and not merely insolvency.

    c. Death of one or more of the partners

    d. Court decree. A court decree can be obtained based on the following:

        (1) If just and equitable to terminate the partnership

        (2) Serious misconduct of a partner—such as habitual drunkenness

        (3) Incapacity of a partner; cannot perform duties—such as insanity

        (4) Business is impractical

        (5) Other partner habitually or purposely commits breach of the partnership contract

5131 Priority of Payments on Dissolution

5131.01 Creditors of the partnership are paid first.

5131.02 Loans made to partnership by partners are next repaid to the extent capital remains.

5131.03 Return of capital contributions made by the partners is next in line of priority.

5131.04 Profits or losses are then divided among the partners as follows:

    a. As agreed upon in the partnership agreement

    b. Equally if there is no partnership agreement to the contrary

    c. Losses are divided the same as profits if there is no partnership agreement to the contrary.

5132 Marshaling of Assets

5132.01 Partnership creditors get first rights on the partnership assets, and individual creditors get first rights on individual partners' assets.

5132.02 Partnership creditors must be completely paid before creditors of individual partners have any rights in partnership assets.

5132.03 Creditors of individual partners must be completely paid before partnership creditors have any rights in the personal assets of the individual partner.

5133 Limited Partnerships

5133.01 Limited partnerships are governed by the Uniform Limited Partnership Act (ULPA) and the Revised Uniform Limited Partnership Act (RULPA). These have been adopted by almost all states.

    a. The limited partnership must have one or more general partners and one or more limited partners.

    b. The limited partnership must file a certificate with the state that lists the following:

        (1) Name of the limited partnership

        (2) Type of business and its location

        (3) General and limited partners

        (4) Contribution of each limited partner (this can be cash or other property)

        (5) Other rights, including rights of limited partners to profits

    c. The name of the partnership cannot use the last name of a limited partner unless a general partner has the same last name.

    d. A limited partner can be given the right to substitute an assignee in their place with no partnership dissolution if the partnership agreement so provides.

    e. One limited partner may obtain priority over other limited partners in distributing profits.

    f. A limited partner who allows the use of his name in the partnership name or who participates in management is liable as a general partner to the creditors of the partnership.

    g. A new general or limited partner cannot be added unless all general and limited partners agree or it is provided for in the partnership agreement.

    h. Order of distribution of assets on dissolution is as follows:

        (1) To creditors

        (2) To limited partners for profit

        (3) To limited partners for return of capital contribution

        (4) To general partners for loans to partnership

        (5) To general partners for profits

        (6) To general partners for return of capital contribution

    i. Sale of a limited partnership interest may be regulated by the federal securities laws.

5134 Joint Ventures

5134.01 Joint ventures are similar to general partnerships in that they involve the co-ownership of a business for profit.

5134.02 Typically, joint ventures are established for conducting a single enterprise or transaction and usually continue for a shorter duration than most general partnerships. Since general partnerships can have the same limitations, however, it is often difficult to distinguish the two types of entities.

5134.03 Most courts hold that joint ventures are governed by partnership law.

    a. Joint venturers, therefore, owe each other fiduciary duties.

    b. Joint venturers generally have the same unlimited liability as general partners.

    c. Joint venturers have equal rights to manage the business; however, they may agree to delegate this power to one participant or employ a third-party manager.

    d. The duration of a joint venture can be specified in the agreement of the parties, terminable at will by any participant, or related to the completion of a specific project such as the purchase and development of a tract of land.

    e. Members of a joint venture do not generally have the same broad implied or apparent authority that a general partner may possess due to the usual limited purpose of a joint venture.

    f. The death of a joint venturer, however, does not automatically dissolve the joint venture.

5135 Limited Liability Company (LLC)

5135.01 An LLC is generally created under state law by filing articles of organization with the secretary of state's office. The articles must include such information as the following:

    a. The name of the LLC

    b. The duration of its existence

    c. The name and address of the LLC's registered agent (for such purposes as service of process)

5135.02 The LLC's name must generally include the words "limited liability company" or similar words that indicate to third parties that the owners of the entity have limited liability.

5135.03 Owners of the interests in an LLC are referred to as members. Most statutes require an LLC to have two or more members; however, some states do allow single member LLCs. Generally, members of an LLC can be individuals, partnerships, corporations, or other LLCs.

5135.04 An LLC is treated as a separate legal entity. Members have no personal liability for any of the LLC's debts simply by reason of being a member.

5135.05 The members of an LLC have a right to manage that which is proportionate to their capital contributions. Members who actually engage in management owe fiduciary duties to the LLC.

5135.06 If the actual authority of a member is not restricted, a member generally may have implied and apparent authority to bind the LLC on contracts entered in the ordinary course of the LLC's business.

5135.07 State LLC statutes generally allow an LLC interest to be transferred as provided in the member's operating agreement.

5135.08 If an LLC interest is transferred, the transferee generally has no right to become a member unless the other LLC members consent. A transferee who does not become a member is still entitled to receive either the return of their capital contribution or the fair market value of their LLC interest.

5135.09 An LLC will generally dissolve upon the death, retirement, bankruptcy, or dissolution of a member. Liquidation of an LLC, however, can generally be avoided by unanimous consent of the remaining members to continue the LLC's business.

5136 Limited Liability Partnership (LLP)

5136.01 An LLP is generally created by filing the required forms with the secretary of state's office.

5136.02 State LLP statutes also generally require that the LLP maintain some specified level of professional liability insurance and pay an annual fee to the state (usually on a per-partner basis).

5136.03 The unique feature of an LLP is that a partner's liability for a fellow partner's professional malpractice is limited to the partnership's assets. In other words, a partner does not have unlimited personal liability for another partner's malpractice.

5136.04 However, partners in an LLP do retain unlimited personal liability for their own malpractice as well as for any other partnership obligations.

5137 Sole Proprietorship

5137.01 A sole proprietorship is a form of business that is simply an extension of the sole, individual owner.

5137.02 No formalities are required for the formation of a sole proprietorship. They are formed very easily and inexpensively. If the individual fails to choose another form in which to operate the business, the business is a sole proprietorship by default.

5137.03 A sole proprietorship is not recognized as a legal entity. Plaintiffs must sue the individual owner, not the sole proprietorship. Also, the sole proprietor must individually sue anyone that causes harm to the business.

5137.04 For federal income tax purposes, the sole proprietorship is not a taxable entity. All of the income and expenses of the business are reported on the sole proprietor's individual federal income tax return.

5140 Corporations

5141 Entity

5141.01 A corporation is an organization formed under state law or federal law that is legally separate and distinct from those persons who own the corporation. This means the shareholders are not liable for corporate obligations except to the extent of their investment in the corporation.

5141.02 Due to its separate legal existence, the corporation is also generally not liable for the personal obligations of its shareholders, directors, officers, or employees.

5141.03 The corporate entity is recognized as being separate except when it is used to defeat public convenience, perpetrate fraud, evade the law, or commit a crime.

5141.04 Ignoring the corporate entity is referred to as "piercing the corporate veil." When this is done, the shareholders can be held liable by the creditors of the corporation for corporate obligations.

5141.05 For courts to ignore the corporate entity and *"pierce the corporate veil,"* two elements must generally be present:

1. **Domination by a shareholder or group of shareholders.** The idea here is that the shareholder or shareholders control the corporation for their own benefit in an attempt to insulate themselves from liability for wrongdoing.

2. **Improper use of the corporation.** Various types of improper use by the dominating shareholder can cause the corporation to be disregarded as a separate entity. For example:

   (a) Using the corporation to perpetrate a fraud

   (b) Thin capitalization of the corporation; here the corporation is formed as a "dummy" entity with insufficient capital to meet reasonably expected business obligations.

   (c) Shareholders looting the corporation to the detriment of the corporation's creditors, such as having the corporation sell assets to a shareholder for a price far below fair market value

5141.06 The corporation can hold property in the corporation's name.

5141.07 The corporation can sue and be sued in the corporation's name.

5141.08 Contracts can be entered in the corporation's name with the corporation as a party to the contract.

5142 Classifications of Corporations

5142.01 **De jure.** A corporation that has generally complied with all the statutory regulations for incorporation except for an insignificant deviation from the statute that causes no harm to the public interest. Corporate existence can generally not be challenged.

5142.02 **De facto.** A corporation that has failed to comply with some provision of the incorporation law. There must be a valid statute under which the corporation could be formed, a good faith attempt to organize under the statute, and an actual use of corporate power. If so, a de facto corporation has the same rights and powers of a de jure corporation insofar as any person or entity, other than the state, is concerned. This recognition prevents harsh rules making the individual owners liable.

5142.03 **Corporation by estoppel.** An organization representing itself to be a corporation or a person contracting with an organization as if it were a corporation is estopped from later denying the corporate existence.

5142.04 **Private.** Organized for private purposes by private parties.

5142.05 **Public (or governmental).** Created by the state to fulfill governmental purposes.

Example: Federal Deposit Insurance Corporation (FDIC)

5142.06 **Quasi-public.** A private corporation furnishing service upon which the public is dependent, such as a public service corporation or utility. It is usually given a special franchise and power.

5142.07 **Profit.** Organized primarily to make a profit for the owners.

5142.08 **Nonprofit.** Formed for religious, charitable, social, educational, or mutual-benefit purposes. They are called eleemosynary (related to, or supported by charity). Examples are athletic clubs, fraternities, hospitals, and private universities. They may be carried on at a profit if the profit is incidental to the main purpose. They must be nonstock.

5142.09 **Domestic.** A corporation is referred to as being a domestic corporation in the state in which it is incorporated.

5142.10 **Foreign.** A corporation is referred to as foreign in a state other than the one in which it is incorporated.

5142.11 **Alien.** Incorporated in a foreign country.

5142.12 **Closely held, closed, close.** A corporation with one or only a few shareholders whose shares are not generally available to the public.

5142.13 **Publicly held.** A corporation whose shares are publicly traded and are generally held by a large number of shareholders.

5142.14 **Professional corporation.** A corporation organized to carry on a profession. Most often these are physicians, CPAs, lawyers, etc.

5142.15 **Stock.** Ownership is evidenced by shares of stock.

5142.16 **Nonstock.** Stock is not issued by the corporation—done only for social or charitable corporations.

5143 Constitutional Rights of a Corporation

5143.01 A corporation has the following constitutional rights:

    a. To be secure from unreasonable searches and seizures

    b. Not to be deprived of life, liberty, or property without due process of law

    c. Not to be tried twice for the same criminal offense (called double jeopardy)

    d. Not to be denied equal protection of the laws

    e. First Amendment right of freedom of speech

5143.02 A corporation does not have the constitutional right against self-incrimination. This right applies only to real persons.

5144 State Incorporation Laws

5144.01 When states first allowed corporations to be formed, it was necessary for the incorporators to appear before the state legislature to ask it to be allowed to form the corporation.

5144.02 If the legislature decided to allow the formation of the corporation, it granted a corporate charter. Legally, this was permission to operate as a corporation in the state.

5144.03 The individual appearances of the incorporators before the legislature became very time-consuming, so the legislatures drafted a general incorporation law and delegated the administrative responsibility to a state official. Most states designate the secretary of state.

5144.04 **Model Business Corporation Act (MBCA)**

   a. The act is the model that most states use as the basis for their incorporation laws.

   b. The MBCA was first drafted in 1946 and has been amended many times. It was completely revised in 1984 and has been amended since then.

   c. The majority of states have adopted the revised MBCA, in whole or in part.

   d. The revised MBCA is used on the CPA Examination to cover the topic of corporation law.

   e. Individual state corporation law may differ somewhat from the revised MBCA. Questions on the CPA Examination, however, should be answered using the rules of the revised MBCA.

5144.05 **Foreign corporations**

   a. All of the states allow foreign corporations to do business in the state.

   b. Foreign corporations doing business in intrastate commerce must qualify to do business in the state and obtain a certificate of authority from the state. Failure to obtain a certificate results in the denial of access to the courts by the corporation as a plaintiff, a statutory penalty, and personal liability of the officers and directors.

   c. A foreign corporation engaged wholly in interstate commerce need not qualify or obtain a certificate of authority.

   d. Only the state of incorporation can regulate the internal affairs of a corporation.

   e. Foreign corporations are treated the same as domestic corporations for regulation purposes. If a state treated foreign and domestic corporations differently, it would be a burden on interstate commerce and, therefore, a violation of the Commerce Clause (unconstitutional).

f. A foreign corporation, registered or unregistered, can always defend itself as a defendant. A state cannot take away this right, because it would be a denial of due process.

g. The following is a diagram of a foreign corporation applying to do business in the state:

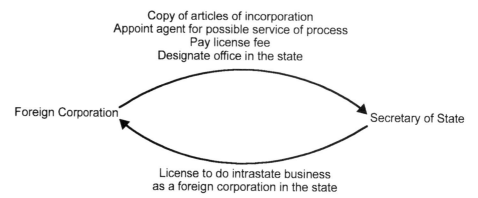

5145   Formation of a Corporation

5145.01 A corporation is formed by applying to the state. The following diagram shows the activities that occur when a corporation is formed. Note that the incorporators do the paperwork with the state, while the promoters sell the stock.

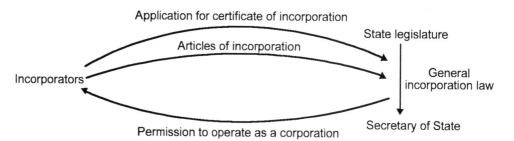

Charter: Old name
Certificate of incorporation: New name

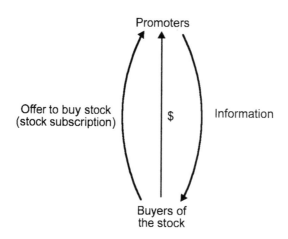

5145.02   **Start of corporate existence.** Issuance of a certificate of incorporation by the secretary of state is considered the start of corporate existence.

5145.03   **Domicile.** A corporation may have only one domicile—its state of incorporation. However, it can qualify to do business in any other state.

5146   Powers of a Corporation

5146.01   A corporation has only the powers expressly given in the law adopted by the legislature (such as the MBCA). Individuals, on the other hand, have any power not denied to them by the Constitution.

5146.02   Corporations derive their power from three sources, as follows:

   a.   **Statutory:** From the state's corporation laws. Examples of this power include the following:

   (1)   Having a corporate name

   (2)   Purchasing and holding property for corporate purposes

   (3)   Making bylaws

   (4)   Borrowing money

   (5)   Making contracts

   b.   **Express:** From the articles of incorporation and the corporate bylaws; cannot conflict with statutory powers.

   c.   **Implied:** Activities needed to carry out the statutory and express powers; these activities fill the gaps that exist in the statutory and express powers.

5146.03   **Corporate liability for wrongful conduct**

   a.   A corporation is liable under the doctrine of *respondeat superior* for the torts of its employees committed within the course of employment. This fact is true even if the activity is beyond the powers of the corporation.

   b.   A corporation can be punished by fine for the criminal conduct of its employees.

   c.   An *ultra vires* act is one beyond the scope of the powers of the corporation. An *ultra vires* act is not necessarily an illegal act, but an illegal act is always an *ultra vires* act.

5146.04   *Ultra vires* can be used only as a defense in limited cases.

   a.   It cannot be used by the corporation to avoid a contract unless it is totally executory.

   b.   It can be used by the following:

   (1)   A shareholder against a corporation to prohibit the corporation from performing a totally executory contract

   (2)   The corporation, or shareholders acting for the corporation, against former or present officers or directors to recover damages

   (3)   The state attorney general against the corporation to stop performance of an *ultra vires* contract or to dissolve the corporation

5147   Incorporators

5147.01   Incorporators are the individuals who apply to the state for incorporation.

5147.02   Incorporators need not have any interest in the corporation. Sometimes the secretaries in the lawyer's office are made the incorporators.

5147.03   Incorporators owe a fiduciary duty to the corporation being formed.

5148   Promoters

5148.01   Promoters are the motivating force in creating the corporation. They do such things as employing services of attorneys and accountants, borrowing funds, and purchasing property for use by the nascent (to be formed) corporation.

5148.02   Promoters owe a fiduciary duty to the corporation being formed.

5148.03   Promoters are liable on preincorporation contracts to third parties unless the following are true:

   a.   The corporation adopts the contract.

   b.   The contract expressly says the promoter is not liable on the contract.

   c.   The contract indicates that neither party is obligated unless the corporation is formed.

5148.04   Promoters are liable on preincorporation contracts if they contract in their own name or in the name of the not-yet-formed corporation, and the corporation is not formed or does not adopt the contract.

5148.05   Promoters cannot make secret profits in forming the corporation.

5149   Initial Issue of Shares

5149.01   After a corporation is formed and the board of directors meets for the first time, one of the first tasks is to accept the offers to buy stock. The board of directors can accept or reject these offers to buy shares.

5149.02   **Preincorporation share subscription**

   a.   **Share subscription:** Offer to buy shares of the corporation not yet formed.

   b.   Irrevocable for six months unless some other provision exists.

   c.   These subscriptions are solicited by the promoters while incorporation is in progress.

5149.03   Payment for shares

    a. Payment may be in money, property, or services already performed.

    b. Payment cannot generally be a promise to pay money in the future (promissory note) or a promise to do services in the future.

    c. The money value assigned by the board of directors or shareholders for property or services shall be conclusive as long as the following are true:

        (1) They acted as prudent directors would act.

        (2) There is a reasonable basis for the valuation (appraisal, etc.).

        (3) They acted in the corporation's best interest.

5149.04   Shares issued but not fully paid

    a. Corporation or corporation creditors can collect the unpaid portion from the original purchaser even if the original purchaser has sold the shares.

    b. Buyer of not fully paid shares is not liable if shares were purchased in good faith and without knowledge from the first person to whom the shares were originally issued by the corporation.

5149.05 Shareholders are liable to the corporation for the difference in value if they purchase shares from the corporation at a discount. At a minimum, the shareholder should pay as follows:

    a. **Par value shares:** Not less than the par value in dollars for the original issue

    b. **No-par shares:** Not less than the dollar amount fixed by the board of directors for the original issue (stated value)

    c. **Treasury shares:** Any dollar amount fixed by the board of directors (this amount can be less than the par value of the shares as originally issued as long as they are sold for FMV)

5150   Corporation Citizenship

5150.01 Citizenship must be determined to see if a federal court has jurisdiction of a case involving the corporation based on diversity of citizenship.

5150.02 The federal courts have jurisdiction only if the parties (plaintiff and defendant) are citizens of different states and the amount in controversy exceeds $50,000.

5150.03 For this purpose, a corporation is a citizen of both the state of incorporation and the state where its principal place of business is located.

5151   Articles of Incorporation

5151.01 The articles of incorporation are like a constitution—they outline the organization of the corporation.

5151.02 Corporate existence starts when the articles of incorporation are filed or when the certificate of incorporation is issued. There is a split of authority. It depends on which view the state selects.

5151.03 The articles are prepared by the promoters or incorporators.

5151.04 The articles of incorporation include the following:

    a. Name of the corporation

    b. Period of time for the corporation's existence—usually is perpetual

    c. Purpose—usually stated as any legal purpose

    d. Share structure, including the number of authorized shares and whether or not there is a preemptive right

    e. Address of registered office

    f. Structure of the board of directors and names and addresses of persons serving as directors until the first annual meeting

    g. Name and address of each incorporator

5151.05 **Amending the articles of incorporation**

    a. All corporations allow for changing, deleting, or adding to their articles of incorporation.

    b. To amend the articles of incorporation, the following must be done:

        (1) The board of directors adopts a resolution and submits it to the vote of the shareholders.

        (2) Shareholders must be given written notice.

        (3) A majority of shares entitled to vote is generally necessary for approval.

5152 Bylaws

5152.01 **Bylaws:** Rules adopted by the corporation's board of directors for regulation and management of the affairs of the corporation

    a. Bylaws are subordinate to the articles of incorporation and the state of incorporation's corporation laws.

    b. Bylaws may not conflict with the articles of incorporation or with the state's corporation laws.

5152.02 Initial bylaws are adopted by the board of directors.

5152.03 Bylaws can be changed by the board of directors unless reserved to the shareholders in the articles of incorporation.

5153 Types of Shares

5153.01 **Authorized:** The maximum number of shares a corporation can issue. The limit is stated in the articles of incorporation.

5153.02 **Issued:** The number of shares actually distributed by the corporation.

    a. Each issue must be approved by the board of directors.

    b. Each issue must be equal to or less than the authorized shares.

5153.03 **Outstanding:** The number of shares owned by shareholders of the corporation.

    a. Outstanding shares must be equal to or less than the issued shares.

5153.04 **Treasury:** The number of shares of the corporation owned by the corporation itself.

    a. These shares are reacquired shares.

    b. They are considered to be authorized and issued but no longer outstanding since they were purchased on the open market by the corporation.

    c. Treasury shares are often held to give stock options to key officers and employees.

    d. Formula: Issued – Outstanding = Treasury

    e. The number of treasury shares must be equal to or less than the number of outstanding shares of the corporation.

5154 Issue of Shares

5154.01 Shares may be issued for any of the following:

    a. Money

    b. Property

    c. Services already performed, but not for services to be performed

5154.02 If money is exchanged for shares:

    a. It cannot be less than the par value or the stated value.

    b. The initial shareholder receiving the shares is liable to the corporation and creditors of the corporation if the money is less than par or stated value.

5154.03 If property or services performed is exchanged for shares:

    a. The value assigned by the board of directors is conclusive as long as the following are true:

        (1) They acted as prudent directors would act.

        (2) There is a reasonable basis for the valuation (appraisal, etc.).

        (3) They acted in the corporation's best interest.

5155 Board of Directors

5155.01 **Board of directors**

    a. Exercises corporate powers and manages the business. They are in a fiduciary relationship with the corporation.

    b. Directors need not be residents of the state of incorporation.

    c. Directors need not be shareholders.

    d. They have authority to fix their own compensation unless the articles of incorporation or bylaws say they are prohibited from doing so.

e. The board can be one or more persons as fixed by the articles of incorporation or bylaws. Traditionally, state statutes required at least three directors. Today most statutes permit fewer than three directors for corporations that have fewer than three shareholders.

f. The board holds office until the next annual meeting or until replaced.

g. It can be divided into classes, with staggered election dates, if there are nine or more directors.

h. It can fill vacancies for the unexpired time by a majority vote of the remaining directors.

i. Directors can be removed by the shareholders' vote with or without cause. Directors serve at the pleasure of the shareholders.

j. The board has a quorum when a majority of the number of directors is present.

k. It can make an act effective if it is passed by the majority of the directors present at a meeting when a quorum exists.

l. The board of directors can divide itself into committees and delegate power to them. Examples are the executive committee and the audit committee.

m. The board can meet anywhere. It need not be in the state of incorporation.

5155.02 Notification to directors of regular or special meetings of the board of directors is specified by the bylaws.

5155.03 Meetings of the board of directors can be conducted via a conference call. They merely have to be able to hear each other at the same time.

5155.04 The board of directors may act without a meeting if all directors consent in writing.

5155.05 **Loans to directors.** Loans to directors are allowed only if authorized by the shareholders.

5155.06 **Liability of directors.** A director is individually liable if the director engages in illegal conduct or conduct that is a breach of fiduciary duty to the corporation. For example, if the director votes:

a. for an illegal dividend, such as a dividend that would make the corporation insolvent,

b. to illegally buy shares of the corporation, or

c. to pay off shareholders before creditors,

then the director would be individually liable.

5155.07 **Business judgment rule.** This rule protects the directors from shareholder lawsuits alleging a lack of due care on the part of the directors in carrying out the corporation's business. This rule will apply as follows:

a. When the board makes an informed decision

b. When there is no conflict of interest

c. When there is a rational basis for the board's decision

5155.08 Dividends

    a. Dividends are declared by the board of directors.

    b. They may be paid in cash, property, or shares of the corporation.

    c. They cannot be declared if the dividend would make the corporation insolvent.

    d. Cash and property dividends are paid out of unreserved and unrestricted earned surplus (retained earnings). Some states allow payment out of net earnings of the current year and the previous year taken together, even if there is a negative earned surplus.

5156 Officers of the Corporation

5156.01 The *officers* are appointed by the board of directors.

5156.02 They are the president, vice president(s), secretary, and treasurer.

5156.03 One person can hold multiple offices, but the president and secretary generally cannot be the same person. Exceptions to this rule exist in some states where "one person corporations" are allowed.

5156.04 The officers can be removed by the board of directors for any reason, but firing an officer may be a breach of an employment contract for which the corporation may be liable.

5156.05 Officers of a corporation owe a fiduciary duty to the corporation.

5157 Managers of the Corporation

5157.01 The *managers* are hired by the officers.

5157.02 The managers serve at the pleasure of the *officers*, unless they have negotiated an employment contract.

5157.03 The managers owe a fiduciary duty to the corporation.

5158 Shareholders

5158.01 **Shareholders** are the owners of the corporation.

5158.02 Shareholders do not generally owe fiduciary duties to the corporation. Controlling shareholders may be deemed to owe fiduciary duties that prevent them from exercising control to further their own interests to the detriment of the corporation and minority shareholders.

5158.03 Shareholders elect the board of directors.

5158.04 **Shareholder voting**

    a. A *quorum* for a meeting is a majority of shares outstanding, unless the articles of incorporation specify otherwise.

    b. A majority of the quorum prevails on votes, unless articles of incorporation specify otherwise.

     c. Treasury shares get no votes. Treasury shares are those owned by the corporation.

     d. A vote can be in person or by proxy. A proxy is a signed document authorizing another person to vote the shareholders' shares of stock. Proxy must be written and is valid for a maximum of 11 months.

     e. **Cumulative voting**

        (1) Applies only for electing the board of directors.

        (2) The number of votes a shareholder gets is determined as follows: Number of shares owned × number of directors being elected.

        (3) A shareholder can distribute votes in any way desired. All the votes can be put on one nominee.

        (4) Cumulative voting increases the chance of minority representation on the board of directors.

        (5) Most states permit cumulative voting if the articles provide for it.

     f. **Straight voting:** One vote for each share for each directorship to be filled.

5158.05 **Voting by proxy**

     a. A shareholder may vote by proxy.

     b. A director is not permitted to vote by proxy.

5158.06 **Shareholder meetings**

     a. Annual meeting details are fixed by the bylaws.

     b. Shareholders are entitled to notice of place, day, and hour of meetings 10 to 50 days before the meeting.

     c. The purpose must also be given for holding special (not annual) shareholder meetings. The meeting is then limited to these stated purposes.

     d. **Notice:** Mailing details by U.S. mail to shareholders of record.

5158.07 **Preemptive right**

     a. Preemptive right is the right of a shareholder to buy a pro rata share of newly issued stock.

     b. The purpose is to allow the current shareholders to maintain their proportionate interest in the corporation.

     c. In most states, a shareholder has no preemptive right unless the right is given in the articles of incorporation.

     d. In some states, a shareholder has a preemptive right unless it is denied in the articles of incorporation.

5158.08   **Dissenting shareholders**

   a. Dissenter's rights exist for shareholders who disagree with certain corporate actions. Shareholders can dissent from the following actions:

   (1) Merger

   (2) Consolidation

   (3) Sale of substantially all the assets of the corporation, not in the usual course of business

   b. To dissent, the shareholder must file a written objection with the corporation, vote against the proposal, and make written demand for payment of the fair value of the shareholders' stock within 10 days of the vote.

   c. Fair value is the stock value on the day before the proposal was voted on by the shareholders.

5158.09   **Shareholders' lawsuits**

   a. If a group of shareholders has been injured, a shareholder may be able to file a *class action suit* on behalf of the class.

   b. Most of these suits arise from violations of federal securities laws and have the following requirements:

   (1) The number in the class is so large it is impractical for all to sue.

   (2) The shareholder suing has substantially the same interest as others in the class.

   (3) The shareholder can fairly and adequately protect and present the interests of the class.

   c. A shareholder may also be able to file a *derivative suit* on behalf of the corporation when the corporation has been injured.

   d. Most of these suits are brought against directors, officers, or someone closely related to them. These suits require that the shareholder is either of the following:

   (1) Currently a shareholder at the time the derivative suit is filed

   (2) Was a shareholder when the wrongful act was committed against the corporation

   e. Generally, a derivative suit can be brought only after the shareholder demands that the board of directors file suit. This demand requirement is excused if it would be futile (e.g., all of the directors have committed fraud against the corporation).

5158.10   **Inspection of records**

   a. At common law, shareholders have certain rights to inspect the books and records of the corporation. Generally, the shareholder right to inspect is found in state corporation statutes.

   b. The MBCA requires that a shareholder must have a proper purpose for an inspection. Also, the right of inspection may be limited to shareholders who own at least 5% of the corporation's stock *or* have owned their stock for at least six months.

   c. The Revised Model Business Corporation Act (RMBCA) gives all shareholders an absolute right to inspect the following:

   (1) Shareholder lists

   (2) Articles of incorporation

---

(3) Bylaws

(4) Minutes of shareholder meetings held during the past three years

d. The RMBCA requires that the shareholder have a proper purpose for inspection of other records such as accounting and tax records, minutes of board of directors' meetings, and minutes of shareholder meetings held more than three years in the past.

e. Officers or agents of the corporation who improperly deny a shareholder's inspection request can be held liable for damages. Under the RMBCA, the shareholder can recover an amount that equals up to 10% of the value of the shares owned in the corporation.

f. The shareholder can appoint an agent, such as an attorney or accountant, to inspect the books and records of the corporation on their behalf.

5159 Suing a Corporation

5159.01 Due process requires that anyone being sued, even a corporation, must be given notice.

5159.02 When a corporation incorporates (for a domestic corporation) or applies to do business in another state (for a foreign corporation), it must designate a registered agent to receive service of process if the corporation is sued.

5159.03 The secretary of state maintains a listing of the registered agents for all corporations in the state.

5160 Permitted Actions of a Corporation

5160.01 **Owning own shares.** A corporation may buy and sell its own shares if cash and retained earnings permit. If insolvent or if the purchase would cause insolvency, the corporation cannot acquire the shares. Shares repurchased by the corporation are called treasury shares.

5160.02 **Indemnification of officers, directors, employees, and agents**

a. A corporation may indemnify an officer, director, employee, or agent of the corporation for any legal action (civil or criminal) done in good faith for the corporation. Generally, indemnification cannot be made if there was negligence or misconduct on the part of the officer, director, employee, or agent.

b. Indemnification is often done through insurance.

5160.03 **Loans to officers and directors**

a. A corporation may make loans to officers and directors. Generally, either the shareholders must approve the loan, or the directors must approve it after finding that approval of the loan will benefit the corporation.

b. The loans can even be without interest.

5160.04 **Employment incentives.** A corporation may offer incentives to officers and key employees. These incentives may include the following:

a. Stock purchase option

b. Bonus

c. Liberal expense account

d. Country club membership

5161 Prohibited Actions of a Corporation

5161.01 The state incorporation law and the corporation's articles of incorporation and bylaws often contain items that cannot be done. These items may include the following:

    a. Paying a dividend that would impair stated capital

    b. Taking advantage of a minority shareholder

5162 Major Changes in Corporate Structure

5162.01 Some major changes in a corporation are permitted only if approved by a majority vote of the shareholders. These changes include the following:

    a. **Merger.** One or more corporations are acquired by another existing corporation, thereby losing their separate corporate existence.

    b. **Consolidation.** Two or more corporations join together as a new corporation, thereby losing their separate corporate existence.

    c. **Sale** of substantially all the assets of a corporation not in the ordinary course of business.

5162.02 **Merger or consolidation**

    a. Two or more corporations can merge or consolidate. To do so, the following must occur:

        (1) The board of directors approves a plan and submits it for shareholder approval.

        (2) Written notice of an annual or special meeting must be given to shareholders at least 20 days prior to the meeting.

        (3) A majority of shares entitled to vote is necessary for approval.

    b. Creditors of the existing corporation are still creditors of the new or surviving corporation.

5162.03 **Merger of subsidiary corporation.** If a corporation owns at least 90% of a subsidiary corporation, it may merge without vote of the shareholders of either corporation.

5162.04 **Sale of substantially all the assets of a corporation**

    a. A sale of assets in the usual course of business can be done by the board of directors alone, without shareholder approval.

    b. A sale of assets not in the usual course of business must be done by resolution of the board of directors, notice to shareholders, and approval by a majority of shareholders.

5163 Accounting vs. Legal Terminology

5163.01 The difference between accounting and legal terminology in the owner's equity section of the balance sheet is shown in the following table:

Accounting Terminology	Corporate Law Terminology
Retained Earnings	Earned Surplus
Additional Paid-in Capital	Capital Surplus
Capital in Excess of Stated Value	Capital Surplus
Par Value of Shares	Stated Capital
Stated Value of Shares	Stated Capital

5163.02 Most of the corporate laws are written using the corporate law terminology rather than the more commonly used accounting terminology.

5164 Amount of Stated Capital

5164.01 **For par shares.** Par value is the stated capital. Any excess received for the shares would be capital surplus.

5164.02 **For no-par shares.** The entire amount received is stated capital, unless the board of directors allocates between stated capital and capital surplus within 60 days.

5165 Books and Records of the Corporation

5165.01 A corporation must keep written records of corporation business, shareholder meetings, board of directors' meetings, and names, addresses, and numbers of shareholders.

5165.02 These records may be examined by a shareholder on written demand. Restrictions may be placed on the right of inspection, such as requiring that the shareholder either:

a. has been a shareholder for six months or more or

b. owns 5% or more of the shares.

5166 Termination of the Corporation

5166.01 Articles of dissolution are filed with the secretary of state after a corporation has been dissolved.

5166.02 Dissolution of a corporation requires the corporation to wind up its business affairs and liquidate its assets.

5166.03 If the corporation has not yet done business or issued shares, it can be dissolved by majority vote of the incorporators or initial directors.

5166.04 A corporation that is doing business can be dissolved by a resolution of the directors approved by shareholder vote.

5166.05 The secretary of state has the power to force a corporation to dissolve involuntarily through administrative or judicial proceedings for such conduct as the following:

a. Failing to file annual reports

b. Failing to pay taxes

    c.   Failing to appoint a registered agent in the state

    d.   Obtaining the articles of incorporation by fraud

5166.06   A shareholder may obtain judicial dissolution of a corporation if any of the following occur:

    a.   The directors are deadlocked, and irreparable injury to the corporation is threatened.

    b.   The directors or those in control of the corporation are acting in a manner which is illegal, oppressive, or fraudulent.

    c.   Shareholders are deadlocked and cannot elect directors for two years.

    d.   Corporate assets are being misapplied or wasted.

5166.07   Creditors may obtain a judicial dissolution if the corporation is insolvent.

5166.08   Termination of the corporation occurs when the assets are liquidated and the proceeds distributed to creditors and shareholders.

5167 S Corporation

5167.01   If certain requirements are met, a corporation and its shareholders can elect to be taxed under Subchapter S of the Internal Revenue Code.

5167.02   For a discussion of the details regarding S corporations, see the taxation material in the Regulation volume.

As a summary, a comparison of various business entities appears in the following tables (section **5168**).

5168   Comparison of Business Entities

Comparison of Business Entity Table

Characteristics	C Corporation	S Corporation	General Partnership	Limited Partnership	Limited Liability Company	Limited Liability Partnership	Sole Proprietorship
Available in all states	Yes	Yes, but state taxation varies	Yes	Yes	Yes	Yes	Yes
Ease of formation	Simple	Simple	Simple to complex	Simple to complex	Simple to complex	More complex	Simple
Governing documents	Articles and bylaws	Articles and bylaws plus "S" elections	Partnership agreement	Partnership agreement	Operating agreement	Partnership agreement	None
Cost of formation	Minimal	Minimal	Moderate to expensive	Moderate to expensive	Moderate to expensive	Moderate to expensive	None
Formal acts required	Yes	Yes	No	Yes; generally must be filed by secretary of state	Yes; generally must be filed by secretary of state	Yes; generally must be filed by secretary of state	No
Existence of uniform act	Yes; Model Business Corporation Act	Not applicable; status as an S corporation is a federal income tax concept	Yes; Uniform Partnership Act (UPA) and the Revised Uniform Partnership Act (RUPA)	Yes; Uniform Limited Partnership Act (ULPA) and the Revised Uniform Limited Partnership Act (RULPA)	Yes; Uniform Limited Liability Company Act (ULLCA)	No	Not applicable
Limited liability of owners	All shareholders	All shareholders	None	None for general partners; limited partners have limited liability unless they significantly participate in the business	All members unless otherwise provided for by statutes	Generally only for debt and obligations arising from action of another partner	None
Number of owners	No limitations	Limited to 100	Minimum of two; no upper limit	Minimum of two; no upper limit	No upper limit; some states permit single-member LLCs	Minimum of two; no upper limit	One

Characteristics	C Corporation	S Corporation	General Partnership	Limited Partnership	Limited Liability Company	Limited Liability Partnership	Sole Proprietorship
Type of owner permitted	No limitations	Basically limited to individual citizens and resident aliens; some corporate and trust ownership permitted	None	No limitations	No limitations	No limitations, except that for professional partnerships each partner may have to be certified or licensed in the profession	No limitations
Multiple classes of ownership	No restrictions	Only one class of stock allowed, but differences in voting rights permitted	No restrictions	No restrictions	No restrictions	No restrictions	No
Permissible businesses	No limitations, except that some states may not allow professional services to be performed through a corporation	No limitations, except that some states may not allow professional services to be performed through a corporation	No limitations	No limitations	No limitations, except that some states may not allow professional services to be performed through an LLC	Most states limit this type of entity to certain professional services	No limitations
Participation in management	No restrictions	No restrictions	No restrictions	Generally restricted to general partners only	No restrictions	No restrictions if formed as a general partnership under state law	No restrictions
Legal title to property	Corporate name	Corporate name	Generally in the partnership name	Partnership name	LLC or member name	Partnership name	Proprietor's name
Transferability of interests	Generally freely transferable	Generally freely transferable, except for limitations as to number and type of shareholders	Transfer generally requires consent of other partners	Transfer generally requires consent of other partners	Follows corporation or partnership, depending on how it is taxed	Transfer generally requires consent of other partners	Freely transferable

Tax Comparison of Business Entity Table

Characteristics	C Corporation	S Corporation	General Partnership	Limited Partnership	Limited Liability Company	Limited Liability Partnership	Sole Proprietorship
Identity of the taxpayer	Corporation	Shareholder, except for built-in gains or passive income	Partners	Partners	Follows corporation or partnership, depending on how it is taxed	Partners	Individual proprietor
Applicable tax rates	Generally, a graduated rate scale from 15% to 35%; but 15% (starting in 2003) on taxable personal holding company income and accumulated taxable income; graduated rates not available to personal service corporations	Individual shareholder tax rates; highest corporate rates on built-in gains or excess passive income	Individual, fiduciary, or corporate tax rates depending on the type of partner	Individual, fiduciary, or corporate tax rates depending on the type of partner	Follows corporation or partnership, depending on how it is taxed	Individual, fiduciary, or corporate tax rates depending on the type of partner	Individual income tax rates
Double taxation	Yes	Generally no	No	No	Follows corporation or partnership, depending on how it is taxed	No	No
Election required	No	Form 2553	No	No	Use Form 8832 if prefer to file as a corporation	No	No
Tax year	Any	Calendar year unless §444 election	The same tax year as a majority of its partners; otherwise calendar unless §444 election	Follows partnership or corporate rules, depending on how it is taxed	Follows partnership or corporate rules, depending on how it is taxed	The same tax year as a majority of its partners; otherwise calendar unless §444 election	Calendar year

Characteristics	C Corporation	S Corporation	General Partnership	Limited Partnership	Limited Liability Company	Limited Liability Partnership	Sole Proprietorship
Contributions of property in exchange for interests in the entity	Generally tax-free under §351	Generally tax-free under §351	Generally tax-free under §721	Generally tax-free under §721	Generally tax-free under §721	Generally tax-free under §721	Not applicable
Contributions of services in exchange for interests in the entity	Taxable unless subject to substantial risk of forfeiture	Taxable unless subject to substantial risk of forfeiture	Generally taxable if made in exchange for capital interest; generally not taxable if made in exchange for profits interest	Generally taxable if made in exchange for capital interest; generally not taxable if made in exchange for profits interest	Follows rules of partnership or corporation, depending on how it is taxed	Generally taxable if made in exchange for capital interest; generally not taxable if made in exchange for profits interest	Not applicable
Method of accounting	Cash method may be permitted except for inventory	Cash method permitted except for inventory	Cash method permitted except for inventory	Cash method generally permitted except for inventory	Generally follows rules for limited partnership unless taxed as a corporation	Generally follows rules for limited partnerships	Cash method permitted except for inventory
Special allocation of tax attributes	Not available	Not available	Very flexible if substantial economic effect	Very flexible if substantial economic effect	Follows corporation or partnership, depending on how it is taxed	Very flexible if substantial economic effect	Not applicable
Retroactive modification to agreement	No	No	Yes	Yes	Follows corporation or partnership, depending on how it is taxed	Yes	Not applicable
Timing of income recognition by owners	When distributed	In year in which S corporation's year ends, whether or not distributed	In year in which partnership's year ends, whether or not distributed	In year in which partnership's year ends, whether or not distributed	Follows corporation or partnership, depending on how it is taxed	In year in which partnership's year ends, whether or not distributed	Based on owner's tax year
Deductibility of losses	Deducted at corporate level	Deduction by shareholders limited to basis in stock plus loans to company	Deduction by partners limited to basis in partnership interest	Deduction by partners limited to basis in partnership interest	Follows corporation or partnership, depending on how it is taxed	Deduction by partners limited to basis in partnership interest	Limited to amount at risk

Characteristics	C Corporation	S Corporation	General Partnership	Limited Partnership	Limited Liability Company	Limited Liability Partnership	Sole Proprietorship
Subject to at-risk provisions	Only if more than 50% of the stock is owned by five or fewer shareholders	Rules applied at shareholder level	Rules applied at partner level	Rules applied at partner level	Follows corporation or partnership, depending on how it is taxed	Rules applied at partner level	Yes
Subject to passive activity rules	Generally no, but exceptions for closely held corporations	Rules applied at shareholder level	Rules applied at partner level	Rules applied at partner level	Follows corporation or partnership, depending on how it is taxed	Rules applied at partner level	Generally no limitations
Treatment of capital losses	Must be used to offset capital gains	Passed through to shareholders	Passed through to partners	Passed through to partners	Follows corporation or partnership, depending on how it is taxed	Passed through to partners	Net $3,000 annual loss allowed after offset of capital gains
Income accumulations within the entity	Reasonable needs of the business	No restrictions	No restrictions	No restrictions	Follows corporation or partnership, depending on how it is taxed	No restrictions	No restrictions
Fringe benefits	No limitations	Owners of more than 2% of the shares cannot receive tax-deductible fringe benefits	Partners are generally not eligible to receive tax-deductible fringe benefits	Partners are generally not eligible to receive tax-deductible fringe benefits	Follows corporation or partnership, depending on how it is taxed	Partners are generally not eligible to receive tax-deductible fringe benefits	Owner is generally not eligible to receive tax-deductible fringe benefits
IRS filing requirements	Files Form 1120	Files Form 1120S and distributes K-1s to shareholders	Files Form 1065 and distributes K-1s to shareholders	Files Form 1065 and distributes K-1s to shareholders	Follows corporation or partnership, depending on how it is taxed	Files Form 1065 and distributes K-1s to shareholders	Proprietor files Schedule C to Form 1040

Characteristics	C Corporation	S Corporation	General Partnership	Limited Partnership	Limited Liability Company	Limited Liability Partnership	Sole Proprietorship
Effect of transfer of interest on the entity	Transfer of more than 50% ownership over a 3-year testing period may limit corporation's use of net operating loss carryovers and other tax attributes	Transfer to an ineligible shareholder may cause termination of "S" election	Transfer of more than 50% of capital and profit interests within 12-month period results in technical termination of the partnership	Transfer of more than 50% of capital and profit interests within 12-month period results in technical termination of the partnership	Follows corporation or partnership, depending on how it is taxed	Transfer of more than 50% of capital and profit interests within 12-month period results in technical termination of the partnership	Not applicable
Character of gain or loss on sale of interest in the entity	Capital	Capital	Capital, except to the extent of partner's allocable share of partnership's ordinary income assets	Capital, except to the extent of partner's allocable share of partnership's ordinary income assets	Follows corporation or partnership, depending on how it is taxed	Capital, except to the extent of partner's allocable share of partnership's ordinary income assets	Not applicable

This page intentionally left blank.

Section 5200
Economic Concepts

5210 Business Cycles and Reasons for Business Fluctuations

5211 Components of the Business Cycle

5211.01 Terminology

    a. Business cycle—A more or less regular pattern of expansion and contraction around the trend of GDP growth.

    b. Potential output—The output, measured as real GDP, that an economy can produce when all its resources are fully employed.

5211.02   Introduction to the Business Cycle

A business cycle is a more or less regular pattern of expansion and contraction around the trend of GDP growth. The concept of the business cycle is designed to help explain the path of the economy and the behavior of certain economic variables such as the economic growth rate as it fluctuates around its long-term trend.

5211.03   The Business Cycle Phases

a.   The business cycle is characterized by four phases:

(1)   The "expansion" phase, where more resources become employed and actual output approaches potential output. In the extreme, there may be over-employment as workers work overtime and the utilization rate for plant and equipment exceeds normal levels. However, this cannot be sustained.

(2)   The "peak," which is the highest point of output during the cycle. The economy is operating above the long-term growth trend of real GDP.

(3)   The "contraction" (or recession) phase, where more resources become unemployed and actual output falls below potential output.

(4)   The "trough," which is the lowest point of output during the cycle. There are large unemployment rates, a decline in annual income, and overproduction. This is the time at which the real GDP stops declining and starts expanding.

b.   A business cycle is measured as the period of time from the peak of one cycle through the four phases to the peak of the next cycle.

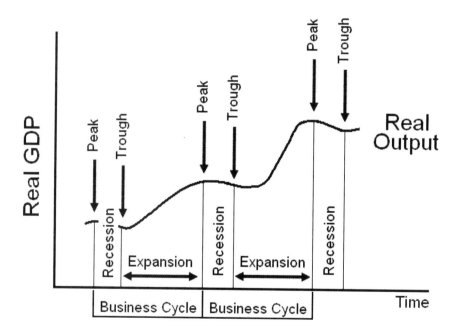

5211.04   Economic Growth

The trend or the path of economic growth measures the level of output (potential output) that could be produced if all the resources were fully employed over time.

a.   The business cycle measures cyclical deviations from the potential output.

b.   If the current level of output is below trend output there is a recessionary gap.

c. If the current level of output is above trend output there is an inflationary gap.

d. Economic growth can occur if a society has access to more or better resources and/or the productivity of existing resources increases, allowing the resources to be used more efficiently.

5212 Circumstances Affecting the Business Cycle

5212.01 Terminology

a. **Aggregate expenditures**—Aggregate spending consists of personal consumption, business investment, government expenditures, and the net difference between exports and imports.

b. **Aggregate Expenditure Model**—A model based on the premise that a business cycle is caused by changes in the level of aggregate spending.

c. **Cyclical unemployment**—Unemployment caused by insufficient spending or aggregate demand.

d. **Discouraged worker**—Workers who have left the labor force because they have been unable to find jobs and have stopped actively looking for work.

e. **Economic growth**—A sustained growth of natural real GDP.

f. **Employment Act of 1946**—Federal legislation that created a commitment for the federal government to develop policies that were designed to promote full employment, stable prices, and reasonable economic growth, thereby promoting economic stability.

g. **Frictional unemployment**—Unemployment that results from workers voluntarily changing jobs, temporary layoffs, and unemployed workers between jobs.

h. **Gross Domestic Product (GDP)**—The total market value of all final goods and services produced within the United States in a given year using either domestic or foreign supplied resources.

i. **Inflationary gap**—The amount by which aggregate demand must shift downward to decrease nominal GDP to its non-inflationary full employment level.

j. **Inventory investment**—Consists of all changes in the stock of raw materials, work-in-process and final goods by a firm in a given time period.

k. **Labor force**—Persons older than 16 years of age who are not institutionalized and who are employed or unemployed and actively seeking employment.

l. **Leading indicators**—One of several tools economic policymakers use to forecast the future direction of GDP. It consists of 10 variables that historically provided advanced notice of a change in the trend of GDP.

m. **Natural rate of unemployment (NRU)**—The unemployment rate that occurs when there is no cyclical unemployment and the economy is producing its potential output.

n. **Political Business Cycle Model**—A model that explains the business cycle as resulting from interactions between economic policy decisions and political decisions designed to influence voter behavior.

o. **Real Business Cycle Model**—A model that explains the business cycle in output and employment as being caused by significant changes in technology and resources or supply shocks. This theory suggests that economic instability arises on the aggregate supply side of the economy.

p. **Real Gross Domestic Product (Real GDP)**—Defined as GDP adjusted for inflation where GDP is divided by the GDP deflator for that year, the index being expressed as a decimal.

q. **Recessionary gap**—The amount by which aggregate demand must shift upward to increase nominal GDP to its non-inflationary full employment level.

r. **Seasonal unemployment**—Unemployment related to seasonal layoffs that occur in regular and recurring patterns in some industries.

s. **Structural unemployment**—Unemployment due to workers not having the skills demanded by employers, and workers who cannot easily move to the location where jobs are available.

t. **Unemployment rate**—The percentage of the labor force that is unemployed at any given point in time.

5212.02 **Theories Explaining Business Cycles**

a. There are several competing theories that economists have developed that try to explain the causes for the business cycle. While there is no universal agreement as to the exact combination of factors that cause business cycles, a brief review of some of the more accepted theories helps to potentially explain how changes at the firm level might affect the economy at the macroeconomic level.

b. The **real business cycle model** is based on the premise that fluctuations in output and employment result from real supply shocks that periodically hit the economy, and that markets adjust rapidly to the shock and always remain in equilibrium.

(1) Monetary policy is assumed to have no real effect on the business cycle.

(2) Toward the end of the expansionary phase of the business cycle, employment is high and jobs are easy to find. The supply of labor is highly elastic with respect to temporary changes in wages as workers are very willing to substitute work for leisure on a short-term basis because wages are high.

(3) The most important shock that can impact the economy is a productivity shock that often results from technological change and leads to an increased level of output from the given amount of inputs. Workers will be willing to work more hours to take advantage of the higher wages caused by the higher productivity.

(4) In the absence of an increase in aggregate demand, the necessary level of output could be produced by a smaller level of inputs, thus increasing unemployment until aggregate expenditures increase. Rising productivity also increases the incentive for business investment.

(5) **Illustration:** Assume that productivity declines significantly because of a supply shock that raises the price of crude oil. This would lead to a dramatic increase in the cost of energy. This in turn would lead to an increase in operating costs for most firms. The cost increases would reduce society's ability to produce real output. At the same time, the increased cost of energy would reduce consumer purchasing power and expenditures on consumer goods. This would further reduce the incentive for businesses to invest.

c. The **political business cycle model** explains the business cycle as resulting from interactions between economic policy decisions and political decisions designed to influence voter behavior.

    (1) Economic policy choices often represent trade-offs between unemployment and inflation.

    (2) Surveys indicate the voters are worried about both issues and perceive rising unemployment to be a problem. Voters are also concerned about the rate of inflation, the rate of increase in the inflation rate, and the effect that inflation could have on their buying power.

    (3) Politicians desire to have the economy "moving in the right direction" as an election approaches.

    (4) Politicians tend to run restrictive fiscal policies early in their terms and to blame the previous administration for current economic problems.

    (5) Fiscal policy tends to become more expansionary as an election year approaches.

    (6) There is little doubt that most administrations tend to pursue certain of these policies; however, it is very difficult for any administration to "fine-tune" fiscal policy since the executive branch does not control all the major policy tools (for example, monetary policy), and the economy may experience macro-shocks such as oil price increases or terrorist attacks.

d. The **insufficient aggregate expenditure model** is based on the premise that a business cycle is caused by inadequate spending. The key components of aggregate expenditure are personal consumption (C), business investment (I), government expenditures (G), and the net difference between exports (X) and imports (M). It is represented by the formula:

$$GDP \;=\; C + I + G + (X - M)$$

Each of these expenditure categories is assumed to be a function of other economic variables:

    (1) The level of personal consumption depends primarily on consumer disposable income and wealth. In addition, the demand for consumer durable goods such as housing and automobiles is influenced by the impact of interest rate changes on monthly payments.

    (2) Business investment depends primarily on the level of interest rates and business expectations concerning the net present value of the cash flows from potential projects. (See section **5311** on Capital Budgeting.)

    (3) Government expenditures are determined by the fiscal policy that is developed by the executive and legislative branches of government.

    (4) Exports are driven by consumer income and wealth in foreign nations as well as foreigners' tastes and preferences for foreign (in this case U.S.) goods. The demand for imports depends primarily on the same factors as personal consumption plus the tastes and preferences U.S. citizens have for foreign goods.

e. The **accelerator model** assumes that the business cycle is caused by the volatility of investment spending.

    (1) Expenditures on capital goods and investment in inventory are related to the rate of change in GDP.

    (2) It assumes that a given level of capital goods is required to produce a given level of output. Also, firms desire a given level of inventory at a given level of demand.

(3) If the economy is operating at full capacity and there is an increase in aggregate demand, then there would be an increase in the demand for capital goods, which stimulates increases in aggregate demand, causing a secondary increase in the demand for capital goods.

(4) With the increase in aggregate demand, inventory levels will fall below desired levels and firms will increase their investment in inventory which will cause an increase in production and employment at the wholesale level.

5212.03 Unemployment

a. The **unemployment rate** measures the percentage of the labor force that is not working. It is calculated as the number of unemployed workers divided by the number of workers in the labor force multiplied by 100. The **labor force** equals all U.S. residents 16 years of age or older who are not institutionalized, who are working, or who are unemployed and actively looking for work. Part-time workers are counted as being employed.

b. **Discouraged Workers** are unemployed workers who are not actively seeking employment, and they are not considered to be part of the labor force. Discouraged workers are also defined as workers who are able and willing to work, but who have not made specific efforts to find work during the past four weeks.

c. **Example:** The data below indicates what happened in the labor market in the United States during the last two months of 2005. The unemployment rate fell from 5.0% to 4.9%. During the month of December some 4,000 discouraged workers who had not been actively seeking employment reentered the labor force.

	November 2005	December 2005
Civilian Labor Force	150,183,000	150,153,000
Employed Workers	142,611,000	142,779,000
Unemployed Workers	7,572,000	7,375,000
Unemployment Rate	5.0%	4.9%
Discouraged Workers	447,000	451,000

5212.04 Types of Unemployment

a. **Frictional Unemployment** occurs due to normal labor turnover. "Search unemployment" includes workers looking for jobs. "Wait unemployment" includes workers waiting to take jobs in the near future. Frictional unemployment is an inevitable and necessary part of well-functioning labor markets.

b. **Seasonal Unemployment** occurs in regular and recurring patterns in some industries (e.g., retail layoffs in January following the holiday season, construction layoffs during the winter in northern areas of the country, or employment patterns in agriculture tied to the harvest season). The key unemployment measure is "adjusted" by using statistical techniques to account for these expected seasonal patterns.

c. **Cyclical Unemployment** is unemployment that is related to the general level of economic activity and tends to rise during the recession phase of the business cycle.

d. **Structural Unemployment** arises when changes in technology and international competitiveness change the skills required to perform jobs and/or change the location of jobs. Workers often find it difficult to obtain jobs without retraining, relocating, or getting additional education.

5212.05   Costs of Unemployment

   a.   Unemployment represents foregone output and causes actual output to be less than potential output.

   b.   There is a social dimension to unemployment, as the loss of a job causes problems with self-esteem. Generally, there is also an increase in domestic violence as the unemployment rate increases and the average time workers remain unemployed increases. Bankruptcy filings also increase as the duration of unemployment increases.

5212.06   Full Employment and the Natural Rate of Unemployment

   a.   **Full employment** is defined as the level of employment where the actual unemployment rate is equal to the natural rate of unemployment (NRU). At this point the economy would be producing its "potential output" with the economy operating at full capacity. The NRU occurs when the number of job seekers is equal to the number of job vacancies, and actual unemployment would be greater than zero due to frictional unemployment.

   b.   Cyclical and structural unemployment would cause the unemployment rate to exceed the NRU.

   c.   The NRU has fluctuated over time. During the 1950s, it was estimated to be in the range of 3.0% to 3.5%. It climbed to approximately 6.5% by the mid-1980s and has declined to the 5.0% range by the end of the 1990s. Key factors explaining the changes were:

   (1)   Demographics—young adults and teenagers spent a larger portion of their time in the labor force looking for jobs, and their percentage of the population rose during the 1970s and then declined in the 1980s and 1990s.

   (2)   Higher rates of imprisonment—the percentage of the male population that was imprisoned almost doubled to 2.3% in the period 1985–1998.

   (3)   Temporary help agencies and Internet—this has helped workers find jobs more rapidly.

5213   The Effect of Business Cycles on Financial Position and Operations

5213.01   Terminology

   a.   **Cyclical unemployment**—Unemployment caused by insufficient spending or aggregate demand.

   b.   **Discouraged worker**—Workers who have left the labor force because they have been unable to find jobs and have stopped actively looking for work.

   c.   **Employment Act of 1946**— Federal legislation that created a commitment for the federal government to develop policies that were designed to promote full employment, stable prices, and reasonable economic growth, thereby promoting economic stability.

   d.   **Frictional unemployment**—Unemployment that results from workers voluntarily changing jobs, temporary layoffs, and unemployed workers between jobs.

   e.   **Gross Domestic Product (GDP)**— The total market value of all final goods and services produced within the United States in a given year using either domestic or foreign supplied resources.

   f.   **Labor force**—Persons older than 16 years of age who are not institutionalized and who are employed or unemployed and actively seeking employment.

g. **Leading indicators**—One of several tools economic policymakers use to forecast the future direction of GDP. It consists of 10 variables that historically provided advanced notice of a change in the trend of GDP.

h. **Natural Rate of Unemployment (NRU)**—The full employment rate that occurs when there is no cyclical unemployment and the economy is producing its potential output.

i. **Unemployment rate**—The percentage of the labor force that is unemployed at any given point in time.

5213.02   Economic Variables

a. The approaches used to forecast the path of the business cycle and the probable future trends provide a sense of the importance of the statistical information that is gathered by various government agencies and business organizations. It is also important to look at how specific economic variables behave during the various phases of the business cycle.

b. Leading economic indicators are a set of variables that historically have demonstrated a high correlation with the level of economic activity. This has allowed economic policymakers to use this data to forecast the future direction of **Gross Domestic Product (GDP)** and to develop and implement appropriate macroeconomic policies. The list below provides a brief explanation as to how these indicators might be changing if they were predicting a contraction in the business cycle.

(1) Average workweek—a decline in the number of hours worked in the average workweek for production workers in the manufacturing sector suggests a downturn in manufacturing output.

(2) Initial claims for unemployment insurance—if the number of first-time claims for unemployment compensation is increasing, it suggests rising unemployment and a subsequent decline in real GDP.

(3) New orders for consumer goods—if manufacturers receive fewer orders from retailers for consumer goods, it suggests that consumer spending is declining and that there will be a decline in future production in the consumer goods sector and therefore a decline in real GDP.

(4) Vendor performance—an improvement in delivery times, such as measured by a survey conducted by the Purchasing Managers Association, ironically suggests an economic slowdown with declines in real GDP.

(5) New orders for capital goods—a decline in the orders for capital goods points to a reduction in business investment and aggregate expenditure and thereby real GDP.

(6) Building permits for residential construction—a decline in building permits suggests a downturn in the construction industry.

(7) Stock prices—sustained declines in stock prices, measured by an index such as the S&P 500, tends to point to declining corporate profits. Additionally, price declines also make it less attractive for firms to issue new stock, and the declines would also lead to a decrease in consumer wealth and consumer spending.

(8) Money supply—actions by the Federal Reserve to reduce the money supply tend to be related to declines in real GDP. As the Fed reduces the money supply, everything else being equal, interest rates would rise, and this would reduce the incentive for business investment and the spending on consumer durables. (Leading indicators such as money supply are forecasts, not measurements.)

(9) Interest rate spread—increases in short-term nominal interest rates generally indicate the monetary authorities wish to slow the level of economic activity. These moves tend to reduce the spread between short-term and long-term interest rates that have a negative impact on business investment. Thus, a restrictive monetary policy is likely to cause a decline in future real GDP.

(10) Consumer expectations—declining consumer optimism, as measured by a consumer survey such as that conducted by the Survey Research Center at the University of Michigan or the Conference Board, suggests declines in consumption and possibly future declines in real GDP.

 c. While none of these indicators in isolation forecasts an economic slowdown, historically a decline in the index of leading economic indicators for three consecutive months has provided advance notice of a decline in real GDP. It is important to note, however, that these forecasts have not been infallible and, at times, have not provided sufficient advance warning for policymakers to be able to respond in a timely manner.

5213.03 Unemployment and the Business Cycle

 a. Unemployment is a lagging indicator in that the unemployment rate lags behind the phase of the business cycle. The rate does not begin to decline significantly until the economy is well into an economic recovery.

 b. Cyclical unemployment rises as the economy moves into the contractionary phase of the business cycle and tends not to decline until the trough is reached and the recovery is well underway.

  (1) Firms tend to have existing workers work overtime or to hire part-time workers during the early stages of a recovery as a means of controlling labor costs until the recovery seems certain.

  (2) During the recessionary phase, a number of workers become what is known as **"discouraged workers"** and drop out of the labor force entirely as they cease to be actively looking for work. As the recovery begins, these people again begin to look for work and re-enter the labor force, thus slowing the decline in the unemployment rate.

5213.04 Inflation and the Business Cycle

 a. Inflation is positively correlated to the business cycle. Policies designed to stimulate aggregate expenditures tend to increase inflationary pressures unless they occur when the economy is experiencing high rates of unemployment. The inflationary pressures increase as the economy gets closer to full employment of labor, machinery, and equipment.

 b. As a general rule, many firms have an ability to pass cost increases (cost-push inflation) on to consumers near the end of the expansionary phase of the business cycle. Even firms with a significant degree of pricing power have difficulty increasing prices near the trough of a business cycle. In today's world, with increased competitive pressures, most firms are facing increased pressures on operating margins, i.e., reduced ability to pass through cost increases, whatever the phase of the business cycle. This has been a major factor in making cost control increasingly important for a firm to maintain profitability.

5213.05   **Inventory Investment and Gross Private Domestic Investment**

   a.   Inventories and utilization of existing plant capacity fluctuate more with the business cycle than any other components of aggregate expenditures. Changes in inventory investment exhibit sharp, but generally short-lived, fluctuations during the business cycle.

   b.   Inventory investment occurs when firms increase their level of inventory. Anticipated (desired) inventory investment must be distinguished from unanticipated (undesired) inventory investment. Inventory investment will tend to be high:

     (1)   If an unanticipated sales increase causes the firm's inventory to decline below desired levels (an unanticipated change).

     (2)   If the firm builds up inventory levels in anticipation of an expected increase in sales (an anticipated change).

   c.   Generally a firm has an inventory policy that sets a target inventory and attempts to maintain that desired level of inventory.

     (1)   Problems often arise as sales begin to increase and the firm finds inventories falling below desired levels. The firm acts to increase inventories to return to the desired level, and then often, because further sales increases are expected, many firms continue to increase inventory levels in anticipation of the increase. When sales first begin to fall, inventory levels rise rapidly (unanticipated), causing a rapid decline in orders for new products.

     (2)   At the trough of the business cycle, inventories tend to be low as firms have sold off inventories and are pessimistic about the possibility of future sales increases. Thus, inventories tend to fall below desired levels as the unanticipated sales increases begin. As firms overcome their pessimism and begin to believe that the sales increase represents a real change in the sales trend, inventory investment begins to climb rapidly.

   d.   **Illustration:** Assume that an auto dealer has sales of 40 cars per month and desires to hold an inventory equal to one month's sales. As long as sales stay stable at 40 units a month, the firm's desired level of inventory will remain unchanged. Now suppose that demand drops to 30 units a month and it takes the firm two months to respond to the change. By the time the change in demand is recognized, inventory will have climbed to 60 units. For the foreseeable future the dealer would want to hold 30 units in inventory. Thus, when responding to the change in demand, the dealer's orders would fall to zero for the next period before stabilizing at the new demand level of 30 units.

     Thus we see that inventory fluctuations can be significant, even if there are only small changes in the level of final demand. Today, many firms are using computer-based tracking programs to be better able to shorten the time between a demand change and their ability to recognize that change and adjust their inventory.

5213.06   Sectors of the Economy and the Business Cycle

There are several sectors of the economy that demonstrate a direct relationship to various phases of the business cycle:

a. Durable goods include capital goods, commercial buildings, and heavy equipment and farm implements.

   (1) During good times the demand for durable goods increases as manufacturing firms order new machinery and equipment to meet demand for their products. New capital goods are purchased before old equipment is fully depreciated. The impact of this new investment is magnified by the multiplier effect (see section **5224.08**), causing an increase in income, employment and output.

   (2) During the contraction phase of the business cycle, there generally is a significant decline in spending on durable goods as firms find they have excess capacity. Rather than purchase new equipment, there is a tendency to continue to use old or existing equipment.

b. Consumer durable goods include things such as homes and automobiles.

   (1) Purchases of these goods tend to be very sensitive to interest rates and consumer income. Near the peak of the business cycle, strong consumer income tends to keep purchases high. Rising interest rates tend to slow the rate of the increase in demand and become a negative factor when income begins to fall as a recessionary phase begins.

   (2) One key driver of the demand for consumer durables is the monthly payment (that is, the fixed expenditure a consumer is committing to make when the good is purchased on credit). When times are good, lenders tend to be willing to accept more risk and make marginal loans by reducing their credit standards. This supports the consumer willingness and ability to buy their products.

   (3) As the contraction phase begins and unemployment begins to climb and income falls, lenders tighten their credit policies. Additionally, there is an increasing concern about possible unemployment among employed workers. These factors cause the demand for consumer durables to fall as these purchases can be postponed. The outcome is an unanticipated increase in inventories in the retail sector.

5220 Economic Measures and Reasons for Changes in the Economy

5221 Reasons for Inflation, Deflation, Expansion, and Recession

5221.01   Terminology

a. Commodity Substitution Bias—A bias introduced into calculating the CPI as consumers have a tendency to cut back on the consumption of relatively more expensive goods and substitute relatively cheaper goods at various stages of the business cycle.

b. Consumer Price Index (CPI)—Widely used index for measuring the rate of inflation. It measures the weighted-average cost of a "market basket" of goods and services purchased by the typical household.

c. Cost-Push Inflation—Inflation caused by rising resource prices that result in an increase in per-unit costs of production.

d. Deflation—A sustained decline in the general price level.

e. Demand-Pull Inflation—Inflation caused by an excess in total spending relative to the economy's current capacity to produce goods and services.

f. GDP Deflator—The price index that is based on all goods and services produced in the economy. It is also known as the implicit price deflator and is the index used to compute real GDP.

g. Hyperinflation—An extremely rapid rate of inflation that usually has a devastating impact on real output and employment.

h. Inflation—A sustained increase in the general price level.

i. New Goods Bias—A bias introduced into calculating the CPI since consumers are constantly replacing old goods with new goods.

j. Outlet Substitution Bias—A bias introduced into calculating the CPI due to the fact that more people begin shopping at discount stores when prices rise.

k. Producer Price Index (PPI)—An index used to measure the rate of inflation for goods used in the production process. It is also known as the wholesale price index.

l. Quality Change Bias—A bias introduced into calculating the CPI since the quality of many items tends to improve each year. This improvement is not accounted for when incorporating the price of the improved good into the index.

5221.02 Inflation

a. Inflation is a sustained increase in the average level of prices and is measured by using a fixed-weight price index. In measuring the consumer price index (CPI), consumers are assumed to buy a specified group of goods and services—a "market basket of goods." The items in the market basket are "weighted" based on their relative importance in terms of consumer spending. The rate at which the weighted-average price for these goods increases is the inflation rate.

b. The inflation rate is determined by comparing the prices paid for the market basket of goods in one period to that paid in another. The CPI is reported by the government every month and is used to adjust Social Security benefits annually and to adjust income tax brackets for inflation.

c. Biases in the CPI calculation include:

    (1) **New goods bias.** New goods constantly replace old goods, and the index does not compare both the price and quality between the old and new goods. This problem is handled by periodically revising the market basket of goods used to calculate the CPI. This factor creates an upward bias in the CPI.

    (2) **Quality change bias.** The quality of many items improves each year and the improvement must be compared to the increase in price of the good. This factor generally creates an upward bias in the CPI.

    (3) **Commodity substitution bias.** Consumers have a tendency to cut back on the consumption of relatively more expensive goods and substitute relatively cheaper goods as prices rise. This factor tends to have increases in the CPI overstate the overall rate of inflation.

    (4) **Outlet substitution bias.** As prices increase, there is a tendency for more people to shop at discount stores, and in recent years, online shopping has allowed consumers to search for lower prices for many products.

d. Other commonly reported measures of inflation include the **producer price index (PPI)** that measures the rate of increase in wholesale prices and the **GDP deflator** that measures the price changes for all goods and serviced included in GDP. It is used when calculating real GDP.

5221.03   Types of Inflation

    a. **Demand-pull Inflation** is caused by an excess in total spending relative to the economy's current capacity to produce goods and services. It is an excess of demand relative to output at the current price level. This is often referred to by the phrase, "too much money chasing too few goods," and will continue as long as there is excess total spending.

    b. **Cost-push Inflation** occurs when rising prices result from an increase in resource costs and thus a rise in per-unit costs of production. Rising per-unit production costs squeeze profits and reduce a firm's willingness and ability to produce goods and services. Examples of factors that might cause cost-push inflation include negotiated increases in wage rates, and supply shocks such as the rapid rise in energy prices during the 1970s and early 1980s as OPEC reduced production. Each of these factors increased the cost of producing and transporting most products, and created a period of rapid cost-push inflation. This type of inflation tends to be self-limiting since the rising prices will cause firms to reduce supply, and this leads to an increase in unemployment and a reduction in demand.

    c. **Hyperinflation** is an extremely rapid rate of inflation that usually has a devastating impact on real output and employment. Creditors avoid debtors to prevent being repaid with cheap money, and money eventually becomes worthless. Examples include Germany where prices increased by 322% per month from late 1922 to late 1923 culminating with a monthly price increase of 32,000% in October 1923. Argentina, Brazil, Bolivia, Nicaragua, Peru, Poland, and Zaire each had a 1000% inflation rate (an average of 22% per month) in at least one year during the 1980s or 1990s.

    d. **Deflation** is a sustained decline in the general price level. Creditors gain at the expense of debtors. Japan has been experiencing deflation on an irregular basis for more than 20 years.

5221.04   Impact of Inflation

    a. **Redistribution Effects of Inflation**—There is a difference between nominal income (the amount of income a household receives as wages, rent, interest, and profit) and the purchasing power of that income (real income). When inflation occurs, not everyone's nominal income rises at the same rate and, therefore, there will be some redistribution of purchasing power as inflation persists. The redistribution effects of inflation are highly dependent on whether or not the inflation was anticipated or unanticipated.

    b. **Illustration:** Assume that Tom's nominal income increases by 3%. If prices rise by 3%, his real income remains the same. However, if prices rise by 5%, his real income will decline by 2%. A simple formula provides an approximation of how much real income will change:

        % change in real income = % change in nominal income - % change in price level

    c. **Who Is Hurt by Inflation:** A key group that is hurt by unanticipated inflation is those individuals who receive a fixed income. They see their real income fall as prices rise. This group would include individuals who receive fixed pension payments, firms that receive fixed lease payments, workers with fixed-step raises that do not keep pace with inflation, minimum wage workers, and families living on welfare. A second group that is hurt by unanticipated inflation is savers. As prices increase, the purchasing power of accumulated savings declines. To the extent that the savings earn interest, part of the impact of inflation can be offset. The third major group hurt by unanticipated inflation are creditors. Ignoring interest payments, the same number of dollars will be repaid as are borrowed. As prices go up, the purchasing power of these dollars goes down. This fact strongly suggests that one component of nominal interest rates would be a premium designed to compensate lenders for the risk of anticipated inflation.

d. **Illustrations:** Assume that a saver has $5,000 deposited in a savings account and is earning 3% on the funds. The nominal value of the account would be $5,150 at the end of the year. If the inflation rate was 2%, the purchasing power of that $5,150 at the end of the year would be approximately $5,050; and if inflation ran at 4%, the purchasing power would be approximately $4,950.

e. **Illustration:** If the bank lent Jane $2,000 that is to be repaid in three years and inflation averages 5% above the loan interest rate during the period, a rough approximation of the purchasing power of the principle amount that is repaid would be $1,700. The bank gets repaid in "cheap dollars."

f. **Who Is Helped (or Unaffected) by Inflation:** Individuals who are fortunate enough to have flexible-income may be able to be less affected by inflation. Some payments are indexed to the CPI. For example, payments to Social Security recipients are adjusted annually for increases in the CPI. Some union contracts have cost-of-living adjustments (COLA) that provide partial protection from the impact of rising prices on the purchasing power of the income received. Property owners are often able to increase rents when inflation is high. Firms with pricing power often are often able to pass through a portion of cost increases on to consumers in the form of higher prices.

Unanticipated inflation provides a benefit to debtors. They are able to pay back the principle and fixed-rate interest with "cheaper dollars." Real income is redistributed from the bank's owners to the borrowers. Inflation during the 1980s helped fuel a rapid increase in housing prices, providing a windfall capital gain to many existing homeowners and reducing the real cost of their fixed-mortgage payments.

The federal government has approximately $6 trillion in outstanding debt. With the government operating at a deficit, the government tends to pay off maturing bonds by issuing new debt, thereby repaying the debt with dollars that had less purchasing power than the dollars originally borrowed.

g. **Anticipated Inflation:** If inflation is anticipated, some individuals and firms may be able to reduce the impact of inflation on their purchasing power. For example, lenders can add an inflation premium to the interest rates they charge, and even may begin to offer variable rate loans to shift the impact that inflation has on interest rates to the borrower. (See section **5324.05**.) Savers might chose to hold their funds in short-term instruments, reinvesting at higher rates as they mature.

h. **Impact of Inflation on Output:** The impact of inflation on the nation's level of real output depends on the type of inflation that is occurring and its severity. Cost-push inflation reduces the level of real output and also redistributes the resulting lower level of real income.

Many economists suggest that having full employment and economic growth depends on a high level of consumer spending. This spending generates profits, leads to low unemployment, and provides an incentive for firms to expand capacity. However, at some point the resulting level of aggregate expenditures might lead to demand-pull inflation.

A commonly held belief is that a low level of inflation is a small price to pay if it supports full employment and continued growth. Moderate inflation also makes it easier for a firm to adjust real wages downward if demand for their product falls. In this case, simply holding nominal wages constant would reduce the firm's real wage costs. From a public relations perspective, reducing costs in this manner would be preferable to highly visible decreases in nominal wages.

5222 Economic Measures

5222.01 Terminology

a. **Capital Consumption Allowance (Depreciation)**—The estimated amount of capital goods used up in the production of GDP through natural wear-and-tear, obsolescence and accidental destruction. The accounting concept of depreciation provides a good proxy for this measure.

b. **Coincident-Indicators**—An index of four economic variables that tend to change in tandem to the change in economic activity.

c. **Consumer Price Index (CPI)**—The price index that measures the weighted-average price of a market-basket of more than 300 goods and services.

d. **Cost of Living Adjustment (COLA)**—An automatic increase in the wages of workers or payments received by Social Security recipients to adjust for the impact of inflation. Some union contracts also contain such protection.

e. **Disposable Income (DI)**—The portion of personal income that is available to be consumed or saved.

f. **GDP Price Deflator**—A price index that measures the geometric average of price changes over hundreds of products that compose GDP. The result is known as chain-weighted real GDP.

g. **Gross Domestic Product (GDP)**—The market value of all final goods and services produced annually within a country's boundaries using either domestic or foreign supplied resources.

h. **Gross National Product (GNP)**—The market value of all final goods and services produced annually by the citizens of a country using domestic-supplied resources.

i. **Gross Private Domestic Investment**—Expenditures for newly produced capital goods such as machinery and equipment, additions to the stock of inventory on hand, and purchases of new residential housing.

j. **Indirect Business Taxes**—Taxes such as sales, excise, and property taxes as well as taxes that are part of a firm's cost of producing a product. Firms attempt to pass these taxes on to the consumers in the form of higher prices.

k. **Intermediate Good**—An output that is used as an input to produce a final good.

l. **Inventory**—Goods produced that remain unsold. A net addition to the stock of goods on hand.

m. **Lagging-Economic Indicators**—An index of seven economic indicators that tend to follow in the same direction as the change in the level of economic activity at some point after the level of economic activity begins to change direction.

n. **Leading-Indicators**—An index of 10 economic variables that have generally provided advance signals of a change in direction of the level of economic activity.

o. **National Foreign Factor Income**—The difference between factor payments received from the foreign sector by domestic citizens and factor payments made to foreign citizens for domestic production. This provides the key difference between GDP and GNP.

p. **National Income (NI)**—The total income earned by U.S. businesses and citizens no matter where they are located or reside. It is the sum of all payments to factors of production for their contribution to the production of GDP.

q. **National Income Accounting**—A technique used to measure the overall output of the economy and other related variables for an economy in a given period of time.

r. Net National Product (NNP)—GDP minus the amount of the year's output that is required to replace that portion of the capital stock that is worn out (or used up) producing that output.

s. Net Private Domestic Investment—Gross private domestic investment less the portion of the existing fixed capital stock used up or consumed in the production of the current year's output.

t. Nominal GDP—The market value of GDP measured in terms of the prices at the time of measurement. It is not adjusted for inflation.

u. Personal Income (PI)—The amount of income individuals actually receive. It includes the earned and unearned income made available to suppliers of the factors of production prior to the payment of taxes.

v. Personal Taxes—Personal taxes include income taxes, excise taxes, real estate taxes, and taxes on personal property.

w. Price Index—An "index number" that describes the manner in which the "weighted-average" price of a market-basket of commodities has changed over time.

x. Producer Price Index (PPI)—The price index that measures the weighted-average price of a market-basket of physical inputs used in the production process.

y. Real GDP—Nominal gross domestic product adjusted for inflation. The GDP produced during a year divided by the GDP deflator for that year expressed as a decimal.

z. Real per Capita Output—An indicator that defines the real output per person in a nation. Real per capita output is defined as the real GDP of a nation, adjusted for changes in the general price level and divided by the nation's population. It is often used to measure a country's standard of living.

aa. Value Added—The dollar value added to a final good at each stage of the production process, or conversely, the value of a product sold by the firm less the value of all the resources used by the firm to produce the product.

5222.02 Economic Indicators

a. Economic Indicators are a set of variables that measure various aspects of economic activity that provide information to policy-makers as to the state of the economy. The best-known set of indices is developed by the Conference Board, a private business research group.

b. Leading-indicators are an index of 10 economic variables that have generally provided advance signals of a change in the level of economic activity. (See section **5213.02** for more detail.)

(1) Average work week for production workers

(2) S&P 500 stock index

(3) Average weekly initial unemployment insurance claims

(4) New orders for consumer goods

(5) New order for nondefense capital goods

(6) Permits for new residential construction

(7) A measure of vendor delivery performance

(8) Growth in the money supply

(9) Consumer sentiment index

(10) Interest rate spread between the 10-T bond and the Fed Funds rate

c. **Coincident-indicators** are an index of four economic variables that tend to change in tandem to the changes in economic activity.

   (1) Number of employees on nonagricultural payrolls

   (2) Personal income minus transfer payments

   (3) Industrial production index

   (4) Manufacturing and trade sales

d. **Lagging-economic indicators** are an index of seven economic indicators that tend to follow in the same direction as the change in the level of economic activity but lag and only begin to change after the level of economic activity has been changing for some period.

   (1) Average duration of unemployment (measured in weeks)

   (2) Changes in per-unit labor costs

   (3) Average prime rate

   (4) Ratio of inventories to sales

   (5) Outstanding volume of commercial and industrial loans

   (6) Ratio of consumer credit outstanding to personal income

   (7) Manufacturing and trade sales

5222.03   Gross Domestic Product

a. **Gross Domestic Product** is a measure of the market value of all final goods and services produced in an economy during a year. It is a monetary measure to value the nation's output. It excludes **intermediate goods**, which are goods that are purchased for resale or for further processing or manufacturing. This is done to prevent double counting. It also excludes non-productive transactions that have nothing to do with the production of final goods and services such as:

   (1) Public transfer payments such as Social Security, welfare, and veteran's payments.

   (2) Transfers such as inter-family gifts and immigrant remittances.

   (3) Buying and selling of stocks and bonds and other financial assets in the financial markets.

   (4) Secondhand sales.

b. The Expenditure Approach for calculating GDP can be summarized as:

$$GDP = C + I_g + G + X_n$$

   (1) Personal Consumption Expenditures (C) are the personal consumption expenditures on durable consumer goods, nondurable consumer goods, and services. Primary determinants of personal consumption are disposable income, consumer wealth, and interest rates on consumer credit. Personal consumption accounts for approximately two-thirds of GDP.

   (2) Gross Private Domestic Investment (I_g) are all final purchases of machinery and equipment, all construction, all changes in inventory, and purchases of new residential housing. This can be summarized as:

   Net Investment = Gross Investment - Capital Consumption Allowance

   Primary determinants of investment spending are interest rates, capacity utilization rates, and a firm's ability to develop projects with a positive net present value.

(3) Government Purchases (G) are the spending for goods and services used in providing government services including spending on social capital such as buildings and highways.

(4) Net Exports (X_n) is equal to exports minus imports or ($X - M$). Primary determinants for exports are similar to those for consumption, and those for exports would include similar measures for citizens of foreign nations.

c. The Income Approach for calculating GDP deals with the income derived or created to produce the output. National Income (NI) is the sum of all payments to factors of production. However, since all the expenditures noted above do not flow directly to factors of production in the form of income, it is necessary to make certain adjustments to (NI) to derive GDP. The process is as follows:

(1) National Income (NI) = Compensation of employees + rental income + interest income + proprietor's income + corporate profits

(2) GDP = NI + indirect business taxes + capital consumption allowance + net foreign factor income

d. There are several other national accounts that provide useful information concerning the economy's performance. Key among them are:

(1) Net Domestic Product (NDP) = Gross Domestic Product - Capital Consumption Allowance

(2) National Income (NI) = NDP - Net Foreign Factor Income - Indirect Business Taxes

(3) Personal Income (PI) = NI - Social Security contributions - corporate income tax - undistributed corporate profits + transfer payments

(4) Disposable Income (DI) = PI - personal taxes

5222.04 Real vs. Nominal Measures

a. **Gross Domestic Product** is the market value of final goods and services and thus is measured in current dollar or nominal terms. In simple terms, it would be measured by multiplying the quantity of goods produced by the prices of the various goods. One of the possible measures of well-being for a society is the growth in GDP. Nominal GDP growth can be the result of either an increase in the quantity of goods produced and/or an increase in the price of goods. Adjusting nominal data for price increases involves the use of a price index.

$$\text{Price Index in a Given Time Period} = \frac{\text{Price of a Market Basket in a Specific Year}}{\text{Price of the Same Market Basket in the Base Year}} \times 100$$

$$\text{Real GDP} = \frac{\text{Nominal GDP}}{\text{GDP Deflator}}$$

b. There are a number of price indices that are used in economic analysis, including the consumer price index (CPI), producer price index (PPI), and GDP deflator.

(1) The CPI is used to calculate real income, to adjust Social Security payments, and as a base for many COLA adjustments.

(2) The PPI is a measure of the increase in prices paid by producers for their inputs.

(3) The GDP deflator is an index that was developed to calculate real GDP given nominal GDP.

c. Possible shortcomings of the use of GDP as a measure of economic well-being include:

(1) It does not account for non-market transactions; for example, services of homemakers and individuals who do their own repairs.

(2) It fails to account for changing attitudes toward leisure, as reflected in the fact that the average workweek has declined as legislation increased vacation time, the number of holidays, and the amount of available leave time. It also does not account for any "psychological income" that some workers derive from their work.

(3) It does not account for improved product quality. This is dealt with by periodically revising the market basket of goods and re-indexing the base year for the index used to calculate real GDP.

(4) It does not account for activities in the underground economy. This would include illegal activities such as the sale of illicit drugs, gambling, and fencing stolen goods, as well as income legally earned, but not reported as income to the IRS.

(5) It does not account for most negative externalities, with the primary example being its failure to account for the economic and social costs of pollution.

5223 Interest Rates

5223.01 Terminology

a. Adjustable Rate Mortgage—A mortgage that has an interest rate that can change. The rate is usually connected to some index rate.

b. Annual Percentage Rate (APR)—The periodic rate compounded by the number of periods in a year.

c. Basic Interest—Interest calculated on an annual basis using the stated rate of interest.

d. Discount Rate—The rate that the Federal Reserve charges on loans it makes to member institutions. This is a relatively little used tool of monetary policy.

e. Disintermediation—The withdrawal of funds from financial intermediaries when market interest rates rise above interest rate ceilings on various deposit accounts. Disintermediation occurred during periods of high interest rates in the early 1980s prior to interest rate deregulation.

f. Effective Annual Interest Rate—The investment's annual rate of interest when compounding occurs more often than once a year.

g. Equilibrium Interest Rate—In economic terms, the interest rate at which the amount of money demanded is equal to the supply of money.

h. Expected Real Interest Rate—The rate that people expect to pay for loans or earn on savings after adjusting for expected inflation.

i. Fed Funds Rate—The interest rate that banks charge each other for the overnight loans of excess reserves held in the Federal Reserve Bank.

j. Interest Rate—The price of money that serves to ration the supply of loanable funds to projects that are expected to have the highest return (NPV).

k. Loanable Funds—Money available for lending and borrowing.

l. Money Market—The securities market dealing with short-term debt instruments that mature in less than one year. Treasury bills are the largest component of the highly liquid money market instruments.

m. Mortgage-Backed Security—An ownership claim in a pool of mortgages or an obligation that is secured by such a pool. These are securities that are issued by organizations such as Government National Mortgage Association (GNMA).

n. **Negative Amortization**—The situation that might arise if the collection of interest is on a loan is front loaded using the Rule of 78s such that the amount of interest due is greater than the amount of the payment received with the difference reducing the amount of equity or being added back to the remaining outstanding balance of the loan.

o. **Nominal Interest Rate**—The rate that is quoted on bank loans and negotiated in financial markets.

p. **Prime Rate**—Traditionally, the interest rate that banks charge to their most creditworthy customers. Changes in this rate tend to mirror changes in the Fed Funds rate.

q. **Pure Rate of Interest**—The interest paid on long-term riskless securities such as the 30-year T-bond.

r. **Real Interest Rate**—The nominal interest rate minus the current rate of inflation.

s. **Realized Compound Yield**—The yield that is received based on the rate at which interest can be reinvested. If the reinvestment rate is equal to yield to maturity, it is equal to the realized compound yield.

t. **Risk-Free Rate**—The rate that can be earned with certainty. Traditionally, this is defined as the rate on short-term T-bills.

u. **Rule of 78s**—Seventy-eight is equal to the sum of the digits from 1 to 12. For an annual installment loan, twelve-seventy eighths (12/78 or 15.4%) of the interest due on the loan would be charged to the first payment before anything was credited to principal. This concept can be applied to installment loans of any maturity by summing the digits of the number of payments. For example, a 15-year loan with monthly payments would sum the digits from 1 to 180.

v. **Simple Interest**—Interest that is not compounded. Interest is calculated only on the remaining principal balance of the loan.

w. **Theory of Loanable Funds**—A theory that states that the equilibrium interest rate at the point where the supply for loanable funds is equal to the demand in loanable funds.

x. **Usury**—Exorbitant interest.

y. **Yield to Call**—The discount rate that makes the present value of a bond's cash on the callable date equal to the call price of the bond.

z. **Yield to Maturity**—The discount rate that makes the present value of a bond's cash flow equal to its price.

5223.02 **Various Interest Rate Formulas and Their Uses**

Short-term debt is that debt that will be repaid within one year. Interest rates on short-term bank debt are calculated in a number of ways, including:

a. **Basic Interest** is calculated on an annual basis using the stated rate of interest.

Illustration: The customer takes out a $10,000 loan with a 1-year maturity and a 10 percent interest rate. The basic interest is:

Basic interest rate $= interest \div amount\ borrowed$
$= \$1,000 \div \$10,000 = 10\%$

b. Interest is discounted (**Discounted Interest**) when the amount of interest to be collected during the life of the loan is subtracted from the loan proceeds, with the customer repaying the loan principal amount.

Illustration: The customer takes out a $10,000 loan with a 1-year maturity and a 10% interest rate. The interest for the year is $1,000 and the individual receives $9,000. The effective interest rate on the loan is 11.11% ($1,000 ÷ $9,000).

The **add-on interest** method is one where interest is calculated on the full amount of the original principal. The calculated interest is added to the principal and the payment is determined by dividing the sum of principal plus interest by the number of payments to be made. The add-on interest rate can be calculated as follows using the following example:

$$(1) \text{ Approximate Add - on Annual Rate} = \text{Interest Paid} \div (\text{Amount Received} \div 2)$$
$$= \$1,000 \div (\$10,000 \div 2)$$
$$= \$1,000 \div \$5,000$$
$$= 20\%$$
$$(2) \text{ Add - on Effective Rate} = (1 + i)^n - 1$$
$$= (1 + .0167)^{12} - 1$$
$$= 1.2199 - 1$$
$$= 22\%$$

(If the approximate annual rate is 20%, then the monthly rate is 1.67% (or 20% ÷ 12)).

Simple Interest is computed on the remaining outstanding balance using the daily periodic rate times the number of days since the prior payment. (See section **5324.02** for a discussion on simple interest.)

c. Under certain situations with add-on loans where interest is paid according to the **Rule of 78s**, the monthly payment is allocated first to the payment of interest and then to principal. If the amount of interest due is greater than the amount of the payment, the difference would be added on to the loan principal and is termed **Negative Amortization**. This can commonly occur on longer term loans such as 15-year mobile home loans.

d. **Miscellaneous Considerations:**

(1) **Compound Interest** involves the paying or charging interest on interest. The most common usage relates to the effective return on deposits. Federal legislation in 1991 (Truth-in-Savings) was designed to provide consumers with information that would allow them to be able to compare the effective yield on alternative instruments.

Illustration: Assume that an individual deposits $10,000 in a 1-year certificate of deposit paying 6% interest. If interest is compounded annually, he would receive $600 in interest. If the interest were compounded semi-annually, there would be two payments received. The first payment would be $300 and the second payment would also include interest on that $300 and the consumer would receive $609. Quarterly compounding would result in interest earnings in the amount of $614, and daily compounding $618.

(2) **360-day vs. a 365-day year.** Many credit card issuers compute the daily periodic rate using a 360-day as opposed to a 365-day year, yet charge interest for 365 days. This has the result of increasing the effective annual rate on a loan.

Illustration: Assume that you have an 18% loan. With a 365-day year, the daily periodic rate would be 0.0493%, while with a 360-day year the daily periodic rate would be 0.05%.

(a) Effective interest rate using a 365-day year with a 365-day daily periodic rate:

$$((1 + 0.000493)^{365} - 1) = 19.71\%$$

(b) Effective interest rate using a 365-day year with a 360-day daily periodic rate:

$$((1 + 0.0005)^{365} - 1) = 20.02\%$$

5223.03 Why Interest Rates Differ

a. There is risk that the borrower will not repay the loan in a timely fashion. The greater the likelihood that the borrower will default on the loan, the higher the interest rates will be in order to compensate the lender for bearing that risk.

b. Interest rates tend to be higher for longer-term loans. Borrowers tend to like the certainty of a known fixed expense. Lenders are concerned about the possibility of an increase in their cost of funds over the period of the loan and charge a premium to compensate for this risk.

c. There are fixed and variable costs associated with making loans. There tend to be high administrative and processing costs associated with making loans. The costs tend to be higher per dollar loaned for smaller loans and for loans that require more frequent payments. This causes interest rates on smaller loans to be higher than on larger loans, and interest rates on short-term loans to be higher than on longer-term loans.

5223.04 Role of Interest Rates

Interest rates have a significant impact on the level and composition of investment goods purchased and the level of spending for research and development (R&D).

a. Lower interest rates encourage an increase in business investment. This would cause a firm to expand output and increase capital spending once the firm no longer has idle capacity. The reverse would be true if interest rates increase. The Federal Reserve can influence rates in an attempt to influence the level of economic activity.

b. Interest rates are the price of money and serve to ration the supply of available loanable funds to projects with the highest rate of return (NPV). The rationing is not perfect, however, because firms with market power and/or a strong financial position are able to obtain funds at lower rates, which gives them an advantage over other firms that might have more profitable projects but a relatively weak financial position.

Lower interest rates tend to make R&D expenditures more profitable. Thus, lower rates would cause firms to increase such expenditures.

5223.05 Determination of Interest Rates

The use of credit has become ubiquitous in the American economy. Individuals and households receive credit when they take out mortgage and auto loans and use credit cards. Many times it is difficult to determine the interest rate being paid on such loans. Truth-in-lending laws, which were passed in 1968, were passed to provide consumers with a method for comparing the true cost of loans.

5223.06 Methods for Quoting Rates of Return

There are a myriad of methods for computing the rate of return on a loan. Returns on loans such as mortgage loans and bonds that have regular periodic payments are quoted in terms of annual percentage rates (APR). This APR can be translated into an effective annual rate (EAR).

a. APR equals period interest rate × number of periods per year. The period interest can be defined as semi-annual, quarterly, monthly, etc. For example, if the monthly rate is 1.5%, then the APR would be 18% (1.5% × 12 months).

b. To compute the Effective Annual Rate (EAR) we would use the following formulas:

$EAR = ((1 + rate\ per\ period)^2 - 1)$, where the rate per period = APR/2, or

$APR = ((1 + EAR)^{1/n} - 1) \times n$, where n is the number of periods

(See section **5324.02** for an example.)

5223.07 Bond Prices and Yields

Since bond cash flows occur in the future, the price an investor is willing to pay for those payments depends on the value that can be received compared to the value of the dollars today. The nominal rate of return is a combination of the risk-free rate plus a premium for expected inflation. The value of a bond can be computed as follows:

Bond value = PV of the interest payments + PV of par value

And, given a particular maturity, t, and a discount rate, r, the bond value can de defined as:

$$\text{Bond Value} = \text{Coupon Payment}\left(\left(1 - \frac{1}{(1+r)^t}\right) \div r\right) + \left(\text{Par Value} \div (1+r)^t\right)$$

Illustration: Assume that there is a bond with a 6% coupon, 20-year remaining maturity with a $1,000 par value, paying 40 semiannual payments of $30 each. If the market interest is equal to the coupon rate (6%), the value of the bond can be calculated as:

$$\text{Bond Value} = \left(\$30\left(1 - \frac{1}{(1+3\%)^{40}}\right) \div 3\%\right) + \left(\$1,000 \div (1+3\%)^{40}\right)$$

$$= 693.44 + 306.56$$

$$= \$1,000$$

The interest payments represent an annuity, and the final payment is a lump-sum payment. If the market interest rate were equal to the coupon rate, the price of the bond would be equal to the par value as shown above. If, however, the market rate was 8%, the value of the bond would decrease due to the fact that the bondholder would still be getting only the $30 semiannual payments. Given these circumstances, the bond's value could be calculated as:

$$\text{Bond Value} = \left(\$30\left(1 - \frac{1}{(1+4\%)^{40}}\right) \div 4\%\right) + \left(\$1,000 \div (1+4\%)^{40}\right)$$

$$= 593.78 + 208.29$$

$$= \$802.07$$

5223.08 Usury Laws

Many states have usury laws that set a maximum rate that can be charged for a certain type of credit. The purpose of usury laws is designed to limit the cost of borrowing, presumably for low-income borrowers. However, if the ceilings fall below market rates, a shortage of loanable funds at that rate will occur:

a. Since price (the interest rate) no longer rations the funds, the banks will make loans only to more creditworthy borrowers. This would tend to exclude the very individuals that the laws purport to be designed to help.

b. Creditworthy borrowers may be able to borrow at below market interest rates.

c. The outcome of usury law may lead to funds not being allocated to where they could be most efficiently used.

5224 The Federal Reserve and the National Economy

5224.01 Terminology

a. **Deposit Expansion Multiplier (Money Multiplier)**—The multiple of excess reserves that can be created by the banking system in the form of checkable deposits and, therefore, the money supply by making loans or purchasing securities. It is equal to (1 ÷ the reserve ratio).

b. **Discount Rate**—The rate charged by the Fed on loans it makes to member institutions.

c. **Equation of Exchange (Quantity Theory of Money)**—The equation of exchange is MV = PT, where M is the supply of money, V is the velocity of money, P is the price level, and T is the physical output of final goods and services.

d. **Excess Reserves**—Any reserves held by a bank or thrift in excess of the amount of required reserves mandated by the Fed.

e. **Federal Funds Rate (Fed Funds Rate)**—The rate banks charge each other when lending excess reserves in the Fed funds market.

f. **Federal Reserve**—The central bank of the United States.

g. **Federal Open Market Committee (FOMC)**—A 12-member policy-making group at the Federal Reserve that is charged with conducting open market activities of buying and selling of government securities.

h. **Interest Rate**—The price of money expressed as an annual percentage of the amount borrowed.

i. **M1**—The most narrowly defined component of the money supply. It consists of coins and currency in the hands of the public and the checkable deposits held in commercial banks and thrift institutions.

j. **M2**—A broader definition of the money supply that is equal to M1 plus noncheckable savings deposits, small time deposits (less than $100,000), and individual money market mutual fund balances.

k. **M3**—The broadest definition of the money supply that is equal to M2 plus time deposits in excess of $100,000.

l. **Monetary Policy**—Actions by the central bank to attempt to influence the level of interest rates with the goal of moving the economy to a position of full employment, stable prices, and reasonable economic growth.

m. **Money**—Anything that is generally accepted for the exchange of goods and services; a social invention designed to facilitate trade.

n. **Nominal Interest Rate**—The market rate of interest paid (or received) on a security in the financial market. It results from the interaction of supply and demand for loanable funds.

o. **Open-Market Operations**—The buying and selling of government securities by the Federal Reserve Bank as one tool for carrying out monetary policy.

p. **Real Interest Rate**—The nominal interest rate minus the expected inflation rate.

q. **Required Reserves**—The mandated level of reserves a bank or thrift must hold as vault cash or in a reserve deposit at the Fed. It is equal to the bank's deposits times the required reserve ratio.

r. **Required Reserve Ratio**—The minimum percentage of checkable deposits mandated by the Fed that a bank or thrift must hold on deposit in a reserve account at the Fed or on their premises as vault cash.

s. **Velocity of Money**—The average number of times each dollar of the money supply is spent to purchase final goods and services in a given time period.

5224.02 **Functions of Money**

a. To serve as a *Medium of Exchange* to facilitate the exchange of goods and services and promote specialization and division of labor.

b. To act as a *Unit of Account* to serve as a common denominator to measure the relative value of goods and services and define debt obligations, taxes owed, and measure the value of economic output.

c. To serve as a *Store of Value;* this allows for the transfer of purchasing power from the present to the future and allows individuals to accumulate wealth in the form of assets that can be converted to money when the individual wishes to spend it.

d. To be used as a *Standard of Deferred Payment* that facilitates the creation of debt.

5224.03 **Components of the Money Supply**

a. **Money** is defined as anything that is readily acceptable as a medium of exchange. In the United States today, the major portion of M1 money supply consists of debt of the U.S. government and financial institutions.

(1) **M1**—The most narrowly defined component of the money supply. It consists of coins and currency in the hands of the public and the checkable deposits held in commercial banks and thrift institutions. Currency and checkable deposits held by the government, the Fed, and other financial institutions are excluded from this figure.

(2) **M2**—A broader definition of the money supply that is equal to M1 plus noncheckable savings deposits, small time deposits (less than $100,000), and individual money market mutual fund balances. It consists of near-monies and highly liquid financial assets that do not serve as a medium of exchange but are readily convertible into currency or checkable deposits.

(3) **M3**—The broadest definition of the money supply that is equal to M2 plus time deposits in excess of $100,000. This includes the most illiquid components of the money supply. While these assets can be converted to cash, they often would not be able to be disposed of quickly at their current market value.

b. Credit cards are a convenient way to make purchases, but these purchases are not included as part of the money supply since when credit cards are used, the transaction creates a short-term loan that allows the consumer to defer the payment for some period of time.

c. Debit cards are the equivalent of an "electronic check" when funds are transferred immediately from the purchaser's account to the merchant's account. Many brokerage firms offer a product to their customers that will allow the payment for the purchases (that is, a debit to their account) to be deferred with the account being debited on a particular day of each month.

5224.04 Creation of Money

To understand the manner in which the Federal Reserve can impact the level of economic activity, the process by which financial intermediaries create money needs to first be understood.

a. Financial intermediaries take in deposits and make loans.

b. The Federal Reserve requires financial intermediaries to hold reserves against their deposits. This creates a *fractional reserve system* in that only a portion of the total money supply must be held as reserve deposits.

   (1) *Reserves = Reserve deposits at the Fed and vault cash.*

   (2) *Required reserves = Required reserve ratio (r) × Checkable deposits.*

   Reserve deposits must be held on deposit with the Federal Reserve Bank or kept within the bank (known as vault cash).

c. Any reserves that the bank has that are more than their required reserves are defined as **excess reserves**.

   Excess reserves = Reserves − Required reserves

d. When a bank makes a loan, it is assumed that the borrower will spend the money, and the funds will then be deposited elsewhere in the financial system.

e. Under these assumptions, a bank can make loans only if it has excess reserves. It is also true that the "banking system" can expand loan balances if, and only if, there are excess reserves somewhere in the banking system.

f. When a bank creates a loan, it generally gives the borrower a demand deposit. Thus the bank "creates money" by creating an asset in the form of the loan and a liability (debt) in the form of a checkable deposit which is defined as part of the money supply.

5224.05 The Money Multiplier

a. Using the **money multiplier**, we can determine the degree to which the banking system can expand the money supply when new deposits or an infusion of reserves are received.

b. **Illustration:** There are the limits to money supply growth when a bank gets a new deposit. Assume that ABC Bank is loaned up; that is, has no excess reserves and receives a deposit of $100,000. Also, assume that the reserve requirement is 10% (0.10). The bank must hold $10,000 in required reserves and would have $90,000 in excess reserves ($100,000 - 10,000 = $90,000). Thus, the bank can lend up to $90,000.

c. **Illustration:** Assume that the proceeds of this new loan ($90,000) are deposited in XYZ Bank. XYZ Bank must hold $9,000 in required reserves and would have $81,000 in excess reserves, which it can lend. The maximum amount the money supply can be expanded can be determined by the following formulas:

   Money multiplier = 1 ÷ Required reserve ratio

   Potential money creation = Excess reserves × Money multiplier

   In our example, the money multiplier = 1 ÷ 0.10 = 10. Thus, since the original increase in the banking system's excess reserves increase was $90,000, as a result of the deposit the potential growth in the money supply would equal $900,000 (10 × $90,000).

d. **Illustration:** Assume that the Federal Reserve wishes to expand the money supply and purchases $10 million in government securities from Bank XYZ. These funds are deposited in Bank XYZ's reserve account.

Bank XYZ now has $10 million in excess reserves with the potential to increase loans by $10M, and if the reserve requirement is 8%, then the potential increase in the money supply for the banking system is:

$$
\begin{aligned}
\textit{Potential money creation} \quad &= \text{Excess reserves} \times \text{Money multiplier} \\
&= \$10M \times (1 \div 0.08) \\
&= \$10M \times 12.5 \\
&= \$125M
\end{aligned}
$$

5224.06   Monetary Policy Tools Available to the Fed

a. The Fed has monetary policy tools available that impact the ability of financial intermediaries to expand the money supply.

b.   Reserve Requirement

(1) All banks are required to hold a percentage of all their deposits on reserve. The amount ranges from 3% to 10%. These required reserves are legally mandated reserves and include cash held in the bank's vault and deposits held at the regional Federal Reserve banks.

(2) A bank is limited to lending their excess reserves, that is, the difference between the bank's total reserves and its required reserves.

(3) The Fed can control the money supply by changing the reserve requirement percentage. This would impact the money multiplier. For example, if the Fed were to increase the reserve ratio from 8% to 10%, the money multiplier would decline from 12.5 to 10, which would reduce the system's ability to expand the money supply from any given level of excess reserves.

(4) The Fed generally does not utilize this tool of monetary control.

c.   Discount Rate

(1) The Fed serves as the "lender of last resort" for commercial banks and thrifts, and the discount rate is the rate the Fed charges when it lends reserves to member institutions. By providing a loan, the Fed would be creating excess reserves that would allow the financial intermediaries to extend additional credit.

(2) Raising the discount rate would make borrowing money from the Fed less attractive, and it also represents a "signal" from the Fed to the banking system that they would prefer to slow the rate of growth of the money supply.

(3) The Fed generally utilizes this tool of monetary control only sparingly.

d.   Open Market Operations

(1) **Open market operations** are transactions involving buying and selling of government securities by the Fed in the open market. They purchase (or sell) the securities from (to) financial institutions and individuals. If purchased from financial institutions, the funds are deposited in the institution's reserve account at the Fed and represents both an increase in the amount of excess reserves in the banking system and the potential for a multiple expansion of the money supply. Funds purchased from individuals result in a deposit of funds into a checkable deposit that would increase the level of required reserves as well as the amount of excess reserves and thus be less expansionary than if the securities were purchased from a bank.

(2) If the Fed wishes to decrease bank reserves, they would sell securities in the open market, draining excess reserves from the system.

(3) This is the most commonly used tool of monetary policy.

5224.07 Fed Funds Market

a. With the continual movement of money through the financial system, it is very unlikely that an individual financial institution would always have an adequate level of reserves to meet their reserve requirements, even though there were excess reserves available within the banking system. As a means of facilitating the efficient allocation of excess reserves, banks lend their excess reserves among and between themselves in the Federal Funds Market.

b. The **Fed Funds Rate** is the interest rate that banks charge each other when they lend their excess reserves. This rate is determined by the interaction of supply and demand for these reserves. Thus, as the Fed moves to change the amount of reserves in the system, it is attempting to change the "Fed Funds rate." For example, an increase in the amount of excess reserves would cause the Fed Funds rate to decline.

c. When a bank borrows in the "Fed Funds market" the funds are simply transferred from one bank's account to another's on the books of the Fed. These loans are generally short-term, often only overnight to allow the borrowing institution to raise their reserve deposits to the required level.

5224.08 Impact of Monetary Policy on Economic Aggregates

a. Monetary policy is one of the key policy tools that is available to attempt to influence the real GDP and the price level. Monetary policy works through the following process:

  (1) Money Market—Nominal interest rates are determined by the interaction of the supply and demand for money in financial markets. Monetary policy can impact the supply of money and therefore nominal short-term interest rates.

  (2) Business Investment—Increasing interest rates makes business investment less attractive by increasing a firm's weighted-average cost of capital, thereby reducing the net present value of a project's future cash flows.

  (3) Equilibrium GDP—If business investment is reduced, then real GDP will decline by some multiple of the decline in investment (multiplier effect).

b. **Monetary Policy to Contain Inflation**

  (1) The Fed would have a restrictive monetary policy and sell bonds.

  (2) Excess reserves would fall, and the money supply would fall.

  (3) Interest rates would rise, and business investment would decline.

  (4) Aggregate demand would fall, and the inflation rate would decline.

c. **Monetary Policy to Deal with Unemployment**

  (1) The Fed would have an expansionary monetary policy and would buy bonds.

  (2) Excess reserves would increase, and the money supply would increase.

  (3) Interest rates would fall and business investment would increase. There is a potential problem here since it is possible firms would not have viable projects at the trough of a business cycle as a decline in the NPV of expected future cash flows might more than offset the positive effect of a lower WACC. Also, banks might have raised their credit standards and not be willing to lend to firms that have had a poor financial performance during the recession.

  (4) Aggregate demand would increase, and real GDP would climb by some multiple of the increase in investment.

5230 Market Influences on Business Strategies

5231 The Effects of Market Issues on Financial Position and Operations

5231.01 Terminology

a. **COLA**—Cost-of-living adjustments.

b. **Nominal Interest Rate**—The percentage return on a loan.

c. **Real Income**—A measure of the amount of goods and services the nominal income can buy.

d. **Real Interest Rate**—The nominal interest rate minus the expected inflation rate.

5231.02 Purchasing Power

a. Inflation hurts many people and leaves some unaffected. By its very nature, inflation has an impact on the purchasing power of a person's income. Income is measured in nominal terms (for example, you earn $30,000 per year). Real income is a measure of the amount of goods and services the nominal income can buy. **Real income** is computed by dividing nominal income by the CPI (measured in hundredths). Real income compares the purchasing power of nominal income at different points in time. Since not all individuals' nominal income rises at the same rate, inflation will redistribute real income from one group of individuals to another.

b. People on a fixed income, for example, an elderly couple receiving a fixed pension, experience a decline in purchasing power with inflation. Also, creditors will find themselves being repaid with dollars that are worth less in terms of purchasing power. Savers are hurt by inflation as the purchasing power of their savings declines.

c. Some fixed income recipients receive protection from inflation due to cost-of-living adjustments (COLA) that are built into their contracts. Social Security recipients receive a COLA adjustment each year based on the CPI for the previous year.

d. Homeowners have tended to benefit from inflation as the price of homes in many areas of the country has generally increased more rapidly than rate of inflation.

5231.03 Costs of Inflation

a. Inflation is the equivalent of a "tax" on money as its purchasing power is reduced.

b. People hold money to finance transactions or for convenience. Since cash is a non-earning asset, higher interest rates increase the opportunity cost of holding money. The result is that inflation causes people to hold less money.

c. Holding less money in the face of inflation causes what is called "shoe-leather" inconvenience of going to a financial institution more often to acquire cash.

d. These problems have been reduced. Deregulation has allowed financial institutions to pay interest on nearly all accounts, and the introduction of debit cards and the now ubiquitous ATM networks has dramatically reduced the "cost" of acquiring cash.

e. An increase in inflation expectations will cause nominal interest rates to increase. If the rate of inflation increases beyond some point, people tend to spend their money more rapidly as it tends to lose its value as a medium of exchange and a store of value. At the extreme of hyperinflation, money tends to be spent as soon as it is received.

5231.04 Inflation and Interest Rates

The **nominal interest rate** is the stated rate on a loan or a deposit. The real interest rate is calculated in terms of purchasing power and is equal to the nominal interest rate minus the expected inflation rate. One way financial institutions can protect themselves against the impact of inflation is by offering variable rate loans to borrowers. Most short-term business loans are variable in nature in that the contract rate is often tied to the prime rate. Therefore, at a minimum, the rate can be adjusted every time the loan is renewed, and at the extreme, immediately as the prime rate is changed.

5231.05 Anticipated (or Expected) Inflation

Forecasts tend to be based on recent behavior of the inflation rate and expectations concerning the money supply and GDP growth. Individuals and firms can achieve some protection if they anticipate inflation. Adding COLAs to union contracts, financial institutions offering variable rate loans to consumers on savings accounts, and financial institutions having loan interest rates that include an inflation premium or have an adjustable rate can help protect against inflation. Retirees receiving Social Security receive a COLA adjustment each year based on the change in the CPI for the previous 12 months.

5231.06 Costs of Unemployment

a. The primary economic cost of unemployment is the loss of output. The economy is not producing its potential output.

b. The burden of unemployment is unequally shared. Lower-skilled workers have higher unemployment rates than higher-skilled workers. They also tend to have longer periods of structural unemployment. Teenagers have higher unemployment rates than adults. Unemployment rates for minorities are higher than those for whites.

c. Unemployment also has non-economic costs. Extended unemployment increases the percentage of the population living in poverty, raises social tensions, and has been linked to increases in domestic violence and mental illness.

5232 Supply Chain Management

5232.01 Terminology

a. **Logistics**—That portion of the supply chain process that plans, implements, and controls the efficient, effective flow and storage of goods and services and related information from point-of-origin to point-of-consumption in order to meet customers' requirements.

b. **Metrics**—Metrics are measurements that are used to quantify results. It is a means to measure progress toward a specific goal.

c. **Supply Chain Network**—The member firms and the links between them.

d. **Supply Chain Management**—Getting the right product to the right place, in the right quantity, at the right time—at minimum cost.

5232.02   Supply Chain Management

Supply Chain Management is simply defined as getting the right product, to the right place, in the right quantity, at the right time, etc. at minimum cost. Alternative definitions of a supply chain might include:

a.   A network of autonomous or semi-autonomous business entities collectively responsible for procurement, manufacturing, and distribution activities associated with one or more families of related products.

b.   A network of facilities that produces raw materials, transforms them into intermediate goods and then final products, and delivers the products to customers through a distribution system.

c.   A network of facilities and distribution options that performs the functions of procurement of materials, the transformation of these materials into intermediate, and then final goods, and the distribution of the final goods to customers.

5232.03   Key Objectives of Supply Chain Management

a.   To improve communications at all levels of the supply chain to create an uninterrupted flow of materials and products.

b.   To reduce inventory levels while improving customer service levels.

c.   To reduce the supplier base while developing supplier relationships.

d.   To standardize parts in order to reduce inventory levels.

5232.04   Supply Chain Business Processes

a.   Successful supply chain management calls for a change from managing individual functions to integrating the activities into key supply chain processes.

b.   **Customer Relationship Management** provides a structure for how the relationships with customers will be developed and maintained. Key customers and potential target customer groups are identified as part of the firm's mission. Service agreements are developed to meet the needs of the key groups.

c.   **Customer Service Management** provides the firm's face to the customer with a key function being to administer the service agreements. Customers are provided with real-time information as to product availability and delivery and providing assistance with product applications.

d.   **Demand Management** is the process that balances the customers' requirements with the capabilities of the supply chain. Customer demand provides the greatest source of variability in inventory stocking. The goal is to synchronize supply and demand to reduce variability and to use point-of-sale data to make flows through the supply chain move efficiently.

 (1)   If lead times are assumed to be constant, then the ability to fill orders is dependent on the level in the supply chain. The levels of all three types of inventory have increasingly indirect effects on the ability to avoid stockouts.

 (2)   The trade-off is between inventories that are too large and those that are too low to prevent stockouts. This is the classic issue relating logistics and supply chain management.

e.   **Customer orders** are what set the supply chain in motion, and fulfilling them efficiently and effectively is the first key step in providing customer service.

f. In traditional manufacturing flow management, firms produced products that were made-to-stock and placed in the distribution channel based on historical forecasts. Often the wrong mix of products was produced, resulting in undesired inventory with all the typical costs. Within supply chain management, production is pulled through the plant in response to specific customer needs and requires that manufacturing processes have the flexibility to respond to market changes.

g. **Supplier Relationship Management** is the process that defines how a company will interact with its suppliers. Strategic alliances are developed with key suppliers to support manufacturing management and product development. Long-term partnerships are developed with a small core group of suppliers, thus controlling costs and assuring input quality and an adequate level of inventory.

h. If new products are essential to the success of the firm, then the firm must have a process in place that will identify existing and potential customer needs. It is also necessary to select materials and suppliers in conjunction with the supplier management process and develop the appropriate production technology to integrate into the best possible supply chain for the product/market combination.

i. **Returns Management** is in a sense reverse logistics in that it is designed to handle a reverse product flow efficiently and, at the same time, identify opportunities to reduce unwanted returns and control reusable assets.

5232.05 Metrics and Data Collection

a. Metrics provide a measure of the performance of the supply chain and form the basis for the control cycle. Determining the appropriate metrics to be developed is highly dependent upon the structure of the supply chain.

b. It is important to have metrics that can measure customer satisfaction. These could include such things as fill-rates, on-time delivery, and average time from order to delivery.

c. Metrics used to monitor the reduction of inventory levels are also important. It is estimated that for many firms 30%–40% of inventory value represents dead inventory and results in end-of-life write-offs.

d. It is important to have metrics that measure the ability of the firm to respond to environmental changes. These would include things such as flexibility to change output in response to demand changes, determining the degree of interdependence between various components of the supply chain, and determining the appropriate level of safety stock.

e. Other problem areas that might create pitfalls to successful supply chain management include:

(1) Having an inadequate information system that would preclude participating in the supply chain of potential suppliers or customers.

(2) Having an incomplete supply chain that is often missing certain key external elements for dealing with suppliers and/or customers.

5233 Supply and Demand

5233.01 Terminology

a. **Average Revenue**—Total Revenue ÷ Quantity Supplied.

b. **Change in Demand**—A change in the quantity demanded of a particular product at all prices.

c. **Change in Supply**—A change in the quantity supplied of a particular product at all prices.

d. **Change in Quantity Demanded**—A change in consumer willingness to purchase more or less of a product due to a change in price of the product with all other demand determinants remaining unchanged.

e. **Change in Quantity Supplied**—A change in producer willingness to offer more or less of a product due to a change in price of the product with all other supply determinants remaining unchanged.

f. **Complementary Goods**—Goods and services that are used in conjunction with each other. When the price of one good falls, the demand for the other good rises.

g. **Cross-Elasticity of Demand**—The ratio of the percentage change in demand for one product divided by the percentage change in price of another product. If the coefficient is positive, it indicates that the two products are substitutes for each other. If the coefficient is negative, then the two products are complementary.

h. **Demand**—A schedule showing consumer willingness and ability to purchase various alternative quantities of a product at various alternative prices at a given moment in time.

i. **Determinants of Demand**—Factors other than the price of the good that determine the quantity demanded of a product at various alternative prices. These determinants include the prices of other goods, disposable income, consumer tastes and preferences, advertising, the number of buyers, and price expectations.

j. **Determinants of Supply**—Factors other than the price of the good that determine the quantity supplied of a product at various alternative prices. These determinants include prices of other goods, resource prices, technology, taxes and subsidies, price expectations, and the number of sellers in the market.

k. **Equilibrium Price**—The price in a competitive market at which quantity supplied equals quantity demanded, and there is no surplus or shortage. It is the market-clearing price.

l. **Income Effect**—The change in demand for a product that results from a change in consumer real income that is the result of a change in the price of the product.

m. **Income Elasticity of Demand**—Measures the responsiveness of consumer purchases to a change in income. It is the ratio of the percentage change in demand for a product to a percentage change in consumer income. If the value is positive, the good is a normal good. If the value is negative, the good is an inferior good.

n. **Inferior Goods**—A good or service whose demand decreases as consumer's income increases, assuming prices remain constant.

o. **Law of Demand**—An inverse relationship between price and the quantity demanded of a product. That is, as the price falls, consumers are willing and able to purchase more of the product and *vice versa*.

p. **Law of Supply**—A direct relationship between price and the quantity supplied of a product. That is, producers are willing and able to offer more of a product as its price rises and *vice versa*.

q. **Law of Diminishing Marginal Utility**—The proposition that as an individual increases the consumption of a particular good or service, the satisfaction (or marginal utility) derived from the consumption of each additional unit of the good or service declines.

r. **Marginal Revenue**—Change in Total Revenue resulting from a one-unit change in quantity sold. Also known as incremental revenue.

s. **Normal Good**—A good or service whose demand increases as consumer's income increases, assuming prices remain constant.

t. Price Ceiling—A legally determined maximum price for a good or service. For example, some cities have imposed rent ceilings.

u. Price Elasticity of Demand—A measure of responsiveness of consumer demand to a change in the price of the product. It is the ratio of the percentage change in the price of the good to the percentage change in quantity demanded.

v. Price Floor—A legally determined floor price for a good or service. For example, the minimum wage law sets a floor for wages.

w. Rationing Function of Prices—The ability of market forces in a competitive market to eliminate shortages and surpluses via the price mechanism. Prices serve to ration goods to consumers who are willing and able to pay.

x. Revenue—Price × Quantity Sold.

y. Shortage—The amount by which quantity demanded exceeds quantity supplied at a price below the equilibrium price.

z. Substitution Effect—The change in demand for a good that is attributable to consumers substituting a product whose price has fallen due to the fact it is now relatively inexpensive compared to other goods.

aa. Substitute Goods—Goods and services that can be used in place of each other. When the price of one good falls, the demand for the other good falls.

ab. Supply—A schedule showing the producer's willingness to offer various alternative quantities of a product at various alternative prices at a given moment in time.

ac. Surplus—The amount by which quantity supplied exceeds quantity demanded at a price above the equilibrium price.

5233.02   Demand

a. Demand is the quantity of goods or services that buyers are willing and able to purchase at various alternative prices at a given moment in time.

(1) A critical point to remember is that consumers must be both "willing and able" to purchase for their desires to be included as demand.

b. Demand schedules are simply tables of information that relate price and quantity demanded. Demand curve is a graphical representation of the information found in the demand schedule.

c. It is key to understand the difference between change in quantity demanded (moving along a given demand curve) and a change in demand (where one of the demand determinants other than the price of the good changes and causes a shift to a new demand curve).

d. The **Law of Demand** states that there is an inverse relationship between price and quantity demanded.

e. Firms try to forecast the demand for their products by:

(1) Using surveys, focus groups and test marketing.

(2) Using information systems and inventory control systems to monitor consumer buying patterns.

5233.03   Change in Demand

    a. A change in quantity demanded relates to movement along a given demand curve when all demand determinants other than the price of the good are held constant. The movement from Point A to Point B on the curve below represents a change in quantity demanded.

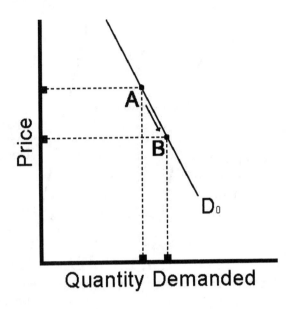

    b. A change in demand is caused by a change in one of the demand determinants other than the price of the good. Examples of demand determinants are:

        (1) The price of other goods.

        (2) Disposable income.

        (3) Consumer tastes and preferences.

        (4) The number of buyers in the market for the product.

        (5) Future price expectations.

        (6) Advertising.

c. A change in demand is a shift in the demand curve. For example, assume that if consumer disposable income increases and the product is a normal good. The demand for the product would increase from D_0 to D_1.

D_1 represents an increase in demand, and D_2 represents a decrease in demand.

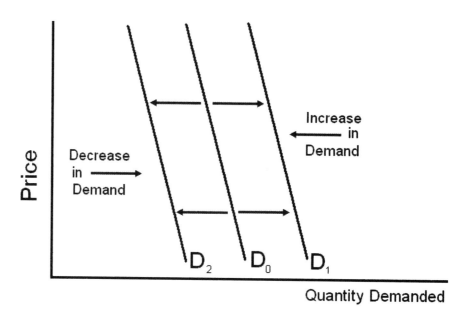

5233.04   Supply

a. **Supply** is the quantity that producers are willing and able to offer for sale at various alternative prices at a given moment in time.

b. Supply schedules are simply tables of information that relate price and quantity supplied. The supply curve is nothing more than the graphical representation of the information found in the supply schedule.

5233.05   **Change in Supply**

a. A change in quantity supplied relates to a movement along a given supply curve when all supply determinants other than the price of the good are held constant. The movement from point A to point B on the supply curve would represent a change in quantity supplied.

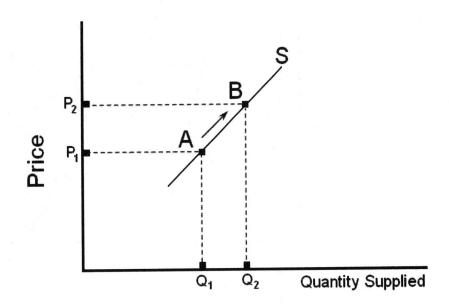

b. A change in supply is caused by a change in one of the supply determinants other than the price of the good. Examples of supply determinants are:

(1) The price of the resources needed to produce the product.

(2) Technology.

(3) Taxes and subsidies.

(4) Prices of other goods.

(5) Future price expectations.

(6) The number of sellers in the market.

c. A change in the supply is a shift in the supply curve. Assume that wages increase (the price of resources). The firm would be less willing and able to offer goods for sale at all prices and supply would decrease from S_0 to S_2. Supply curve S_1 represents an increase in supply and supply curve S_2 represents a decrease in supply.

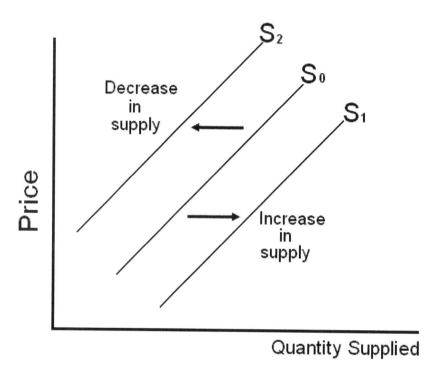

5233.06   Market Equilibrium

a. A market is the place where buyers and sellers interact.

b. The intersection point of the demand curve and supply curve represents the market equilibrium price. This is the point where the market is cleared and there is no shortage or surplus. At this point, quantity demanded equals quantity supplied.

c. A change in demand or a change in supply creates a surplus or a shortage of goods at the current equilibrium price.

d. If the market is allowed to function, there will be a tendency for a new equilibrium to be created.

(1) If there is an increase in demand, both equilibrium price and equilibrium quantity will increase.

(2) If there is an increase in supply, equilibrium quantity increases and equilibrium price falls.

(3) If there is a decrease in demand, both equilibrium quantity and equilibrium price fall.

(4) If there is a decrease in supply, equilibrium quantity falls and equilibrium price increases.

e. The market equilibrium occurs where quantity supplied equals quantity demanded. In the event there is a price floor, that is, a price above the equilibrium price, then the quantity supplied is greater than quantity demanded and there would be a surplus of the product at that price ceiling. On the other hand, at a price below the equilibrium price (a price ceiling), the quantity demanded is greater than quantity supplied and there is a shortage of the product at that price. For example, looking at the graph below, if the price were fixed at a price (P_2) that is above the equilibrium price, then there would be a surplus (equal to $s_2 - d_2$) in the market. Alternatively, if the price ceiling were set at a price (P_1) that is below the equilibrium price, then there would be a shortage ($d_1 - s_1$) in the market.

$d_1 - s_1 =$ shortage at a price below the market equilibrium price
$s_2 - d_2 =$ surplus at a price above the market equilibrium

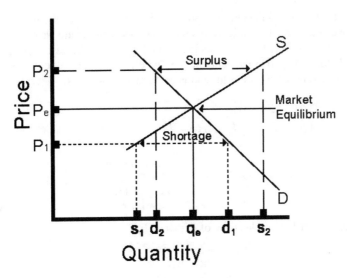

f. The table below provides a summary of the impact on equilibrium price and quantity demanded for the various situations where there are changes in **both** demand and supply at the same time.

	Change in Supply	Change in Demand	Effect on Equilibrium Price	Effect on Equilibrium Quantity
1	Increase	Decrease	Decrease	Indeterminate
2	Decrease	Increase	Increase	Indeterminate
3	Increase	Increase	Indeterminate	Increase
4	Decrease	Decrease	Indeterminate	Decrease

5233.07   **Price Elasticity of Demand**

a. The **Price Elasticity of Demand** is a measure of the responsiveness of consumers to a change in a product's price.

b. The law of demand states that there is an inverse relationship between the price and quantity demanded of a product. However, it does not provide the information about the relationship between the two variables.

c. The formula for measuring the price elasticity of demand is:

$$E_d = \frac{\%Q\Delta_d}{\%P\Delta}$$

Δ = the change in the particular variable

d. The law of demand states that price and quantity move in opposite directions. In other words, as price increases, quantity demanded falls. By convention, economists use the absolute value of the measure rather than using the minus sign when stating price elasticity of demand.

e. A problem arises depending upon which value is used as the base value when performing the calculation. The following situation could arise. If the base price is $10 and the price increases to $12, the price has increased by 20%. If the base were $12 and the price fell to $10, then the percentage change would be 16.67%. To solve this problem, the formula is modified to use a mid-point and is calculated as follows:

$$E_d = \frac{(Q_0 - Q_1) \div ((Q_0 + Q_1) \div 2)}{(P_0 - P_1) \div ((P_0 + P_1) \div 2)}$$

Q_0	=	Original Quantity
Q_1	=	New Quantity
P_0	=	Original Price
P_1	=	New Price

f. Summary of price elasticity of demand (E_d):

Condition	
Elastic	$E_d > 1$
Inelastic	$E_d < 1$
Unit elastic	$E_d = 1$
Perfectly elastic	$E_d = \infty$
Perfectly inelastic	$E_d = 0$

5233.08   Determinants of Elasticity of Demand

a. The larger the number of substitutes generally available for the product, the greater its price elasticity of demand.

(1) Narrowness of definition of the product has a significant impact on the number of substitutes that are available. For example, the demand for Hondas would be more elastic than the demand for automobiles. There are other brands that are readily substitutable for Hondas, but there are few, if any, good substitutes for automobiles for most types of individual transportation.

b. All other things being equal, the higher the price of the good relative to the consumer's income, the more elastic the demand for the product. Everything else being equal, the demand for a new automobile would be more responsive to a price change than the demand for clothing.

    c.   Generally speaking, the more the consumer considers the good to be a "luxury" rather than a "necessity," the greater the price elasticity of demand. Everything else being equal, the demand for entertainment would be more responsive to price changes than the demand for food.

    d.   Generally, the longer consumers have to respond to a price change, the more elastic the demand would be. A classic example relates to the demand for gasoline. When gasoline prices rise, in the short-run consumers have little opportunity to respond; however, if prices remain high, over the long run they can replace their automobiles and trucks with more fuel-efficient vehicles.

5233.09   **Price Elasticity and Total Revenue (The Total Revenue Rule)**

Firms are interested in being able to estimate their revenue from sales. The concept of elasticity provides one method to facilitate making such measurement. In the simplest case, revenue is defined as the price of the product times the quantity sold.

    (1)   If demand is elastic at the current price, then reducing the price will increase the total revenue and vice versa.

    (2)   If demand is inelastic at the current price, then increasing the price will increase total revenue and vice versa.

    (3)   If demand is unitarily elastic, then changing the price will have no impact on total revenue.

This set of relationships is known as the "total revenue rule" and allows a firm to determine the general impact that a price change would have on the firm's revenue if the product's elasticity of demand can be estimated.

5233.10   **Other Measures of Elasticity**

    a.   There are other measures of elasticity that could help a firm estimate the demand for their product as other demand determinants change. These measures are used to define various relationships among and between products.

    b.   **Income elasticity** of demand measures the responsiveness of consumer demand for a product relative to a change in income.

    c.   The formula for calculating income elasticity of demand is:

$$E_y = \frac{\textit{Percentage Change in Demand for the Good}}{\textit{Percentage Change in Income}}$$

    d.   When $E_y > 0$, then the product is a normal good. If E_y is < 0, then the product is an inferior good.

    e.   Summary of income elasticity of demand (E_y):

Condition	
Normal good	$E_y > 0$
Inferior good	$E_y < 0$

    f.   **Cross-elasticity of Demand** measures responsiveness of consumer demand for a product relative to the change in the price of another product. If consumers buy less of the original product, then the goods are complements.

g. The formula for calculating cross-elasticity of demand is:

$$E_{Py} = \frac{\textit{Percentage Change in the Demand for One Good}}{\textit{Percentage Change in the Price of Another Good}}$$

h. If $EP_y > 0$, then the goods are substitutes. If $EP_y < 0$, then the goods are complements. A summary of elasticity:

Condition	
Compliments	$E_{py} < 0$
Substitutes	$E_{py} > 0$
Unrelated	$E_{py} = 0$

5233.11   Other Supply and Demand Topics

a. **Complementary goods** are goods and services that are used in conjunction with each other. When the price of one good falls and the quantity demanded of that good rises, the demand for the other good rises. The cross-elasticity of demand of complementary goods is negative since as the price of product A declines, the more of product B will be purchased at any price. For example, if the price of hot dogs falls, consumers will purchase more hot dogs, and they will also purchase more hot dog buns, a complementary good.

b. **Inferior goods** are goods or services whose demand decreases as a consumer's income increases, assuming prices remain constant. The "inferiority" being described has nothing to do with the actual quality of the item but with the consumer's ability to purchase needed items. For example, when consumers have limited incomes, canned vegetables will often be purchased rather than fresh vegetables; however, as incomes rise, less canned vegetables will be purchased as the consumer substitutes fresh vegetables for the "inferior product" that was purchased only because of the consumer's limited income. Inferior goods have a negative income elasticity of demand.

c. **Normal goods** are good or services whose demand increases as consumer's income increases, assuming prices remain constant. Normal goods have a positive income elasticity of demand.

d. **Substitute goods** are goods and services that can be used in place of each other in at least some of their uses. When the price of one good falls, the quantity demanded of that good increases and the demand for the other good without a price decrease falls. If goods are perfect substitutes, the consumer is indifferent as to which product to purchase and will purchase the one with the lower price. If goods are imperfect substitutes, the purchase decision would be based on the price change of one good relative to trade-offs being made such as differences in quality between the two goods. For example, a consumer may believe a Ford truck is of better quality that a Toyota truck, but at some difference in price, some consumers would substitute the Toyota truck. A substitute good is the opposite of a complementary good.

e. **Law of diminishing marginal utility** is a proposition that describes how an individual's satisfaction (or marginal utility) derived from the consumption of each additional unit of the good or service declines as consumption of that good or service increases. For example, a guest may desire a piece of pie at the end of dinner on Thursday evening and derives a level of "satisfaction" from consuming it. The host offers the guest a second piece of pie and the "satisfaction" the guest receives from consuming that piece of pie is less than that received from consuming the first.

5234 Costs of Production

5234.01 Terminology

a. Accounting Profit—Revenue minus explicit costs.

b. Average Fixed Costs—Total fixed costs divided by quantity.

c. Average Total Costs—Total costs divided by quantity; ATC = AFC + AVC.

d. Average Variable Costs—Total variable costs divided by quantity.

e. Cost of Capital—The opportunity cost of acquiring the funds necessary to support the asset base of the firm.

f. Diseconomies of Scale—Increases in a firm's capacity and output accompanied by increases in the firm's long-run average cost of production.

g. Economic Profit—Revenue minus explicit costs minus implicit costs.

h. Economies of Scale—Increases in a firm's capacity and output accompanied by decreases in the firm's long-run average cost of production. This represents the economies achieved by mass production.

i. Explicit Costs (Accounting Costs)—The cash expenditures that a firm makes to acquire the resources owned by others necessary for production.

j. Fixed Costs—Those costs that do not vary with output and cannot be avoided in the short run.

k. Implicit Costs (Economic Costs)—The earnings that the resources provided to the firm could have received had they been used in their next best alternative use.

l. Law of Diminishing Marginal Return—States that as a firm adds additional units of a variable resource to a fixed resource, output (marginal product) will first increase at an increasing rate, then it will then increase at decreasing rate and, at some point, may become negative.

m. Long Run—The time period long enough that all factors of productions are variable.

n. Marginal Costs—The change in total costs associated with producing one more unit of output.

o. Marginal Product—The change in total output associated with adding one more unit of variable input.

p. Minimum Efficient Scale—The lowest output level at which average total costs are minimized.

q. Normal Profit—The amount necessary for the firm to be willing to keep the resources deployed in the firm.

r. Short Run—The time period so short that at least one input is fixed.

s. Total Costs—All the costs that are attributed to the production of a product or service; TC = FC + VC.

t. Variable Costs—Costs that change as the level of output changes.

5234.02 Short-Run vs. Long-Run

a. Short-Run is a time period so short that at least one input is fixed. It is usually assumed that plant and equipment is the fixed factor. A firm can change the amount of labor, material, and other factors. The time period is a function of the nature of the industry and the level and type of plant capacity they hold.

(1) The short-run for a utility wishing to construct a nuclear plant may be more than 10 years while a small retail firm can add to (or dispose of) its capacity nearly instantaneously.

The short run is also known as the "operating period" where a firm makes decisions related to determining what level of output to produce.

b. **Long-Run** is a time period where all inputs are variable. The long-run is also known as the "planning period" where the entrepreneur or the firm makes decisions such as whether to enter or exit an industry, whether to expand or contract plant capacity, or whether or not to adopt new technology. Once the firm has made the decision concerning plant capacity, they are then "operating in the short-run."

5234.03 **Law of Diminishing Marginal Returns**

The **Law of Diminishing Marginal Returns** states that as a firm adds additional units of a variable resource to a fixed resource, output (marginal product) will first increase at an increasing rate, then it will then increase at a decreasing rate, and at some point may become negative.

5234.04 **Cost of Capital**

a. The **cost of capital** is the opportunity cost of acquiring the funds necessary to support the asset base of the firm.

b. The sources of funds are:

(1) Debt—provided by borrowing from financial institutions or by issuing bonds.

(2) Equity—funds provided by the owners of the firm, either directly by the purchase of common stock, or through retaining profits earned from operations.

5234.05 **Explicit/Implicit Costs**

a. **Explicit Costs (Accounting Costs)** are cash expenditures that a firm makes to acquire the resources necessary for production that are owned by others.

b. **Implicit Costs (Economic Costs)** are the opportunity costs of using the resources provided by the owner of the firm. They represent the earnings that these resources could have received had they been used in their next best alternative use. They could include rental or lease income that is forgone if the owner of a business uses a building for the firm, the lost wages that could have been earned if an individual were employed by an outside firm, or interest that is forgone when funds that were invested elsewhere are now being used by the business.

5234.06 **Various Types of Profits**

a. **Accounting Profit** is revenue minus explicit costs.

b. **Economic Profit** is accounting profit minus implicit costs. It is the residual amount that goes to the owners of the firm. Its existence provides a strong signal to other firms to enter the industry.

c. **Normal Profit** is defined as the amount necessary for the firm to be willing to keep the resources deployed in the firm. Normal profit is also defined as the point where the firm's economic profit is equal to zero; that is, it is covering all its explicit costs and implicit costs (and the owners are making a return sufficient to cover the opportunity cost of the resources they are providing to the firm).

5234.07   Profit Maximizing Rule (MR = MC)

Marginal cost represents the change in total cost associated with producing one additional unit. **Marginal revenue** represents the change in total revenue derived from selling one more unit. If the marginal revenue from selling one more unit is greater than the marginal cost of producing the unit, it makes sense to produce and sell the unit as doing so will increase the firm's profit.

If marginal revenue is greater than marginal costs, then producing more will increase profits. However, if marginal revenue is less than marginal cost, then producing more will lower profit. Thus, profit is at a maximum when marginal revenue equals marginal cost: MR = MC.

5234.08   Shape of and Relationship Between the Various Cost Curves

a.   **Average Fixed Cost (AFC)** declines as output increases. It is defined as Fixed Costs ÷ Quantity.

b.   **Average Variable Cost (AVC)** is a U-shaped curve. It reflects the operation of the Law of Diminishing Returns. Since the marginal returns of adding variable resources initially increase, the variable costs per unit decrease. At some point, as diminishing returns require more units of the variable factor for each additional unit of output, AVC begins to rise. It is defined as Variable Costs ÷ Quantity.

c.   **Average Total Cost (ATC)** is AFC + AVC. It is also U-shaped but turns up at a slower rate than AVC since, for some number of units, AFC will decline by more than AVC increases. It is defined as Total Cost ÷ Quantity.

d.   **Marginal Cost** is the change in total costs associated with producing one more unit of output. Marginal costs are the costs that the firm can control directly; for example, the firm cannot incur them simply by choosing not to produce the last unit of output. (**Note:** Only variable costs are relevant when marginal cost is calculated.)

e.   **Illustration**: A relationship exists between MC, AVC, and ATC. The marginal cost curve always intersects the AVC and the ATC at their minimum points. For example, a basketball player has 23.4 points per game (PPG) average. When she plays an additional (marginal) game, if she scores more than 23.4 points, her (PPG) average will rise. If the marginal is greater than the average, then the average rises. If the marginal is less than the average, then the average falls. Therefore, if the average is neither rising nor falling, the marginal equals the average.

f.   Cost curves will shift if the firm is faced with increased resource costs or if the firm changes its technology.

5234.09   Economies of Scale

a.   **Economies of Scale** occur when increases in a firm's capacity and output are accompanied by decreases in the firm's long-run average cost of production. These are the economies provided by mass production.

b.   The law of diminishing returns does not exist in the long-run since all factors are variable.

c.   Primary causes for economies of scale include:

1.   Increased labor and managerial specialization.

2.   The ability to use more efficient equipment and generally larger facilities.

3.   Ability to spread costs such as R&D expenditures and advertising expenditures over larger volumes of output.

d. **Diseconomies of Scale** occur when increases in a firm's capacity and output are accompanied by increases in the firm's average cost of production in the long-run.

e. Primary causes for diseconomies of scale include:

1. Increased difficulty in efficiently controlling coordinating the firm's operations due to the expansion of management hierarchy.

2. Reduced decision-making flexibility.

3. Potential for increased worker alienation that would require increased management supervision.

f. The graph below pictures a firm's long-run average cost curve that shows the range for economies of scale and diseconomies of scale. It also shows the minimum efficient scale, which is the range of output over which the firm can achieve its minimum average cost.

SAC = Short-Term Average Costs

LRAC = Long-Run Average Costs

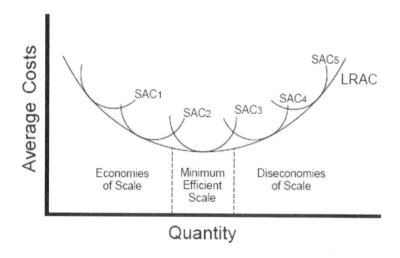

5235 Market Structure

5235.01 Terminology

a. **Consumer Surplus**—The result of a consumer being able to buy the product at the equilibrium price when that price is below what the consumer would be willing to pay for the product.

b. **Kinked-Demand Curve**—The demand curve facing a firm in a non-collusive oligopoly that is based on the assumption that competitors will not follow a price increase and will follow a price decrease.

c. **Monopolistic Competition**—The market structure characterized by many small sellers who produce differentiated products. The firm has some degree of control over product price.

d. **Non-Price Competition**—Competition that is based upon advertising and distinguishing features of a differentiated product.

e. **Oligopoly**—The market structure characterized by a few large firms that produce either a standardized or differentiated product, where entry into the industry is difficult, and where there is a great deal of interdependence between the decisions made by the firms.

f. **Perfectly Elastic Demand**—The demand for the product is perfectly responsive to a price change and suggests that the producer can sell whatever amount they wish at that price.

g. **Perfectly Elastic Demand Curve**—A curve that is horizontal at the market price.

h. **Price Discrimination**—The practice of selling a product or service at different prices to different consumers when those price differences are not justified by cost differences. It can occur when different consumers have different elasticities of demand for the product.

i. **Price War**—Successive rounds of price-cutting by firms in an attempt to maintain market share.

j. **Producer Surplus**—A situation that exists when producers are able to sell their product above the price they would have been willing to accept.

k. **Pure (Perfect) Competition**—The market structure characterized by a large number of sellers producing a standardized product with easy entry and exit into and out of the industry, and information that is free and readily available. The seller has no ability to influence the product price.

l. **Pure Monopoly**—The market structure within the industry consisting of one firm producing a unique product. The firm tends to have a significant amount of pricing power and control over the supply of the product.

5235.02 **Perfect Competition**

a. The market structure of **Perfect Competition** is characterized by a large number of sellers producing a standardized product with easy entry and exit into and out of the industry. The seller has no ability to influence the product price.

b. There are a number of assumptions involving perfect competition:

(1) There are many small independently acting buyers and sellers, none of whom can influence price.

(2) Firms produce a standardized or homogeneous product.

(3) Each firm produces such a small portion of total output that they have no influence over price. The firm is a price taker, that is, the firm must accept the market price.

(4) There is free entry into and exit from the industry. There are no significant legal, technological, or financial barriers to entry.

(5) Information is free and readily available.

(6) Firms face a **perfectly elastic** demand curve at the market price that is determined where consumer demand equals industry supply.

(7) For the perfectly competitive firm, Price = Average Revenue = Marginal Revenue.

(8) If the firm is making an economic profit, there is an incentive for new firms to enter the market. The entry of new firms will increase supply and shift the industry supply curve to the right, reducing the equilibrium price. Entry will continue until there is no economic profit, that is, the firm is earning only a normal profit.

c. The market equilibrium occurs where price equals marginal cost at the minimum point on the average cost curve. This means that in equilibrium, a firm is operating at its most efficient level of output. The following graph represents the equilibrium position in a perfectly competitive industry. Marginal revenue equals marginal cost as minimum average cost. At this point, the firm is making only a normal profit.

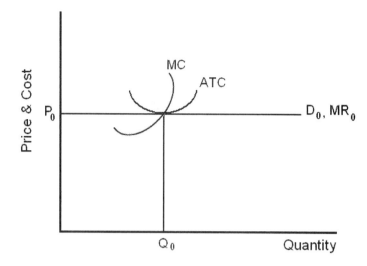

$$
\begin{array}{lcl}
P_0 & = & \text{Price} \\
Q_0 & = & \text{Quantity Demanded} \\
D_0 & = & \text{Demand} \\
MR_0 & = & \text{Marginal Revenue} \\
MC & = & \text{Marginal Cost} \\
ATC & = & \text{Average Total Cost}
\end{array}
$$

5235.03   Monopolistic Competition

a. The market structure for **Monopolistic Competition** is characterized by having many small firms that produce differentiated products. The firm has some degree of control over product price.

b. There are a number of assumptions for monopolistic competition:

(1) There are a relatively large number of independent and small buyers and sellers.

(2) There is free entry into and exit from the industry.

(3) Firms are producing a differentiated product. The differences may be found in product attributes such as materials, design and workmanship, varying degrees of customer service, convenient location, packaging, and brand image.

c. In monopolistic competition:

(1) The firm faces a downward-sloping demand curve and marginal revenue is less than price.

(2) There tends to be significant use of advertising as a form of non-price competition. The goal of advertising is to shift the firms demand curve to the right and to make demand less elastic; that is, to make consumers less responsive to price changes.

(3) Product differentiation leads to firms competing on quality, price, and marketing.

(4) Firms can make an economic profit in the short-run.

(5) The existence of economic profit provides an incentive for firms to enter the industry, shifting the industry supply curve to the right.

(6) Entry will continue until economic profit disappears.

d. Firms in markets that are imperfectly competitive face a downward sloping demand curve, which implies that marginal revenue is less than price. In the graph below, the firm would maximize price at the point where marginal revenue equals marginal cost. At the profit maximizing level of output (Q_o), the firm would change price (P_o) and make an economic profit as shown in the area $P_o ABP$.

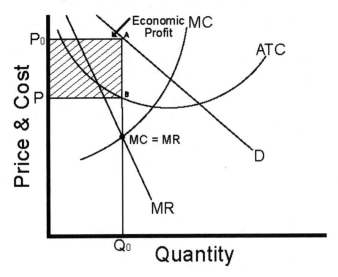

P	=	Price
Q	=	Quantity Demanded
D	=	Demand
MC	=	Marginal Cost
MR	=	Marginal Revenue
ATC	=	Average Total Cost

5235.04 Oligopoly

a. Oligopoly is a market structure characterized by a few firms that sell either a standardized or differentiated product and where entry into the industry is difficult.

b. There are a number of assumptions for an oligopoly:

(1) There are a small number of relatively large firms.

(2) Firms may produce either a standardized or differentiated product.

(3) Firms in the industry are interdependent.

(4) Firms tend to engage in non-price competition.

c. In oligopolies:

(1) Firms face a downward-sloping demand curve and have some degree of control over price.

(2) There generally are barriers to the entry for new firms into the industry, including economies of scale (that is, the firm must be large to be efficient), ownership of raw materials, patents, and brand image.

(3) Firms can benefit from collusion. A cartel is one form of collusion where producers create formal agreements specifying how much each member will produce and charge. OPEC is an example of a cartel. Such collusion is illegal in the United States.

d. A **Kinked Demand Curve** is one type of demand curve that a firm operating in an oligopoly might face. One strategic assumption is that competitors will follow a price reduction but will not follow a price increase. Under these circumstances prices would tend to remain relatively stable.

(1) A firm will not gain market share by lowering prices and thus revenue would fall.

(2) A firm would lose market share if it raises prices, and thus revenue would fall if the firm were operating on the elastic portion of its demand curve.

(3) If competitors fail to understand this logic, there is a strong possibility of a **price war** as firms engage in successive rounds of price cutting in an attempt to maintain market share.

e. If a firm in an oligopoly faces a kinked demand curve, demand is relatively more elastic in response to a price increase and more inelastic if the firm reduces price. The theory indicates that in the range of costs between points A and B on the graph, the firm would not change price or output even though marginal costs increased.

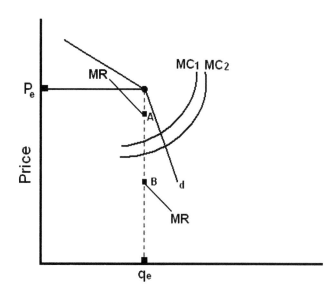

P	=	Price
q	=	Quantity
MR	=	Marginal Revenue
d	=	Demand
MC	=	Marginal Cost

f. Since firms in an oligopoly prefer to engage in non-price competition, advertising wars often occur. Product improvements and successful advertising campaigns cannot be easily replicated by the competition. Since many oligopolies have sufficient resources to finance advertising, an increase in advertising expenditures on the part of one firm may force competitors to respond or lose market share. This would be one example of a barrier to entry for competitors.

This often is akin to the inverse of a price war in that, in the end, advertising is self-canceling, and firms have increased cost without increasing revenue.

Price Leadership is another form of competition in oligopoly. It often results in an implicit agreement that coordinates prices without having the firms engage in illegal collusion. Basic tactics of leadership include the following:

(1) Infrequent price changes. The firm does not respond immediately to day-to-day fluctuations in demand. Price tends to change only when costs have increased significantly (an industry-wide wage increase or increases in energy costs).

(2) Potential impending price changes are usually "announced" by the price leader.

(3) The goal is not to maximize short-term profit but rather to discourage the entry of new firms into the industry and protect long-term profitability. The price leader often has a cost advantage over other firms in the industry and can still be profitable at a price level that smaller, higher-cost firms could not.

5235.05   Monopoly

a. In a **Monopoly**, there is a single seller of a product for which there are no close substitutes. The firm has considerable control over price and is a price maker.

b. A monopolist:

(1) has strong barriers to entry that keep competitors out of the industry. These barriers might include economies of scale, legal barriers such as patents and licenses, advertising or competitive pricing strategies, and control of existing resources.

(2) faces a downward-sloping demand curve with marginal revenue less than price.

(3) may have its monopoly position derived from government action. In this instance, the firm may go to great limits to maintain that monopoly by engaging in rent-seeking activities such as lobbying legislators.

(4) will tend to set price in the elastic range of their demand curve.

(5) tends to have less incentive to innovate and improve efficiency than firms in monopolistically competitive or oligopolistic industries.

A public utility is a common example of a regulated monopoly.

c. Natural monopolies arise when economies of scale extend beyond the market's size and total costs are minimized by having only one firm in the industry. Conditions often exist for local public utilities where competition is impractical.

(1) Often the government regulates the industry with a key form of regulation being the setting of prices that can be charged.

(2) In some instances in the United States, natural monopolies have been moved to private ownership. For example, the U.S. Postal Service has been privatized.

(3) Some regulation (for example, early regulation of the airline industry) was designed to prevent creation of a natural monopoly.

5235.06   Consumer Surplus and Producer Surplus

The demand curve and supply curve show what consumers and producers are willing and able to buy or offer for sale at various alternative prices at a given moment in time. The interaction of buyers and sellers in the marketplace determines an equilibrium price. If a consumer is able to buy the product at the equilibrium price, and that price is below what the consumer would be willing to pay for the product, a "consumer surplus" exists. The same would be true for producers who are able to sell their product above the price they would have been willing to use. This difference is known as a "producer surplus." The graph below demonstrates the degree of consumer and producer surplus at a market equilibrium.

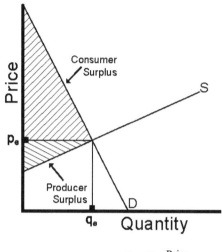

p = Price
q = Quantity
D = Demand
S = Supply

5235.07   Price Discrimination

a.   A firm can increase profits if different prices can be charged to different buyers. This would be price discrimination. Price Discrimination is the practice of selling a product or service at different prices to different consumer when those price differences are not justified by cost differences.

b.   Price discrimination is possible when:

(1) the firm is able to have some degree of control over output and price.

(2) buyers can be segregated into distinct classes that have different abilities (or willingness) to pay for the product or service often based upon different elasticities of demand. Prices are often varied for different age groups. For example, admission to entertainment facilities often varies with age, with children and senior citizens receiving discounts.

(3) purchasers from the lower-priced market would not have the ability to resell to purchasers from the higher-priced market. Examples would be airline tickets and legal or medical services. Price discrimination is widely used in the airline industry. For example, the business traveler often has an inelastic demand when the need for traveling arises. The vacationer, however, has a more elastic demand and is willing to buy advance purchase tickets to obtain lower fares.

c.   The logic of price discrimination is to attempt to segment the market and, change the price consumers would be willing to pay, and recapture a portion of the consumer surplus.

5236　Differentiation Strategies Creating a Competitive Advantage

5236.01　Terminology

   a.　Acquisition—One organization purchases another for cash, debt securities, or equity securities by purchasing the majority of the common stock of the other firm. Both companies continue to operate separately.

   b.　Best-Cost Provider—Firms that attempt to provide a product with superior quality, features, durability, service, etc. at a price below that charged by competitors.

   c.　Differentiation Strategy—A strategy that seeks to create a competitive advantage by developing a product that has unique attributes that are not offered by the competition.

   d.　Low-Cost Provider—Firms that are able to provide a standardized product to the consumer for a price less than competitors due to their lower production costs.

   e.　Merger—A business combination where one or more companies are merged into the surviving organization.

   f.　Niche Strategy—Focusing on either low-cost or differentiation in a particular market niche by doing something different than competitors.

   g.　Outsourcing—The purchasing of component parts and services from outside firms as opposed to producing the part or providing the service in-house.

   h.　Strategic Alliance—Flexible and often cost-effective arrangements where unrelated companies share technology, expertise, and business capabilities with each other. This often involves arrangements with suppliers, distributors, and makers of complementary products or providers of complementary services.

5236.02　Introduction to the Challenge of Creating Competitive Strategies

   a. The focus when developing differentiation strategies is to create a competitive advantage for the firm. This can be done through a variety of means as long as the firm is favorably positioned in the marketplace in comparison to the competition. The firm needs to create a competitive edge that successfully attracts customers by providing products that fit the needs and wants of the consumer.

   b. Companies that are successful in creating sustainable competitive advantages are likely to have above-average profits.

5236.03　The Low-Cost Provider

   a. The **Low-Cost Provider** has the ability to reduce non-value added costs better than the competition, and at least a portion of those costs savings are passed on to the consumer in the form of lower prices. Firms that successfully lower costs must examine the entire value chain looking for imaginative ways to reduce costs and to control the use of activities that drive costs. The successful low-cost provider continually looks for ways to reduce costs year-after-year in areas as diverse as the purchasing of raw materials to the delivery of the finished goods. This would be an example of continuous improvement.

   b. In a market that is extremely price sensitive, the low-cost provider is in a superior position to attract customers as well as to earn a profit.

   c. The low-cost provider strategy works best in markets where:

      (1) the products produced by all firms in the industry are essentially identical. The consumers have common uses and needs for the product, and product differentiation is minimal.

---

(2) buyers tend to be price sensitive and have the ability to shop for the best price. The use of the Internet has made comparison shopping easier for many products and has expanded the search possibilities for individuals in non-urban areas as well.

(3) consumers can easily switch from one product to another and see few differences between the various alternatives offered by different companies within the industry.

5236.04   The Best-Cost Provider

a.   The **Best-Cost Provider** attempts to provide a product with superior quality, features, durability, service, etc. at a low price. In other words, the strategy is to give consumers more value for their money. This is done by matching or beating the competition's product attributes while being able to produce the product at a lower cost.

b.   The firm that successfully competes using the best-cost provider strategy needs to be able to incorporate upscale product attributes while still aggressively controlling costs. The most successful firms using this strategy have unique proficiencies and abilities that allow them to produce high-caliber products while controlling costs at the same time. The better a firm does at successfully balancing these two important aspects of production, the more advantage it has over competitors.

5236.05   The Differentiation Strategy

a.   A **differentiation strategy** seeks to create a competitive advantage by developing a product that has unique attributes that are not offered by the competition. The firms that are the most successful using the differentiation strategy develop products that provide value to customers and cannot be easily duplicated by the competition. Generally product features that can be easily duplicated, improved upon, or replaced by a substitute do not provide sustainable differentiation. Unfortunately, any differentiation strategy that works well for a company will attract imitators.

b.   In order for a differentiation strategy to be successful, it must be tied to something that cannot be easily copied, such as core competencies, available resources, or other internal attributes that cannot be easily copied.

c.   A variation on the differentiation strategy is for a firm to make a product that requires replacement parts that are slightly different than standard parts available made by other companies. Once the product is sold, the consumer is "locked into" purchasing the specific replacement part produced by the original firm. Often these replacement parts have high mark-ups.

5236.06   The Niche Strategy

a.   A **niche strategy** can either focus on low-cost or differentiation in a particular market niche by doing something different than competitors. The firm can be small and often unable to compete in the total market, but if there is a substantial product competitive strength and unique features that are attractive to the niche members, it can still be highly successful.

b.   The niche strategy can work best if:

(1) the niche market is large enough to be profitable, if sustainable, and offers growth potential.

(2) the market leaders have little interest in the niche. This could be due to the fact that it would be difficult or costly to meet the expectations of the mainstream market as well as the expectations of the niche.

(3) few, if any, other competitors are focusing on the particular niche in question.

(4) the firm supplying the niche has developed facilities and resources particularly to service the niche market and has developed significant customer relations.

5236.07 Creating Strategic Alliances

a. As the global market becomes smaller, many firms are turning to strategic alliances in order to gain a competitive advantage in new markets. As technologies, resources, skills, and competitive capabilities become more complex, it has become more difficult for one organization to "do it all." By developing strategic alliances, companies can gain access to needed technology, business capabilities, resources, and markets that would not have been cost effective to obtain. There is often synergy in the collection of the various organizations' expertise that allows for a competitive advantage to develop that a single firm on its own would have been unable to obtain. These developing alliances in the current world market are creating competition between various sets of firms forming alliances.

b. Alliances are beneficial in gaining access to international markets. It is not unusual for alliances to include suppliers, producers, distributors, or makers of companion products. One of the difficulties in maintaining alliances is the possibility of conflicts and unresolved differences among the alliance members often relating to control of proprietary technologies.

5236.08 Mergers and Acquisitions

a. Mergers and acquisitions can also be used to create competitive advantages. By acquiring a firm in another country, a company can gain access to a new market and take advantage of the acquired organization's reputation. Needed technology or resources are often acquired through mergers and acquisitions, allowing an organization to strengthen market segments where they are weak or allowing that organization to enter new segments.

b. Either domestic or global mergers/acquisitions allow an organization to:

(1) lower risk by diversifying into additional industries.

(2) enter new markets.

(3) provide possible opportunities to more rapidly reach profitability in new areas.

(4) take advantage of economies of scale.

(5) potentially lower costs along the value chain of activities.

(6) strengthen its resource base and production capabilities.

c. Diversification often becomes the best means to expand when the firm has run out of reasonable growth opportunities in the core business.

5236.09 Other Differentiation Strategies

a. Outsourcing various activities can provide a strategic advantage, providing the outsourced activity can be performed better or more cost effectively by an outside firm.

(1) When outsourcing an activity, it is important that the firm's core competencies not be diminished.

(2) Outsourcing can provide access to greater competencies and capabilities as well as better technology. For example, many organizations are currently outsourcing human resource activities. Employment laws and requirements are complex, and often, small firms do not have the expertise to run their own human resource departments in an efficient and effective manner.

(3) Outsourcing can improve flexibility and reduce production cycles. Often a component part can be produced faster and with a higher quality by a firm that specializes in the production of that part.

(4) Outsourcing allows a firm to reduce costs, lowers labor costs in various countries, and has created an opportunity for some firms to outsource production and, therefore, jobs.

b. E-commerce technology has allowed many organizations to reach new markets in an efficient and effective manner; however, it has also allowed easier entry into a firm's current markets by new competitors. It has allowed some organizations to sell directly to the consumer. Since consumers can now quickly compare prices from a number of competitors, price competition has increased in many cases.

c. A firm can offset domestic disadvantages by using many of the strategies discussed. A global competitive advantage can be achieved by:

(1) having alliances (or mergers/acquisitions) that allow for the transfer of competitive competencies and capabilities as they relate to the world market.

(2) developing value chain activities that lower costs and/or achieve greater product differentiation.

(3) outsourcing production to take advantage of lower labor costs.

5240 Implications to Business of Dealing in Foreign Currencies, Hedging, and Exchange Rate Fluctuations

5241 Circumstances Giving Rise to Exchange Rates

5241.01 Terminology

a. **Arbitrage**—An action undertaken to capitalize on inefficiencies in financial markets.

b. **Exchange Rate**—The price of one currency expressed in terms of another currency.

c. **MNC**—Multinational corporations.

d. **Speculation**—An attempt to use what is believed to be relevant information to "outguess the market."

5241.02 General Concepts

a. **Arbitrage** is an action undertaken to capitalize on inefficiencies in financial markets. It is a response to the belief in the "law of one price" that states that a product should sell for the same price in all markets, less the cost of transfer between markets. Arbitrage involves buying in the low-priced market and reselling in the high-priced market. The increased demand in the low-priced market causes the price to increase and the increased supply in the high-priced market causes the price to decline. Arbitrage profits are available until the two prices are equal.

b. **Speculation** is an attempt to use what is believed to be relevant information to "outguess the market." Financial transactions in foreign exchange markets are very sensitive to market expectations regarding exchange rates. The decision to hold securities denominated in any particular currency is generally tied to expectations concerning the market value of the currency. If news causes expectations concerning currency values to change, it will affect the supply or demand for the particular currency, and thereby exchange rates.

5241.03   Exchange Rate Systems and Practices

    a. The exchange rate is simply the price of one currency expressed in terms of another. For example assume that the exchange rate between the dollar and the yen is expressed as $1 = 120 yen. This could also be expressed as 1 yen = $0.008333 ($1/120).

    b. Exchange rates are determined by the interaction of supply and demand for the various foreign currencies in foreign exchange markets. If the demand for a nation's currency increases, the price of the currency will appreciate. If a currency appreciates, it increases in value in terms of the other currencies. In this instance, if the yen were to appreciate, it would take fewer yen to buy a dollar. For example, as the yen appreciates, the exchange rate might fall to $1 = 110 yen. This would make Japanese exports more expensive for American consumers. If the supply of the nation's currency increases, the price of the currency will depreciate or decline in value in terms of other currencies.

    c. Exchange rate determinants include:

        (1) **Changes in consumer tastes** for the products of a particular country. If consumers wish to buy more products from a country, they will increase the demand for that country's currency.

        (2) **Relative income changes.** If, for example, disposable income rises more rapidly in Europe than in the United States, all other things being equal, Europeans will demand more American goods. The demand for dollars will increase and the supply of Euros that will be required to purchase the additional dollars will increase.

        (3) **Relative interest rates.** Suppose that real interest rates rise in the United States while they stay constant in Europe. Europeans will find the U.S. a more attractive place to make financial investments in fixed income securities and will increase the supply of Euros.

    d. Over time flexible exchange rates will adjust and eliminate balance-of-payments surpluses or deficits between two nations. Disadvantages of flexible exchange rate systems include:

        (1) A flexible exchange rate produces uncertainty in the future price of a foreign currency and reduces the amount of trade.

        (2) If a country's currency strengthens, it will need to export fewer goods and services to get a specific level of imports from another country. Thus, in this instance, it would be said that the country's terms-of-trade has improved.

5241.04   Fixed Exchange Rate System

    a. Governments determine specific boundaries within which they will allow their currency's exchange rate to fluctuate and commit to making economic policy adjustments which maintain the exchange rate within those limits. A government cannot do anything directly to stop changing patterns of the supply and demand for its currency in international financial markets.

    b. The advantage of a fixed rate system is that MNCs would be able to engage in international trade without worrying about exchange risk.

    c. A key disadvantage of the fixed exchange rate system is that a government, faced by economic pressures, will choose to alter the value of its currency. While the exchange rate does not fluctuate on a regular basis, it may be revalued or devalued by a significant amount unexpectedly.

5241.05   **Managed Float System**

Today most countries allow the value of their currency to float, but at times intervene in the market when exchange rate changes are counter to national objectives. Some nations peg their currency to the dollar and then allow their currency to fluctuate against other currencies as the dollar fluctuates. The key reasons for intervention are:

a.   to maintain the boundaries that have been defined above.

b.   to smooth exchange rates, that is to minimize volatility.

c.   to respond to temporary disturbances that cause undesired exchange rate movements.

5241.06   **Exchange Rate Determinants**

a.   Changes in demand and/or supply of the currency—As the demand for a currency increases, the exchange rate will also increase. As the supply of a currency increases, the exchange rates will decrease.

b.   Changes in consumer tastes—If consumers desire a foreign product, the demand for that product and the resulting increase in demand for the foreign currency will affect exchange rates.

c.   Relative income changes—As incomes rise, the demand for imports increases, thus having an affect on exchange rates.

d.   Relative price changes—As prices decrease for a particular foreign product relative to domestic prices, the demand for that product will increase thus having an effect on exchange rates.

e.   Relative interest rates—As interest rates increase in a given country, interest in investing in securities in that country rises. As investing activities increase, the supply and demand for those currencies are affected as well as the exchange rates.

f.   Relative inflation rates—Changes in inflation can have an effect on international trade activity. The changes in this activity will in turn influence the supply and demand for various currencies, resulting in changes in exchange rates.

g.   Government controls—Governments can influence exchange rates by imposing exchange and trade barriers, buying and selling securities in foreign exchange markets, and changing interest rates in their home country.

5242   Hedging

5242.01   **Terminology**

a.   **Covered Interest Arbitrage**—Investment in a foreign money market instrument with a simultaneous forward sale of the currency in which the security is denominated.

b.   **Currency Correlations**—The degree to which the two currencies move in relation to each other.

c.   **Currency Option Hedge**—Options provide the owner with the right, but not the obligation, to purchase a given quantity of foreign exchange at a given price at some time in the future. The buyer of the option pays a premium for the option and does not have to exercise the option if the currency does not move in a favorable direction. The buyer can participate in any gains that might result from any unexpected favorable current fluctuations.

d.   **Economic Exposure**—The degree to which a firm's present value of expected future cash flows can be impacted by unanticipated exchange rate fluctuations.

e. **Forward Hedge**—Uses a forward exchange contract that is tailor-made for the specific amount of the currency required. These contracts are generally written by commercial banks for their clients.

f. **Forward Rate**—The rate at which a bank is willing to exchange one currency for another on some specified future date.

g. **Fundamental Forecasting**—Forecasting based on the presumed relationship between exchange rates and economic variables such as money supply growth, inflation rates, and the level of economic activity between two countries.

h. **Future Hedges**—Standardized contracts used to either purchase or sell foreign currency. These contracts are purchased on an exchange, written for a fixed amount of foreign currency with specific maturity dates, and require an initial margin. These contracts also are marked-to-market daily.

i. **Hedge**—A strategy to insulate a firm from exposure to foreign exchange fluctuations.

j. **Hedging Exchange Rate Exposure**—The use of transactions to protect a firm from loss due to changes in the future exchange rates.

k. **Interest Rate Parity**—The suggestion that forward rates differ from spot rates by an amount that reflects the interest differential between the two currencies. If this were not the case, then arbitrage opportunities would exist.

l. **Market-Based Forecasting**—Forecasting starting from the premise that financial markets provide an unbiased estimate of future events.

m. **MNC**—Multinational corporations.

n. **Money Market Hedge**—A hedge using borrowing and lending in domestic and international money markets to match future cash inflows and outflows in a given currency.

o. **Option**—The right to buy (call option) or sell (put option) an asset at a specified exercise price on or before a specified expiration date.

p. **Spot Rate**—The price at which foreign currency can be purchased or sold for immediate delivery.

q. **Technical Forecasting**—Forecasting that involves anticipation of previous patterns of exchange rate movements and projects them into the future to generate a forecast.

r. **Transactions Exposure**—The degree to which the value of a firm's future cash transactions can be affected by exchange rate fluctuations. The sensitivity of the actual (or realized) domestic currency values of a firm's contractual cash flows that are denominated in foreign currencies to unexpected exchange rate changes.

s. **Translation Exposure**—The exposure of the MNC's consolidated financial statements to foreign exchange fluctuations.

5242.02   The Hedging Decision

MNCs constantly face the decision as to whether or not to hedge future payables and receivables. Often these decisions are based on the magnitude of the potential risks and the firm's forecast of future foreign exchange rates.

a.   Short-term financing decisions—firms that borrow often have access to loans denominated in several currencies. A favorable choice would be to borrow in the currency where market interest rates are low and the value of the currency is expected to weaken in value over the term of the loan.

b.   Short-term investment decisions—firms often have significant amounts of excess cash available for short periods of time and can choose to make their deposits in a variety of currencies. A favorable choice for the deposit would be in a market with high interest rates where the value of the currency is expected to strengthen during the term of the deposit.

c.   Capital budgeting decision—as an MNC assesses the viability of investing in a foreign project, it must account for the fact that the project may generate cash flows that periodically must be converted to another currency. The analysis can only be completed when the estimated cash flows are ultimately measured in the parent's local currency.

d.   Long-term financing decisions—corporations that issue bonds may wish to consider denominating the bonds in a foreign currency. Their preference would be to have the bonds denominated in a currency that would depreciate over time against the currency they are receiving from the sale. Exchange rate forecasts are needed to estimate the expected cost differential from borrowing in different currencies.

e.   Earnings assessment—when earnings are reported, subsidiary earnings are consolidated and translated into the currency of the parent's home country.

5242.03   Forecasting Techniques

The fact that firms must make decisions that can be impacted by exchange rate movements suggests that they either explicitly or implicitly make forecasts about exchange rate movements in the decision-making process. If the firm engages in explicit forecasts, the basic techniques for forecasting include:

a.   **Technical forecasting** involves the use of historical exchange rate data to predict future values. This type of forecasting is generally limited to forecasting the near future, which is often not effective for developing corporate policies. This type of forecasting is generally more relevant for speculators who are concerned with day-to-day exchange rate movements.

b.   **Fundamental forecasting** is based on the presumed relationship between exchange rates and economic variables. This forecasting methodology is subject to a series of limitations, including:

(1)   The precise timing of the relationships predicted by the regression model cannot be determined.

(2)   Some of the data for which relationships have been determined cannot be obtained in a timely manner so that it would be usable for current forecasts.

(3)   The probability of many events that have an impact cannot be readily quantified.

(4)   Regression coefficients that are obtained from the forecasting model are often not constant over time.

    c. **Market-based forecasting** starts from the premise that financial markets provide an unbiased estimate of future events, and uses either the spot rate or the forward rate.

        (1) **Illustration:** For example, if the current spot rate shows that the Japanese yen is expected to appreciate against the dollar in the very near future, this should encourage speculators to buy the yen with U.S. dollars today in anticipation of its appreciation. These purchases would tend to drive the yen's value up at once and therefore, the current value of the yen should reflect its expected value in the very near term.

        (2) The forward rate that is quoted for a specific date in the future is commonly used as a proxy for the forecasted future spot rate on that date. An example would be as follows: if speculators expect the spot rate on the Japanese yen in 60 days to be $1 = 122 yen and the 60-day forward rate is $1 = 119 yen, they might simply buy yen 60-days forward at $1 = 119 yen, and then sell them when they are received at the spot rate. If this is the common speculator strategy, then the forward purchases of yen will cause the forward rate to increase until the speculative demand runs its course. Thus, the forward rate reflects the market's expectations of the spot rate at the end of the period. To the degree that the forward rate is shown to be an unbiased estimate of the future spot rate, then corporations can monitor the forward rate as they develop their exchange rate expectations. Arbitrage activity would tend to eliminate any differential.

5242.04 **Exposure**

    a. The rationale for forecasting foreign exchange rates is to help the firm make decisions as to whether they should remain exposed to exchange rate fluctuations or if they should attempt to hedge their foreign exchange positions. Forecasting methodologies can be evaluated over time by comparing the actual values of the currencies to those predicted by the forecast over long periods of time.

    b. While exchange rates cannot be forecasted with perfect accuracy, a reasonable forecast can allow a firm to estimate its exposure to exchange rate fluctuations. To the degree that a firm discovers that it is highly exposed, it then can begin to consider approaches to reduce the exposure.

    c. **Transactions exposure** is simply defined as the degree to which the value of a firm's future cash transactions can be affected by exchange rate fluctuations. It can be measured by determining (1) the projected net amount of inflows or outflows in a particular foreign currency and then (2) the overall risk of exposure for each of the currencies.

        (1) Exposure to "net" cash flows—Forecasts of net cash flows tend to be for relatively short periods where the anticipated cash flows can be predicted with reasonable accuracy. Such predictions require a reasonably sophisticated information system to track the positions in the various currencies.

        The firm needs to project a consolidated "net" position in the currency. These positions must be converted into dollars so that the firm can measure the exposure in each currency using a standardized measure. Since the actual level of period cash flows and end-of-period exchange rates are unknown, it would be reasonable to construct a range of estimates for both cash flows and exchange rates.

        (2) The firm may not have its own method for forecasting end-of-period exchange rates, but at a minimum the firm can use historical data to measure the degree of currency variability. The standard deviation measure is a common way to define the variability of a particular currency. Currency variability can change over time, and use of this method would require periodic updating of the measure.

The key is to determine how each individual currency could affect the firm by assessing the standard deviations and correlations between the various currencies over the period of the transaction.

d. Managing Transactions Exposure

(1) The firm should identify the net transaction exposure on a currency-by-currency basis. This data would be gathered from all subsidiaries.

(2) If possible, a firm may be able to modify its pricing policy. For example, by invoicing its exports in the same currency that would be needed to pay for imports, or in its domestic currency, the exchange rate risk could be shifted to the foreign firm.

(3) To the degree that the firm cannot match the inflows and outflows with foreign currencies, hedging should be considered.

e. Currency correlations—The correlation coefficient measures the degree to which the two currencies move in relation to each other. Over the long-run, the correlations tend to be positive, which indicates that currencies tend to move in the same direction against the dollar, albeit not in the same magnitude. This information would help the firm determine the degree to which they have transaction risk among and between various currencies to which they might be exposed. For example, if the firm has exposure with the Swiss franc and the Japanese yen, and those two currencies are correlated vis-a-vis the dollar, then an expected inflow of Swiss francs can serve as a partial offset against an expected outflow of Japanese yen.

f. An alternative method to assess exposure would be the value-at-risk (VAR) measure that would combine the methods above to predict the potential maximum one-day loss for a firm that is exposed to exchange rate fluctuations. In this instance, the firm might have a policy that would trigger hedging activities if the VAR reaches a certain magnitude.

g. Economic exposure measures the degree to which a firm's present value of expected future cash flows can be impacted by exchange rate fluctuations. As an example, a firm's local sales in its home country would be expected to decrease if its home currency appreciates because the firm will face increased foreign competition as foreign substitute products will now be cheaper in terms of the local currency. At the same time, cash inflows on exports denominated in the local currency will decline due to the appreciation of the currency since foreign importers will need more of their currency to pay for their imports.

h. We must note that if a firm's local currency depreciates, it would be impacted in the opposite direction from when the currency appreciates. Local sales would be expected to increase due to reduced foreign competition, and their exports denominated in local currency will appear cheaper to importers, which will lead to increased foreign demand for their products.

On the cost side with regard to cash outflows, imported supplies denominated in the local currency will not be directly affected by exchange rate movements. However, the cost of supplies denominated in foreign currencies will rise because more of the depreciated currency will be needed to acquire the foreign currency needed to make the purchase.

i. Even firms that are not involved in foreign sale of goods or purchase of foreign supplies may be subject to economic exposure due to the impact of exchange rate movements on the price of substitute goods offered by foreign competitors in their local markets. The degree of economic exposure is likely to be much greater for MNCs. An MNC needs to assess the degree to which economic exposure exists and then make a determination as to whether or not they wish to attempt to insulate themselves against it. Economic exposure can be measured by:

(1) Sensitivity of earnings to exchange rates—This method involves classifying cash flows into specific income statement items and then making a subjective prediction about the value of these items based on an exchange rate forecast. The base forecast then can be compared with alternative exchange rate forecasts. Comparing the resulting income statements would allow the firm to assess the impact of exchange rate movements on earnings and cash flows.

(2) Sensitivity of cash flows to interest rates—This method involves using regression analysis of historic cash flows and comparable exchange rates. The following formula illustrates:

$$PCF_t = \alpha_o + a_1 e_t + \mu_t$$

PCF_t = percentage change of inflation-adjusted cash flows measures in the home country currency over period t.

e_t = percentage change in exchange rate of the currency over period t.

μ_t = random error term

α_0 = y-intercept

a_1 = slope coefficient

The regression coefficient (a_1) indicates the sensitivity of PCF_t to e_t. This method is valid if the firm expects no major adjustments to its operating structure.

j. **Translation Exposure** is the exposure of the MNC's consolidated financial statements to foreign exchange fluctuations. A subsidiary's earnings are translated into the reporting currency and, therefore, are subject to exchange rate fluctuations.

There are some questions concerning the relevance of translation exposure, with arguments in favor including:

(1) Cash flow perspective—The key consideration is the degree to which a subsidiary would remit earnings to the parent. If the earnings are retained by the subsidiary and reinvested if feasible investment opportunities exist, then the earnings would not be converted and sent to the parent. If a portion of the earnings are remitted, or expected to be remitted in the future, then it could be expected that future cash flows could be adversely affected if the foreign currency is weakening.

(2) Stock price perspective—Investors tend to use expected future earnings forecasts to derive an expected value per share. If an MNC conducts a large portion of its business in foreign countries that have changing exchange rates that are expected to negatively affect the translation of future earnings, then it is likely that the market stock price for the MNC will decline.

k. Determinants of translation exposure:

(1) Proportion of business conducted through foreign subsidiaries—The larger the percentage of the firms business conducted by foreign subsidiaries, the larger the percentage of a given financial statement item that is likely to be susceptible to translation exposure.

(2) Location of foreign subsidiaries—Since the financial statements of a subsidiary are typically measured in the subsidiary home currency, the correlation between that currency and the parent's home currency will determine the degree to which translation exposure is likely to become a problem.

(3) Accounting methods used—Many of the important rules for financial statement consolidation for U.S.-based firms are found in SFAS 52 (FASB Statement 52). Under SFAS 52, consolidated earnings are sensitive to the functional currency's weighted-average exchange rate.

l. Managing translation exposure:

As we noted earlier, translation exposure exists when the future cash transactions of a firm are impacted by exchange rate fluctuations. The problem arises when a firm knows the amount of the foreign currency it will need to complete the transaction but not the amount of domestic currency that will be required to purchase it. Once the degree of transaction exposure is measured, if the firm decides to hedge all or part of the exposure, it must then choose among the various hedging techniques that are available.

There is one possible non-hedging possibility that might be available to the firm to manage the exposure. Depending on the negotiating strength of the two parties involved in the transaction, it might be possible for the firm to invoice the transaction in the currency that will be used to pay for the import, effectively shifting the transaction exposure to the exporter.

Techniques to eliminate all or part of transaction exposure:

(1) **Future hedges**—A firm buys a currency futures contract that gives the firm the right to receive a specified amount of a specified currency for a given price on a specific date. By buying such a contract, the firm is able to lock-in the amount of the foreign currency needed to make the expected payment. These contracts are designed to hedge currency needs in the short term.

A firm could sell a futures contract if it desired to sell a specific amount of a specified currency for a stated price on a specific date. This type of hedge might be used to hedge future receivables denominated in a foreign currency.

(2) **Forward hedge**—A forward hedge is very similar to a futures hedge except that it is designed to be used by large corporations who have relatively large positions to hedge. These hedges are negotiated between the corporation and a commercial bank with the contract specifying the currency, the exchange rate, and the settlement date. These contracts may be used to either purchase or sell foreign currency with a company that needs foreign currency in the future. A company expecting to need to sell currency in the future would negotiate a contract to sell the currency forward to lock in the rate at which the currency can be sold.

(3) **Money market hedge**—This type of hedge involves the firm taking a position in domestic or foreign money markets to hedge a payables or receivables position.

(4) **Currency option hedge**—This type of hedge ideally would insulate the firm from adverse foreign exchange movements, but also allow the firm to benefit from favorable exchange rate movements if the currency does not move in the expected manner during the hedging period. This could create a situation where not hedging a position could produce a better outcome than hedging. A currency option hedge resolves this problem by allowing the firm to hedge the exchange risk, and at the same time participate in any gains that might result from unexpected currency fluctuations.

m. The above techniques could be used in the following fashions to hedge specific transaction exposures:

Hedging Technique	Hedging Receivables	Hedging Payables
Futures Hedge	A currency futures contract could be sold in the local currency in the amount of the particular receivable.	A currency futures contract could be purchased in the local currency in the amount of the particular payable.
Forward Hedge	A forward contract could be negotiated in the foreign currency to sell the amount of the receivable.	A forward contract could be negotiated in the foreign currency to purchase the amount of the payable.
Money Market Hedge	Borrow funds in the denominating currency of the receivable, convert the loan to the local currency, and invest it. When the receivables are received, the loan is then paid off with the cash inflows.	Borrow funds in the local currency of the payables, and invest the funds until they are needed to meet the payable obligation.
Currency Option Hedge	A currency put option is purchased in the local currency for the amount related to the receivables.	A currency call option is purchased in the local currency for the amount related to the payables.

5243 Transfer Pricing

5243.01 Terminology

a. Transfer price—The price charged for goods or services provided by one segment of a company to another segment of the company.

5243.02 General Approaches to Transfer Pricing

a. Special problems arise when applying the rate of return or residual income approaches to performance evaluations whenever segments of a company do business with each other. One of the difficult issues has to do with the establishment of transfer prices for intracompany sales. A **transfer price** is the price charged for goods or services by one segment of a company for those goods or services to another segment of the company (intra-company sale).

b. The determination of the transfer price can:

(1) Include a "profit,"

(2) Include only the accumulated costs to that point, or

(3) Be negotiated between the two segments.

c. The problems arise when a division sells the product or service in question to outside companies as well as the sister organization. Since the price charged by one division becomes the cost to the second division, the purchasing division would like the price to be low while the selling division would like the price to be high.

5243.03 General Approaches to Transfer Pricing

    a. Transfer prices can be set using:

        (1) variable costs only, or

        (2) full absorption costs.

    b. Transfer prices can equal current market prices.

    c. Transfer prices can be set at a negotiated market price agreeable to both business segments. The negotiated price could be less than, equal to, or more than the current market price. Many times when a negotiated price is used, the selling segment does not have an outside market for the particular product or service.

5243.04 Transfer Prices at Cost

    a. When transfer prices are set at cost, there will be no profits for the selling division for the sale.

    b. When cost-based transfer prices are used, dysfunctional decisions can result since there are no built-in mechanisms for telling the manager when it is in the best interest of the organization for transfers to be made between divisions. As a result, profits for the company as a whole may be adversely affected if the savings to one segment is less than losses to the other.

    c. **Illustration:** XYZ Company has two divisions—Relay and Motor. The Motor division needs 50,000 relays a year and could purchase them from the Relay division. The following information is available:

Relay Division:

(1) Sells relays to the outside for $20 each.

(2) Has $12 of variable costs per relay.

(3) Has the capacity to produce 50,000 relays a year.

(4) Could produce relays for the Motor division for $10 of variable costs per relay since there would be no selling or marketing expenses.

(5) There is only capacity to produce 50,000 relays a year, so production can either be sold to the outside or internally, but not both.

Motor Division:

(1) Needs 50,000 relays a year.

(2) Can purchase relays from the outside for $15 each.

(3) Adds $25 of additional variable costs to each motor.

(4) Sells the motors for $60 each.

(5) Has variable costs of $40 per relay.

	Relay Division	Motor Division	Total
Sales ($20, $60)	$1,000,000	$3,000,000	$4,000,000
Less variable ($12, $40)	600,000	2,000,000	2,600,000
Contribution Margin	$400,000	$1,000,000	$1,400,000

If the Motor division purchases the relays from the Relay division for $12 each (the Relay division's variable costs), the contribution margins of the divisions and the total organization will be changed to:

Sale of 50,000 units	Relay Division	Motor Division	Total
Sales ($12, $60)	$600,000	$3,000,000	$3,600,000
Less Variable ($12, $35)	600,000	1,750,000	2,350,000
Contribution Margin	$ -0-	$1,250,000	$1,250,000
Decrease in Contribution Margin			$ 150,000

This situation, however, would potentially be different if the Relay division had excess capacity, and the sales to the Motor division at $12 each would not have an adverse effect on the outside sales. (See section **5243.06** for a discussion of setting transfer prices when the selling division has idle capacity.)

d. Another problem with the above illustration is that the only division to show a profit is the one that makes the final sale to an outside party. Thus, there is little incentive for the first division to control costs since all of the costs are simply passed on to another division. Unless costs are subject to some type of competitive pressure at transfer points, waste and inefficiency almost invariably develops.

e. Despite the shortcoming of setting transfer prices at cost, this method is frequently used. It is easy to understand and highly convenient to use. If, however, transfer prices are based upon costs, standard costs should be used. This will avoid passing on inefficiencies from one division to another.

f. Transfer prices at cost frequently use a cost that includes at least some level of fixed costs. However, there are numerous variations of the definition of fixed costs:

(1) Only selling division fixed costs.

(2) Only manufacturing fixed costs for the selling division.

(3) Selling division's fixed costs and corporate costs allocated to the selling division.

Obviously, there would need to be an annual allocation rate for the fixed costs in question applied to the units transferred from one division to another if some level of defined fixed costs were to be included in the transfer price.

5243.05 **Developing a Formula for Negotiated Transfer Prices**

a. One method for developing transfer prices between divisions is to set the transfer price equal to the variable costs of the goods being transferred plus the contribution margin per unit that is lost to the selling division as a result of giving up the outside sales. The transfer price computed by this formula is a price based on competitive market conditions.

b. An important point to consider is that the price set by the transfer price formula represents the lower limit for the transfer price. In other words, the selling division must be at least as well off as if it only sold to outside customers.

c. Whenever the selling division must give up outside sales in order to sell internally, it has an opportunity cost that must be considered in setting the transfer price. The opportunity cost is the contribution margin that will be lost as a result of giving up outside sales. Unless the transfer price can be set high enough to cover this opportunity cost along with the variable costs associated with the sale, then no transfers should be made.

d. Illustration: The pump division needs 20,000 special valves per year, requiring an unusual production process. The variable costs to manufacture the valve in the valve division would be $20 per unit. To produce the special valve that requires a complicated production process, the valve department would have to give up the production of 50,000 normal valves per year sold to the outside that would provide a contribution margin of $14 per unit. What would be the lowest price that the valve division would be willing to sell the special valve to the pump division?

Solution: The contribution margin that would be lost would be $700,000 (50,000 valves × $14 per unit). Spreading the lost contribution margin over the 20,000 special valves, it can be determined that the lost contribution would be $35 per unit ($700,000 lost contribution margin ÷ 20,000 special valves).

Using the transfer pricing formula:

$$\textit{Transfer Price} = \textit{Variable costs per unit} + \textit{Lost contribution margin}$$
$$= \$20 + \$35$$
$$= \$55 \textit{ per unit}$$

The valve division would be indifferent to selling the special valve to the pump division and selling the other normal valves to the outside if it received a minimum of $55 per unit. Providing that the pump division cannot purchase the special valve for less that $55 on the outside, it should accept the $55 per unit price.

5243.06 Production for Internal Transfer by a Division with Idle Capacity

a. When idle capacity exists, the selling division's opportunity cost may be zero. Depending upon what alternative uses this division might have for its idle capacity it may be advantageous to sell to the purchasing division.

b. Under the idle capacity condition, as long as the selling division can receive a price greater than its variable costs, it will be better off—at least in the short run. As long as the purchasing division can purchase the product for less from the sister division than the current purchase price from the outside, it will be better off and, thus, the corporation as a whole will benefit.

Illustration: Returning to our original illustration, the Motor division (purchasing division) can purchase from the outside for $15. If the Relay division (selling division) has enough idle capacity to meet the purchasing division's needs and there are no additional outside sales prospects at the current $20 per unit, then the organization will benefit from the transfer. Using the transfer price formula:

Transfer price = Variable costs per unit + Lost contribution margin per unit

It can be determined that the minimum transfer price should be $12, the variable costs to produce the relays, since there is no lost contribution margin for sales that would not otherwise have occurred. The organization as a whole will benefit if the transfer price is set anywhere within the range of $12 and $15. If the Relay division (selling division) refuses to sell to the Motor division (purchasing division), the company as a whole will lose up to $3 of contribution margin on each unit. This can be summarized as follows:

Sale of 100,000 units (50,000 to the outside and 50,000 to the Motor Division)	Relay Division	Motor Division	Total
Original Sales ($20, $60)	$1,000,000	$3,000,000	$4,000,000
Additional internal sales	500,000	-0-	500,000
Total Sales	1,500,000	3,000,000	4,500,000
Less outside sales variable costs ($12)	(600,000)		(600,000)
Less variable costs for internal sales ($10, $35)	(500,000)	(1,750,000)	(2,250,000)
Contribution Margin	$400,000	$1,250,000	$1,650,000
Original Contribution Margin			$1,400,000
Increase in Contribution Margin			$250,000

5243.07   International Issues and Transfer Pricing

a.   Many multinational corporations (MNCs) have international sales among the components of the organization. That means that transfer prices must be set between divisions and/or subsidiaries that reside in different countries. The MNCs have the same basic transfer pricing issues just discussed; however, there is an additional issue of taxes. Not all governments have identical tax rates; therefore, it is in the best interest of an MNC to use transfer pricing to shift the profit to subsidiaries in countries with lower tax rates when possible.

b.   The flexibility to shift profit through the use of transfer pricing may be limited due to the fact that some host governments restrict such transfers when the intent is to avoid taxes. In other words, sales/purchases between subsidiaries of a firm are expected to use the principle of an arm's-length transaction when setting prices. There is still, however, a bit of flexibility in setting transfer prices without violating laws or regulations. Even though there is a limited range for setting transfer prices, subsidiaries often can shift costs for technology, research and development, etc. to subsidiaries in countries with high tax rates.

c.   Currently, the U.S. tax code requires that transfer prices are "arm's-length transactions." On March 12, 2003, the Pacific Association of Tax Administrators (PATA) reached an agreement for a final Transfer Pricing Documentation Package. The result is the PATA members have agreed to certain principles that allow taxpayers to prepare one set of documentation to meet the transfer pricing documentation provisions of each country. If a taxpayer complies with the provisions under the agreement, the taxpayer is shielded from transfer documentation penalties that might otherwise apply in each of the four jurisdictions (Australia, Canada, Japan, and the United States). The IRS extended the tax code to include transfer pricing of services as well as products in 2004.

d. **Illustration:** Two subsidiaries located in different counties transfer products. Subsidiary A supplies materials to subsidiary B. Subsidiary B has a higher tax rate (50%) than Subsidiary A (30%). Subsidiary A is currently charging $200,000 to Subsidiary B for a component part.

	Subsidiary A	Subsidiary B	Total
Sales	$200,000	$400,000	$600,000
COGS	100,000	200,000	300,000
Gross Profit	100,000	200,000	300,000
Operating Expenses	40,000	150,000	190,000
Earnings before taxes	60,000	50,000	110,000
Income Tax (50%, 30%)	30,000	15,000	45,000
Net Income	$30,000	$35,000	$65,000

If the transfer price is changed to favor Subsidiary B (only charging $150,000 for the component part), the total net income will increase due to the fact that Subsidiary B has a lower tax rate.

	Subsidiary A	Subsidiary B	Total
Sales	$150,000	$400,000	$550,000
COGS	100,000	150,000	250,000
Gross Profit	50,000	250,000	300,000
Operating Expenses	40,000	150,000	190,000
Earnings before taxes	10,000	100,000	110,000
Income Tax (50%, 30%)	5,000	30,000	35,000
Net Income	$5,000	$70,000	$75,000
Increase in Total Net Income			$10,000

5310 Financial Management

5311 Capital Budgeting Tools

5311.01 Terminology

a. Accounting Rate of Return—A project's annual accounting operating income divided by the initial investment required (or average investment). This is also known as the simple rate of return.

b. Annuity—Cash flow of a constant sum of money at equal intervals of time for a specified period.

c. Annuity Due (Annuity in Advance)—An annuity in which cash flows occur at the beginning of all periods.

d. Annuity in Arrears (Regular Annuity)—An annuity in which cash flows occur at the end of all periods.

e. Benefit-Cost Ratio—Also known as the profitability index.

f. Breakeven Point—The level of sales at which costs equal revenues (a special case of CVP analysis). Costs can be defined as including or not including financial costs.

g. **Capital Budget**—An outline for planned expenditures for fixed assets.

h. **Capital Budgeting**—Analysis of investment decisions, usually for plant or equipment, to determine whether a project should be included in the firm's capital budget.

i. **Cost of Capital**—The rate that a company must pay to obtain funds from creditors and stockholders.

j. **Cost-Volume-Profit Analysis (CVP)**—The analysis of the effects of changes in sales volume on revenue, costs, and income.

k. **Discount Rate**—The rate of return used when determining the present value of a future cash flow.

l. **Discounted Payback Period**—The length of time required to recover the initial cash investment using the accumulated sum of the annual discounted cash flows.

m. **Discounting**—The practice of determining the net present value of a single payment or series of payments to be received in the future.

n. **Hurdle Rate**—A company-determined minimum accepted rate of return that is used to discount future cash flows using the NPV method and the rate that is compared to using the IRR method. A high rate is used when there is a higher risk.

o. **Internal Rate of Return (IRR)**—The discount rate at which the net present value of the investment equals zero. Also called the Time-Adjusted Rate of Return. It measures the rate of return on a project and assumes that all cash flows can be reinvested at the IRR.

p. **Margin of Safety**—The excess sales over the breakeven sales point.

q. **Net Present Value (NPV)**—The difference between the present value of the inflows and outflows for an investment project.

r. **Opportunity Cost**—The return available from alternative choices that are rejected. The maximum contribution that is foregone by using limited resources in a particular manner.

s. **Payback Period**—Period of time required to recover the initial investment without considering the time value of money.

t. **Profitability Index (Excess Present Value Index)**—The present value of the cash flows divided by the project's initial cost (or average cost). If the profitability index is greater than one, then a project's NPV is positive.

u. **Project Profitability Index**—A method used to compare the NPVs of projects with different initial investments.

v. **Required Rate of Return**—The minimum rate of return acceptable compared to returns available on other investments.

w. **Simple Rate of Return**—A project's annual accounting operating income divided by the initial investment required (or average investment). This is also known as the accounting rate of return.

x. **Sunk Cost**—A cost that has already occurred and is not affected by a capital budgeting decision.

y. **Time-Adjusted Rate of Return**—The interest rate that equates the present value of the cash inflows and outflows. Also called the Internal Rate of Return.

5311.02   Capital Budgeting Basics

   a.   **Capital Budgeting** is the analysis of investment decisions that have a useful life longer than one year. Management uses capital budgeting to allocate resources to investment opportunities in an attempt to obtain the maximum value for the firm. Investment decisions are project oriented. Poor capital budgeting decisions can often be difficult to reverse. Questions such as the following are addressed:

   (1)   Should machinery be replaced by more expensive but more efficient models?

   (2)   Should a new product or market be added?

   (3)   Should existing debt be extinguished or refinanced?

   (4)   How can a constrained resource best be used?

   b.   The relevant data in capital budgeting is cash-flow oriented. Regardless of the approach used, the following items are essential:

   (1)   Initial investment

   (2)   Future net cash inflows or net savings in cash outflows

   c.   Data for capital budgeting is relevant only if it affects the cash flows. Some data accumulated for financial reporting is either not useful or must be adjusted to be useful for capital budgeting purposes. Financial accounting is primarily concerned with computing periodic earnings using the accrual basis of accounting for the firm or a reportable segment of the firm. Accrual accounting is not relevant in capital budgeting. The decision is project oriented, and relevant data includes the expected cash flows associated with that project. Items such as the depreciation expense are sunk costs as they relate to capital decisions, and only become relevant as they relate to tax consequences.

   d.   Because capital budgeting is long-term oriented, the time value of money is very important. Some approaches to capital budgeting account for the time value of money and some do not. Those that account for it are considered preferable because of the difference between a $1 investment today and a $1 return sometime in the future. Inflation that persists and the opportunity cost of having money sit idle make present and future earnings unequal. Present-value techniques are useful in adjusting dollar amounts received or paid at different points in time to a common point in time. A brief review of the time value of money is provided in section **5311.03**.

   e.   There are several techniques for capital budgeting. These approaches are often used, first to screen project possibilities, and second to rank existing choices. Those commonly used techniques include:

   (1)   Payback Method (see section **5311.04**)

   (2)   Discounted Payback (see section **5311.05**)

   (3)   Accounting Rate of Return (see section **5311.06**)

   (4)   Net Present Value (see section **5311.07**)

   (5)   Internal Rate of Return (see sections **5311.08** and **5311.09**)

   (6)   Profitability Index (see section **5311.10**)

   (7)   CVP Analysis/Margin of Safety (see section **5311.11**)

5311.03   Time Value of Money

a. Cash received at different points in time is not comparable because of the time value of money. Money held today has a greater value than money that will be received tomorrow. The time value of money is determined by the price of the money (interest) and the length of the time period. Present value or future value computations are made to adjust for time and interest so that all cash flows are set at a common point in time. There are two basic questions involving the time value of money computations. First, what is the future value (value at some specified point in the future) of a sum of money to be received today? Second, what is the present value (value today) of a sum of money received in the future? These questions can be answered for a single, lump-sum cash flow or a series of cash flows. A series of equal cash flows is called an annuity.

b. **Future value of a $1 sum.** A sum of money (P) invested today at a given interest rate (i) will increase in value over time (n). The future value (F) of that sum can be computed as:

$$F = P(1+i)^n$$

Factors have been computed for various combination of i and n where the interest factor is specified as $f_{in} = (1 + i)^n$ and are contained in future value tables. A portion of a future value table is shown below.

Period	8%	10%	12%
1	1.0800	1.1000	1.1200
2	1.1664	1.2100	1.2544
3	1.2597	1.3310	1.4049
4	1.3605	1.4641	1.5735
5	1.4693	1.6105	1.7623

When using the factors from the table, the equation $F = P(f_{in})$ is used.

Illustration: How much will $10,000 be worth in four years if the interest rate is 10%?

Formula solution: F = P (1 + i)n
                           = $10,000 (1 + .10)^4
                           = $14,641
Table solution: F = P(f_{in}) when i = 10% and n = 4
                           = $10,000 (1.4641)
                           = $14,641

c. **Present value of a $1 sum:** The method for computing the present value or discounted value of a $1 sum is just the opposite of future value. The question is, what amount (P) must be invested today at a given interest rate (i) to be worth a specified amount (F) in a given number of years (n)? The present value equation can be solved for P to obtain the following:

$$P = F\left(\frac{1}{(1+i)^n}\right)$$

Where the PV factor for a sum received in the future is specified as:

$$P_{in} = \frac{1}{(1+i)^n}$$

The present value tables contain various combinations of i and n. Note that P_{in} is the reciprocal of f_{in}. A portion of the PV tables are shown below.

Period	8%	10%	12%
1	0.9259	0.9091	0.8929
2	0.8573	0.8264	0.7972
3	0.7938	0.7513	0.7118
4	0.7350	0.6830	0.6355
5	0.6806	0.6209	0.5674

Illustration: An investment will pay $15,000 in four years. What is the present value of the payout if the interest rate is 10%? In other words, what amount of money would have to be invested today to pay $15,000 in four years?

Formula Solution:

$$P = F \times \left(\frac{1}{(1+i)^n} \right)$$

$$= \$15,000 \times \left(\frac{1}{1.10^4} \right)$$

$$= \$15,000 \times (0.6830)$$

$$= \$10,245$$

Table Solution

$P = F(P_{in})$ where i = 10% and n = 4

$= \$15,000(0.6830)$

d. **Annuity:** An **ordinary annuity** (annuity in arrears) is a series of equal cash flows received at the end of equal intervals of time. An annuity due (annuity in advance) is a series of equal cash flows received at the beginning of equal intervals of time. The difference between these two cash flows is that no interest is computed on the last payment of an annuity in arrears. When dealing with future value/present value tables, care must be taken that the correct annuity table is used.

An example of an annuity in arrears (regular, ordinary, or deferred annuity) with 3 annual payments of $1,000 each would be:

Time Period	Payment
0	0
1	$1,000
2	$1,000
3	$1,000

An example of an annuity due (annuity in advance) with 3 annual payments of $1,000 each would be:

Time Period	Payment
0	$1,000
1	$1,000
2	$1,000
3	0

e. **Future Value of an ordinary annuity:** The future value of an ordinary annuity represents equal annual payments received at the end of the period that are accumulated and earn interest. In other words, what will be the value of a series of payments that are compounded at a given rate of interest at a point in the future? There will be no interest earned until the first payment is made, and no interest will be earned on the last payment. (FVA = future value of an annuity, PMT = the payment)

$$FVA = PMT\left(\frac{(1+i)^n - 1}{i}\right)$$

As with future value and present value of a $1 sum, there are tables available to speed the calculation of the future value of an annuity. A portion is shown below:

Period	8%	10%	12%
1	1.0000	1.0000	1.0000
2	2.0800	2.1000	2.1200
3	3.2464	3.3100	3.3744
4	4.5061	4.6410	4.7793
5	5.8666	6.1051	6.3528

Illustration: What is the future value of a 3-year, ordinary $1,000 annuity when money is worth 10%?

Formula Solution:

$$FVA = PMT\left(\frac{(1+i)^n - 1}{i}\right)$$

$$= \$1,000\left(\frac{(1+.10)^3 - 1}{.10}\right)$$

$$= \$1,000(3.3100)$$

$$= \$3,310$$

Table Solution:

FVA = PMT(FVIFA$_{in}$) where i = 10% and n = 3

$$= \$1,000(3.3100)$$

$$= \$3,310$$

The future value of an annuity due has a similar formula to the one above. Remember, an annuity due has the cash flow occurring at the beginning of the period.

$$FVA_{due} = PMT\left(\frac{(1+i)^n - 1}{i}\right)(1+i)$$

There are also annuities due tables available in order to make calculations easy.

f. **Present Value of an Annuity:** The present value of an annuity is the value today of a future series of payments discounted at a particular interest rate. The present value of an annuity can be computed by restating each of the annuity amounts to the present time period using the present value of an annuity formula or the factor from a table of present values of an annuity of $1. Remember to be careful to determine whether an annuity in arrears (ordinary annuity) or an annuity in advance (annuity due) is appropriate.

The formula for the present value of an ordinary annuity is:

$$PVA_n = PMT\left(\frac{1-(1+i)^{-n}}{i}\right)$$

There are tables available to speed the calculation of the present value of an annuity. A portion for an annuity due is shown below:

Period	8%	10%	12%
1	0.9259	0.9091	0.8929
2	1.7833	1.7355	1.6901
3	2.5771	2.4869	2.4018
4	3.3121	3.1699	3.0373
5	3.9927	3.7908	3.6048

Illustration: What is the present value of a $1,000 annuity received at the end of the year for three years when interest is 10% and payments are made at the end of the period?

Formula Solution: PVA_n = $\$1,000 \quad \left(\dfrac{1-(1+i)^{-n}}{i}\right)$

= $\$1,000 \quad \left(\dfrac{1-(1+.10)^{-3}}{.10}\right)$

= $\$1,000\ (2.4869)$

= $\$2,489$

Table Solution: PVA_n = $PMT\ (PVIFA_{in})$ where $i = 10\%$ and $n = 3$

= $\$1,000\ (2.4869)$

= $\$2,489$

The present value of an annuity due has a similar formula to the one above. Remember, an annuity due has the cash flow occurring at the beginning of the period.

$$PVA_{due} = \$1,000\left(\frac{1-(1+i)^{-n}}{i}\right)(1+i)$$

There are also annuities due tables available in order to make calculations easy.

g.   **Compound interest:** When dealing with capital budgeting problems, assume that interest is compounded annually. However, it is not unusual to have interest stated at an annual rate but paid semi-annually (bonds), quarterly, or even monthly. In these cases, the interest rate and number of periods must be adjusted when making the calculation by using the following steps:

(1)   Adjust the interest rate according to the compounding period. For example, 16% interest compounded semi-annually is 8% each period.

(2)   Adjust n from the number of years to the number of compounding periods. For example, five years compounded semi-annually is 10 periods.

5311.04 Payback Method

a. The **payback period method** does not adjust for the time value of money. It computes the length of time required to recover the initial cash investment with net cash flows. When the annual cash flows are equal, the payback period is computed by dividing the initial investment by the annual cash flow.

$$\text{Payback Period} = \frac{\text{Initial Investment}}{\text{Annual Cash Flow}}$$

If the annual cash flows are not equal, they are accumulated until the cumulative amount equals the initial investment. The payback period is the length of time required to accumulate cash that equals the amount of the initial investment.

b. When several investment alternatives are being considered, they can be ranked according to the payback period. The investment alternatives with the shortest period are considered most desirable. This method is simple to compute and easy to understand and explain. Early paybacks provide managers with the flexibility to reinvest funds at an earlier date; therefore, managers who are uneasy about predicting cash flows into the distant future will often choose projects with early paybacks. Managers who expect to be transferred in the near future may also seek projects that will provide quick results.

c. The chief limitation is that the payback method emphasizes liquidity and disregards profitability. This method is most appropriate when precise estimates of profitability are not crucial. Its use often occurs when a firm has a weak cash and/or credit position, or if there is considerable risk involved in the proposed project. The time value of money is not considered. For example, two projects each requiring an initial investment of $1 million and yielding cash inflows of $250,000 a year would be considered to be identically attractive even if the first project has cash inflows for 5 years and the second project for 10 years.

d. The payback method can be a good screening tool but as a general rule should not be used as the primary investment evaluation tool.

e. **Illustration:** Payback Method

Problem: Compute the payback period for an investment opportunity that costs $20,000 and provides equal annual cash flows of $4,000 per year for eight years.

> **Solution:** $\dfrac{\$20,000}{\$4,000}$ = 5 years

Notice how the payback method does not even consider the cash flows between the end of the payback period and the end of the investment's useful life - in this case, between years 5 through 8.

5311.05 Discounted Payback

a. The **Discounted Payback** is the length of time required to recover the initial cash investment using a sum of the discounted future cash flows.

Since the discounted annual cash flows will not be equal, they are accumulated until the cumulative sum equals the initial investment. The discounted payback period is the length of time required to accumulate the amount of the initial investment using the discounted cash flows.

b. As with the payback method, the investment alternative with the shortest payback period is considered the most desirable. This method is simple to compute, easy to understand and explain, and also takes the time value of money into consideration, albeit in a very limited manner. The chief limitation is that the discounted payback method also emphasizes liquidity and disregards profitability.

c. **Illustration:** Discounted Payback Method

Problem: Compute the discounted payback period for an investment opportunity that costs $10,000 and provides equal annual cash flows of $5,000 per year for three years given an expected 10% return.

First the cash flows need to be discounted.

Cash Flows:

Initial Investment	Annual Cash Flows	Discounted Value
$10,000.00		$10,000.00
	$5,000 × .9091	4,545.50
	5,000 × .8264	4,132.00
	5,000 × .7513	3,756.50

Solution: $10,000 - [$4,545.50 (Year 1) + $4,132.00 (Year 2) + $1,322.50 (Year 3)] = 0

Since the discounted cash flows for Year 3 equal $3,756.50 and only $1,322.50 is needed in Year 3 to complete the payback, it can be extrapolated that approximately 2.4 years will be needed to pay back the initial investment in discounted terms. Note that using the traditional payback method, the payback period would be only 2 years. When using the discounted payback method, the payback period increases.

5311.06   Accounting Rate of Return (Simple Rate of Return)

a. The **accounting rate of return** does not consider the time value of money. The annual net cash inflow is adjusted for depreciation to arrive at annual accounting income and divided by the investment. It focuses on the average income generated by a project in relation to the investment. Unlike other methods, it focuses on income and not cash flows.

$$\text{Accounting Rate of Return} = \frac{\text{Net Cash Inflow} - \text{Depreciation}}{\text{Investment}}$$

b. The average annual profits (or increased income) is the numerator. This method does not differentiate between projects that have high early cash inflows and projects that have high late cash inflows. Thus, the time value of money is not taken into account.

c. There is not unanimous agreement as to how the investment should be defined. Some alternatives include (a) initial cost, (b) average book value, or (c) annual book value. Either (a) or (b) is preferable to (c). The use of annual book value results in an increasing rate of return over the life of the investment, providing the accounting income was relatively stable over the life of the project, since the book value would decrease as accumulated depreciation increases.

d. When using this method as a screening tool, the accounting rate of return must be equal to or greater than the company's hurdle rate for the project to be acceptable.

e. This method is popular due to consistency with financial reporting techniques commonly used to evaluate company and divisional performance; however, it does bring all of the accrual income problems into the formula. It is also simple and easy to understand.

f. **Illustration:** Accounting Rate of Return Method (Simple Rate of Return)

Problem: Compute the accounting rate of return for an investment opportunity that costs $100,000 and provides equal net cash inflows of $20,000 per year for 10 years. Straight-line depreciation is used in calculating net income; therefore annual depreciation will be $10,000 ($100,000 ÷ 10 years). The average investment will be the initial investment divided by 2, or $50,000.

Solution:

$$\text{Accounting Rate of Return} = \frac{\text{Net Cash Inflow} - \text{Depreciation}}{\text{Investment}}$$

$$= \frac{\$20,000 - \$10,000}{\$50,000}$$

$$= 20\%$$

5311.07 **Net Present Value**

a. The **Net Present Value Method** adjusts for the time value of money. It seeks to determine whether the present value of the estimated net future cash inflows at a desired (or required) rate of return will be greater or less than the cost of the proposed investment. Using this method, initial investment, net cash inflows (or cash savings), and the discount rate are givens. The present value (PV) of the net cash inflows is calculated and compared to the initial investment. An investment proposal is desirable if its net present value (NPV) is positive. In other words, the present value of the future cash inflows is greater than the cost of the investment.

b. When several investments proposals with reasonably similar investment sizes are being considered, they can be ranked by net present values. The proposal with the highest NPV should be chosen. An implicit assumption of this method is that all net cash inflows can be reinvested at the discount rate used in computing NPV. If the proposals have unequal investments, they should be ranked according to their profitability index. The profitability index is computed by dividing the present value of the cash flows by the initial investment. (See section **5311.10** for more information on the Profitability Index.)

The Net Present Value method can also be used when examining cost-saving projects. For example, when considering projects that would replace equipment with newer, more efficient models, the costs with the lowest NPV would be the most desirable alternative.

c. **Illustration:** Net Present Value.

Problem: An investment costing $20,000 will reduce production costs by $5,000 per year. The useful life will be eight years, and there will be a zero salvage value. The desired minimum rate of return of 12% is used for capital budgeting purposes. Should this investment be considered?

Solution: The NPV is calculated by determining the PV of the $5,000 annual cash savings for 8 periods using a 12% rate. The present value factor for eight periods at 12% is 4.968.

Net Present Value:
Cash flows ($5,000 × 4.968)	$ 24,840
Initial Investment	(20,000)
Net Present Value	$ 4,840

Since the NPV is positive, this is a desirable investment at a 12% return.

d. The NPV method can easily be applied if the annual cash flows are not equal.

Illustration: An investment alternative costs $10,000 and results in cash flows of $5,000, $4,000 and $3,000, respectively, for three years. The desired minimum rate of return is 14%. In this case, the PV of cash flows for each year is calculated, summed, and compared to the cost of the investment. If the NPV is negative, the investment is rejected.

Solution: The NPV is calculated by determining the PV of the cash flows for each year using a 14% discount rate.

Net Present Value:
Cash Flows	
Year 1: $5,000 × .877	$4,385.00
Year 2: $4,000 × .769	3,076.00
Year 3: $3,000 × .675	2,025.00
Total PV of cash flows	9,486.00
Initial Investment	(10,000.00)
Net Present Value	(514.00)

Since the NPV is negative, this is **not** a desirable investment at a 14% return.

e. **The discount rate (or hurdle rate)** is the required internal rate of return for projects considered by a company or investor. This rate is often based upon a company's weighted-average cost of capital, incorporating a risk premium related to the riskiness of the project in question. In other words, this rate must reward the investor for the risk that is being assumed when undertaking the investment.

5311.08 Internal Rate of Return (Time-Adjusted Rate of Return)—Equal Annual Cash Flows

a. **The Internal Rate of Return** (IRR) is the rate of discount (interest) that equates the present value of the net cash flows including the initial cash outlay to zero. This method can be used when the cost of the investment and annual cash flows are known, and the calculated rate of return is then compared to the firm's desired rate of return (hurdle rate). If the return is less than the desired rate of return, the project should be rejected. This method is also known as the Time-Adjusted Rate of Return.

$$\frac{\text{Investment Required}}{\text{Net Annual Cash Inflow}} = \text{Factor of the Internal Rate of Return}$$

b. After the Factor of the Internal Rate of Return is calculated, the present value tables of an annuity are used in order to determine the rate of return that equates the present value of the cash inflows and outflows to zero. Since the discount factors frequently do not coincide with the annuity table, interpolation is often necessary.

c. The IRR can be interpreted as the highest rate of interest an investor could pay for borrowed funds to finance the investment being considered and be no worse off than if the investment were not undertaken. In other words, the investment equals the present value of the payoff.

d. When more than one project is being considered, they are ranked according to their projected rate of return. Those with the highest rate of return are the most desirable. An implicit assumption of this method is that all net cash inflows from the project under consideration can be reinvested at the computed rate of return, and the method is, therefore, a less reliable method than the NPV method for ranking investments. This method is a good tool for making an accept/reject decision for potential projects that have met the initial requirements for consideration. Using this method, all projects that have a return greater than the company's hurdle rate should be given further consideration.

e. The NPV and IRR methods will potentially rank projects differently if the initial investment differs and/or the timing of the cash flows differs between the projects. The NPV method is the better method since the reinvestment assumption is the cost of capital as opposed to the IRR assumption of reinvestment at the computed rate of return on the cash flows for the particular project.

f. The payback reciprocal can be used to approximate a project's internal rate of return if the cash flow pattern is relatively stable.

g. **Illustration:** Internal Rate of Return.

Problem: The company is considering the acquisition of a new machine that costs $20,000. It will provide a savings of $5,000 per year over its useful life of eight years. The salvage value is expected to be zero. What is the internal rate of return, and should the machine be acquired?

Solution: The cash flows are charted as follows:

Initial Cash Outflow	$20,000
Cash Inflows	
Year 1	$5,000
Year 2	$5,000
Year 3	$5,000
Year 4	$5,000
Year 5	$5,000
Year 6	$5,000
Year 7	$5,000
Year 8	$5,000

When the cash flows are an annuity, the present value factor can be determined by dividing the initial investment by the annuity:

$$\frac{\text{Investment Required}}{\text{Net Annual Cash Inflow}} = \text{Factor of the Internal Rate of Return}$$

$$= \frac{\$20,000}{\$5,000}$$

$$= 4.0000 \text{ Present Value Factor}$$

The internal rate of return (time-adjusted rate of return) can be obtained from the present value table for an annuity in arrears (since it is assumed that the cash flows occur at the end of the period) by finding the rate for the number of periods (in this case 8) that has a factor closest to 4.000. In this case, the rate is approximately 18.5%. This project would be desirable if the minimum acceptable rate of return (hurdle rate) is less than 18.5%.

Period	17%	18%	19%	20%	21%
8	4.207	4.078	3.954	3.837	3.726

5311.09   Internal Rate of Return (Time-Adjusted Rate of Return)—Unequal Annual Cash Flows

a.   The internal rate of return is not easily applied when the cash flows are not equal annuity payments. A trial-and-error method must be used to obtain the rate of return when hand-calculated; however, computer software is available to compute the IRR that frequently uses an iterative trial-and-error method. Required inputs to such a program are cash flows (both inflows and outflows) by period and a seed internal rate of return. The computer program uses the seed (rough approximation) IRR on the initial calculation and refines the rate on subsequent calculations until it has a rate that produces a net present value of zero (or very close to zero).

b.   **Illustration:** An investment opportunity costs $10,000 and returns $5,000, $4,000, and $3,000 respectively, the first three years. What is the internal rate of return (IRR)?

(1)   First Attempt: Using an interest rate of 10%, the net present value is $105, computed as follows:

Cash Flows:

$5,000 × .9091	$4,545.50
4,000 × .8264	3,305.60
3,000 × .7513	2,253.90
Present value cash inflows	10,105.00
Cash investment	(10,000.00)
Net Present Value	$105.00

Since this is a positive amount, a higher interest rate is selected.

(2)   Second Attempt: Using an interest rate of 11%, the net present value is ($55.50), computed as follows:

Cash Flows:

$5,000 × .9009	$4,504.50
4,000 × .8116	3,246.40
3,000 × .7312	2,193.60
Present value cash inflows	9,944.50
Cash investment	(10,000.00)
Net Present Value	($55.50)

Since the NPV is a negative amount, the interest rate is somewhat less than 11%. By extrapolation, a rate of approximately 10.7% is obtained. If the desired minimum rate of return is greater than 10.7%, the project should be rejected.

5311.10   Profitability Index (Excess Present Value Index)

a.   The **Profitability Index** takes both the size of the original investment and the value of the discounted cash flows into account. This is calculated by dividing the present values of the cash flows after the initial investment by that investment.

$$\frac{\text{Present Value of Cash Flows Not Including the Initial Investment}}{\text{Initial Investment}} = \text{Profitability Index}$$

This allows for the comparison of various projects with differing initial investment amounts. Note that any project with a positive NPV will, by definition, have a Profitability Index greater than 1. The Present Value of Cash Flows Not Including the Initial Investment equals the NPV of that project plus the initial investment.

b.   The Profitability Index is often used to compare two or more mutually exclusive projects. Potential projects might be mutually exclusive in that they represent viable options to accomplish the same task. Other constraints might include a limited capital budget or lack of adequate resources to accomplish multiple projects. The alternative project with the highest profitability index is the most desirable.

c. **Example:** Assume that the information is available on two mutually exclusive projects:

	Project 1	**Project 2**
Initial Investment	$50,000	$75,000
NPV	$20,250	$25,000

Calculate the Profitability Index:

Project 1: $\dfrac{\$20,250 + \$50,000}{\$50,000}$ = 1.41

Project 2: $\dfrac{\$25,000 + \$75,000}{\$75,000}$ = 1.33

Assuming that funds are available, the most desirable project based upon the Profitability Index would be Project 1. Note that the profitability index uses the PV of the cash flows and not the NPV; therefore the initial investment amount must be added back to the NPV.

d. The Profitability Index is also known as the **Benefit-Cost Ratio**.

e. An alternative formula used to calculate the profitability index is:

$$\frac{\text{Net Present Value of the Project}}{\text{Initial Investment}} + 1 = \text{Profitability Index}$$

Using this alternative formula and the above data for Project 1, the profitability index would be calculated as:

$$\frac{\$20,250}{\$50,000} + 1 = 0.41 + 1 = 1.41$$

f. The **Project Profitability Index** is an additional variation of the profitability index. When an organization with limited funds is considering projects that require different initial investments, the NPV of one project cannot be directly compared to the NPV of another potential project. If the NPV of each project is divided by the required investment of that project, the project profitabilities can then be compared. The project with the highest project profitability index would be the most desirable project.

$$\text{Project Profitability Index} = \frac{\text{Net Present Value of the Project}}{\text{Investment Required}}$$

g. **Example**: Look at the following information regarding two possible investment opportunities.

	Project 1	**Project 2**
NPV of proposed project (a)	$8,000	$4,500
Investment Required (b)	$10,000	$5,000
Project profitability index (a ÷ b)	0.80	0.90

Since the project profitability is higher for Project 2 than Project 1, Project 2 is the more desirable choice.

h. An additional variation of the profitability index is used when there is a constrained resource that can be used to produce incremental profits in multiple segments. Here the profitability index formula is:

$$\text{Profitability Index} = \frac{\text{Incremental Profit from the Segment}}{\text{Constrained Resource Required by the Segment}}$$

If machine hours were the constraint (bottleneck) and multiple segments of the organization could use the limited machine hours to produce incremental profits, then by determining the profitability of one unit of the constraint, management can determine the most profitable way to use the constraint.

This formula is really the basis for the formula shown in section (a) to be used for projects of a more long-term nature. For that formula, the *incremental profits from the segment* are defined as the positive net present values of the cash flows after the initial investment, and the amount of the *constrained resource* is defined as the investment required by the project.

i. **Example:** The following information is available regarding incremental profits that could be produced by two different segments using a constrained resource (machine hours).

	Product 1	Product 2
Incremental profit possible	$250,000	$400,000
Amount of machine hours necessary to produce the incremental profit	100 hours	200 hours

Segment 2 may appear to be more attractive since an additional $400,000 of profit is possible; however, more machine hours (constraint) are necessary for each dollar of profit; therefore, the constraint of machine hours can be best be utilized in producing Product 1 than Product 2.

	Product 1	Product 2
Incremental profit possible (a)	$250,000	$400,000
Amount of machine hours necessary to produce the incremental profit (b)	100 hours	200 hours
Profitability index (a ÷ b)	$2.50 per hour	$2.00 per hour

5311.11   CVP Analysis/Margin of Safety

a. In the context of capital budgeting, Cost/Volume/Profit analysis (CVP) is often used to determine the margin of safety for a project. In other words, how much could projected sales fall and still not fall below the breakeven point?

b. The CVP formula:

Profit = Sales – Variable Costs – Fixed Costs

Sales = Number of units sold times sales price per unit

Variable Costs = Number of units sold times variable costs per unit

Fixed Costs = Total fixed costs for anticipated range

The breakeven point is a special case of CVP analysis where the profit equals zero. In other words, sales revenue equals total costs.

Illustration: Product A sells for $5 per unit. Variable production costs are $3 per unit and fixed costs per period are $50,000. What will the profit be if 100,000 units are produced and sold? What is the breakeven point?

Solution:

Profit	=	Sales - Variable Costs - Fixed Costs
	=	($5 × 100,000) - ($3 × 100,000) - $50,000
	=	$150,000

Breakeven in units:	$0 = \$5x - \$3x - \$50,000$
	$x = 25,000$ units

c. **Margin of safety** is the excess sales over the breakeven sales point. This can be important when looking at projects with projected sales. The methods used to evaluate capital budgeting decisions use projected sales (savings). If, however, the projections are incorrect, then there could be significant changes in the calculations of the payback period, NPV, and IRR. When evaluating a project, the likelihood that the sales/production projected will be achieved needs to assessed.

Illustration: Using the above illustration, calculate the margin of safety:

Margin of safety	= 100,000 projected unit - 25,000 breakeven units
	= 75,000 units

This could also be expressed in term of dollars. The margin of safety for sales is $375,000 ($5 per unit × 75,000 units). In this case, sales could fall significantly (by 75%), and there would still be a profit.

5311.12   The Implications of Tax on Capital Budgeting Decisions

a. Many items in capital budgeting have related tax effects. Items that do not affect cash flows such as depreciation are not relevant in basic PV calculations. They must, however, be taken into consideration when income taxes are relevant or the present value of the cash flows related to taxes is relevant. Items that do not affect cash flows except as they relate to the payment of income taxes include depreciation and gains and losses on asset dispositions.

b. The implications of income tax on capital budgeting include:

(1) Cash flows in the form of revenue are taxable. Revenues must be computed net of tax. This can have a dramatic effect on the NPV of a project.

(2) Cash outflows in the form of expenses are deductible in computing taxes payable. These cash outflows must be computed net of tax.

(3) Depreciation is not a cash flow, but it affects the amount of taxes payable. The reduction in taxes payable due to depreciation is a cash inflow item that must be included in the analysis.

(4) Gain or loss on the disposition of an existing facility (piece of equipment) is a taxable gain or a deductible loss for computing income tax.

(5) Salvage value at book value results in no gain (loss) and has no tax consequences.

c. The generally accepted approach is to compute all items net of tax and apply one of the capital budgeting approaches described previously. The marginal tax rate is most often used.

Illustration: ABC Company is considering the replacement of the current machine with a new one. The old machine has a book value of $0 and a salvage value of $8,000. The new machine would cost $30,000 and will result in an annual savings of $10,000 per year because of improved operating efficiency. It has a useful life of 6 years and an expected salvage value of $6,000. Straight-line depreciation is used, and the company has a marginal tax rate of 40%. The desired minimum rate of return is 20%. (Note, when evaluating a project that would increase sales or reduce costs, the marginal tax rate should be used.)

Solution

(1) After-tax cash flow from selling the old machine:

Sales price	$ 8,000
Book value	0
Gain	8,000
Taxes (40%)	3,200
Net Cash Inflow	$ 4,800

(2) Net cash outflow to purchase the new machine:

Cost of new machine	$30,000
Cash available from sale of old machine after tax	4,800
Net initial investment	$25,200

(3) Annual cash inflows or cash savings:

$$\text{Depreciation} = \frac{\text{Cost} - \text{Salvage Value}}{\text{Life}} = \frac{\$30,000 - \$6,000}{6 \text{ years}} = \$4,000/\text{year}$$

Operating savings	$10,000
Less depreciation	4,000
Taxable savings	6,000
Taxes (40%)	2,400
Net savings	$3,600

   (c) Total annual cash flows:

Net savings	$3,600
Add back depreciation	4,000
Annual cash flow	$7,600

(4) The salvage value of the new machinery has no tax consequences in Year 6 since the salvage value will equal book value. The cash flows for the six years will look like:

Period	Cash Flow
0	($25,200)
1	7,600
2	7,600
3	7,600
4	7,600
5	7,600
6	7,600 + 6,000

The calculation of Net Present Value at 20% for six years:

Cash savings	
Annual:	$7,600 × 3.326 = $25,278
Salvage, Year 6:	6,000 × 0.335 = 2,010
Present Value of Cash Flows	27,288
Less: Initial investment	25,200
Net Present Value	$2,088

Since the NPV is positive, replacing the old machine would be a desirable investment.

5312 Using Capital Budgeting Tools for Decision Making

5312.01 Terminology

a. **Avoidable Cost**—A cost that could be eliminated in whole or in part if a different course of action is taken that would either end the need for the activity or increase efficiency.

b. **Common Cost**—A cost that is incurred to support a number of activities and cannot be directly traced to any of them.

c. **Constraint**—A limited resource that limits an organization's ability to produce enough to satisfy demand.

d. **Differential Cost**—A cost that differs between alternatives. Also known as incremental cost or relevant cost.

e. **Historic Cost**—The acquisition cost of assets. Also called acquisition or original cost.

f. **Imputed Cost**—A relevant cost in decision making but one for which information might not be available. A value will need to be imputed generally based upon management's judgment.

g. **Incremental Cost**—A cost that is expected to differ among alternative future courses of action. Also known as differential cost and relevant cost.

h. **Joint Product Costs**—Costs of a single process or a series of processes that simultaneously produce two or more products of significant value.

i. **Opportunity Cost**—A net cash inflow that will be lost if a particular course of action under consideration is taken as compared to another possibility.

j. **Outsourcing**—The strategic use of outside resources by organizations to perform tasks or produce products traditionally handled by or produced using internal staff and resources.

k. **Relevant Cost**—A cost that is expected to differ among alternative future courses of action. Also known as incremental cost or differential cost.

l. **Relevant Range**—Limits within which the volume of activity can vary and cost relationships still remain valid.

m. **Split-Off Point**—The point in the manufacturing process where the joint products produced become individually identifiable.

n. **Sunk Cost**—A cost that has already occurred and is not affected by a capital budgeting decision.

5312.02 **Relevant Costs for Decision Making**

a. The function of decision making is to select future courses of action that will achieve maximum profits (highest net revenue) for the firm in the future. The analysis can be based on an individual project approach or an incremental cost or revenue approach. Under the individual project approach, the total costs or revenues of each project are first computed, and the project with the lowest cost or highest revenue is selected. When the incremental approach is used, the incremental or added costs to move to the alternative proposal are subtracted from the incremental revenue provided by it. If the result is positive, it is considered a desirable alternative.

b. Critical in management decision making is the understanding that sunk (past) costs are irrelevant. Relevant costs for decision making are expected future costs that will differ among alternatives available to the firm. Historical costs are useful only as they help predict the future.

(1) The book value of old equipment is not relevant since it is an historic cost. Nothing can change what has already been spent.

(2) The current disposal price of old equipment is relevant since expected future cash flows will differ among alternatives. (Replacing vs. Keeping)

(3) The gain or loss on sale (or disposal) of equipment is irrelevant to decision making since this is merely an algebraic difference between book value and disposal price. Note, however, that any tax consequences resulting from the gain or loss from the sale would be relevant.

(4) The cost of new equipment is relevant since expected cash outflows will differ between alternatives.

(5) Fixed costs that will not change among alternatives are irrelevant. Fixed costs that will be eliminated or added due to the project under consideration are relevant.

(6) Variable costs are relevant if they differ among alternatives (per unit cost) or if production volume is changed (change in total cost).

(7) The timing of expected future costs and revenues is relevant to decision making due to the time value of money. The use of discounted cash flow methods will take timing issues into consideration.

(8) **Illustration:** An uninsured machine costing $50,000 is destroyed the first day. There are two alternatives—(a) dispose of it for $5,000 and replace it with another machine for $51,000 or (b) rebuild it to original state for $45,000. Which alternative should be selected?

Solution: Rebuild, based on the following analysis. The $50,000 original cost is a sunk cost and irrelevant.

(a)	New	$51,000	(b) Rebuild	$45,000
	Less Salvage	5,000		
	Net Cost	$46,000		

In this situation, it would cost less to rebuild the equipment than replace it.

c. Steps to use in the decision-making process:

(1) Define the problem. Replace equipment, make or buy a component part, expand or contract, accept a special order, etc.

(2) Determine possible alternatives and compare each to the firm's goals for congruence.

(3) Prepare estimates of costs/revenues, benefits, and risks for each alternative that is complementary to the firm's goals.

(4) Identify and estimate possible constraints such as availability of funds, capacity, availability of raw materials, and skilled labor.

(5) Select the alternative that will most likely maximize the present value of the company's future cash flows without violating any of the constraints.

d. Since cash is the most important aspect of running a business, decision making leans toward defining cost and benefits in terms of cash flows—positive, negative, or both. Since the choice of one action will potentially prevent another from being taken, the decision should be based on perceived differences among the alternatives being considered—the incremental approach. When future cash is affected, the PV of the incremental cash flows should be used.

e. An **opportunity cost** is a net cash inflow that will be lost if the course of action under consideration is pursued. An action that eliminates a cash inflow is equivalent to an action that produces a cash outflow.

Illustration: An overstock of 5,000 widgets could be sold as a special promotion at $100 each. If the action is rejected, the incremental cash inflow of ($500,000) represents the opportunity cost of not selling the widgets.

f. Any past cash outflow (or committed future cash outflow) that is not affected by the decision to pursue the course of action under consideration is a sunk cost to the decision at hand. In the example used above, the cost of the widgets would be a sunk cost.

Some managers would choose not to replace an old machine with current depreciable book value greater than zero due to the fact that they do not want to recognize a loss on disposal. "Depreciation expense" over the next few years is often considered to be more appealing than a "loss on disposal." For many, there appears to be a psychological issue regarding the appearance of "loss on disposal" on the income statement even though it would be in the best interest of the organization to replace current production assets with new ones.

g. Pitfalls of relevant costing:

    (1) Assuming that all variable costs are relevant. For example, normal variable marketing costs may not be relevant for a special order, or there might be incremental marketing costs associated with the proposed alternative.

    (2) Assuming that all fixed costs are irrelevant. If a proposal would require operating outside the relevant range, fixed costs could increase or decrease. When purchasing new equipment, fixed costs are likely to change.

    (3) The use of unit costs can be misleading. Original unit costs could contain a combination of both relevant and irrelevant costs.

5312.03   Make/Buy Decision (Insourcing vs. Outsourcing)

a. Management may be faced with a decision as to whether or not to outsource production of a component. One of the costs that often makes the decision difficult is fixed overhead costs that are allocated to parts produced internally and would remain if the component is outsourced. These costs should be excluded from the decision since there are no incremental costs involved. However, any incremental cost associated with the outsourcing or opportunity costs related with the idle capacity should be included when comparing the cost of producing the component internally with the price of the outsourced part.

b. The main idea behind these decisions is to use the available resources as efficiently and effectively as possible, taking into consideration the possibility of outsourcing.

c. There are other qualitative issues such as supplier relationships, the need for skilled labor/supervision, labor relations, etc. that may be important in the final decision, and ultimately may be the deciding factor in the decision.

d. **Illustration:** A company currently makes a component part that another firm has offered to provide for $250 per unit. Currently 1,000 units are produced at the following costs:

Direct Materials	$50,000
Direct Labor	75,000
Manufacturing Overhead	
Variable	30,000
Fixed	80,000
Total Costs for 1,000 units	$235,000 or $235 per unit

Additionally, if the part was purchased, fixed costs of $25,000 would be eliminated and the current production space could be rented for $30,000 a year. Should the company make or buy the part?

Solution:

The opportunity costs associated with not renting the space are additional costs added to the cost of making the part due to the "lost opportunity." The relevant fixed costs are those that will differ among the alternatives; therefore, the fixed costs that would continue under either circumstance need to be removed from the cost of producing the product in order to compare the cost of making the product to that of buying the component part. In this scenario, it would be $40,000 more expensive for the company to purchase the part than to make it.

Solution Using Relevant Cost Approach:

	Total Costs	Per Unit Cost
Original cost to produce 1,000 units (from the illustration)	$235,000	$235
Lost opportunity cost for not renting space	30,000	30
Non-relevant fixed costs	(55,000)	(55)
Total relevant costs to produce units	210,000	210
Cost to purchase 1,000 units (from the illustration)	250,000	250
Cost to make units is less than cost to purchase	$(40,000)	$(40)

Alternative Solution Using Full Cost Approach:

	Cost to Make	Cost to Purchase	Difference
Direct materials	$ 50,000		
Direct labor	75,000		
Variable overhead	30,000		
Fixed overhead – relevant	25,000		
Fixed overhead – not relevant	55,000	55,000	
Cost to purchase		250,000	
Rental income		(30,000)	
	$235,000	$275,000	$(40,000)

e. **Outsourcing** is the purchasing of goods and services as opposed to producing the goods and services internally (insourcing). The make or buy decision shown above would be equally valid for services—human resources, accounting, maintenance, etc. Often the most important elements of a make/buy decision are non-quantifiable variables such as quality or dependability.

5312.04 Replace Equipment

a. Applying the concept of relevance to decisions regarding equipment replacements highlights the fact that past expenditures (sunk costs) are irrelevant. Therefore, the book value—original cost minus accumulated depreciation—of the current equipment is irrelevant when considering replacements. Nothing can be done when replacing the equipment to change what was spent in the past on the original asset.

b. Likewise, the gain or loss on the disposal of equipment is irrelevant since the gain or loss is merely the difference between the disposal value and the book value. Unfortunately, managers frequently will avoid replacing equipment that would create a loss on disposal since a "loss" looks bad on the department income statement.

c. The disposal value of the old equipment is relevant since it is a benefit to be received if the replacement occurs.

d. The cost of the new equipment is relevant since it is a future cost that can be accepted or avoided by a future decision.

e. Only future costs (revenues) that will differ between the alternatives of keeping or replacing the old equipment are relevant to the decision-making process.

f. Ideally, replacement decisions will take taxes into account. The gain or loss on the disposal of equipment is a taxable event and, therefore, will affect future cash flows. Increased revenues and/or decreased costs will increase taxes.

g. Ideally, replacement decisions will take the time value of money into account. When the cash inflows are greater in later years for an equipment replacement, this situation is less desirable than when cash inflows are greater in earlier years.

h. **Illustration:** A company is considering replacing an older piece of equipment with a more efficient machine. Cost of Capital is 10%. Available data is as follows:

	Old Equipment	New Equipment
Original Cost	$500,000	$600,000
Useful Life	10 years	5 years
Remaining Life	5 years	5 years
Accumulated Depreciation	250,000	N/A
Current Disposal Value	175,000	N/A
Disposal Value in 5 Years	0	0
Annual Revenues	400,000	400,000
Annual Operating Costs	150,000	50,000
Average Tax Rate	40%	40%

Solution without tax and PV considerations:

(1) First, the book value of $250,000 and the potential loss on disposal of $75,000 are irrelevant.

(2) The current disposal value of $175,000 is relevant as well as the cost of the new machine ($600,000).

(3) Analysis of the cash (outflows) and inflows for the 5-year period is:

	Keep	Replace	Difference
Total Operating Costs Outflow			
($150,000 × 5)	($750,000)		($750,000)
($50,000 × 5)		($250,000)	(250,000)
			(500,000)
Disposal Value	0	175,000	(175,000)
Cost of New Machine	0	(600,000)	600,000
Total Relevant Costs	($750,000)	($675,000)	($75,000)

Given this analysis, it would appear that replacing the equipment would save the company $75,000 before taxes due to lower annual operational cost outflows. For this case, the alternative with the least amount of cash outflows is the most desirable.

Solution with tax and PV considerations:

(1) In this analysis, the assumption is made that all tax payments occur at the end of the period as well as revenues and related costs.

(2) The gain/loss is not relevant in itself; however, the tax consequences of that event are relevant.

(3) Annual cash flows:

	Keep	Replace
Revenues	$400,000	$400,000
Cash Operating Expenses	(150,000)	(50,000)
Depreciation	(50,000)	(120,000)
Taxable Income	200,000	230,000
Tax (40%)	80,000	92,000
Net Income	120,000	138,000
Add Back Depreciation	50,000	120,000
Annual Cash Flow	170,000	258,000
PV of Annual Cash Flow *	$644,436	$978,026

* PV of an annuity at 10% for 5 periods is 3.7908.

(4) There is a tax effect on the loss at the time of disposal if the equipment is replaced. The book value of $250,000 and the disposal value of $175,000 result in a loss of $75,000. This will result in a tax savings of $30,000 ($75,000 × 40%) at the end of the first year. This tax savings will have a PV of $27,273 ($30,000 × .9091).

(5) The original analysis can now be modified taking tax and PV into consideration:

	Keep	Replace	Difference
PV of Annual Cash Flows	$644,436	$978,026	($333,590)
Disposal Value (year 0)	0	175,000	(175,000)
Cost of New Machine (year 0)	0	(600,000)	600,000
PV of Tax Savings on Disposal	0	27,273	(27,273)
Total Relevant Cash Flows	$644,436	$580,299	$64,137

Looking at this replacement decision taking taxes and PV into consideration provides a different outcome. The PV of the available cash flows would be higher if the equipment is retained. Therefore, this would be the alternative that adds the most value to the firm.

5312.05   One-Time Special Orders

a.   Occasionally, a request is received to manufacture a product and sell it below the normal sales price. It is generally assumed that the special order will not encroach on existing sales. If it does, the order is generally rejected because the regular price is established to provide long-run profitability based on normal demand for the product.

If the assumption that existing sales would be unaffected by the special order is valid, then profitability can be increased by accepting the special order as long as the selling price per unit exceeds the variable costs. Fixed costs normally allocated to all units produced can be excluded from the decision because they will be absorbed by the normal production run and not change if the special order is accepted or not.

b.   **Illustration:** Gyro Gear Company produces a special gear used in automatic transmissions. Each gear sells for $28, and the company sells approximately 500,000 units each year. Unit cost data for the current year are presented below:

Unit Costs for Gears

	Variable Costs	Fixed Costs	Total Unit Cost
Direct Material	$6.00		$6.00
Direct Labor	5.00		5.00
Mfg. Overhead	2.00	$7.00	9.00
Distribution	4.00	3.00	7.00
Total Unit Costs	$17.00	$10.00	$27.00

Gyro has received an offer from a foreign manufacturer to purchase 25,000 gears. Domestic sales would be unaffected by this transaction and excess capacity is available.

If the offer is accepted, variable distribution costs will increase $1.50 per gear for insurance, shipping, and import duties. What is the relevant unit cost to a pricing decision on this offer?

Solution: The first step is to determine what costs are relevant. The variable manufacturing costs per unit (material, labor, and overhead) will remain unchanged, and due to the increased volume, these variable costs are relevant. The variable distribution costs will increase to $5.50 per unit and are also relevant. The total fixed indirect and distribution costs will remain unchanged whether the special order is accepted or not; therefore, they are not relevant. The relevant costs can be summarized as follows:

Variable Costs

Direct Materials	$6.00
Direct Labor	5.00
Overhead	2.00
Distribution	5.50
Total Costs	$18.50

If the special order is priced more than $18.50 per unit, the profitability of the firm will increase. The original unit costs of $27.00 per unit had included the fixed costs in calculating unit costs, and, therefore, included irrelevant costs that could have caused a desirable alternative to be rejected. A general rule involving special orders is that if the incremental revenue exceeds the incremental costs, then the special order will be profitable. A word of caution, if idle capacity does not exist, the special order will cut into normal orders or require overtime to complete, thus increasing costs. If the firm is working at full capacity, opportunity costs would have to also be taken into consideration. Also, the firm must be concerned about the possibility that existing customers may be upset if they found out that differential pricing is being used and demand similar discounts.

5312.06   Dropping Product Lines and Other Segments

a. Some segments may report a loss when reports are prepared showing net income by segment. Based on this type of analysis, some managers will suggest that the segment be discontinued to increase overall enterprise profit. This often overlooks the fact that all costs have been allocated to the various segments, and some common costs would not be avoided by eliminating the segment. With this type of decision, the segment should not be discontinued immediately as long as the segment's margin over direct division costs is positive; however, a more productive use of this capacity could be found in the future.

b. Obviously, if a product line, division, or business segment is discontinued, all variable costs relating to that segment will be dropped. In the area of fixed costs, each cost must be examined item by item in order to determine what costs could be eliminated and what costs will continue.

c. **Illustration:** The Gentry Company currently has two divisions that had operating results as follows for last year.

	Division 1	Division 2	Total
Sales	$300,000	$150,000	$450,000
Variable Costs	155,000	100,000	255,000
Contribution Margin	145,000	50,000	195,000
Direct Fixed Costs for Division	55,000	30,000	85,000
Margin Over Direct Division Costs	90,000	20,000	110,000
Allocated Corporate Costs	50,000	30,000	80,000
Operating Income (Loss)	$40,000	($10,000)	$30,000

Since Division 2 sustained an operating loss during the year, the president is considering the elimination of this division. Assume that the direct fixed costs of Division 2 could be avoided if the division is eliminated. Should the division be eliminated?

Solution: If Division 2 is eliminated, all of the variable costs for the division as well as the direct fixed costs for the division would also be eliminated. However, the allocated corporate costs would not be eliminated; thus, total corporate income would decrease by $20,000 ($30,000 of current net income - $20,000 of lost division margin). Currently Division 2 contributes $20,000 toward covering the corporate costs. Division 2 should be continued until some other more profitable manner to absorb the $20,000 in allocated corporate costs can be found.

5312.07   Expansion

The decision-making process when considering adding a customer, division, or business segment is similar to the disposal decision. As long as the revenues for the new segment are larger than the directly related costs of that segment, a positive contribution will be made to the organization as a whole, thus increasing profits. The fact that a portion of the current corporate-office costs will be allocated to the new segment is irrelevant since these costs existed prior to the consideration of the new segment. Only revenues and costs that will change as a result of the expansion need to be considered.

5312.08   Effective Use of a Constrained Resource

a. Relevance applies to product mix decisions in the short-run if there are capacity constraints. (Note that in the long-run, expansion can eliminate this constraint.) Each product provides a contribution margin, and choosing the product that produces the highest contribution per unit within the constraint will maximize income. In many cases, however, it is necessary to carry (produce) a variety of products since customers desire choice.

b. **Illustration:** A company can produce two touring bikes, regular and deluxe. Factory capacity in terms of time available for assembly is the constraint. Only 2,000 hours are available. The following information is available:

	Regular	**Deluxe**
Contribution Margin (CM) Per Unit	$250	$330
Assembly Time Required	2 Hours	3 Hours

Solution: Analyzing the contribution margin per machine hours yields the following results:

	Regular	**Deluxe**
CM Per Machine Hour (Calculation)	$125 ($250 ÷ 2)	$110 ($330 ÷ 3)
Contribution Available for 2,000 Assembly Hours (Calculation)	$250,000 ($125 × 2,000)	$220,000 ($110 × 2,000)

Due to the assembly constraint (and assuming sufficient consumer demand), the regular racing bike should be produced in order to maximize profits. The contribution margin per machine hour for each model is the relevant item in this case - not the contribution margins of the separate models.

c. Capacity can possibly be increased within the constraint in the short-run by:

   (1) working overtime at the constraint providing the CM minus the increased wages due to overtime is still greater than zero.

   (2) subcontracting some of the constraint area output. Again the cost must be less than the benefit.

d. Capacity can possibly be increased within the constraint in the long-run by:

   (1) reengineering the process in the constraint area.

   (2) investing in additional capacity.

5312.09 **Sell or Process Further Decisions**

a. Joint product costs are the costs of a single process or a series of processes that simultaneously produces two or more products of significant value. Joint costs can be allocated to the products in a variety of ways, but all joint cost allocations are irrelevant in a decision whether to sell the product at the split-off point or process it further. This type of decision should be based on incremental revenues and incremental costs after the split-off point. If incremental revenue exceeds incremental cost, the additional processing will always be profitable.

b. **Illustration:** An organization has three joint products (copper, silver, lead) made from copper ore that can each be processed further after the split-off point or sold without further processing. The question is which sales point - with or without further processing - is most beneficial to the company. Data regarding overall profitability is shown below if all products are processed further after the split-off point.

Final Sales Revenue		$500,000
Less Cost of Producing End Products		
Cost of Copper Ore	$200,000	
Cost of Separating Ore	60,000	
Cost of Further Processing	150,000	410,000
Profit		$ 90,000

As can be seen, the company is making a profit; however, the question is whether or not the organization is maximizing profit by the further processing of all three joint products or could increase profits by further processing only one or two of the joint products.

Solution: In order to make the best choice, an incremental approach needs to be used. Are the incremental revenues of further processing greater than the incremental costs of that processing? Each product needs to be examined individually in order to determine whether further processing of that particular product is maximizing revenues. This could be done as follows:

	Copper	Silver	Lead
Final Sales Revenue - After Processing	$150,000	$260,000	$90,000
Less Sales Value at Split-Off Point	100,000	180,000	70,000
Incremental Revenue Provided by Further Processing	50,000	80,000	20,000
Less Cost of Further Processing	40,000	95,000	15,000
Profit (Loss) from Further Processing	$10,000	($15,000)	$ 5,000

As can be seen in this instance, the company would increase profits by $15,000 if the silver ore is sold at the split-off point and not processed further; however, the other two products, copper and lead, should continue with further processing.

5313 Financial Modeling

5313.01 **Terminology**

a. **Capital Intensity Ratio**—The dollar value of assets that is required to create a dollar of sales.

b. **Corporate Strategies**—Broad, long-range plans such as developing new technologies in a particular field.

c. **Capital Structure**—Percentage of debt, preferred stock, and common stock used for financing the firm's assets.

d. **Free Cash Flow**—The cash flow actually available for distribution to investors after the firm has made all necessary investments in fixed assets and permanent working capital necessary to support on-going operations.

e. **Mission Statement**—A statement defining the general purpose of the company.

f. **NOPAT (net operating profit after taxes)** —The profit that a firm would make if there were no debt and no non-operating assets. [EBIT (1-Tax Rate)]

g. **Operating Plans**—The plans used to implement the corporate strategy involving the identification of the responsibility for implementation, specific tasks to be accomplished, and revenue and costs targets, among other things.

h. **Proforma Financial Statements**—Projected financial statements based on a given set of assumptions.

i. **Sales Forecast**—The projection of both volume and dollar value of sales for a future period.

5313.02   Introduction to Financial Planning Models

a. Managers use projected financial statements to:

(1) Plan future performance and compare the projections to goals.

(2) Plan future financing needs.

(3) Look at effects of proposed changes in operations.

b. A **mission statement** defines the general purpose of the company. Such things as the purpose of the firm's existence (often maximizing stockholder wealth), the scope of the company (defining the industry and location of operations), and the objectives of the organization (general philosophy) are presented in the mission statement.

c. **Corporate strategies** are then developed. They are broad, long-range plans such as developing new technologies in a particular field. These strategies need to be realistically obtainable in the long-term and attuned with the organization's purpose, scope and objectives.

d. **Operating plans** are used to implement the corporate strategy, and are usually 1–5 years in length with the first year of the plan being the most detailed. The plan will identify responsibility for implementation, specific tasks to be accomplished, revenue and costs targets, among other things.

5313.03   The Financial Planning Process

a. The **Financial Planning Process** involves taking the operating plans and developing proforma financial statements, forecasting financing needs, and measurement (control) criteria.

b. The proforma financial statements are used to project the results of the operating plans and to determine if those plans provide realistic results. These statements are also used to monitor results in order to determine whether the anticipated results of operations actually occurred.

c. As part of the planning process, the funds necessary to support the operating plans need to be determined (generally for a period of five years). This would include requirements for research and development, expansion, working capital, marketing, and production.

d. Management must determine whether the needed funds will be generated internally or whether outside financing will be required. Any constraints on the availability of funds must be realistically woven into the operating plans. If funds are projected to be unavailable, plans may need to be scaled back. If expected borrowing would include covenants, then the potential constraints (current ratio, debt/equity ratio, compensating balance) would need to be included in the development of the proforma statements.

e. System controls need to be developed to oversee the procurement, allocation, and use of funds relating to the operating plans as developed.

f. Since forecasts are nothing more than projections, they are potentially subject to error. Procedures need to be developed to monitor and adjust the operating plan should actual performance be different than projected performance. In that case, the firm would need to modify the original financial plan to compensate for actual conditions. Since forecasts are based upon anticipated economic conditions and expected customer needs and wants, adjustments are often necessary as circumstances change. (Strong vs. weak economy, response by the competition, natural events such as floods, disasters, etc.)

g. A performance-based compensation system may need to be developed in order to ensure that management is rewarded for the accomplishment of goals related to the attainment of strategic goals.

5313.04   The Sales Forecast

a. Today, most forecasting is done using computer-based models; thus, various inputs can be readily changed to test various assumptions, and the projected results in the form of financial statement are instantaneously available. Models are based upon revenue/cost relationships and can be quite sophisticated. This makes planning quicker and easier for management.

b. The **Sales Forecast** is the projection of both volume and dollar value of sales for a future period. It is based upon economic conditions, customer-anticipated product/service needs and wants, recent industry trends, assumed expected marketing efforts, and the products (new and old) to be sold. This forecast is extremely important since nearly all other parts of the operating and financial budgets are based upon the sales forecast. If the sales forecast is too low, the company may not have enough production capacity to meet customer demands. If the sales forecast if too high, the organization may end up with excess inventory and/or excess capacity - both potentially costly mistakes. For example, expansion without increased sales could result in fixed financing charges without generating the cash flow needed to make interest and principal repayment.

c. The sales forecast begins with a study of sales from the last 5–10 years. Although the past cannot be projected directly into the future, it is often a good source of information regarding recent trends. Care must be taken to determine whether significant recent events or recent product changes make the projection of the past sales data into the future invalid. If conditions are expected to be similar to those of prior years, regression analysis can be a useful tool for projecting future sales.

d. Some factors to be considered when developing a sales forecast:

(1) Sales forecasts for each division and each product within each division provide a more realistic total sales projection than merely projecting total sales for the company.

(2) Sales forecasts for various marketing regions - foreign, domestic, regional - provide superior total estimates. This would include looking at the market share and anticipated marketing efforts within each region.

(3) Exchange rates also must be projected if some portion of projected sales will be in foreign markets.

(4) Economic conditions (inflation, deflation, expansion, recession) need to be predicted as well as their potential effect on sales in the various marketing regions.

(5) With the introduction of a new product, a firm can often have a competitive advantage with increased market share until the competition can develop similar products.

5313.05 Percent of Sales Method to Forecast Financial Statements

a. Some variation of the Percent of Sales Method is the most commonly used method to forecast financial statements. It starts with the sales forecast and then expresses many of the financial statement accounts as a percentage of sales. Note that these relationships can be constant or may change over time. Many income statement and balance sheet items have proportional relationships to sales. For example, sales increase and accounts receivable will likely have the same relative rate of increase. Some items on the financials do not have direct relationships with sales, and judgment is necessary to set them at reasonable levels.

If sales and accounts receivable are projected to increase at the same rate, then the accounts receivable turnover ratio will remain constant. Adjustments would need to be made in the relationship percentage if, for example, the firm were considering a change in its credit policy.

b. Using computer models, the relationships between sales and financial statement items can easily be set and modified if necessary.

5313.06 Forecasting the Income Statement

Relationships between sales or another financial statement item need to be established as part of the modeling process. Simple models may combine all costs of goods sold except depreciation; however, more accurate budgets would separate variable and fixed expenses. Relationships could be expressed as follows:

	Actual Current	Forecasted Relationship	Projected
Sales	$110,000	110% of current	$121,000
Costs except Depr.	80,000	73% of sales	88,300
Depreciation	12,000	15% of P&E	15,200
EBIT	18,000		17,500
Interest	5,000	Same as current	5,000
EBT	13,000		12,500
Taxes (40%)	5,200		5,000
NI before dividends	7,800		7,500
Dividends	1,000	Same as current	1,000
Addt's to RE	$6,800		$6,500

EBIT = Earnings before Interest & Taxes
EBIT = Earnings before Taxes
P&E = Profits and Earnings

5313.07 **Forecasting the Balance Sheet**

a. If sales increase, there are a number of items on the balance sheet that will increase such as working capital items that are related to sales/production. See section **5314** for a discussion on projecting cash flows.

b. Unless the credit policy is changed, the relationship between sales and receivables will increase proportionately. Thus, sales increase by 10%, and then accounts receivable will increase by 10%. Inventory also generally holds a similar proportional relationship to sales. Care must be taken, however, if suppliers are expected to change prices.

c. Spontaneous funds are generated through the use of credit. As inventory purchases and production increase (driven by increased sales), current liabilities such as accounts payable and accrued labor also increase. There is a direct relationship between many current liabilities and projected sales.

d. The relationship between sales and property plant and equipment (PP&E) is often not as clear as the relationships between working capital items and sales. For example, companies often build facilities with capacities greater than current needs; thus, sales increases for a limited number of years can often be handled by current PP&E. In the long-run, however, no organization can increase sales indefinitely without increasing capacity. When projecting necessary increases in capital items, management must look closely at current facilities and the efficiency of operations in relation to projected sales. Increases in PP&E are likely to be "lumpy" and occur as the firm reaches capacity constraints.

e. Increases in long-term debt are closely tied to permanent increases in working capital and PP&E. For example, higher sales must be supported by a higher level of assets (current and long-term). Some of this support comes from the spontaneous credit just discussed, and any remaining shortfalls must come from additional short-term debt, long-term debt, or stock issues. Management must decide whether to use debt or equity for additional financing needs. (See sections **5321**, **5322**, and **5323** for discussions on the use of financing options.)

Note that additional interest-bearing financing will change the interest expense on the income statement.

f. Projected retained earnings (RE) is current RE plus forecasted net income less projected dividends to be paid.

5313.08 **Examining the Forecast**

a. Once the preliminary forecast is complete, it must be examined in order to determine whether the goals of management and requirements of current lenders have been met and whether the projected health of the organization has been maintained (or improved, if necessary). Various ratios such as the current ratio, debt/equity, and ROA (Return on Assets) need to be computed and compared to management's expectations, lender's requirements, and possibly industry standards.

For example, if the projected debt to equity ratio is 60% and a current lender requires a maximum of a 50% ratio, then management will have to make a revision in the projected plans - either substituting equity for debt or finding a way to reduce the need for additional funds.

b. Spreadsheet models allow management to test the results of their projections against standards, requirements, and expectations. The inflows and outflows of cash can be predicted providing the necessary information for management to make important financing decisions. Dividend and financing policies can also be examined as to their effect on the amount of external funds necessary for expansion.

5313.09 Projecting Free Cash Flow

a. **Free cash flow** is the cash flow actually available for distribution to investors after the firm has made all necessary investments in fixed assets and working capital required to support the on-going operations. For a growth company, there may be a negative free cash flow. This is not necessarily bad, providing that growth can ultimately provide value for the investors as well as the cash flow necessary to service the long-term debt.

b. Since the income statement uses accrual accounting, income must be converted to the cash basis. Investors include debt holders as well as stockholders; therefore, income needs to be calculated as if there no were debt by calculating NOPAT (net operating profit after taxes).

$$NOPAT = EBIT(1 - Tax\ Rate)$$

NOPAT still includes items that did not use cash; therefore, non-cash items must be added back in order to arrive at operating cash flow:

$$Operating\ cash\ flow = NOPAT + Depreciation\ and\ amortization$$

c. The information found on the balance sheets provides us with the data necessary to compute the net investment for the period (ending net PP&E less beginning PP&E); however, annual depreciation is also included in the change in the beginning and ending net PP&E figures. Gross investment in operating for a period can be summarized as follows:

$$Gross\ Investment\ in\ Operating\ Capital = Net\ Investment\ for\ the\ Period + Depreciation\ and\ Amortization$$

d. Free Cash Flow can be expressed in an equation form as follows:

$$Free\ Cash\ Flow = Operating\ Cash\ Flow - Gross\ Investment\ in\ Operating\ Capital$$

If Operating Cash Flow and Gross Investment in Operating Capital equations are substituted in the above formula, the result is:

$$Free\ Cash\ Flow = NOPAT - Net\ Investment\ in\ Operating\ Capital$$

e. When planning, the calculation of Free Cash Flow can be an important analytical tool. With the planned level of capital expenditures for expansion, will there be enough cash available for debt and equity investors? The results for a single year are not important in isolation. This is an equation that draws importance over time and allows a firm to answer the question as to whether an expansion today can be expected to provide the cash flow necessary to satisfy investors in the future.

5313.10 Capital Intensity Ratio

The **Capital Intensity Ratio** measures the dollar value of assets that are needed to create a dollar of sales. Obviously, this ratio varies from industry to industry and has a major effect on capital requirements. Companies that have higher asset to sales ratios need more assets to increase sales levels and will generally require a greater amount of external financing.

$$Capital\ Intensity\ Ratio = \frac{Assets\ Tied\ to\ Sales}{Sales}$$

This ratio can be very helpful when determining estimates of funds that will be necessary to support increased sales volumes.

5313.11 The AFN (Additional Funds Needed) Formula

a. As a company grows, additional funding is often necessary. Sales are forecasted, and the total assets necessary to support those sales are estimated. For example, increased sales often necessitate increased inventory levels, and those same increased sales result in increased receivables. A portion of the higher asset levels are funded through the spontaneous liabilities that result due to the increased sales, and a portion of the increased income will possibly be available to support the higher asset base. Long-term debt, however, is not considered to be spontaneous and does not vary with sales. In most forecasts, the increase in assets needed due to increased sales will exceed the spontaneous funds created by the higher activity levels; therefore, it is necessary to determine the additional funds needed (AFN). The formula used to determine the AFN only calculates the funds needed. Management would then have to decide whether to raise those funds through debt or equity.

The formula for AFN is as follows:

$$\text{Additional Funds Needed} = \text{Required Increase in Assets} - \text{Spontaneous Increase in Liabilities} - \text{Increase in Retained Earnings}$$

Where:

$$\text{Required Increase in Assets} = \frac{\text{Assets}_0}{\text{Sales}_0} \times \text{Change in Sales}$$

$$\text{Spontaneous Increase in Liabilities} = \frac{\text{Liabilities}_0}{\text{Sales}_0} \times \text{Change in Sales}$$

$$\text{Increase in Retained Earnings} = \text{Profit Margin} \times \text{Sales}_1 \times \text{Retention Percentage}$$

Note that in these formulas, assets and liabilities relative to sales in Year 0 are expected to increase in proportion to sales in the projected coming period. The retention percentage is a management decision as to what percentage of the profits to pay out in dividends and what percentage of those same profits to retain in the company.

b. The required increase in assets can be calculated by using the capital intensity ratio:

$$\text{Required Increase in Assets} = \text{Capital Intensity Ratio} \times \text{Increase in Sales}$$

Assets in this equation are defined as all assets necessary to support increased sales - both working capital and capital assets. **Note:** Increases in capital assets may be "lumpy" in nature, and, therefore, this number represents only a reasonable approximation of the amount of the increase in the asset base in any particular period.

c. The spontaneous increase in liabilities can also be calculated using existing relationships. The relationship between spontaneous liabilities such as accounts payable and accrued liabilities related to sales must be determined. As sales increase, these spontaneous liabilities will increase in relation to sales. This can be expressed as:

$$\text{Spontaneous Increase in Liabilities} = \text{Spontaneous Liabilities to Sales Ratio} \times \text{Increase in Sales}$$

d. The increase in retained earnings can be calculated providing anticipated profit retention has been determined by management. The increase in retained earnings is dependent upon projected sales, expected profit margin, and retention policy.

Given: M = Profit Margin
S_1 = Projected Sales
RR = Retention Ratio (percent of net income to be retained)
     This can also be expressed as $(1 - \text{payout ratio})$.

$$\text{Increase in Retained Earnings} = MS_1(RR)$$

e. There are five important elements of the AFN formula:

(1) Predicted sales growth.

(2) The assets needed to produce each sales dollar (capital intensity ratio).

(3) The relationship between spontaneous liabilities and sales.

(4) The profit margin, since the higher the profit level, the less need for financing.

(5) Profit retention, since the more funds retained, the less need for additional financing.

5313.12 Projecting Excess Capacity

a. One of the decisions necessary when preparing projections is whether capacity needs to be increased. The sales at full capacity can be projected by dividing actual sales by the percentage of capacity used to create those sales.

$$\text{Full Capacity Sales} = \frac{\text{Actual Sales}}{\text{Percentage of Capacity Used to Create Sales}}$$

For example, if sales were at $500,000 and 80% of capacity was used to produce those sales, then the amount that sales could increase before expansion could be estimated as follows.

$$\text{Full Capacity Sales} = \frac{\$500,000}{80\%} = \$625,000$$

Thus, sales could increase by $125,000 ($625,000 at full capacity - $500,000 at 80% capacity) before plant expansion would be necessary.

b. This information can also be used to project the necessary increase in production capacity for a given sales level given the following relationship:

$$\frac{\text{Actual Fixed Assets}}{\text{Full Capacity Sales}} = \frac{\text{Targeted Fixed Assets}}{\text{Projected Sales}}$$

Using the above example, if $200,000 of production assets would be needed to support $625,000 of full capacity sales, then what would the target fixed assets be for $750,000 of projected sales?

$$\text{Target Fixed Asset} = \frac{\text{Actual Fixed Assets} \times \text{Projected Sales}}{\text{Full Capacity Sales}}$$

$$= \frac{\$200,000 \times \$750,000}{\$625,000} = \$240,000$$

In reality, indicating a need to increase assets by $40,000 may not be absolutely correct since additions to production assets might not show a linear relationship due to increased efficiency of new equipment. Management's judgment may be essential when estimating the actual additional assets that would be required and determining the timing of those additions.

5314 Projecting Cash Flows

5314.01 Terminology

a. **Cash Budget**—The projections of sources and uses of funds for a specified period of time.

b. **Cash Flow Cycle**—The continuous cycle of issuing stock or borrowing, purchasing assets, producing the product, selling the product, and collecting the cash payments for possible reinvestment.

c. **Target Cash Balance**—The desired cash balance necessary to safely conduct business.

5314.02   The Cash Budget

a.   The **Cash Budget** is the projection of sources and uses of funds for a specified period of time. All of the operating budgets affect the flow of cash; therefore, they must be prepared prior to the creation of the cash budget. After the projected cash inflows and outflows are determined and the scheduled outflows for repayments for prior financing and necessary interest payments are accounted for, and a cash balance target is determined, then the necessary future financing needs can be projected.

b.   The Cash Budget is divided into four main sections: Cash receipts, Cash disbursements, Cash surplus or deficit, and Cash financing.

c.   The Cash receipts include all cash inflows except those resulting from financing activities. In most cases, the major source of cash inflows is from operating revenues; however, it is important to remember that projected sales are not the same as projected cash inflows from operations. Credit sales are an important source of revenue for most firms; therefore, the operating period cash inflows are the cash sales and the collections on client accounts during the period. The cash receipt section of the cash budget is actually a bridge between the sales budget and the accounts receivable balances on the beginning balance sheet and the projected ending balance sheet.

Beginning Accounts Receivable Balance
+ Projected Sales on Account
− Projected Cash Collections
= Projected Ending Accounts Receivable Balance

In order to determine the projected cash collections for the period, it is necessary to know the projected sales as well as the beginning accounts receivable aging and the expected collection pattern.

Illustration: The Timely Corporation had an accounts receivable balance on December 31st comprised of the following:

Sales Source	Amount
From October Sales of $450,000	$ 40,500
From November Sales of $550,000	173,250
From December Sales of $700,000	401,625
Total Accounts Receivable 12/31	$615,375

It is expected that 10% of the sales for each month will be cash sales. Of the remaining sales, 15% will be collected the month of the sale, 50% the month following the sale, 25% the second month following the sale, and the remaining 10% in the third month.

Projected total sales for January are $500,000. What are the projected cash inflows for the month of January?

Solution:

	Cash Inflows
10% of January sales of $500,000 as cash sales	$ 50,000
15% of January credit sales of $450,000 ($500,000 × 90%)	67,500
50% of December credit sales of $630,000 ($700,000 × 90%)	315,000
25% of November credit sales of $495,000 ($550,000 × 90%)	123,750
10% of October credit sales of $405,000 ($450,000 × 90%)	40,500
Total Projected Cash inflows in January	$596,750

d.   Other anticipated cash receipts from interest, dividends, sale of marketable securities or other investments, proceeds from the sale of property, plant, and equipment, and proceeds from the company's own stock issues are also listed as cash receipts. Many of these inflows are discretionary and result from decisions made by management.

e. The cash disbursements section itemizes all of the cash outflows except those due to financing that are expected during the period. Major sources for outflows are expected payments for materials (merchandise), labor, overhead, selling, and administrative expenses. Again, the various operating expense budgets do not represent the flow of cash due to the use of the accrual method of accounting. Each listed expense category needs to be converted from an accrual to a cash basis in order to project the related expected cash outflows. The disbursement section of the cash budget is a bridge between the beginning balance sheet and the projected ending balance sheet. This can be summarized by:

```
  Beginning Accounts Payable Balance
+ Projected Purchases on Account
- Projected Cash Payments on Account
= Projected Ending Accounts Payable Balance
```

In order to determine the projected cash payments, it is necessary to know the credit terms as well as the payment philosophy of the organization. Are obligations paid within the credit terms? Are discounts generally taken?

Illustration: The Johnson Company adheres to credit terms in the payment of accounts payable of either 2/10, net 30 (when offered) or simply net 30. Discounts of 2% are offered on 20% of all purchases. The remaining 80% have terms net 30. Assume that purchases are made evenly throughout the month. Purchases of $310,000 are projected to be made March and $360,000 during the month of April. What are the projected cash disbursements for April?

Solution:

Average daily purchases for March = $310,000 ÷ 31 = $10,000

Average daily purchase for April = $360,000 ÷ 30 = $12,000

April Cash Disbursement Items	Projected Disbursement
80% of March sales with net 30 terms ($310,000 × 80%)	$248,000
Since payments taking discounts are paid on the 10th day, nine days of March purchases qualifying for discounts are outstanding on April 1st. [($10,000 × 20%) × 9 days] × 98%	17,640
Since payments taking discount are paid on the 10th day, 21 days of April purchases qualifying for discounts are paid in April. [($12,000 × 20%) × 21 days] × 98%	49,392
Total Projected April Disbursement for Accounts Payable	$315,032

Outstanding accounts payable at the end of the month would be:

80% of the April purchases of $360,000	$288,000
9 days of April purchases qualifying for discounts (($12,000 × 9 days) × 20%)	21,600
Total Accounts Payable April 30th	$309,600

The outstanding accounts payable at the end of April could also be calculated in the following manner:

80% of the April purchases with the terms net 30 will be outstanding on April 30th ($360,000 × 80%).	$288,000
The remaining portion of the $72,000 of 2/10, net 30 purchases will be outstanding at the end of the month ($72,000 − $50,400).	21,600
Total Accounts Payable at the end of April	$309,600

f. Other disbursements such as capital purchases, dividend payments, stock repurchases, purchases of investments, or other various disbursements other than for financing are also listed as cash outflows. Many of these items are discretionary payments and can vary from period to period.

g. The cash inflows before financing are added to the beginning cash balance for the period from which the cash outflows before financing are deducted to arrive at the excess cash (or deficit) available.

> Beginning Cash Balance
> + Projected Cash Receipts Other Than Financing
> − Projected Cash Disbursement Other Than Financing
> = Excess (Deficit) Cash Available Over Disbursements

h. The financing section summarizes the borrowing, repayments, and cash interest payments deemed to be necessary during the period. Most organizations have a **target cash balance** that is the desired cash assumed to be necessary to safely conduct business. If the excess (deficit) cash is less than the target cash balance and required interest payments, then it is necessary to finance the cash needs of the organization. If there is an amount in excess of the target cash balance after interest payments at the end of the projected period, previous financing can be repaid or the funds can be invested.

The cash inflows before financing are added to the beginning cash balance for the period from which the cash outflows before financing are deducted to arrive at the excess cash (or deficit) available.

> Excess (Deficit) Cash Available Over Disbursements
> + New Borrowing
> − Repayments
> − Interest Payments
> = Target Cash Balance

Illustration: A firm has an opening cash balance of $25,000 and outstanding long-term financing (due in 3 years) of $60,000 at a 10% interest rate at the beginning of the year. It is projected that cash receipts will equal $750,000 and that cash disbursements will equal $739,250. The desired target cash balance at the end of the year is $32,000. Will the company have to borrow funds in order to meet the desired target cash balance? Assume that all additional financing will be acquired at the beginning of the period at a 10% rate and that all repayments will be at the end of the period.

Solution:

Beginning Cash Balance	$25,000
+ Projected Cash Receipts	750,000
- Projected Cash Disbursements	(739,250)
= Excess (Deficit) Cash Available	35,750
Projected Additional Financing	?
Projected Repayments	?
Projected Interest Payments	?
Projected Ending Cash Balance	$ 32,000

If there is no additional financing, then $6,000 of interest payments ($60,000 × 10%) will be paid out, leaving a balance less than the desired target cash balance of $32,000. (Projected Excess Cash Available of $35,750 less Projected Interest Payments of $6,000 is $29,750.) Therefore, additional financing will be necessary. The equation needed to determine the additional cash needed is as follows:

Projected Excess Funds + Projected Additional Financing − 10% (Original Financing + Projected Additional Financing) = Target Cash Balance

$35,750 + Pro. Add't Financing − 10% ($60,000 + Pro. Addt'l Financing) = $32,000

Solving for the Project Additional Financing, it can be determined that an additional $2,500 will need to be borrowed. The projected interest payments will be $6,250 [10% ($60,000 + $2,500)].

Beginning Cash Balance	$25,000
+ Projected Cash Receipts	750,000
- Projected Cash Disbursements	(739,250)
= Excess (Deficit) Cash Available	35,750
Projected Additional Financing	2,500
Projected Repayments	0
Projected Interest Payments	(6,250)
Projected Ending Cash Balance	$32,000

i. Most organizations have a master cash budget that is then broken down into monthly or even weekly mini-budgets due to the fact that cash flows and disbursements do not occur evenly throughout the year. The need for financing and/or the repayment of prior financing will often vary from month-to-month depending upon the business cycle. The target cash balance may also be varied during the year.

j. Certain items such as depreciation add complexity to the cash budget. Even though depreciation does not require the use of cash, it does have an effect on taxable income and ultimately the taxes paid.

5314.03   The Cash Flow Cycle

a. The cash balance is the focal point of the cash flow cycle. Inflows and outflows are related and often dependent upon each other. Cash is increased by the issuance of stock and borrowing. These funds are then used to purchase material, labor and capital assets necessary to produce the product. The product is then sold and ultimately cash is collected to replenish the cash account. This is a continuous cycle, and if any one of the segments falls behind projections, the cash account will ultimately be affected negatively. Funds must continually be available to purchase material and labor so new products can be produced and sold, and new cash inflows generated.

b. If higher sales are projected, it is often necessary to increase purchases thus increasing raw materials inventory and accounts payable (a spontaneous source of financing). Increased production often requires additional funds to pay for labor on a timely basis as well as to cover the increased investment in the work-in-process inventory and ultimately the finished goods inventory. It is also possible that additional capital equipment will need to be purchased. All of these cash needs occur before the sales and the cash inflows resulting from those sales occur. Depending upon the length of the cycle - capital expansion, production, sales, collection—and how quickly obligations have to be met (A/P, accrued wages), the firm may be required to finance a considerable amount through the use of debt and/or equity.

c. Sale revenues will exceed costs for a profitable firm, and ultimately cash inflows will exceed cash outflows, allowing for the repayment of the original financing and/or for dividend payments to the shareholders. A profitable firm will frequently have to finance large portions of its cash demands that are caused by rapid expansion due to the lag in the cash flow cycle.

d. Costs will exceed revenues for an unprofitable firm. Since cash outflows will exceed cash inflows, more borrowing will be necessary in order to meet current obligations. That borrowing will carry greater risk and, therefore, demand higher interest costs, thus increasing cash outflows even further. Uncontrolled expansion can also have a significant negative impact on cash balances, and a once healthy firm can begin to have serious cash flow problems. Once the payment for current obligations begins to slow (e.g., not meeting terms of creditors or payroll), the material and labor necessary to produce the product can become difficult to procure.

5314.04   Predicting Cash Flow for Capital Projects

a. It can often be difficult to estimate the cash flows expected to result from a proposed capital project. Outflows can result from:

(1) Capital purchases

(2) Anticipated increases in working capital

(3) Projected costs related to the costs of additional production inputs (variable and fixed).

(4) Research, development, and engineering costs

(5) Marketing expenses

(6) Taxes on additional revenue (or cost savings)

Inflows can come from:

(1) New or additional revenues

(2) Cost savings

(3) Disposals of assets

From the estimates of the above items, cash flows relating to the life of the project can be developed. The longer the project, the less likely that the estimates will be accurate; therefore, it is not unusual for a company to prepare multiple cash flow estimates based upon different economic assumptions concerning alternative economic scenarios.

b. Cash flows are not the same as accounting income due to the use of the accrual method. The most dramatic difference is frequently seen in the handling of depreciation. The cash flow model for capital projects recognizes the purchase of capital assets at the time that they are acquired. Accounting income expenses that same amount over the life of the asset. Depreciation, however, does affect the taxes paid on an annual basis that are a part of the cash outflows. The following chart shows a comparison of accounting earnings and annual cash flow for a particular project, providing all sales and expenses are in cash other than depreciation.

	Accounting Earnings	Cash Transactions
Sales	$100,000	$100,000
Less:		
Cost of Good Sold (Excluding Depr.)	65,000	65,000
Depreciation	15,000	
Gross Margin	20,000	
Less: Selling and Admin.	15,000	15,000
Operating Profit	$5,000	
Less: Taxes (40%)	2,000	2,000
Net Income	$ 3,000	
Cash Flow		$ 18,000

Another method of determining the cash flow for a particular project is through the use of the following equation:

Cash Flow = (Revenue - Cash Expenses) × (1 - Tax Rate) + (Depreciation × Tax Rate)

Using the above example, the cash flow of the proposed project can be calculated:

Cash Flow   = [$100,000 - ($65,000 + $15,000)] × (1 - .40) + ($15,000 × .40)
             = $18,000

The use of this formula does not include any financing expenses since the manner of the financing is not relevant when evaluating/comparing projects for acceptance. When using a discounted cash flow method of evaluation, the cost of capital is taken into account; therefore, if financing costs were included in the projected cash flows that are then discounted, the financing costs would be doubled counted. After a project is potentially accepted, the best financing method can then be chosen.

5320 Strategies for Long- and Short-Term Financing Options

5321 Determine Appropriate Short-Term and Long-Term Strategies

5321.01 Terminology

a. **Aggressive Approach to Financing Short-Term Debt**—The financing of part of the permanent current assets with spontaneous credit.

b. **Conservative Approach to Financing Short-Term Debt**—The use of permanent assets to finance some of the seasonal needs and spontaneous credit (accounts payable) to finance the remaining seasonal needs.

c. **Financial Leverage**—The extent that fixed-income securities (debt and preferred stock) are used in a firm's capital structure.

d. **Maturity Matching Approach to Financing**—The matching of assets to liability maturities. Also known as the "self-liquidating approach" to financing.

e. **Net Operating Working Capital (NOWC)**—Operating current assets minus operating current liabilities.

f. **Permanent Current Assets**—Assets that are permanent in nature in that they are carried even at the low points of the business cycle.

g. **Temporary Current Assets**—Assets that fluctuate with the business cycle as sales vary.

5321.02 Financing with Short-Term Debt

a. Assets are generally divided into current and long-term, or permanent assets. Current assets can be further divided into:

(1) **Temporary current assets** that would include assets that would fluctuate with the business cycle as sales vary with the corresponding changes in the levels of accounts receivable and inventory between the maximum and minimum levels over the annual business cycle.

(2) **Permanent current assets** that would include assets that are more permanent in nature in that they are carried even at the low points of the business cycle such as the minimum accounts receivable and inventory levels during the lowest part of the business cycle.

b. The **conservative approach** to financing short-term debt uses permanent assets to finance all of the permanent operating assets requirements and also some of the seasonal needs. Spontaneous credit (accounts payable) is used to finance the remaining seasonal needs. A firm using this approach would hold liquid assets in marketable securities during the low points of the seasonal cycle.

c. The **maturity matching approach to financing** matches assets to liability maturities. This approach minimizes default risk and is considered to be a moderate approach to financing.

Illustration: If a new factory is financed with short-term funds, it is unlikely that the new facility would have been built and produced a large enough cash flow at the end of one year in order to repay the loan at maturity. In this scenario, if the lender refused to renew the loan, the company would be in a difficult position. If the new facility had been financed with long-term debt, the cash flows provided by the new operation would have more closely matched the repayment cash outflows, and the need for refinancing is less likely to arise.

d. The difficulty with maturity matching is that imperfect estimates are used in determining the lives of assets. In reality, firms tend to attempt to develop a reasonable approximation of matching. Also, it is necessary to have some percentage of the financing come from equity that has no maturity.

e. The **aggressive approach** to financing short-term debt would be to finance part of the permanent current assets with spontaneous credit such as accounts payable. The aggressive approach can be carried to a high degree by also financing part of the fixed assets with short-term borrowing. Such a firm would be at risk if interest rates increase as well as face possible difficulties with loan renewals. The degree of aggressiveness is defined by the degree to which permanent NOWC (net operating working capital) and fixed assets are funded by spontaneous credit and/or short-term debt.

5321.03   Financing with Long-Term Debt

a. Financial leverage is created through the use of debt. If the firm has superior profits (excess return on total assets above the cost of debt), the return above the cost of the debt accrues to the shareholder. Thus assets financed through debt can provide increased worth to the stockholder. (See section **5327.03** for a discussion on financial leverage.) Borrowed funds generally require a fixed payment (interest) so debt holders cannot share in superior profits after receiving the necessary interest payments.

b. Financial structure (use of debt and equity) is influenced by:

(1) management's attitude toward risk.

    (a) Smaller firms are not likely to want to use additional equity sold to new shareholders as a source of financing due to the diluting effect; however, large firms generally will not be opposed to selling additional stock since a stock sale will have little effect on company control.

    (b) A small firm may be reluctant to use debt as a source of funds due to the extreme risk that failure of one product or a slight down-turn in the economy may have on cash flow. Default is more likely in a small firm than a large one.

(2) the industry norms.

Debt service is related to sales volume and the control of costs leading to profitability. Growth industries tend to have high profit margins. Mature industries tend to have stable sales and profit margins. Lenders are concerned about a specific company's ability to make necessary payments. Generally, debt holders will not lend funds to a firm that has a debt to equity ratio above the normal range for the industry or a times interest earned ratio below the normal range for the industry without higher interest rates to compensate for the additional risk. Lenders are particularly interested in an organization's solvency ratios as compared to the industry norms when deciding whether additional funds should be lent to the firm in question.

(3) the anticipated future growth rate.

If new financing is used to expand, it is important to estimate the future growth of sales in order to determine whether cash flows resulting from the new productive assets will create a cash flow large enough to service the debt.

(4) lenders' attitudes toward the industry and the specific firm.

Lenders' attitudes play an important role in capital structure. As lenders become concerned about rising debt levels, they will either demand higher interest rates to compensate for the additional risk, or they may refuse to lend the necessary funds. A firm's ability to grow may often be limited to the funds available through the use of debt.

c. Whenever additional long-term funds are needed, management can choose between debt and equity. Long-term debt is likely to be used when:

(1) sale and profits are estimated to be stable or increasing.

(2) anticipated profits are sufficient to make good use of leverage.

(3) control (through voting privileges) is important.

(4) the existing capital structure has a low use of debt.

(5) requirements or covenants of debt issues are not arduous.

5322 Identify Advantages and Disadvantages of Short-Term and Long-Term Financing

5322.01 Terminology

a. **Long-Term Debt**—Obligations expected to have a maturity of more than one year.

b. **Short-Term Debt**—Obligations expected to have a maturity of one year or less. Much of this debt is "unfunded."

5322.02 Advantages of Short-Term Debt

a. A short-term loan can generally be obtained quickly.

b. Cost of obtaining short-term debt is generally low since the lender tends to only do a minimal financial examination of the firm applying for funds.

c. There are generally no prepayment penalties.

d. Short-term debt generally has few restrictions.

e. Since the yield curve is typically upward sloping, short-term interest rates are generally lower than long-term interest rates.

f. Interest expense is tax deductible and, therefore, provides financial leverage.

g. Accounts payable is a primary source of short-term debt and it is spontaneously created when inventory is purchased.

5322.03 Disadvantages of Short-Term Debt

a. Short-term interest rates can vary widely over time subjecting the firm to refinancing risk.

b. An unexpected need for cash during a recession could cause cash flows to be insufficient to meet the short-term obligations.

    c.   Due to changing financial conditions, short-term debt may not be renewable and thus, depending upon the level of short-term debt may put a firm in an illiquid position that could lead to bankruptcy.

5322.04   **Advantages of Long-Term Debt**

    a.   A firm's interest cost is fixed for the maturity of the loan, thus protecting the firm from interest rate changes (or within a limited range for a variable interest rate).

    b.   Interest expense is tax deductible and, therefore, provides financial leverage.

    c.   The yield required by providers of long-term debt is lower than required by providers of equity due to the fact that the risk is lower.

    d.   The control of the firm is not shared by long-term debt holder.

5322.05   **Disadvantages of Long-Term Debt**

    a.   Long-term debt frequently has various restrictive covenants that can dramatically limit choices available to management. Examples include setting dividends, obtaining additional debt, holding compensation balances, maintaining levels of liquidity and/or solvency ratios, and prepayment penalties.

    b.   If interest rates fall, a firm could be locked into a high interest rate.

    c.   If profits (cash flows) fall, interest expenses still have to be paid.

    d.   Long-term debt has a maturity date at which time the principal needs to be repaid.

    e.   A firm generally has a limit as to the amount of funds that can be raised through the issuance of long-term debt.

5323 Forms of Financing

5323.01   **Terminology**

    a.   **Bond**—A publicly offered form of long-term debt where the borrower agrees to makes payments of interest and principal on specific dates to the bond holder.

    b.   **Call Provision**—The right of the issuer to redeem (call) the bond issue prior to the maturity date under certain circumstances.

    c.   **Cash Conversion Cycle**—The difference between the cash collection period and cash payment period.

    d.   **Coupon Rate**—Stated rate of interest for a bond.

    e.   **Factoring**—A form of short-term financing that involves selling accounts receivable to a factor.

    f.   **Financial Leases (Capital Leases)**—Leases that do not provide for maintenance of the asset, that are not cancelable, and for which the lessor receives payments equal to the full price of the asset over the term of the lease.

    g.   **Funded Debt**—Long-term debt.

    h.   **Indenture**—The legal document that contains the terms of the bond issues.

    i.   **Inventory Conversion Period**—The average time in days that inventory is held before being sold.

    j.   **Lease**—A form of long-term financing on property, plant, and equipment without traditional transfer of ownership.

k. **Letter of Credit**—An international financing tool that guarantees payment to an international supplier upon the safe arrival of the goods by issuing a loan to the purchaser to be paid by a transfer from the seller's bond.

l. **Line of Credit**—An agreement with a bank to have up to a specific amount of funds available as a short-term loan during a particular period.

m. **Net Working Capital**—Current assets less current liabilities.

n. **Off-Balance Sheet Financing**—A leased asset that does not appear on the balance sheet as either a leased asset (long-term asset) or a lease obligation (long-term liability).

o. **Operating Leases (Service Leases)**—Leases that include both financing and maintenance. Lease payments are considered to be period expenses; however, the leased asset does not appear on the balance sheet as either a leased asset or a lease obligation.

p. **Payables Deferral Period**—The average time that short-term obligations related to the purchase/production of inventory is outstanding.

q. **Pledging**—The use of accounts receivable as collateral in order to obtain a short-term loan.

r. **Receivables Collection Period**—The average time that receivables are outstanding before they are turned into cash.

s. **Revolving Credit Agreement**—An agreement to extend credit by a bank to a company over a specified period of time that involves an annual commitment fee. The company has the right to periodic advances throughout the period of the loan.

t. **Sinking Fund**—Requires the issuer to retire a portion of the bond issue each year or deposit funds into a restricted account to be accumulated for the retirement of the bonds.

u. **Restrictive Covenant**—Conditions that must be met by the issuer during the life of the bond issue.

v. **Term Loan**—Legal agreement between a borrower and lender where the borrower promises to make interest and principal payments at specific times to the lender for the use of borrowed funds.

w. **Unfunded Debt**—Short-term debt.

x. **Working Capital**—Short-term assets such as cash, receivables, and inventory.

y. **Zero Working Capital**—When inventories + receivables – payables equal zero.

5323.02 Working Capital

a. **Working Capital** is short-term assets such as cash, receivables, and inventory. **Net Working Capital** is current assets less current liabilities. Working capital is tied to the cash conversion cycle where inventory is purchased or produced and sold on account, and payments are made. It focuses on the difference between the cash collection period and cash payment period.

(1) The **inventory conversion period** is the average time that inventory is held in days before being sold. (Average inventory ÷ Average sales per day)

(2) The **receivables collection period** is the average time that receivables are outstanding before they are turned into cash. (Average accounts receivable ÷ Average sales per day)

(3) The **payables deferral period** is the average time that short-term obligations related to the purchase/production of inventory are outstanding. (Average payables ÷ Average purchases per day)

(4) The **cash conversion cycle** is the inventory conversion period and the receivable collection period less the payables deferral period. It represents the amount of time that funds are tied up in non-cash current assets.

Illustration: If the inventory conversion period is 45 days, the receivable collection period is 35 days, and the payable deferral period is 30 days, what is the cash conversion cycle?

Solution: The cash conversion cycle is simply:

Inventory conversion period + Receivable collection period - Payable deferral period = 45 days + 35 days - 30 days = 50 days

Thus cash is tied up in non-cash current items for 50 days. This represents a permanent financing need.

b. As long as the cash conversion cycle can be shortened without encroaching on sales or increasing costs, a firm should attempt to do so since that will mean that a lower amount of permanent financing will be necessary, and there is a cost to any financing. This can be done by:

(1) Selling products more quickly

(2) Collecting receivable more quickly

(3) Slowing down payments (See the discussion on discounts in section **5332.05**.)

Illustration: Using the above example, if $25,000 of obligations related to the purchase/production of inventory are created each day, the necessary working financing needs would be $1,250,000 given the cash conversion cycle of 50 days ($25,000 × 50 days). If products could be sold on average 2 days earlier, receivables collected on average 3 days earlier, and payments on payables delayed on average 1 day more, then the conversion cycle would be decreased by 6 days. That translates into a decrease of $150,000 tied up in non-cash current assets. If the cost of borrowing is 6%, that would mean that the organization would save $9,000 per year ($150,000 × 6%).

c. The concept of **zero working capital** is when inventories + receivables - payables equal zero. This equation can be translated as the use of payables for the sole source of financing for inventories and receivables. If a company moves to zero working capital, there are two results:

(1) There is a one-time infusion of cash as either inventory and/or receivables are decreased or payables increased.

(2) Income is permanently increased on an annual basis due to the fact that financing is no longer needed to support working capital (higher level of inventory and receivables including the costs of carrying inventory and receivables). The costs of financing operating assets are shifted to suppliers. Inventory reductions can often be accomplished through the use of JIT (Just-in-Time).

d. If working capital is reduced, the amount of financing decreases; thus, EVA (economic value added) will increase since the after-tax dollar cost of operating capital will decrease.

5323.03   Letter of Credit

A letter of credit is an international financing tool that guarantees payment to an international supplier upon the safe arrival of the goods by issuing a loan to the purchaser. A letter of credit can be irrevocable (not subject to cancellation if the specific conditions are met), or revocable.

5323.04 Line of Credit

a. A **line of credit** is an agreement with a bank to have up to a specific amount of funds available as a short-term loan during a particular period. If the line of credit is for $100,000, a firm can borrow $20,000 in January, borrow an additional $35,000 in May, repay $40,000 in July, and borrow $50,000 in September, etc. As long as the total amount borrowed at a given point in time remains under $100,000 during the period of the agreement, the firm will continue to have access to additional funds. Interest is usually paid monthly and calculated on the average outstanding balance during the period. This method of financing allows a firm to smooth out the business cash flow cycle as well as to have funds available for possibly both precautionary and speculative needs.

b. The use of the Line of Credit affects both current assets and current liabilities equally. They increase and decrease in a parallel fashion; however, as long as the current ratio is greater than one, an increase in a line of credit (increase to cash and an increase to current liabilities) will decrease the current ratio.

Illustration: A firm has $100,000 of current assets, $50,000 of current liabilities, and a current ratio of 2 to 1 ($100,000 ÷ $50,000). If $25,000 is borrowed on the line of credit, current assets will increase to $125,000, current liabilities to $75,000, and the current ratio will become 1.7 to 1 ($125,000 ÷ $75,000).

c. A variation on the line of credit is the revolving credit agreement that is generally used by large corporations. This is an agreement by a bank to extend credit to a company over a specified period of time; however, if the firm does not make use of the revolving credit, it still has to an annual commitment fee. For example, the approved revolving credit could be for three years to allow a corporation to borrow up to $50 million. Even if the company does not use any of the credit during the year, it will still have to pay a significant commitment fee expressed in terms of a percent (for example, a quarter of 1% or $125,000 annually in the above illustration). If the corporation borrows $25 million on the revolving credit agreement, the commitment fee would drop to a percent of the unused portion of the agreement ($62,500 in this illustration), and the corporation would pay interest on the outstanding borrowed balance as well.

The biggest difference between a line of credit and a revolving credit agreement is that there is a legal obligation with a revolving credit agreement that does not exist with a simple line of credit. This legal obligation guarantees the company access to the funds over the life of the agreement.

5323.05 Pledging and Factoring of Accounts Receivables

a. **Pledging** is the use of accounts receivable as collateral in order to obtain a short-term loan. If the purchaser of the goods that created the receivable does not honor the obligation, the risk of default remains with the borrower who pledged the receivables. The lender will generally only accept pledged receivables for strong customers and often will only lend up to 75% of the pledged amount as a further protection.

b. **Factoring** involves selling accounts receivable to a factor as a form of short-term financing. The factor assumes the risk of collection, and the purchaser is notified of the factoring arrangement and usually remits payments directly to the factor. (In some instances factoring can be done with recourse.) Since the risk is shifted to the factor, the factor will take over the responsibility of doing the credit check on a potential customer. Therefore, functions performed by the factor include credit checks, lending, and bearing of default risk. Generally the selling firm receives funds from the sale immediately upon shipment of goods to the purchaser. The amount received is the full amount of the sale less a factor fee (usually a percentage of the total sale). The fee incorporates a reserve for sales returns and allowances, interest costs, and profit for the factor. At the end of a specified period, the reserve amount is paid to the seller providing there have not been sales returns and allowances. It is not uncommon for factoring arrangements to be on-going.

Illustration: A company sells $50,000 of goods with the terms net/30. The receivable is immediately factored with a 3% factor fee, 10% interest, and a reserve of 8%. How much does the selling firm immediately receive from the factor?

Solution: The factor fee will be $1,500 (3% of $50,000). The reserve will be $4,000 (8% of $50,000). The interest will be calculated on 10% of the balance available to the seller and adjusted for a monthly period length.

This can be summarized as follows:

Sales:		$50,000
Less:		
Factor Fee (3% × $50,000)	$1,500	
Reserve (8% × $50,000)	4,000	5,500
Amount due firm		44,500
Less interest on amount for		
30 days (10% × $44,500 × 30/360)		371
Amount paid to seller		$44,129

After 30 days, any remaining part of the reserve (maximum of $4,000 in this case) that was not absorbed by returns and allowances will be remitted to the seller.

The cost of factoring needs to be compared to the costs of running a credit department when making a decision as to which alternative to pursue.

5323.06 Leasing Options

a. A lease is a form of long-term financing on property, plant, and equipment without traditional ownership. When reviewing leasing options, the cost of the lease needs to be compared with the cost of ownership. The cost of the lease is also influenced by the fact that the lessor is concerned about earning a reasonable rate of return on the asset.

b. Operating leases (service leases) include both financing and maintenance. Lease payments are considered to be period expenses; however, the leased asset does not appear on the balance sheet as either a leased asset or a lease obligation. This is considered to be off-balance sheet financing. Generally the cost of financing and maintenance is built into the lease contract. Often the full cost of the leased property will not be recovered by the lessor during the initial lease period, and the lessee commonly contains a right-to-cancel clause.

c. Off-balance sheet financing allows a firm to have use of an asset without decreasing the balance sheet solvency.

Illustration: The comparison of leasing and purchasing capital assets:

Firm A and B before purchasing or leasing capital asset:

Current Assets	$100	Debt		$150
Long-term Assets	200	Equity		150
Total:	$300	Total:		$300
		Debt Ratio		50%

Firm A purchasing a capital asset for $100 using financing:

Current Assets	$100	Debt ($150 + $100)	$250
Long-Term Assets ($200 + $100)	300	Equity	150
Total:	$400	Total:	$400
		Debt Ratio	62.5%

Firm B leasing a capital asset using an operating lease:

Current Assets	$100	Debt (No Change)	$150
Long-Term Assets (No Change)	200	Equity	150
Total:	$300	Total:	$300
		Debt Ratio	50%

Both firms have identical production assets; however, the financial solvency of Firm B appears to be superior to that of Firm A (debt ratio of 50% vs. 62.5%). Note that due to SFAS 13, information regarding operating leases must be included in the notes to the financial statements, and can be useful when determining the true solvency of an organization. This would make the cause for these differences transparent to the analyst.

d. **Financial leases (capital leases)** do not provide for maintenance of the asset and are not cancelable, and the lessor receives payments equal to the full price of the asset over the term of the lease. They are basically installment purchases. The balance sheet would show both the leased asset as well as the lease obligation similar to a firm that purchased a capital asset as required by SFAS 13.

e. The evaluation of leasing vs. purchase decision can be done by using the PV of the cash flows. The option with the lowest PV of the costs for obtaining and using the capital asset would be most desirable. (See section "f" below.)

Illustration: A firm has the choice to purchase a 3-year asset for $21,000 or lease it for $8,500 per year. If the asset is purchased, maintenance cost will be $1,000 per year and the tax saving from depreciation will be $2,800. If the asset is leased, maintenance costs will be $1,000 per year, and the tax savings from leasing will be $3,400. There will be no value left at the end of the 3-year period. Which alternative is a better choice when considering cash flows if the cost of capital is 8%? Assume that all payments are due at the end of the period except the purchase price under the purchase option.

Solution: The present values of the cash flows need to be determined. Note that since the maintenance costs are the same for both options, they are not relevant in this decision.

Purchase Option:			
	Cash Flows	**PV Factor**	**PV Cash Flows**
Purchase Price	($21,000)	1.00	($21,000)
Annual cash flows:			
Tax Savings from Depr.	2,800	2.5771	7,216
PV of relevant cash flows			($13,784)
Lease Option:			
	Cash Flows	**PV Factor**	**PV Cash Flows**
Annual Lease Pmts	($8,500)	2.5771	($21,905)
Tax Savings from Lease Pmts	3,400	2.5771	8,762
PV of relevant cash flows			($13,143)

In this example, it would be better to lease since the PV of the net cash outflows of the relevant items are less for the leasing option than the purchase option.

 f. The availability of credit is sometimes a major part of the decision to purchase or lease. If an organization wishes to maximize financial leverage while maintaining a high level of (superficial) solvency, operating leases may be chosen. It is often thought that firms can obtain a greater amount of financing through the use of leases as opposed to debt.

5323.07 **Term Loan**

 a. A **Term Loan** is a legal agreement between a borrower and lender where the borrower promises to make interest and principal payments at specific times to the lender for the use of borrowed funds. It is a form of funded debt (long-term debt).

 b. Term Loans have advantages over the issuance of bonds and equity.

  (1) Term loans can be drawn up quickly since the borrower and lender work directly together.

  (2) The terms of the loan can have more flexibility since they are not registered with the SEC. Also, modifications can potentially be made during the life of the loan.

  (3) Term loans have low issuance costs.

 c. Generally, term loans are paid off in equal installments. This is a protection to both the lender and the borrower that funds will be available for repayment. When funds from the loan are used to purchase equipment, the repayment schedule is frequently matched to the productive life of the equipment.

 d. Interest rates can be either fixed or variable.

5323.08 **Debentures and Bonds**

 a. A bond is generally a publicly offered form of long-term debt where the borrower agrees to makes payments of interest and principal on specific dates to the bond holder. Most bond issues are advertised and held by many different investors as opposed to the one lender of a term loan. The bonds have a coupon rate (rate of interest) that is generally fixed.

b. An indenture is the legal document that contains the terms of the bond issues. This document is approved by the SEC before the bond issue is offered to the public. It will clearly state the provisions of the issue. Common provisions include:

(1) Call provision - The right of the issuer to redeem the bond issue prior to the maturity date under certain circumstances.

(2) Sinking fund - Requires the issuer to retire a portion of the bond issue each year or deposit fund into a restricted account to be accumulated for the retirement of the bonds.

(3) Restrictive Covenants - Conditions that must be met by the issuer during the life of the bond issue such as maintaining a debt ratio no higher than a specified amount, possibly restricting dividend payments, maintaining a minimum current ratio, as well as other conditions.

c. Bond ratings are determined using the Standard & Poor's rating system based upon the probability that the issuing corporation will go into default. These ratings range from AAA (very strong) to D (in default). AAA and AA are considered to be of a high quality, A and BBB are considered to be investment grade, BB and B are considered to be substandard, and CCC to D are considered to be speculative.

The rating is based upon the financial health of the issuing organization (capital structure as well as stable profitability), bond provisions, pending legal actions, and time to maturity. The rating is done by rating agencies using subjective judgment. The bond rating has a direct effect on the bond's interest rate, and thus the firm's cost of capital if a firm wishes to issue new debt. Since many bonds are purchased by institutional investors who are generally restricted to no lower than investment-grade bonds, this rating is extremely important.

d. The value of bonds is based upon the present value of discounted future cash flows comprised of an annuity plus a lump sum. The bond's market value fluctuates with changes in the market interest rates. If the coupon rate equals the market interest rate, then the market value of the bond will be equal to the face value (par value). If the market interest rate is above the coupon rate, the bond will be selling at a discount to par. The bond's cash flows, interest and lump-sum payment, are set, so by selling the bond at a discount, PV of the future cash flows equal at return at the market rate for the discounted amount. If the market interest rate is lower than the coupon rate, the bond will sell at a premium to par.

As the bond approaches maturity, its market value will approach par. Changing interest rates will have an impact on the market value of the bond, the impact being greater the longer the remaining maturity of the bond. The issuing corporation, however, will be required to make the same semi-annual interest payment no matter what changes occur in the interest rate over the life of the bond. When bonds are issued, the coupon rate on the bond generally is set close to the current market rate.

Illustration: A $1,000 bond with a 7% coupon rate, maturing in 10 years is selling in a 6% market. What is the current market value of the bond?

Solution: The bond is valued by determining the PV of the future cash flows (maturity value of $1,000 and semi-annual interest payments of $35 each ($1,000 × 3.5%)). Using present value tables for 3% (due to semi-annual interest payments), 20 periods, the value of the bond can be calculated:

PV of maturity ($1,000 × .5537) =	$553.70
PV of interest pmts ($35 × 14.8775) =	520.71
Present Value	$1,074.41

Due to the fact that the coupon rate is higher than the current market rate, the bond will sell at a premium.

e. Bonds are a major source of financing for many corporations. There are both advantages and disadvantages to this form of raising capital:

(1) Advantages:

(a) No matter how profitable an organization is, the bond holder will still only receive the same semi-annual interest payment over the life of the bond. Operating income in excess of the bond interest goes to the equity holder.

(b) Bond interest is a taxable deduction, thus lowering taxes paid.

(c) Bond holders are not allowed to participate in the control of the corporation through voting for directors. Some bond issues can be convertible to common stock as a right but not an obligation on the part of the shareholder.

(d) Some bond issues can be callable prior to the maturity date given a specific set of circumstances. This gives management some degree of flexibility.

(2) Disadvantages:

(a) The semi-annual interest payments are due even during a period of low profitability or loss. The bonds must be retired at maturity. There is always risk that the corporation will not have the funds available or be able to refinance when needed. The use of sinking fund or amortization payments helps to eliminate some of the risk.

(b) There is very little flexibility in the indenture provision, and since a bond issue may be in existence for 10 to 20 years, bond terms cannot be changed to reflect changing economic conditions.

(c) There is a limit on the amount of funds that are available through the use of long-term debt based upon generally accepted norms of debt to equity ratios for each industry. If a firm's ratios fall outside the limits, the cost of the additional debt, if available, increases to match the risk.

(d) In times of economic downturn, it is often difficult to raise capital through the use of long-term debt.

5323.09 **Equity Financing**

a. Preferred stock is a hybrid between bonds and common stock. The dividend is generally a fixed amount expressed in terms of a percentage of the par value of the preferred stock and cannot be changed in the future. This is similar to the interest payments on bonds. If, however, the profitability of the firm is down, the company does not have to pay a current preferred dividend payment. This is like the dividend payments on common stock. Many preferred stocks are cumulative, so that if dividend payments are missed (in arrears) then unpaid preferred dividends must be paid in the future before common dividends can be distributed. Although preferred stock is issued with the intent of making the expected dividend payment on a timely basis, failure to make preferred dividend payments will not force bankruptcy. However, issuing new bonds, preferred stock, or common stock would potentially be difficult if a corporation was in arrears. Preferred dividends are not deductible for tax purposes.

b. Investors regard preferred stock as a riskier investment than bonds since:

(1) bondholders are in a superior position in the event of liquidation.

(2) bondholders are more likely to continue to receive interest payments during a period of economic downturn.

c. There are a number of varieties of preferred stock.

    (1) Participating preferred stock allows for a limited participation in dividend increases based on a stated formula.

    (2) Dividends on preferred stock can be cumulative or noncumulative.

d. As with bonds, there are both advantages and disadvantages to financing with preferred stock.

    (1) Advantages:

        (a) No matter how profitable an organization is, the preferred stockholder will receive only a maximum dividend payment that is either fixed or has a limited participation.

        (b) Most preferred stock issues do not allow for participation in the control of the corporation through voting for directors.

        (c) In a period of low profitability or loss, preferred dividends do not have to be paid or at minimum can be delayed if there is a cumulative feature. Failure to pay dividends will not lead to bankruptcy.

        (d) Preferred stock generally does not have a maturity date, and some issues are convertible into common stock and some have a callable feature.

        (e) Preferred stock increases the equity position of the corporation.

        (f) The convertible feature coupled with the callability feature can be used to force conversion. This gives management some degree of flexibility.

    (2) Disadvantages:

        (a) Preferred stockholders' claims are before that of common stockholders in the event of liquidation and dividend payments.

        (b) Preferred dividends are not a deductible expense for tax purposes.

e. Common stock represents the ownership of a firm and can be a major source of financing. Common stock:

    (1) Gives shareholders the right to share in the residual value of the firm after creditors and preferred shareholders are paid.

    (2) Gives shareholders the right to vote for the board of directors.

    (3) Does not give shareholders the right to dividends. Dividends are only distributed to shareholders if declared by the board of directors.

    (4) Does not provide a tax deduction through the issuance of dividends.

    (5) Gives shareholders the right to share in the profits of the firm after creditors and preferred stockholders. There is no limit to this participation.

f. The issuance of common stock involves a number of steps, including filing with the SEC, publishing a prospectus, and choosing an investment banker. This can involve significant costs that ultimately reduce the amount of funds available from a given offering. These costs are knows as flotation costs.

g. The source of financing through common stock only comes from the original issuance of that stock and has no relationship to the current market price.

h. Similar to debt and preferred stock, the issuance of common stock has advantages and disadvantages.

    (1) Advantages:

        (a) In a period of low profitability or loss, common dividends do not have to be paid. Failure to pay dividends will not lead to bankruptcy. Growth companies also frequently do not pay dividends.

        (b) There is no maturity for common stock since it represents permanent ownership.

        (c) Common stock increases the equity position of the corporation and can provide a basis for increasing debt.

    (2) Disadvantages:

        (a) Common stockholders require a greater return to compensate for the additional risk of the investment.

        (b) Common dividends are not a deductible expense for tax purposes.

        (c) The issuance of new stock dilutes ownership.

5324 Interest Rates

5324.01   Terminology

a. Add-on Interest Loans—Loans where the interest is calculated and added to the amount received by the borrower when determining the loan's face value.

b. Annual Compounding—When interest is compounded (calculated) once a year (or in other words, annually).

c. Annual Percentage Rate (APR)—The periodic rate times the number of periods per year.

d. Compound Interest—The process of paying interest on the prior interest of an investment.

e. Coupon Rate—The stated annual interest rate on bonds.

f. Discounted Interest—When the interest on a loan is calculated in advance and subtracted from the proceeds of the loan.

g. Effective Interest Rate—The rate of interest that will produce the same future value of cash using frequent compounding as compared to annual compounding at a given stated rate.

h. Floating Interest Rates—An interest rate that is tied to some market rate of interest (or index) such as the prime rate.

i. Installment Loans—Loans where the borrower makes the payments in regular installments and that frequently use the add-on interest method.

j. Nominal Interest Rate—The stated interest rate.

k. Periodic Interest Rate—The rate charged by the lender for each period.

l. Prime Rate—A published rate that is charged by commercial banks to their best and strongest customers.

m. Regular Interest—The same as simple interest where interest is not compounded.

n. Semi-annual Compounding—When interest is credited twice a year.

o. **Simple Interest**—Interest that is not compounded. Interest is calculated only on the remaining principal balance of the loan.

p. **Stated Interest Rate**—The nominal interest rate.

5324.02 Simple Interest

a. **Simple interest** is when interest is not compounded. In other words, interest is not earned on interest. This is also known as **regular interest**. To calculate simple interest, the nominal interest rate is divided by the number of days in a year in order to get the rate per day. Note that banks often use a 360-day year that results in a slightly higher loan rate.

$$\text{Interest Rate Per Day} = \frac{\text{Nominal Rate}}{\text{Days in Year}}$$

The interest rate per day is then multiplied by the number of days in loan period and times the outstanding balance of the loan. The result of this calculation is the simple interest.

b. **Illustration:** $50,000 is borrowed at 10% with interest payments due on a monthly basis. The interest payment for the month of March would be calculated as follows using a 365-day year:

$$\text{Interest Rate Per Day} = \frac{10\%}{365 \text{ Days}} = 0.00027397$$

$$\text{Interest Charge for March} = \text{Days in Period} \times \text{Interest Rate Per Day} \times \text{Amount of Loan}$$

$$= 31 \text{ Days} \times 0.00027397 \times \$50,000 = \$424.65$$

c. The actual effective interest rate for simple interest depends upon how often the interest must be paid. The more often that interest is paid, the higher the effective amount. This is due to the time value of money. If the interest is only paid at the end of the loan period using simple interest, then the effective rate equals the stated rate. If, however, the interest payments are paid on a monthly basis for a 10% simple loan, then the effective rate would be slightly higher than the stated rate.

Illustration: If interest is paid only at the end of the year for a $50,000 1-year loan at 10%, then the effective interest rate is 10%. $5,000 of interest will be paid at the end of the year:

$$\frac{\$5,000}{\$50,000} = 10.00\%$$

If the interest is paid quarterly for a $50,000 1-year loan at 10%, then the effective interest rate is 10.35%. There are 91 days in a quarter; thus, the periodic interest rate for 91 days is 2.4925% (daily rate × 91). The effective annual rate with quarterly payments can be expressed as:

$$\text{Effective annual rate paid quarterly} = (1 + 0.024925)^4 - 1 = 10.35\%$$

If this same calculation were done using a monthly payment, the effective rate would be higher due to the time value of money. The more often the interest is paid, the higher the effective rate.

5324.03 **Compound Interest**

a. **Compound Interest** is the process of paying interest on the prior interest in an investment. For example, $100 is deposited in a bank earning an annual interest of 10%. The $10 of interest earning at the end of the first year is left in the bank. The interest earned during the second year will be based upon the investment of $110 ($100 initial investment + the $10 interest from the first year). By the end of the second year, the original investment of $100 will have grown to $121.

Original deposit	$100
Interest for the 1st year:	
$100 × 10%	10
Balance at the end of the 1st year	110
Interest for the 2nd year:	
$110 × 10%	11
Balance at the end of the 2nd year	$121

b. The balance in the investment after a given number of periods (n) can be calculated using the following formula:

$$FV_n = PV(1+r)^n$$

Note that this is the formula used in future value tables.

c. **Example:** If $n = 5$ years and the interest rate is 8% a year, the balance at the end of the 5th year in the investment will be:

$$F_5 = \$100 \, (1 + .08)^5$$
$$= \$147$$

(See section **5311.03** for the use of future value tables.)

d. Annual compounding is when interest is compounded (calculated) once a year (or in other words, annually).

e. Semi-annual compounding is when interest is credited twice a year. This allows for a greater compounding effect since the interest credited at six months earns interest during the second six months. If the interest rate is 8%, then the interest compound each six months is based on 4% of the balance in the account.

f. **Illustration:** Compare annual compounding and semi-annual compounding given an opening balance of $100,000 left in an account for five years earning 8%. (Use future value tables for the calculation.)

Solution: Annual compounding results in a value of $146,930 ($100,000 × 1.4693) since the future value factor of 8% for five periods is 1.4693. Thus, annual compounding results in $46,930 of interest.

Semi-annual compounding results in a value of $148,802 ($100,000 × 1.4802) since the future value factor of 4% for 10 periods is 1.4802. Thus semi-annual compounding results in $1,872 additional interest or a total of $48,802 of interest. Note when using semi-annual compounding, 4% interest is paid 10 times during the 5-year period.

5324.04 **Effective Interest**

a. The effective interest rate is the rate of interest that will produce the same future value of cash using frequent compounding as compared to annual compounding at a given stated rate. The stated rate (nominal rate) is thus converted to an effective rate.

b. The formula for compounding that occurs more frequently than annually is a variation of the compound interest formula where "*m*" is the number of compounding periods and I_{Nom} is the nominal interest rate.

$$\text{Effective Annual Rate} = \left(1 + \frac{i_{nom}}{m}\right)^m - 1$$

Illustration: If the interest rate is 10% and compounding occurs on a monthly basis, the effective interest rate would be:

$$\text{Effective Annual Rate} = \left(1 + \frac{0.10}{m}\right)^m - 1 = \left(1 + \frac{0.10}{12}\right)^{12} - 1 = 10.47\%$$

5324.05 **Market Interest Rates**

a. The stated or nominal interest rate on a fixed-income security is composed of several elements: a real risk-free rate of interest (r*) plus several premiums for various types of risk, including inflation, potential default, the securities marketability (liquidity), and maturity risk (or interest rate risk).

b. The stated or nominal interest rate (r) can be expressed by the following formula:

$$r = r^* + IP + DRP + LP + MRP$$

(1) The risk-free rate of interest (r*) is generally considered to be the rate of interest paid on U.S. Treasury securities.

(2) The inflation premium (IP) is not the current rate of inflation, but rather represents the expected average inflation over the life of the security.

(3) The default risk premium (DRP) is the premium for the risk that a borrower will not make principal and interest payments in a timely fashion. Treasury securities have a default risk of zero. Corporate bonds are rated, with the rating defining the security's default risk. The DRP would be the difference between the rate on a corporate security and a government security for instruments that have similar maturity and liquidity characteristics.

Illustration: The data in the table below shows representative yields and yield spreads (DRP) for variously rated securities for early January 2004.

	Yields	DRP
U.S. Treasury	4.09	
AAA	4.60	51
AA	4.80	71
A	5.01	92
BBB	5.56	147
BB+	8.29	420

(4) The liquidity premium (LP) relates to the ease with which a security can be converted to cash. The liquidity premium is very difficult to measure; however, estimates suggest that the premium can range from two to perhaps four to five percentage points between the most and least liquid financial assets with similar default risk and maturity characteristics. The differential would tend to be higher the riskier the asset and the more uncertainty there is in the market.

(5) The prices of any long-term bonds can decline sharply when interest rates rise. This is what is known as interest rate risk (MRP). The risk is higher the longer the remaining years to maturity. This factor raises interest rates on long-term bonds relative to short-term bonds. It is difficult to measure, but tends to be higher when interest rates are volatile and uncertain, and it is estimated to have been in the range of one to three percentage points in recent times.

5324.06   **Risk-Free Rate of Interest**

a. The **Risk-Free Rate of Interest** is the nominal risk-free rate (r_{RF}) that is paid on U.S. Treasury securities. It is assumed that these securities have no default risk and no liquidity risk. As we noted above, long-term government securities are subject to maturity risk.

b. The risk-free rate of interest can also be defined as the real risk-free interest rate (r^*) plus the inflation premium (IP).

c. In 1997, the U.S. Treasury began issuing indexed bonds with interest payments linked to the rate of inflation. In mid-January 2004, the yield on these bonds ranged from 0.48% to 2.39%, with the higher yields coming on the longer-term securities because they have a maturity risk associated with them.

d. The risk-free rate is used to help determine the cost of equity when using the capital asset pricing model (CAPM).

5324.07   **Discounted Interest**

a. When a loan is discounted, the interest is deducted in advance. For example, a $10,000 loan at 10% will have $1,000 of interest. When a loan is discounted, $9,000 would be received at the inception of the loan, and $10,000 will be repaid. The borrower receives the face value of the loan less the interest.

b. Since the borrower does not receive the use of the face value of the loan, the effective interest is always higher than the stated rate.

Illustration: Using the example above, a $10,000 loan with a 10% nominal rate discounted at $1,000 will have an effective interest rate of:

$$\text{Effective Interest Rate} = \frac{\$1,000}{\$9,000} = 11.11\%$$

5324.08   **Installment Loan Interest**

a. Installment loans typically use add-on interest. Add-on interest loans calculate the interest and then add that number to the face value of the loan. The loan is then repaid in equal installments. This method is sometimes used in car or major appliance loans.

b. **Illustration:** $12,000 is borrowed at 10% interest to be paid back in 12 monthly installments. The interest would be $1,200 ($12,000 × 10%). The face value of the loan would become $13,200 ($12,000 + $1,200). The monthly installments would be $1,100 ($13,200 ÷ 12 months). The borrower would only have the use of the full amount of the loan for the 1st month since there are 12 monthly installments. In reality, the borrower would, on average, only have use of about half of the loan's face value. Therefore, the annual rate could be calculated to be **approximately**:

$$\text{Approximate Annual Rate} = \frac{\text{Interest Paid}}{\text{Amount Received} \div 2} = \frac{\$1,200}{\$6,000} = 20\%$$

c. Using the above example, the effective interest rate can be calculated. Using a financial calculator, the monthly interest can be determined to be 1.5%. This, however, is a monthly rate. The effective rate is:

$$\text{Add-on Effective Rate} = \left(1 + k_d\right)^n - 1.0 = \left(1 + .015\right)^{12} - 1.0 = 19.56\%$$

d. Before the passage of the truth-in-lending law in the 1970s, installment loans such as the one shown above would have been listed at 10%. Now the APR (annual percentage rate) of 19.56% would have to be listed in the loan document.

5324.09   **Other Interest Topics**

a. The **annual percentage rate (APR)** is the periodic rate times the number of periods per year. It is required to be reported when the nominal rate of interest is less than the effective interest rate. APR is a term often used in conjunction with the interest rate charged on credit cards. For example, the monthly interest rate of 1.5% is multiplied by 12 to provide an APR of 18%. This, however, is not the actual effective rate. Using the effective annual interest formula shown in section **5324.04**, the effective rate for the loan with an APR of 18% would be 19.56%.

   APR = Periods per year × Rate per period

b. The **Nominal or Stated Rate** of interest is the rate that is frequently used in advertising as the rate that is being charged on loans or credit cards. It is a simple annual rate that does not take into account the time value of money, so loans that are compounded more frequently than on an annual basis will have a higher effective interest rate than the stated (nominal) rate. Quoted nominal rates can only be compared if the loans being contrasted have the same number of compounding periods on an annual basis. The best way to compare different loans is to use effective interest rates.

c. The **Periodic Interest Rate** is the rate charged by the lender for each period. A 12% annual rate implies a 3% quarterly rate (12% ÷ 4). A 1.5% monthly rate translates into an 18% annual rate (1.5% × 12). If there is only one payment made per year, then the periodic interest rate equals the nominal rate.

d. The **Coupon Rate** is the stated annual interest rate on bonds. This is the fixed amount of interest expressed in terms of a percent that is determined at the time of issuance of the bonds and generally remains fixed during the life of the bond issue.

e. **Floating Interest Rates** are variable rates of interest that are tied to some market interest rate and are adjusted periodically in tandem with changes in that market index. Generally such rates are tied to a market rate such as the prime rate. This allows the lender to receive the highest possible interest rate given the market conditions.

f. The **Prime Rate** is a published rate that is charged by commercial banks to their best and strongest customers. In the past, this has been the lowest rate charged by banks; however, in recent years, competition from the commercial paper market has forced banks to offer lower rates to customers who can readily access the commercial paper market. Frequently loan rates are stated as a percentage over the prime rate.

5325　Weighted-Average Cost of Capital

5325.01　Terminology

a.　**CAPM (Capital Asset Pricing Model)** —A model used to estimate the required return on a firm's cost of capital: $R_i = R_F + \beta_i (R_m - R_F)$.

b.　**Dividend Growth Model**—A model used to estimate the cost of equity.

c.　**Weighted-Average Cost of Capital (WACC)**—The weighted average of the cost of debt and the various equity components of the firm's capital structure.

5325.02　Weighted-Average Cost of Capital

a.　The cost of capital is an important element in making investment decisions as projects with a higher rate of return than the firm's cost of capital will increase the value of the firm. The relevant cost of capital is the firm's long-term cost of capital since we are evaluating long-term projects or investments.

b.　**The Weighted-Average Cost of Capital** is the weighted average of the cost of debt and the various equity components of the firm's capital structure. It is preferable to use weights based on the market value of the items or the firm's target capital structure.

(1) The cost of debt (k_d) is the expected interest cost on new debt times one minus the marginal tax rate due to the fact that interest payments are tax deductible.

(2) The cost of preferred stock (k_{ps}) is determined by dividing the preferred dividend by the net issuance price for the preferred stock. Preferred dividends are not tax deductible.

(3) The cost of retained earnings is the opportunity cost that stockholders of a firm could earn elsewhere if they made investments of comparable risk. This figure would need to be imputed.

(4) The cost of equity (k_e) is more expensive than the cost of debt since stockholders are subject to more risk than debt holders. There are a number of ways to estimate the cost of equity, and one commonly used method to obtain the estimate is the **dividend growth model**. The formula used is:

$$k_e = (D_1 \div P_o (1 - F)) + g$$

This formula assumes that the firm pays a dividend equal to D_1, would issue new stock at price P_o, and would pay a flotation cost (F) that is equal to some percentage of the value of the stock being issued. It is assumed that the firm's dividend will grow at a constant rate (g).

Illustration: The firm's dividend was $1.50 and is expected to grow 6% per year. They expect to be able to sell new stock at a price $30 per share and flotation costs are expected to be 10% of the value of the stock issue. What is the firm's cost of equity?

$$
\begin{aligned}
k_e &= (\$1.50 \div \$30 (1 - 0.10)) + 6.0\% \\
&= (\$1.50 \div \$27.00) + 6.0\% \\
&= 5.56\% + 6.0\% \\
&= 11.56\%
\end{aligned}
$$

c. Most analysts use the **CAPM (Capital Asset Pricing Model)** to estimate the required return on a firm's cost of equity. The basic equation for estimating the required return on equity (R_i) is:

$$R_i = R_F + \beta_i (R_m - R_F)$$

The beta coefficient is the amount of risk that an individual stock contributes to the market portfolio and is a measure of the correlation between the volatility of the price of the individual stock and the volatility of the stock market. The market risk premium ($R_m - R_F$) is the premium that common stocks have returned over time in excess of the risk-free rate (R_F). Generally the current Treasury bill rate is used as the risk-free rate. Some analysts would use the 10-year Treasury Bond rate for the risk-free rate when evaluating long-term capital projects.

d. The primary conclusion of the **capital-asset pricing model (CAPM)** is that the relevant risk on any security is its contribution to the risk of a well-diversified portfolio. A commonly used benchmark portfolio for the market portfolio is the S&P 500.

e. **Illustration:** Assume that the current T-bill rate is 3.35% and the market risk premium is 7% for a diversified market portfolio.

$$\begin{aligned} R_i \quad &= R_F + \beta_i (R_m - R_F) \\ &= 3.35\% + 1.0\,(7.0\%) \\ &= 10.35\% \end{aligned}$$

Under this scenario, investors would expect to earn 10.35% on a diversified market portfolio. [Note: The beta coefficient for the diversified market portfolio is 1.0.]

Given the information in the example above and assuming that the beta coefficient for an individual security is 1.4, what return would investors require to hold this security?

Solution: Using the formula from (c) above, that is, $R_i = R_F + \beta_i (R_m - R_F)$, the return required by investors would be 13.15%.

$$\begin{aligned} R_i \quad &= R_F + \beta_i (R_m - R_F) \\ &= 3.35\% + 1.4\,(7.0\%) \\ &= 13.15\% \end{aligned}$$

f. The weighted-average cost of capital can be computed as follows:

$$WACC = (wt_d \times k_d) + (wt_{pf} \times k_{pf}) + (wt_e \times k_e)$$

Example: Assume that the firm can issue new debt at 5% and that the marginal tax rate is 40%. The firm has $1,000 par preferred stock that pays a dividend of 4%. Using the CAPM, it is estimated that investors require a 16% return to purchase the firm's stock. The firm has a target capital structure of 30% debt, 10% preferred stock and 60% equity. What is the firm's WACC?

Solution:

$$\begin{aligned} WACC \quad &= (.30 \times [.05 \times (1 - .40)]) + (.10 \times .04) + (.60 \times .16) \\ &= .009 + .004 + .096 \\ &= .109 \text{ or } 10.9\% \end{aligned}$$

5325.03 Optimal Capital Structure

a. Finance theory indicates that the goal for a firm should be to minimize its weighted-cost of capital, and it can do so by achieving its optimal capital structure.

b. The tax shield for debt makes debt a very attractive component of the capital structure. However, increasing the amount of debt in the structure beyond some point causes increasing financial distress costs that would cause the cost of additional debt to climb. Theoretically, the firm should continue to issue debt until the increasing financial distress costs offset the positive value of the tax shield.

c. It is very difficult to accurately determine the optimal capital structure, and in practice a firm attempts to find an optimal range of debt-to-equity that would minimize the weighted-average cost of capital.

d. Key elements in making capital structure decisions include:

(1) Sales stability - a firm whose sales are stable can take on more debt than a firm with unstable sales.

(2) Asset structure - firms with assets that are suitable to be pledged as security for a loan can use debt more heavily than firms with special purpose assets.

(3) Operating leverage - firms with less operating leverage are better able to employ financial leverage.

(4) Growth rate - faster-growing companies are more likely to rely more heavily on debt.

(5) Profitability - firms with high profitability are better able to support more of their financing needs with internally generated funds.

(6) Taxes - the higher a firm's marginal tax rate, the greater the advantages of using debt.

(7) Management attitude - management can exercise judgment as to the appropriate capital structure.

e. As shown by the following graphs, the lower the firm's weighted-average cost of capital (WACC) the greater the value of the firm since the WACC is used to discount the firm's expected cash flows. Thus, many firms are concerned about creating a capital structure that minimizes its cost of capital. As a firm moves from being an all equity firm (that is, with debt equal to zero) to adding debt to the capital structure the firm's WACC will being to decline. This is true because debt is less risky than equity (demanding a lower return) and debt has a "tax shield" in that the interest cost is tax deductible. Therefore, adding debt to the capital structure mix reduces WACC. This decline will continue until financial markets perceive that the firm's debt-to-asset (or equity) ratio has reached a point where additional debt will increase the firm's "financial distress costs" (that is, the possibility of bankruptcy) and require a higher return on the debt to compensate for the increased risk. At this point, the firm's WACC will begin to rise. A firm's "optimal capital structure" is the ratio that minimizes WACC, in the example found in Graph B it is found to be 40%.

Graph A

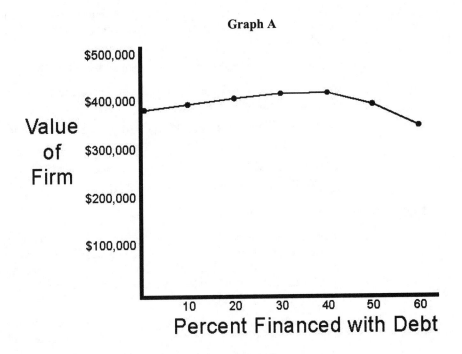

Graph B

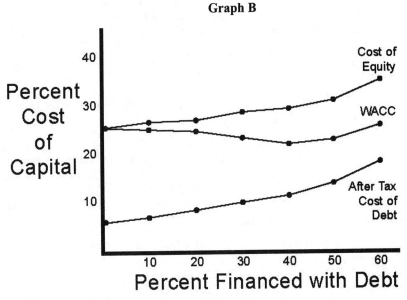

5326   Business Risk

5326.01   Terminology

a. **Business Risk**—The uncertainty associated with the ability to forecast EBIT due to such things as sales variability and operating leverage.

b. **Credit Risk**—The risk that receivables will not be collected in full on a timely basis.

c. **Company Risk** (Company Specific Risk)—Risk that is specifically associated with a particular firm due to mix of products, new products, competition, patents, lawsuits, etc.

d. **Default Risk**—The risk that the borrower will be unable to make interest and/or principal payments as scheduled on the obligation.

---

e. **Interest Rate Risk**—The risk of holding fixed interest-bearing instruments such as a bond when interest rates are changing that will result in the change of the market value of the debt instrument.

f. **Liquidity Risk**—The risk that an asset cannot be sold for market value on short notice.

g. **Market Risk**—The risk measured by the beta coefficient, associated with a security that cannot be eliminated by diversification.

h. **Purchasing Risk (Purchasing Power Risk)**—The risk that inflation will result in less purchasing power for a given sum of money.

i. **Reinvestment Risk**—The risk that interest rates will have declined when short-term investments must be rolled over.

5326.02   Interest Rate Risk

a. **Interest Rate Risk** is the risk of holding fixed interest-bearing instruments such as a bond when interest rates are changing. The price of long-term bonds is more sensitive to changes in interest rates than the price of short-term securities; thus, a rise in interest rates would cause the price of a fixed interest-bearing instrument to drop. Generally, the longer the maturity value, the greater the interest rate risk.

b. **Illustration:** 8%, 20-year bonds are purchased at par for $100,000 when the market was yielding 8%. If interest rates rise to 10%, the price of the bond will decrease so that the actual yield will equal 10% to match the current market rate. The market value is the PV of the future cash flows, and for a bond that matures in 20 years and pays $8,000 of interest annually to yield 10%, the PV would be calculated as follows:

$$\begin{array}{rl} \$100,000 \times .1486 = & \$14,860 \\ + \$8,000 \times 8.5136 = & \underline{68,109} \\ & \underline{\$82,969} \end{array}$$

The potential drop in market value is the risk associated with holding a long-term fixed interest-bearing instrument.

c. If a short-term Treasury bill is held during a period of rising interest rates, the loss in market value related to that increase in interest rates is much less significant. For example, given the same interest rate scenario described above, the price of a $100,000, 180 T-bill would decline to $99,069.

5326.03   Reinvestment Risk

Reinvestment Risk arises when investments must be rolled over. If rates have declined, the interest earned will decline.

5326.04   Liquidity Risk (Marketability Risk)

a. A highly liquid asset can be sold on short notice for close to its market value; however, an asset that changes hands infrequently often does not have a ready market. Therefore, a price reduction is often necessary if the asset is sold on short notice. **Liquidity risk** is the risk that an asset cannot be sold for market value on short notice.

b. Securities such as U.S. Treasury bills or stock in major corporations have a ready market and can be sold quickly for the quoted market price. Bonds issued by an obscure firm would probably have to be sold at a discount over market price in order to find a willing buyer on short notice. Bonds such as these have a high level of liquidity risk.

5326.05 Market Risk

Market risk is the risk associated with a security that cannot be eliminated by diversification. This includes such things as recessions, inflation, and changing interest rates that affect all firms. This is also known as systematic risk.

5326.06 Company Risk (Company-Specific Risk)

Company Risk is risk that is specifically associated with a particular firm due to mix of products, new products, competition, patents, lawsuits, etc. Within a portfolio, Company Risk can be eliminated by proper diversification.

5326.07 Credit Risk

a. **Credit Risk** is the risk that receivables will not be collected in full on a timely basis. Increased risk includes costs related to bad debt losses, higher receivable balances resulting in higher carrying costs, higher customer investigation fees, and collection costs.

b. Credit risk can be evaluated by looking into the customer's:

   (1) character. Will the customer make an honest effort to pay all obligations?

   (2) capacity. Does the customer have the ability to make necessary payments on a timely basis?

   (3) capital position. Does the customer have a good financial position such as discovered or measured through ratio analysis?

   (4) collateral. Are assets pledged as security on the obligation?

   (5) general conditions. What are the probable economic conditions and how might they affect the customer's ability to pay?

5326.08 Default Risk

a. **Default Risk** is the risk that the borrower will be unable to make interest and/or principal payments as scheduled on the obligation. The higher the possibility of default, the greater the return required by the lender.

b. U.S. Treasury Bonds are considered to be default risk free. Securities and bonds do have some degree of risk, and several organizations such as Moody's Investment Service and Standard & Poor's Corporation rate bonds for default risk. The lower the quality of the bonds, the greater the interest rate the issuing firm is required to pay in order to compensate for the risk.

5326.09 Business Risk

Business Risk is the uncertainty associated with the ability to forecast EBIT (earnings before interest and taxes). Business risk is dependent upon a number of factors that can be affected by the industry, the region, or the specific firm. Generally the smaller firms and/or companies that rely heavily on a small number of customers have greater business risk.

a. The more volatile the demand for the organization's product or service, the greater the risk.

b. The higher the fixed cost of the firm (operating leverage), the greater the risk that the breakeven point will not be reached.

c. The more variable the sales price for the firm's products, the greater the risk.

d. The more volatile the cost of inputs, the greater the risk.

e.   The greater the firm's ability to pass on price increases for materials, the lower the risk.

f.   The greater the firm's ability to develop new products in a timely, cost-effective manner, the lower the risk.

5326.10   Purchasing Risk

Purchasing Risk (Purchasing Power Risk) is the risk that inflation will result in less purchasing power for a given sum of money. Assets that are expected to rise in value during a period of inflation have a lower risk. For example, real estate often appreciates during an inflationary period; however, cash loses value during that same period.

5327   Risk and Return Trade-Offs

5327.01   Terminology

a.   **Degree of Financial Leverage**—The percentage change in profits available to common stockholders that is associated with a particular percentage change in EBIT.

b.   **Degree of Operating Leverage**—The percentage change in operating income compared to the percentage change in sales.

c.   **Degree of Total Leverage**—The percentage change in net profit related to a percentage change in revenue.

d.   **Financial Leverage**—The extent to which debt and preferred stock (fixed securities) are used in the capital structure.

e.   **Operating Leverage**—The extent to which fixed costs are used in the operating structure.

f.   **Target Capital Structure**—The balance of debt and equity financing where the value of the firm is maximized.

5327.02   Operating Leverage

a.   Business risk is built partially on the degree a company uses fixed costs in its operations. The higher the fixed costs, the greater the risk that the breakeven point will not be reached given a drop in sales. When fixed costs are high, a small drop in sales can result in a loss for the period. **Operating leverage** relates the percentage changes in EBIT to the percentage change in revenue. The greater the operating leverage, the greater the change in operating income will be given a particular change in sales. Therefore, a company with a high degree of operating leverage would have a large change in operating income for a relatively a small change in sales.

b.   The **degree of operating leverage** is the percentage change in EBIT related to a given percentage change in revenue.

$$\text{DOL} = \frac{\text{\% Change in Net Operating Income}}{\text{\% Change in Sales}} = \frac{\text{Contribution Margin}}{\text{Contribution Margin} - \text{Fixed Costs}}$$

A DOL of 2 means that the percentage change of EBIT will be twice the size of the percentage change in sales. If sales increase by 20%, then EBIT will increase by 40%; however, if sales decrease by 20%, then EBIT will decrease by 40%.

c. A firm can change the DOL by changing the proportion of fixed costs to variable costs. The larger the proportion of fixed costs, the higher the DOL and the higher the breakeven point. The higher the proportion of variable costs, the lower the DOL and the lower the breakeven point.

Also, notice that after the breakeven point is reached with a high DOL, the operating profit increases quickly; thus, the additional risk associated with high fixed costs also contains the possibility of higher profits in the event of a positive sales outcome. The following diagram shows how income can increase rapidly after reaching the breakeven point if high fixed costs and low variable costs are used in the production process.

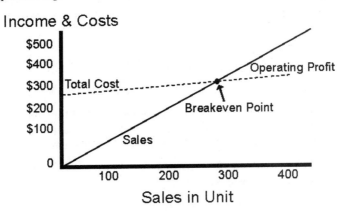

The lower the fixed costs, the lower the DOL and breakeven point will be. Given the same sales as in the above diagram, a lower percentage of fixed cost will cause the breakeven point to be reached at an earlier sales level; however, the operating profit will increase slowly in relation to increased sales. The operating profit (loss) is the difference between the sales and total costs.

d. Illustration: Tally Company has the following information available regarding sales and costs from the last period:

Sales in Units	10,000
Selling Price per Unit	$10.00
Variable Costs per Unit	$6.00
Fixed Costs for Period	$20,000

What is the DOL?

Solution:

$$\text{DOL} = \frac{\text{Contribution Margin}}{\text{Contribution Margin - Fixed Costs}}$$

$$= \frac{10,000 \text{ Units } (\$10.00 - \$6.00)}{10,000 \text{ Units } (\$10.00 - \$6.00) - \$20,000} = 2$$

5327.03 Financial Leverage

a. Financial Leverage refers to the extent to which debt and preferred stock (fixed income securities) are used in the capital structure. The larger the percentage of debt and preferred stock that is used for financing, the greater the risk that the company will not earn enough to cover the fixed interest and preferred dividend payments. The more leverage, the greater the risk, and the higher the cost of capital.

b. **Degree of Financial Leverage** is the percentage change in earnings available to common stockholders related to a given percentage change in EBIT.

$$DFL = \frac{\% \text{ Change in Net Income}}{\% \text{ Change in Net Operating Income}} = \frac{EBIT}{EBIT - Interest}$$

When there is no debt financing used, the DFL will equal 1. When debt does exist, a change in EBIT will result in a greater proportional change in the earnings per share.

If the DFL were 2, then a 10% increase in EBIT would result in a 20% (10% × 2) increase in earnings per share.

If the organization has preferred stock, the DFL equation is modified to:

$$DFL = \frac{EBIT}{EBIT - Interest \, Expense - \dfrac{Preferred \, Dividends}{1 - Tax \, Rate}}$$

c. If a firm has no debt and begins to substitute debt for equity, at first the value of the firm will rise, reach a peak, and then begin to fall due to the increased risk of additional debt. This peak in maximized value is the target capital structure.

d. **Illustration:** Tally Company has the following information available about sales and costs from the last period:

Sales in Units	10,000
Selling Price per Unit	$10.00
Variable Costs per Unit	$6.00
Fixed Costs for Period	$20,000
Interest Costs for Period	$15,000

What is the DFL?

Solution:
$$DFL = \frac{EBIT}{EBIT - Interest \, Expense}$$
$$= \frac{10,000 \, Units \, (\$10.00 - \$6.00) - \$20,000}{[10,000 \, Units \, (\$10.00 - \$6.00) - \$20,000] - \$15,000}$$
$$= 4$$

5327.04 **Total Leverage (Degree of Combined Leverage)**

a. If a company used both high degrees of operating and financial leverage, only small changes in sales will result in large fluctuations in EPS. This can be shown in equation form:

$$\text{Degree of Total Leverage} = \frac{\% \text{ Change in Net Income}}{\% \text{ Change in Sales}} = DOL \times DFL$$

b. This ratio can be used to predict the effect of a change in sales on income and ultimately the earnings available to common stockholders.

c. This ratio is determined by the relationship between operating and financial leverage. For example, if risk is lowered by reducing the degree of operating leverage, then the firm would be in a better position to increase the use of debt thus increasing the financial leverage.

d. The financial statement effects of DOL and DFL can be shown by using the income statement format:

			Previous	Percentage Increase	Resulting Change
DTL of 8	**DOL of 2**	Sales	$100,000	10%	$110,000
		Variable Costs	60,000		66,000
		Fixed Costs	20,000		20,000
		EBIT	20,000	20%	24,000
	DFL of 4	Fixed financing costs	15,000		15,000
		EBT	5,000		9,000
		Taxes (40%)	2,000		3,600
		Net Income	$3,000	80%	$5,400

Please note that the results were based on the assumptions that the cost relationships remain unchanged (fixed and variable) as well as the firm's capital structure, including the amount of the fixed financing payments. As the relationships change, the DOL, DFL, and DTL would also change.

e. **Illustration:** Tally Company has the following information available about sales and costs from the last period:

Sales in Units	100,000
Selling Price per Unit	$10.00
Variable Costs per Unit	$6.00
Fixed Costs for Period	$20,000
Interest Costs for Period	$15,000

What is the DTL?

Solution: DTL = DOL × DFL

$$= \frac{10,000\ (\$10 - \$6)}{10,000\ (\$10 - \$6) - \$20,000} \times \frac{10,000\ (\$10 - \$6) - \$20,000}{10,000\ (\$10 - \$6) - \$20,000 - \$15,000}$$

$$= 2 \times 4 = 8$$

5330 Financial Statement Implications of Liquid Asset Management

5331 Cash Management Techniques

5331.01 Terminology

a. **Cash Budget**—A cash management tool that details cash inflows and outflows over a specified period of time.

b. **Certificate of Deposit**—A time deposit with a financial institution for a specified period of time. Interest rates will vary depending upon the amount of the deposit and the time to maturity.

c. **Collection Float**—The different between the checks that have been received and those credited by the bank and the related funds available for use.

d. **Commercial Paper**—Short-term, unsecured promissory notes issued by large firms.

    e. **Compensating Balances**—Minimum account balances required to be kept by a firm in a bank in order to obtain bank services without additional fees or a loan.

    f. **Disbursement Float**—The amount of the checks issued that have yet to clear the bank.

    g. **Float**—The difference between bank cash and book cash.

    h. **Line of Credit**—An agreement where a firm has arranged to borrow from a bank up to a specific amount within a defined period of time.

    i. **Marketable Securities**—Low-risk investments that can be quickly turned into cash.

    j. **Net Float**—The sum of the disbursement float and the collection float.

    k. **Netting**—A cash management technique that maximizes cash flow by reducing the administrative and transaction fees for currency conversion.

    l. **Precautionary Balances**—Cash balances held as a reserve for random or unexpected fluctuations in cash inflows or outflows.

    m. **Speculative Balances**—Cash available to the firm to take advantage of business opportunities.

    n. **Synchronizing Cash Flows**—The matching of the timing of cash outflows with the timing of cash inflows.

    o. **Target Cash Balance**—The desired cash balance that the firm believes is necessary to safely conduct business.

    p. **Transaction Balances**—Cash available to make expected day-to-day payments of various obligations.

    q. **Treasury Bonds**—Bonds issued by the U.S. government.

5331.02 **Reasons to Hold Cash**

There are four primary reasons for a company to hold cash.

    a. Transactions purposes: Cash is necessary for a company to conduct its day-to-day business.

    b. Precaution purposes: Since cash flows do not flow evenly over time and often cash inflows are not matched with cash outflows (a business cycle consideration), it is necessary to have enough cash on hand to compensate for unanticipated fluctuations in cash flows.

        (1) Precautionary cash is often held in highly liquid marketable securities. This provides security and additional interest income.

        (2) Today, most companies have a line-of-credit arrangement to cover the precautionary needs.

    c. Speculative purposes: Cash balances are also necessary to allow a firm to take advantage of potential business opportunities such as bargain purchases.

        (1) Near-Cash is advisable for speculative purposes so that additional interest/dividend income can be earned.

        (2) Organizations often do not hold cash for speculative purposes if they have a readily available source of funds such as a line-of-credit.

    d. To meet compensating balance requirements: **Compensating balances** are amounts required to be kept in an account by a bank and are often mandatory in order to obtain a loan or to avoid paying fees for individual bank services.

5331.03   **The Cash Budget**

 a. The **cash budget** is a cash management tool that details cash inflows and outflows over a specified period of time. It can be prepared on a yearly, quarterly, monthly, weekly, or even daily basis. Since cash inflows and outflows are not necessarily uniform throughout the year, the cash budget highlights when cash shortages are likely to occur, allowing management to plan necessary borrowing, and also highlights when cash surpluses will be available for repayments or investments.

 b. The cash budget is based upon estimates of sales, credit terms, and bad debt levels (cash collections); estimates for purchases and payment terms (cash payments); estimates for production and payment terms for conversion costs (cash payments); estimates for borrowings (cash inflows), repayments, and associated interest payments (cash outflows); estimates for capital purchases (possible cash outflows) and disposals (possible cash inflows); and potential dividend payments (cash outflows). Since this budget is based upon estimates, it is necessary to update the cash budget on a regular basis when data on actual inflows and outflows become available.

 c. The **target cash balance** is the desired cash balance management believes to be necessary to safely conduct business. This amount may vary during the year due to the cyclical nature of many industries. When estimated cash inflows exceed estimated cash outflows for a given period including planned capital expenditures, the excess can be used to repay short-term credit and/or be invested. When estimated cash outflows exceed estimated cash inflows for a given period, investments can be turned into cash to meet these cash needs, or short-term borrowing can be arranged. Many companies have line-of-credit arrangements to help them smooth out cash flows throughout the year.

5331.04   **Synchronizing Cash Flows**

Synchronizing cash flows matches the cash outflows with the timing of the receipt of cash inflows. This allows firms to keep transaction balances to a minimum. Many companies stagger the billing of customers throughout the month in an attempt to create fairly even daily cash inflows while planning the timing of payments for various obligations so that due dates are during various weeks of the month. The lower the target cash balance, the more funds that are available for productive uses.

5331.05   **Speed of Cash Collections and Disbursements**

 a. From the perspective of an individual firm, collections need to be made as quickly as possible and disbursements delayed as long as possible, providing discounts are not lost nor unnecessary interest charges incurred. This allows for the maximum cash balance at any given time.

 b. When a check is received from a customer, it does not mean that funds are necessarily available at the time of receipt. Due to the check clearing process, it may be one to three days before the funds are available. The difference between the checks that have been received and those credited by the bank is the **collection float**. The goal of management is to keep this float as low as possible.

 c. Techniques such as the use of lockboxes (see section **5335.07**) and electronic fund transfers (see section **5335.06**) allow firms to speed up the collection process.

    d. The **net float** is the difference between the firm's checkbook balance and the balance of the account in the bank's records. The difference is due to the collection float and the disbursement float. The **disbursement float** is the amount of the checks written but that have yet to clear the bank. The disbursement float allows a firm to have lower cash balances.

    e. Techniques such as the use of zero balance accounts (see section **5335.05**) allow a firm to not hold funds in non-interest-bearing accounts to meet anticipated disbursement needs.

5331.06   **Use of Marketable Securities**

    a. **Marketable securities** are generally low-risk investments that can be quickly turned into cash. Marketable securities include:

       (1) U.S. Treasury Bills

       (2) Bank Certificates of Deposit

       (3) Commercial Paper

    Since most firms attempt to minimize cash balances, excess cash is often invested in marketable securities that are purchased with maturities that coincide with seasonal needs, maturing debt, tax payments, or other potential needs.

    b. Marketable securities have low risk and high liquidity.

       (1) Since safety is an important factor, short-term marketable securities are generally lower yielding since safety is traded for higher yield and minimizes default risk.

       (2) Short-term investments also minimize interest rate risk since their market values do not show a high degree of price fluctuation related to interest rate changes.

    c. Marketable securities are held as a substitute for cash. By transferring excess cash to interest-bearing investments, the surplus can add value to the firm. The funds are still readily available to meet transaction, precautionary and speculative needs.

    d. Marketable securities are held as temporary investments to be used to meet seasonal needs or to protect against business downturns.

    e. Marketable securities are held to meet planned financial needs such as a maturing bond issue, upcoming tax payments, or a possible expenditure for plant or equipment.

    f. Marketable securities can be used as a temporary place for funds received but yet to be invested in long-term investments or capital additions.

    g. With the use of lines-of-credit, the need for marketable securities has diminished for companies that have access to such financing options.

    By using a line-of-credit to meet short-term needs for funds as opposed to marketable securities:

       (1) A firm's current ratio could be lower without indicating a greater risk that the obligations would not be repaid on a timely basis. There is however a risk that funds available from this method of financing might not meet all of the firm's actual short-term needs.

       (2) If excess cash is not expected to be needed for precautionary and speculative purposes, it might be feasible to put these additional funds to better use, such as by investing them in higher-yield, medium-term investments or to fund capital enhancements to improve the productivity of the existing capacity.

5331.07 Cash Management and the Multi-Company, International Firm

   a. A multi-company firm has additional cash management issues. Each subsidiary needs to manage cash on an individual basis; however, a centralized cash management group needs to manage the cash flows between the parent-subsidiary and within inter-subsidiaries in order to optimize cash flows. Such management can benefit subsidiaries in need of funds by supplying the needed cash from excess funds from another subsidiary or the parent.

   b. The need to increase the speed of cash inflows is magnified in the international setting due to increased mailing times. The use of lockboxes around the world is one method of speeding up collection. Another method is to have preauthorized payments where the firm can charge a customer's account up to a specified limit. Today, most large firms use an electronic method such as the Internet to transfer funds.

   c. International cash flows result in the need for currency conversions. By using a tool called **netting**, administrative and transaction costs resulting from currency conversions can be reduced. For example, if two subsidiaries are located in different countries and A purchases parts from B, transactions resulting from the sale of the parts from B to A are "netted" for a period of time (generally a month), and one net payment involving currency exchanges is made per period thus reducing conversion costs.

   A more complex multilateral netting system is used when there are a parent and several subsidiaries. The transactions among the various entities are netted so that conversion costs are minimized.

   d. The use of various cash transfers for international organizations may be hampered by foreign government restrictions and characteristics of the banking systems in less developed countries

5332 Accounts Receivable Management Techniques

5332.01 Terminology

   a. **Cash Discount**—A percentage or dollar reduction on an invoice designed to encourage early payment.

   b. **Collection Procedures**—The steps taken by a firm to collect past-due accounts.

   c. **Collection Policy**—The tough or lax procedures used to see that credit accounts are collected.

   d. **Credit Period**—The length of time for which credit is extended without an interest penalty.

   e. **Credit Policy**—The credit standards, credit period, available discounts, and collection procedures for trade accounts receivable.

   f. **Credit Quality**—The ability to collect receivables in full and in a timely manner.

   g. **Credit Standards**—The firm-developed benchmarks used to determine the minimum financial strength needed to provide credit to a customer.

   h. **Incremental Profit**—The difference between incremental sales and incremental costs.

   i. **Quality of Credit**—The ability to collect receivables in full and in a timely manner.

5332.02 **Introduction to Accounts Receivable Management**

a. Firms extend credit on sales in order to increase revenues. Since the objective of increased sales is to increase profit, a firm will theoretically extend credit until the cost of offering additional credit equals the costs incurred in generating those sales (incremental analysis).

b. The value of the trade accounts receivable at any given time is directly tied to sales volume, which in turn is influenced by factors some of which management has control of such as product price and quality and advertising. Another major controllable factor influencing sales is the firm's credit policy that consists of:

   (1) **Credit period**—the length of time the customer is given to pay for the purchases. For example, credit terms of "3/10, net 30" allows buyers to take up to 30 days to pay without incurring interest charges.

   (2) **Discounts**—the credit terms "3/10, net 30" allow customers to take a 3% discount if the payment is received within 10 days of the invoice. The full amount would be due in 30 days if the discount opportunity was not taken.

   (3) **Credit Standards**—the required financial strength of acceptable customers. Relaxing the standards is likely to boost sales, but also to increase bad debt losses.

   (4) **Collection Policy**—how tough or lax the firm is in terms of attempting to collect slow-paying accounts. Again, there is a trade-off between attempting to speed up the collection of an account and possibly losing a customer.

c. The credit manager is generally responsible for administering a firm's credit policy. However, credit policy is generally set at an administrative level with the firm.

d. A change in credit policy involves the interaction between several variables. Below are some of the issues management would need to analyze when considering a change in the credit policy.

   (1) Sales—What is the projected increase in the level of gross sales that would result from the change?

   (2) Account Receivable—There is generally a proportional relationship between an increase in sales and an increase in accounts receivable. An increase in accounts receivable would mean that additional funds would be tied up until collection. Increasing accounts receivable would require increasing funding (debt or equity) with a possible increase in interest costs.

   (3) Discounts and Bad Debt Losses—What proportion of customers would be expected to take the discount? What proportion of the additional receivable would become bad debts?

   (4) Costs of Running a Collection Department—Would more staff (higher costs) be needed to run collection department due to higher volume? Would there be fixed costs associated with the expansion of the credit collection efforts?

   (5) Management would have to compare the increased revenues expected with the increased costs to determine whether the firm would be better off on an incremental profit basis.

e. A firm's **credit policy** includes the credit standards, credit period, available discounts, and collection procedures.

f. The **quality of credit** is defined as the ability to collect receivables in full and in a timely manner.

g. A firm's credit policy is often dictated or strongly influenced by competitors since unless the firm's policies are competitive, sales will often be lost.

5332.03 Credit Standards

Credit standards are the firm's standards by which potential customers are measured in the process of being approved for credit. The lower the standards, the higher the sales and the higher the associated costs such as bad debt losses that come from extending credit to less creditworthy customers. Optimal credit standards allow for the marginal cost of extending the additional credit to equal the margin profits produced by the increased sales resulting from to the relaxed credit standards. (See section **5326.07** for a discussion on credit risk.)

5332.04 Credit Period

a. The **credit period** is the length of time for which credit is extended. It is the time that elapses between the sale and the expected collection of funds. Lengthening the credit period often encourages sales, but also increases financing needs due to the fact that additional funds will be tied up in the additional receivables. Longer credit periods are also associated with higher bad debt expenses.

b. If the credit period is extended, trade accounts receivable will increase due to the increased holding time of receivables as well as increased credit sales.

c. The cost of extending the credit period can be calculated by multiplying the increase in accounts receivable by the marginal cost of capital.

Illustration: If a firm increases its credit period from 30 to 45 days, average accounts receivable are predicted to increase from $400,000 to $500,000. If the cost of capital is 10%, then the marginal cost of changing the credit period is $10,000 ($100,000 × 10%).

d. In poor economic times, a firm needs to be concerned that customers will unilaterally extend the credit period.

5332.05 Available Discounts

a. Discounts are used as an incentive to get the customer to make an early payment. This would reduce the cash outflow needed by the customer to meet the obligation. A common discount would be stated as "2/10, net 30". This is interpreted to mean that the customer may take a 2% discount if the payment is received within 10 days, with the full amount due and deemed current if received between 11 to 30 days.

b. Discounts provide:

(1) a price reduction for customers.

(2) a means to attract new customers.

(3) a way to reduce the average collection period.

c. Seasonal discounts are also offered by some organizations. By placing an order by a specified date, customers are offered discounts even if the merchandise is shipped months later. This is a tool designed to lock-in sales that would help to facilitate scheduling production.

5332.06   Collection Procedures

Collection procedures are steps that a firm takes to collect past-due accounts. These steps might include a series of increasingly severe letters or telephone calls with the account ultimately turned over to a collection agency. Collection procedures are expensive and can often be reduced by screening customers more carefully or by tightening credit standards. These choices generally involve a cost/benefit issue.

5332.07   Alternative Credit

The acceptance of bank credit cards and debit cards is an alternative to providing in-house credit to customers and can often be less expensive. Retail organizations are often forced into accepting this form of payment due to widespread consumer use and the acceptance by competitors.

   a.   Charge tickets can be deposited daily, much like a check.

   b.   Funds are available immediately for debit card transactions and almost immediately for credit card transactions.

   c.   Banks charge fees in the range of 3% to 10% of the dollar sales volume based upon average transaction amount and total dollar volume. The higher the volumes and the larger the average per transaction, the lower the fee would be.

5333 Inventory Management Techniques

5333.01   Terminology

   a.   **Carrying Costs**—The costs to hold inventory, such as the costs of storage, warehouse rent or depreciation, insurance, interest, obsolescence, and spoilage, opportunity costs of funds tied up to finance the inventory.

   b.   **Economic Order Quantity**—The optimal quantity of inventory that can be ordered given various costs.

   c.   **Just-In-Time (JIT) Production System**—A production system where raw material and component parts are purchased just as they are needed in the production process, thus potentially reducing raw material inventory close to zero.

   d.   **Lead Time**—The time that will transpire between placing an order and the receipt of that order.

   e.   **Nonvalue-Adding Activity**—Activities that could be eliminated without detracting from customer satisfaction.

   f.   **Order Lead Time**—The time interval between placing an order and receiving the items.

   g.   **Ordering Costs**—The costs associated with placing and receiving orders.

   h.   **Reorder Point**—The point where inventory drops to the number of units that are expected to be sold or used during the lead time plus any safety stock that the firm deems to be necessary.

   i.   **Safety Stock**—A level of inventory that is held in excess of the desired inventory level to cover unanticipated demand.

j. **Stockout Costs**—The costs related to lost sales and/or rush orders when an outage occurs.

k. **Value-Adding Activities**—Activities that would reduce customer satisfaction if eliminated.

5333.02 The Importance of Inventory

Inventories can take many forms—raw materials, work-in-process, finished goods, supplies - and inventories are extremely important to many organizations. Without the appropriate inventories, there will possibly not be an adequate level of goods available to meet demand. Thus, it is important that management prepare adequate sales forecasts in order to assure that enough inventory will be available to meet the forecasted demand. Without the necessary inventory, sales are lost. On the other hand, excessive inventories lead to high carrying costs.

There are two major issues involved in inventory management—having the right inventory at the right place at the right time and not having too much inventory, which would result in excessive carrying costs.

5333.03 Just-In-Time

a. A **Just-In-Time (JIT) Production System** purchases raw materials and component parts just as they are needed in the production process, thus reducing raw material inventory close to zero. It is part of a manufacturing philosophy that promotes the simplest, least costly means of production. Under ideal conditions, the company would receive raw materials just in time to go into production, manufacture parts just in time to be assembled into products, and complete products just in time to be shipped to customers. JIT shifts the production philosophy from a push approach to a pull approach.

(1) The push approach begins with the acquisition of raw materials that are pushed into production through the various stages of production, and finally into finished goods inventory. The goal is to have finished goods ultimately sold to customers without deep discounting.

(2) The pull approach starts with the demand for finished goods from a customer. The customer's order triggers the production of the goods. Inventories are acquired only to meet production needs.

b. Under ideal conditions, the company would attempt to create a situation where both raw material inventory as well as finished goods inventory would be eliminated and work-in-process inventory kept to a minimum.

c. Raw materials are delivered just in time to meet the production schedule, with a guaranteed high level of product quality so that they can bypass inspection and go directly to production. This requires long-term purchase agreements with suppliers and coordination between purchasing and production. The result is a virtual elimination of raw material inventory. The cost of carrying inventory is shifted to the supplier.

d. The rate of production for individual departments is determined by the needs of each succeeding department. Inventory buffers with a predetermined size are used to signal when a department should be working. The department works as long as the buffer is less than the desired level. This eliminates most work-in-process inventory.

e. As soon as products are finished, they are immediately shipped to the customer, thus eliminating finished goods inventory and immediately converting the product into cash or accounts receivable. Close supplier/customer relations can allow both supplier and customer to use JIT systems.

f. Generally there are changes required in several areas of the manufacturing process to make JIT successful.

(1) Activities that do not add value need to be eliminated. Activities are identified as value-adding activities and nonvalue-adding activities. A **nonvalue-adding activity** is any activity that could be eliminated without detracting in any way from customers' satisfaction with the final product. Moving time, inspection time, and times in queues are all nonvalue-adding activities and should be eliminated as much as possible. Machining, milling, and polishing of products are all value-adding activities, as customer satisfaction would be reduced without them.

(2) Supplier relationships are of key importance. It is important to select a small number of suppliers who can guarantee both the quality and timely delivery of raw materials. Raw materials are usually delivered in small quantities as needed for production. Responsibility for raw material quality is also shifted to the supplier.

(3) Manufacturing cells are developed. Traditional departments and processes are replaced with manufacturing cells that contain families of machines typically spread through several departments. A component or a complete product can be produced within one cell rather than being transferred between several departments.

(4) The workforce is highly trained and flexible. The cellular manufacturing environment requires a labor force that is capable of operating several different machines. The workforce must be capable of servicing the machines and performing inspections on finished products.

(5) Total quality control is implemented at the inventory and production level. The streamlined flow of raw materials and components through the production process does not allow for product defects. No defects can be allowed in parts or raw materials received from suppliers, in work-in-process, or in finished goods. Emphasis is placed on doing things right the first time and avoiding rework or waste of any type. Products are inspected for quality at each stage of the process. When a defect is discovered, the production process is halted until the problem is corrected. Responsibility for inspecting products is shifted from inspectors to production workers. There is a commitment for continuous improvement in all aspects of the company.

(6) Set-up time is reduced. Set-up time is the time required to change equipment, move materials, and obtain forms needed to shift production from one product to another. Meeting customer demand on short notice without any finished goods inventory requires the ability to shift production from one product to another with a short set-up time.

g. When using JIT methods, the differences between net operating income using the absorption method or variable costing method will be reduced since the differences relating to the costing of inventory are eliminated with the elimination of the finished goods inventory. If inventories are almost non-existent, then differences in inventory valuations will be extremely small, bringing the results of net income using absorption or variable costing extremely close.

h. Advantages of JIT production systems:

(1) Funds are no longer tied up in inventories and can be more effectively used elsewhere.

(2) Warehouses formerly used to store inventory can be put to more productive use.

(3) As defects are reduced, less waste occurs and customers' satisfaction is increased.

(4) As production time is decreased, a greater output potential is created.

(5) Customers' satisfaction is increased due to the shorter delivery time from the point the order is received (order lead time).

i. Disadvantages of JIT production systems:

(1) Increased possibility of stockouts if delivery of a critical part is delayed due to strikes, disasters, or other unexpected occurrences.

5333.04 Economic Order Quantity

a. The **economic order quantity** is the least amount of inventory that should be ordered given the various costs involved. The Economic Order Quantity Model (EOQ) provides a formula for determining the quantity of a particular inventory item that should be ordered in order to minimize inventory costs.

$$EOQ = \sqrt{\frac{2DS}{Ci}}$$

b. Relevant items in determining the economic order quantity:

D = The demand per year in units

S = Setup or ordering cost per order or batch

C = The cost per unit

i = The carrying costs expressed as a percentage of inventory cost

c. Inventory decision models contain costs that move in opposite directions. Carrying costs increase as the size of the order increases. Set-up or ordering costs, however, decrease as the size of the production run or order increases. The EOQ model seeks to minimize the combined total of these two costs, as illustrated in the following graph.

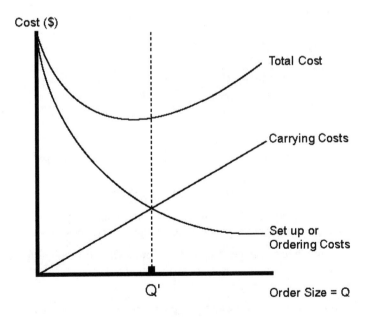

d. Assuming that there is constant demand and no change in lead time, the reorder point is equal to the sum of expected units of demand during the lead time plus any required safety stock. This relationship can be illustrated as follows:

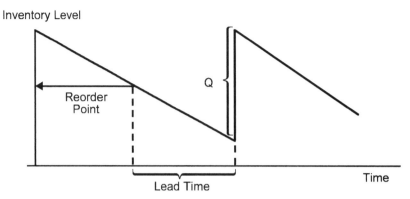

The formula for the reorder point (RP) is:
$$RP = D_{LT} + SS$$

D_{LT} is the average demand during the lead time period. This can be calculated by determining the demand per day and multiplying that result by the number of days in the lead time. SS is the safety stock required.

e. **Illustration:** Use the following data to compute the economic order quantity and reorder point assuming 300 business days per year.

Demand (D)	40,000 units per year
Unit Cost (C)	$50
Carrying Cost Rate (i)	20% per year
Order Cost (S)	$115 per order
Lead Time (LT)	3 days
Safety Stock (SS)	500 units

Solution:

$$EOQ = \sqrt{\frac{2DS}{Ci}}$$
$$= \sqrt{\frac{(2)(40,000)(\$115)}{(\$50)(20\%)}}$$
$$= 960 \; units$$

$$RP = D_{LT} + SS$$
$$= [(40,000 \; units / 300 \; days) x \; 3 \; days] + 500 = 900 \; units$$

5333.05 **Reasons for Not Minimizing Inventory Levels**

a. Larger inventory levels can guarantee the availability of inventory as needed. When stockout costs are high, carrying a larger safety stock may be appropriate.

b. Through use of large discounts or more favorable credit terms, customers may be convinced to purchase larger quantities. Thus, inventory policy needs to be coordinated with other policies such as credit policies.

c. If competition is very high, suppliers may feel the need to increase inventory levels to insure prompt deliveries to customers.

d. Inventories can be a good hedge against inflation if cost of replacing inventory is increasing.

e. **Safety stock** is a level of inventory that is held in excess of the desired inventory level to cover unanticipated demand. This additional inventory provides security from stock-outs and lost sales when the time to replace inventory exceeds the anticipated period. The level of safety stock is determined by a balancing of the cost of holding additional inventory items and the cost, or lost revenue, associated with not having goods available for the customer when they wish to purchase them.

5334 Accounts Payable Management Techniques

5334.01 Terminology

a. **Free Trade Credit**—Credit received during the discount period.

b. **Trade Credit**—A spontaneous source of financing created when goods and services are purchased on account in the normal course of business.

5334.02 Trade Credit

a. Most companies purchase on credit, making trade credit a significant part of current liabilities. **Trade credit** is a spontaneous source of financing created when goods and services are purchased on account in the normal course of business. If a firm purchases $10,000 of goods per day on average, at the end of 30 days, $300,000 ($10,000 × 30) of financing has been created. If suppliers' credit terms increase to 45 days, an additional $150,000 [$10,000 × (45 days - 30 days)] of credit can be generated.

b. As a general rule, firms will hold cash payments until the last minute that an obligation is due in order to increase their average cash balance. This is the case unless the cost of making an early payment is less than the firm's cost of capital.

5334.03 Free Trade Credit

a. Firms frequently have credit terms that include offering a discount on invoices if paid within the discount period. "2/10, net 30" provides a discount of 2% if the invoice is paid within 10 days and full payment is expected within 30 days if the discount is not taken.

b. **Free trade credit** is credit received during the discount period. In the example mentioned above, the discount period would be the first 10 days of the net purchase period.

c. **Illustration:** A firm purchases $50,000 of merchandise on credit with the terms 2/10, net 30. What amount is paid to satisfy the obligation if the payment is made by the 10th day of the net 30 period?

Solution: $50,000 - ($50,000 × 2%) = $49,000 with the firm gaining a $1,000 discount.

5334.04 Cost of Trade Credit

a. If payment is not made on trade credit within the discount period, the discount is lost, and the full amount of the credit is paid within 30 days. The results of this lost discount are:

(1) The savings of the discount are lost.

(2) The size of trade credit increases, thus increasing the debt load.

b. **Illustration:** A firm purchases $2 million of merchandise throughout the year (assuming a 360-day year) and is offered a 2% discount on all invoices paid within 10 days. If all invoices are paid within the discount period, the full amount paid will be $1,960,000 ($2 million × 98%). This results in a savings of $40,000 per year.

If all discounts are taken, payables at any given time will average $54,444 [($1,960,000 ÷ 360 days) × 10 days)]. If the discounts are not taken and payment is made within the 30-

day period, then average accounts payable will increase to $163,333 (($1,960,000 ÷ 360 days) × 30 days). That is an additional $108,889 of trade credit that is being used.

There is a cost to this additional credit—the lost $40,000 in discounts. The lost discounts represent increased cost for the merchandise; therefore the price of the additional $108,889 of trade credit is $40,000. The cost of this credit is computed as follows:

$$\frac{\text{Lost Discount}}{\text{Additional Credit Supplied}} = \frac{\$40,000}{\$108,889} = 36.7\%$$

c. If a firm can borrow funds at an interest rate lower than the cost of the foregone discount, then the funds should be borrowed and the discounts taken. If the firm above can borrow $108,889 at 10% for an annual interest cost of $10,889, then $29,111 would be saved on an annual basis ($40,000 - $10,889).

d. The return on taking discount can also be calculated using the following formula:

$$\frac{360}{\text{Total Credit Period} - \text{Discount Period}} \times \frac{\text{Percentage of Discount}}{100\% - \text{Percentage of Discount}}$$

Using the above illustration, the return can be calculated:

$$\frac{360}{30 \text{ days} - 10 \text{ days}} \times \frac{2\%}{100\% - 2\%} = 36.7\%$$

e. Payment of trade credit beyond the normal credit terms' will likely result in interest charges thus increasing the cost of credit as well as hurting relations with the supplier. Firms that do not take advantage of discounts are generally in a weaker financial position with poor cash flow and/or limited access to other sources of funds.

5334.05   Trade Credit and Financial Statements

a. Not taking discounts can have a dramatic effect on the financial statements—affecting profitability as well as liquidity.

b. The effect on profitability can be shown in the following tables comparing the results on income of a firm taking vs. not taking trade discounts. In this example, it is assumed that a company will have to borrow at 10% ($10,889 annual interest) in order to take advantage of the available discounts (see above information).

	Do Not Take Discounts	Take Discounts
Sales	$4,000,000	$4,000,000
Purchases	1,960,000	1,960,000
Other Costs	1,500,000	1,500,000
Interest	0	10,889
Discounts Lost	40,000	0
Total Costs	3,500,000	3,470,889
Income before Tax	500,000	529,111
Tax (40%)	200,000	211,644
Net Income after Tax	$ 300,000	$ 317,467

Since the discounts exceed the cost of the interest expense, net income is increased by taking the discounts. In this case, income is increased by $17,467 or approximately 6%.

c. Assuming that the firm goes to the bank to finance a note payable so that funds are available to take advantage of the discounts, the liability/equity sections of the balance sheet will have the following comparison when taking vs. not taking trade discounts:

	Do Not Take Discounts	Take Discounts
Accounts Payable	$163,333	$54,444
Note Payable		108,889
Accruals	50,000	50,000
Long-Term Debt	75,000	75,000
Equity	250,000	250,000
Total Liab. & Equity	$538,333	$538,333

Thus, the Total Liabilities & Equity will be the same. The only difference is that the firm will be able to choose how to finance the amount needed to take advantage of the discount for early payment and reduce the cost of financing—short-term loan, long-term loan, or equity. This example was presented using a short-term note. The nature of the spontaneity of the trade credit financing often causes these cost-saving options to be missed.

5335   Short-Term Tools

5335.01   Terminology

a. **Commercial Paper**—Short-term, unsecured, promissory notes that are offered by financially strong companies.

b. **Compensating Balance**—Amounts required to be kept in an account by a bank in order for a firm to obtain a loan or bank services.

c. **Deposit Transfer Check**—An official bank check that provides a means of moving funds from one account to another within the banking system.

d. **Float**—Funds represented by checks that have been written but are still in the process of being cleared through the banking system. The difference between the bank and book balances.

e. **Lockbox**—A mailbox set up to intercept accounts receivable payments with the goal of speeding up the collection of cash.

f. **Official Bank Check**—Checks that provide a means of moving funds from one account to another within the banking system.

g. **Trade Credit**—A source of funds that is spontaneously created as a result of the purchase transaction.

h. **Zero Balance Account**—Bank accounts held at zero until checks are cleared and then sufficient funds are transferred from another account in an amount large enough to cover the checks presented.

5335.02   Compensating Balances

    a.   A **Compensating Balance** is a cash balance required to be held in an account by a bank in order to obtain a loan or to avoid paying directly for certain bank services. Required balances are either a fixed minimum amount or a minimum average balance for a given period such as a month.

    b.   Compensating balances increase the cost of a loan or impart a cost to services provided.

        (1) **Illustration:** If a compensating balance of $10,000 is required in order to receive free bank services, the company would not hold these funds otherwise, and the money could be invested receiving a 5% return; then the actual cost of those services would be $500 per year ($10,000 × 5%). This could be compared with the actual cost of the services to determine if it would be less expensive to pay for the services directly.

        (2) **Illustration:** If a compensating balance of $10,000 is required in order to receive a $100,000 bank loan at 10%, then the effective cost of that loan will be increased, since only $90,000 will actually be available for use. The stated rate of interest on a $100,000 loan at 10% would be $10,000 per year. The effective rate of interest would then be 11.1% ($10,000 ÷ $90,000).

5335.03   Trade Credit

Trade Credit is a source of funds that is spontaneously created as a result of the purchase transaction. Trade credit (accounts payable) is often the largest short-term debt item held by firms. If a firm purchases an average of $10,000 a day under the terms of net 30, then financing of $300,000 has been spontaneously supplied to that firm providing the payment terms are met. (See section **5334** for a discussion of the use and cost of trade discounts.)

5335.04   Commercial Paper

    a.   **Commercial Paper** is short-term, unsecured notes that are offered by stable companies. These are in large amounts with short-term maturities generally ranging from one month to a maximum of 270 days. Access to the market for commercial paper is limited to a small number of companies that are exceptionally good credit risks. The interest rates on commercial paper tend to be somewhat below the prime rate.

    b.   The advantages of commercial paper include:

        (1) Providing the firm an additional source for funds that is readily accessible once the firm's paper has been rated.

        (2) Lower rates than are available with traditional bank loans—generally ranging from 1½ to 3½ percentage points below the prime rate.

        (3) Absence of costly financing arrangements and the need for potential compensating balances.

        (4) The repeated issuance of successful commercial paper improves a borrower's reputation in the financial markets.

    c.   The primary disadvantage of commercial paper is that if a firm is facing temporary financial difficulties, it would not be able to utilize this source of funding.

5335.05 Zero Balance Accounts (Sweep Accounts)

    a. **Zero Balance Accounts** are held at zero until a claim is made against the account. At that time, the holding bank transfers sufficient funds from an interest-bearing account to the zero balance account. The firm must have at least one additional account with the bank, and there is generally a small fee associated with transfers.

    b. A zero balance account can be effectively used by an organization when the interest earned in the interest-bearing account is greater than the fees associated with the transfers of funds. Operationally, it reduces the need for the firm to monitor daily fund flows.

    c. A hybrid of the zero balance account is a payroll account where funds necessary to cover payroll are transferred automatically as the payroll checks are being issued.

5335.06 Electronic Fund Transfers

    a. Firms are increasingly expecting payment of large bills by use of automatic electronic debits. Funds are automatically deducted from one account and added to another. This is the ultimate in terms of speeding up the collection process. Today, many electronic transfers are done on the Internet.

    b. The use of debit cards by individuals is an example of the application of this technology for small payments made by consumers.

5335.07 Lockbox Systems

    a. A **lockbox** is a system where checks are sent to post office boxes rather than corporate headquarters. The checks are collected several times a day by a local bank, and the funds are immediately deposited into the company's local account.

    b. A lockbox system can significantly reduce the time required to receive funds and make them available for use, often by two or three days, since multiple lockboxes can be located throughout the U.S. and internationally.

    c. Today, the bank generally notifies the firm with a daily record of receipts collected via an electronic data transmission system and wires funds to the firm's cash concentration account.

5335.08 Official Bank Checks (a.k.a. Depository Transfer Checks)

    a. **Depository Transfer Checks** are official bank checks that provide a means of moving funds from one account to another within the banking system. A DTC is payable to a particular account in a particular bank.

        (1) The payer prepares and mails a DTC.

        (2) The DTC is deposited by the payee (often through the use of a lockbox).

        (3) The DTC is sent to a concentration bank that serves as a clearing house for funds within the banking system. Often the lockbox is located at the concentration bank as a means of speeding up the collection process.

        (4) The concentration bank begins the clearing process by sending the check to the central bank.

        (5) Ultimately, the funds are deducted from the payer's account when the payer's bank is notified of the funds transfer.

    b. **Float** is the difference between the company's checkbook balance and the bank's balance. It represents the net effect of checks in the process of collection. Checks written by the firm create disbursement float and reduce the book cash. Checks received and deposited by the firm create collection float and increase the book balance. As checks are cleared, the bank cash position is reconciled to the book cash position.

5336   Fixed and Variable Loan Rates

5336.01   Terminology

    a. **Collateral**—Assets that are used to secure repayment of a loan.

    b. **Compensating Balance**—A minimum cash balance that must be maintained during the life of a loan, usually expressed in terms of a percentage of the loan amount.

    c. **Discounted Loan**—A loan where the interest is calculated on the face amount and deducted in advance from the loan proceeds.

    d. **Fixed Rate Debt**—Debt where the nominal interest rate remains constant throughout the life of the debt instrument.

    e. **Floating Interest Rate (Variable Rate)**—A debt interest rate that is linked to a market measure such as the prime rate or the rate on U.S. Treasury securities and varies through the life of the debt instrument.

    f. **Loan Covenant**—A defined legal right available to the lender under defined conditions.

    g. **Nominal Rate**—Stated rate of interest.

    h. **Pledging**—The use of receivables or inventory as collateral on a loan.

    i. **Prime Rate**—The published interest rate charged by commercial banks to large, financially strong companies.

5336.02   Introduction to Loans

    a. Loan rates vary by maturity, size of the loan, and riskiness of the borrower.

        (1) Over time, changes in inflation expectations cause nominal interest rates for new loans to change.

        (2) The size of the loan has an effect on the cost of the borrowing. Smaller loans have higher rates due to the fact that there are fixed costs that are incurred in underwriting and servicing the loan. Often these costs are recovered by the lender in the form of fees.

        (3) Since the lender needs to be compensated for the risk of lending, riskier borrowers are charged higher interest rates. Large, healthy companies can borrow at the prime rate, and some of the strongest organizations can actually acquire financing below prime. However, given their riskiness, most firms borrow at an interest rate of prime plus a risk premium.

    b. Interest rates can vary over time. When the economy is weak and inflation is low, demand for loans tends to be low since companies do not have the need or desire to expand. The Federal Reserve will generally make money readily available under these conditions, and as a result, interest rates are low. However, when the economy is strong and inflation is high, the reverse will hold true and interest rates tend to be higher.

c. The terms of loans can have an effect on both the working capital and solvency of an organization.

    (1) The nominal or stated rate of interest can be either fixed or floating. (See section **5336.03**.)

    (2) Loans can be interest-only loans that require only interest payments to be made until maturity. It is not unusual for loans to be renewed at maturity providing that the creditworthiness of the borrower does not deteriorate; therefore, even short-term loans may end up effectively having more of a long-term character for a firm with a strong financial position.

    (3) The nominal or stated rate of interest is not necessarily the effective interest rate due to such things as the timing and frequency of interest payments, discounted interest, add-on interest, and compensating balance. (See the interest rate discussion in section **5324**.)

    (4) Loan covenants, commitment fees, interest rate structures, and servicing costs can also increase the effective interest cost of loans.

5336.03   **Fixed Rates**

a. Nominal interest rates for new debt fluctuate over time; therefore, there is a risk to having a fixed rate loan. When a firm takes out a fixed rate loan, they are locking in the interest rate for the maturity of the loan. This would allow the firm to have a fixed interest rate. Generally, fixed rate loans are used to finance additions to fixed assets or to finance the permanent portion of working capital.

b. The fixed rate loan provides the borrower with a fixed interest expense and the lender with a fixed interest income. The firm takes a risk that rates might fall during the term of the loan, but since rates might also rise, many firms deem it prudent to convert the interest expense into a fixed cost. Lenders take a risk that rising market interest rates will raise their costs of funds and reduce the profitability of the loan.

c. There is risk in delaying long-term financing in favor of short-term.

    (1) There are no guarantees that interest rates will fall. In fact, they could continue to rise and remain high for a significant period of time.

    (2) There are no guarantees that short-term financing will continue to be available. If short-term loans cannot be obtained, a firm may be forced into selling off productive assets to meet obligations.

5336.04   **Variable Rates**

a. Floating rate financing involves tying the lending rate to a market measure such as the prime rate or yield on U.S. Treasury securities. When interest rates are rising, floating rates become extremely attractive to lenders since the floating rate will minimize their interest rate risk. The variable rate debt allows the borrower to borrow during periods of higher interest rates without being locked into that rate should rates fall before the maturity date. However, the firm absorbs the interest rate risk and might find its interest expense rising if short-term rates increase. Companies whose revenues tend to vary with the market interest rates while costs tend to remain stable (such as capital intensive firms) can use variable rate loans to provide some degree of stability in net earnings.

b. A characteristic of a fixed-rate bond is that the market value of the bond moves in the opposite direction as interest rates. As interest rates rise, the value of the bond falls. As interest rates fall, the market value of the bond increases. Some investors wish to reduce this risk and would prefer to hold variable rate bonds. Since the variable rate bond interest payments will change in response to changes in market interest rates, its market value will tend to be stable and thus be less risky from the investor's point of view.

c. Often variable rate debt has a floor below which the interest rate cannot fall.

d. If the movement of interest rates is positively correlated to a firm's operating income, then the use of variable rate loans will reduce the risk to borrowers. When interest rates are high, the firm's income will tend to be increasing. Therefore, the use of floating rates could help a firm to stabilize income and decrease the effects of leverage. For firms that have a negative correlation between interest rates and operating income, the use of variable rate loans is ill-advised, since risk will be increased.

e. **Illustration:** The following two tables show the effect of using floating rate financing in periods of both boom and recession to a company with a positive correlation between operating income and interest rates.

Boom Period	Fixed Rate Financing	Flexible Rate Financing
Total Assets	$750,000	$750,000
Variable rate debt at 14%		400,000
Fixed rate debt at 11%	400,000	
Equity	350,000	350,000
Total Debt and Equity	$750,000	$750,000
Sales	$1,000,000	$1,000,000
Operating Expenses	800,000	800,000
Net Operating Income	200,000	200,000
Less Interest	44,000	56,000
Taxable Income	156,000	144,000
Less Taxes (40%)	62,400	57,600
Net Income	93,600	86,400
Return on Equity	26.7%	24.7%

Recession Period	Fixed Rate Financing	Flexible Rate Financing
Total Assets	$750,000	$750,000
Variable rate debt at 8.5%		400,000
Fixed rate debt at 11%	400,000	
Equity	350,000	350,000
Total Debt and Equity	$750,000	$750,000
Sales	$800,000	$800,000
Operating Expenses	670,000	670,000
Net Operating Income	130,000	130,000
Less Interest	44,000	34,000
Taxable Income	86,000	96,000
Less Taxes (40%)	34,400	38,400
Net Income	51,600	57,600
Return on Equity	14.7%	16.5%

Comparison of Fixed and Flexible Rate financing:

	Fixed Rate Financing	Flexible Rate Financing
ROE in Boom	26.7%	24.7%
ROE in Recession	14.7%	16.5%
Average ROE	20.7%	20.6%
Range of ROE	12 points	8.2 points

f. The comparative data suggests that over a long time, the average ROE using either variable rate or fixed rate financing would tend to be about equal. However, the variability of ROE would tend to be lower over the business cycle if the firm uses variable rate financing. These are the type of results that would hold if a firm's operating profits are closely correlated to changes in interest rates. Thus, a firm would need to determine if reducing interest rate risk (fixed rate financing) is more or less desirable than interest expense-variability (variable rate financing) when making a choice between loan alternatives.

5336.05 Loan Covenants

Lenders will look carefully at a company's financial health, and particularly its solvency, before granting loans. As an additional measure of security, loan covenants are frequently required. A **loan covenant** is a legal means by which the lender has a specific right under defined conditions. The covenant clearly defines default and the remedies available to the lender if default should occur. The default provision is generally defined in a manner that would allow discovery of potential problems at an early stage so the lender is alerted to the potential deteriorating financial health of the lendee and can begin to take remedial action. Typical loan covenants include:

1. The maintenance of a current ratio or quick ratio no lower than a specified level. This guards against a deteriorating liquidity position. This covenant could require a firm to hold more assets in cash or near-cash assets than perhaps would otherwise be the case.

2. The maintenance of a debt-to-equity ratio no higher than a specified level. This keeps the company from adding significant additional debt without increasing equity, which would put the current lender in a less secure position. A covenant of this type might preclude a firm from taking advantage of business opportunities that would require additional borrowing.

3. Not allowing dividends to be paid above a specific amount. This ensures that the assets of the firm cannot be disbursed in an attempt to avoid paying creditors.

4. The pledging of receivables or inventory as collateral for a loan. If the firm defaults on the loan, the ownership of the pledged asset reverts to the lender. This is a protection provided to the lender so that at least a portion of the obligation will be honored in the case of default. By pledging receivables or inventory, the cash that could be obtained from these assets will no longer be available to meet general current liabilities, thus lowering the effective current ratio. Generally a loan secured by collateral is filed with the state in which the collateral is located in order to protect the lender's security interest. This provides the lender with a legal guarantee and prevents the borrower from using the same collateral on more than one loan.

5. Compensating balances are often required when the ability to make the necessary payments in a timely manner is in question. The lender requires the firm to hold a particular amount (usually a percentage of the loan) as cash or near-cash. The use of such balances raises the effective interest rate of the loan since those funds are not available for use until the obligation has been honored. For example, an 8% loan for $50,000 is granted with the loan covenant that a 10% compensating balance ($5,000) is held during the life of the loan, and then only $45,000 will actually be available for use ($50,000 - $5,000). This makes the effective interest rate 8.9% ($4,000 annual interest ÷ $45,000 usable loan balance).

6. Occasionally, if the borrowing firm is a small corporation, the lender will require major stockholders to personally guarantee the loan. This keeps the major stockholder (often upper management) from diverting funds to another company and defaulting on the original loan.

7. **Illustration:** A firm is granted a $75,000 discounted loan at 10% with a 20% compensating balance. What is the effective interest rate?

Solution: With a discounted loan, the interest is calculated and deducted in advance.

Interest = 10% of face value of loan = 10% of $75,000 = $7,500

The compensating balance is calculated on the face value of the loan.

Compensating balance = 20% of $75,000 = $15,000

The usable funds are the amount actually received less the compensating balance:

Usable funds = $75,000 - $15,000 = $60,000
The effective interest = Interest paid ÷ Usable funds = $7,500 ÷ $60,000 = 12.5%

Due to the use of a discounted loan and a compensating balance, a nominal interest rate of 10% becomes an effective interest rate of 12.5%.

5337 Ratio Analysis

5337.01 Terminology

a. **Liquidity**—A firm's ability to satisfy short-term obligations.

b. **Gross Margin**—(Net Sales minus Cost of Goods Sold).

c. **Market Measures**—Ways to measure price and yield behaviors of securities.

d. **Net Working Capital**—(Current Assets minus Current Liabilities).

e. **Profitability**—The measure of success in terms of income defined in various manners over a period of time.

f. **Solvency**—A firm's ability to meet long-term obligations.

g. **Working Capital**—Current assets.

5337.02 General Comments

a. The analysis and interpretation of financial statements are carried out in part through ratio analysis that relates different financial statement elements in meaningful ways. A particular ratio is not significant by itself. The importance of ratio analysis lies in the relationship between ratios (inter-company comparisons, peer group comparisons) and their changes from one point to another for a given firm (intra-company comparisons). Ratios are computed and analyzed on a comparative basis as follows:

(1) Comparing operating characteristics of an enterprise over a series of successive years.

(2) Comparing operating characteristics of an enterprise with other similar enterprises, pre-established standards (target ratios), or legal/contractual requirements.

b. Ratios can be divided into major categories:

(1) Liquidity/Activity

(2) Solvency/Coverage

(3) Profitability/Asset Utilization

(4) Market Measures

c. Many ratios, especially the Profitability/Asset Utilization ratios, compare elements from the balance sheet to elements from the income statement. In these cases, the balance sheet element that is used should be an average for the period. For example, the inventory turnover ratio should use the average inventory level for the period. If the beginning and ending inventory levels are not representative of the entire period, then a rolling, monthly or weighted average should be used.

5337.03 General Limitations

a. While ratio analysis can be very helpful, the user must be aware of its limitations and make adjustment as necessary. Judgment must be used in interpreting the results of ratio analysis.

b. Ratio analysis tends to be more useful for narrowly focused firms as it is difficult to develop industry averages for large firms that have different divisions in different industries.

c. Since the goal for most firms is to be better than average, merely attaining average performance generally is not deemed to be satisfactory. One alternative is to attempt to benchmark performance against industry leaders' ratios.

d. Inflation may cause balance sheet distortion making book values significantly different from market values. Inflation may also have a significant impact on depreciation charges, inventory costs and/or profitability.

e. Seasonal factors might also distort ratio analysis. This problem can be minimized by using monthly averages for the variables that are subject to seasonal fluctuation.

f. Analysts need to be aware that firms may use "window dressing" to attempt to improve the appearance of their financial position. This could cause a firm to manipulate data to show positive short-term effects that would, in reality, produce negative long-term results.

g. Different accounting practices can distort ratios and/or comparisons between companies. For example, a firm that leases assets rather than purchasing them can artificially improve fixed asset turnover and debt ratios. Also, different fiscal years, different markets, different locations (affecting taxation, labor costs, governmental regulation, etc.), different sizes, different stages of development (growth vs. mature), different dividend payment policies, use of LIFO vs. FIFO, differences in the use of operational and financial leverage, and different industries can make intercompany comparisons difficult.

h. There is often disagreement among analysts as to what constitutes a "good" or "bad" value for a ratio. For example, underlying circumstances such as the availability of an unused line-of-credit may allow for a particular company to have a low current ratio that is not considered to be "inadequate" if the line-of-credit was not available.

i. Firms often have a mix of ratios, some of which would present a "good" picture and others that might present a "bad" picture. This requires an analyst to use some form of statistical technique such as discriminate analysis to assess the probability that the firm would have financial trouble based upon the particular mix.

j. Some balance sheet and income statement accounts are based on estimates and judgments (receivables and inventory), and some ratios are based upon arbitrary assumptions (EPS).

k. For some ratios, there is a lack of uniformity in the formula used in calculating the ratio. Different formulas for identical ratios may be used by different firms, as well as before-versus after-tax figures as ratio components, thus leading to an inability to make inter-firm comparisons. The use of a 360-day year (for computational convenience) as opposed to a 365-day year also can lead to different results; however, the actual sales days of the year for many non-retail companies is usually less than 300.

l. Accrual income does not necessarily indicate the availability of cash, and current liabilities may understate short-term demands on cash due to such items as operating leases.

m. Unless data from an adequate number of years is used, performance measures and trends may be misinterpreted and/or misstated.

n. Some ratios include the use of external market values such as the price of stock and are influenced by numerous variables over which management has little influence or control.

5337.04 **Sample Data**

Many different ratios are computed and used to analyze the operating characteristics of enterprises by investors and creditors, both present and potential, as well as management. Some of the frequently used ratios are described in the next sections using hypothetical information for the Sample Company for the years 2005 and 2006.

Sample Company Comparative Balance Sheets December 31, 2005 and 2006	12/31/2006	12/31/2005
Assets		
Cash	$250,000	$200,000
Net Accounts Receivable	200,000	100,000
Inventories	100,000	150,000
Total Current Assets	550,000	450,000
Net Plant and Equipment	400,000	450,000
Goodwill	100,000	100,000
Total Assets	$1,050,000	$1,000,000
Liabilities and Equities		
Accounts Payable	$200,000	$150,000
Long-Term Debt	450,000	500,000
Preferred Stock, $100 par	100,000	100,000
Common Stock, $10 par	200,000	200,000
Retained Earnings	100,000	50,000
Total Liabilities and Equities	$1,050,000	$1,000,000

```
┌─────────────────────────────────────────────────────────────────┐
│                        Sample Company                             │
│                       Income Statement                            │
│                 For the Year Ended December 31, 2006              │
│                                                                   │
│   Net Sales                                        $1,000,000     │
│   Cost of Goods Sold                                  600,000     │
│   Gross Profit on Sales                               400,000     │
│   Selling and Administrative Expenses                 225,000     │
│   Income from Operations                              175,000     │
│   Interest on Long-Term Debt                           50,000     │
│   Income Before Taxes                                 125,000     │
│   Income Taxes                                         50,000     │
│   Net Income                                          $75,000     │
│                                                                   │
│   Dividends Declared on Preferred Stock               $15,000     │
│   Dividends Declared on Common Stock                  $10,000     │
│   Net Earnings Per Common Share                            $3     │
│   Market Price Per Share on December 31, 2006             $17     │
└─────────────────────────────────────────────────────────────────┘
```

5337.05 **Liquidity (Activity)**

    a. **Liquidity** measures a firm's ability to satisfy short-term obligations. It implies that the company has the ability to turn assets into cash or the ability to obtain cash. It is also related to the speed within which given assets can be converted into cash.

    b. Lack of liquidity:

        (1) is a matter of degree as opposed to being strictly liquid or non-liquid.

        (2) may mean that an organization is unable to take advantage of favorable discounts.

        (3) may mean that an organization might be unable to take advantage of profitable business opportunities.

        (4) limits management's flexibility.

        (5) may cause lower profitability.

5337.06 **Working Capital**

    a. The concept of **Net Working Capital** assumes that all current assets are liquid and may readily be turned into cash that can be used to satisfy all current liabilities.

        Current Assets - Current Liabilities = Net Working Capital

    b. Working Capital is expressed in absolute dollars, and in that form, it would be difficult to judge the adequacy of the measure when making inter-firm comparisons. It also has limited value when judging adequacy of Working Capital.

    c. Working Capital only has significance when related to other variables such as sales, total assets, etc.

    d. Care should be used in determining the actual *availability* of current assets. For example, cash held as a compensating balance under a bank loan should not be considered to be available.

    e. Calculation using data from the Sample Company for December 31, 2006.

        Net Working Capital = Current Assets - Current Liabilities
        $350,000 = $550,000 - $200,000

    f. Working Capital equals Current Assets.

5337.07   Current or Working Capital Ratio

    a. The **Current Ratio** is a relative comparison of current assets to current liabilities. It calculates the number of dollars of current assets that are available to cover each dollar of current liabilities.

$$\text{Current Ratio} = \frac{\text{Current Assets}}{\text{Current Liabilities}}$$

    b. The higher the ratio, the more likely that current obligations can be met (safety issue). A current ratio below the industry average suggests to potential lenders that the firm might have difficulty meeting its current obligations and, if the problems were severe enough, a low current ratio could limit access to additional external funds.

    c. A higher than average current ratio could be positive, or it might mean that the firm is holding idle cash, has slow-paying customers, or is having problems moving inventory. This could mean that too much capital is tied up in receivables and inventory, which might lead to a decrease in net income. These factors might be viewed as indicating an increasingly risky position, and banks might become hesitant to lend to the firm except at higher rates.

    d. The current ratio can easily be manipulated in the short term ("window dressing"); however, a higher manipulated ratio is difficult to sustain over the long term. This is done by using cash to pay current liabilities, thus increasing the current ratio.

    e. In determining the adequacy of the current ratio, some consideration must be given to the relationship between the current ratio and the operating cycle. If the cycle is relatively short, a lower current ratio may be adequate. Conversely, a lower accounts receivable turnover and/or inventory turnover would necessitate the need of a higher current ratio to provide the same level of safety.

    f. If a line of credit is available, a lower current ratio would be acceptable.

    g. If LIFO is used and there are old LIFO layers in inventory, the current ratio will be understated if inflation has occurred.

    h. Calculation using data from the Sample Company for December 31, 2006.

$$\text{Current Ratio} = \frac{\text{Current Assets}}{\text{Current Liabilities}}$$

$$= \frac{\$550,000}{\$200,000} \qquad = 2.75 \text{ to } 1$$

5337.08   Quick or Acid-Test Ratio

    a. The **Quick Ratio (Acid-Test Ratio)** is a sterner test for liquidity than the current ratio due to the fact that it includes only the more liquid of the current assets in the calculation. It is a measure of the ability to discharge currently maturing obligations based on the most liquid (quick) assets.

$$\text{Quick Ratio} = \frac{\text{Cash} + \text{Marketable Securities} + \text{Net Accounts Receivable}}{\text{Current Liabilities}}$$

    b. Since inventory is not included, the problems with inventory valuation are avoided as well as the additional business cycle issues related to turning inventory into cash.

    c. This ratio might still need to be adjusted if receivables are subject to a lengthy collection period (dollars may not be available as needed), or if they might be factored at less than the carrying value (fewer dollars will be available).

d. Calculation using data from the Sample Company for December 31, 2006:

$$\text{Quick Ratio} = \frac{\text{Cash} + \text{Marketable Securities} + \text{Net Accounts Receivable}}{\text{Current Liabilities}}$$

$$= \frac{\$250,000 + \$200,000 \text{ Receivable}}{\$200,000} = 2.25 \text{ to } 1$$

5337.09   Accounts Receivable Turnover Ratio

a. The **Accounts Receivable Turnover Ratio** measures both the quality and liquidity of the accounts receivable.

$$\text{Accounts Receivable Turnover} = \frac{\text{Net Credit Sales}}{\text{Average Accounts Receivable}}$$

b. The quality of the receivables is defined as collection without losses. It is assumed that the longer that receivables are outstanding, the more likely it is that they will not be collected.

c. The turnover is an indicator of the age of the receivables. It indicates how many times, on average, the receivables are generated and collected during the year.

d. Credit terms should provide an approximation of an expected turnover rate. For example, if the credit terms are net 60, it would be expected that the turnover would be 6 times if receivables were actually collected within the 60 days. A ratio lower than 6 in this case suggests the possibility of collection problems.

e. This ratio would be affected by significant seasonal fluctuations unless the denominator is a weighted-average.

f. It is frequently necessary to use net sales due to the fact that specific information concerning credit sales is not available.

g. Calculation using data from the Sample Company for 2006:

$$\text{Accounts Receivable Turnover} = \frac{\text{Net Credit Sales}}{\text{Average Accounts Receivable}}$$

$$= \frac{\$1,000,000}{\frac{\$200,000 + \$100,000}{2}} = 6.67 \text{ times}$$

5337.10   Number of Days Sales in Trade Accounts Receivable (Average Collection Period)

a. The **Number of Days Sales in Trade Accounts Receivable** measures the number of days on average that it takes to collect accounts receivable.

$$\text{Number of Days Sales in Accounts Receivable} = \frac{360}{\text{Accounts Receivable Turnover}}$$

$$\text{Or}$$

$$= \frac{\text{Average Accounts Receivable}}{\frac{\text{Credit Sales}}{360}}$$

b. This ratio can easily be compared to the credit terms in order to evaluate the performance of the receivables department.

c. Significance is gained when comparing the ratio to credit terms or to industry averages.

d. Significantly higher than expected ratios could mean the firm:

(1) has poor collection procedures.

(2) has difficulty in obtaining prompt payment from customers even though they have made diligent collection efforts.

(3) has customers that are experiencing financial difficulty.

e. The best way to investigate a problem is to do a comparative aging of receivables.

f. Calculation using data from the Sample Company for 2006:

$$\text{Number of Days Sales in Accounts Receivable} = \frac{360}{\text{Accounts Receivable Turnover}}$$

$$= \frac{360}{6.67 \text{ times}} = 54 \text{ days}$$

or

$$= \frac{\frac{\text{Average Accounts Receivable}}{\text{Credit Sales}}}{360} = \frac{\frac{\$200,000 + \$100,000}{2}}{\frac{\$1,000,000}{360}} = 54 \text{ days}$$

5337.11   Inventory Turnover Ratio

a. The **Inventory Turnover Ratio** measures the speed with which inventory can be converted into sales. In other words, the control that management has over inventory is assessed. The quality of the inventory is determined by the company's ability to use and dispose of inventory without a loss.

$$\text{Inventory Turnover} = \frac{\text{Cost of Goods Sold}}{\text{Average Inventory}}$$

b. Since inventories are purchased or produced for the purpose of obtaining a return, it is extremely important to determine if corrective action needs to be taken. A low turnover can be caused by a variety of factors, some of which are anticipated and based upon management's actions, and others that are unanticipated and require corrective action. These factors include:

(1) Obsolete items

(2) Unanticipated weak demand

(3) Build-up to meet expected future demand or firm commitments

(4) Build-up to avoid future price increases

(5) Build-up in anticipation for a strike or material shortages

c. Excessive inventories can lead to:

(1) high storage and insurance costs.

(2) a greater risk of obsolescence, physical deterioration, or theft.

(3) tying up funds that could be used in a more productive fashion, thus leading to decreased profitability.

d. A high turnover may be an indication that:

   (1) the firm is managing its inventory well and thereby achieving higher productivity.

   (2) the inventory that is held is highly marketable.

   (3) obsolete inventory does not appear to be a problem.

   However, an extremely high turnover suggests a higher probability of stock-outs.

e. Different inventory cost flow assumptions (FIFO vs. LIFO) can produce widely different inventory valuations and thus turnover ratios. This can make comparisons between organizations difficult.

f. For seasonal businesses, it is best to use a monthly average inventory figure in the calculation of this ratio, since that is generally more representative of what has actually occurred.

g. Calculation using data from the Sample Company for 2006:

$$\text{Inventory Turnover} = \frac{\text{Cost of Goods Sold}}{\text{Average Inventory}}$$

$$= \frac{\$600,000}{\dfrac{\$150,000 + \$100,000}{2}} = 4.8 \text{ Times}$$

5337.12 Number of Days Sales in Inventory

a. The **Number of Days Sales in Inventory** measures the number of days it takes to sell the inventory.

$$\text{Number of Days Sales in Inventory} = \frac{360}{\text{Average Inventory}}$$

Or

$$= \frac{\text{Average Inventory}}{\dfrac{\text{Cost of Sales}}{360}}$$

b. This ratio converts the Inventory Turnover into days and is also a good indicator of how well inventory is managed.

c. The conversion of Inventory into cash is the total of the Number of Day's Sales in Inventory and the Number of Day's Sales in Accounts Receivable. In other words, how quickly can inventory be turned into cash? These ratios are likely to fluctuate at various points in the business cycle.

d. Calculation using data from the Sample Company for 2006:

$$\text{Number of Days Sales in Accounts Receivable} = \frac{360}{\text{Inventory Turnover}}$$

$$= \frac{360}{4.8 \text{ times}} = 75 \text{ days}$$

Or:

$$= \frac{\text{Average Inventory}}{\text{Cost of Sales} \div 360} = \frac{(\$150,000 + \$100,000) \div 2}{\$600,000 \div 360}$$

$$= 75 \text{ days}$$

5337.13   Solvency (Coverage)

   a.   **Solvency** is the organization's ability to meet long-term obligations (repayment of principal as well as interest) through the use of cash or by converting non-cash assets into cash.

   b.   Solvency ratios are related to questions about the firm's long-term viability.

   c.   Solvency is closely related to financial risk. As the financing of the organization shifts from equity financing toward debt financing, the risk that the firm could default on its long-term obligations increases.

   d.   Solvency is also measured on a continuum. A lack of solvency could lead to:

      (1) the inability to refinance long-term debt at favorable rates thus leading to lower profitability.

      (2) a greater risk of defaulting on current maturities that could ultimately lead to bankruptcy and liquidation.

   e.   Leverage is created when a portion of the company's assets are acquired by issuing debt rather than using equity to finance the purchase; therefore, solvency is also related to the use of leverage. (See section **5327.03** for a discussion on financial leverage.)

   f.   The use of debt tends to reduce a firm's cost of capital. Since debt tends to be less risky then equity, it has a lower cost. This advantage is enhanced by the fact that interest on debt is tax deductible (creating what is know as the "tax shield" on debt) while dividends paid on common equity are not. (See section **5321.03** for a discussion on prudent debt levels.)

5337.14   Debt to Total Assets

   a.   The **Debt to Total Assets Ratio** indicates the extent that leverage has been used to finance the assets held and the degree to which creditor protection is provided in the case of insolvency. It is also called the Debt Ratio. It indicates the percentage of assets financed through debt.

$$\text{Total Debt to Total Assets} = \frac{\text{Total Debt}}{\text{Total Assets}}$$

   b.   Since creditors are concerned about a firm's ability to repay long-term debt and their protection in the case of liquidation, they prefer that this ratio is within the acceptable range in order to provide a cushion against potential loss. Generally, the lower the ratio, the greater is the firm's solvency.

   c.   A higher ratio indicates:

      (1) more leverage has been used.

      (2) there is a greater risk to the creditor.

      (3) there is a greater risk that the firm would not be able to meet its long-term obligations under adverse conditions.

    d. Care needs to be taken with this ratio since there are many possible definitions for the variables used in both the numerator and denominator. Also, the denominator reflects the historical cost of assets and not their current market values.

    e. Calculation using data from the Sample Company for December 31, 2006:

$$\text{Total Debt to Total Assets} = \frac{\text{Total Debt}}{\text{Total Assets}}$$

$$= \frac{\$200,000 + \$450,000}{\$1,050,000} = 62\%$$

5337.15 **Debt to Equity**

    a. The **Debt to Equity Ratio** is an alternative used to measure the relationship of debt to capital. In this ratio, the dollars of debt per dollar of equity are measured. It clearly shows whether creditors or stockholders have a bigger stake in the organization.

$$\text{Debt to Equity} = \frac{\text{Total Debt}}{\text{Total Stockholders' Equity}}$$

    b. The Debt to Equity Ratio measures the company's ability to meet long-term obligations. As with the previous ratio, care must be used when comparing the results to other organizations since there are a variety of definitions for the variables used in both the numerator and denominator. The conservative approach is to use total debt as the numerator.

    c. From a creditor's point of view, the lower the ratio, the less the risk of insolvency.

    d. Calculation using data from the Sample Company for December 31, 2006:

$$\text{Debt to Equity} = \frac{\text{Total Debt}}{\text{Total Stockholders' Equity}}$$

$$= \frac{\$200,000 + \$450,000}{\$100,000 + \$200,000 + \$100,000} = 1.63 \text{ to } 1$$

5337.16 **Times Interest Earned**

    a. The **Times Interest Earned Ratio** measures a firm's ability to cover interest charges. This is important since, at minimum, a company would need to pay current interest charges in a given period. This is also known as the Interest Coverage Ratio.

$$\text{Times Interest Earned} = \frac{\text{Net Income Before Tax} + \text{Interest Expense}}{\text{Interest Expense}}$$

    b. A higher ratio is associated with greater solvency and demonstrates a greater margin of safety for meeting fixed interest payments.

    c. This ratio measures the ability to add new debt in the future.

    d. A concern is that accrual income is not necessarily representative of the cash available to pay the interest obligations.

    e. Since interest is tax deductible, both interest and taxes are added back to net income indicating the amount available to cover the fixed interest payments.

    f. Calculation using data from the Sample Company for 2006:

$$\text{Times Interest Earned} = \frac{\text{Net Income Before Tax} + \text{Interest Expense}}{\text{Interest Expense}}$$

$$= \frac{\$125,000 + \$50,000}{\$50,000} = 3.5 \text{ Times}$$

5337.17 Profitability (Asset Utilization)

Profitability is the measure of success in terms of income defined in a variety of ways over a period of time. In analyzing profitability, earnings are compared to a base such as sales, productive assets, or equity. Increased profitability provides the potential for increased dividend payments as well as from stock appreciation. Increased profitability also provides greater security for debt holders.

5337.18 Gross Margin

a. The **Gross Margin Ratio** compares the gross margin (gross profit) generated by the net sales revenue. In other words, what percentage of the sales dollars were used to cover the cost of goods sold? The remaining amount is left to cover the general and administrative expenses as well as to provide a profit. This is also known as the gross profit ratio.

$$\text{Gross Margin in Ratio} = \frac{\text{Gross Margin}}{\text{Net Sales Revenue}}$$

b. This ratio is generally more useful to management than to creditors or investors since the data necessary to analyze why changes occurred in the ratio are only available internally. Changes are caused by one of the following elements or a combination of the following items.

(1) Increase/decrease in unit sales price

(2) Increase/decrease in cost per unit

c. Calculation using data from the Sample Company for 2006:

$$\text{Gross Margin in Ratio} = \frac{\text{Gross Margin}}{\text{Net Sales Revenue}}$$

$$= \frac{\$400,000}{\$1,000,000} = 40\%$$

5337.19 Profit Margin

a. The **Profit Margin Ratio** calculates the percentage of each dollar of sales that is recognized as net income. In other words, it measures the efficiency of earnings as compared to sales. It indicates how well management has controlled expenses in relationship to revenues earned. This ratio is an excellent way to compare the profits of companies of varying sizes. This is also known as the return on sales ratio.

$$\text{Profit Margin Ratio} = \frac{\text{Net Income}}{\text{Net Sales}}$$

b. In alternative definitions, the numerator for this ratio can take a variety of forms—operating income, net income, income available to stockholders, or income from recurring operations.

c. The use of accrual income includes estimates and items over which management has little or no control.

d. Calculation using data from the Sample Company for 2006:

$$\text{Profit Margin Ratio} = \frac{\text{Net Income}}{\text{Net Sales}}$$

$$= \frac{\$75,000}{\$1,000,000} = 7.5\%$$

5337.20   Asset Turnover

a. The **Asset Turnover Ratio** indicates how many dollars of sales were created by each dollar of total assets. It helps to determine whether the available assets were used efficiently to create sales. One goal of management is to generate the highest possible amount of sales per dollar of invested capital. Note that different industries tend to have different reasonable ranges for this ratio.

$$\text{Asset Turnover} = \frac{\text{Net Sales Revenue}}{\text{Average Total Assets}}$$

b. As in all turnover ratios, a high asset turnover is a desirable outcome since it results from an effective use of available assets; however, it is not unusual for a company that has recently expanded to see a drop in asset turnover until the new facility is fully utilized.

c. For internal use, it is desirable to calculate this ratio comparing divisional sales to divisional assets.

d. Comparison between firms within an industry can be difficult due to the fact that the age of the assets used in the production of the sales may vary. This is a limitation caused by the use of historical costs as opposed to fair market values for the productive assets. There is also a problem when comparing a capital-intensive firm to a labor-intensive firm.

e. There are also problems created due to the fact that the generally used formula does not take into account that certain assets make no tangible contribution to sales. It is assumed that an asset's participation in generating sales is related to its recorded amount. Adjustments to the asset figure are used in attempts to compensate for this problem. For example, long-term investments are not involved in the production and sale of the product and are often not included in the calculation.

f. Calculation using data from the Sample Company for 2006:

$$\text{Asset Turnover} = \frac{\text{Net Sales Revenue}}{\text{Average Total Assets}}$$

$$= \frac{\$1,000,000}{\dfrac{\$1,050,000 + \$1,000,000}{2}} = 0.98$$

5337.21   Return on Assets (ROA)

a. The **Return on Assets Ratio** measures the productivity of assets in terms of producing income. This ratio depends upon the organization's ability to get a high profit from each sales dollar while generating high sales per dollar of invested capital. A consistently high ROA is an indication that management is making effective decisions and that the organization is a growth company.

$$\text{Return on Assets} = \frac{\text{Net Income}}{\text{Average Total Assets}}$$

b. The DuPont Equation breaks ROA down to the Asset Turnover and Profit Margin.

$$\text{Return on Assets} = \frac{\text{Net Income}}{\text{Net Sales}} \times \frac{\text{Net Sales}}{\text{Average Total Assets}}$$

Through the use of the DuPont Equation, ROA is broken down to the profit margin showing the effective control of cost (Net Income/Net Sales) and the asset turnover showing the efficient use of assets (Net Sales/Average Total Assets).

c. Since neither profit margin nor asset turnover can increase indefinitely, at some point, the only way to create further increases in earnings is to increase the asset base by adding to production capacity.

d. Limitations specific to this ratio include the use of accrual net income that is subject to estimates and does not reflect actual cash return. The rate of return is also based upon historical asset costs that do not reflect current market values.

e. The numerator can use a variety of income figures including EBIT. The philosophy behind the use of EBIT is that the earnings available to three parties, stockholders, creditors, and the government (taxes) is created through the use of the assets available to the organization. The denominator is often restricted to only income producing assets by excluding long-term investments and intangibles.

f. Calculation using data from the Sample Company for 2006:

$$\text{Return on Assets} = \frac{\text{Net Income}}{\text{Average Total Assets}}$$

$$\frac{\$75,000}{(\$1,050,000 + \$1,000,000) \div 2} = 7.3$$

5337.22   Return on Equity (ROE)

a. The **Return on Equity Ratio** measures the return to common stockholders. The ratio calculates how many dollars were earned for each dollar of common equity. When comparing this ratio with ROA, the investment of the creditors is removed. This ratio is affected by the net income available to the stockholders (net income – preferred dividends), the profit margin available to the stockholders, the asset turnover, and the extent to which assets are financed by common stockholders. The method of financing used (debt vs. equity) has a major effect on this ratio.

$$\text{Return on Equity} = \frac{\text{Net Income - Preferred Dividends}}{\text{Average Common Equity}}$$

or, using the DuPont Equation

$$\text{ROE} = \frac{\text{Net Income – Preferred Dividends}}{\text{Sales}} \times \frac{\text{Sales}}{\text{Average Assets}} \times \frac{\text{Average Assets}}{\text{Average Stockholders' Equity}}$$

b. The denominator consists of the average of the total equity less preferred shares and minority interest. One of the major problems with this ratio is that the historical issue price is used as opposed to the current market value.

c. The **Common Stockholders' Leverage Ratio** (Average Assets/Average Stockholders' Equity used above) measures the portion of assets that are financed through common equity (also called the Equity Multiplier). The larger this ratio, the greater the financial leverage will be. Various organizations within an industry will have potentially dramatic differences in ROE resulting from financing decisions—debt vs. equity. If ROA is greater than the cost of borrowing, then ROE will be higher than ROA due to the impact of financial leverage.

d. Calculation using data from the Sample Company for 2006:

$$\frac{\text{Net Income - Preferred Dividends}}{\text{Average Common Equity}} = \text{Return on Equity}$$

$$\frac{\$75,000 - \$15,000}{(\$300,000 + \$250,000) \div 2} = 22\%$$

5337.23   Market Measures

Investors use a variety of ratios to analyze the price and yield behavior of securities. These measures use a variety of market data as well as financial statement information.

5337.24 **Price-Earnings Ratio**

a. The **Price-Earnings Ratio** indicates the relationship of common stock to net earnings. The market price is the investors' perception of the future; therefore, this ratio combines the performance measure of the past (EPS) to perceptions of the future.

$$\text{Price Earnings Ratio} = \frac{\text{Price Market of Stock}}{\text{Earnings per Share}}$$

b. The Earnings per Share computation is subject to arbitrary assumptions and accrual income. EPS is not the only factor affecting market prices.

c. A high P/E ratio is a possible indication of a growth company and/or of a low-risk organization.

d. Calculation using data from the Sample Company for 2006:

$$\text{Price Earnings Ratio} = \frac{\text{Price Market of Stock}}{\text{Earnings per Share}}$$

$$= \frac{\$17.00}{\$3.00} = 5.67$$

5337.25 **Dividend Yield**

a. The **Dividend Yield Ratio** shows the return to the stockholder based on the current market price of the stock.

$$\text{Dividend Yield} = \frac{\text{Dividend per Common Share}}{\text{Market Price per Common Share}}$$

b. Dividend payments to stockholders are subject to many variables. The relationship between dividends paid and market prices is a reciprocal one.

c. This ratio is calculated using the current market price; however, most of the shareholders did not purchase their shares at the current price thus making their personal yield different than the calculated yield.

d. Calculation using data from the Sample Company for 2006:

$$\text{Dividend Yield} = \frac{\text{Dividend per Common Share}}{\text{Market Price per Common Share}}$$

$$= \frac{\$10,000 \div 20,000 \text{ shares}}{\$17.00 \text{ per Share}} = 2.9\%$$

5337.26 **Payout Ratio to Common Shareholders**

a. The **Payout Ratio to Common Shareholders** measures the portion of net income to common shareholders that is paid out in dividends.

$$\text{Payout Ratio Common Shareholders} = \frac{\text{Common Dividends}}{\text{Net Income} - \text{Preferred Dividends}}$$

b. Income does not necessarily measure cash available for dividend payment. Payments are heavily influenced by management policy, the nature of the industry, and the stage of development of the particular firm. All of these items diminish comparability between companies.

c. Organizations that have high growth rates generally have low payout ratios since most earnings are kept as retained earnings with the funds being reinvested in the company instead of providing cash dividends. A firm that has consistently paid a dividend and suddenly lowers its dividend payout often is signaling a lack of available cash and the existence of liquidity or solvency problems.

d. Calculation using data from the Sample Company for 2006:

$$\text{Payout Ratio Common Shareholders} = \frac{\text{Common Dividends}}{\text{Net Income - Preferred Dividends}}$$

$$= \frac{\$10,000}{\$75,000-\$15,000} = 16.67\%$$

Section 5400
Information Technology (IT)

5410 Introduction to Information Systems

5410.01   In the Statement of Financial Accounting Concepts No. 2, the Financial Accounting Standards Board defined accounting as being an information system (IS). It also stated that the primary objective of accounting is to provide information useful to decision makers. This means that accounting is an information identification, development, measurement, and communication process.

The Institute of Management Accountants (IMA) conducted an intensive analysis of the job duties of corporate accountants. Respondents clearly indicated that work relating to accounting systems was the single most important activity performed by corporate accountants.

A system is a set of two or more interrelated components that interact to achieve a goal. Systems are almost always composed of smaller subsystems, each performing a specific function important to and supportive of the larger system of which it is a part. Accounting systems generally consist of several accounting subsystems, each designed to process transactions of a particular type. Although they differ with respect to the type of transactions processed, all accounting subsystems follow the same sequence of procedures. These procedures are referred to as accounting cycles.

An effective information system is essential to any organization's long-run success. Without a means of monitoring the events that occur, there is no way to determine how well the organization is performing or to track the effects of various business activities on company resources.

5411 IS Components

5411.01 An Information System has five components:

1. The people who operate the system and perform various functions.

2. The procedures, both manual and automated, involved in collecting, processing, and storing data about the organization's activities.

3. The data about the organization's business processes.

4. The software used to process the organization's data.

5. The information technology infrastructure, including computers, peripheral devices, and network communications devices.

5411.02 The accounting information system (AIS) is a subset of the management information system (MIS). The AIS is composed of both the human and capital resources within an organization that are responsible for:

1. the preparation of financial information and

2. the information obtained from collecting and processing company transactions.

The AIS performs several important functions in an organization:

1. It collects and stores data about activities and business transactions.

2. It processes data into information and provides reports that are useful for making decisions.

3. It provides adequate controls to safeguard the organization's assets.

5412 IS Objectives

5412.01 According to the AICPA, an AIS has five primary objectives:

1. Identify and record all valid transactions. For example, if a company intentionally records a fictitious sale, it can overstate revenues and income. If a company forgets to record some expenses or understates expenses at the year's end, it can overstate net income.

2. Properly classify transactions. For example, improperly classifying an expense as an asset overstates assets and net income.

3. Record transactions at their proper monetary value. For example, an account receivable that becomes uncollectible should be written off.

4. Record transactions in the proper accounting period. Recording 200Y sales in 200X overstates sales and net income for 200X and has the opposite effect for 200Y.

5. Properly present transactions and related disclosures in the financial statements. Failing to disclose a lawsuit or a contingent liability could mislead the reader of a financial statement.

5413 IS Functions

5413.01   An Information System should fulfill several important functions:

a. Provide adequate controls to:

    (1) Safeguard the organization's assets and data.

    (2) Ensure that the information produced is both reliable and accurate.

b. Collect and store data. Data is any and all of the facts that are collected, stored, and processed by an information system. Data is one of an organization's most valuable assets. Data includes both quantitative and qualitative items and may be financial or operational in nature.

c. Transform data into information. Once collected, it is the job of the IS to transform data into information so it can be used to make decisions. Thus, information is data that has been organized and processed to provide meaning.

d. There are several characteristics that make information useful and meaningful for decision making.

    (1) Relevant – Information is relevant if it reduces uncertainty, improves decision makers' ability to make predictions, or confirms or corrects their prior expectations.

    (2) Reliable – Information is reliable if it is free from error or bias and accurately represents the events or activities of the organization.

    (3) Complete – Information is complete if it does not omit important aspects of the underlying events or activities that it measures.

    (4) Timely – Information is timely if it is provided in time to enable decision makers to use it to make decisions.

    (5) Understandable – Information is understandable if it is presented in a useful and intelligible format.

    (6) Verifiable – Information is verifiable if two knowledgeable people acting independently would each produce the same information.

e. There are limits to the amount of information that the human mind can effectively absorb and process. Information overload occurs when those limits are passed. Information overload is costly, because decision-making quality declines while the costs of providing that information increase. Thus, information overload reduces the value of information.

f. Information systems must use advances in IT to filter and condense information, thereby avoiding information overload. An important decision involves identifying which potential IS improvements are likely to yield the greatest return. Making this decision wisely requires an understanding of an organization's overall business strategy.

g. There are costs associated with producing information, including the time and resources spent in collecting, processing, and storing data, and in distributing information to decision makers.

h. Improve decision making. An information system should provide feedback on the results of actions so it can be used to improve future decisions. For example:

    (1) Reports can help to identify potential problems that require management action.

    (2) Query languages can facilitate the gathering of relevant data upon which to make decisions.

    (3) Tools (such as graphical interfaces, decision models, and analytical tools) can help the decision maker interpret information and evaluate and choose among alternative courses of action.

5414 How an IS Can Add Value to an Organization

5414.01 An information system adds value to an organization by:

    a. improving the quality and reducing the costs of products or services.

    b. improving efficiency of operations by providing more timely information.

    c. improving decision making by providing accurate information in a timely manner.

    d. sharing knowledge and expertise, thereby improving operations and providing a competitive advantage.

    e. improving the efficiency and effectiveness of its supply chain.

5415 Types of Management Information Systems

5415.01 **Accounting Information System (AIS):** The AIS includes the human and capital resources within an organization that are responsible for (a) the preparation of financial information and (b) the information obtained from collecting and processing company transactions. The AIS is a subset of the Management Information System.

5415.02 **Decision Support System (DSS):** A DSS is an extension of a management information system. It is designed to aid in semi-structured decision making. Some processes and functions are preprogrammed in a DSS; the decision is not made by the system. Instead, the decision maker must apply insight and exercise judgment while interacting with the system.

5415.03 **Executive Information System (EIS):** An EIS is an information system designed to provide executives with the needed information to make strategic plans, to control and operate the company, to monitor business conditions in general, and to identify business problems and opportunities.

5415.04 **Expert System (ES):** An ES is a computerized information system that allows non-experts to make decisions about a particular problem that are comparable with decisions of experts in the area. These systems include knowledge bases that represent facts and inferences they know. They use heuristics (rules of thumb) in processing information.

5415.05 **Strategic Information System (SIS):** An SIS provides information that may allow an organization to make strategic, competitive decisions.

5415.06 **Transaction Processing System (TPS):** A TPS is a completely programmed and automated system, treating every problem in exactly the same way. This type of system is used in AISs so that each transaction is processed in an identical manner.

5416 Hardware and Software Concepts

5416.01 **Access Time:** The time it takes a program (software) and device (hardware) to retrieve data and make it available to the microprocessor.

5416.02 **ASCII:** Acronym for American Standard Code for Information Interchange. ASCII provides a standard representation for English characters, with each letter assigned a number from 0 to 127. These codes enable data to be exchanged from one computer to another.

5416.03 **Assembly Language:** A programming language in which each machine language instruction is represented by mnemonic characters. It is a symbolic language, an English-like and understandable alternative to basic machine language.

5416.04 **Bar Codes:** Special identification labels found on most merchandise. A code includes vertical lines of differing widths that represent binary information that is read by an optical scanner.

5416.05 **Bulletin Board System (BBS):** A computer system that functions as a centralized information source and message switching system for a particular interest group.

5416.06 **CD-ROM:** A storage device that uses laser optics for reading data rather than magnetic storage devices. Although CD-ROM discs are "read only," the disks are useful for storing large volumes of data (roughly 600 megabytes per disk).

5416.07 **Central Processing Unit (CPU):** The hardware that contains the circuits that control the interpretation and execution of instructions and that serves as the principal data processing device. Its major components are the arithmetic-logic unit, the memory, and the control unit.

5416.08 **Checkpoint:** Any one of a series of points during a long processing run at which an exact copy of all the data values and status indicators of a program are captured. Should a system failure occur, the system could be backed up to the most recent checkpoint and processing could begin again at the checkpoint rather than at the beginning of the program. (Also see section **5451.07**.)

5416.09 **Compiler:** A computer program that converts a source program (e.g., COBOL) into an object program (i.e., machine language). Compilers permit programmers to use procedural languages, such as COBOL, which reduce programming effort.

5416.10 **Computer-Integrated Manufacturing (CIM):** A manufacturing approach in which much of the manufacturing process is performed and monitored by computerized equipment, in part through the use of robotics and real-time data collection on manufacturing activities.

5416.11 **Cooperative Processing:** A system that permits the computers in a distributed processing network to share the use of another end user's application program.

5416.12 **Data Buffer:** A temporary storage area, usually in RAM, that holds data before or after being processed by the microprocessor. The buffer compensates for the differences in the rates of data flow from input/output devices to the central processing unit.

5416.13 **Database Management Systems (DBMS):** A complex software package that permits users to access information from the database. In addition to basic data movement services, the DBMS provides for access and identification security, concurrent use of data, and backup and recovery. The DBMS is "application-independent" and does not actually run application programs.

5416.14 **Decision Table:** A table that indicates the alternative logic conditions and actions to be taken in a program.

5416.15 **Direct Conversion:** An approach to converting from one system to another in which the old system is discontinued, after which the new system is started (also known as "burning the bridges" or "crash conversion").

5416.16 **Docking Station (aka Port Replicator):** These devices allow a user to plug in a laptop and use it with input/output devices similar to a desktop computer. When the laptop is docked, a full-size monitor and keyboard are used with the computer.

5416.17 **Embedded Audit Module:** Special portions of application programs that track items of interest to auditors, such as any unauthorized attempts to access the data files.

5416.18 **Facilities Management Organization:** Manages an organization's in-house data processing facilities under the user's guidelines.

5416.19 **Fuzzy Logic:** Systems suitable for dealing with imprecise (ambiguous) data and problems that have many solutions.

5416.20 **Generalized Audit Software (GAS):** Designed to allow auditors to select sample data from files and check computations.

5416.21 **Hardware Controls:** Controls built into the computer by the manufacturer to detect computer failure. Hardware controls include duplicate circuitry, echo checks, and dual reading.

5416.22 **Indexed-Sequential-Access Method (ISAM):** A file organization and access approach in which records are stored in sequential order by their primary key on a direct access storage device. An index file is created, which allows the file to be accessed and updated randomly.

5416.23 **Input Device:** Hardware used to enter data into the computer system. Input devices include the keyboard, mouse, light pens, optical scanners, and magnetic ink character readers.

5416.24 **Integrated Test Facility (ITF):** A testing technique in which a dummy company or division is introduced into the company's computer system. Test transactions may then be conducted on these fictitious master records without affecting the real master records. These test transactions may be processed along with the real transactions, and the employees of the computer facility need not be aware that testing is being done.

5416.25 **Language Processor:** A type of conversion program. It converts a source program (such as a COBOL program) into instruction codes that the CPU can execute.

5416.26 **Linked List:** A file structure that contains a field that has the address of the next record.

5416.27 **Machine Language:** Programs or data that have been converted into binary code. Machine language is the language that is used directly by the computer. The binary code is usually arranged as a hexadecimal (base 16) code.

5416.28 **Macro:** A series of keystrokes or commands that can be given a name, stored, and activated each time the keystrokes must be repeated.

5416.29 **Magnetic Disk:** A round plate on which data can be encoded. Magnetic disks, such as floppy disks, can be erased and recorded over. Random access is possible with magnetic disks. A floppy disk is more portable than a hard disk. However, the hard disk has a much faster access time and greater storage capacity than a floppy disk.

5416.30 **Magnetic Ink Character Recognition (MICR):** The recognition of characters printed by a machine that uses special magnetic ink. Commonly used in the banking industry.

5416.31 **Magnetic Tape:** A secondary storage medium that is about ½ inch in width and that has a magnetic surface on which data can be stored. The most popular types are seven-track and nine-track tapes. Access to data stored on magnetic tape is sequential.

5416.32 **Modem:** Modulator/demodulator, a communications device that converts the computer's digital signals into analog signals that can be sent over phone lines. The modem can be internal (mounted on a board within the computer) or external (a freestanding unit).

5416.33 **Multiprocessor Computer System:** A computer that allows multiple processing units to function simultaneously, therefore allowing simultaneous execution of two or more tasks.

5416.34 **Multiprogramming:** A technique used to enable an operating system to handle two or more independent programs by overlapping their execution. There is the appearance of simultaneous execution of programs but in reality the single processing unit is switching back and forth between the programs.

5416.35 **Object Technology:** Permits developers to reuse portions of program code (the objects) and thus decrease the amount of new program code that is required for an application.

5416.36 **Operating System:** A software program that controls the overall operation of a computer system. Its functions include controlling the execution of computer programs, scheduling, debugging, assigning storage areas, managing data, and controlling input and output.

5416.37 **Optical Character Recognition (OCR):** The use of light-sensitive hardware devices to convert characters readable by humans into computer input. Since OCR readers can read only certain items, a special machine-readable font must be used.

5416.38 **Parallel Conversion:** A systems conversion approach in which the new and old systems are run simultaneously until the organization is assured that the new system is functioning correctly.

5416.39 **Performance Monitoring:** The systematic measurement and evaluation of operating results such as transaction rates, response times, and incidence of error conditions.

5416.40 **Pilot Conversion:** The implementation of a system in just one part of the organization, such as a branch location. This approach localizes conversion problems and allows training in a live environment. Disadvantages are the long conversion times and the need to interface the old system with the new system.

5416.41 **Point-of-Sale Recorders (POS):** Electronic devices that function as both a terminal and a cash register. They are used commonly in retail stores to record sales information at the time of the sale and to perform other data processing functions.

5416.42 **Random Access Memory (RAM):** A temporary storage location for computer instructions and data. RAM may have data both written to it and read from it.

5416.43 **Read-Only Memory (ROM):** Internal CPU memory that can be read but usually may not be changed. The operating system and language translator programs are permanently stored in ROM.

5416.44 **Service Programs:** Application programs that can be called in by the user's programs to perform some common, subordinate function. They are sometimes referred to as "canned" programs.

5416.45 **Software Monitor:** Collects data on the use of various hardware components during a computer run.

5416.46 **Spreadsheet:** A table of values, arranged in rows and columns, where some of the cells' values are the result of a calculation performed on other cells. Should the value of one of the cells change, the resulting values would also change. Designing spreadsheet models involves defining the problem, identifying inputs and outputs, developing assumptions and decision criteria, and documenting formulas.

5416.47 **Storage:** Placement of data in internal memory or on a medium such as magnetic disk or magnetic tape, from which it can later be retrieved.

5416.48 **Systems Software:** Software that interfaces between the hardware and the application program. Systems software can be classified as operating systems, database management systems, utility programs, language translators, and communications software.

5416.49 **Teleconferencing:** An electronic meeting conducted among several parties at remote sites.

5416.50 **Trojan Horse:** A set of unauthorized computer instructions in an authorized and otherwise properly functioning program. It performs some illegal act at a pre-appointed time or under a predetermined set of conditions.

5416.51 **Usenet groups:** Public electronic discussion groups in which anyone on the Internet can participate.

5416.52 **Windowing:** A characteristic of a microcomputer system that can display more than one program on the screen at the same time, where each program is in its own area of the screen, or *window*, although only one program is active at a time.

5420 Data Processing Cycle and Developing Information Systems

5420.01 The data processing cycle consists of four steps (as shown in Figure 1):

Figure 1

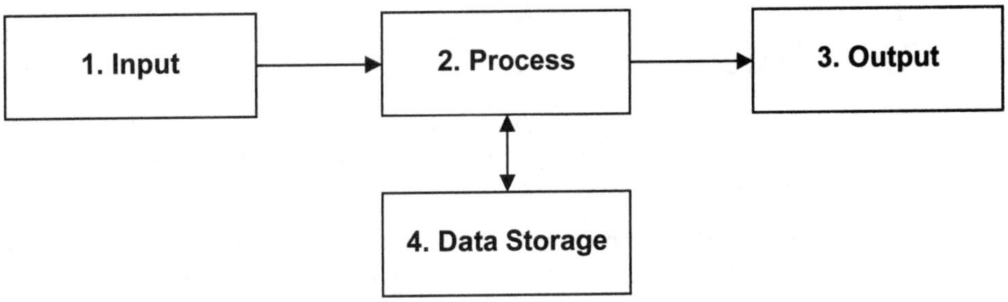

5421 Data Input

5421.01 Historically, paper source documents have been used to collect data about business activities. This data was later entered into the computer.

Today, as much business activity data as possible is recorded directly into computers, often through a computer data entry screen that retains the same name as the paper source document it replaced.

5421.02 Data such as the following is collected about each business activity or transaction:

a. Date and time it occurs

b. Employees involved

c. Location of the activity or transaction

d. Item(s), such as inventory, that is (are) involved

e. Quantity and price of each item

f. Total amount of the business activity or transaction

g. Bill-to and ship-to addresses

h. Any special delivery or receiving instructions

i. Customer or vendor name

5421.03 The accuracy, control, and efficiency of data input are improved by:

a. using well-designed source documents and data entry screens.

b. grouping logically related data close together.

c. using appropriate shading and borders to clearly separate data items.

d. using prenumbered source documents or by having the system automatically assign a sequential number to each new transaction. This makes it easier to verify that all transactions have been recorded and that none of the documents have been misplaced.

e. providing instructions or prompts about the data collected.

f. using check-off boxes or pull-down menus to present the available options.

g. using machine-readable turnaround documents, which are records of company data sent to an external party and then returned to the system as input to facilitate data processing.

Example: A utility bill that is read by a special scanning device when it is returned with a payment.

h. using source data automation devices (ATMs, point-of-sale (POS) scanners, and bar code scanners) that capture transaction data in machine-readable form at the time and place of their origin.

5422 Data Processing

5422.01 The most common data processing activity is data maintenance, which is the periodic processing of transactions to update stored data. There are four basic types of data maintenance:

1. Additions (Insert new records into a master file.)
    Example: Add a new customer to the customer master file.

2. Deletions (Remove records from a master file.)
    Example: Purge the vendor master file of all inactive vendors.

3. Updates (Revise current balances in master files, generally by adding or subtracting a transaction record amount.)
    Example: Sales data is used to reduce inventory quantities on hand and increase the customer's account balance.

4. Changes (Modify data in master files.)
    Example: Change customer credit ratings and addresses.

5422.02 Following are the data maintenance steps required to update an accounts receivable master file record to reflect a sales transaction (as shown in Figure 2):

a. The account number field is used to match each transaction file record with the appropriate record in the master file. In this example, account 0123 is being updated to reflect the effects of a sales transaction that occurred on February 19, 20XX, as recorded on invoice number 9876.

b. The sale amount ($360) is added to the existing account balance ($1,500) to produce the updated current account balance ($1,860).

c. The current balance on the old master file ($1,500) is the new previous balance (replacing $1,000) in the new master file record.

Figure 2

TRANSACTION DATA (record in transaction file)

Account Number	Transaction Type	Transaction Date	Document Number	Transaction Amount
0123	Sale	02/19/XX	9876	$360.00

FILE UPDATE PROCESS   (repeated for all transactions)

- Verify data accuracy of transaction record
- Match primary key (account number) of transaction file record with master file record
- Update account balances

ACCOUNTS RECEIVABLE RECORD (old master file)

Account Number	Credit Limit	Previous Balance	Current Balance
0123	$2000.00	$1000.00	$1500.00

UPDATED ACCOUNTS RECEIVABLE RECORD   (new master file)

Account Number	Credit Limit	Previous Balance	Current Balance
0123	$2000.00	$1500.00	$1860.00

5422.03   Master files can be updated in three ways:

1. **Batch Processing** is updating master files periodically to reflect all transactions that occurred during a given time period. The master file is updated at set times (such as hourly or daily) or whenever a manageable number (50 to 100, for example) of transactions are gathered. Transaction data can be entered as a batch or as each transaction occurs (called on-line batch processing).

   The first step in batch processing is to sort the transaction file so it is in the same sequential order as its corresponding master file. For example, before updating the accounts receivable master file, the transaction file containing sale and payment transactions should be sorted so that it is in customer number order. Then the computer:

   a. reads a transaction file record and/or an old master file record.

   b. when the primary keys match, updates the old master file record.

   c. creates a new master file with the updated master file records and the old master file records that are not updated.

   d. repeats the update process.

   Batch processing is primarily used for applications, like payroll, where all or most records need to be updated. Its advantage is efficiency in processing. Its disadvantage is that the only time the master files are current is immediately after the update.

2. On-Line, Real-Time Processing

    a. On-line, real-time processing is where the computer:

        (1) captures data electronically, edits it for accuracy and completeness, and updates the master file as each transaction occurs.

        (2) processes information requests from users by locating the desired information in the data files and displaying it in the specified format.

    Unlike batch processing, transaction file records can be in any order. When a transaction occurs, the computer uses the primary key of the transaction file (such as account number) to search the master file for the desired record. The appropriate record is retrieved, updated, and written back to the master file. Unlike batch processing, which creates a new master file, on-line processing does not create a new master file—it merely updates the existing master file.

    b. Most companies use on-line, real-time processing for most applications because:

        (1) master file information is always current and results in better decision making.

        (2) on-line data entry is more accurate than batch processing because:

            (a) the system can refuse incomplete or erroneous entries.

            (b) since data is entered as the transaction occurs, errors can be easily corrected.

3. On-Line Batch Processing is a combination of the above two approaches, where transaction data are entered when the event occurs but processed later in batches.

5423 Data Output

5423.01 When displayed on a monitor, output is referred to as a soft copy. When printed on paper, it is referred to as a hard copy.

5423.02 Information output is presented in three forms:

1. Documents are records of transactions or other company data.

    a. They can be printed out or stored as electronic images in a computer.

    b. Some are meant for external parties, such as checks and invoices. Others are used internally, such as receiving reports and purchase requisitions.

    c. Source documents are used at the beginning of a process.

    d. Operational documents are generated at the end of a transaction processing activity.

2. Reports are prepared for both internal and external users.

    a. Many different people use reports. For example:

        (1) Employees use reports to control operational activities.

        (2) Managers use reports to make decisions and develop business strategies.

        (3) External parties use reports to comply with regulatory requirements, make decisions (such as judging creditworthiness), and evaluate company operations (profitability, etc).

    b. Reports are produced on a regular basis, on an exception basis to call attention to unusual conditions, and on demand.

    c. Companies should periodically reassess the need for each report produced. All too often, reports are prepared long after their need disappears, wasting time, money, and computer resources.

3. **Queries** are requests for a specific piece of information.

   a. Queries arise from problems and questions that need rapid action or answers and information needs that are not satisfied by documents or periodic reports.

   b. When a query is made, the system finds the information, retrieves it, and displays or analyzes it as requested.

   c. Since many queries are repetitive, users can have a predetermined set of queries available to them that are developed by information system (IS) specialists. Unusual or one-time queries are usually developed by the users themselves.

   Some companies allow suppliers to query their databases so the suppliers can better meet their needs. This allows the supplier to gauge how well a product is selling and maximize sales by stocking and promoting the items that are selling well.

5423.03 The information an IS provides falls into three main categories:

1. Financial statements. Financial statements are used by:

   a. external parties to make decisions about extending credit to or investing in the organization.

   b. internal parties to meet stewardship requirements.

2. Managerial reports. An IS should provide managers with detailed operational information to measure organizational performance. For example:

   a. Budgets are financial planning tools that express goals in financial terms. For example, a cash budget shows projected cash inflows and outflows and provides advance warning of cash flow problems in time to permit corrective action to be taken.

   b. Performance reports are financial controls because they list the budgeted and actual amounts of revenues and expenses and show the variances, or differences, between these two amounts. If differences are minor, the item is under control and no action is needed. If significant deviations occur, the discrepancy should be investigated and the problem corrected.

   c. Examples of managerial reports include:

      (1) Relative profitability of products or performance of salespeople

      (2) Cash flow projections (collections and pending obligations)

      (3) Sales forecasts

      (4) New product revenue and cost estimates

      (5) Production and delivery schedules

      (6) Open purchase orders

      (7) Inventory stock status reports

3. External reports.

   To comply with legal requirements, income tax returns and 10-K filings with the Securities and Exchange Commission are produced.

5423.04   **XBRL: An IT Opportunity to Improve Financial Reporting**

    a.   Until recently, disseminating financial and nonfinancial information electronically was a cumbersome, inefficient process because:

        (1) recipients had different requirements for the way information was delivered to them. As a result, organizations spent a great deal of time and incurred significant expense to format the same information a number of different ways.

        (2) the organizations that received the data had to manually reenter much of it into their own information systems.

    The problem is caused by the way information is displayed on the Internet. HTML code specifies how data is displayed; it does not provide information about data content. Extensible business reporting language (XBRL) was developed to provide a way to communicate the content of data. XBRL uses tags to identify the contents of each data item. For example, an XBRL tag might indicate that a data item represents accounts receivable.

    b.   There are several benefits to creating and electronically disseminating financial data using XBRL:

        (1) Organizations can publish information once, using XBRL tags, in a format that anyone can use as they see fit.

        (2) Information systems and analysis tools can interpret the XBRL tags. Recipients do not need to manually reenter data they obtain electronically. Instead, they can be fed directly into any information system or analysis tool that understands XBRL.

        (3) XBRL tags result in more efficient and accurate Internet searches.

5424 Data Storage

5424.01   **Manual Systems**

    a.   In a manual system, the files that store cumulative information about company resources are called ledgers. Ledgers are books; "keeping the books" refers to maintaining and updating the ledgers. Most companies have:

        (1) a general ledger that contains summary-level asset, liability, equity, revenue, and expense account data.

        (2) a subsidiary ledger that records the detailed data for general ledger accounts that have subaccounts (accounts receivable, inventory, fixed assets, and accounts payable).

    b.   For example:

        (1) The general ledger contains an Accounts Receivable account that summarizes the amount all its customers owe the company.

        (2) The subsidiary accounts receivable ledger contains a record with detailed information (name, address, account balance, credit limit, etc.) about each individual customer.

    c. The general ledger account that summarizes a subsidiary ledger is called a control account. The relationship between the general ledger control accounts and individual subsidiary account balances has important control implications and helps organizations maintain the accuracy of stored data.

        (1) The sum of all subsidiary ledger accounts should equal the corresponding general ledger control account amount. A discrepancy between the two indicates a recording error has occurred.

        (2) Example: The inventory subsidiary ledger contains a dollar balance for each inventory item. The inventory subsidiary ledger total should be the same as the general ledger inventory control account total.

5424.02 **Chart of Accounts**

    a. All general ledger accounts are numbered and the chart of accounts is a list of all general ledger account numbers and names. The chart of accounts structure is important because:

        (1) it is used to prepare financial statements and reports.

        (2) it should contain sufficient detail to meet an organization's information needs.

            (a) Data stored in individual accounts can easily be summed for presentation in reports.

            (b) Data stored in summary accounts cannot be easily broken down and reported in more detail.

    b. In a chart of accounts, each account number digit serves a specific purpose. For example, in a three-digit account number:

        (1) The first digit represents major financial statement categories: current assets, noncurrent assets, liabilities, equity accounts, revenues, expenses, etc. Each category is assigned a separate block of numbers, based on financial statement order: current assets are the 100s, noncurrent assets the 200s, and so on.

        (2) The second digit represents subaccounts, with numbers assigned to match financial statement appearance order: 110 is accounts receivable and 140 is inventory.

        (3) The third digit could identify specific accounts: 511 could represent cash sales and 512 credit sales.

    c. Charts of accounts differ, depending on the nature and purpose of the organization. For example:

        (1) A corporation would have accounts for common stock and retained earnings, while a partnership would have separate capital and drawing accounts for each partner.

        (2) A retail company has only one type of inventory account, while a manufacturing company has separate accounts for raw materials, work in process, and finished goods.

    d. A chart of accounts should provide room for growth in the form of gaps that allow for later insertion of additional accounts.

      Subsidiary ledger accounts usually have longer account codes than those in the general ledger. For example, each individual account receivable could have a seven-digit code.

        (1) The first three digits could be 120, the general ledger accounts receivable code.

        (2) The next four digits could identify up to 10,000 individual customers.

226

5424.03   Data Storage Organization Concepts

Information in a computer must be organized such that it can be easily and efficiently stored and retrieved. Figure 3 summarizes basic data storage concepts and definitions, using accounts receivable information as an example.

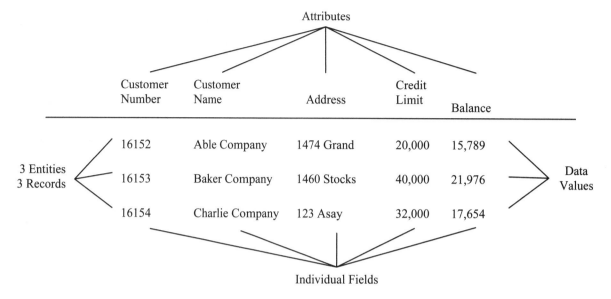

As this accounts receivable file stores information about three separate entities (Able, Baker, and Charlie Companies) there are three records in the file. As each record has five separate attributes (customer number, customer name, address, credit limit, and balance), there are five different fields in each record. Each field stores a data value that describes an attribute of a particular entity (customer). For example, 16154 is the customer number of Charlie Company.

In a spreadsheet, each row represents a different record and each column represents an attribute. Each cell represents a field. Thus, each intersecting row and column in a spreadsheet is a field within a record, the contents of which are called a data value.

These data hierarchies are shown in Figure 4.

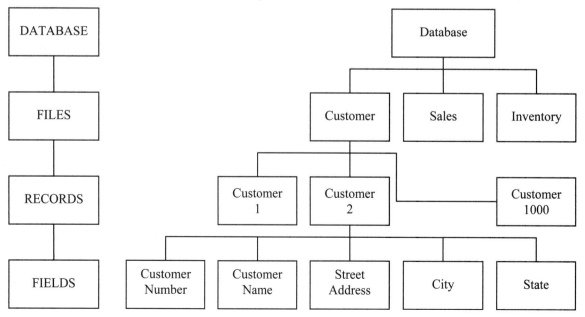

5424.04 **Basic Data Storage Concepts**

Database creation begins with identification of the entities about which data should be captured. Next, the attributes of those entities can be determined.

The following are basic data storage concepts and definitions:

a. An entity, sometimes called a variable, is something about which information is stored (employees, inventory items, customers).

b. Each entity has attributes, or characteristics of interest, which are stored (employee pay rates, customer addresses).

c. Each entity type has the same set of attributes. (All employees have an employee number, pay rate, and home address.)

d. A data value is a specific instance of an attribute. (The data value for Able Company's customer number is 16152.)

e. Data values are stored in a physical space called a field. A customer number, such as 16152, will be stored in a field named "Customer Number." For each entity, there is a field for each attribute of interest (customer name field, customer address field, etc). Attribute data values will differ. (One employee's pay rate is $8.00, another's is $8.25.)

f. A set of fields is called a record. (A customer record could have many fields, such as customer number, customer name, address, and balance.)

g. Related records are grouped to form a file (all customer receivable records are stored in an accounts receivable file).

h. A set of interrelated, centrally coordinated files is referred to as a database (the accounts receivable file is combined with customer, sales analysis, and related files to form a customer database).

5424.05 **Types of Files**

a. A master file stores cumulative information about an organization and is similar to a ledger in a manual system. For example:

(1) The inventory and equipment master files store information about important organizational assets.

(2) The customer and vendor master files store information about important outside companies.

b. While master files are permanent and extend across many fiscal periods, individual records within a master file are constantly changing as:

(1) They are updated to reflect transactions that take place. For example, customer account balances are updated to reflect new sales transactions and payments received.

(2) Records are added to or deleted from a master file as needed.

c. A **transaction file** contains data about transactions that occur during a specific period of time and is similar to a journal in a manual system. Transaction files are not permanent, but are maintained for a period of time for back-up purposes.

Examples include a sales transaction file and a customer payments transaction file. Both files are used to update individual customer account balances in the customer master file.

d. Archive files are records of past transactions, including those of past periods.

e. Reference files are files that are referred to during processing. These would include items such as price lists and tax rates.

f. A flat file is a traditional file system characterized by having only fixed-length "flat" files. All files are of equal length.

5425 Databases

5425.01 Historically, new files and programs were created each time an information need arose. This resulted in a proliferation of master files and the same data stored in two or more separate master files. When data was updated on one file and not on the other, data inconsistencies arose. This led to the creation of databases that are an organizational resource managed for the entire organization, not just a department or function.

A database is a set of interrelated, centrally coordinated files:

(1) Their use minimizes or eliminates the proliferation of master files and data redundancies.

(2) Data integration and data sharing is accomplished by combining master files into larger databases accessed by many application programs.

(3) A database management system (DBMS) coordinates user-computer interfaces.

(4) A database system consists of the database, the DBMS, and application programs that access the database through the DBMS.

(5) The data dictionary contains a description of all data elements, stores, and flows in a system. Typically, a master copy of the data dictionary is maintained to ensure consistency and accuracy throughout the development process. The data dictionary is created using a data definition language (DDL).

(6) The data query language (DQL) is used to interrogate the database.

(7) The data manipulation language (DML) provides programmers with a facility to update the database.

(8) Data control language (DCL) is used to specify privileges and security rules.

5425.02 **Views of Data**

a. In a database system, data can be viewed two ways:

(1) The logical view is the way a user or programmer organizes and understands the data conceptually. For example, a sales manager will view information about customers as being stored in a table.

(2) The physical view is how data is physically arranged and where it is stored (CPU, tape, CD-Rom, or other media).

b. Database systems separate the logical and physical views of data. This:

(1) makes it easier to develop new applications. Programmers can concentrate on telling the computer what to do (program logic) without worrying about how and where the data is stored and accessed.

(2) allows users to change the way they view data relationships (their logical view of the task) without changing how the data are stored physically. Database administrators can also make changes to the way data is physically stored to improve system performance and not have the change affect users or application programs.

c. The term "schema" was coined to describe the logical structure of a database. In a database there are several levels of schemas. Two that are important to accountants are:

(1) the conceptual-level schema lists all data elements and the relationships between them. As a result, it is referred to as the organization-wide view of the database.

  (2) an external-level schema is the portion of the database that is of importance to an individual user. Each external-level schema is referred to as a subschema.

 d. The difference between the two schema levels is illustrated using the revenue cycle.

  (1) The conceptual schema contains information about all revenue cycle data such as customers, sales, cash receipts, salespeople, cash, and inventory.

  (2) Each external-level subschema meets the needs of a particular user and is designed such that users only have access to the data they need to do their job. Access to other data items is prohibited.

  For example, the sales order entry subschema allows access to customer credit limits and current balances as well as inventory quantities and prices. It would not allow access to inventory costs or company bank account balances.

5425.03 **Relational Databases**

 a. Most new database systems are relational databases that store data as tables. Each row in a relational table contains data about a separate entity. For example:

  (1) Each inventory table row contains data about a particular inventory item.

  (2) Each customer table row contains data about a specific customer.

Each column in a table contains information about entity attributes. For example, in a sales table, the columns represent specific sales transaction characteristics (date, amount, customer number).

 b. Relational database tables have three types of attributes:

  (1) A primary key uniquely identifies a specific row in a table. For example, the primary key in an inventory table is item number. In some tables, the primary key is two or more attributes.

  (2) A foreign key is an attribute in one table that is a primary key in another table. A foreign key is used to link tables.

  Customer number can be a foreign key in a sales table that links a particular sales transaction with information about the customer who participated in the transaction.

  (3) Other non-key attributes in each table store important information about that entity.

  An inventory table contains information about the description, quantity on hand, and list price of each inventory item the company sells.

 c. Normalization is the process of following the guidelines for properly designing a relational database that is free from delete, insert, and update anomalies. It involves breaking the database into logical tables that can then be joined to create new tables with the information of interest.

5425.04 **ERP Systems**

Traditionally, the accounting information system was called a transaction processing system because its only concern was financial data and accounting transactions. Useful nonfinancial information, such as the time of day it occurred, was collected and processed outside of the accounting information system. It was difficult to effectively integrate data from the financial and non-financial systems and to eliminate data redundancies.

Enterprise resource planning (ERP) systems are designed to overcome these problems.

They integrate all aspects of a company's operations with its traditional IS. For example, when an order is entered, transaction data automatically flows to all affected parts of the company. Inventory is updated, production schedules are adjusted, and purchase orders are initiated to acquire any needed raw materials and supplies.

 a. Collect and store important nonfinancial data, such as the time the activity occurred.

---

    b. Integrate financial and nonfinancial operating data, as both are required for proper and complete performance evaluation.

    c. Collect and store data from external sources, such as data about customer satisfaction, to determine if the company is meeting its customer's requirements and expectations.

5426 Developing Information Systems

5426.01   Three factors influence the design of an information system:

1. **Developments in information technology (IT).** IT has had a significant impact on accounting and other business activities. In today's world, one must continually strive to implement new IT developments. This implementation requires an understanding of those developments and how they can be used to modify business strategies. This is illustrated by the growth of the Internet, which can:

    a. change the way products are distributed (digitized products, such as software, are distributed electronically).

    b. cut costs dramatically, thereby helping companies implement a low-cost strategy.

    c. make more information available, allowing companies to adopt new strategies.

2. **Organizational strategy.** Companies must develop an effective strategy and use IT to help them achieve their objectives. Two basic strategies organizations use to achieve their goals are:

    a. product differentiation, which is developing products or services not offered by competitors.

    b. low-cost, which is trying to be the most inexpensive and most efficient producer of a product.

3. **Organizational culture.** An IS operates within an organization and should reflect the values and culture of that organization. IS design can influence organizational culture by controlling the flow of the organization's information.

5426.02   **Why Information Systems Change**

Since organizations continually need faster and more reliable information, an information system continually undergoes changes. These changes can be minor adjustments, so extensive the old system is replaced by a new one, or somewhere between the two extremes. Change is so constant and frequent that most organizations are undergoing some form of system improvement or change at any point in time. Among the reasons companies change their systems are the following:

1. Need for new or different information (Increased competition, business growth or consolidation, mergers and divestitures, new regulations, etc.)

2. Technological changes (To use technology advances or existing IT that was previously too expensive.)

3. Need for improved business processes (Updating inefficient business processes.)

4. Competitive advantage (Increased quality, quantity, or speed of information can result in an improved product or service and may lower costs.)

5. Productivity gains (Automate clerical and repetitive tasks, significantly decrease the performance time of other tasks.)

6. Growth (Upgrade or replace outgrown systems.)

7. Downsizing (Move from centralized mainframes to networked PCs or to Internet-based systems to reduce costs and push decision making as far down the organization chart as possible.)

5426.03   **Systems Development: The People Involved**

Many people play strategic roles in systems development, including:

1. **Top Management.** The role of top management is to:

   a. align the organization's information systems with its corporate strategies.

   b. establish goals and objectives for the information system.

   c. help make important information systems decisions.

   d. support and encourage systems development projects.

   e. establish project selection priorities and set organizational policies.

   f. review IS department performance and motivate IS leaders.

2. **User Management.** The role of user management is to:

   a. help determine information requirements.

   b. help estimate project benefits and costs.

   c. assign appropriate staff to development projects.

   d. allocate the funds needed to develop and operate the system.

3. **Accountants.** During systems design, accountants:

   a. as users, determine their information needs and system requirements and communicate them to system developers.

   b. as members of project development teams or the IS steering committee, help manage systems development.

   c. as control experts:

      (1) take an active role in designing system controls.

      (2) periodically test the system to determine whether controls are implemented and functioning properly.

4. **Information systems steering committee.** Organizations usually establish an executive-level steering committee that crosses function and divisional boundaries in order to:

   a. plan and provide oversight to the information systems function.

   b. set IS policies.

   c. ensure that top management participates in, guides, and controls system development.

   d. coordinate information systems activities.

5. **Project development team.** A team made up of systems specialists, managers, accountants, and users guides each development project. Their function is to:

   a. plan and supervise each project.

   b. monitor projects to ensure that they are completed on time and within budget.

   c. help manage change and help ensure proper consideration is given to the people involved in the change.

   d. keep top management and the steering committee informed of the project's progress.

    e. interact frequently with users to ensure their needs are met.

    f. meet regularly to plan, control and monitor project progress.

6. **Systems analysts.** As analysts design information systems, they:

    a. study the existing information systems.

    b. work with users to make sure the system meets their needs.

    c. prepare the specifications that computer programmers need to write the new system.

    d. monitor IT improvements.

    e. help management, users, and other company employees successfully use technology.

7. **Computer programmers.** Programmers:

    a. write computer programs using specifications the systems analysts develop.

    b. make changes to existing computer programs to keep up with changing information needs.

5426.04   **The Systems Development Life Cycle (SDLC)**

Most information systems changes proceed through a five-step systems development life cycle shown in Figure 5.

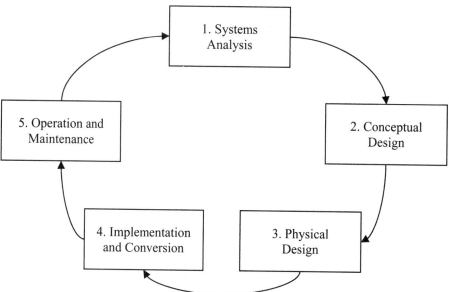

5426.05   **Systems analysis.** During systems analysis, information to purchase or develop a system is gathered.

    a. Systems development requests are received and prioritized so limited development resources are maximized.

    b. A system survey is conducted to:

        (1) define the nature and scope of the project.

        (2) identify project strengths and weaknesses.

    c. An in-depth feasibility study is conducted.

    d. Information needs of users and managers are identified and documented. This is a critical part of systems analysis, as these needs are used to develop and document the systems requirements used to select or develop a new system.

    e. A report summarizing systems analysis results is prepared for the steering committee.

5426.06 **Conceptual design.** During conceptual design, the company performs the following steps to determine how to meet user needs:

    a. Identify and evaluate appropriate design alternatives, such as:

        (1) buying software

        (2) developing software in-house

        (3) outsourcing software development to someone else

    b. Develop detailed specifications that describe what the system should accomplish and how it will be controlled.

    c. Communicate conceptual design requirements to the information systems steering committee.

5426.07 **Physical design.** The company uses the conceptual design requirements to:

    a. design input and output documents.

    b. write computer programs.

    c. create files and databases.

    d. develop policies and procedures.

    e. build controls into the new system.

After the new system is designed and created, physical system design results are communicated to the steering committee.

5426.08 **Implementation and conversion.** During this phase all physical design components are assembled and the system is put into place.

    a. An implementation and conversion plan is created and implemented.

    b. Hardware and software are installed and tested.

    c. Employees are hired and existing employees are relocated.

    d. Employees are trained.

    e. Processing procedures are developed and tested.

    f. Standards and controls are established and implemented.

    g. System documentation is completed.

    h. The organization converts to the new system and discontinues the old system.

    i. Fine-tuning adjustments are made.

    j. A post-implementation review is conducted to detect and correct any design deficiencies.

    k. The new system is complete when the operational system is delivered to the organization.

    l. The steering committee is sent a final report.

5426.09 **Operation and maintenance.** The new, operational system is used as needed.

    a. The system is periodically reviewed.

    b. Modifications are made as problems arise or needs change.

    c. At some point the company will need to make major modifications or replace the system and the SDLC begins again.

In addition, three activities (planning, assessing project feasibility, and managing change) are performed throughout the life cycle.

5427 Planning Systems Development

5427.01 At various times during the SDLC it is important to prepare systems development plans so that:

    a. systems goals and objectives are aligned with the organization's strategic plan.

    b. the system is more efficient.

    c. there is co-ordination between subsystems.

    d. the organization has a strategy for deciding which new systems to develop.

    e. the company keeps up with IT changes.

    f. systems are not duplicated.

    g. cost and time overruns are avoided.

    h. development efforts are not wasted.

    i. the system can be easily maintained.

    j. management is aware of future resource needs.

    k. employees are better prepared for the changes that take place.

5427.02 Two types of systems development plans are used:

    1. Master plan. Many organizations develop 5-year master plans that are updated at least yearly. The master plan specifies:

        a. the system's objectives and contents.

        b. how the system is to be developed and who will develop it.

        c. how the needed resources will be acquired.

        d. the status of development projects in process.

        e. the priority of planned development projects and the criteria for prioritization.

        f. development timetables. (Highest priority projects should be developed first.)

    2. Project development plan. Each project development plan contains:

        a. an analysis of the project's anticipated benefits and costs.

        b. the human, hardware, software, and financial resources needed to develop and operate the system.

        c. a project development schedule that lists the activities the development team must follow to create and operate the new system.

5427.03 **Feasibility Analysis**

    a. A feasibility study is prepared during systems analysis and updated as needed during the SDLC.

        (1) A large-scale system often requires a fairly extensive feasibility study.

        (2) A desktop system may get by with an informal analysis or no analysis at all.

    b. Development projects can be terminated at any time if it becomes evident that the project will not succeed. As each SDLC phase is completed, the steering committee uses the updated feasibility analysis to decide whether to:

        (1) proceed with the project.

        (2) proceed if specific problems are resolved.

        (3) terminate the project.

    c. Early go-no-go decisions are particularly important, as each subsequent SDLC step requires more time and monetary commitments.

        (1) As projects progress through the SDLC phases they are less likely to be canceled if a proper feasibility study has been prepared and updated.

        (2) Occasionally, systems are scrapped after implementation because they do not meet an organization's needs.

    d. There are five types of feasibility:

        (1) Technical: The system can be developed and implemented with existing technology.

        (2) Operational: People are available to design, implement, and operate the system and users can and will use the system.

        (3) Legal: Federal and state laws and statutes, administrative agency regulations, and the company's contractual obligations can be complied with.

        (4) Scheduling: The system can be developed and implemented on time.

        (5) Economic: System benefits exceed the costs of developing, implementing, and operating the system.

5427.04   Economic Feasibility

The capital budgeting model is the basic framework for an economic feasibility study in which benefits and costs are translated into dollar estimates and compared to determine if the system is cost beneficial.

    a. Benefits can be either tangible or intangible and include:

        (1) Cost savings

        (2) More efficient data processing

        (3) Improved customer service

        (4) Better management control

        (5) Increased job satisfaction and employee morale

        (6) Increased productivity

    b. Costs include:

        (1) Hardware, including equipment replacement and expansion

        (2) Site preparation (raised floors, air conditioning, special fire extinguishers)

        (3) Software acquisitions and updates

        (4) Designing, programming, testing, and documenting software

        (5) Maintenance and support

        (6) Operating the system

        (7) Hiring, training, and relocating staff

        (8) Installing the new system

        (9) Converting data files to a new format and storage media

      (10) Salaries of systems analysts, programmers, operators, data entry operators, and management

      (11) Supplies and overhead

      (12) Financing charges

5427.05 Three capital budgeting techniques are used to evaluate the economic feasibility of new systems:

1. Payback period: the time it takes for savings from the new system to equal the initial investment.

2. Net present value (NPV): estimated future cash flows (benefits less costs) discounted back to the present using a discount rate that reflects the time value of money. Alternatives with a positive NPV are economically feasible.

3. Internal rate of return (IRR): the interest rate that results in an NPV of zero. To be acceptable, the IRR of the project must meet or exceed a minimum acceptable rate.

When comparing projects, the proposal with the shortest payback period, highest positive NPV, or highest IRR is usually selected.

5428 Change Management

5428.01 Systems development personnel are agents of change. Companies need to be sensitive to and consider the feelings and reactions of those affected by change. They have to learn to manage people's reactions and overcome their resistance to change. Change management is essential because the best system fails without the support of the people it serves.

    a. People consider change to be good or bad depending on how they are personally affected by it.

        (1) Management views change positively if it increases profits or performance or if it reduces costs.

        (2) Employees view the same change as bad if their job is terminated or adversely affected.

    b. Some important reasons why resistance to change takes place include:

        (1) Younger, more highly educated, or more technologically aware people are more likely to accept and less likely to oppose change to an IS.

        (2) People object to the way changes are made as much as the change itself.

    c. Employees are more likely to resist change if:

        (1) They sense top management does not support the change.

        (2) The reasons behind it are not explained.

        (3) They have had negative experiences with prior IS changes.

        (4) They have emotional attachments to their duties or coworkers.

    d. Change is not easy because people fear the unknown, the uncertainty accompanying change, losing their jobs, losing respect or status, failure, technology, and automation.

    e. Initial resistance to change is often subtle:

        (1) Tardiness, leaving work early, or taking longer than authorized breaks.

        (2) Subpar performance and work slow-downs.

        (3) Reluctance to provide developers with information.

    f. Major resistance to change usually occurs after a new system is implemented and people have to use the system. It often takes one of three forms:

        (1) Aggression – Destroying, crippling, or weakening the system's effectiveness (increased error rates, disruptions, deliberate sabotage).

(2) Projection – blaming the new system for any and all difficulties.

(3) Avoidance – ignoring the system, hoping it will eventually go away.

5428.02 Behavioral problems related to change can be overcome by observing the following guidelines:

a. Develop systems that meet user needs.

b. Allay fears, to the extent possible, that no major job losses or responsibility shifts will occur.

c. Inform employees of changes as soon as possible to reduce uncertainty.

d. Maintain a safe and open atmosphere that promotes an attitude of trust and cooperation.

e. Obtain management support for the project. When possible, obtain a powerful champion who will supply needed resources and motivate others to assist and cooperate with the new system.

f. Solicit user participation. Ask users to provide data, make suggestions, and help make decisions.

g. Provide honest and timely feedback.

h. Humanize the system and help users understand it. Explain how the systems will affect them personally.

i. Build excitement about the system by describing the opportunities the new system provides and emphasizing important and challenging tasks that can be performed with the new system.

j. Make sure performance evaluations are in line with the new system.

k. Test system integrity prior to implementation to minimize initial bad impressions.

l. Allow the emotional issues related to change to cool, then handle them in a nonconfrontational manner, or sidestep them.

m. Control user's expectations and avoid unrealistic expectations of system capabilities and performance.

5429 Documenting Information Systems

5429.01 Documentation is the explanation of what, how, who, why, when, and where of an information system. It is especially important to document the data processing cycle steps (data input, data processing, data storage, information output) and information systems controls.

There are several regulatory acts that make documentation skills important.

a. **SAS 94, "The Effect of Information Technology on the Auditor's Consideration of Internal Control in a Financial Statement Audit"** requires external auditors to understand the automated and manual procedures of the company being audited. Internal controls weaknesses and strengths are more easily spotted using flowcharts and other graphic portrayals.

b. **The Sarbanes-Oxley Act (SOX)** requires:

(1) Public company management must include an internal control report in its annual report that:

(a) states management is responsible for establishing and maintaining an adequate internal control structure.

(b) assesses the effectiveness of the internal control system.

(2) External auditors must evaluate management's assessment of their internal control structures and attest to its accuracy.

(3) In other words, both the company and its auditors have to document and test the company's internal controls. This means that company employees as well as auditors must be able to prepare, evaluate, and read different types of documentation, such as flowcharts.

5429.02 Information systems are documented using the following methods:

a. Narrative documentation is a written, step-by-step explanation of system components and interactions.

b. A flowchart graphically describes an information system in a clear, concise, and logical manner. Flowcharts use a standard set of input/output, processing, storage, and data flow symbols to pictorially describe the system.

   (1) A document flowchart graphically describes the flow of documents and information among areas of responsibility within an organization. Document flowcharts trace a document from its cradle to its grave. They show where each document originates, its distribution, the purposes for which it is used, its ultimate disposition, and everything that happens as it flows through the system.

   (2) An internal control flowchart is particularly useful in analyzing the adequacy of control procedures in a system, such as internal checks and segregation of duties. It can reveal weaknesses or inefficiencies in a system, such as inadequate communication flows; unnecessary complexity in document flows; or procedures responsible for causing wasteful delays.

   (3) A system flowchart graphically describes the relationship among the input, processing, and output functions of an AIS. A system flowchart begins by identifying both the inputs that enter the system and their origins. The input is followed by the processing portion of the flowchart; that is, the steps performed on the data. The logic the computer uses to perform the processing task is shown on a program flowchart. The resulting new information is the output component, which can be stored for later use, displayed on a screen, or printed on paper. In many instances, the output from one process is an input to another.

   (4) An internal control flowchart is particularly useful in analyzing the adequacy of control procedures in a system, such as internal checks and segregation of duties. It can reveal weaknesses or inefficiencies in a system, such as inadequate communication flows; unnecessary complexity in document flows; or procedures responsible for causing wasteful delays.

c. Diagrams. A data flow diagram (DFD) graphically describes the source of data, the flow of data in an organization, the processes performed on the data, where data is stored in the organization, and the destination of data. It is used to document existing systems and to plan and design new ones.

d. Dictionaries. A data dictionary contains a description of all data elements, stores, and flows in a system. Typically, a master copy of the data dictionary is maintained to ensure consistency and accuracy throughout the development process.

e. Other written material that explains how a system works.

f. Operating documentation is all information required by a computer operator to run a program, including the equipment configuration used, variable data to be entered on the computer console, and descriptions of conditions leading to program halts and related corrective actions.

5430 E-Business

5430.01 E-business (or e-commerce) is using information technology (IT) advances, particularly networking and communications technology, to improve business processes. This includes using IT to improve external interactions (with suppliers, customers, investors, creditors, government, and media) and redesign its internal processes.

Before the widespread use of the Internet, organizations could choose whether or not to engage in e-business. Some companies did so, as a way to gain a competitive advantage. In today's world, e-business initiatives are often a necessity rather than a choice or an attempt to gain a competitive advantage.

5430.02 There are two principal forms of e-business:

1. **Business-to-consumer (B2C)**, where individuals purchase items (books, music, airline tickets) on the Internet.

    a. Most B2C transactions are straightforward and do not involve a great deal of money.

        (1) A consumer visits a company website, decides what to purchase, places an order, and pays using a credit card.

        (2) The seller ships the goods to complete the transaction.

    b. Trust and confidence are important in B2C transactions because the parties do not have long-term relationships; they usually have not done business with each other before. Consumers need confidence that:

        (1) a company's website represents a legitimate electronic "storefront."

        (2) their orders will be filled correctly.

        (3) the vendor can and will keep the personal information they provide private.

        Services such as WebTrust (developed by the AICPA) have been designed to provide these assurances.

    c. In B2C e-commerce, payments are made using:

        (1) credit cards.

        (2) electronic bill payments, which are electronic checks that function like paper checks, but are less costly to process.

        (3) electronic cash, which is stored as tokens in an electronic wallet or on a smart card. It avoids credit card and electronic check fees.

2. **Business-to-business (B2B)**, where organizations do business with one another.

    a. Most B2B transactions occur between organizations with established relationships so there is less need for third-party assurance services.

    b. In B2B transactions, large dollar amounts are usually involved.

        (1) The selling organization extends credit to customers.

        (2) Partial payments on accounts are permitted, which makes accounting for and controlling sales and customer payments more challenging.

5431 Using E-Business to Improve Business Processes

5431.01 Technological advances have made e-business possible. They have also reduced the costs and increased the speed and accuracy with which business processes are executed. For example:

a. Businesses can identify suppliers, compare prices, and negotiate prices more effectively and efficiently.

b. Reverse auctions, where suppliers bid against each other to provide goods or services, can be used to produce cost savings.

c. Companies have access to more accurate and timely information, which:

(1) allows organizations to better manage inventory.

(2) allows sellers to reduce transportation costs by combining shipments.

(3) significantly improves planning.

(4) allows organizations to improve the effectiveness of advertising and reduce its costs.

5431.02 For products and services that can be digitized:

a. The receiving function is performed electronically, yielding tremendous cost savings (the buyer does not have to spend time and money receiving goods and routing them to the person who ordered them).

b. The delivery function is performed electronically, which eliminates transportation cost and avoids the expense of selecting and packing goods for shipment.

5431.03 The human resources department can be more efficient and effective by allowing employees to make changes, such as new withholdings, changes in retirement allocations, and name changes.

a. This empowers employees, increases morale, and can generate cost savings by reducing HR staff.

b. The effectiveness of the HR function is improved as staff focuses on value-added activities rather than clerical tasks.

5431.04 Companies can use web pages to:

a. create electronic catalogs and automate sales order entry. This allows customers to place orders at their conveniences. It also significantly reduces staff as there is no need to enter telephone, mail, or fax sales orders.

b. make sure customers receive consistent information.

c. electronically "interview" customers using a sequence of menu-driven forms. Only the most complex problems are routed to a customer service representative.

5431.05 **E-Business Success Factors**

1. The success of e-business initiatives is determined by the degree to which e-business:

a. activities are aligned with and support the organization's overall business strategy.

Implementing e-business processes is not a basic strategy; it is using networking and communications technology to more efficiently and effectively carry out the organization's business processes.

b. processes embody three key business transaction characteristics.

(1) Validity. Both transaction parties need to know the identity of the other to make sure a transaction is authentic, valid, and enforceable.

(2) Integrity. Both parties want assurance that transaction information is accurate and has not been altered during transmission.

(3) Privacy. If either party so desires, transaction information should be kept private and confidential.

2. In traditional business processes:

    a. authorizations and approvals (signatures, notarizations, and signature guarantees) help ensure validity.

    b. manual and automated error detection and correction techniques (signatures across sealed envelopes, certified or hand-delivered communications) help ensure accuracy and provide assurance that the contents of a message have not been altered.

    c. privacy is achieved by using techniques such as sealed envelopes and courier delivery.

3. In e-business processes, concerns and objectives are the same but the ways they are achieved differ. The controls section (**5450**) discusses control techniques that can provide more assurance about validity, integrity, and privacy than is possible in traditional business processes.

5432 E-Business Communications

5432.01 The following communications and networking technology are used in e-business.

5432.02 **Internet Technologies**

    a. The **Internet** is a worldwide web of interlinked computers and networks. An incredible amount of information and services are available to Internet users. The Internet facilitates e-business and makes it more cost effective by eliminating the need for companies and consumers to use VANs and special telephone lines to exchange information.

    b. **Internet service providers (ISPs)** own and maintain portions of the Internet backbone and provide access to the Internet.

    c. **Browsers** make it possible for users to easily navigate through vast amounts of information found on the Internet.

    d. An **intranet** is a company-specific internal network that is navigated with Internet browser software. Intranets significantly reduce the costs of disseminating and sharing information and increase the effectiveness of operations. These benefits can be magnified by giving suppliers and customers limited access to company intranets.

    e. **Extranets** link the intranets of two or more companies. Access to extranets is typically limited to trusted trading partners.

    f. A **gateway**, often implemented via software, translates between two or more different protocol families and makes connections between dissimilar networks possible.

    g. An **application service provider (ASP)** uses the Internet to rent software programs to its customers.

        (1) Using an ASP has several advantages:

            (a) Customers significantly reduce the costs associated with purchasing software because the ASP spreads its costs among its many customers.

            (b) Customers do not have to purchase expensive hardware to run the latest and greatest software.

            (c) Customers can always have the most current software.

(d) Customers can achieve greater security and privacy protection if the ASP uses better and more elaborate controls than does the customer.

(2) The major disadvantages of the ASP model are:

(a) Customers must rely on the ASP for essential business services. If an ASP goes out of business, its customers are in a very precarious position.

(b) Customers face the very real risk that sensitive data can be compromised since ASPs serve many different customers (possibly even direct competitors).

5432.03 Languages and Technologies Used for Information Exchange

a. **eXtensible Markup Language (XML)** is a set of standards for defining the content of data on web pages.

b. **ebXML** is a variation of XML that sets standards for coding common business documents. Because it eliminates the need for proprietary software to translate documents created by different companies, it is easier to use and less expensive than EDI.

c. **Electronic funds transfer (EFT)** is disbursing cash electronically, rather than by check. EFT is made possible by the Automated Clearing House (ACH) network created by the banking system.

d. **Electronic data interchange (EDI)** is used to electronically transfer information between and within organization computers.

(1) This eliminates the need to manually reenter data, improves accuracy, and cuts costs associated with mailing, processing, and storing paper documents.

(2) With the advent of the Internet, third-party networks are no longer needed to transmit EDI messages.

e. **Financial electronic data interchange (FEDI)** integrates EFT with EDI.

(1) The buyer's IS sends orders and delivery instructions to the seller's IS.

(2) The seller delivers the goods.

(3) The buyer's IS sends a message, containing both the remittance data and EFT instructions, to its bank.

(4) The buyer's bank forwards that message to the seller's bank.

(5) The seller's bank deposits money electronically into the seller's account.

(6) The seller's bank sends the remittance data and the notification of the funds transfer to the seller.

5433 E-Business Networking Technologies

5433.01 A **financial value-added network (FVAN)** is an independent organization that provides hardware and software that allow the various EDI networks to communicate with the ACH network.

a. The buyer's IS sends the remittance data and funds transfer instructions together to the FVAN.

b. The FVAN translates the payment instructions from EDI format into ACH format and sends that information to the buyer's bank.

c. The buyer's bank makes a traditional EFT payment to the seller's bank, and the FVAN sends the remittance data to the seller in EDI format.

d. As the seller receives the EFT and EDI portions separately, both must contain a common reference number to facilitate proper matching.

  e. Although the buyer realizes the full advantage of FEDI, the seller does not.

5433.02 A **value-added network (VAN)** offers specialized hardware, software, and long-distance communications to private networks so they can exchange data.

5433.03 A **virtual private network (VPN)** uses the Internet to create a privately owned network that:

  a. Provides a secure, cost-effective method of providing remote access to an organization's network.

  b. Saves companies money, as the cost of the VPN software and higher-capacity lines linking the organizational network to the Internet is less than the leased lines and toll-free phones that the Internet replaces.

5433.04 A **local area network (LAN)** links computers and other devices located close to each other, such as in the same building. These devices are connected to the network using a network interface card (NIC). LANs can be configured in one of three basic ways:

  a. In a **star configuration**, each device is connected to a central server that controls all communications between devices. Devices send messages to the server, which forwards it to the appropriate device.

  b. In a **ring configuration**, each device is linked to two other devices. To control data flow, a software token (these LANs are often called token ring networks) is continually passed around the ring. To send a message, a device grabs the token and attaches a message. Each device checks for messages as the token travels around the ring.

  c. In a **bus configuration**, each device is connected to a main channel called a bus. A software algorithm controls communications between devices. To send a message, a device waits until the bus is free. The other devices check the message to see if it is for them.

5433.05 A **wide area network (WAN)** covers a wide geographic area. There are three ways to configure a WAN:

  a. Centralized, where all devices are linked to a mainframe.

    (1) Advantages: better control, more experienced IT staff, economies of scale.

    (2) Disadvantages: greater complexity, higher communications costs, less flexibility in meeting department and user needs.

  b. Decentralized, where each department has its own computer and LAN.

    (1) Advantages: meets department and user needs better, lower communication costs, and locally stored data.

    (2) Disadvantages: coordinating data stored at many locations, higher hardware costs, implementing effective controls.

  c. Distributed data processing (DDP) system, where computers at each location handle local processing and are also linked to the corporate mainframe.

    (1) Advantages: local computers back each other up, risk of catastrophic loss is reduced, and local systems can easily be added, upgraded, or deleted.

    (2) Disadvantages: coordinating the system, maintaining hardware and software, difficulty standardizing documentation and control, more difficult to achieve adequate security controls and separation of duties, data duplication and inconsistencies.

  d. Downsizing is a procedure of shifting data processing and problem solving from mainframes to smaller computer systems. Downsizing saves money and allows the end user to be more involved in the processing of the data.

  e. A metro-area network (MAN) connects multiple sites with multiple workstations for shared use of common resources.

              Section 5400

5433.06 A **communications channel** connects sending and receiving devices. A communications network often uses several different channels, as each possesses characteristics that affect the network's reliability, cost, and security.

    a. Common channels include telephone lines, fiber optic cables, terrestrial microwaves, satellite, and cellular radio frequencies.

    b. A channel's information carrying capacity is measured by its bandwidth. The greater the bandwidth, the greater the capacity and speed of transmission.

5433.07 In a **client/server system** a desktop computer, referred to as the client, sends a data request to a server. The server retrieves the relevant subset of data from the database and sends it to the client. Client/server systems can be configured in two ways.

    a. A two-tiered system, where the central database is stored on the server and each client has its own application software.

        (1) Advantages: better able to meet user needs, easier to design and control.

        (2) Disadvantages: powerful clients, with abundant disk storage, are needed for local processing; applications software must be purchased and maintained for each client.

    b. A three-tiered client/server system, where a top-tier server stores the central database and a second-tier server uses applications programs to do most of the data processing. All the client has to do is request data from the servers and format data.

        (1) Advantages: inexpensive "thin clients" or network PCs can be used, less applications software to purchase and maintain, lower data transmission costs.

        (2) Disadvantages: high cost, more complex applications development is required.

5433.08 E-business applications require **communications software** that:

    a. controls network access (link and disconnect devices, dial and answer telephones automatically, restrict access to authorized users).

    b. manages the network (determine if network devices are ready to send or receive data, queue input and output, determine system priorities, route messages, log network use and errors).

    c. controls the transfer of data, files, and messages among the various devices and protects them from unauthorized access.

    d. detects and controls errors.

    e. works with protocols, which are rules and procedures for exchanging data. The Internet protocol is called Transmission Control Protocol/Internet Protocol (TCP/IP). When a file, document, or e-mail is ready to be sent over the Internet:

        (1) the TCP protocol breaks it up into small packets, gives each a header that contains the destination address, and sends the packets over the Internet.

        (2) the IP protocol guides the packets to the proper destination using the packet header information.

        (3) The TCP protocol reassembles the packets into the original message.

5440 Information System Control

5440.01 As companies become more reliant on information systems that become ever more complex to meet growing needs for information, they face an ever-present risk of their systems being compromised.

    a. Organizations experience major control failures because:

        (1) the loss of crucial information is viewed as a distant, unlikely threat, so control problems are underestimated and downplayed.

        (2) companies do not understand the control implications of moving from secure, highly controlled, and centralized computer systems to a less secure network or Internet-based system.

        Client/server systems, which make much more information available to many more workers, are harder to control than centralized mainframe systems.

        (3) companies do not fully realize that information is a strategic resource, and protecting it is crucial to their survival.

        (4) time-consuming control measures are not put in place due to productivity and cost pressures.

        (5) confidentiality becomes a major concern when companies give customers and suppliers access to their system and data.

    b. Companies are increasing computer control and security by taking the following, proactive steps:

        (1) Hiring full-time security and control staff

        (2) Making control problems and solutions a major part of employee training

        (3) Establishing formal information security policies and enforcing them

        (4) Building controls into systems during the initial design stage rather than adding them after the fact

        (5) Moving sensitive data to a safe and secure environment

5440.02 **Threats, Risks, and Exposures**

A threat is any event that could damage or harm an information system.

An exposure is the potential dollar loss that could result should a threat occur.

A risk is the likelihood or probability that a threat will actually occur.

Companies face the following four threats.

    1. **Natural and political disasters** (fires, floods, earthquakes, high winds, excessive heat, and war). Disasters can destroy an information system, cause companies to fail, and affect many companies at the same time.

    2. **Software errors and equipment malfunctions** (software errors, operating system crashes, hardware failures, power outages and fluctuations, and data transmission errors)

    3. The greatest risks to information systems, and the greatest dollar losses, are **unintentional acts** (accidents or innocent errors and omissions) resulting from poorly trained personnel, human carelessness, and failure to follow established procedures. For example:

        a. Users lose or misplace data or enter erroneous input.

        b. Files, data, and programs are accidentally erased or altered.

    c. Computer operators use the wrong version of a program or the wrong data files, or misplace files.

    d. Systems analysts develop systems that do not meet company needs or do not perform their intended tasks.

    e. Programmers make logic errors.

4. Intentional acts or computer crimes. For example:

    a. Sabotage, which is destroying a system or some of its components.

    b. Computer fraud, which is stealing money, data, or computer time or services, or falsifying financial statements.

When companies do not protect their systems from these four threats, they may face an additional threat—a lawsuit.

5440.03   **Overview of Control Concepts**

    a. Historically, internal control has been defined as the plan of organization and the methods a business uses to:

      (1) safeguard assets

      (2) provide accurate and reliable information

      (3) promote and improve operational efficiency

      (4) encourage adherence to prescribed managerial policies

    b. An internal control structure is the policies and procedures an organization establishes to provide reasonable assurance that organizational objectives are achieved. A system that provides complete assurance is difficult, if not impossible, to design and is prohibitively expensive.

5440.04   Internal controls can be classified in three ways:

1. Preventive controls, which eliminate problems before they occur. For example:

    a. Hiring highly qualified personnel and training them well

    b. Segregating employee duties so no one can commit and conceal a fraud

    c. Controlling physical access to buildings, assets, and information

2. Detective controls, which uncover problems as they occur (not all control problems can be prevented, and preventive controls cannot eliminate all problems). For example:

    a. Having a second person check all important calculations

    b. Preparing bank reconciliations and monthly trial balances

3. Corrective controls, which help solve problems after they are discovered. For example:

    a. Store backup copies of important files in a secure, off-site location

    b. Establishing procedures to make sure errors are corrected and properly resubmitted for processing

    c. Establish and practice a disaster recovery plan and an emergency incident response plan

    d. Create a computer emergency response team (CERT) to react to security breaches and take corrective action in a timely basis. A CERT consists of technical specialists to solve security problems and senior operations management to make critical business decisions. For each incident, the team needs to:

      (1) determine that a problem exists, often through preventive and detective controls.

      (2) contain the problem as soon as possible to minimize the damage.

(3) identify why the problem occurred.

(4) repair the damage and correct the problem, such as restoring data from backup files and reinstalling corrupted programs.

(5) determine how to prevent the problem in the future or detect it sooner. It may be necessary to implement new controls or modify existing security policies and procedures.

(6) determine whether or not to try and catch and prosecute the perpetrator. If they do, a forensic expert can help make sure all available evidence is gathered, stored, and presented such that it is admissible in court.

5440.05   Levers of Control

Some people believe that there is an inherent conflict between controls and creativity. In order to help companies manage this conflict, Robert Simons, a Harvard business professor, has advocated the implementation of four levers of control:

1.   A **belief system** conveys key company values to employees and motivates them to adhere to such ideals.

(a)   A belief system should be broad enough to appeal to employees at all levels of the organization.

(b)   The belief system should help employees comprehend the direction management wants the company to take.

2.   A **boundary system** promotes ethical behavior by setting limits beyond which an employee must not pass.

(a)   A boundary system should not tell employees exactly what they must do in every situation, as this can discourage creativity and initiative.

(b)   Employees should be allowed to meet customer needs and solve problems using their own ingenuity, as long as they operate within certain limits.

3.   A **diagnostic control system** compares actual performance to planned performance in order to evaluate company progress.

(a)   A diagnostic control system facilitates the monitoring of critical performance outcomes and the progress of individuals, departments, or locations as they endeavor to attain strategically important goals.

(b)   This system provides feedback that enables management to modify and fine-tune inputs and processes so future outputs will more closely match goals.

4.   An **interactive control system** helps top-level managers with high-level activities that require frequent attention, such as setting company objectives and developing company strategy.

(a)   An interactive control system generates data that should be analyzed and discussed in meetings with superiors, subordinates, and peers present.

5440.06   COBIT: A Security and Control Framework

a.   Control Objectives for Information and Related Technology (COBIT) was developed by the Information Systems Audit and Control Foundation (ISACF). COBIT consolidates standards from 36 different sources into a single framework of generally applicable IT security and control practices that:

(1)   helps balance risk and controls in information systems.

(2)   provides assurance that security and IT controls are adequate.

(3)   guides auditors as they form opinions and advise management on internal controls.

b. The COBIT framework looks at controls in three different ways:

    (1) Business Objectives. Information must conform to seven distinct, but overlapping business requirements:

        (a) Availability

        (b) Compliance with legal requirements

        (c) Confidentiality

        (d) Effectiveness (relevant, pertinent, and timely)

        (e) Efficiency

        (f) Integrity

        (g) Reliability

    (2) IT resources, which include:

        (a) Application systems

        (b) Data

        (c) Facilities

        (d) People

        (e) Technology

    (3) IT processes, which include:

        (a) Acquisition and implementation

        (b) Delivery and support

        (c) Monitoring

        (d) Planning and organization

5440.07 COSO's Internal Control Framework

a. The Committee of Sponsoring Organizations (COSO) studied internal controls and issued a report that:

    (1) defined internal controls as the process implemented by the board of directors, management, and those under their direction to provide reasonable assurance that the following control objectives are achieved:

        (a) Effectiveness and efficiency of operations

        (b) Reliability of financial reporting

        (c) Compliance with applicable laws and regulations

    (2) provided guidance for evaluating internal control systems.

    (3) has been widely accepted as the authority on internal controls.

b. COSO defines internal control as a process because it permeates an organization's operating activities and is an integral part of basic management activities. Internal control does not provide absolute assurance because the possibilities of human failure, collusion, and management override of controls make the internal control process an imperfect one.

c. There are five components of COSO's internal control model:

    (1) Control environment. The foundation of a business is its people and the environment in which it operates.

    (2) Control activities. Policies and procedures are needed to make sure control objectives are effectively carried out.

(3) **Risk assessment.** Organizations must set objectives to identify, analyze, and manage their risks.

(4) **Information and communication.** Organizations should create and use information and communication systems to plan, conduct, manage, evaluate, and control their operations.

(5) **Monitoring.** Information systems and internal control policies and procedures must be monitored so that needed modifications can be made.

5441 COSO's Enterprise Risk Management Framework

5441.01 Nine years after COSO released the internal control framework, it began investigating how organizations could improve the risk management process by effectively identifying, assessing, and managing risk. The result was an enhanced corporate governance document, called **Enterprise Risk Management—Integrated Framework (ERM).**

The ERM framework takes a risk-based, rather than a controls-based, approach. It expands on the elements of the internal control integrated framework and is much more comprehensive. The objective is to achieve all the goals of the control framework and help the organization to:

a. attain reasonable assurance that company objectives and goals are achieved and problems and surprises are minimized,

b. continuously assess risks and identify the appropriate action to take and the resources to allocate to overcome or mitigate risk,

c. achieve its financial and performance targets, and

d. avoid adverse publicity and damage to the entity's reputation.

5441.02 There are eight components of COSO's ERM framework:

1. **Internal environment.** The people in a business and the environment in which they operate are the foundation for all other ERM components.

2. **Objective setting.** Management must put into place a process to formulate objectives in order to help the company assess and respond to risks.

3. **Event identification.** Certain events can affect the company's ability to implement its strategy and achieve its objectives. Management must identify these events and determine whether they represent risks or opportunities.

4. **Risk assessment.** Identified risks are evaluated to determine how they affect the company's ability to achieve its objectives and how to manage them. Both qualitative and quantitative methods are used to assess risks.

5. **Risk response.** Management can choose to avoid, reduce, share, or accept risks after careful analysis.

6. **Control activities.** To ensure that management's risk responses are effectively carried out, policies and procedures should be implemented.

7. **Information and communication.** Information about ERM components needs to be communicated through all levels of the company and with external parties.

8. **Monitoring.** ERM processes must be monitored, deficiencies reported to management, and modifications performed when required.

Each of these eight components is discussed in the following sections.

5442 Internal Environment

5442.01 According to COSO, an internal environment consists of the following seven factors.

5442.02 **Commitment to Integrity, Ethical Values, and Competence.** To accomplish this, management should:

    a. foster an organizational culture based on integrity and ethical values.

    b. make integrity a basic operating principle by consistently encouraging and rewarding honesty and verbally labeling honest and dishonest behavior. Punishing or rewarding honesty without labeling or explaining it or using an inconsistent standard of honesty will result in inconsistent moral behavior.

    c. actively teach and practice integrity.

    d. establish policies that clearly and explicitly describe honest and dishonest behaviors, especially for uncertain or unclear issues such as conflicts of interest and accepting gifts.

    e. thoroughly investigate all dishonest acts.

    f. dismiss employees found guilty of dishonesty and prosecute enough of them so that the remaining employees know dishonesty is not tolerated and will be punished.

    g. require employees to report any incidents of dishonest, illegal, or unethical acts and discipline employees who knowingly fail to report violations.

    h. make a commitment to competence, and this begins with having competent employees. Competence is a factor of knowledge, experience, training, and skills.

5442.03 **Management's Philosophy, Operating Style, and Risk Appetite.** If management behaves responsibly and honestly, employees are more likely to do so. When management does not comply with internal controls, employees are not likely to comply with the company's internal controls. Management must also decide how much risk the company is willing to accept, referred to as "risk appetite," in order to achieve its goals and objectives. To assess management's philosophy, operating style, and risk appetite, ask questions such as:

    a. Does management assess risks and rewards as part of their decision-making process or do they take undue risks to achieve their objectives?

    b. Is the company's risk appetite in alignment with company strategy?

    c. Does management manipulate performance measures to make them more favorable?

    d. Does management demand ethical behavior or do they pressure employees to achieve results regardless of the methods?

    e. Does management have the attitude that the ends justify the means?

5442.04 **Organizational Structure.** An organizational structure defines lines of authority, responsibility, and reporting. An overly complex or unclear organizational structure may indicate more serious problems. Important aspects of organizational structure include:

    a. what the company's overall framework is for planning, directing, and controlling its operations.

    b. how a company defines lines of authority and responsibility.

    c. whether authority is centralized or decentralized.

    d. how responsibility is assigned for specific tasks.

    e. how the allocation of responsibility affects management's information requirements.

    f. how the accounting and information system functions are organized.

5442.05 **The Audit Committee of the Board of Directors.** All publicly held companies are required to have an audit committee made up of outside board of directors members that oversee:

    a. its internal control structure.

    b. its financial reporting process.

    c. its compliance with laws, regulations, and standards.

    d. the hiring, compensating, and work of external and internal auditors.

    e. independent reviews of management to evaluate their integrity and to increase the investing public's confidence in the accuracy of the company's financial reporting process.

5442.06 **Methods of Assigning Authority and Responsibility.** High-level corporate executives should make individual departments or individuals responsible for specific business objectives or processes and then hold them accountable. They can do this with:

    a. formal job descriptions.

    b. a formal code of conduct that covers ethical behavior standards, conflicts of interest, acceptable business practices, and regulatory requirements.

    c. a written policy and procedures manual that:

        (1) explains proper business practices.

        (2) documents how transactions and errors are to be processed and handled.

        (3) contains the chart of accounts.

        (4) contains example copies of forms and documents.

        (5) can be used to train new and existing employees.

    d. employee training programs.

    e. operating plans, schedules, and budgets.

5442.07 **Human Resources Policies and Practices.** Appropriate policies and procedures for managing employees include:

    a. Hire employees based on how well they meet written job requirements.

    b. Check resumes and reference letters and perform background checks when evaluating job applicant qualifications.

    c. Promote employees based on merit and performance.

    d. Train the members of the organization.

        (1) All employees

            (a) Why security measures are important to the organization's long-run survival

            (b) Safe computing practices, such as not opening unsolicited e-mail attachments, only using approved software, not sharing or revealing passwords, and physically protecting laptops when traveling

            (c) How to prevent attacks that use deception to obtain unauthorized access to passwords or other information about their accounts or computers

            (d) To not allow outsiders or unauthorized employees to follow them through restricted access entrances such as computer rooms, data storage areas, inventory storage areas, and any other internally or externally locked doors

        (2) New and existing employees

        In their responsibilities and in organizational policies and procedures

    (3) Computer security professionals

        (a) In new IT developments that create new security threats and make old solutions obsolete

        (b) To keep abreast of recent hacking developments. White-hat hackers monitor hacker activities and publish on web pages how to perpetrate all known hacking activities and how to protect systems from each hacking approach.

    (4) Top management

    To support training efforts and the enforcement of sanctions against employees who willfully violate security policies

e. Establish formal compensation, job incentive, career advancement, and working condition policies.

f. Enforce mandatory annual vacations and assign employees' jobs to others during their absence.

g. Require all employees, suppliers, and contractors to sign and abide by a confidentiality agreement.

h. Rotate sensitive duties among key employees.

i. Purchase fidelity bond insurance for all key employees.

j. Prosecute and incarcerate hackers and fraud perpetrators.

k. Remove discharged and disgruntled employees from sensitive jobs and deny them access to the information system to prevent retaliation.

5442.08 **External Influences.** An organization is influenced by:

a. requirements imposed by the:

    (1) stock exchanges,

    (2) Financial Accounting Standards Board (FASB),

    (3) Securities and Exchange Commission (SEC), and

    (4) PCAOB (Public Company Accounting Oversight Board).

b. regulatory agency requirements, such as those for banks, utilities, and insurance companies.

5443 Objective Setting

5443.01 Companies should formulate a mission statement or corporate vision and use it as a foundation to establish and prioritize more specific sub-objectives throughout the firm. Management must meet four types of objectives in order to achieve company goals:

5443.02 **Strategic objectives** are high-level goals that are aligned with and support the company's mission.

a. Strategic objectives should be set before all other objectives.

b. They are intended to create shareholder value.

c. They require management to identify alternative ways to accomplish the objectives and carefully identify and assess the risks involved before making a decision.

5443.03 **Operations objectives** deal with the effectiveness and efficiency of company operations, such as performance and profitability goals and safeguarding assets.

a. Operations objectives are a product of management preferences, judgments, and style.

     b.   They may vary significantly among entities.

     c.   They must be relevant to the company's industry and economic conditions.

     d.   They give a clear direction as to how to allocate resources.

5443.04   **Reporting objectives** help ensure the accuracy, completeness, and reliability of internal and external company reports, of both a financial and nonfinancial nature.

     a.   Reporting objectives are usually imposed by external entities, such as the IRS and other governmental regulators.

5443.05   **Compliance objectives** help the company comply with all applicable laws and regulations.

     a.   Most compliance objectives are imposed by external entities.

     b.   They can have a significant impact on the company's reputation.

5444 Event Identification

5444.01   Event identification is the third ERM component. According to COSO, an **event** is "an incident or occurrence emanating from internal or external sources that affects implementation of strategy or achievement of objectives. Events may have positive or negative impacts or both." It is important to remember that events:

     a.   represent uncertainty,

     b.   may or may not occur,

     c.   are difficult to foretell,

     d.   can have an unforeseeable impact on a company,

     e.   may trigger other events, and

     f.   can occur individually or concurrently.

5444.02   It is imperative that management anticipate all possible events that could affect the company, both positive and negative, and understand the interrelationship of events. Some of the more common techniques companies use to identify events include the following:

     a.   Using comprehensive lists of potential events

     b.   Performing an internal analysis

     c.   Monitoring leading events and trigger points

     d.   Conducting workshops and interviews

     e.   Performing data mining and analysis

     f.   Analyzing business processes

5445 Risk Assessment and Risk Response

5445.01   There are two types of risk. **Inherent risk** is the risk that exists before management takes any steps to control the likelihood or impact of a risk. **Residual risk** is the risk that remains after management reacts to the risk, such as by implementing internal controls.

     An internal control risk assessment has six steps and is performed as follows. (Also see Figure 6.)

5445.02   Identify threats. Companies face the following types of threats:

     a.   Strategic (doing the wrong things)

b. Operating (doing the right things, but in the wrong way)

c. Financial (financial resources are lost, wasted, or stolen; inappropriate liabilities are incurred)

d. Information (incorrect input data, faulty or irrelevant stored information, an unreliable system, incorrect or misleading reports)

5445.03 Estimate risk, which is a measure of how likely an error is to occur. Errors are more likely than fraud.

5445.04 Estimate exposure, which is a measure of the magnitude of an error. For example, there is a small risk of an earthquake, but the exposure is enormous if it destroys the information system.

5445.05 Identify controls. One or more controls should be identified to protect the company from each threat. Preventive, detective, and corrective controls complement each other, and a good internal control system employs all three.

a. A preventive control is superior to a detective one.

b. If preventive controls fail, detective controls are essential for discovering the problem.

c. Corrective controls help recover from the problem.

5445.06 Estimate costs and benefits. The following principles should govern this analysis:

a. An internal control system provides reasonable assurance that control problems do not take place; no system can provide foolproof protection, as the cost would be prohibitive.

b. Too many controls slow the system down and negatively affect operational efficiency.

c. The benefits of an internal control procedure must exceed its cost.

d. The benefit of a control procedure is the difference between the expected loss with the control procedure(s) and the expected loss without it.

Expected loss is the mathematical product of risk and exposure. (Expected loss = risk × exposure)

5445.07 Respond to risk.

a. **Reduce** the risk. Implementing an effective system of internal controls is the most effective way to reduce the likelihood and impact of risk.

b. **Accept** the risk by not acting to prevent the risk or lessen its impact.

c. **Share** some of the risk or transfer it to another party by outsourcing an activity, acquiring insurance, or hedging transactions.

d. **Avoid** the risk by not engaging in the activity that produces the risk.

Figure 6

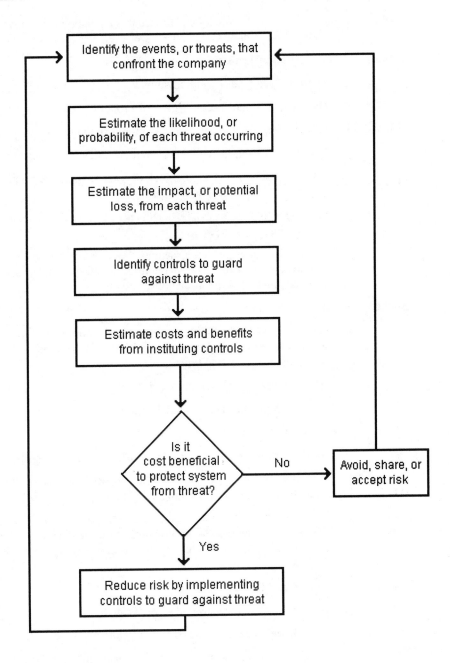

5446 Control Activities

5446.01 Control activities are policies and procedures that help management achieve control objectives. According to COSO, there are seven categories of control activities:

5446.02 **Authorization of Transactions and Activities**

    a. There are two types of authorizations.

        (1) General authorization is given for routine transactions.

        (2) Specific management authorization is required for certain activities or transactions.

    b. Under either method, it is important to document authorization as follows:

        (1) Employees should sign, initial, or enter an authorization code on a paper-based transaction document or record.

        (2) The authorization can be documented using a digital signature (or fingerprint) in computer systems.

    Employees who process transactions should verify the presence of the appropriate authorization(s). Employees in the information systems department should not be allowed to initiate or authorize transactions.

5446.03 **Separation of Duties**

    a. No employee should be in a position to both commit and conceal fraud or unintentional errors. This can be prevented by an effective segregation of duties, which is achieved by separating the following functions:

        (1) Authorizing transactions and decisions

        (2) Recording transactions and decisions

        (3) Custody of assets

    If a person can perform two or more of these functions, problems can arise.

    b. With effective separation of duties, it is difficult for a single employee to perpetrate fraud. Detecting fraud where two or more people are in collusion to override the controls is more difficult.

    c. Computers can be used to perform some of these functions. The principle of separating duties remains the same; the only difference is that the computer, not a human, performs the function.

5446.04 **Documents and Records**

    a. Well-designed documents and records can:

        (1) help organizations quickly identify potential problems.

        (2) be used to verify that assigned responsibilities are completed correctly

        (3) ensure transaction accuracy.

    b. To maximize their internal control value, documents should:

        (1) be easy to fill out, maximize efficiency, minimize recording errors, and facilitate transaction review and verification.

        (2) have a space for authorizations, where such is required.

        (3) be sequentially prenumbered to facilitate accounting for each document.

        (4) provide an audit trail, to make it easier to:

            (a) trace individual transactions through the system.

            (b) correct errors.

            (c) verify system output.

5446.05   **Asset and Record Safeguards**

To safeguard assets from theft and unauthorized use:

a. restrict physical access to computer rooms and equipment.

b. restrict logical access to computer files and information.

c. restrict physical access to assets by using safes, lockboxes, safety deposit boxes, cash registers, and restricted storage areas.

d. protect records and documents using fireproof storage areas and off-site backup, restricting access to blank checks and documents and locked filing cabinets.

e. supervise employees effectively.

f. maintain complete and accurate records of all assets, including information.

g. control the environment using air conditioners, fire retardants, raised floors to protect computer equipment from flooding, and reinforced rooms to protect computers from falling objects.

h. segregate duties as discussed earlier.

5446.06   **Independent Checks on Performance**

Independent checks include:

a. reconciling independently maintained records.

b. comparing actual quantities and recorded quantities.

c. using double-entry accounting (debits equal credits) to make sure both sides of a transaction are recorded. In addition, comparing total debits with total credits is an important test of the accuracy of allocating items to various asset, expense, revenue, and liability accounts.

d. top-level reviews of planned performance, prior period performance, and performance of competitors.

e. analytical reviews that examine the relationship between different sets of data.

f. Using batch totals.

    (1) In batch processing:

        (a) Source documents are assembled in groups.

        (b) Batch or control totals are manually computed before entering data into the system.

        (c) Control totals are generated during each subsequent process.

        (d) Someone other than the person who prepared the original batch total compares the two totals.

        (e) Discrepancies indicate a processing error. The cause of the discrepancy is identified and corrected before the transaction is reprocessed.

    (2) Limiting batch sizes reduces the time required to find the cause of any individual discrepancy. Five batch totals are used in computer systems:

        (a) Financial totals (the sum of a dollar field, such as total inventory or total cash disbursements)

        (b) Hash totals (the sum of a field not normally totaled, such as inventory item number)

        (c) Record counts (how many transactions are processed)

        (d) Line counts (how many lines of data are entered)

        (e) Cross-footing balance tests (The grand total of all the row totals is compared to the grand total of all the column totals to make sure they are equal.)

g. Independent review. After one person processes a transaction, a second person:

    (1) reviews the work of the first.

    (2) checks for proper authorization.

    (3) examines supporting documents.

    (4) tests whether prices, quantities, and extensions are accurate.

5446.07 Project Development and Acquisition Controls. In order to manage the development, acquisition, implementation, and maintenance of information systems, it is crucial to have a formal, appropriate, and proven methodology. Appropriate controls contained in the methodology to monitor systems development include the following:

a. A **strategic master plan** that aligns an organization's information system with its business strategies.

b. A **project development plan** outlining significant project milestones, how the project will be completed, and project costs.

c. A **data processing schedule** that maximizes computer resources by organizing all data processing tasks.

d. A **steering committee** that supervises systems development and acquisition.

e. **System performance measurements** to accurately evaluate a system. Conventional measurements include:

   (1) **throughput** (output per unit of time),

   (2) **response time** (time it takes the system to respond), and

   (3) **utilization** (percentage of time the system is used productively).

f. A **post-implementation review** that determines if the projected benefits were attained.

As an alternative to developing systems internally, companies may employ a **systems integrator**, a vendor who manages the systems development efforts of external parties.

5446.08 **Change Management Controls.** New business practices and advances in information technology require organizations to constantly revise their information systems. **Change management** ensures that such modifications do not adversely affect the following system principles:

a. Reliability

b. Security

c. Confidentiality

d. Integrity

e. Availability

5447 Information and Communication

5447.01 The primary purpose of an IS is to produce information that improves decision making. This requires an understanding of how:

a. transactions are initiated, authorized, and handled.

b. data is captured in electronic form or converted from source documents to an electronic format.

c. data is processed.

d. computer files are updated.

e. data is stored and retrieved.

f. data is summarized and formatted as output.

g. information is reported to internal and external users.

5447.02 These items form what is referred to as an audit trail. An audit trail must go two directions:

a. Individual transactions can be traced from the point where they occur through the system to the financial statements.

b. Financial statement numbers can be traced back through the system to individual transactions.

5448 Monitoring Performance

5448.01 Key methods of monitoring performance include the following.

5448.02 Effective supervision. Supervision is important in all companies, but especially important in companies too small to have adequate segregation of duties. Effective supervision involves:

    a. training employees to effectively and efficiently complete their jobs.

    b. monitoring employee performance to spot and correct problems and errors.

    c. safeguarding assets by overseeing employees who have access to them.

    d. correcting errors as soon as possible.

    e. safeguarding assets.

5448.03 Responsibility accounting, which includes:

    a. the use of budgets, schedules, plans, standard costs, and quality standards.

    b. performance reports that compare planned and actual performance.

    c. procedures for investigating and correcting significant variances.

5448.04 Internal auditing, which involves:

    a. reviewing the reliability and integrity of financial and operating information.

    b. testing internal control effectiveness and recommending control improvements.

    c. determining whether employees comply with management policies and procedures.

    d. ensuring that all applicable laws and regulations are followed.

    e. evaluating management efficiency and effectiveness.

        (1) Internal audit should be organizationally independent of accounting and operating functions.

        (2) The director of internal audit should report to the audit committee of the board of directors.

    f. reviewing and evaluating system development projects for appropriateness and completeness. This review is especially important during:

        (1) feasibility study.

        (2) systems design.

        (3) program design.

        (4) testing the system.

        (5) conversion and implementation.

5448.05 Log analysis. Most systems create a log of who accesses the system and the specific actions each user performs.

    a. Log analysis is examining the audit trail created by the logs to monitor system security.

    b. It should be done regularly to detect problems in a timely manner.

    c. Since logs quickly grow in size, system administrators use software tools to find log entries that might be intrusions.

5448.06 Managerial reports, which provide information about key performance indicators that are used to monitor and access control effectiveness such as:

    a. downtime caused by security incidents.

    b. time to react to security incidents once detected.

5448.07 Vulnerability scans which identify whether a system possesses any well-known vulnerabilities.

5448.08 Penetration tests or authorized attempts to break into an organization's information system.

    a. The testers, usually an internal audit team or a security consulting firm, try everything possible to compromise the system.

    b. To get into office to locate passwords or access computers, they masquerade as janitors, temporary workers, or confused delivery personnel. They also use sexy decoys to distract guards, climb through roof hatches, and drop through ceiling panels.

    c. Some consultants claim they can penetrate more than 9 out of 10 companies attacked.

5448.09 Actions by the chief security officer (CSO), who:

    a. conducts vulnerability tests and risk assessments.

    b. audits security measures implemented by the company.

    c. helps the chief information officer create and put into place sound security policies and procedures.

    d. promotes security efforts and disseminates information about fraud, errors, security breaches, and other improper system uses and their consequences.

5448.10 Patch management, which is fixing known system vulnerabilities and installing the latest software updates for security programs (anti-virus, firewall, etc.), operating systems, and other application programs.

    a. Highly skilled hackers and security consulting firms search for vulnerabilities in widely used software.

    b. Hackers publish instructions for exploiting a vulnerability (called an exploit) on the Internet. These instructions are easy to follow and the published code can be automatically executed by the attackers called "script kiddies."

    c. When vulnerabilities are found, software developers release a patch (code that fixed the vulnerability).

    d. Patch management is the process of regularly applying patches and updates to software.

Because unanticipated side effects of patches can create new problems, patches software must be carefully tested before being used so that important applications are not compromised or crashed.

Organizations may have to apply hundreds of patches to thousands of computers as multiple patches are released each year for each software program used by an organization.

5448.11 ERM evaluations. Internal auditors or others within the firm can gauge ERM effectiveness by conducting an ERM evaluation.

    a. This can be a formal evaluation or a self-assessment process.

5448.12 Tracking purchased software. Companies should regularly conduct software audits to ensure that they are not violating software license agreements. Specifically, they should make certain that:

    a. there are adequate licenses for all users,

    b. the company is not paying for more licenses than are necessary, and

    c. all employees are informed of the consequences of using unlicensed software.

5448.13 Engaging forensic specialists, which includes:

   a. forensic accountants, who specialize in fraud detection and investigation.

   b. computer forensics specialists, who deal with computer crimes and are instrumental in discovering, extracting, safeguarding, and documenting evidence that can be used as a basis for legal action.

5448.14 Installing fraud detection software, which is special software designed to recognize patterns and clues that fraudsters tend to leave behind.

   a. Other companies use **neural networks** that mimic the brain, have learning capabilities, and are surprisingly accurate in identifying suspected fraud.

5448.15 Implementing a fraud hotline.

   a. Sarbanes-Oxley requires companies to establish mechanisms for employees to report abuses such as fraud.

   b. Fraud hotlines allow employees to anonymously report fraud.

   c. Not all calls are legitimate, and some callers have alternative motives.

   d. Using a fraud hotline set up by a trade organization or commercial company can overcome the risk of hotline operators reporting to people involved in top-management fraud.

5450 Using Computers to Implement Controls

5450.01 In today's world, information systems have become increasingly more vulnerable. Among the reasons are:

   a. Organizations are increasingly dependent on their information systems to manage their businesses, manufacture goods, and render services.

   b. We live in an inter-connected world and it is often not possible to lock others out of our information systems. Increasingly, a company's success is dependent on the ability to quickly and efficiently communicate with customers, vendors, employees, business partners, shareholders, and various governmental entities.

5450.02 One of management's major responsibilities is to make sure a company's information resources are secure and adequately controlled. The advent of computer-based information systems has not changed basic internal control objectives. However, the extensive use of information technology and the changes in the way companies operate have changed the ways these internal control objectives are achieved. Internal control systems have evolved to parallel the involvement in information systems.

5450.03 IT advancements make it possible for an organization to strengthen its internal control structure.

   a. New controls were developed to eliminate or minimize the risks introduced when companies moved to a mainframe-based computer system from a paper-based system.

   b. New controls were also developed when businesses moved to a distributed, client/server system from a centralized, mainframe-based system.

   c. Now, new controls are needed to control the risks that arise as we move into an Internet-based, e-commerce environment.

5450.04 The AICPA has introduced SysTrust, a new evaluation service that independently tests and verifies a system's reliability. SysTrust uses the following four principles to determine if a system is reliable:

   a. **Availability:** Users can enter, update, process, and retrieve data as needed.

b. **Security:** The system is protected from unauthorized physical and logical access to prevent or minimize the theft, improper use, alteration, destruction, or disclosure of data and software.

c. **Maintainability:** Authorized, tested, and documented changes can be made and the changes communicated to management and authorized users, without affecting system availability, security, and integrity.

d. **Integrity:** The system accomplishes its objectives in an unimpaired manner: processing is complete, accurate, timely, and free from unauthorized or inadvertent system manipulation.

5450.05 Ensuring system reliability is a top management issue, not an information technology issue. Management is responsible for the reliability and accuracy of the organization's information. The Sarbanes-Oxley Act requires:

a. the CEO and CFO to certify that financial statements accurately represent company activities.

b. an annual report on the company's internal controls. Included in the report is:

   (1) a management acknowledgement that it is responsible for designing and maintaining internal controls.

   (2) management's assessment of the effectiveness of those controls.

5450.06 To successfully implement systems reliability principles, a company must:

a. develop and document a comprehensive set of control policies before designing and implementing specific control procedures. Otherwise, they will most likely end up purchasing a mish-mash of products that do not protect every information system resource.

b. effectively communicate policies to all employees, customers, suppliers, and other authorized users. All users should be sent regular, periodic reminders about security policies and be trained in how to comply with them.

c. design and employ appropriate and cost-beneficial control procedures to implement the policies.

d. monitor the system and take corrective action to maintain compliance with policies. System reliability is a moving target as IT advances create new threats, alter the risks associated with existing threats, and provide new ways to deal with threats.

5450.07 To ensure system reliability, companies must implement a set of preventive controls and supplement them with methods for detecting incidents and procedures for taking corrective remedial action. A company must also employ multiple layers of controls so that if one control fails or is circumvented, another control will prevent, detect, or correct the reliability breakdown.

5450.08 **Controls Related to More than One Reliability Principle.** Management must make sure that each of the four reliability objectives is achieved. There are four categories of controls that are used to achieve two or more of these objectives related to more than one reliability principle:

5450.09   Strategic Planning and Budgeting

   a.   Organizations face several threats related to strategic planning and budgeting:

      (1) The information system does not support business strategies.

      (2) Resources are not used efficiently or effectively.

      (3) Information needs are not met or are unaffordable.

   b.   Several controls can eliminate or minimize these threats:

      (1) Develop a multiyear (3- to 5-year) strategic plan that shows how the organization will achieve its long-range goals and the role information technology will play in meeting those goals.

         (a) Management should update the plan at least twice a year.

         (b) Top management should review and approve the strategic plan at least yearly.

      (2) Establish a research and development group that is responsible for assessing how emerging technologies will impact business operations. Use their findings to update the plan.

      (3) Budget resources to support the strategic plan.

5450.10   Develop a System Reliability Plan

One reason some organizations can not ensure system reliability is they lack a plan to achieve this objective. To develop and implement a systems reliability plan, an organization should:

   a.   assign plan responsibility and accountability to a top-level manager.

   b.   review and update the plan regularly.

   c.   make management, users, and all personnel with system reliability responsibilities aware of the plan.

   d.   require all new and existing employees to follow all security procedures.

   e.   identify, document, and test:

      (1) availability, security, maintainability, integrity, and user reliability requirements.

      (2) performance objectives, policies, and standards for the reliability requirements.

   f.   determine ownership, custody, access, and maintenance responsibility for information resources (hardware, software, data, infrastructure, and people).

   g.   develop a security awareness program and use it to train employees.

   h.   document and report all system reliability problems and analyze them, looking for causes and possible trends.

   i.   identify and review all new or changed legal requirements for their impact on system reliability.

   j.   log and review all changes requested by users for their impact on system reliability.

   k.   assess system reliability risks each time the system is changed, modified, or updated.

5450.11   Documentation

It is hard to ensure systems reliability without proper documentation, as this can result in ineffective system design, operation, review, audit, and modification. Documentation can also be used in training system users. It is important to develop and maintain three different types of documentation:

   a.   Administrative (standards and procedures for analysis, design, programming, processing file handling, and storage)

b. Systems (input, processing, output, and error handling procedures for each application)

c. Operating (equipment configurations, programs, files, setup and execution procedures, and corrective actions for each program)

5450.12   Training

Organizations should spend the time and money necessary to make sure the people who design, develop, implement, and operate the company's information system are qualified and well trained. There should be an adequately staffed information center help desk to deal with errors in user interactions with the information system. The same holds true for those in charge of any aspect of system security.

5451 Availability

5451.01   Systems need to be protected from things like software and hardware failures, sabotage, political and natural disasters, and power outages. As management relies more on information systems for support, system downtime has the potential to interrupt business operations. Three categories of controls are used to ensure information system availability: (1) minimizing system downtime, (2) disaster recovery plan, and (3) data and program file backups.

5451.02   Minimizing System Downtime

a. When an information system goes down:

(1) significant financial losses are often incurred,

(2) critical business operations are interrupted, and

(3) data can be lost or destroyed.

b. Several controls can eliminate or minimize system downtime:

(1) Establish policies and procedures to deal with hardware failures, power outages, unintentional errors, loss or destruction of data, sabotage, and other problems.

Train employees so they can understand, follow, and implement them.

(2) Perform regular preventive maintenance on key system components.

(3) Install an uninterruptible power supply (UPS). This auxiliary power supply:

(a) prevents data loss from power surges or dips and

(b) keeps computers operating for a limited time when there is a power failure.

(4) Install redundant system components so the system can continue operating if system components fail.

(5) Obtain disaster and business interruption insurance so the company can recover from downtime failures.

5451.03   Disaster Recovery Plan

A disaster recovery plan is used to smoothly and quickly restore data processing capacity when there is a disaster. A recovery plan has the following objectives:

a. Minimize the disruption, damage, and loss from the disaster.

b. Establish a short-term data processing alternative so the company can quickly resume normal operations.

c. Train and familiarize personnel with emergency procedures.

5451.04 Disaster recovery plans should contain the following:

a. Recovery priorities. The plan should identify and prioritize:

    (1) hardware, software, applications, and data necessary to sustain the most critical applications.

    (2) sequence and timing of all recovery activities.

b. Insurance to:

    (1) replace equipment lost in the disaster.

    (2) compensate for business interruptions.

c. Specific assignments. A plan coordinator should:

    (1) be responsible for implementing the recovery plan.

    (2) assign individuals and teams specific recovery responsibilities such as finding new physical facilities, operating the system, installing software, setting up data communications linkages, recovering data, and procuring forms and supplies.

d. Backup computer and telecommunications facilities, which can be arranged by:

    (1) establishing reciprocal agreements with companies with compatible facilities so each company can use the other's computers if an emergency occurs.

    (2) signing a contract for a contingent site. A hot site is configured to meet user requirements. A cold site has everything needed (power, air conditioning, and support systems) to quickly install a computer. Cold site users rely on their computer vendors for prompt delivery of equipment and software if an emergency occurs.

    (3) distributing processing capacity in a multilocation organization so other facilities can take over if one location is damaged or destroyed.

    (4) investing in duplicate hardware, software, or data storage devices for critical applications.

e. Periodic testing and revision. A recovery plan must be:

    (1) regularly tested with a simulated disaster, with each disaster recovery team carrying out its assigned activities.

    (2) constantly improved, since most plans fail their initial test and tested plans rarely anticipate and deal with all real-life disaster problems.

    (3) reviewed to make sure it reflects current computer application changes, equipment configurations, and new personnel assignments.

f. Complete documentation of all aspects of the system.

    (1) Copies of the documentation should be stored securely at multiple locations.

    (2) One copy should be some distance from the system.

5451.05 **Data and Program File Backups**

    a. All program and data files should be backed up regularly and frequently.

    b. A copy should be stored on-site and another at a secure site some distance away.

    c. Backup files can be transported to the remote site in two ways:

        (1) Physically, by mailing, shipping, or delivering them

        (2) Electronically, by way of electronic vaulting. There are two main electronic vaulting approaches: (1) the push approach, where a company electronically sends the items to be backed up, and (2) the pull approach, where the electronic vaulting service installs its software on company computers and uses Internet connections to periodically contact company computers and automatically back up data. If data is lost or needs to be accessed, the Internet connection provides prompt on-line access to the backup data.

    d. To protect data privacy, all data should be encrypted before being transmitted.

5451.06 As shown in Figure 7, batch processing files are backed up using the grandfather-father-son concept.

    Figure 7

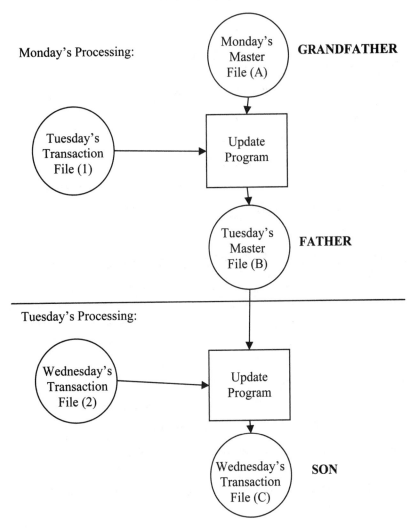

When a master file is updated, a new master file is created.

A destroyed master file can be recreated using prior generations of the master file and the appropriate transaction file. For example, if Wednesday's master file is destroyed it could be recreated using Tuesday's master file and Wednesday's transaction file. If Tuesday's master file was also destroyed, it could be recreated using Monday's master file and Tuesday's transaction file.

5451.07 On-line databases are also backed up.

 a. Periodically during processing, a checkpoint (a copy of the database at that point in time and the information needed to restart the system) is created.

 b. The checkpoint data is stored on a separate storage medium.

 c. The database is recreated by determining the last checkpoint and reprocessing all subsequent transactions.

 d. Between checkpoints, a rollback (a pre-updated copy of each record created prior to processing a transaction) is created. If a problem occurs, records are rolled back to the pre-update value and the transaction is reprocessed.

5451.08 PC hard drives can be backed up on CDs, diskettes, and tape files.

 Do not store the on-site backup copy next to the PC, as it can be destroyed by any disaster that wipes out the PC.

5451.09 The company should periodically practice restoring a system from the backup data so employees know how to quickly restart the system if a failure occurs.

5452 Security

5452.01 The following five classifications of controls are used to make systems more secure:

 1. Segregation of systems duties

 2. Physical access controls

 3. Logical access controls

 4. Personal computers and client/server network protection

 5. Internet and telecommunication controls

5453 Segregation of Systems Duties

5453.01 In a highly integrated system, a person with unrestricted access to the computer, its programs, and live data may be able to perpetrate and conceal fraud. To prevent this, organizations must effectively segregate the following information system duties:

5453.02 Systems administrators, who make sure the information system operates efficiently and effectively.

5453.03 Network managers, who make sure:

 a. the organization's networks operate continuously and properly, and

 b. all applicable devices are linked to the organization's internal and external networks.

5453.04 Security management, who make sure all system components are secure and protected from any and all internal as well as external threats.

5453.05 Change management, who make sure all organizational changes are made effectively and efficiently.

5453.06   Users, who:

    a.   authorize and record transactions,

    b.   use system output, and

    c.   are responsible for correcting errors.

5453.07   Systems analysts, who:

    a.   help users analyze their information needs and

    b.   design information systems that meet those needs.

5453.08   Programmers, who:

    a.   use the design developed by the analysts to develop an information system and

    b.   write computer programs.

5453.09   Computer operators, who make sure:

    a.   data is properly entered into the computer,

    b.   data is processed correctly, and

    c.   needed output is produced.

5453.10   Information system librarians, who maintain company databases, files, and programs in a separate and secure storage area.

5453.11   A data control group, which makes sure:

    a.   a log is kept of all inputs, data processing operations, stored data, and system output;

    b.   source data has been properly approved;

    c.   transactions are processed correctly;

    d.   input and output are reconciled;

    e.   records of input errors are maintained so they can be corrected and resubmitted;

    f.   data-related errors are sent to the users who originated the transaction for correction;

    g.   systems output is distributed to the intended and proper user; and

    h.   there is adequate rotation of operator duties.

5453.12   Analysts, programmers, and other non-operations system personnel should not be allowed to operate the computer or be in the computer room while a program is being run. Application programs that are on the server should be stored as object code to prevent computer operators from making changes to the programs during execution. Object code is created when a program written in the source language such as COBOL has been compiled. Changes cannot be made directly to the object code. Source code is the language that programmers use to write the programs. Some source code is interpreted, or executed line-by-line by the computer and can be edited at any time. Source code should only be used when in a secure development and/or testing environment.

5454 Physical Access Controls

5454.01 When actual, physical access to computer equipment is not restricted, computers, files, and data can be damaged or accessed by unauthorized parties. Physical access security can be achieved using the following controls:

5454.02 Where possible, there should only be one unlocked building entrance during normal business hours. Emergency exits should not permit outside entry and an alarm should sound when the exit is opened.

5454.03 A security guard or receptionist should be stationed at the main entrance to:

    a. verify the identity of employees,

    b. require all visitors to sign in, and

    c. have an employee escort visitors to their building destination.

5454.04 Locate sensitive computer equipment, programs, and data in locked rooms.

    a. Securely lock all entrances to the computer room.

    b. Use security guards and closed-circuit television systems to monitor all entrances.

    c. Require proper employee ID to gain access to the computer room. Security badges that have photos and magnetic, electric, or optical codes can be used to automatically log each employee's entry and exit. This log should be reviewed periodically by supervisory personnel.

    d. Multiple failed access attempts should trigger an alarm.

    e. Rooms where sensitive hardware, software, or data are stored should supplement locks with other security technologies such as card readers, numeric keypads, or various biometric devices such as retina scanners, fingerprint readers, or voice recognition.

5454.05 Monitor all visitor access to sensitive company sites.

    a. Log them in and out.

    b. Brief them on company security policies.

    c. Require them to wear a visitor badge.

    d. Escort them to their destinations.

5454.06 Install security alarms that can detect unauthorized, off-hours access.

5454.07 Lock PCs, laptops, and other computer devices when they are not in use.

5454.08 Place hardware and critical system components away from hazardous or combustible materials.

5454.09 Restrict access to private, secured telephone lines and to authorized terminals or PCs. Restrict access to telephone and LAN wiring to prevent wiretapping. Do not expose cables and wiring to areas accessible to the public. Disconnect wall jacks not in current use. Securely lock wiring closets containing telecommunications equipment.

5454.10 Laptops, cell phones, and PDA devices require special attention to prevent their theft and the loss of the data they contain.

    a. Employees should always lock their laptops to an immovable object.

    b. Store sensitive data on removable media, rather than the hard drive, in an encrypted format and lock it up at night.

    c. Installing software on laptops so that if it is stolen the laptop will automatically dial a toll-free number and reveal its current location when the thief attempts to use it to connect to the Internet.

5454.11 Restrict access to network printers, because they often store document images on their hard drives. There have been cases where intruders have stolen the hard drives in those printers, thereby gaining access to sensitive information.

5454.12 Install fire and smoke detectors and use fire extinguishers that do not damage computer equipment.

5455 Logical Access Controls

5455.01 People can damage information systems without having physical access to the system. They only need to be able to reach the systems electronically. Several levels of logical access are needed:

    a. Authentication, which ensures that unauthorized users and devices are not allowed to access any part of the system.

    b. Authorization, which makes sure the system can recognize authorized users, but restrict their access to:

        (1) data they are not allowed to use and

        (2) those functions (reading, copying, updating, adding, deleting, modifying, downloading, printing) they are authorized to perform.

5455.02 Inadequate logical access controls leave a company vulnerable to the unauthorized access and use of systems software, application programs, data files, and other system resources.

5455.03 The following controls are used to restrict logical access: user identification numbers and passwords, physical possession identification, and biometric identification.

5455.04 **User identification numbers and passwords**. This is also known as knowledge identification.

Identification numbers and passwords are used to access a system:

    a. Users enter a unique user ID, such as an employee number, and a password (letters and numbers known only to the user and the system).

    b. The user ID and password are compared to user ID numbers and passwords stored in the system to see if they are valid.

    c. If they are valid, the system assumes an authorized user.

    d. The disadvantage of passwords is they can be guessed, lost, or given away, allowing an unauthorized person to access the system.

5455.05 To minimize risks associated with passwords:

    a. Assign passwords randomly to users, as user-selected passwords are easy to guess. The passwords should not be related to the employee's personal interests or hobbies.

    b. Change passwords frequently, as often as every 90 days.

    c. Passwords should be at least 8 characters long and use a mixture of upper- and lower-case alphabetic, numeric, and special characters so they cannot be easily guessed or cracked using special software. They should not be words found in dictionaries or words with either a preceding or following numeric character. Longer passwords such as "LongpasswordsRharder2crack&easier2remember" are harder to crack and easier to remember. In fact, passwords this long that follow the other guidelines can be virtually impossible to guess.

    d. Users should be held accountable for keeping their user IDs and passwords confidential and for the actions of anyone using them.

    e. Program the system to not display ID numbers or passwords as they are entered.

    f. Automatically log users off the system after 15 minutes of inactivity.

g. Do not leave computers unattended if they have accessed confidential corporate databases.

h. Assign electronic ID numbers to each authorized system device.

i. Only allow authorized devices to communicate with the system.

j. Only allow authorized devices to access the data they are authorized to use.

k. Restrict user and terminal interaction to business hours, or some other appropriate time frame.

l. Terminate system access requests if a valid ID number and password is not entered within three attempts to prevent an unauthorized user from trying many combinations of user IDs and passwords.

m. Investigate devices that repeatedly attempt to use invalid ID numbers or passwords to access the system.

n. Immediately cancel a terminated employee's user ID and password.

o. Reassess a transferred employee's rights to access data.

p. Use smart cards that continuously generate new and unique passwords.

5455.06 **Physical possession identification.** Employees are often identified by something they possess, such as an ID badge or a smart card.

a. Computers and security devices (door locks, etc.) read the ID cards.

b. Security is strengthened if an ID card and a password are both required to access a system.

c. Their disadvantage: They can be lost, stolen, or given away.

5455.07 **Biometric identification.** Unique physical characteristics (fingerprints, voice patterns, retina prints, facial patterns and features, body odor, signature dynamics, and keyboarding patterns) can all be used to identify people. A device reads a user's biometrics and compares it against those stored in the computer.

a. Biometric devices should be able to adapt to slight personal changes, such as bloodshot eyes.

b. Remote users must posses a biometric identification device to use the system.

c. Their disadvantage: they are expensive, can be hard to use, and are not 100% accurate.

    (1) They may reject legitimate users (voice recognition systems may not recognize an employee who has a cold).

    (2) They may allow access to unauthorized people.

    (3) Some, such as fingerprints, have negative connotations that hinder their acceptance.

    (4) The biometric templates (the digital representation of an individual's fingerprints or voice) must be stored. Any compromise of those templates would cause serious problems for people.

5455.08 Since no single authentication method is foolproof, multi-factor authentication, such as requiring a smart card and a password, provides much stronger authentication than either method alone.

5455.09 Authorization controls are implemented using compatibility tests and access control matrices.

a. Compatibility tests. Companies should classify data based on how its loss or unauthorized use would impact it and determine the data and program access privileges of employees and outsiders. When users request access to data or programs or try to operate the system, a compatibility test can determine if the user is authorized to perform the desired action. This prevents unintentional errors and deliberate attempts to manipulate the system. Several confidentiality levels are defined and used:

      (1) Some data does not need to be restricted and is put on a website.

      (2) Some data is restricted to employees.

      (3) Confidential data is restricted to owners and appropriate top management and employees. Confidential data is restricted to owners and appropriate top management and employees.

      (4) No one should be able to read, add, delete, and change data without someone reviewing their activities.

  b. Access control matrix. Compatibility tests use an access control matrix, which is:

      (1) a list of authorized user ID numbers and passwords and

      (2) a list of all files, data, and programs and the access each user has to them.

5455.10 Authentication and authorization controls are also used for computing devices.

  a. Each device (PC, workstation, printer, etc.) requires a network interface card (NIC) to connect to a company's internal network.

  b. Each NIC has a unique identifier, called a media access control (MAC) address.

  c. Access should be restricted to devices with a recognized MAC addresses. The MAC addresses can also be used for authorization. For example, only devices in the payroll department and belonging to appropriate top management should have access to payroll data.

5456 Personal Computers and Client/Server Network Protection

5456.01 Companies that do not adequately protect their personal computers and client/server networks are vulnerable to the following threats and risks:

  a. Unauthorized access to confidential data

  b. Damage to computer files and equipment

  c. Theft of information assets

5456.02 Personal computers (PCs) and networks are more vulnerable than mainframes because:

  a. Physical access is more difficult to control:

      (1) PCs are everywhere, and many people are familiar with their use and operation.

      (2) Networks have many PCs connected to them that must be controlled, and this increases the risk that a network can be attacked.

  b. PC users are usually not as security and control conscious as mainframe users.

  c. It is difficult to segregate duties in a PC and network environment, and one person may be responsible for both developing and operating a PC system.

  d. End user computing (EUC) allows user to develop their own information systems. These systems are often difficult to integrate with the organizational information system.

  e. Networks can be remotely accessed from almost anywhere using modems and phone lines, the Internet, and EDI.

  f. PCs and laptops are portable and subject to theft.

5456.03 Many mainframe control policies and procedures apply to PCs and networks. Other important controls include:

    a. Train PC users:

        (1) in control concepts and their importance.

        (2) to test and document the application programs they develop themselves.

        (3) to protect their computers from viruses.

    b. Install locks on PCs to protect against theft and unauthorized access.

    c. Label PCs with nonremovable tags.

    d. Establish and enforce policies and procedures to:

        (1) restrict the data that is stored on or downloaded to PCs. Store sensitive data in a secure environment (on a server or mainframe) rather than on a PC, or on a diskette or disk drives that are removed and stored in a locked safe.

        (2) minimize the theft of PCs and laptops. For example, do not leave or store laptops in cars, and carry laptops onto airplanes rather than checking them.

        (3) prohibit putting personal software on company PCs, copying company software for personal use, and using the system in unauthorized ways.

    e. Back up hard drives and other storage medium regularly.

    f. Password protect or encrypt files so stolen data cannot be used.

    g. Use a utility program to wipe a disk clean when confidential data is deleted.

    Most PCs erase the index to the data, rather than the data itself, and utility programs can retrieve data deleted in this way.

    h. Use several different levels of passwords to restrict access to incompatible data.

    i. Use specialists and security programs to:

        (1) mimic an intruder.

        (2) provide valuable information about network security.

        (3) detect network weaknesses.

        (4) determine where the system can be improved.

    j. Log and audit user access and actions so it is easier to trace and correct security breaches.

    k. When PCs are part of a local or wide area network many of these control procedures can be enforced and monitored at the network level.

5456.04 All host devices (PCs and servers where programs reside) and applications (software on those hosts) should be hardened.

    a. The default configurations of host devices and operating systems often turn on many optional settings or special purpose services that are never used or are not essential. This maximizes the likelihood of successful installation without the need for customer support but creates security weaknesses because they have flaws, called vulnerabilities, which can be exploited to either crash the system or take control of it.

    b. Hardening is the process of modifying the configuration of hosts and application software and deleting, or turning off, unused and unnecessary programs that represent potential security threats.

Every host should have regularly updated anti-virus software and a software-based firewall program. Security software can be used to control access to information system resources such as data files, software, and program libraries.

5457 Internet and Telecommunication Controls

5457.01   Companies need to exercise caution when conducting business on the Internet because:

    a. many websites have serious security flaws.

    b. hackers are attracted to the Internet and frequently try and break into company systems linked to the Internet.

    c. many websites are run by fraudsters that lure people into divulging confidential information which they use or sell to others. Others offer to sell people goods, take their money, and never deliver the goods.

    d. before it arrives at its destination, an Internet message can easily pass through 6 to 10 computers that can read or electronically copy the message. Even messages sent on a company's secure intranet can be read.

5457.02   The following controls can improve Internet and telecommunications security:

5457.03   Encryption is transforming data, called plaintext, into unreadable gibberish, called ciphertext. Decryption reverses this process, transforming ciphertext back into plaintext.

    a. Both a key and an algorithm are used to encrypt plaintext into ciphertext and to decrypt the ciphertext back into plaintext.

        (1) The key is a fixed length string of binary digits (a 128-bit key has 128 0s and 1s). The longer the key, the less likely it is that someone can break the encryption code.

        (2) The algorithm is a formula that combines the key and the text. A strong algorithm that has been rigorously tested is difficult, if not impossible, to break by using brute-force guessing techniques.

    b. To encrypt a document:

        (1) the data to be encrypted is divided into blocks the same length as the key.

        (2) the formula is applied to each block of data, producing a ciphertext version of the data that is the same size as the original.

    c. To decrypt a document, the computer divides the ciphertext into 128-bit blocks and then applies the decryption key to each block.

    d. Data is encrypted using one of the following encryption systems:

        (1) A symmetric, or single key system, uses the same key to encrypt and decrypt a message.

        (2) An asymmetric, or public key infrastructure (PKI), system uses two keys. The public key, as the name implies, is publicly available. The private key is kept secret, and only the owner of that pair of keys knows what it is. Either key can be used to encode a message, but only the other key can be used to decode it.

    e. A symmetric key is simple, fast, and efficient but has the following disadvantages.

        (1) Since the sender provides the recipient with the secret key, the two parties need to have some method for securely exchanging the key. System effectiveness depends on controlling who knows the secret key.

        (2) It requires a secret key for each different party with whom the company communicates.

        (3) Since both parties have the same secret key, there is no way to prove who created a specific document and therefore no way to create legally binding agreements.

    f.   The PKI approach has the following advantages over single key systems:

        (1) It eliminates problems with exchanging keys, and companies only need one key.

        (2) It is more secure, because two different keys are used to encode and decode a message.

        (3) Anyone can use the organization's public key to encrypt a message, but only the organization can use its private key to decode the message.

        (4) Data can be encrypted with the private key and decrypted with the public key. Since this makes it possible to prove who created a document, legally binding electronic agreements can be created.

        (5) The main drawback to asymmetric encryption systems is that it is much slower than single key systems - too slow to be used to exchange large amounts of data over the Internet.

5457.04   Hashing is taking plaintext of any length and transforming it into a short code called a hash. Hashing differs from encryption in two important aspects.

    a.   Encryption always produces ciphertext similar in length to the original plaintext, but hashing always produces a hash that is of a fixed short length, regardless of the length of the original plaintext.

    b.   Encryption is reversible, but hashing is not. Given the decryption key and the algorithm, ciphertext can be decrypted back into the original plaintext. In contrast, it is not possible to transform a hash back into the original plaintext, because hashing throws away information.

5457.05   A digital signature uniquely identifies the sender of an electronic message, similar to how a handwritten signature identifies the signer of a paper document.

    a.   In a PKI system, a digital signature is created when the sender's private key encrypts the sender's message. The message can only be decoded using the corresponding public key.

    b.   A valid digital signature does not verify the identity of the private key's owner. It only proves that the message was sent by the owner of the private key that corresponds to the public key used to decode the message.

5457.06   A digital summary, called a digest, creates a digital signature.

    a.   A common utility program creates the digest by calculating the digital values of every character in the document.

    b.   If a character in the original document changes, the digest value changes. This helps detect whether business document contents are altered or garbled during transmission.

5457.07   A digital certificate is an electronic document.

    a.   It is created and digitally signed by a trusted third party, which certifies the identity of the owner of a particular public key.

    b.   It contains that party's public key and can be stored on websites.

        (1) Browsers are designed to automatically obtain a copy of that digital certificate and use the public key contained therein to communicate with the website.

        (2) Thus, digital certificates provide an automated method for obtaining an organization's or individual's public key.

    c.   It functions like a driver's license or passport. It is used to identify:

        (1) The owner of a private key and its corresponding public key.

        (2) The amount of time the certificate is valid.

5457.08   A certificate authority issues public and private keys, records the public key in a digital certificate, and otherwise manages digital certificates.

    a.   The certificate authority's digital signature is included in the digital certificate so a certificate's validity can be verified.

    b.   This functions like a hologram, watermark, or other device that verifies the validity of a driver's license or passport.

5457.09   Routers control the flow of information sent over the Internet or an internal local area network.

    a.   Data to be sent is divided into packets and transmitted, and the device receiving the packets reassembles the packets to recreate the original message or data.

    b.   Two important protocols, referred to as TCP/IP, govern the process for transmitting information over the Internet.

        (1)   The Transmission Control Protocol (TCP) specifies the procedures for dividing data into packets and reassembling them.

        (2)   The Internet Protocol (IP) specifies the structure of the packets and how to route them to the proper destination.

    c.   Every IP packet consists of two parts: a header and a body.

       The header contains the packet's origin and destination addresses, as well as information about the type of data contained in the body of the packet.

    d.   A router reads the destination address field in an IP packet header to determine where it is to be sent.

       Rules, referred to as an access control list (ACL), determine which packets are allowed into a system.

    e.   A border router connects an organization's information system to the Internet.

        (1)   It checks the contents of the destination address field of every packet it receives. If the address is not that of the organization, the packet is forwarded on to another router on the Internet.

        (2)   If the destination address matches that of the organization, the source and destination fields in the IP packet header undergo a number of tests before being allowed in.

        (3)   Packets that fail a test are not allowed into the system. Those that do not fail the tests are passed on to the firewall, where they will be subjected to more detailed testing before being allowed to enter the organization's internal network.

5457.10   A firewall prevents outsiders and employees from gaining unauthorized access to a system.

    a.   It consists of hardware and software that control communications between:

        (1)   an external, or untrusted network, such as the Internet or a value-added network, and

        (2)   an internal network, often called the trusted network. The firewall prevents unwanted information from flowing into and out of the trusted network.

    b.   Firewalls also separate internal networks to protect sensitive data from unauthorized internal use.

    c.   A firewall must be able to protect itself from attack, hostile traffic, and unauthorized modification.

    d.   Firewalls often use redundant hardware, software, and other information technology to reduce outages and failures.

    e.   Like the border router, firewalls use ACLs (access control lists) to determine what to do with each packet that arrives.

Firewalls act as filters and only permit packets that meet specific conditions to pass. Packets not allowed to enter by a firewall rule are dropped.

    f. Firewalls can be penetrated or bypassed, so:

        (1) all communication network links should be continuously monitored to determine whether a firewall was bypassed by wireless communications links between the IS and outside parties.

        (2) intrusion detection and prevention systems should be used to detect any penetrations.

    g. Internal firewalls are often used to segment different departments within an organization. This increases security and strengthens internal control, as there is a way to enforce segregation of duties.

5457.11 An intrusion prevention system (IPS) identifies and drops packets that are part of an attack.

    a. An IPS examines the data in the body of an IP packet and therefore is more effective than routers and firewalls that merely look at data in an IP header. There are several ways to check the packet contents:

        (1) Checking packet contents against a database of patterns (signatures) of known attack methods

        (2) Developing a profile of normal traffic and using statistical analysis to identify packets that do not fit that profile

        (3) Using rule bases that specify acceptable standards for specific types of traffic and drop all packets that do not conform to those standards

    b. The disadvantages of an ISP are that it is:

        (1) slow, as it takes more time to examine the body of an IP packet than an IP packet header and

        (2) prone to false alarms, which results in rejecting legitimate traffic.

5457.12 The border router, firewall, and intrusion prevention system are complementary tools to control which information is allowed to enter and leave the organization's information system. Multiple filtering devices are more efficient than any one device.

    a. Border routers quickly filter out obviously bad packets.

    b. Firewalls only allow packets to enter that appear to contain specific types of data for specific types of programs.

    c. The IPS verifies that packet contents actually conform to the organization's security policies.

5457.13 Tunneling can be used to create a virtual private network without the cost of leased private lines. Tunneling is also used to safeguard internal networks in organizations. In tunneling:

    a. networks are connected—firewall to firewall—via the Internet.

    b. data are split into small Internet Protocol (IP) packets.

    c. the packets are encrypted, mixed with millions of other IP packets, and sent over the Internet.

    d. at their destinations, packets are decrypted and the original message is reassembled.

5457.14 Control dial-in access using modems.

    a. Modems create a huge hole in systems security as they often by-pass organization firewalls, and users seldom use good authentication controls.

      This creates a "back door" attackers can use to compromise system security.

    b. This can be controlled in two ways:

      (1) After users connect to their company's remote access server, their login data is sent to a Remote Authentication Dial-In User Service (RADIUS) server, where user identity is authenticated.

      (2) Computer security or internal audit periodically checks for rogue modems and sanctions employees responsible for installing them.

5457.15 Control the risks associated with wireless access.

    a. Authenticate all devices attempting to establish wireless access by routing them through a RADIUS server or other authentication device.

    b. Treat all wireless access as if it was coming from the Internet and force all wireless traffic to go through the main firewall and the intrusion prevention system.

    c. Turn on the security features in wireless equipment when it is installed. Normally this equipment comes with the security features disabled.

    d. Configure all authorized wireless NICs such that they can only connect to wireless access points. If wireless NICs can connect with other devices that have a wireless NIC, a peer-to-peer network is created that has little or no authentication controls.

    e. Make unauthorized connections and eavesdropping more difficult by:

      (1) reducing the broadcast strength of wireless access points so it does not bleed out of the building.

      (2) placing wireless access points in the interior of the building and use directional antennas.

      (3) configuring wireless access points to only accept connections to authorized MAC addresses.

      (4) not automatically broadcasting the access point's address, called a service set identifier (SSID). This forces users to manually enter the SSID.

      (5) having computer security or internal audit periodically find and disable rogue access points and discipline the employees who installed them.

5457.16 Electronic envelopes are used to protect e-mail messages. The envelope is created using private or public key encryption technique and sent over the Internet.

    a. The envelope containing the e-mail is opened using the keys and the message is decrypted.

    b. Encrypted e-mail message authenticity and integrity is guaranteed if the secrecy of the keys is maintained.

5457.17 Restrict access to the Internet.

    a. To avoid hackers, viruses, and other Internet problems, some companies do not allow employees to access the Internet or use outside e-mail.

    b. Others have a one-way, outgoing Internet connection so employees can access the Internet to do research, but outsiders cannot access their system.

    c. Some companies use Internet servers with no connection to other company systems. Data the company wants Internet users to have is stored on the server. If hackers damage the system, the company merely reloads the data and restarts the system.

5458 Maintainability

5458.01   Two categories of controls are used to make sure a system can be adequately maintained:

1. Project development and acquisition controls

2. Change management controls

5458.02   **Project Development and Acquisition Controls**

   a.   When project development and acquisition controls are not used, the results are:

     (1)   poorly managed development or acquisition projects and

     (2)   large sums of money wasted.

   b.   The following project development and acquisition controls can help minimize failures:

     (1)   Use a proven methodology for developing, acquiring, implementing, and maintaining information systems and related technologies.

     (2)   Develop and use a strategic master plan.

     (3)   Develop and use project development plans that:

       (a)   detail how projects are to be completed, including the modules or tasks to be performed.

       (b)   list project milestones (significant points when progress is reviewed).

       (c)   show who will perform each task.

       (d)   list project completion dates.

       (e)   itemize the cost of each project and its component parts.

     (4)   Assign each project to a manager and team and hold them responsible for the project's success or failure.

     (5)   Prepare a data processing schedule so scarce computer resources can be maximized.

     (6)   Develop system performance measurements so the system can be properly evaluated. Common measurements include:

       (a)   throughput (output per unit of time).

       (b)   utilization (percentage of time the system is being productively used).

       (c)   response time (how long it takes the system to respond).

     (7)   Conduct a post-implementation review to:

       (a)   determine if the project's anticipated benefits were achieved.

       (b)   encourage accurate and objective initial cost and benefit estimates.

5458.03   **Change Management Controls**

   The following change management control policies and procedures can help control information system changes:

   a.   Look for needed changes by periodically reviewing all systems.

   b.   Require all information system change requests to be submitted using a standardized format. Log and review all change requests.

   c.   Require IT management to review, monitor, and approve all change requests.

   d.   Assess what impact each change will have on system availability, security, maintainability, and integrity.

e. Use the strategic master plan to prioritize all change requests.

f. Assign specific responsibilities to the people making the change and monitor their work. Make sure that the assignments do not violate segregation of duties requirements.

g. Prevent unauthorized systems and data access by controlling system access rights.

h. Develop a plan to back out of any unsuccessful mission-critical system change.

i. Create a quality assurance function to:

    (1) make sure all standards and procedures are followed.

    (2) make sure changes do not skip any appropriate system development steps (development, testing, and implementation).

    (3) test all hardware, infrastructure, and software changes extensively in a separate, nonproduction environment before the change is put into live production mode.

    (4) determine if changes achieved their stated objectives.

    (5) keep management and those who requested the change informed of all changes.

    (6) update all documentation and procedures after a change is implemented.

j. Log all emergency changes that do not follow standard procedures.

    (1) Have management review and approve them as soon as possible after they are made.

    (2) Make sure there is an audit trail for all urgent matters.

k. After a new system has been placed in operation, all subsequent program changes should be approved before implementation to determine whether they have been authorized, tested, and documented.

    (1) The operations group may request changes to improve operational efficiency, but the group should not have final authority to approve changes.

    (2) Operations personnel should have sole authority to place changed programs into production status.

    (3) Temporary changes (patch programs) to a program to permit completion of a production run should be forbidden, unless specific authorization of EDP management is obtained.

    (4) All program changes should be thoroughly tested before implementation.

5459 Integrity

5459.01 General controls make sure an organization's overall control environment is secure and well managed.

5459.02 Application controls:

a. are designed to prevent, detect, and correct transaction errors;

b. ensure the integrity of a specific application's inputs, stored data, programs, data transmissions, and outputs; and

c. are much more effective when there are good general controls.

When application controls are weak, the information system is more likely to produce information that contains errors and leads to poor management decisions. This can negatively affect relationships with customers, suppliers, and other external parties.

The following six categories of controls can improve system integrity:

1. Source data controls

2. Input validation routines

3. On-line data entry controls

4. Data processing and storage controls

5. Output controls

6. Data transmission controls.

5459.03 **Source Data Controls**

The following controls make sure source documents and other input data are authorized, accurate, complete, accounted for properly, entered into the system, and sent to their intended destination in a timely manner. They should also make sure the data has not been suppressed, duplicated, or otherwise improperly changed.

a. Design source documents such that they minimize errors and omissions.

b. Prenumber all documents and have the system identify and report any missing or duplicate numbers.

c. Restrict source document preparation to authorized personnel.

d. Require all source documents, where required, to be properly authorized before processing them.

e. Use machine-readable turnaround documents (company data sent to an external party and returned to the system as input) to reduce data input time, effort, expense, and errors.

f. Cancel documents that have been entered into the system so they cannot be reused.

    (1) Deface paper documents by marking them paid or perforating them.

    (2) Flag electronic documents to show they have been canceled.

g. Retain original source documents long enough to satisfy legal requirements.

h. Use check digit verification.

    (1) ID numbers can have a check digit computed from the other digits. For example, a six-digit account number can have a seventh digit, which is the check digit.

    (2) Data entry devices verify the check digit each time the ID number is entered by using the six digits to recalculate the seventh check digit.

    (3) The verification calculation will not match the check digit if an error is made in entering the six digits or the check digit.

i. Use key verification.

    (1) An employee rekeys data entered through a keyboard.

    (2) The system compares the two sets of keystrokes.

    (3) Discrepancies are highlighted for correction.

    (4) Key verification is used for crucial input such as customer numbers and amounts.

5459.04   **Input Validation Routines**

Input validation routines, called edit programs, test input data as it is entered into a system to make sure it is accurate and valid. These tests are called edit checks. In on-line processing, edit checks are performed during the source data entry process, and incorrect data is not accepted until corrected. In batch processing, a separate program performs the edit checks on the input data before it is processed.

a. The following edit checks are used in input validation routines.

    (1) Capacity checks, to test whether data will fit into a field.

    (2) Field checks, to test whether characters are the proper type. A field check on a numerical field would indicate an error if it contains blanks or alphabetic characters.

    (3) Limit checks, to make sure a numerical amount does not exceed an upper or lower limit.

    (4) Range checks, to test for both an upper and a lower limit.

    (5) Reasonableness test, to make sure data makes sense when compared to other data.

    (6) Redundant data checks, to determine whether two identifiers in a transaction record match.

    (7) Sequence checks, to test whether input data is in the proper numerical or alphabetical sequence.

    (8) Sign checks, to test data for the appropriate arithmetic sign. (An inventory balance should never possess a negative sign.)

    (9) Validity checks, or existence checks, to compare ID numbers or transaction codes to those stored in the system. When vendor 12612 is entered, the computer locates that vendor in its database to confirm that vendor is valid.

    (10) Hash total: a set of nonfinancial numbers not normally totaled (e.g., invoice numbers) are totaled by the system after input and are compared to the total generated by the documents themselves.

b. Companies also need to establish procedures to record, correct, and report all input validation errors.

    (1) Enter all error data (date occurred, cause, date corrected, date resubmitted) in an error log.

    (2) Investigate, correct, and resubmit errors on a timely basis.

    (3) Use the normal input validation routine to reedit the corrected transactions.

    (4) Review the log periodically to make sure all errors were corrected.

    (5) Summarize errors by record type, error type, cause, date, and disposition in an error report sent to management.

5459.05   **On-Line Data Entry Controls**

The following on-line data entry controls help ensure the integrity, accuracy, and completeness of transaction data entered from on-line devices:

a. Field, limit, range, reasonableness, redundant data, sign, and validity checks as previously described

b. User ID numbers, passwords, and compatibility tests to make sure employees are authorized to enter, access, or view data

c. Automatic entry of transaction data, where possible, to reduce keying time and errors

d. Prompt feature, to request input data (the system waits for an acceptable response)

e. Preformatting, to display highlighted blank spaces in a document (the system waits for data to be entered)

f. Completeness checks, to make sure all required input is entered

g. Closed-loop verification, to test input data accuracy

    (1) When an account number is entered, the system displays the corresponding account name so users can make sure the account number is correct.

    (2) It can be used in place of redundant data checks to make sure a valid, but incorrect, identification number is not entered.

h. Transaction logs, to reconstruct on-line files when they are damaged. The log, which can help make sure transactions are not lost or entered twice, should include:

    (1) a unique transaction identifier,

    (2) date and time the transaction occurred,

    (3) the terminal, transmission line, and operator associated with the transaction, and

    (4) the sequence the transactions were entered.

i. Clear error messages that indicate:

    (1) when an error has occurred.

    (2) which item is in error.

    (3) what the operator should do to correct it.

j. Retain data needed to reproduce on-line data entry documents as long as needed to satisfy legal requirements.

5459.06   **Data Processing and Storage Controls**

The following controls are used to help ensure data processing integrity (all transactions are processed as authorized, no authorized transactions were omitted, and no unauthorized transactions were added) and to safeguard stored data.

a. Develop policies and procedures for:

    (1) computer operators, data libraries, and data control personnel,

    (2) scheduling data processing tasks, so data is not processed without authorization, and

    (3) maintaining an audit trail, so the system can track people who have access to confidential data.

b. Require employees to sign confidentiality agreements.

c. Create a data control function that:

    (1) logs input data as it is received, entered into the system, processed, and dispersed as output,

    (2) checks to make sure all transactions are authorized,

    (3) monitors data processing activities for errors and problems,

    (4) develops control totals over input and reconciles them to the totals from each subsequent processing activity,

    (5) notifies users of input errors and problems, and

    (6) reenters all errors that have been corrected.

    d. Perform the following reconciliation procedures on a periodic and regular basis:

        (1) Reconcile all system updates to control reports, file status/update reports, or other control reports.

        (2) Reconcile general ledger accounts to subsidiary account totals.

        (3) Reconcile database totals with data maintained outside the system.

    e. Test stored data to determine whether it is out of date (employees retire or quit; suppliers and customers move or fail). Unneeded data should be purged.

    f. Use the following file labels to protect data files from inadvertent misuse:

        (1) External labels that contain the file name, contents, and date processed

        (2) Internal labels, such as (1) volume labels that identify the data recording medium (hard disks, diskettes, and tapes), (2) header labels that contain the file name, expiration date, and other identification data, and (3) trailer labels that contain file control totals. These totals are compared to those calculated during data processing.

    g. Use write protection mechanisms that protect files from being accidentally destroyed or erased.

        (1) A tape file protection ring prevents a tape file from being written upon.

        (2) Diskettes have on/off switches that accomplish the same thing.

    h. Implement the following database protection mechanisms.

        (1) Procedures for accessing and updating the database

        (2) A data dictionary to make sure data is defined and used consistently

        (3) Concurrent update controls to prevent problems when multiple users simultaneously update a record (Lock other users out of the system until one has finished updating the file.)

    i. Use data conversion controls to make sure new files and databases are free from errors when data from old files and databases are converted to the new format.

        (1) Process data using both the old and new system at least once.

        (2) Compare the results to identify differences and problems.

        (3) Have internal auditors carefully supervise and review data conversion activities.

    j. Protect stored data.

        (1) Use a data library, where data files are logged in and out by a librarian.

        (2) Back up data files and store a copy at a secure off-site location.

        (3) Protect the data library from conditions that harm stored data such as fire, dust, and excess heat or humidity.

5459.07 **Output Controls**

The following controls help make sure data output is accurate and is only made available to authorized output users.

    a. Review and reconcile data.

        (1) Have data control compare output control totals to input and processing control totals and investigate any differences.

        (2) Have data control review all output to make sure it is reasonable and in the proper format.

        (3) Require users to carefully review computer output to make sure it is complete and accurate.

b. Establish procedures to make sure output is:

(1) distributed to an authorized individual in the appropriate user department.

(2) protected from unauthorized access, modification, and misrouting.

(3) stored in a safe and secure area.

(4) corrected when errors are discovered.

(5) properly disposed of after it is no longer needed.

5459.08 Data Transmission Controls

The following controls reduce the risk of data transmission errors and failures:

a. Monitor the data communicator network, looking for weak points that need to be improved.

b. Make sure networks have enough capacity to handle peak processing demands.

c. Create more than one communication path between important network components so the system can continue to function if a path fails.

d. Use faster, more efficient, and higher-grade telecommunications lines that are less likely to fail and have fewer static problems.

e. Use encryption to:

(1) make sure data transmissions and transactions are limited to authorized users.

(2) protect data from electronic eavesdropping.

(3) prevent unauthorized tampering.

(4) determine, with a high level of certainty, who sent a message.

f. Use routing verification procedures to make sure messages are sent to the right place:

(1) Use a header label to identify transmitted data and its destination.

(2) Use mutual authentication schemes that require both sending and receiving computers to exchange passwords before initiating a data communication.

(3) Use a callback system where (1) a password is entered to identify authorized users, (2) the computer disconnects, and (3) the system calls the user back to verify the user's identity, password, telephone number, and/or location.

g. Use parity checking.

(1) Computers use 8 bits (0s or 1s) to represent a single character.

(2) Transmitted bits may be lost or received incorrectly.

(3) To detect these errors, a parity bit (a ninth bit) is added to every character.

(4) In even parity, each bit has an even number of ones; in odd parity, there are an odd number of ones.

(5) To check parity, devices that receive data verify that there are an even (or odd) number of ones.

(6) Two-dimensional parity checking tests parity both vertically and horizontally. Dual checking is important in telecommunications, because noise bursts frequently cause two or more adjacent bits to be lost.

h. Use message acknowledgment techniques so the device that sends an electronic message knows that it was received.

(1) Use an echo check that calculates a summary statistic, such as the number of bits in the message, before sending data. The receiving unit calculates the same summary statistic and sends it to the sending device (hence the name "echo check"). If the counts do not agree, an error has occurred.

(2) Have the receiving unit make sure the entire message was received by checking for a trailer label. The receiving unit signals the sending unit when a data transmission error occurs, and the data is resent. If the system cannot automatically resend the data, it will ask the sending device to retransmit the data.

5460 Basic Business Processes

5460.01 Many business activities are repetitive and engaged in frequently. For example, a retail company sells merchandise to customers in exchange for cash on a daily basis. It frequently buys inventory from suppliers to replenish the merchandise that is sold.

5460.02 These basic exchanges can be grouped into several transaction cycles or business processes. The most common are:

    a. The revenue cycle, where goods or services are sold in exchange for cash or a promise to pay cash.

    b. The expenditure cycle, where goods or services are purchased in exchange for cash or a promise to pay cash.

    c. The production cycle, where raw materials are turned into products that can be sold.

    d. The human resources (payroll) cycle, where people are hired, trained, compensated for time and effort they expend, and dismissed.

    e. The financing cycle, where companies obtain funds from investors and creditors and pay dividends and repay borrowings.

5460.03 While the basic cycles do not change, there are differences in cycles among companies. For example:

    a. Some organizations do not use every cycle. For example, retail stores do not have a production cycle.

    b. Some organizations have unique requirements. For example, financial institutions have demand deposit and customer loan cycles.

    c. Transaction cycles differ depending upon the type of organization. For example, the expenditure cycles of a service company (CPA or law firm) do not purchase, receive, or pay for merchandise to resell to customers.

5460.04   The transaction cycles are implemented as separate modules in most accounting software packages.

Figure 8 uses a merchandising company to show how these transaction cycles relate to one another and their relationship with the general ledger and reporting system, which is used to generate information for internal and external parties.

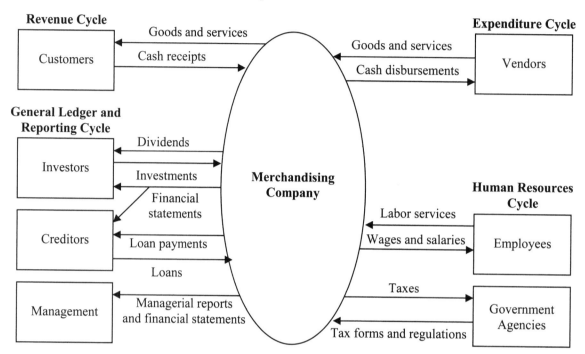

Transaction Cycle	Transactions (Business Activities)
Revenue	Customer orders, sales, shipping/delivery, cash receipts, sales discounts, sales returns and allowances, bad debts.
Expenditure	Purchase requisitions, purchases, receipt of inventory, cash disbursements, purchase returns and allowances, purchase discounts.
Human resources	Hiring, training, promotion, firing, payroll, and taxes.
General ledger and reporting	Nonroutine transactions, adjusting entries, closing entries, managerial reports and financial statements.

5460.05   Objectives

a.   Each cycle has specific objectives that it needs to accomplish. Each cycle also faces a number of threats that put company assets at risk. Controls are put in place to eliminate or minimize these risks. There are several objectives, threats, and controls that apply to all the cycles.

All cycles have the following objectives:

(1)   Data must be available when it is needed.

(2)   All activities must be performed efficiently and effectively.

5460.06   Threat

Multi-Cycle Threat: Loss or unauthorized disclosure of data. Data can be lost, resulting in:

a.   inaccurate external and internal reporting,

b.   inaccurate responses to customer and vendor inquiries,

    c.   customer or vendor information leaked to competitors,

    d.   inventory and fixed assets not being monitored effectively,

    e.   manufacturing activities not being performed efficiently and effectively,

    f.   morale problems,

    g.   lawsuits, or

    h.   the potential demise of the entire organization.

5460.07   **Controls**

    a.   Back up all master and transaction files regularly, including the general and subsidiary ledgers.

        (1) Keep one back-up copy on-site so it can be immediately accessed if the original is damaged or destroyed.

        (2) Store another back-up copy off-site as insurance against a major disaster such as a fire or earthquake.

    b.   Develop, implement, and periodically test a disaster recovery plan to handle major disasters that can destroy a computer system.

    c.   Use external and internal file labels on all disks, tapes, and other storage media:

        (1) to reduce the possibility of accidentally erasing important files and

        (2) to make sure the correct version of the master file is updated.

    d.   Use physical security controls to restrict physical access to data and computer equipment.

    e.   Use passwords, user IDs, and an access control matrix to limit logical access to sensitive files, data items, and terminals to authorized employees. For example:

        (1) Only sales staff should be allowed to create sales orders.

        (2) Only the cashier should be able to indicate that an invoice has been paid.

        (3) Sales staff should have read-only access to customer credit limits and current account balances.

        (4) Access controls should exist for individual terminals so the terminal can only process transactions its department is authorized to perform.

    f.   Encrypt data to make it unintelligible to anyone able to get unauthorized access to files or data.

    g.   Use simple, easy-to-complete documents with clear instructions so transaction data can be recorded accurately and efficiently.

    h.   Record who completed and who reviewed a document as evidence of proper transaction authorization.

    i.   Prenumber documents to make sure all transactions are recorded.

    j.   Restrict access to blank documents and to programs that create documents to reduce the risk of unauthorized transactions.

    k.   Log all activities, especially actions involving managerial approval (e.g., extending credit limits), so they can be reviewed later as part of the audit trail.

5460.08   **Threat**

Multi-Cycle Threat: Poor performance. It is important that all business activities be performed efficiently and effectively.

5460.09   **Controls**

a. Prepare and review performance reports to assess the efficiency and effectiveness of cycle activities and to look for inefficient or ineffective performance. For example:

     (1) Assess sales force effectiveness by breaking sales down by salesperson, region, or product.

     (2) Assess marketing performance by breaking down the marginal profit contribution of each territory, customer, distribution channel, salesperson, or product.

     (3) Evaluate the frequency and size of back orders to determine how well inventory management policies satisfy customer needs.

     (4) Identify slow-moving products to avoid excessive inventory levels.

     (5) Prepare an accounts receivable aging schedule to monitor accounts receivables collections, estimate bad debts, and evaluate credit policies.

     (6) Prepare cash budgets to know when to borrow funds to meet short-term cash shortages and when to invest excess funds.

     (7) Monitor vendor performance using vendor performance reports.

b. Track employee knowledge and skills so they can be shared and used to provide a sustainable competitive advantage.

c. Monitor employees who telecommute to make sure they are:

     (1) working the hours for which they are being paid.

     (2) not using company-provided computing resources inappropriately:

         (a) visiting pornographic websites, sending or forwarding offensive e-mail, or storing and using pirated copies of software.

         (b) operating a personal business on the side, using company-provided assets for personal use.

d. Train employees to maximize the efficiency and effectiveness of business processes and keep abreast of changes in information technology and legal requirements.

Each of the major business cycles is discussed in the following sections.

5461 The Revenue Cycle

5461.01   The revenue cycle is a recurring set of business and data processing activities associated with selling goods and services to customers in exchange for cash.

The revenue cycle produces information that is used by other accounting cycles:

a. Both the expenditure and the production cycles use sales information to purchase or produce additional inventory.

b. The payroll cycle uses sales information to compensate employees (calculate sales commissions and bonuses).

c. The general ledger and reporting function uses revenue cycle information to prepare financial statements and performance reports.

As shown in Figure 9, there are four basic business activities in the revenue cycle. Each of these activities, the threats the activities face, and the controls used to eliminate or minimize these threats are now discussed.

Figure 9

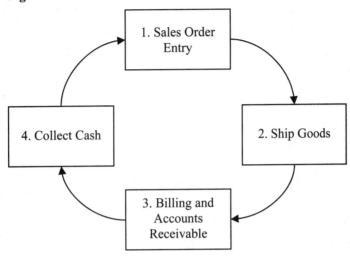

5461.02   Sales Order Entry

The revenue cycle begins when customer orders are received. The primary objectives of the sales order entry process are to:

a.   Accurately and efficiently process customer orders.

b.   Make sure all sales are legitimate.

c.   Make sure the company gets paid for all credit sales.

As shown in Figure 10, the sales order entry process consists of three steps:

Figure 10

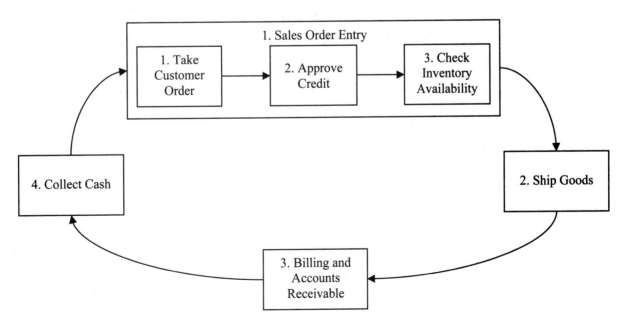

5461.03 The three steps in the sales order entry process are take customer orders, approve credit, and check inventory availability.

5461.04 **Take customer orders.** Customer orders are received in the store, by mail, by phone, or from a salesperson in the field. Companies have used information technology advancements to improve the efficiency and effectiveness of the sales order entry process. For example:

 a. Customers can enter sales order data themselves on a company website.

 b. Customers can use interactive sales order entry websites called choiceboards to design their own products.

  For example, Dell customers can mix and match parts and features to create a computer to meet their needs at an affordable price.

 c. Electronic data interchange (EDI), where suppliers and customers are linked, eliminates the need for data entry and improves the efficiency and effectiveness of the sales order process.

 d. E-mail can be used to communicate price changes, special needs and interests, and sales promotions.

5461.05 **Threats and Controls in Taking Customer Orders**

 1. **Threat:** Incomplete or inaccurate customer orders.

  a. This results in inefficiencies (the customer must be contacted and data re-entered).

  b. This can negatively affect customer perceptions and adversely affect future sales.

 2. **Controls**

  a. Use automatic data lookups to retrieve data already stored in the customer master file, thereby preventing data entry errors.

  b. Perform validity checks of customer account numbers and inventory item numbers (to make sure the numbers entered match information in the customer and inventory master files).

  c. Use reasonableness tests to compare items and quantities ordered with past sales history for these items and customers.

  d. Use completeness tests to make sure all required information is entered.

 3. **Threat:** Orders that are not legitimate.

 4. **Control:**

  a. Require a signed purchase orders from customers.

  b. Require a digital signature and digital certificate for all e-business transactions.

5461.06   **Approve credit.** A credit sale should be approved before goods are released from inventory.

5461.07   **Threat and Controls in Making Credit Sales**

1.   **Threat:** Credit sales that later become uncollectible.

2.   **Controls**

   a. Set credit limits for each customer based on their credit history and ability to pay.

   b. Give sales order personnel general authorization to approve an order if its total plus the customer's existing balance does not exceed the customer's approved credit limit.

   c. Have someone other than the salesperson approve special circumstances (new customer, exceeding credit limits), especially if sales personnel are paid on commission.

   d. Do not allow sales order entry clerks or sales personnel to change a customer's credit limit.

   e. Maintain accurate and current customer account balances and credit limits.

5461.08   **Check inventory availability.** There are several steps to this process:

   a. Have the system find out if there is enough inventory on hand to fill the order. If so:

      (1) notify shipping, inventory control, and billing of the sale,

      (2) create an order and enter it into the system, and

      (3) let the customer know the expected delivery date.

   b. If there is insufficient inventory, back order the item so the production department can produce the requested item or purchasing can order it.

5461.09   **Threat and Controls in Inventory Availability**

1.   **Threat:** Stockouts, carrying costs, and markdowns.

   a. Sales are lost when stockouts occur.

   b. Excess inventory increases carrying costs and may require significant markdowns.

2.   **Controls**

   a. Make periodic physical inventory counts to verify the accuracy of recorded amounts.

   b. Create accurate systems for sales forecasting and inventory control.

      (1) Develop sales forecasts (review them regularly for accuracy and revise them as needed) to predict the demand for goods.

      (2) Develop ordering procedures (reorder points, economic order quantities, etc.) that ensure that sufficient inventory is on hand to meet forecasted needs.

   c. Monitor supplier performance, such as:

      (1) on-time delivery rates.

      (2) defect rates and other quality measures.

5461.10   Ship Goods

The second revenue cycle activity is filling customer orders and shipping merchandise. This process has two steps (as shown in Figure 11):

Figure 11

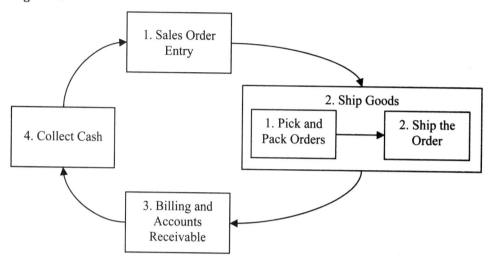

5461.11   Pick and pack orders. After the sales order is entered, a picking ticket that lists the items and quantities to be shipped is printed. Warehouse employees:

a.   use it to identify the items and quantities to remove from inventory,

b.   record quantities picked on the picking ticket (or enter them into the system), and

c.   forward the inventory to shipping.

5461.12   Ship the order.

a.   Shipping:

(1)   counts the inventory to be shipped.

(2)   compares their counts to:

(a)   quantities on the picking ticket and

(b)   quantities on the sales orders copy that was sent to shipping.

(3)   initiates a back order for any missing items.

(4)   enters the correct quantities shipped on the packing slip.

(5)   enters the sales order number, item number(s), and quantities into the system. This:

(a)   updates the quantity-on-hand field in the inventory master file.

(b)   produces a packing slip that lists the quantity and description of each shipment item.

(c)   produces multiple copies of the bill of lading (a legal contract that states who is responsible for goods in transit; specifies the carrier, sources and destination of the shipment, and special shipping instructions; and indicates whether the customer or vendor is to pay the carrier).

5461.13 **Threats and Controls in Shipping Goods**

1. **Threat:** Shipping errors. Shipping incorrect items, incorrect quantities, or sending the shipment to the wrong address can:

   a. negatively impact customer satisfaction and future sales.

   b. result in the loss of assets if the erroneously shipped goods are not paid for.

2. **Controls**

   a. Require shipping personnel to enter quantities to be shipped into the system before the goods are shipped to detect and correct mistakes prior to shipment. Print packing slips and bills of lading after the system has verified shipment accuracy.

   b. Use bar code scanners to record picked and shipped inventory.

   c. Use field checks and completeness tests to ensure data accuracy.

3. **Threat:** Inventory theft. This results in:

   a. reduced profitability.

   b. lost assets.

   c. inaccurate inventory records, which can cause problems with filling customer orders.

4. **Controls**

   a. Keep inventory in a secure location and restrict physical access to that location.

   b. Document all inventory transfers. Require warehouse and shipping employees to sign the document transferring inventory to shipping (or make the appropriate acknowledgment of the transfer on-line).

   c. Release inventory to shipping employees only when there is an approved sales order and a system-generated picking ticket.

   d. Periodically count physical inventory on hand and reconcile it to recorded inventory.

   e. Hold the employees who are responsible for storing inventory accountable for any shortages.

5461.14 **Billing and Accounts Receivable**

   a. The primary objectives of the billing and accounts receivable functions are to ensure that:

   (1) customers are billed for all sales,

   (2) invoices are accurate, and

   (3) customer accounts are accurately maintained.

b. There are two steps in the Billing and Accounts Receivable Activity (as shown in Figure 12).

Figure 12

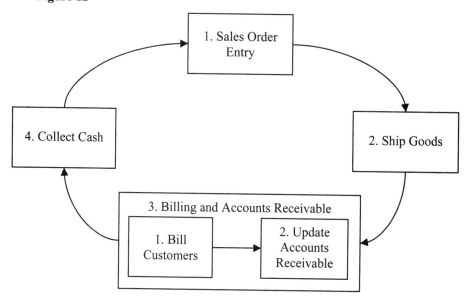

(1) Bill customers. After goods are shipped, a sales invoice is sent to customers to let them know how much they owe and where to send payment. EDI and EFT technology is often used to reduce billing costs and the time required to send invoices and receive payment.

(2) Update accounts receivable. Sales invoice information is used to update customer accounts.

    (a) There are different ways to maintain accounts receivable depending on when customers remit payments, how payments are updated on the accounts receivable master file, and monthly statement format.

        1. With the open-invoice method, customer payments are applied against specific invoices. Two invoice copies are mailed to the customer. One serves as a remittance advice and is returned with the payment.

        2. With the balance-forward method, customers pay the balance shown on a monthly statement that lists all sales and payment transactions that occurred during the past month.

        Cycle billing can be used to spread out billing and cash receipts. Monthly statements are prepared and mailed at different times for subsets of customers. For example, the master file could be divided into four parts, and each week monthly statements sent to one-fourth of the customers.

    (b) As part of the update process, adjustments to customer accounts are sometimes needed due to:

        1. items that are returned.

        2. allowances for damaged goods.

        3. customer's accounts that must be written off.

        In such cases, the credit manager fills out a credit memo. When the credit memo is for damaged or returned goods, the customer is sent a copy.

5461.15 **Threats and Controls in Billing and Accounts Receivable**

1. **Threat:** Failure to bill customers for items shipped. When this occurs:

   a. companies suffer financial loss due to cash not being collected, and

   b. sales, inventory, and accounts receivable data are inaccurate.

2. **Controls**

   a. Segregate shipping and billing to prevent an employee from shipping merchandise and then not billing the customer.

   b. Prenumber all documents sequentially.

   c. Match sales orders and packing slips to sales invoices to make sure shipments have been billed.

   d. Make sure every shipment is recorded in an information system that does not produce invoices.

3. **Threat:** Billing errors. This includes pricing mistakes and billing customers for items not shipped or on back order.

   a. Overbilling can result in customer dissatisfaction.

   b. Underbilling results in the loss of assets and reduced profitability.

4. **Controls**

   a. Have the computer retrieve inventory prices from the inventory master file rather than having employees enter them into the system.

   b. Reconcile packing slip quantities with sales order quantities to avoid shipping mistakes.

   c. Use bar code scanners to minimize data entry errors.

5. **Threat:** Errors in customer accounts. This can:

   a. decrease future sales.

   b. lead to the theft of cash.

6. **Controls**

   a. Use validity checks to make sure all customer numbers and invoice numbers are valid.

   b. Use closed-loop verification tests (enter the customer number and the system retrieves the customer name) to make sure the proper account is being credited.

   c. Use field checks on payment amounts to make sure all values entered are numeric.

   d. Use batch totals when customer payments are processed in batches. Have someone other than the person processing the original transactions reconcile the batch totals.

   e. Compare the accounts receivable subsidiary file balance to the general ledger accounts receivable control account balance after customer payments are processed. If they are not equal, a posting error has occurred and should be corrected.

   f. Compare the number of customer accounts updated with the number of checks received to make sure all remittances were processed.

   g. Mail monthly statements to all customers so they can do an independent review of their accounts (customers will complain if their accounts are incorrect).

5461.16 **Collect Cash**

Companies use a variety of cash receipt processes to collect and identify where cash remittances come from and to determine what account or invoice to credit.

a. Two copies of each invoice can be mailed to customers; one is returned with the payment.

(1) Accounts receivable is sent either the copy returned in the mail or a remittance list that identifies the names and amounts of all customer payments. Customer payments are sent to the cashier.

(2) Companies can use a bank lockbox, which is a postal address that customers use to mail in their payments. The bank:

(a) gets the mail from the post office;

(b) deposits the checks in the company's account; and

(c) sends the remittance advice, an electronic list of all remittances, and photocopies of all checks to the company.

(3) An electronic lockbox has an additional advantage:

The bank electronically sends information about customer account numbers and amounts remitted as soon as checks are received and scanned.

(4) Electronic funds transfer (EFT) is used to electronically send customer payments to their supplier's bank.

(5) EFT with EDI can be integrated (called financial electronic data interchange [FEDI]) to automate the billing and cash collections processes.

5461.17 **Threat and Controls in Collecting Cash**

1. **Threat:** Theft of cash. An employee intent on stealing company assets is most likely to go after cash, as it is the most liquid asset.

2. **Controls**

a. Segregate duties so employees with custody of (physical access to) cash do not record or authorize any cash transactions. It is especially important to segregate the following duties:

(1) Handling cash or checks and posting remittances to customer accounts, as employees could lap customer accounts.

(2) Handling cash or checks and authorizing credit memos, as employees could issue a credit memo to conceal embezzlement.

(3) Issuing credit memos and maintaining customer accounts, as employees could write off amounts owed by friends or customers they collude with.

b. Minimize the amount and extent of money and checks that are handled.

(1) Use a bank lockbox, EFT, or FEDI for customer payments when the benefits of reduced processing costs, lower thefts, and faster access to customer payments outweigh their costs.

c. Promptly document all remittances, as cash is most likely to be lost at the time it is received.

(1) Have two people open all incoming mail to minimize the risk of cash or checks being stolen.

(2) Prepare a list of all checks received as the mail is opened.

(3) Restrictively endorse each check after it is removed from the envelope.

   d. Segregate the recording and custody functions by sending remittance data to accounts receivable and customer payments to the cashier. Use the following control checks:

      (1) Compare accounts receivable credit totals to cash deposited totals.

      (2) Have internal audit compare remittance lists with validated deposit slips and bank statements to make sure all checks and cash were deposited.

   e. Send monthly statements to customers, as they will complain if there are errors.

   f. Use cash registers that record all cash receipts when cash is received directly from customers.

   g. Encourage customers to watch their purchase being rung up and to ask for a receipt by using signs to let them know that:

      (1) their purchase is free if they are not given a receipt, or

      (2) they are entitled to a discount if their receipt has a red star on it.

   h. Deposit all customer receipts daily to:

      (1) reduce the amount of cash and checks that can be stolen.

      (2) make it easier to reconcile bank statements with sales, accounts receivable, and cash collection records.

   i. Make sure the bank statement is reconciled by someone who has no other cash handling and recording duties. This:

      (1) provides an independent check on the cashier, and

      (2) prevents bank statement manipulations that conceal cash embezzlements.

   j. Make sure accounts receivable (a recording function) does not have physical access to cash or checks.

5462 The Expenditure Cycle

5462.01   The expenditure cycle is a recurring set of business and data processing activities associated with purchasing and paying for goods and services. A primary objective of the cycle is to minimize the cost of acquiring and maintaining inventories, supplies, and other needed organizational services.

There are several information flows in the expenditure cycle (as shown in Figure 13):

Figure 13

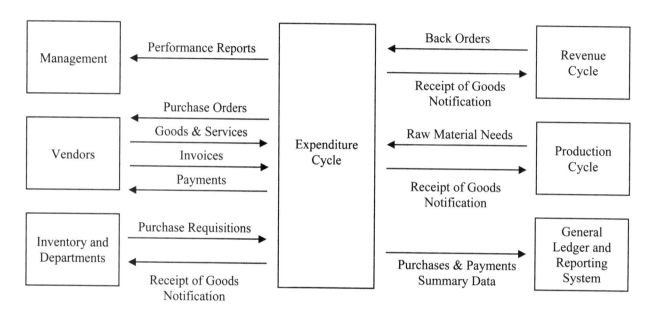

Information technology can be used to improve the efficiency and effectiveness of expenditure cycle activities. A company can also require customers to modify their own expenditure and revenue cycles. In other words, changes in one company's operations may necessitate IS changes in companies they do business with. For example, the major automobile manufacturers may require suppliers to transmit invoices via EDI and receive payments using EFT.

5462.02 Expenditure Cycle Business Activities

There are three expenditure cycle business activities and they interact with the four activities of a vendor's revenue cycle (as shown in Figure 14). We will now discuss the expenditure cycle activities, the threats that these activities face, and the controls used to eliminate or minimize these threats.

Figure 14

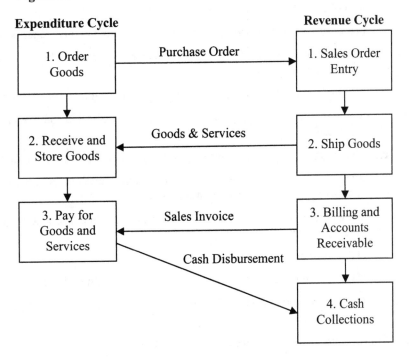

5462.03 Order Goods

The first expenditure cycle activity is ordering raw materials, inventory, or supplies. There are two steps in the order goods activity.

1. **Requisition Goods.** When the inventory control function or company employees notice that goods are needed, they create a purchase requisition (either a document or an electronic form) that identifies:

   a. the person making the request;

   b. delivery location and date;

   c. item numbers, descriptions, quantity, and price of each item requested; and

   d. in some cases, a suggested supplier.

2. **Prepare Purchase Order.** Purchase requisitions are sent to a purchasing agent who purchases the goods.

   The purchasing agent:

   a. selects an approved supplier that sells the desired items.

      (1) Supplier selection depends on factors such as price, quality, and reliability.

      (2) To monitor suppliers, organizations track and periodically evaluate supplier performance.

   b. prepares a purchase order and sends it to the chosen supplier. A purchase order:

      (1) is a formal request to sell and deliver specified products at designated prices.

    (2) is a promise to pay.

    (3) becomes a contract once the supplier accepts it.

    (4) includes supplier and purchasing agent's names, order and delivery dates, delivery location, shipping method, and information about the items ordered.

5462.04 Information technology can be used to improve the purchasing process by:

  a. using EDI or the Internet to communicate electronically.

    (1) Costs can be reduced by eliminating printed and mailed paper documents.

    (2) Stockouts can be minimized or reduced by eliminating the delivery time associated with paper documents.

  b. developing vendor-managed inventory programs to minimize or eliminate stockouts.

    Suppliers access inventory data in company databases and automatically ship inventory when needed.

  c. running reverse auctions where suppliers compete to sell goods at the lowest price.

  d. using trading exchanges (electronic marketplaces) that link buyers and sellers of commodity-type goods that are differentiated by price.

  e. using procurement cards (corporate credit cards) to improve efficiency and reduce purchasing costs.

    (1) Each card has a spending limit.

    (2) All employee purchases are summarized on one monthly bill.

    (3) The purchases from each card can be allocated to appropriate general ledger accounts.

5462.05 **Threats and Controls in Ordering Goods, Part 1**

  1. **Threat:** Stockouts and excess inventory.

    a. Stockouts result in lost sales and customer dissatisfaction.

    b. Excess inventory incurs carrying costs, causes cash flow problems, may result in obsolete inventory, and reduces profitability.

  2. **Controls**

    a. Develop an accurate sales forecast system to know the demand for each product.

    b. Develop an accurate perpetual inventory control system to make sure inventory information is always current. Periodically count inventory and reconcile the counts to the perpetual records.

    c. Select suppliers that meet delivery commitments, monitor supplier performance, and select new suppliers when performance falls below acceptable levels.

    d. Prepare performance reports to highlight deviations in product quality, prices, and delivery commitments. Review them periodically.

    e. Use bar code technology to eliminate human data entry and improve perpetual inventory record accuracy.

3. **Threat:** Purchasing errors. This includes:

    a. buying unnecessary items, and

    b. failure to take advantage of available volume discounts.

4. **Controls**

    a. Develop an accurate perpetual inventory control system to make sure inventory information is always current. Periodically count inventory and reconcile the counts to the perpetual records.

    b. Have department supervisors review and approve all purchase requisitions before they are sent to the purchasing department.

    c. Integrate subunit databases so items do not have different numbers in various databases and make the database available to all who need it.

    d. Prepare reports that link item descriptions to part numbers.

5462.06   Threats and Controls in Ordering Goods, Part 2

1. **Threat:** Purchasing goods at inflated prices.

2. **Controls**

    a. Store the prices of frequently purchased items in the computer and require purchasing agents to consult them when ordering goods.

    b. Require competitive, written bids for high-priced as well as specialized items.

    c. Charge purchases to the budget of the department requesting the goods.

    d. Periodically compare actual costs with budget allowances and investigate any significant deviations.

    e. Review purchase orders to make sure the policies mentioned above are followed.

3. **Threat:** Purchasing goods of inferior quality. Substandard products can result in:

    a. costly production delays, and

    b. high scrap and rework costs.

4. **Controls**

    a. Monitor supplier prices to determine which provide the highest-quality goods at the most competitive prices.

    b. Create a list of approved suppliers known to provide goods of acceptable quality. Collect and periodically review supplier performance data to:

        (1) keep approved supplier lists current, and

        (2) drop suppliers if the quality of their goods fall.

    c. Review purchase orders to make sure approved suppliers are used.

    d. Hold purchasing managers responsible for all purchase costs, including scrap and rework costs.

5462.07   Threats and Controls in Ordering Goods, Part 3

1. **Threat:** Purchasing from unauthorized suppliers. This can result in:

    a. inferior quality goods,

    b. overpriced goods, or

    c. legal problems (such as violating import quotas).

2. **Controls**

    a. Review all purchase orders to make sure that only approved suppliers are used.

    b. Develop a process for adding suppliers to the approved list.

        (1) Limit the number of people who can add suppliers.

        (2) Require approval of all additions to the list of authorized suppliers.

    c. Restrict access to the approved supplier list and periodically review it for unauthorized changes.

3. **Threat:** Kickbacks. Suppliers may give purchasing agents gifts to persuade them to buy from the supplier. This can:

    a. impair buyer objectivity, or

    b. result in inflated prices or inferior quality goods.

4. **Controls**

    a. Do not allow purchasing agents to accept gifts from potential or existing suppliers.

    b. Have purchasing agents sign a conflict of interest statement each year that discloses any and all direct or indirect financial interests in current or potential suppliers.

    c. Conduct supplier audits, where company personnel visit suppliers to check their records and determine their policies and practices.

5462.08   **Threats and Controls in Ordering Goods, Part 4**

1. **Threat:** EDI-related risks.

2. **Controls**

    a. Use passwords, user IDs, access control matrices, and physical access controls to limit logical and physical access to equipment, files, and data items to authorized personnel.

    b. Establish procedures to verify and authenticate all EDI transactions. Send transaction acknowledgements to help ensure transaction accuracy.

    c. Time-stamp and number all EDI transactions to prevent orders from being lost.

    d. Maintain a log of all EDI transactions. Periodically review them to make sure they have all been processed according to established policies.

    e. Use data encryption to ensure EDI transaction privacy.

    f. Use digital signatures to make sure transactions are authentic.

3. **Threat:** Purchase of phantom services. When fraud perpetrators set up fictitious vendors they are likely to use a vendor that provides services, as they do not require purchase orders or result in receiving reports. Therefore, different procedures are needed to control the purchase of services, such as lawn maintenance or maintenance work. A major challenge is verifying that the services were actually performed.

4. **Controls**

    a. Make visual inspections to make sure the service was rendered where possible.

    b. Hold department supervisors responsible for all service costs they incur.

    c. Charge the services to accounts for which the requesting department is responsible.

    d. Compare actual and budgeted expenses and investigate any discrepancies.

5462.09 **Receive and Store Goods**

During this activity:

a. goods are accepted only when a valid purchase order indicates they were ordered.

b. the receiving department accepts deliveries from suppliers and counts the goods to make sure all ordered items were received.

It is important to verify the quantity and quality of goods delivered, so the company pays only for goods actually received.

c. a receiving report is completed for all accepted deliveries. It contains delivery details, such as date received, shipper, supplier, purchase order number, the items received, and the quantity of each item received.

The person inspecting and approving the receipt of goods should initial the receiving order.

d. the received goods are sent to stores to be stored until needed.

5462.10 Information technology advancements can be used to improve the efficiency and effectiveness of the receiving and inventory storage functions:

a. Companies can minimize data entry errors by:

(1) requiring suppliers to bar code their products and receiving clerks to scan the bar codes to get product numbers and quantity of items received.

(2) requiring vendors to attach, to each crate of goods, a radio frequency identification tag that emits a signal and installing a receiving unit at the company that can read the radio signal.

b. Trucks can be equipped with data terminals linked to satellites that track the exact location of all incoming shipments.

5462.11 **Threats and Controls in Receiving and Storing Goods**

1. **Threat:** Receiving unordered goods. This incurs unnecessary costs related to storing and returning goods.

2. **Controls**

a. Require the receiving department to accept only deliveries for which there is an approved copy of the purchase order.

(1) The receiving clerk should make sure the purchase order number on the vendor's packing slip matches an unfilled purchase order.

(2) For this to happen, the receiving department needs access to the open purchase order file.

3. **Threat:** Errors in counting goods received. This results in:

a. inaccurate perpetual inventory records, and

b. paying for goods not received.

4. **Controls**

a. Use bar codes to improve the efficiency and accuracy of receiving counts.

b. Do not let receiving clerks know order item quantities. Otherwise, the receiving clerk could simply do a quick visual comparison of quantities received with those indicated on the packing slip.

(1) Let receiving clerks know how important it is to carefully and accurately count all deliveries.

    (2) Require receiving clerks to sign the receiving report (or enter their employee ID numbers in the system) so they can be held accountable.

    (3) Offer bonuses to receiving clerks who catch discrepancies between the packing slip and actual quantity received before the delivery person leaves.

    (4) Require inventory stores to count all items from receiving and hold stores responsible for any subsequent shortages.

    (5) Require receiving clerks to check for inventory damage while making their counts.

5. **Threat:** Losing inventory.

6. **Controls**

    a. Store inventory in secure locations and restrict access to the storage area.

    b. Document all intra-company inventory transfers to know who to hold responsible for shortages and to make sure all inventory movements are recorded accurately. For example:

        (1) Receiving and inventory stores should acknowledge the transfer of goods from the receiving dock into inventory.

        (2) Inventory stores and production should acknowledge the release of inventory into production.

    c. Take physical inventory counts regularly. Critical items should be counted frequently and less critical items counted less often. Reconcile the counts with the inventory records.

5462.12 Pay for Goods and Services

The third expenditure cycle activity involves two steps: approve and pay vendor invoices for payment and pay approved invoices.

5462.13 Approve vendor invoices for payment.

    a. Accounts payable should authorize payment for goods and services only if they were ordered and actually received.

        (1) A valid purchase order is evidence that the goods or services were actually ordered.

        (2) A valid receiving report is evidence the goods were received.

    b. Most companies record accounts payable after a supplier invoice has been received and approved. Vendor invoices are processed in two ways:

        (1) In a nonvoucher system approved invoices are posted to the appropriate supplier record in the accounts payable file and stored in an open-invoice file.

        When an invoice is paid, it is removed from the open-invoice file, marked paid, and stored in the paid-invoice file.

        (2) In a voucher system a disbursement voucher is created to summarize one or more vendor invoices and specify which general ledger account to debit.

        The voucher identifies the supplier, lists all outstanding invoices, and indicates how much is to be paid after applicable discounts and allowances are deducted.

    c. Information Technology advancements can help improve the accounts payable process by:

        (1) requiring invoices to be submitted electronically (by EDI or the Internet) and using the system to automatically match invoices to appropriate purchase orders and receiving reports.

      (2) using an "invoiceless" approach, called evaluated receipt settlement (ERS), that replaces the traditional three-way matching process (vendor invoice, receiving report, purchase order) with a two-way match (purchase order, receiving report).

      (3) using procurement cards or corporate credit cards to eliminate most small invoices.

      (4) using electronic forms for submitting travel expenses.

5462.14 **Pay approved invoices.** A voucher package consists of a vendor invoice, a purchase order, and a receiving report. After voucher packages are approved, funds are disbursed by check or EFT and sent to suppliers.

5462.15 **Threats and Controls in Paying for Goods and Services, Part 1**

1. **Threat:** Errors in vendor invoices. These errors include:

    a. discrepancies between quoted and actual prices charged, and

    b. errors in calculating the total amount due.

2. **Controls**

    a. Have an independent person, or the system:

      (1) verify prices and quantities on vendor invoices and compare them with those on the purchase order and receiving report.

      (2) verify the mathematical accuracy of vendor invoices.

    b. Require employees who have procurement cards to keep receipts and verify monthly statement accuracy.

    c. Adopt ERS to eliminate vendor invoices errors (companies pay after matching receiving reports with purchase orders).

    d. Train purchasing and accounts payable staff on transportation practices and terminology so the company does not pay unnecessary transportation costs.

    e. Negotiate significant discounts with designated carriers to reduce costs.

    f. Capture data on carriers, so reports identifying suppliers who fail to comply with shipping instructions can be prepared.

3. **Threat:** Paying for goods not received.

4. **Controls**

    a. Compare vendor invoice quantities with the quantities the inventory control person entered into the system.

      (1) Inventory control should make sure that when goods are transferred from receiving, their count agrees to receiving's count.

    b. Use budgetary controls and careful reviews of departmental expenses to find potential problems when purchasing services.

5462.16 **Threats and Controls in Paying for Goods and Services, Part 2**

1. **Threat:** Failing to take available purchase discounts.

2. **Controls**

    a. Set up procedures to make sure approved invoices are filed by due date.

    b. Have the system track invoice due dates and print a list of all outstanding invoices by due date.

    c. Use a cash flow budget that indicates expected cash inflows and outstanding commitments so the company can plan to take advantage of purchase discounts.

3. **Threat:** Paying the same invoice twice. An invoice can be paid more than once.

    a. A duplicate invoice could be sent after the company's check is in the mail.

    b. An invoice could become separated from the documents in the voucher package.

    Duplicate payments are usually detected by the supplier, who may or may not return the duplicate payment. Duplicate payments affect a company's cash flow needs and result in incorrect financial records until the duplicate payment is detected.

4. **Controls**

    a. Approve invoices for payment only when accompanied by a purchase order and receiving report.

    b. Only pay based on an original copy of an invoice; do not authorize payment based on a photocopy.

    c. When payment is made, invoices and voucher packages should be canceled (marked "paid") so they cannot be resubmitted for payment.

    d. Automate accounts payable, to eliminate most clerical errors associated with processing invoices.

    e. Use invoiceless accounts payable systems to improve efficiency.

        (1) Control access to the supplier master file and monitor all changes made to it.

        (2) The supplier master file contains the prices of goods being purchased and unauthorized changes to those prices can result in overpayments to suppliers.

    f. Use internal auditors to detect and recover overpayments to suppliers.

5462.17   **Threats and Controls in Paying for Goods and Services, Part 3**

1. **Threat:** Accounts payable recording and posting errors. This can result in:

    a. errors in financial and performance reports, and

    b. poor decisions.

2. **Controls**

    a. Compare supplier account balances before and after processing checks with the total amount of invoices processed.

    b. Reconcile the accounts payable control account balance in the general ledger to one of the following:

        (1) The total of all supplier account balances.

        (2) Unpaid vouchers.

3. **Threat:** Misappropriated cash, checks, or EFTs.

4. **Controls**

    a. Restrict access to cash and blank checks.

    b. Pre-number checks sequentially and periodically account for them.

    c. Restrict access to the check-signing machine.

    d. Require two signatures for checks in excess of a certain amount, to provide an independent review of the expenditure.

    e. Have the cashier or treasurer mail signed checks, rather than returning them to accounts payable, to make sure checks are mailed to the intended recipients.

    f. Segregate duties.

    (1) Have accounts payable assemble voucher packages and authorize payments.

    (2) Have the treasurer or cashier sign checks.

g. Have internal auditors periodically review the supplier master file to check for duplicate supplier entries.

h. Have someone who has no involvement in processing cash collections or disbursements reconcile all bank accounts promptly.

    (1) This provides an independent check on accuracy.

    (2) It prevents someone from misappropriating cash and concealing the theft by manipulating the bank reconciliation.

i. To prevent check alteration and forgery:

    (1) Use check-protection machines that print check amounts in distinctive colors.

    (2) Use special inks that change colors if altered.

    (3) Print checks on special paper that contains watermarks.

    (4) Send a list of all legitimate checks to the bank, which will clear only those checks appearing on the list.

j. For minor purchases, use a petty cash fund managed by an employee with no cash-handling or accounting responsibilities.

    (1) The petty cash fund should be an imprest fund for a small, fixed amount.

    (2) Require vouchers for every disbursement so that, at all times, the sum of cash plus vouchers equals the imprest fund balance.

    (3) When needed, turn the vouchers in to accounts payable to get the fund replenished.

    (4) Cancel petty cash fund vouchers so they can not be reused.

    (5) Have internal auditors make periodic, unannounced counts of the fund balances and vouchers.

    (6) Hold the person in charge of the petty cash fund responsible for any shortages.

k. To control electronic funds transfers:

    (1) Implement strict access controls such as passwords and user IDs that are changed regularly.

    (2) Record the user and the location of the originating terminal to monitor the adequacy of access controls.

    (3) Encrypt EFT transmissions to prevent alteration.

    (4) Time-stamp all EFT transactions and number them to facilitate subsequent reconciliation.

    (5) Establish a control group and have them monitor EFT transactions for validity and accuracy.

    (6) Use special programs, called embedded audit modules, to monitor all transactions and flag these with specific characteristics for further review.

5470 The Production Cycle and Human Resources Cycle

5471 The Production Cycle

5471.01 The production cycle is a recurring set of business and data processing activities associated with manufacturing products. The production cycle interacts with the other cycles as indicated in Figure 15:

Figure 15

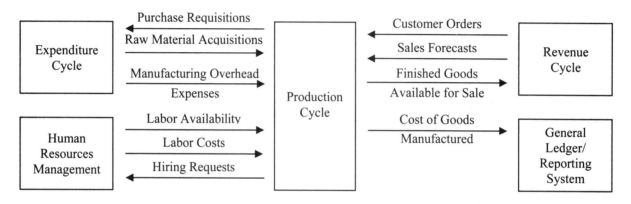

There are four basic activities in the production cycle (as shown in Figure 16). Each of these activities is briefly explained. The threats a system faces during each activity are also explained, along with the controls used to prevent the threat.

Figure 16

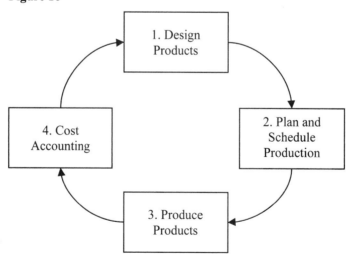

5471.02 **Design Products**

Products are designed to meet customer requirements at the lowest possible production costs. Two main documents are produced during product design:

a. **Bill of materials,** which lists the part number, description, and quantity of each item used in a finished product.

b. **Operations list,** which lists labor and machine requirements for manufacturing the product.

5471.03 **Threat and Controls in Designing Products**

1. **Threat:** Poor product design, which drives up costs in several ways:

   a. Too many unique components, which increases costs associated with purchasing and maintaining raw materials inventories

   b. Inefficient production processes, which makes moving from producing one product to another overly complex and costly

   c. Poorly designed products, which results in excessive warranty and repair costs, an impaired reputation, and a reduction in future sales

2. **Controls**

   a. Use complete and accurate data about the relationships between components and finished goods.

   b. Analyze warranty and repair costs to find out why products fail, and redesign the products to increase quality.

5471.04 **Plan and Schedule Production**

a. An efficient production plan helps organizations:

   (1) fill existing orders,

   (2) have sufficient product to meet anticipated short-term demand, and

   (3) avoid excess finished goods inventories.

b. Two common production planning methods are:

   (1) **Manufacturing resource planning (MRP-II):**

      (a) Meets forecasted sales demands by balancing existing production capacity and raw materials needs.

      (b) Since goods are produced based on sales forecasts, it is often referred to as push manufacturing.

   (2) **Just-in-time (JIT) manufacturing systems:**

      (a) JIT minimizes or eliminates raw materials, work in process, and finished goods inventory.

      (b) Since goods are produced in response to customer demand, JIT is often referred to as pull manufacturing.

c. The planning and scheduling activity produces several documents:

   (1) **Master production schedule (MPS):**

      (a) MPS shows how much product to produce and when to produce it.

      (b) Customer orders, sales forecasts, and finished goods inventory quantities are used to determine production amounts.

      (c) The bill of materials is "exploded" to determine the raw materials needed to meet the MPS production goals.

      - Raw material requirements are compared with current inventory levels.

      - Purchase requisitions are generated for needed materials and sent to the purchasing department.

(2) Production order:

    (a) Authorizes a specified amount of product to be produced.

    (b) Lists the operations to be performed, how much product to produce, and where to deliver the finished product.

(3) Materials requisition:

    (a) Authorizes the storeroom to release the specific quantity of raw materials.

    (b) Contains the production order number, date of issue, and the part numbers and quantities of all necessary raw materials.

(4) Move tickets:

Identify the raw materials moved within the factory, where they are moved to, and the time of transfer.

5471.05   **Threats and Controls in Planning and Scheduling Production**

1. **Threat:** Over or Under Production.

    a. Overproduction results in too many goods, cash flow problems, reduced profitability, and obsolete inventory.

    b. Underproduction results in lost sales and customer dissatisfaction.

2. **Controls**

    a. Develop an accurate sales forecast system to know the demand for each product.

    b. Develop an accurate perpetual inventory control system to make sure inventory quantities are always correct.

        (1) Periodically count inventory and reconcile the counts to the perpetual records.

        (2) Use bar code technology to eliminate human data entry and improve perpetual inventory record accuracy.

    c. Prepare production performance evaluation reports to evaluate production quantities, product quality, and delivery schedules.

    d. Require approval and authorization of production orders:

        (1) Use passwords and an access control matrix to restrict access to the production scheduling program.

        (2) Use closed-loop verification to make sure correct production orders are released. The production planner enters the product number.

            (a) The system retrieves the description, order quantity, and other relevant data.

            (b) The system requests the user to verify that the correct production order is being released.

    e. Select suppliers that meet delivery commitments, monitor supplier performance, and select new suppliers when performance falls below acceptable levels.

3. **Threat:** Unauthorized acquisition of fixed assets. This can result in:

    a. overinvestment in fixed assets and

    b. reduced profitability.

4. **Controls**

    a. Require supervisory personnel to recommend large capital expenditures and do a feasibility analysis of the proposed expenditure.

b. Require a capital investments committee to review acquisition recommendations and prioritize them.

c. Require small capital expenditures to be purchased directly out of departmental budgets.

d. Hold managers accountable for their department's return on fixed assets.

e. Send potential suppliers a request for proposal (RFP) that specifies the desired asset properties and invite them to send in a bid.

f. Require the capital investments committee to review RFP responses and select the best bid.

5471.06   Produce Products

This is the production cycle step where products are actually manufactured.

Using information technology, such as robots and computer-controlled machinery, is referred to as computer-integrated manufacturing (CIM) and can significantly reduce production costs.

5471.07   Threat and Controls in Producing Products

1.   Threat: Theft or overstatement of inventories and fixed assets.

2.   Controls

b. Limit physical access to inventories and fixed assets.

c. Use access controls and compatibility tests to restrict access to information about inventories and fixed assets to authorized personnel.

d. Document all internal movements of inventory through the production process.

(1) Use materials requisitions to authorize the release of raw materials to production.

(2) Require inventory control clerks and production employees receiving raw materials to sign the materials requisition to acknowledge that goods were released to production.

(3) Document and authorize requests for materials in excess of the amounts specified in the bill of materials.

(4) Use move tickets to document the movement of inventory through the production process.

(5) Document any return of materials not used in production.

e. Segregate duties.

(1) Have the inventory stores department be responsible for maintaining physical custody of raw materials and finished goods inventories.

(2) Have department or factory supervisors be responsible for work-in-process inventories.

(3) Have production planners and the production information system be responsible for preparing production orders, materials requisitions, and move tickets.

f. Use bar code scanners and on-line terminals to record inventory movement and help maintain accurate perpetual inventory records.

g. Have an employee without any custodial responsibility count inventory on hand periodically. Discrepancies between physical counts and recorded amounts should be investigated and corrected.

h. Identify and record all fixed assets.

(1) Make managers responsible and accountable for fixed assets under their control.

(2) Authorize and document all disposals of fixed assets.

(3) Prepare a report of all fixed asset transactions periodically and send it to the controller, who should verify the proper authorization and execution of each transaction.

i. Maintain adequate insurance to cover losses and replace assets.

5471.08 **Cost Accounting**

a. The final production cycle step is cost accounting, which has two objectives:

(1) Provide the information to plan, control, and evaluate production operation performance. To make timely and accurate decisions, management needs the information system to collect real-time data about production activity performance.

(2) Provide accurate cost data about products, and collect and process the information needed to calculate inventory and cost of goods sold. To assign costs to specific products and organizational units, the IS must categorize costs. This requires cost data to be carefully coded during collection, as costs may be allocated in multiple ways, for several different purposes.

For example, factory supervision costs are assigned to departments for performance evaluation purposes and to specific products for pricing and product mix decisions.

b. Most companies use either job-order or process costing to assign production costs.

(1) Job-order costing:

(a) assigns costs to specific production batches or jobs and

(b) is used when a product or service consists of discretely identifiable items.

(2) Process costing:

(a) assigns costs to processes and calculates the average cost for all units produced and

(b) is used when similar goods or services are produced in mass quantities and discrete units are not readily identified.

5471.09 **Threats and Controls in Cost Accounting**

1. **Threat:** Production activity data is not recorded or processed accurately, resulting in:

a. erroneous decisions about which products to produce and how to price products.

b. inaccurate inventory records that lead to overstocking or shortages of goods.

c. errors in financial statements and managerial reports that misrepresent performance and lead to poor decisions.

2. **Controls**

a. Automate data collection (bar code scanners, badge readers) to improve accuracy.

b. Use passwords, user IDs, and an access control matrix to restrict access to production data to authorized personnel.

c. Use check digits and closed-loop verification to make sure data about raw materials used, operations performed, and employee numbers are entered correctly.

d. Use validity checks to make sure that requested materials are on the bill of materials.

e. Count physical inventory and periodically compare the counts to recorded quantities.

3. **Threat:** Inefficiencies in production operations and quality control problems.

4. **Controls**

    a. Monitor manufacturing activities closely and take prompt action to correct any deviations from standards.

    b. Prepare appropriate performance reports.

    c. Maintain and carefully review measures of throughput (number of good units produced in a given period of time).

    d. Maintain quality control measures such as:

        (1) Productive capacity (maximum number of units that can be produced with current technology). To increase productive capacity: improve labor or machine efficiency, rearrange the factor floor to expedite material movements, or simplify product design.

        (2) Productive processing time (percentage of total production time used to manufacture a product). To improve productive processing time: improve maintenance to reduce machine downtime and schedule new material deliveries more efficiently to reduce wait time.

        (3) Yield (percentage of nondefective units produced). To improve yield: use higher-quality raw materials and improve worker skills.

    e. Develop information about the following quality control costs and use that information to minimize the costs.

        (1) Prevention costs (production process changes that reduce product defect rates)

        (2) Inspection costs (tests to make sure products meet quality standards)

        (3) Internal failure costs (reworking or scrapping defective products)

        (4) External failure costs (selling defective products, which results in product liability claims, warranty and repair expenses, loss of customer satisfaction, and damage to the company's reputation)

5472 The Human Resources Cycle

5472.01 The human resources management (HRM)/payroll cycle is a recurring set of business and data processing activities associated with managing employee information and compensating employees.

a. The more important tasks include:

(1) Recruiting and hiring new employees

(2) Training new and existing employees

(3) Assigning jobs to employees

(4) Compensating employees

(5) Evaluating employee performance

(6) Voluntary and involuntary terminations

The first and last activities are performed once for each employee. The other activities are performed periodically for as long as the person is employed.

b. Compensating employees is the payroll system's main function. The HRM system takes care of the other tasks. These two systems are organizationally separate in larger organizations. The director of human resources manages the HRM system and the controller manages the payroll system.

The main inputs to the payroll system and their sources are:

(1) The HRM department provides data about hirings and terminations as well as pay-rate changes.

(2) Employees make changes to their files (deductions, address changes, dependents).

(3) Departments send data about how many hours each employee works.

(4) Government agencies are the source of tax rate changes and instructions for meeting regulatory requirements.

(5) Other organizations provide information on calculating various withholdings (insurance, union dues).

c. The principal outputs of the payroll system are paper checks or electronic remittance and reports.

(1) Paychecks are sent to employees or their pay is sent by direct deposit to their bank accounts.

(2) A payroll check transfers funds from the company's payroll account.

(3) Checks are sent to government agencies, insurance companies, and other organizations for amounts withheld from gross pay.

(4) Reports are sent to management and external parties.

d. Payroll is usually processed in batch mode because:

(1) paychecks are prepared periodically (weekly, biweekly, or monthly), and

(2) most employees are paid at the same time.

5472.02 Payroll Cycle Activities

There are seven common payroll cycle activities (as shown in Figure 17). These activities, along with threats the organization faces in these activities and the controls used to minimize or eliminate the threats, are now discussed.

Figure 17

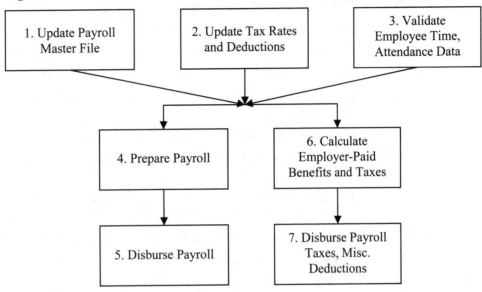

5472.03 Update Payroll Master File

The HRM department authorizes and oversees payroll file updates, including:

a. new hires.

b. terminations.

c. changes in pay rates and discretionary withholdings.

5472.04 Threat and Controls in Updating Payroll Master File

1. **Threat:** Unauthorized changes to the payroll master file. This can:

   a. be costly if the data used to calculate employee pay (wages, salaries, commissions) is fraudulently inflated and

   b. make labor cost reports unreliable and result in erroneous decisions.

2. **Controls**

   a. Restrict authority to update the payroll master file to the HRM department.

   b. Prohibit HRM personnel from processing payroll or distributing paychecks.

   c. Have someone other than the person recommending a payroll master file change review and approve the change.

   d. Use passwords, user IDs, and an access control matrix to restrict access to payroll files and data to authorized personnel. The system should verify the identity and authority of anyone making and approving payroll master file changes.

   e. Require each department supervisor to review reports documenting changes that affect their employees or department.

5472.05 **Update Tax Rates and Deductions**

The payroll department makes these infrequent changes when they receive:

a. tax rate changes from government agencies or

b. payroll deduction changes from insurance companies, unions, etc.

5472.06 **Validate Employee Time and Attendance Data**

This information comes from various sources:

a. Hourly employees punch a time card to record arrival and departure times.

b. Production employees complete job-time tickets to record the jobs they perform.

   (1) These labor costs are allocated among various departments, cost centers, and production jobs.

   (2) Professionals record time spent so they can bill clients.

   (3) Salaried employees are paid a fixed wage and supervisors monitor their time and attendance.

   (4) Sales staff may be paid a fixed wage, a commission, or a wage plus commission. In addition, they may be paid bonuses for meeting or exceeding targets.

5472.07 **Threat and Controls in Validating Employee Time and Attendance Data**

1. **Threat:** Inaccurate time data. This can result in:

   a. inaccurate labor expenses and labor expense reports,

   b. poor decisions, and

   c. hurt employee morale, if paychecks are incorrect or not prepared.

2. **Controls**

   a. Use badge readers, bar code scanners, and on-line terminals to:

      (1) collect data on employee time and attendance electronically and

      (2) collect job-time data and send it to the payroll processing system.

   b. Include edit checks in data entry programs:

      (1) Field checks, for numeric data in fields such as employee number and hours worked

      (2) Limit checks, on the hours worked field

      (3) Validity checks, on the employee number field

   c. Restrict payroll master file changes to someone not directly involved in processing payroll.

   d. Require payroll master file changes to be approved by appropriate supervisors.

   e. Reconcile time clock data to job-time ticket data.

      (1) This should be done by someone who does not generate the data.

      (2) All time card hours should be accounted for on the job-time tickets.

5472.08 Prepare Payroll

To prepare payroll:

a. Departments provide data about the hours their employees work. The time should be approved by a supervisor.

b. Gross pay is calculated using the payroll master file and the transaction file containing time and wage information for the period.

c. Net pay is calculated by subtracting all payroll deductions, tax withholdings, and voluntary deductions from gross pay.

d. Gross pay, deductions, and net pay year-to-date fields in each employee's record in the payroll master file are updated.

e. The following items are printed:

   (1) Employee paychecks and earnings statements (gross pay, deductions, net pay, and year-to-date totals).

   (2) Payroll register (a list of each employee's gross pay, deductions, and net pay). The payroll register authorizes the transfer of funds to the company's payroll bank account.

   (3) Deduction register (voluntary deductions for each employee).

f. Labor costs are allocated to appropriate general ledger accounts and a running total of these allocations is maintained.

g. A summary journal entry is posted to the general ledger using total labor costs and the column totals in the payroll register.

5472.09 Threat and Controls in Preparing Payroll

1. **Threat:** Inaccurate payroll processing. This can:

   a. be costly if the company overpays its employees,

   b. hurt employee morale, particularly if paychecks are late or not ready on time, and

   c. result in penalties if an incorrect payroll tax amount is sent to the government.

2. **Controls**

   a. Calculate batch totals prior to data entry.

      (1) Check them against totals calculated during each subsequent processing stage.

      (2) If original and subsequent totals agree, all payroll records were processed, data input was accurate, and bogus time cards were not entered during processing.

   b. Cross-foot the payroll register to make sure the total of the net pay column equals the total of gross pay less the total deductions column.

   c. Use a payroll clearing account (a zero-balance account) to verify payroll cost recording accuracy and completeness, and to allocate costs appropriately.

      (1) Debit gross pay to the payroll control account.

      (2) Credit net pay to cash and credit the various withholdings.

      (3) Cost accounting distributes labor costs to appropriate expense categories and credits the payroll control account for the allocation total. The payroll control account credit should equal the previous debit to net pay and the various withholdings.

      (4) The payroll control account should be zero after posting both entries.

   d. Properly classify workers as employees or independent contractors. Misclassification can result in back taxes, interest, and penalties.

   e. Have the HRM department review decisions to hire temporary or outside help.

5472.10   **Disburse Payroll**

Employees are paid by check or direct deposit. To disburse payroll:

a. The payroll register is sent to accounts payable for review and approval.

b. Accounts Payable prepares a disbursement voucher to authorize a funds transfer from the organization's general account to its payroll account.

c. The disbursement voucher and payroll register are sent to the cashier, who:

   (1) reviews the document,

   (2) prepares and signs a check (or electronic disbursement) transferring funds to the payroll bank account,

   (3) reviews, signs, and distributes employee paychecks,

   (4) redeposits unclaimed paychecks in the company's general bank account, and

   (5) sends a list of the unclaimed paychecks to the internal audit department for review and follow-up.

d. The payroll register is returned to the payroll department where it is filed by date along with the time cards and job-time tickets.

e. The disbursement voucher is sent to the accounting clerk, who uses it to update the general ledger.

5472.11   **Threat and Controls in Disbursing Payroll**

1.   **Threat:** Paychecks are prepared and disbursed for fictitious or terminated employees.

2.   **Controls**

   a. Segregate duties.

     (1) Have Accounts Payable authorize and record payroll transactions.

     (2) Have someone who does not authorize or record payroll distribute paychecks (such as the cashier) to prevent a supervisor from not reporting employee terminations and keeping their paychecks.

     (3) Make sure someone independent of the payroll process reconciles the payroll bank account.

   b. Restrict access to blank payroll checks and the check signature machine.

   c. Periodically account for sequentially prenumbered payroll checks.

   d. Make sure the cashier does not sign payroll checks until he/she checks and reviews the payroll register and disbursement voucher.

   e. Use a separate payroll bank account to limit payroll check fraud.

     (1) Use an imprest fund (fund deposits are for the net pay for that period) so when all paychecks are cashed, the payroll account will have a zero balance.

     (2) When the account is reconciled, fraudulent checks can be spotted easily.

   f. Require positive identification when distributing paychecks.

   g. Require internal audit to periodically observe paycheck distributions.

   h. Make sure unclaimed paychecks are:

      (1) returned to the treasurer's office for prompt redeposit,

      (2) traced back to time records, and

      (3) compared to the employee master payroll file to make sure they are for legitimate employees.

    i. Deposit employee paychecks directly into employee accounts.

5472.12   **Calculate Employer-Paid Benefits and Taxes**

    a. Employers are required by law to pay certain taxes and benefits, including:

      (1) payroll taxes,

      (2) Social Security taxes, and

      (3) a percentage of employee gross pay (capped at a maximum annual limit) to unemployment compensation insurance funds.

    b. Employers voluntarily pay for certain benefits, including:

      (1) all or a portion of employee health, disability, and life insurance premiums;

      (2) flexible benefit plans that provide:

        (a) minimal medical insurance and pension contributions and

        (b) benefit credits that can be used for vacation time or health insurance; and

      (3) savings plan contributions.

    Providing these benefits and services, and making employee-requested changes on a timely basis, can be expensive and time consuming. To provide better service without increasing costs, companies can have employees make the changes themselves using the company's intranet.

5472.13   **Disburse Payroll Taxes and Miscellaneous Deductions**

    Companies periodically pay the various tax liabilities they have incurred by check or electronic funds transfer.

5472.14   **Threats and Controls in Disbursing Payroll Taxes and Miscellaneous Deductions**

    1. **Threat:** Hiring unqualified or dishonest employees. This can result in:

      a. increased production expenses and

      b. theft of assets.

    2. **Controls**

      a. Explicitly state skill qualifications in the job postings for each open position.

      b. Require candidates to sign a statement on the job application form that:

        (1) confirms the accuracy of the information on the form.

        (2) gives permission to do a thorough background check.

      c. Perform thorough background checks to verify:

        (1) the applicant does not have a prior criminal record.

        (2) job applicant skills and references.

        (3) college degrees earned.

        (4) actual job titles of people listed as references.

3. **Threat:** Employment law is violated. This can result in:

   a. stiff penalties from the government and

   b. civil suits by alleged victims of employment discrimination.

4. **Controls**

   a. Carefully document all actions and decisions relating to advertising, recruiting, and hiring new employees. This demonstrates compliance with applicable government regulations.

   b. Send employees to training courses that keep them current with employment law.

5472.15   Outsourcing Payroll and HRM Functions

a. Some organizations outsource their payroll and HRM functions to reduce costs. There are two types of outsourers:

   (1) Payroll service bureaus process payroll.

   (2) Professional employer organizations (PEO) process payroll and also provide HRM services (employee benefits plans, etc.).

b. Both options are attractive to smaller businesses because:

   (1) their fees are less than the cost of doing payroll in-house due to the economies of scale that come from preparing paychecks for many companies.

   (2) the need for tax law expertise is eliminated.

   (3) a wide range of benefits can be offered because the costs of administering benefits can be spread across all of the PEO's clients.

   (4) computer resources are freed up by eliminating payroll and HRM applications. They can be used to improve service in other areas.

5480 General Ledger and Reporting System

5480.01 The general ledger and reporting system plays a central role in a company's Information System.

    a. Primary functions of this system are to collect and organize:

        (1) data from each of the accounting cycle subsystems,

        (2) data from the treasurer about financing and investing activities,

        (3) data from the budget department, and

        (4) adjusting entries from the controller.

    b. In the general ledger and reporting system, data is organized and stored such that the information needs of internal and external users can be met. Examples of these information needs are:

        (1) Managers need information to plan, control, and evaluate their operations.

        (2) Users need regular reports, as well as information to meet their real-time inquiry needs.

        (3) Investors and creditors need financial statements, as well as more detailed and more frequent reports, to evaluate organizational performance and make investment and credit-granting decisions.

        (4) Government agencies require periodic reports of organization performance to evaluate compliance with laws and regulations.

    c. There are four basic activities in the general ledger and reporting system (as shown in Figure 18). Each of these activities is briefly explained. The threats a system faces during each activity are also explained, along with the controls used to prevent the threat.

        Figure 18

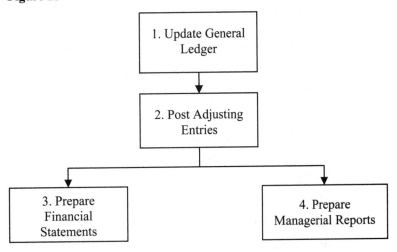

5480.02 **Activities in General Ledger and Reporting System**

a. **Update General Ledger.** These updates are journal entry postings that originate from:

(1) accounting subsystems. These are summary journal entries of transactions that took place during a specific period of time.

(2) treasurer. These are individual journal entries for nonroutine transactions and are often documented using journal vouchers. Examples include:

(a) issuance or retirement of debt,

(b) purchase or sale of investment securities, and

(c) acquisition of treasury stock.

b. **Post Adjusting Entries.** The controller's office makes the following types of adjusting entries:

(1) End-of-period accruals, to record events where cash has not yet been received or disbursed. Examples include:

(a) interest revenue earned and

(b) wages payable.

(2) End-of-period deferrals, to record that cash has been exchanged, but services or goods have not been. Examples include:

(a) recognizing the portion of advance payments from customers earned during a specific period and

(b) expensing the portion of prepaid assets (e.g., rent, interest, and insurance) used this period.

(3) Estimates of expenses that occur over several accounting periods. Examples include:

(a) depreciation and

(b) bad debt expense.

(4) Evaluations to reflect differences between the actual and recorded value of an asset or a change in accounting principle. Examples include:

(a) changing inventory valuation methods,

(b) reducing inventory due to obsolescence, and

(c) adjusting inventory records based on physical counts of inventory.

(5) Correcting general ledger errors.

c. **Prepare Financial Statements.** Most companies prepare three basic financial statements:

(1) Income Statement

(2) Balance Sheet

(3) Statement of Cash Flows

d. **Produce Managerial Reports.** Several general ledger control reports are used to verify the accuracy of the posting process.

(1) Examples include:

(a) general ledger account balances and

(b) journal vouchers listed by date, numerical sequence, or account number

(2) A number of budgets are produced for planning and evaluating performance:

    (a) Operating budgets show planned revenues and expenditures.

    (b) Cash flow budgets show estimated cash inflows and expenditures.

5480.03   **Threats and Controls in General Ledger and Reporting System, Part 1**

1. **Threat:** An error in updating the General Ledger produces incorrect information, which can result in:

    a. misleading reports and

    b. poor decisions.

2. **Controls**

    a. Input controls, such as:

      (1) Making sure summary journal entries represent actual reporting period activity

      (2) Validity checks to make sure a general ledger account exists for each journal entry account number

      (3) Field checks to make sure amount fields in a journal entry contain only numeric data

      (4) Zero-balance checks in journal entries to make sure total debits journal entries equal total credits

      (5) Completeness tests to make sure all pertinent journal entry data is entered

      (6) Closed-loop verification tests to make sure account numbers match account descriptions, so that the correct general ledger account is accessed

      (7) Adjusting entry files for standard recurring adjusting entries, such as depreciation expense

        (a) Because the entries are not keyed in each time, this improves input accuracy.

        (b) Because the entries are not forgotten, this improves input completeness.

      (8) Signing checks on general ledger account balances to make sure the balance is of the appropriate nature (debit or credit)

      (9) Run-to-run totals to verify batch processing accuracy

        (a) Calculate new general ledger account balances, based on beginning balances and total debits and credits applied to the account.

        (b) Compare that total with the actual account balance in the updated general ledger.

        (c) Investigate any discrepancies, as they indicate a processing error that must be corrected.

    b. Reconciliations and controls that help detect general ledger updating errors.

      (1) Compare total debit balances to total credit balances in a trial balance to determine if a posting error has occurred.

      (2) Determine if clearing and suspense accounts have end-of-period zero balances.

      (3) Determine if general ledger control account balances agree to corresponding subsidiary ledger totals.

      (4) Examine end-of-period transactions to make sure they are recorded in the proper time period.

    c. An audit trail provides the information needed to:

        (1) trace transactions from source documents to the general ledger and any report or document using that data,

        (2) trace items on reports back through the general ledger to the original source document, and

        (3) trace general ledger account changes from their beginning to their ending balance.

5480.04   Threats and Controls in General Ledger and Reporting System, Part 2

1. **Threat:** Unauthorized access to the general ledger, which can result in:

    a. confidential data leaks to competitors,

    b. corruption of the general ledger, and

    c. concealing asset theft.

2. **Controls**

    a. User IDs, passwords, and access control matrix to:

        (1) control general ledger access and

        (2) enforce proper segregation of duties, by limiting the functions legitimate users may perform.

    b. Limit the functions performed at a terminal. For example, entering adjusted entries can be restricted to terminals in the controller's office.

    c. Check for a valid authorization code for each journal voucher record before posting that transaction to the general ledger.

        (1) This authorization code is part of the audit trail.

        (2) Inspecting the audit trail can detect unauthorized general ledger access.

5490 EDP Terminology: Important IT Terms to Know

In order to answer many of the multiple-choice questions pertaining to information technology (IT) on the CPA Examination, you must develop knowledge of IT terminology. The purpose of the following glossary is to provide a good working base of IT terms. Half the battle in understanding the intricacies of IT is to understand the terminology and the unique jargon associated with IT. The terms that you need to understand are presented in alphabetical order. The order of presentation should facilitate future reference when actual CPA Examination multiple-choice questions are studied.

5491 Abort to Conceptual Design Specifications

5491.01 **Abort:** A deliberate or unexpected termination of a program. A program may be instructed by the user to suspend during long operations such as printing or searching the database. Programs may also unexpectedly abort due to bugs in the software, incorrect input, or a hardware malfunction.

5491.02 **Acceptance Tests:** Tests of new systems using specially developed transactions and acceptance criteria. The test results are evaluated to determine if the system is acceptable.

5491.03 **Access Control List:** Rules that determine which packets are allowed into a system.

5491.04 **Access Control Matrix:** An internally maintained list that the computer uses to verify that the person attempting to access system resources is authorized to do so. The matrix usually consists of a list of user codes, a list of all files and programs maintained on the system, and a list of the accesses each user is authorized to make.

5491.05 **Access Time:** The time it takes a program (software) and device (hardware) to retrieve data and make it available to the microprocessor.

5491.06 **Accounting Business Cycle:** The activities corresponding to an organization's major accounting transactions. There are five major accounting cycles: acquisition and cash disbursements, payroll and personnel, sales and collection, capital acquisition and repayment, and inventory and warehousing.

5491.07 **Accounting Information System (AIS):** The human and capital resources within an organization that are responsible for (1) the preparation of financial information and (2) the information obtained from collecting and processing company transactions. The AIS is a subset of the management information system.

5491.08 **Ad Hoc Queries:** Nonrepetitive requests for reports or answers to specific questions about the contents of the system's data files.

5491.09 **Adapter:** An expansion board that provides specialized processing and control for the microprocessor. An adapter fits in the computer's expansion slot and supports devices such as a monitor or mouse, or connects the computer to a network.

5491.10 **Administrative Documentation:** A description of the overall standards and procedures for the data processing facility, including policies relating to justification and authorization of new systems or systems changes; standards for systems analysis, design, and programming; and procedures for file handling and file library activities.

5491.11 **Alphanumeric:** The complete set of letters (A-Z) and numeric characters (0-9). In addition to these, @, #, and $ are considered alphanumeric characters.

5491.12 **Application:** The problem or data processing task to which a computer's processing power is applied.

5491.13 **Application Controls:** Controls that relate to the data input, files, programs, and output of a specific computer application, rather than the computer system in general. Contrast with general controls.

5491.14 **Application Programmer:** A person who formulates a logical model, or user view, of the data to be processed and then writes an application program using a programming language.

5491.15 **Application Service Provider (ASP):** A company that provides access to and use of application programs via the Internet. The ASP owns and hosts the software; the contracting organization accesses the software remotely via the Internet.

5491.16 **Application Software:** The programs that perform the data or information-processing tasks required by the user. Common types of application software in accounting include accounts receivable and payable, inventory control, and payroll.

5491.17 **Artificial Intelligence (AI):** A field of study in which researchers are attempting to develop computers that have the ability to reason, think, and learn like a human being.

5491.18 **ASCII:** Acronym for American Standard Code for Information Interchange. ASCII provides a standard representation for English characters, with each letter assigned a number from 0 to 127. These codes enable data to be exchanged from one computer to another.

5491.19 **Asymmetric Encryption:** Using two keys to encrypt and decrypt a message. A public key is publicly available to everyone, and the private key is kept secret. Either key can be used to encode a message, but only the other key can be used to decode it. It eliminates problems with exchanging keys, and companies only need one key. Since data can be encrypted with the private key and decrypted with the public key, it is possible to prove who created a document, so legally binding electronic agreements can be created. An asymmetric encryption system is much slower than single key systems.- too slow to exchange large amounts of data over the Internet.

5491.20 **Asynchronous Transmission:** Data transmission in which each character is transmitted separately. A start bit is required before the character and a stop bit after it because the interval of time between transmission of characters can vary. Contrast with synchronous transmission.

5491.21 **ATM Card:** A bank card that many businesses accept in lieu of credit and debit cards.

5491.22 **Attributes:** Characteristics of interest in a file or database; the different individual properties of an entity. Examples of attributes are employee number, pay rate, name, and address.

5491.23 **Audit Hooks:** Concurrent audit techniques that embed audit routines into application software to flag certain kinds of transactions that might be indicative of fraud.

5491.24 **Audit Log:** A log kept on magnetic tape or disk of all computer system transactions that have audit significance.

5491.25 **Audit Trail:** The trail or path left by a transaction when it is processed. The trail begins with the original documents; proceeds with transactions, entries, and posting of records; and is complete with the report. The traditional audit trail is illustrated as follows:

Source document ⟶ Journal ⟶ Ledger ⟶ Report

The traditional audit trail is characterized by accessible records, observable activities, source documents, detailed chronological journals, and ledger summaries. IT has impacted the audit trail in the following ways:

a. Source documents once transcribed into machine-readable form are no longer used in processing. Documents may be filed in a manner that makes subsequent access difficult.

b. Some systems (real time) may eliminate traditional source documents.

c. Ledger summaries may be replaced by master files.

d. Printed-out data may not be available.

e. Processing activities are difficult to observe because much of the data activities are contained within the system.

5491.26 **Authentication:** Ensuring that unauthorized users and devices do not access any part of the system.

5491.27 **Authenticity:** Being able to determine, with almost absolute certainty, who sent a message.

5491.28 **Authorization:** Making sure the system can recognize authorized users, but restricting their access to data they are not allowed to use and to those functions (reading, copying, updating, adding, deleting, modifying, downloading, printing) they are authorized to perform.

5491.29 **Auxiliary Storage:** Supplementary or secondary storage that usually has a larger capacity, but longer access time, than primary on-line storage.

5491.30 **Backup File:** Duplicate copy of a current file.

5491.31 **Bandwidth:** The data transmitting capacity of a communication channel.

5491.32 **Bar Codes:** Special identification labels found on most merchandise. A code includes vertical lines of differing widths that represent binary information that is read by an optical scanner.

5491.33 **Batch Processing:** Accumulating transaction records into groups or batches for processing at some regular interval such as daily or weekly. The records are usually sorted into some sequence (such as numerically or alphabetically) before processing.

5491.34 **Batch Totals:** Sums of the instances of numerical items, calculated for a batch of documents. These totals are calculated prior to processing the batch and are compared with machine-generated totals at each subsequent processing step to verify that the data was processed correctly.

5491.35 **BCD (Binary Coded Decimal):** A method for representing each of the decimal digits 0 through 9 by a distinct group of binary digits. For example, in the 8-4-2-1 BCD notation, the decimal number 49 is 0100 (4) 1001 (9). The decimal number 5 is 0101.

330

5491.36 **Benchmark Problem:** A data processing task that is executed by different computer systems. The results are used to measure systems performance and to make comparative evaluations among systems.

5491.37 **Biometric Identification:** Using unique physical characteristics such as fingerprints, voice patterns, retina prints, signature dynamics, and the way people type certain groups of characters to identify people.

5491.38 **BIOS (Basic Input/Output System):** An interface between the hardware and the operating system that interprets the electronic signals sent from the software applications to hardware devices. The BIOS allows software to operate efficiently regardless of the type of hardware that is used.

5491.39 **Bits Per Second (BPS):** A unit of measurement describing the number of bits of data transmitted electronically in one second.

5491.40 **Bits:** Binary digits that are the smallest storage location in a computer. A bit may be either "on" or "off," or "magnetized" or "nonmagnetized." A combination of bits (usually eight) is used to represent a single character of data.

5491.41 **Boot:** The process of starting up the computer, which involves a self-checking diagnostic and progressive loading of the operating system. A cold boot occurs when the computer is turned on from the off position. A warm boot occurs when a computer that is already on is reset.

5491.42 **Border Router:** A device that connects an organization's information system to the Internet. It tests the contents of the destination address field of every packet it receives. Packets that fail a test are not allowed into the system. Those that do not fail the tests are passed on to the firewall, where they will be subjected to more detailed testing before being allowed to enter the organization's internal network.

5491.43 **Boundary Protection:** On a magnetic disk, more than one file may be stored on a single disk. Likewise, in multiprogramming computer operations, several programs may be in core storage at one time. In both cases, boundary protection prevents the intermixing or overlapping of data.

5491.44 **Broadband Lines:** Communications channels that are capable of handling high-speed data transmissions, usually in the range of 20,000 to 500,000 bps. Their primary use is for high-speed data transmission between computer systems.

5491.45 **Browser:** Software that allows a user to access and navigate the Internet and display the contents of Internet sites.

5491.46 **Buffer:** A temporary storage area, usually in RAM, that holds data before or after being processed by the microprocessor. For example, changes made to a file are not written back to the disk as they are made, but instead are held in a buffer and sent to the disk when the file is saved. The buffer allows changes to be recorded much more efficiently than accessing the file on the disk each time a change is made.

5491.47 **Buffer Storage:** Secondary storage used to facilitate the transfer of data between internal and external storage. It is used to facilitate transfers between devices whose input and output speeds are not synchronized.

5491.48 **Bug:** A malfunction (mistake) in a program, system, or equipment.

5491.49 **Bus Network:** Type of network organization in which all devices are attached to a main channel called a "bus." Each network device can access the other devices by sending a message to its address. Each device reads the address of all messages sent on the bus and responds to the messages sent to it.

5491.50 **Business Intelligence:** The process of accessing the data contained in a data warehouse and using it for strategic decision making. There are two main techniques used in business intelligence: online analytical processing (OLAP) and data mining.

5491.51 **Business Process Reengineering (BPR):** The thorough analysis and complete redesign of business processes and information systems to achieve dramatic performance improvements.

5491.52 **Byte:** A group of adjacent bits that is treated as a single unit by the computer. The most common size for a byte is 8 bits. An 8-bit byte can be used to represent an alphabetic, numeric, or special character, or two numeric characters can be "packed" into a single 8-bit byte.

5491.53 **Cache:** A location for storing information once it has been accessed in order to quickly access it again.

5491.54 **Callback System:** A routing verification procedure. After the user dials in and is authenticated, the computer disconnects and calls the user back as an additional security precaution.

5491.55 **Canned Software:** Programs written by computer manufacturers or software development companies for sale on the open market to a broad range of users with similar needs.

5491.56 **Capacity Check:** An input validation routine that ensures that data will fit into its assigned field.

5491.57 **Cathode Ray Tube (CRT):** A type of monitor used in some personal computers and computer terminals.

5491.58 **CD-ROM:** A storage device that uses laser optics for reading data rather than magnetic storage devices. Although CD-ROM discs are "read only," the discs are useful for storing large volumes of data (roughly 600 megabytes per disc).

5491.59 **Cell:** The intersection of a row and a column in spreadsheets. Usually identified by the row/column coordinates.

5491.60 **Central Processing Unit (CPU):** The hardware that contains the circuits that control the interpretation and execution of instructions and that serves as the principal data processing device. Its major components are the arithmetic-logic unit, the memory, and the control unit.

5491.61 **Centralized Data Processing System:** All the data processing equipment, personnel, and controls located in the same geographical area.

5491.62 **Centralized Network:** A large, centralized computer system that handles a company's data processing needs. Such a system requires complex software and is designed to provide a company with an "economy of scale" advantage in data processing operations.

5491.63 **Centralized System:** Data processing is done at a centralized processing center. User terminals are linked to the centralized host computer so that users can send data to the host computer for processing and access data as needed.

5491.64 **Certificate Authority:** An independent organization that issues digital certificates.

332

5491.65   **Character:** Letters, numeric digits, or other symbols used for representing data to be processed by a computer.

5491.66   **Chart of Accounts:** A listing of all balance sheet and income statement account number codes for a particular company.

5491.67   **Check Digit:** A redundant digit in a data field that provides information about the other digits in the data field. It is used to check for errors or loss of characters in the data fields as a result of data transfer operations. If data is lost or erroneously changed, the fact that the check digit does not match the other data in the field will signal that an error has occurred.

5491.68   **Check Digit Verification:** The edit check in which a check digit is recalculated to verify that an error has not been made. This calculation can be made only on a data item that has a check digit.

5491.69   **Checkpoint:** Any one of a series of points during a long processing run at which an exact copy of all the data values and status indicators of a program are captured. Should a system failure occur, the system could be backed up to the most recent checkpoint and processing could begin again at the checkpoint rather than at the beginning of the program.

5491.70   **Chief Security Officer (CSO):** A person who conducts vulnerability tests and risk assessments, audits security measures implemented by the company; helps the chief information officer create and put into place sound security policies and procedures; promotes security efforts; and disseminates information about fraud, errors, security breaches, and other improper system uses and their consequences.

5491.71   **Client/Server System:** An arrangement of a LAN where information requested by a user is first processed as much as possible by the server and then transmitted to the user. Contrast with fileserver.

5491.72   **Clock Speed:** The speed at which a microprocessor executes instructions. An internal clock synchronizes the various parts of the computer. The CPU requires a fixed number of clock cycles to execute an instruction. The faster the clock, the more the CPU can execute per second.

5491.73   **Closed-Loop Verification:** An input validation method in which data that has just been entered into the system is sent back to the sending device so that the user can verify that the correct data has been entered.

5491.74   **CMOS:** A type of memory chip powered by a small battery on the motherboard that retains its data when the power is turned off. It contains the hard drive specifications, types of floppy drive, the clock information, and the amount of memory, among other pieces of information.

5491.75   **Coding:** (1) Assigning numbers, letters, or other symbols according to a systematic plan so that a user can determine the classifications to which a particular item belongs. (2) Writing program instructions that direct a computer to perform a specific data processing task.

5491.76   **Cold Site:** A location that provides everything necessary to quickly install computer equipment in the event of a disaster-stricken organization.

5491.77   **Command:** An instruction to the computer to perform a specific task. Commands may be special words that the computer understands, function keys, or menu choices.

5491.78   **Committee of Sponsoring Organizations (COSO):** A private sector group consisting of the American Accounting Association, the AICPA, the Institute of Internal Auditors, the Institute of Management Accountants, and Financial Executives International.

5491.79 **Communications Channel:** The line, or link, between the sender and the receiver in a data communications network.

5491.80 **Communications Network:** An information system consisting of one or more computers, a number of other hardware devices, and communication channels linked into a network.

5491.81 **Communications Software:** A program that controls the transmission of data electronically over communications lines.

5491.82 **Compatibility:** The ability of a device or program to work with another device or program.

5491.83 **Compatibility Check (or Compatibility Test):** A procedure for checking a password to determine if its user is authorized to initiate the type of transaction or inquiry he or she is attempting to initiate.

5491.84 **Compensating Controls:** Control procedures that will compensate for the deficiency in other controls.

5491.85 **Compiler:** A computer program that converts a source program (e.g., COBOL) into an object program (i.e., machine language). Compilers permit programmers to use process-orientated languages such as COBOL, which reduce the programming effort.

5491.86 **Completeness Test:** An on-line data entry control in which the computer checks if all data required for a particular transaction has been entered by the user.

5491.87 **Computer Emergency Response Team (CERT):** A team that reacts to security breaches and takes corrective action on a timely basis. A CERT consists of technical specialists to solve security problems and senior operations management to make critical business decisions.

5491.88 **Computer Fraud:** Any illegal act for which knowledge of a computer is essential for the crime's perpetration, investigation, or prosecution.

5491.89 **Computer Operator:** Person who maintains and runs the daily computer operations.

5491.90 **Computer Programmers:** Persons who develop, code, and test computer programs.

5491.91 **Computer Programming:** The process of writing software programs to accomplish a specific task or set of tasks.

5491.92 **Computer Security:** The policies, procedures, tools, and other means of safeguarding information systems from unauthorized access or alteration and from intentional or unintentional damage or theft.

5491.93 **Computer Security Officer:** An employee independent of the information system function who monitors the system and disseminates information about improper system uses and their consequences.

5491.94 **Computer System:** The input/output devices, data storage devices, CPU, and other peripheral devices that are connected together. The software necessary to operate the computer is also considered a part of the system.

5491.95 **Computer-Aided Software (or Systems) Engineering (CASE):** Software used by analysts to document and manage a systems development effort.

5491.96 **Computer-Based Information System:** Information system in which a computer is used as the data processor; the equipment, programs, data, and procedures for performing a set of related tasks on a computer.

5491.97 **Computer-Integrated Manufacturing (CIM):** A manufacturing approach in which much of the manufacturing process is performed and monitored by computerized equipment, in part through the use of robotics and real-time data collection on manufacturing activities.

5491.98 **Concatenated Key:** The combination of two fields in a database table that together become a unique identifier or key field.

5491.99 **Conceptual Design Specifications:** Once a conceptual design alternative has been selected, systems requirements are specified for systems output, data storage, input, and processing procedures and operations.

5492 Conceptual Systems Design to Entity

5492.01 **Conceptual Systems Design:** A phase of the systems development life cycle in which the systems designer proposes a systems design without considering the physical restrictions of particular hardware and software.

5492.02 **Conceptual Systems Design Report:** A document specifying the details of the conceptual systems design that is used by physical systems designers to identify the hardware, software, and procedures necessary to deliver the system.

5492.03 **Conceptual-Level Schema:** The organization-wide schema of the entire database. It lists all data elements in the database and the relationships between them. Contrast with external-level schema and internal-level schema.

5492.04 **Concurrent Audit Techniques:** A software routine that continuously monitors an information system as it processes live data in order to collect, evaluate, and report to the auditor information about the system's reliability.

5492.05 **Concurrent Update Controls:** Controls that lock out one user to protect individual records from potential errors that could occur if two users attempted to update the same record simultaneously.

5492.06 **Configuration:** For a network, the entire interrelated set of hardware. For a microcomputer, the configuration references the complete internal and external components of the computer including peripherals.

5492.07 **Console:** A hardware device that computer operators use to interact with large computer systems.

5492.08 **Context Diagram:** A data flow diagram that provides a summary-level view of a system. It shows the data processing system, the input and output of the system, and the external entities that are the sources and destinations of the system's input and output.

5492.09 **Continuous and Intermittent Simulation (CIS):** A concurrent audit technique that embeds an audit module into a database management system, rather than the application software.

5492.10 **Control Account:** The general ledger account that summarizes the total amounts recorded in the subsidiary ledger. Thus, the accounts payable control account in the general ledger represents the total amount owed to all vendors. The balances in the subsidiary accounts payable ledger indicate the amount owed to each specific vendor.

5492.11   **Control Environment**: The organization's environment as related to controls. It consists of many factors, including management's philosophy, the audit committee, and the organizational structure.

5492.12   **Control Risk:** The risk that a significant control problem will fail to be prevented or detected by the internal control system.

5492.13   **Control Totals:** Batch totals used to ensure that all data is processed correctly. Examples are the number of transactions processed and the dollar amount of all updates.

5492.14   **Controller:** A device that relieves the microprocessor of some control responsibility (e.g., the transfer of data from the computer to a peripheral device such as a printer).

5492.15   **Conversion:** The process of changing from one form or format to another. See also data conversion, media conversion, software conversion, system conversion, and hardware conversion.

5492.16   **Cookies:** Pieces of data sent by a web server to be stored on a computer's hard drive. Cookies contain information about the computer user, such as a user name, password, or some other identification, and allow a website to recognize the computer on subsequent visits.

5492.17   **Corrective Controls:** Procedures established to remedy problems that are discovered through detective controls.

5492.18   **Cross-Footing Balance Test:** A procedure in which worksheet data is totaled both across and down, and then the total of the horizontal totals is compared to the total of the vertical totals to ensure the worksheet balances.

5492.19   **Custom Software:** Computer software that is developed and written in-house to meet the unique needs of a particular company.

5492.20   **Data:** Characters that are accepted as input to an information system for further storing and processing. After processing, the data become information.

5492.21   **Data Communications Network:** Communication system that bridges geographical distances, giving users immediate access to a company's computerized data. It also allows multiple companies or computer services to be linked for the purpose of sharing information.

5492.22   **Data Communications:** The transmission of data from a point of origin to a point of destination.

5492.23   **Data Definition Language (DDL):** A database management system language that is used to create the database, to describe the schema and subschemas, to describe the records and fields in the database, and to specify any security limitations or constraints imposed on the database.

5492.24   **Data Dictionary:** A description of all data elements, stores, and flows in a system. Typically, a master copy of the data dictionary is maintained to ensure consistency and accuracy throughout the development process.

5492.25   **Data Diddling:** Changing data before it is entered, as it is entered, or after it has already been entered into the system. The change can be made to delete data, to change data, or to add data to the system.

5492.26 **Data Encryption (or Cryptology):** The translation of data into a secret code for storage or data transmission purposes. Encryption is particularly important when confidential data is being transmitted from remote terminals, because data transmission lines can be electronically monitored without the user's knowledge.

5492.27 **Data Flow Diagram (DFD):** A graphical description of the source of data, the flow of data in an organization, the processes performed on the data, where data is stored in the organization, and the destination of data. It is used to document existing systems and to plan and design new ones.

5492.28 **Data Independence:** A data organization approach in which the data and the application programs that use the data are independent. This means that one may be changed without affecting the other.

5492.29 **Data Leakage:** The unauthorized copying of company data, often without leaving any indication that it was copied.

5492.30 **Data Maintenance:** The periodic processing of transactions to update stored data. The four types of data maintenance are additions, deletions, updates, and changes.

5492.31 **Data Manipulation Language (DML):** A database management system language that is used to update, replace, store, retrieve, insert, delete, sort, and otherwise manipulate the records and data items in the database.

5492.32 **Data Mart:** A smaller data warehouse that is built by an organization for various functions such as finance and human resources.

5492.33 **Data Mining:** A method for accessing information stored in a data warehouse by using statistical analysis or artificial intelligence techniques to "discover" relationships in the data.

5492.34 **Data Model:** An abstract representation of the contents of a database.

5492.35 **Data Modeling:** The process of defining a database so that it faithfully represents all key components of an organization's environment. The objective is to explicitly capture and store data about every business activity that the organization wishes to plan, control, or evaluate.

5492.36 **Data Processing Center:** The room that houses a company's computer system (the hardware, software, and people who operate the system).

5492.37 **Data Processing Cycle:** The operations performed on data in computer-based systems to generate meaningful and relevant information. The data processing cycle has four stages: data input, data processing, data storage, and information output.

5492.38 **Data Processing Schedule:** A schedule of data processing tasks designed to maximize the use of scarce computer resources.

5492.39 **Data Query Language (DQL):** A high-level, English-like command language that is used to interrogate a database. Most DQLs contain a fairly powerful set of commands that are easy to use, yet provide a great deal of flexibility.

5492.40 **Data Redundancy:** The storage of the same item of data in two or more files within an organization.

5492.41 **Data Transmission Controls:** Methods of monitoring the network to detect weak points, maintain backup components, and ensure that the system can still communicate if one of the communications paths should fail.

5492.42 **Data Value:** The actual value stored in a field. It describes a particular attribute of an entity.

5492.43 **Data Warehouses:** Very large databases.

5492.44 **Database:** A set of interrelated, centrally controlled data files that are stored with as little data redundancy as possible. A database consolidates many records previously stored in separate files into a common pool of data records and serves a variety of users and data processing applications.

5492.45 **Database Administrator:** The person responsible for coordinating, controlling, and managing the data in the database.

5492.46 **Database Management System (DBMS):** The specialized computer program that manages and controls the data and interfaces between the data and the application programs.

5492.47 **Database Query Language:** Easy-to-use programming language that lets the user ask questions about the data stored in a database.

5492.48 **Debugging:** The process of checking for errors in a computer program and correcting the errors that are discovered.

5492.49 **Decentralized System:** An information processing system that has an independent CPU and a data processing manager at each location.

5492.50 **Decision Support System (DSS):** An interactive computer system designed to help with the decision-making process by providing access to a computer-based database or decision-making model.

5492.51 **Default Value:** A control that helps preserve the integrity of data processing and stored data by leaving a field blank if a standard value is to be used.

5492.52 **Demand Reports:** Reports that have a prespecified content and format but are prepared only in response to a request from a manager or other employee.

5492.53 **Denial-Of-Service Attack:** An attack that bombards the receiving server with so much information that it shuts down.

5492.54 **Desk Checking:** A visual and mental review of a newly coded program to discover keying or program errors.

5492.55 **Detective Controls:** Controls designed to discover control problems soon after they arise.

5492.56 **Dialog Box:** An on-screen display that presents information and/or requests that the user make a choice.

5492.57 **Digital Certificate:** Identifies the owner of a particular private key and the corresponding public key and the time period during which the certificate is valid.

5492.58 **Digital Fingerprint:** A hash number that identifies and validates a digital certificate.

5492.59 **Digital Signature:** A piece of data signed on a document by a computer. A digital signature cannot be forged and is useful in tracing authorization.

5492.60   **Direct Access:** An access method that allows the computer to access a particular record without reading any other records. Because each storage location on a direct access storage device has a unique address, the computer can find the record needed as long as it has the record's address.

5492.61   **Direct Access Storage Device (DASD):** A storage device (such as a disk drive) that can directly access individual storage locations to store or retrieve data.

5492.62   **Direct Conversion:** An approach to converting from one system to another in which the old system is discontinued, after which the new system is started (also known as "burning the bridges" or "crash conversion").

5492.63   **Directory:** A file used to organize other files into a hierarchical structure.

5492.64   **Disaster Recovery Plan:** Plan that prepares a company to recover its data processing capacity as smoothly and quickly as possible in response to any emergency that could disable the computer system.

5492.65   **Disk:** A round plate on which data can be encoded. Magnetic disks, such as floppy disks, can be erased and recorded over.

5492.66   **Disk Drive:** A device equipped with one or more heads that read and write data.

5492.67   **Diskette:** A round piece of flexible magnetic film enclosed within a protective cover. It is a popular storage medium for microcomputers.

5492.68   **Distributed Data Processing (DDP):** A system in which computers are set up at remote locations and then linked to a centralized mainframe computer.

5492.69   **Document**: Record of a transaction or other company data such as a check, invoice, receiving report, and purchase requisition.

5492.70   **Document Flowchart:** A diagram illustrating the flow of documents through the different departments and functions of an organization.

5492.71   **Documentation:** Written material consisting of instructions to operators, descriptions of procedures, and other descriptive material. Documentation may be classified into three basic categories: administrative, systems, and operating.

5492.72   **Download:** To transmit data or software maintained on a large host (mainframe) computer to a personal computer for use by an individual working at the personal computer.

5492.73   **Downsizing:** Shifting data processing and problem solving from mainframes to smaller computer systems. Downsizing saves money and allows the end user to be more involved in the processing of the data.

5492.74   **Eavesdropping:** When a computer user observes transmissions intended for someone else. One way unauthorized individuals can intercept signals is by setting up a wiretap.

5492.75   **E-business:** All uses of advances in information technology, particularly networking and communications technology, to improve the ways in which an organization performs all of its business processes.

5492.76   **Echo Check:** A hardware control that verifies transmitted data by having the receiving device send the message back to the sending device so that the message received can be compared with the message sent.

5492.77   **Economic Espionage:** The theft of information and intellectual property.

5492.78   **Economic Feasibility:** The dimension of feasibility concerned with whether the benefits of a proposed system will exceed the costs.

5492.79   **Economic Order Quantity (EOQ):** The optimal order size so as to minimize the sum of ordering, carrying, and stockout costs. Ordering costs include all expenses associated with processing purchase transactions. Carrying costs are the costs associated with holding inventory. Stockout costs represent costs, such as lost sales or production delays, which result from inventory shortages.

5492.80   **Edit Checks:** Accuracy checks performed by an edit program.

5492.81   **Edit Programs:** Computer programs that verify the validity and accuracy of input data.

5492.82   **Electronic Commerce:** The use of advances in networking and communications technology to improve the ways in which a company interacts with its suppliers and customers.

5492.83   **Electronic Data Interchange (EDI):** The use of computerized communication to exchange business data electronically in order to process transactions.

5492.84   **Electronic Data Processing (EDP):** Processing data utilizing a computer system. Little or no human intervention is necessary while data is being processed.

5492.85   **Electronic Envelope:** A method for protecting e-mail messages by using public or private key techniques to encrypt and decrypt the messages.

5492.86   **Electronic Funds Transfer (EFT):** The transfer of funds between two or more organizations or individuals using computers and other automated technology.

5492.87   **Electronic Lockbox:** A lockbox arrangement in which the bank electronically sends the company information about the customer account number and the amount remitted as soon as it receives and scans those checks. This enables the company to begin applying remittances to customer accounts before the photocopies of the checks arrive.

5492.88   **Electronic Mail:** Also called e-mail, is an application that allows messages to be sent, stored, and received between users of computers on a network or over the Internet.

5492.89   **Electronic Vaulting:** Electronically transmitting backup copies of data to a physically different location. Electronic vaulting permits on-line access to backup data when necessary.

5492.90   **E-mail Bomb:** A type of denial-of-service attack in which the receiver's e-mail server is bombarded with hundreds of e-mail messages per second.

5492.91   **E-mail Forgery:** Altering e-mail to make it appear that it came from a different source.

5492.92   **E-mail Threats:** Unwarranted threats sent to victims by e-mail. The threats usually require some follow-up action, often at great expense to the victim.

5492.93   **Embedded Audit Modules:** Special portions of application programs that track items of interest to auditors, such as any unauthorized attempts to access the data files.

5492.94   **Encryption/Decryption:** Encryption is transforming data, called plaintext, into unreadable gibberish, called ciphertext. Decryption reverses this process, transforming ciphertext back into plaintext.

5492.95 **End-User Computing (EUC):** The creation, control, and implementation by end users of their own information system.

5492.96 **End-User Development (EUD):** When information users develop applications on their own, rather than going through the information systems department.

5492.97 **End-User System (EUS):** Information system developed by the users themselves, rather than professionals in the information systems department, to meet their own operational and managerial information needs. An EUS draws upon the information in existing corporate databases to meet users' information needs.

5492.98 **Enterprise Resource Planning (ERP) System:** A system that integrates all aspects of an organization's activities into one accounting information system.

5492.99 **Entity:** The item about which information is stored in a record. Examples include an employee, an inventory item, and a customer account.

5493 Entity Integrity Rule to Internal Control Structure

5493.01 **Entity Integrity Rule:** A design constraint in a relational database, requiring that the primary key have a non-null value. This ensures that a specific object exists in the world and can be identified by reference to its primary key value.

5493.02 **Entity-Relationship (E-R) Diagram:** A graphical depiction of a database's contents. It shows the various entities being modeled and the important relationships among them. An entity is any class of objects about which data is collected. Thus, the resources, events, and agents that comprise the REA data model are all entities. An E-R diagram represents entities as rectangles; lines and diamonds represent relationships between entities.

5493.04 **Error Log:** The record of data input and data processing errors.

5493.05 **Error Message:** A message from the computer indicating that it has encountered a mistake or malfunction.

5493.06 **Error Report:** A report summarizing errors by record type, error type, and cause.

5493.07 **Evaluated Receipt Settlement (ERS):** An "invoiceless" approach to the accounts payable process. ERS replaces the traditional three-way matching process (vendor invoice, receiving report, and purchase order) with a two-way match of the purchase order and receiving report. ERS saves time and money by reducing the number of potential mismatches. ERS also saves suppliers the time and expense of generating and tracking invoices.

5493.08 **Executive Information System (EIS):** Information system designed to provide executives with the needed information to make strategic plans, to control and operate the company, to monitor business conditions in general, and to identify business problems and opportunities.

5493.09 **Expansion Board:** A circuit board that may be installed in an expansion slot in the computer to give it added capabilities.

5493.10 **Expansion Slot:** An opening in the computer where the circuit board can be inserted to add additional capabilities to the computer.

5493.11 **Expected Loss:** A measure of loss based on (1) the potential loss associated with a control problem and (2) the risk, or probability, that the problem will occur.

5493.12 **Expenditure Cycle:** A recurring set of business activities and related data processing operations associated with the purchase of and payment for goods and services.

5493.13 **Expert System (ES):** A computerized information system that allows nonexperts to make decisions about a particular problem that are comparable with those of experts in the area.

5493.14 **Exporting:** The formatting of data in such a way that it can be immediately processed by another application.

5493.15 **Exposure:** A measure of risk derived by multiplying the potential magnitude of an error, in dollars, by the error's estimated frequency (probability) of occurrence.

5493.16 **External Label:** A label on the outside of a magnetic storage medium (e.g., tape or disk) that identifies the data contained on the storage medium.

5493.17 **External Modem:** A modem that is not contained within the computer system.

5493.18 **External-Level Schema:** An individual user's or application program's view of a subset of the organization's database. Each of these individual user views is also referred to as a subschema. Contrast with conceptual-level schema and internal-level schema.

5493.19 **Extranet:** The term used for the linked intranets of two or more companies.

5493.20 **Fault Tolerance:** The capability of a system to continue performing its functions in the presence of a hardware failure.

5493.21 **Feasibility Study:** An investigation to determine if the development of a new application or system is practical. This is one of the first steps in the systems evaluation and selection process.

5493.22 **Feedback:** Informational output of a process that returns as input to the process, initiating the actions necessary for process control.

5493.23 **Field:** The part of a data record that contains the data value for a particular attribute. All records of a particular type usually have their fields in the same order. For example, the first field in all accounts receivable records may be reserved for the customer account number.

5493.24 **Field Check:** An edit check in which the characters in a field are examined to ensure they are of the correct field type (e.g., numeric data in numeric fields).

5493.25 **File:** A set of logically related records, such as the payroll records of all employees.

5493.26 **File Access:** The way the computer finds or retrieves each record it has stored.

5493.27 **File Maintenance:** The periodic processing of transaction files against a master file. This maintenance, which is the most common task in virtually all data processing systems, includes record additions, deletions, updates, and changes. After file maintenance, the master file will contain all current information.

5493.28 **File Organization:** The way data is stored on the physical storage media. File organization may be either sequential or direct (random, nonsequential, or relative).

5493.29 **File-Server:** An arrangement of a LAN where an entire file is sent to the user and then processed by the user, not the server. Contrast with client/server system.

5493.30 **Financial Electronic Data Interchange (FEDI):** The combination of EFT and EDI that enables both remittance data and funds transfer instructions to be included in one electronic package.

5493.31 **Financial Total:** The total of a dollar field, such as total sales, in a set of records. It is usually generated manually from source documents prior to input and compared with machine-generated totals at each subsequent processing step. Any discrepancy may indicate a loss of records or errors in data transcription or processing.

5493.32 **Financial Value-Added Network (FVAN):** An independent organization that offers specialized hardware and software to link various EDI networks with the banking system for EFT.

5493.33 **Financing Cycle:** A recurring set of business activities and related data processing operations associated with obtaining the necessary funds to run the operations, repay creditors, and distribute profits to investors.

5493.34 **Firewall:** A combination of security algorithms and router communications protocols that prevent outsiders from tapping into corporate databases and e-mail systems.

5493.35 **Floppy Disk:** A portable, magnetic-coated disk that can be written on and read from using a basic form of storage media.

5493.36 **Flowchart:** A graphical description of an information system in a clear, concise, and logical manner. Flowcharts use a standard set of input/output, processing, storage, and data flow symbols to pictorially describe the system.

5493.37 **Flowcharting Symbols:** A set of objects that are used in flowcharts to show how and where data moves. Each symbol has a special meaning that is easily conveyed by its shape.

5493.38 **Flowcharting Template**: A piece of hard, flexible plastic on which the shapes of flowcharting symbols have been die cut.

5493.39 **Foreign Key:** An attribute appearing in one table that is itself the primary key of another table.

5493.40 **Format:** Preparing a disk for reading and writing information. Disks must be formatted before they can be used.

5493.41 **General Authorization:** When regular employees are authorized to handle routine transactions without special approval.

5493.42 **General Controls:** Controls that relate to all or many computerized accounting activities, such as those relating to the plan of organization of data processing activities and the separation of incompatible functions. Contrast with application controls.

5493.43 **General Journal:** The general journal is used to record infrequent or nonroutine transactions, such as loan payments and end-of-period adjusting and closing entries.

5493.44 **General Ledger and Reporting System:** The information-processing operations involved in updating the general ledger and preparing reports that summarize the results of the organization's activities.

5493.45 **General Ledger:** Contains summary-level data for every asset, liability, equity, revenue, and expense account of the organization.

5493.46   **Generalized Audit Software (GAS):** A software package that performs audit tests on the data files of a company.

5493.47   **Gigabyte:** One billion bytes or, more precisely, 1,024 MB when referring to computer storage.

5493.48   **Grandfather-Father-Son Concept:** A method for maintaining backup copies of files on magnetic tape or disk. The three most current copies of the data are retained, with the son being the most recent.

5493.49   **Graphical User Interface (GUI):** Operating environment where the user selects commands, starts programs, or lists files by pointing to pictorial representations (icons) with a mouse. A Macintosh computer, Microsoft's Windows, and IBM's OS/2 are all GUI environments.

5493.50   **Group Decision Support Software (GDSS):** Software that encourages and allows everyone in a group to participate in decision making. A GDSS brings a group of people together to share information, exchange ideas, explore differing points of views, examine proposed solutions, arrive at a consensus, or vote on a course of action.

5493.51   **Groupware:** Software that combines the power of computer networks with the immediacy and personal touch of the face-to-face brainstorming session. Groupware lets users hold computer conferences, decide when to hold a meeting, make a calendar for a department, collectively brainstorm on creative endeavors, manage projects, and design products.

5493.52   **Hacker:** A person who gains unauthorized access to a computer network.

5493.53   **Hacking:** Unauthorized access and use of computer systems, usually by means of a personal computer and telecommunications networks.

5493.54   **Hard Copy:** A printed report produced from a master file or transaction file dump. It is used primarily for "auditing around the computer."

5493.55   **Hard Disk:** A magnetic storage disk made of rigid material and enclosed in a sealed disk unit to reduce the chances of the magnetic medium being damaged by foreign particles. A hard disk has a much faster access time and greater storage capacity than a floppy disk.

5493.56   **Hardening:** Modifying the configuration of hosts and application software and deleting, or turning off, unused and unnecessary programs that represent potential security threats.

5493.57   **Hardware:** Physical EDP equipment (such as printers, tape drives, CPUs, etc.) that inputs, transmits, processes, stores, and outputs data. Contrast with software.

5493.58   **Hardware Controls:** Controls built into the computer by the manufacturer to detect computer failure.

5493.59   **Hash Total:** A total generated from values for a field that would not usually be totaled, such as customer account numbers. It is usually generated manually from source documents prior to input and compared with machine-generated totals at each subsequent processing step. Any discrepancy may indicate a loss of records or errors in data transcription or processing.

5493.60   **Hashing:** Taking plaintext of any length and transforming it into a short code called a hash. Hashing differs from encryption in that encryption always produces encrypted text similar in length to the original text, but hashing always produces a hash that is of a fixed short length, regardless of the length of the original plaintext. In addition, encryption is reversible, but hashing is not.

5493.61 **Header Label:** Type of internal label that appears at the beginning of each file and contains the file name, expiration date, and other file identification information.

5493.62 **Help Desk:** An in-house group of analysts and technicians that answers employees' questions with the purpose of encouraging, supporting, coordinating, and controlling end-user activity.

5493.63 **Hierarchical Program Design:** The process of designing a program from the top level down to the detailed level.

5493.64 **Home Page:** A "storefront" or site on the Internet that is set up by individuals and firms to provide useful and interesting information about the individual or firm.

5493.65 **Host:** A device, such as a PC or server, where programs reside.

5493.66 **Hot Site:** Completely operational data processing facility configured to meet the user's requirements that can be made available to a disaster-stricken organization on short notice.

5493.67 **Human Resources (Payroll) Cycle:** The recurring set of business activities and related data processing operations associated with effectively managing the employee workforce.

5493.68 **Hyperlink:** A text phrase or a graphic that conceals the address of a website. A hyperlink allows a user to go directly to another location within the same website or to another website.

5493.69 **Hypertext Markup Language (HTML):** A programming language that defines the format and display of text and graphics when viewing a website.

5493.70 **Implementation:** The process of installing a computer. It includes selecting and installing the equipment, training personnel, establishing operating policies, and getting the software onto the system and functioning properly.

5493.71 **Implementation and Conversion:** The capstone phase in the SDLC where the elements and activities of the system come together. Implementation includes installing and testing new hardware and software, hiring and training employees, and testing new processing procedures. Standards and controls must be established and documented. The final step, conversion, consists of dismantling the old system and converting it into the new one.

5493.72 **Implementation Plan:** A written plan that outlines how the new system will be implemented. The plan includes a timetable for completion, who is responsible for each activity, cost estimates, and task milestones.

5493.73 **Index File:** A master file of record identifiers and corresponding storage locations.

5493.74 **Index Sequential Access Method (ISAM):** A file organization and access approach in which records are stored in sequential order by their primary key on a direct access storage device. An index file is created, which allows the file to be accessed and updated randomly.

5493.75 **Information:** Data that has been processed and organized into output that is meaningful to the person who receives it. Information can be mandatory, essential, or discretionary.

5493.76 **Information Overload:** The state in which additional information cannot be used efficiently and has no marginal value.

5493.77 **Information Processing:** The process of turning data into information. This process has four stages: data input, data processing, data storage, and information output.

5493.78   **Information System:** An organized way of collecting, processing, managing, and reporting information so that an organization can achieve its objectives and goals. Formal information systems have an explicit responsibility to produce information. In contrast, an informal information system is one that arises out of a need that is not satisfied by a formal channel. It operates without a formal assignment of responsibility.

5493.79   **Information Systems Audit:** Reviews the general and application controls of an AIS to assess its compliance with internal control policies and procedures and its effectiveness in safeguarding assets.

5493.80   **Initial Investigation:** A preliminary investigation to determine if a proposed new system is both needed and possible.

5493.81   **Input:** Data entered into the computer system either from an external storage device or from the keyboard of the computer.

5493.82   **Input Controls:** Ensure that only accurate, valid, and authorized data is entered into the system.

5493.83   **Input Controls Matrix:** A matrix that shows the control procedures applied to each field of an input record.

5493.84   **Input Device:** Hardware used to enter data into the computer system.

5493.85   **Input Validation Routines:** Computer programs or routines designed to check the validity or accuracy of input data.

5493.86   **Input/Output Bound:** Describes a system that can process data faster than it can receive input and send output. Consequently the processor has to wait on the I/O devices.

5493.87   **Inquiry Processing:** Processing user information queries by searching master files for the desired information and then organizing the information into an appropriate response.

5493.88   **Integrated Circuit:** Also known as a chip, this is a small electronic device that houses thousands of millions of individual circuits.

5493.89   **Integrated Services Digital Network (ISDN):** An extensive digital network with built-in intelligence to permit all types of data (voice, data, images, facsimile, video, etc.) to be sent over the same line.

5493.90   **Integrated System Processing:** A data processing system that coordinates a number of previously unconnected processes (i.e., applications) to improve processing efficiency by reducing or eliminating redundant data entry. In integrated data processing, a single input record describing a transaction initiates the updating of all files associated with the transaction.

5493.91   **Integrated Test Facility:** A testing technique in which a dummy company or division is introduced into the company's computer system. Test transactions may then be conducted on these fictitious master records without affecting the real master records. These test transactions may be processed along with the real transactions, and the employees of the computer facility need not be aware that testing is being done.

5493.92   **Integration:** The combining of subsystems.

5493.93   **Integrity:** Protecting data from unauthorized tampering.

5493.94   **Interface:** The common boundary between two pieces of hardware or between two computer systems. It is the point at which the two systems communicate with each other.

5493.95   **Interface Devices:** Devices used by computer systems to communicate with each other. Examples include modems, hubs, and network interface cards.

5493.96   **Internal Control:** Controls within a business organization that ensure information is processed correctly.

5493.97   **Internal Control Flowchart:** A flowchart used to analyze the adequacy of control procedures in a system. It can reveal weaknesses or inefficiencies in a system, such as inadequate communication flows; unnecessary complexity in document flows; or procedures responsible for causing wasteful delays.

5493.98   **Internal Control Structure:** The plan of organization and all the coordinate methods and measures adopted within a business to safeguard its assets, check the accuracy and reliability of its accounting data, promote operational efficiency, and encourage adherence to prescribed managerial policies.

5494   Internal Labels to Patch Management

5494.01   **Internal Labels:** Labels written in machine-readable form on a magnetic storage medium (e.g., tape or disk) that identify the data contained on the storage medium. Internal labels include volume, header, and trailer labels.

5494.02   **Internal Modem:** A modem that resides on an expansion board within the computer.

5494.03   **Internal-Level Schema:** A low-level view of the entire database describing how the data are actually stored and accessed. It includes information about pointers, indexes, record lengths, and so forth. Contrast with external-level schemas and conceptual-level schemas.

5494.04   **Internet:** An international network of independently owned computers that operates as a giant, seamless computing network. No one owns it, and no single organization controls its use. Data is not centrally stored but is stored on computers called web servers.

5494.05   **Internet Misinformation:** False or misleading information spread using the Internet.

5494.06   **Internet Protocol (IP):** The protocol that specifies the structure of IP packets and how to route them to the proper destination.

5494.07   **Internet Service Providers (ISPs):** Companies that provide connections to the Internet for individuals and other companies. Major ISPs include MCI, GTE, and Sprint.

5494.08   **Internet Terrorism:** Crackers (hackers intending to cause harm) using the Internet to disrupt electronic commerce and destroy company and individual communications.

5494.09   **Interrupt:** An event or signal that stops data processing. Interrupts are typically used in multiprogramming or real-time processing. An interrupt is usually caused by a signal from an external source.

5494.10   **Intranet:** An internal network that can connect to the main Internet and be navigated with simple browser software. It is usually closed off from the general public.

5494.11 **Intrusion Prevention System (IPS):** A program that identifies and drops packets that are part of an attack. An IPS examines the data in the body of an IP packet and therefore is more effective than routers and firewalls that merely look at data in an IP header. An ISP is slow, as it takes more time to examine the body of an IP packet than an IP packet header. It is also prone to false alarms, which result in rejecting legitimate traffic.

5494.12 **IP Packet:** Data to be sent over a network is divided into packets, and transmitted, and the device receiving the packets reassembles the packets to recreate the original message or data. Every packet consists of two parts. The header contains the packet's origin and destination addresses, as well as information about the type of data contained in the body of the packet. The body contains the data.

5494.13 **Job Control Language:** A programming language devised to prepare the operating system for an application to be processed.

5494.14 **Just-In-Time (JIT) Inventory System:** A system that minimizes or virtually eliminates manufacturing inventories by scheduling inventory deliveries at the precise times and locations needed. Instead of making infrequent bulk deliveries to a central receiving and storage facility, suppliers deliver materials in small lots at frequent intervals to the specific locations that require them.

5494.15 **Just-In-Time Manufacturing:** Manufacturing systems with short planning horizons whose goal is to minimize or eliminate inventories of raw materials, work in process, and finished goods. It is often referred to as pull manufacturing because goods are produced in response to customer demand. Theoretically, JIT manufacturing systems produce only in response to customer orders.

5494.16 **Key:** A unique identification code assigned to each data record within a system.

5494.17 **Key Verification:** Method used to check the accuracy of data entry by having two people enter the same data using a key-operated device. The computer then compares the two sets of keystrokes to determine if the data was entered correctly.

5494.18 **Key-To-Disk Encoder:** Several keying stations are linked to a minicomputer that has an attached disk memory. Data may be entered simultaneously from each of the key stations and pooled on the disk file.

5494.19 **Key-To-Tape Encoder:** A device for keying in data and recording the data on magnetic tape.

5494.20 **LAN Interface:** The hardware device that interfaces between the local area network (LAN) cable and the hardware devices (computers, printers, etc.) connected to the LAN.

5494.21 **Laptop:** A small, portable computer that can be powered by a rechargeable battery pack as well as by using a regular electrical outlet.

5494.22 **Legal Feasibility:** The dimension of feasibility that determines if there will be any conflicts between the system under consideration and the organization's ability to discharge its legal obligations.

5494.23 **Library:** A collection of files, records, and programs. Program documentation is usually also contained in and secured by the library function.

5494.24 **Limit Check:** An edit check to ensure that a numerical amount in a record does not exceed some predetermined limit.

5494.25 **Line Count:** Total number of lines entered during a data processing session.

5494.26 **Local Area Network (LAN):** A network that links microcomputers, disk drives, word processors, printers, and other equipment located within a limited geographical area, such as one building.

5494.27 **Lockbox:** A postal address to which customers send their remittances. This post office box is maintained by the participating bank, which picks up the checks several times each day and deposits them to the company's account. The bank then sends the remittance advices, an electronic list of all remittances, and photocopies of all checks to the company.

5494.28 **Log:** A record of the operations of data processing equipment that lists each job run, the time it required, operator actions, and other pertinent data.

5494.29 **Log Analysis:** Examining the audit trail created by system logs that record who accesses the system and the specific actions each user performs, to monitor the system security.

5494.30 **Logic Errors:** Errors that occur when the instructions given to the computer do not accomplish the desired objective. Contrast with syntax errors.

5494.31 **Logic Time Bomb:** A program that lies idle until some specified circumstance or a particular time triggers it. Once triggered, the bomb sabotages the system by destroying programs or data.

5494.32 **Logical Access:** The ability to use computer equipment to access company data.

5494.33 **Logical Models:** Descriptions of a system that focus on the essential activities and flow of information in the system, irrespective of how the flow is actually accomplished.

5494.34 **Logical View:** The manner in which users conceptually organize, view, and understand the relationships among data items. Contrast with physical view.

5494.35 **Looping:** A sequence of program instructions that can be executed repetitively. Each repetition is called a cycle.

5494.36 **Machine Language:** Programs or data that have been converted into binary code. Machine language is the language that is used directly by the computer. Contrast with source program.

5494.37 **Machine-Readable:** Data that is in a form that can be read by a data processing machine. Data on magnetic tape or disk can be read directly by the computer, while data on paper using specific formats (input sheets) can be read by an optical character reader.

5494.38 **Macro:** A series of keystrokes or commands that can be given a name, stored, and activated each time the keystrokes must be repeated.

5494.39 **Magnetic Disks:** Magnetic storage media consisting of one or more flat round disks with a magnetic surface on which data can be written.

5494.40 **Magnetic Ink Character Recognition (MICR):** The recognition of characters printed by a machine that uses special magnetic ink.

5494.41 **Magnetic Tape:** A secondary storage medium that is about 1/2 inch in width and that has a magnetic surface on which data can be stored. The most popular types are seven-track and nine-track tapes.

5494.42 **Main Memory:** The internal memory directly controlled by the CPU, which usually consists of the ROM and RAM of the computer.

5494.43 **Mainframe Computers:** Large digital computers, typically with a separate stand-alone CPU. They are larger than minicomputers.

5494.44 **Management Control:** Activities by management designed to motivate, encourage, and assist officers and employees to achieve corporate goals and objectives as effectively and efficiently as possible and to observe corporate policies.

5494.45 **Management Information System:** The set of human and capital resources in an organization that are dedicated to collecting and processing data so that all levels of management have the information they need to plan and control the activities of the organization.

5494.46 **Manual Information System:** Information system in which most of the data processing load is completed by people without the use of computers.

5494.47 **Manufacturing Resource Planning (MRP-II):** A comprehensive, computerized planning and control system for manufacturing operations. It is an enhancement of materials requirements planning that incorporates capacity planning for factory work centers and scheduling of production operations.

5494.48 **Mapping Programs:** Programs activated during regular processing that provide information as to which portions of the application program were not executed.

5494.49 **Masquerading:** When a perpetrator gains access to a system by pretending to be an authorized user. This approach requires that the perpetrator know the legitimate user's identification numbers and passwords.

5494.50 **Master File:** A permanent file of records that reflects the current status of relevant business items such as inventory and accounts receivable. The master file is updated with the latest transactions from the current transaction file.

5494.51 **Master Plan:** A document specifying the overall information system plan of an organization.

5494.52 **Memory:** Memory includes disk, core, and drum storage devices. Memory is a device into which a unit of information can be copied and stored for future reference.

5494.53 **Message:** (1) The data transmitted over a data communication system. (2) The instructions that are given to an object in object-oriented languages.

5494.54 **MHz:** Abbreviation for megahertz, or million cycles per second. The speed of microprocessors is measured in megahertz.

5494.55 **Microprocessor:** The silicon chip containing the central processing unit or CPU. Executes the instructions that perform arithmetical and logic operations on data held in memory.

5494.56 **Modem:** Modulator/demodulator, a communications device that converts the computer's digital signals into analog signals that can be sent over phone lines. The modem can be internal (mounted on a board within the computer) or external (a freestanding unit).

5494.57 **Modular Conversion:** An approach for converting from an old system to a new system in which parts of the old system are gradually replaced by the new until the old system has been entirely replaced by the new.

5494.58 **Monitor:** A video display unit or CRT.

5494.59 **Motherboard:** The main circuit board of the computer that contains the microprocessor, memory, and disk drives, among other items.

5494.60 **Multimedia:** Computer-based applications that combine text, 3-D graphics, full-screen video, sound, and animation.

5494.61 **Multiprogramming:** A technique used to enable an operating system to handle two or more independent programs by overlapping their execution.

5494.62 **Multitasking:** The ability of the computer to execute more than one program at a time.

5494.63 **Mutual Authentication Scheme:** A routing verification procedure that requires both computers to exchange their passwords before communication takes place.

5494.64 **Narrative Documentation:** Written, step-by-step explanation of the system components and how the components interact.

5494.65 **Narrowband Lines:** Phone lines designed to accept data transmissions of up to 300 bps. This type of line is not suitable for transmitting audible or voice-like signals.

5494.66 **Network:** Two or more computers linked together for data and resource sharing. These include local area networks (LANs), wide area networks (WANs), virtual area networks (VANs), intranet, extranet, central/decentralized processing, distributed daily processing, client/server computing, and end-user computing.

5494.67 **Network Administrator:** One who installs, manages, and supports a LAN. The network administrator also controls access to the system and maintains the shared software and data.

5494.68 **Network Interface Card (NIC):** The device needed to connect a computer or peripheral to a data communications network.

5494.69 **Neural Networks:** Computing systems that imitate the brain's learning process by using a network of interconnected processors that perform multiple operations simultaneously and interact dynamically. Neural networks recognize and understand voice, face, and word patterns much more successfully than do regular computers and humans.

5494.70 **Nonoperational (or Throwaway) Prototypes:** Prototypes that are discarded, but the system requirements identified from the prototypes are used to develop a new system.

5494.71 **Normalization:** The process of following the guidelines for properly designing a relational database that is free from delete, insert, and update anomalies.

5494.72 **Object (Machine) Language:** Synonymous with machine language. A COBOL source program that has been compiled into machine language is referred to as an object deck.

5494.73 **Off-Line Devices:** Devices that are not connected to or controlled by the main CPU. Off-line devices are used to prepare data for entry into the computer system (e.g., key-to-tape encoder, keypunch/verification equipment). Contrast with on-line devices.

5494.74 **On-Line Analytical Processing (OLAP):** Tools that provide access to information stored in a data warehouse by using queries to investigate hypothesized relationships.

5494.75 **On-Line Batch Processing:** Processing in which the computer captures the data electronically and stores it so that it can be processed later.

5494.76 **On-Line Devices:** Hardware devices that are connected directly to the CPU by cable or telephone line (e.g., CRT terminal, disk drive).

5494.77 **On-Line Processing:** Processing individual transactions as they occur and from their point of origin rather than accumulating them to be processed in batches. Online processing requires the use of online data entry terminals and direct access file storage media so that each master record can be accessed directly.

5494.78 **On-Line, Real-Time (OLRT):** An operation in which data input is obtained directly from measuring devices, and the computer results are thereby obtained during the processing of the event. For example, in airline reservation control, a real-time system provides an instantaneous picture of seat availability, cancellations, sales, and flight data.

5494.79 **Operating Documentation:** All information required by a computer operator to run a program, including the equipment configuration used, variable data to be entered on the computer console, and descriptions of conditions leading to program halts and related corrective actions.

5494.80 **Operating System:** A software program that controls the overall operation of a computer system. Its functions include controlling the execution of computer programs, scheduling, debugging, assigning storage areas, managing data, and controlling input and output.

5494.81 **Operational Control:** Decisions that are concerned with the efficient and effective performance of specific tasks in an organization.

5494.82 **Operational Document:** A document that is generated as an output of transaction processing activities. Examples include purchase orders, customer statements, and employee paychecks. Contrast with source document.

5494.83 **Operational Feasibility:** The dimension of feasibility concerned with whether a proposed system will be used by the people in an organization. It also is concerned with how useful the system will be within the operating environment of the organization.

5494.84 **Operational Prototypes:** Prototypes that are further developed into fully functional systems.

5494.85 **Operations and Maintenance:** The last phase of the system development life cycle where follow-up studies are conducted to detect and correct design deficiencies. Minor modifications will be made as problems arise in the new system.

5494.86 **Optical Character Recognition (OCR):** The use of light-sensitive hardware devices to convert characters readable by humans into computer input. Since OCR readers can read only certain items, a special machine-readable font must be used.

5494.87 **Optical Disk:** A mass storage medium that is capable of storing billions of bits. Lasers are used to write to and read from an optical disk.

5494.88 **Optical Scanner:** A device that reads text or illustrations on paper and digitizes the images to create a graphics file.

5494.89 **Output:** The information produced by a system. Output is typically produced for the use of a particular individual or group of users.

5494.90 **Output Controls:** Controls that regulate system output.

5494.91 **Outsourcing:** Hiring an outside company to handle all or part of the data processing activities.

5494.92   **Parallel Conversion:** A systems conversion approach in which the new and old systems are run simultaneously until the organization is assured that the new system is functioning correctly.

5494.93   **Parallel Port:** A connector transmits several bits of data across eight parallel lines simultaneously.

5494.94   **Parallel Simulation:** An approach auditors use to detect unauthorized program changes and data processing accuracy. The auditor writes his or her own version of a program and then reprocesses data. The output of the auditor's program and the client's program are compared to verify that they are the same.

5494.95   **Parity Bit:** An extra bit added to a byte, character, or word. The parity bit is magnetized as needed to ensure that there is always an odd (or even) number of magnetized bits. The computer uses the odd (or even) parity scheme to check the accuracy of each item of data.

5494.96   **Parity Checking:** As a computer reads or receives a set of characters, it sums the number of 1-bits in each character to verify that it is an even number. If not, the corresponding character must contain an error.

5494.97   **Password Cracking:** Using illicit means to steal a file containing passwords and then using them.

5494.98   **Password:** A series of letters, numbers, or both that must be entered to access and use system resources. Password use helps prevent unauthorized tampering with hardware, software, and the organization's data.

5494.99   **Patch Management:** Process of regularly applying patches to software to fix known system vulnerabilities and installing the latest software updates for security programs, operating systems, and other application programs. Organizations may have to apply hundreds of patches to thousands of computers as multiple patches are released each year for each software program used by an organization.

5495   Penetration Test to Service Center (Bureau)

5495.01   **Penetration Test:** An authorized attempt to break into an information system.

5495.02   **Peripherals:** The hardware devices (such as those used for input, output, processing, and data communications) that are connected to the CPU.

5495.03   **Personal Digital Assistant (PDA):** A handheld computer that has had a significant impact on personal productivity.

5495.04   **Personal Identification Number (PIN):** A confidential code that allows an individual to gain access to a system and the data or resources stored in that system.

5495.05   **Phreaker:** A hacker who attacks phone systems.

5495.06   **Physical Access:** Ability to physically use computer equipment.

5495.07   **Physical Design:** A phase of the system development life cycle where the broad, user-oriented requirements of the conceptual design are implemented by creating a detailed set of specifications that are used to code and test the computer programs.

5495.08 **Physical Model:** The description of physical aspects of a database (e.g., field and file sizes, storage and access methods, and security procedures).

5495.09 **Physical Possession Identification:** A method of identifying people by an item they physically possess, such as an ID card.

5495.10 **Physical Systems Design:** The phase of the systems development life cycle in which the designer specifies the hardware, software, and procedures for delivering the conceptual systems design.

5495.11 **Physical Systems Design Report:** A report prepared at the end of the physical design phase that describes the system. Management uses this report to decide whether or not to proceed to the implementation phase.

5495.12 **Physical View:** The way data is physically arranged and stored on disks, tapes, and other storage media. EDP personnel use this view to make efficient use of storage and processing resources. Contrast with logical view.

5495.13 **Piggybacking:** When a perpetrator latches on to a legitimate user who is logging in to a system. The legitimate user unknowingly carries the perpetrator with him as he is allowed into the system.

5495.14 **Pilot Conversion:** The implementation of a system in just one part of the organization, such as a branch location. This approach localizes conversion problems and allows training in a live environment. Disadvantages are the long conversion times and the need to interface the old system with the new system.

5495.15 **Pixel:** A single point in a graphic image. The computer monitor displays images by dividing the screen into millions of pixels, which are so close together that they appear to the human eye to be a solid image.

5495.16 **Point-Of-Sale (POS) Recorders:** Electronic devices that function as both a terminal and a cash register. They are used commonly in retail stores to record sales information at the time of the sale and to perform other data processing functions.

5495.17 **Policy and Procedures Manual:** A management tool for assigning authority and responsibility. It details management's policy for handling specific transactions.

5495.18 **Postimplementation Review:** Review made after a new system has been operating for a brief period. The purpose is to ensure that the new system is meeting its planned objectives, to identify the adequacy of system standards, and to review system controls.

5495.19 **Postimplementation Review Report:** A report that analyzes a newly delivered system to determine if the system achieved its intended purpose and was completed within budget.

5495.20 **Preformatting:** An on-line data entry control in which the computer displays a form on the screen and the user fills in the blanks on the form as needed.

5495.21 **Preventive Controls:** A control system that places restrictions on and requires documentation of employee activities so as to reduce the occurrence of errors and deviations. Because preventive controls operate from within the process being controlled, they are perhaps the type of control most consistent with the original meaning of the term "internal control."

5495.22 **Preventive Maintenance:** A program of regularly examining the hardware components of a computer and replacing any that are found to be weak.

5495.23 **Primary Key:** A unique identification code assigned to each record within a system. The primary key is the key used most frequently to distinguish, order, and reference records.

5495.24 **Printed Circuit:** A plate on which computer chips and other devices are mounted.

5495.25 **Private Key System:** An encryption system in which both the sender and the receiver have access to the key but do not allow others access to the same key.

5495.26 **Process:** A set of actions, automated or manual, that transforms data into other data or information.

5495.27 **Processing Controls:** Controls that ensure that all transactions are processed accurately and completely and that all files and records are properly updated.

5495.28 **Processing of Test Transactions:** Running hypothetical transactions through a new system to test for processing errors.

5495.29 **Production Cycle:** The recurring set of business activities and related data processing operations associated with the manufacture of products.

5495.30 **Program:** A set of instructions that can be executed by a computer.

5495.31 **Program Evaluation and Review Technique (PERT):** A commonly used technique for planning, coordinating, controlling, and scheduling complex projects such as systems implementation.

5495.32 **Program Flowchart:** A graphical description of the operations performed by a computer program. An approved program flowchart serves as the blueprint for coding a computer program.

5495.33 **Program Maintenance:** The revision of a computer program to meet new program instructions, satisfy system demands such as the need for a new report, correct an error, or make changes in file content.

5495.34 **Program Tracing:** A technique used to obtain detailed knowledge of the logic of an application program, as well as to test the program's compliance with its control specifications.

5495.35 **Programmer:** A person who develops the program flowchart, writes the program, and debugs the program.

5495.36 **Project Development Plan:** A proposal to develop a particular computer system application. It contains an analysis of the requirements and expectations of the proposed application.

5495.37 **Project Development Team:** A group of people consisting of specialists, management, and users that develop a project's plan and direct the steps of the systems development life cycle. The team monitors costs, progress, and employees, and gives status reports to top management and to the steering committee.

5495.38 **Project Milestones:** Significant points in a development effort at which a formal review of progress is made.

5495.39 **Prompting:** An on-line data entry control that uses the computer to control the data entry process. The system displays a request to the user for each required item of input data and then waits for an acceptable response before requesting the next required item.

5495.40 **Proposal to Conduct Systems Analysis:** A document calling for the analysis of either an existing or a proposed system. This document is prepared by a user or department and requests the information systems function to analyze the feasibility of developing a system to perform a specific function.

5495.41 **Protocol:** The set of rules governing the exchange of data between two systems or components of a system.

5495.42 **Prototyping:** An approach to systems design in which a simplified working model, or prototype, of an information system is developed. The users experiment with the prototype to determine what they like and do not like about the system. The developers make modifications until the users are satisfied with the system.

5495.43 **Public Key Infrastructure (PKI):** An approach to encryption that uses two keys: a public key that is publicly available and a private key that is kept secret and known only by the owner of that pair of keys. With PKI, either key (the public or private) can be used to encode a message, but only the other key in that public-private pair can be used to decode that message.

5495.44 **Public Key System:** An encryption system that uses two separate keys: a public key that is available to everyone and a private key known only to the user.

5495.45 **Query:** A request for specific information from a computer. Queries are often used with a database management system to extract data from the database.

5495.46 **Query-By-Example (QBE) Languages:** Graphical query languages for retrieving information from a relational database.

5495.47 **Query Languages:** Languages used to process data files and to obtain quick responses to questions about those files.

5495.48 **Random Access Memory (RAM):** A temporary storage location for computer instructions and data. RAM may have data both written to it and read from it.

5495.49 **Range Check:** An edit check designed to verify that a data item falls within a certain predetermined range of acceptable values.

5495.50 **Read-Only Memory (ROM):** Internal CPU memory that can be read but usually may not be changed.

5495.51 **Real-Time Notification:** A variation of the embedded audit module in which the auditor is notified of each transaction as it occurs by means of a message printed on the auditor's terminal.

5495.52 **Real-Time System:** A system that is able to respond to an inquiry or provide data fast enough to make the information meaningful to the user. Real-time systems are usually designed for very fast response.

5495.53 **Reasonableness Test:** An edit check of the logical correctness of relationships among the values of data items on an input record and the corresponding file record. For example, a journal entry that debits inventory and credits wages payable is not reasonable.

5495.54 **Record:** A set of logically related data items that describes specific attributes of an entity, such as all payroll data relating to a single employee.

5495.55 **Record Count:** A total of the number of input documents to a process or the number of records processed in a run.

5495.56 **Record Layout:** A document that illustrates the arrangement of items of data in input, output, and file records.

5495.57 **Recovery Procedures:** A set of procedures that is followed if the computer quits in the middle of processing a batch of data. The procedures allow the user to recover from hardware or software failures.

5495.58 **Redundant Data Check:** An edit check that requires the inclusion of two identifiers in each input record (e.g., the customer's account number and the first five letters of the customer's name). If these input values do not match those on the record, the record will not be updated.

5495.59 **Reengineering:** The thorough analysis and complete redesign of all business processes and information systems to achieve dramatic performance improvements. Reengineering seeks to reduce a company to its essential business processes.

5495.60 **Referential Integrity Rule:** A constraint in relational database design requiring that any non-null value of a foreign key must correspond to a primary key in the referenced table. This constraint ensures consistency in the database.

5495.61 **Relational Data Model:** A database model in which all data elements are logically viewed as being stored in the form of two-dimensional tables called "relations." These tables are, in effect, flat files where each row represents a unique entity or record. Each column represents a field where the record's attributes are stored. The tables serve as the building blocks from which data relationships can be created.

5495.62 **Relations:** The tables used to store data in a relational database.

5495.63 **Remote Batch Processing:** Accumulating transaction records in batches at some remote location and then transmitting them electronically to a central location for processing.

5495.64 **Report:** System output organized in a meaningful fashion. Used by employees to control operational activities, by managers to make decisions, and by investors and creditors to gather information about a company's business activities. Prepared for both internal and external use.

5495.65 **Report Writers:** Software that lets a user specify the data elements to be printed. The report writer searches the database, extracts the desired items, and prints them out in the user-specified format.

5495.66 **Reprocessing:** An approach auditors use to detect unauthorized program changes. The auditor verifies the integrity of an application program and then saves it for future use. At subsequent intervals, and on a surprise basis, the auditor uses the previously verified version of the program to reprocess data that has been processed by the version used by the company. The output of the two runs is compared and discrepancies are investigated.

5495.67 **Request For Proposal (RFP):** A request by an organization or department for vendors to bid on hardware, software, or services specified by the organization or department.

5495.68 **Request For Systems Development:** A written request for a new or improved system. The request describes the current system's problems, why the change is needed, and the proposed system's goals and objectives as well as its anticipated benefits and costs.

5495.69   **Requirements Costing:** A system evaluation method in which a list is made of all required features of the desired system. If a proposed system does not have a desired feature, the cost of developing or purchasing that feature is added to the basic cost of the system. This method allows different systems to be evaluated based on the costs of providing the required features.

5495.70   **Response Time:** The amount of time that elapses between making a query and receiving a response.

5495.71   **Revenue Cycle:** The recurring set of business activities and related information-processing operations associated with providing goods and services to customers and collecting cash in payment for those sales.

5495.72   **Ring Network:** A configuration in which the data communications channels form a loop or circular pattern when the local processors are linked together. Contrast with star network.

5495.73   **Risk:** The likelihood that a threat or hazard will actually come to pass.

5495.74   **Rollback:** A process whereby a log of all pre-update values is prepared for each record that is updated within a particular interval. If there is a system failure, the records can be restored to the pre-update values and the processing started over.

5495.75   **ROM (Read Only Memory):** Computer memory on which data has been prerecorded.

5495.76   **Round-Down Technique:** A fraud technique used in financial institutions that pay interest. The programmer instructs the computer to round down all interest calculations to two decimal places. The fraction of a cent that was rounded down on each calculation is put into the programmer's own account.

5495.77   **Routers:** Devices that control the flow of information sent over the Internet or a local area network. A router reads the destination address field in an IP packet header to determine where to send it.

5495.78   **Routing Verification Procedures:** Controls to ensure that messages are not routed to the wrong system address. Examples are header labels, mutual authentication schemes, and dial-back.

5495.79   **Sabotage:** An intentional act where the intent is to destroy a system or some of its components.

5495.80   **Salami Technique:** A fraud technique in which tiny slices of money are stolen from many different accounts.

5495.81   **Sarbanes-Oxley Act (SOX):** A law passed in 2002 that requires public company management to include an internal control report in its annual report that states management is responsible for establishing and maintaining an adequate internal control structure and that they have assessed the effectiveness of the internal control system. The law also requires external auditors to evaluate management's assessment of their internal control structures and attest to its accuracy. SOX also requires The CEO and CFO to certify that financial statements accurately represent company activities.

5495.82   **Scanning Routines:** Software routines that search a program for the occurrence of a particular variable name or other combinations of characters.

5495.83   **Scavenging:** The unauthorized access to confidential information by searching corporate records. Scavenging methods range from searching trash cans for printouts or carbon copies of confidential information to scanning the contents of computer memory.

5495.84   **Scheduling Feasibility:** The dimension of feasibility that determines if the system being developed can be implemented in the time allotted.

5495.85   **Schema:** A description of the types of data elements that are in the database, the relationships among the data elements, and the structure or overall logical model used to organize and describe the data.

5495.86   **Search Engine:** A tool for navigating the World Wide Web that allows a user to search for a website by keywords.

5495.87   **Secondary Key:** A field that can be used to identify records in a file. Unlike the primary key, it does not provide a unique identification.

5495.88   **Secondary Storage:** Storage media, such as magnetic disks or magnetic tape, on which data that is not currently needed by the computer can be stored. Also called auxiliary storage.

5495.89   **Security Measures and Controls:** Controls that are built into an information system to ensure that data is accurate and free from errors. Security measures also protect data from unauthorized access.

5495.90   **Segregation Of Duties:** The separation of assigned duties and responsibilities in such a way that no single employee can both perpetrate and conceal errors or irregularities.

5495.91   **Semiconductor:** A tiny silicon chip upon which a number of miniature circuits have been inscribed.

5495.92   **Sequence Check:** An edit check that determines if a batch of input data is in the proper numerical or alphabetical sequence.

5495.93   **Sequential Access:** An access method that requires data items to be accessed in the same order in which they were written.

5495.94   **Sequential File:** A way of storing numeric or alphabetical records according to a key. To access a sequential file record, the system starts at the beginning of the file and reads each record until the desired record is located.

5495.95   **Sequential File Processing:** Processing a master file sequentially from beginning to end. The master and transaction files are processed in the same predetermined order, such as alphabetically.

5495.96   **Serial Port:** A connector that transmits data one bit at a time over a single one-way wire.

5495.97   **Server:** High-capacity computer that contains the network software to handle communications, storage, and resource-sharing needs of other computers in the network. The server also contains the application software and data common to all users.

5495.98   **Service Center (Bureau):** Organizations specifically designed to process computer data for a fee. This service varies from the use of generalized software (programs) adapted to each customer's application to the processing of programs developed by either the customer or by the service bureau specifically for the customer.

5496   Sign Check to World Wide Web (WWW)

5496.01   **Sign Check:** An edit check that verifies that the data in a field has the appropriate arithmetic sign.

5496.02 **Single Key Encryption Systems:** Encryption systems that use the same key to encrypt and decrypt a message.

5496.03 **Smart Cards:** Plastic cards that contain a microprocessor, memory chips, and software; can store up to three pages of text. Used in Europe as a credit or ATM card.

5496.04 **Snapshot Technique:** An audit technique that records the content of both a transaction record and a related master file record before and after each processing step.

5496.05 **Social Engineering:** Fraudulently gaining information to access a system by fooling an employee.

5496.06 **Software:** A computer program that gives instructions to the CPU; also used to refer to programming languages and computer systems documentation.

5496.07 **Software Agents:** Computer programs that learn how to do often-performed, tedious, time-intensive tasks.

5496.08 **Software Piracy:** The unauthorized copying of software.

5496.09 **Source Code (or Source Program):** A computer program written in a source language such as BASIC, COBOL, or assembly language. The source program is translated into the object (machine language) program by a translation program such as a compiler or assembler.

5496.10 **Source Data Automation (SDA):** The collection of transaction data in machine-readable form at the time and place of origin. Examples of SDA devices are optical scanners and automated teller machines.

5496.11 **Source Documents:** Contain the initial record of a transaction that takes place. Examples of source documents, which are usually recorded on preprinted forms, include sales invoices, purchase orders, and employee time cards. Contrast with operational document.

5496.12 **Spamming:** E-mailing the same message to everyone on one or more Usenet newsgroups or LISTSERV lists.

5496.13 **Specific Authorization:** When an employee must get special approval before handling a transaction.

5496.14 **Spreadsheet:** A table of values, arranged in rows and columns, where some of the cells' values are the result of a calculation performed on other cells. Should the value in one of the cells change, the resulting values would also change.

5496.15 **Star Network:** A configuration in which there is a centralized real-time computer system to which all other computer systems are linked. Contrast with ring network.

5496.16 **Steering Committee:** An executive-level committee to plan and oversee the information systems function. The committee typically consists of management from the systems department, the controller, and other management affected by the information systems function.

5496.17 **Storage:** Placement of data in internal memory or on a medium such as magnetic disk or magnetic tape, from which they can later be retrieved.

5496.18 **Strategic Plan:** An organization's multiple-year plan that serves as a technological road map and lays out the projects the company must complete to achieve its long-range goals.

5496.19 **Structured Programming:** A modular approach to programming in which each module performs a specific function, stands alone, and is coordinated by a control module. Also referred to as "GOTO-less" programming because modular design makes GOTO statements unnecessary.

5496.20 **Structured Query Language (SQL):** The standard text-based query language provided by most, but not all, relational DBMSs. Powerful queries can be built using three basic keywords: SELECT, FROM, and WHERE.

5496.21 **Structured Walkthrough:** A formal review process in program design in which one or more programmers walk through the logic and code of another programmer to detect weaknesses and errors in program design.

5496.22 **Subdirectory:** A directory that is under another directory. Every directory except the root directory is a subdirectory.

5496.23 **Subschema:** (1) A subset of the schema that includes only those data items used in a particular application program or by a particular user. (2) The way the user defines the data and the data relationships.

5496.24 **Subsystems:** Smaller systems that are a part of the entire information system. Each subsystem performs a specific function that is important to and that supports the system of which it is a part.

5496.25 **Superzapping:** The use of a special system program to bypass regular system controls to perform unauthorized acts. A superzap utility was originally written to handle emergencies, such as restoring a system that had crashed.

5496.26 **Symbolic (Source) Language:** A language that is input into the compilation process.

5496.27 **Symmetric Encryption:** Using a single key to encrypt and decrypt a message. A symmetric key is simple, fast, and efficient but requires a way to securely exchange the key, requires a secret key for each different party with whom the company communicates, and there is no way to prove who created a document and therefore no way to create legally binding agreements.

5496.28 **Synchronous Transmission:** Data transmission in which start and stop bits are required only at the beginning and end of a block of characters. Contrast with asynchronous transmission.

5496.29 **Syntax Errors:** Errors that result from using the programming language improperly or from incorrectly typing the source program.

5496.30 **System Control Audit Review File (SCARF):** A concurrent audit technique that embeds audit modules into application software to continuously monitor all transaction activity and collect data on transactions having special audit significance.

5496.31 **System Flowchart:** A graphical description of the relationship among the input, processing, and output functions of an AIS. A system flowchart begins by identifying both the inputs that enter the system and their origins. The input is followed by the processing portion of the flowchart; that is, the steps performed on the data. The logic the computer uses to perform the processing task is shown on a program flowchart. The resulting new information is the output component, which can be stored for later use, displayed on a screen, or printed on paper. In many instances, the output from one process is an input to another.

5496.32   **System Performance Measurements:** Measurements used to properly evaluate and assess a system. Common measurements include throughput (output per unit of time), utilization (percentage of time the system is being productively used), and response time (how long it takes the system to respond).

5496.33   **System Review:** A step in internal control evaluation in which it is determined if the necessary control procedures have been prescribed.

5496.34   **System:** (1) An entity consisting of two or more components or subsystems that interact to achieve a goal. (2) The equipment and programs that comprise a complete computer installation. (3) The programs and related procedures that perform a single task on a computer.

5496.35   **Systems Analysis:** (1) A rigorous and systematic approach to decision making, characterized by a comprehensive definition of available alternatives and an exhaustive analysis of the merits of each alternative as a basis for choosing the best alternative. (2) Examination of the user information requirements within an organization to establish objectives and specifications for the design of an information system.

5496.36   **Systems Analysis Report:** Comprehensive report prepared at the end of the systems analysis and design phase that summarizes and documents the findings of analysis activities.

5496.37   **Systems Analysts:** The people who are responsible for developing the company's information system. The analyst's job generally involves designing computer applications and preparing specifications for computer programming.

5496.38   **Systems Approach:** Way of handling systems change by recognizing that every system must have an objective, a set of components, and a set of interrelationships among the components. The systems approach proceeds step by step, with a thorough exploration of all implications and alternatives at each step.

5496.39   **Systems Concept:** A systems analysis principle that states that alternative courses of action within a system must be evaluated from the standpoint of the system as a whole rather than from the standpoint of any single subsystem or set of subsystems.

5496.40   **Systems Design:** The process of preparing detailed specifications for the development of a new information system.

5496.41   **Systems Development Life Cycle (SDLC):** Five procedures and steps that a company goes through when it decides to design and implement a new system. The five steps are systems analysis, conceptual design, physical design, implementation and conversion, and operation and maintenance.

5496.42   **Systems Documentation:** A complete description of all aspects of each systems application, including narrative material, charts, and program listings.

5496.43   **Systems Implementation:** The task of delivering a completed system to an organization for use in day-to-day operations.

5496.44   **Systems Software:** Software that interfaces between the hardware and the application program. Systems software can be classified as operating systems, database management systems, utility programs, language translators, and communications software.

5496.45   **Systems Survey:** The systematic gathering of facts relating to the existing information system. A systems analyst generally carries out this task.

5496.46 **Systems Survey Report:** The culmination of the systems survey. It contains documentation such as memos, interview and observation notes, questionnaire data, file and record layouts and descriptions, input and output descriptions, and copies of documents, flowcharts, and data flow diagrams.

5496.47 **SysTrust:** An information systems assurance service introduced by the AICPA and the Canadian Institute of Chartered Accountants (CICA) that independently tests and verifies a system's reliability. SysTrust uses four principles to determine if a system is reliable: availability, security, maintainability, and integrity.

5496.48 **Tagging:** An audit procedure in which certain records are marked with a special code before processing. During processing, all data relating to the marked records is captured and saved so that the auditors can verify it later.

5496.49 **Tape Drive:** The device that controls the movement of the magnetic tape and that reads and writes on the tape.

5496.50 **Tape File Protection Ring:** A circular plastic ring that determines when a tape file can be written on. When the ring is inserted on a reel of magnetic tape, data can be written on the tape. If the ring is removed, the data on the tape cannot be overwritten with new information.

5496.51 **TCP/IP:** Two important protocols that govern the transmission of information over the Internet.

5496.52 **Technical Feasibility:** The dimension of feasibility concerned with whether a proposed system can be developed given the available technology.

5496.53 **Terminal:** An input/output device for entering or receiving data directly from the computer. Also referred to as cathode ray tube (CRT) or visual display terminal (VDT).

5496.54 **Test Data:** Data that has been specially developed to test the accuracy and completeness of a computer program. The results from the test data are compared with hand-calculated results to verify that the program operates properly.

5496.55 **Test Data Generator Program:** A program that takes the specifications describing the logic characteristics of the program to be tested and automatically generates a set of test data that can be used to check the logic of the program.

5496.56 **Threats:** Potential losses to an organization arising from hazards such as embezzlement, employee carelessness or theft, or poor management decisions.

5496.57 **Throughput:** (1) The total amount of useful work performed by a computer system during a given period of time. (2) A measure of production efficiency representing the number of "good" units produced in a given period of time.

5496.58 **Time Sharing:** A computing technique in which numerous devices can utilize a central computer concurrently for input, processing, and output functions.

5496.59 **Token Ring:** A LAN configuration that forms a closed loop. A token is passed around the ring to indicate that a device is free to send or receive a message.

5496.60 **Trailer Label:** Type of internal label that appears at the end of each file and serves as an indicator that the end of the file has been reached.

5496.61   **Transaction Cycles:** A group of related business activities (e.g., the set of business activities consisting of sales order entry, shipping, billing, and cash receipts constitutes the revenue cycle). The five major transaction cycles are revenue, expenditure, production, human resource management/payroll, and general ledger and reporting.

5496.62   **Transaction File:** A relatively temporary data file containing transaction data that is typically used to update a master file.

5496.63   **Transaction Log:** A detailed record of every transaction entered in a system through data entry.

5496.64   **Transaction Processing:** A process that begins with capturing transaction data and ends with an informational output.

5496.65   **Transcription Error:** An error occurring during data conversion from a manual to an automated environment in which one digit of a number is written incorrectly during the conversion. For example, a "4" in the tens position transcribed as a "9" ("140" transcribed as "190") would cause an error of 50 in the value of the number.

5496.66   **Transmission Control Protocol/Internet Protocol (TCP/IP):** The protocol that specifies the procedures for dividing data into packets and reassembling them. It creates what is called a packet-switching network. When a message is ready to be sent over the Internet, the TCP breaks it up into small packets. Each packet is then given a header, which contains the destination address, and the packets are then sent individually over the Internet. The IP uses the information in the packet header to guide the packets so that they arrive at the proper destination. Once there, the TCP reassembles the packets into the original message.

5496.67   **Transposition Error:** An error that results when the numbers in two adjacent columns are inadvertently exchanged (for example, 64 is written as 46).

5496.68   **Trap Door:** A set of computer instructions that allows a user to bypass the system's normal controls.

5496.69   **Trojan Horse:** A set of unauthorized computer instructions in an authorized and otherwise properly functioning program. It performs some illegal act at a preappointed time or under a predetermined set of conditions.

5496.70   **Tunneling:** An Internet security approach in which data is sent between firewalls in small encrypted segments called "packets."

5496.71   **Turnaround Document:** A document, readable by humans, that is prepared by the computer as output, sent outside the system, and then returned as input into the computer. An example is a utility bill.

5496.72   **Turnkey System:** A system that is delivered to customers is ready (theoretically) to be turned on. A turnkey system supplier buys hardware, writes application software that is tailored both to that equipment and to the specific needs of its customers, and then markets the entire system.

5496.73   **Uninterruptible Power System (UPS):** An alternative power supply device that protects against the loss of power and fluctuations in the power level.

5496.74   **Universal Product Code (UPC):** A machine-readable code that is read by optical scanners. The code consists of a series of bar codes and is printed on most products sold in grocery stores.

5496.75 **Universal Resource Locator (URL):** An address that is used to find a unique location on the World Wide Web.

5496.76 **UNIX:** A flexible and widely used operating system for 16-bit machines.

5496.77 **Updating:** Changing stored data to reflect more recent events (e.g., changing the accounts receivable balance because of a recent sale or collection).

5496.78 **Usenet Newsgroups:** Public electronic discussion groups in which anyone on the Internet can participate.

5496.79 **User:** All people who interact with the system. Users are those who record data, manage the system, and control the system's security. Those who use information from the system are end users.

5496.80 **User ID:** A knowledge identifier such as an employee number or account number that users enter to identify themselves when signing on to a system.

5496.81 **User Identification (ID) and Authentication System:** A system that requires users to identify themselves by entering a unique user ID when they sign on to the system.

5496.82 **Utility Programs:** A set of prewritten programs that perform a variety of file and data-handling tasks (e.g., sorting or merging files) and other housekeeping chores.

5496.83 **Utilization:** The percentage of time a system is being productively used.

5496.84 **Validity Check:** An edit test in which an identification number or transaction code is compared with a table of valid identification numbers or codes maintained in computer memory.

5496.85 **Value-Added Network (VAN):** Public network that adds value to the data communications process by handling the difficult task of interfacing with the multiple types of hardware and software used by different companies.

5496.86 **Virtual Private Network (VPN):** A network that controls access to an extranet by encryption and authentication technology.

5496.87 **Virus:** A code that is passed from one computer to another, via disks or a network, that interferes with the normal operation of the computer. Viruses duplicate themselves and consume all available memory, which brings the machine to a halt and may corrupt or delete files.

5496.88 **Voice Input:** A data input unit that recognizes human voices and converts spoken messages into machine-readable input.

5496.89 **Volume Label:** A type of internal label that identifies the contents of each separate data recording medium, such as a tape, diskette, or disk pack.

5496.90 **Vulnerability Scan:** A test to identify whether a system possesses any well-known vulnerabilities.

5496.91 **Walk-Throughs:** Meetings, attended by those associated with a project, in which a detailed review of systems procedures and/or program logic is carried out in a step-by-step manner.

5496.92 **War Dialing:** Searching for an idle modem by programming a computer to dial thousands of phone lines. Finding an idle modem often enables a cracker to gain access to the network to which it is connected.

5496.93 **Warm Boot:** Resetting the computer after it has already been turned on. A warm boot is normally used to clear memory after a system crash.

5496.94 **Web Servers:** Large computers on the Internet that are scattered worldwide and contain every imaginable type of data. Each web server can have tens of thousands of networks and users attached to it.

5496.95 **Website:** A collection of information on the World Wide Web, organized into a number of documents related to a common subject or set of subjects.

5496.96 **Wide Area Information Servers (WAIS):** Tools for searching the Internet's huge information libraries.

5496.97 **Wide Area Network (WAN):** A telecommunications network that covers a large geographic area anywhere in size from a few cities to the whole globe. A WAN uses telephone lines, cables, microwaves, or satellites to connect a wide variety of hardware devices in many different locations.

5496.98 **Wiretap:** To listen (eavesdrop) in on an unprotected communications line.

5496.99 **World Wide Web (WWW):** The universe of global network accessible information.

5497 WORM to Zip Drive

5497.01 **WORM:** "Write once, read many." For example, an optical disk can be written on once, but later read many times.

5497.02 **Worm:** Similar to a virus except that it is a program rather than a code segment hidden in a host program. A worm also copies itself and actively transmits itself directly to other systems.

5497.03 **Write Protect:** Marking a file or disk so that its contents cannot be deleted. Disks that have been write-protected can only be read; they cannot be modified or deleted.

5497.04 **Zero-Balance Check:** An internal check that requires the balance of the payroll control account to be zero after all entries to it have been made.

5497.05 **Zip Drive:** A computer drive used to compress a file so that large amounts of data can be stored using a small amount of disk space.

This page intentionally left blank.

Section 5500
Planning and Measurement

5501 General Introduction

5501.01 Cost and managerial accounting are distinguished from financial accounting by the users of the information. Financial accounting is primarily concerned with providing information to external decision makers including stockholders, creditors, and governmental agencies. Cost and managerial accounting are concerned mainly with providing managers with information that will assist them in operating the enterprise efficiently and effectively. **Cost accounting** is historically oriented; it is a process of accumulating costs by department or function and by product to compute the cost of the goods manufactured or the services provided. A major objective of this process for manufacturing firms is to value inventories in the balance sheet and to compute cost of goods sold in the income statement. **Managerial accounting** is concerned with providing information to management that will be useful in making decisions about the operations of the business. This may include some historical information; however, most of it is current and projected information.

Generally accepted accounting principles, as outlined by the authoritative bodies of the accounting profession, are very important in all aspects of financial accounting. They are relevant in cost accounting only to the extent that some of the cost accounting data is used in external reporting. Other areas of cost accounting and almost all aspects of managerial accounting are not controlled by generally accepted accounting principles. The underlying principles in these cost and managerial accounting areas include (a) identifying the decisions to be made, (b) identifying the information that is relevant to the decision-making process, and (c) organizing the information so that it is most useful to management.

Quantitative methods are frequently employed by accountants to model, quantify, and evaluate decision alternatives. Accountants must be familiar with the quantitative techniques available, be able to recognize when their use is appropriate, and be able to perform the calculations required for their use. This section covers cost accounting, managerial accounting, and quantitative methods.

A careful study of the basic concepts covered in this section and an application of those concepts to problem situations will prepare you for the cost/managerial accounting portion of the CPA Exam.

5501.02 This section has been divided into the following areas:

Paragraph	Topic
5510	Manufacturing Accounting; Cost Estimation, Determination, and Drivers
5520	Job Order Costing, Process Costing, and Activity-Based Costing (ABC)
5530	Standard Costs and Variance Analysis
5540	Joint Costs, Byproducts, Spoilage, Waste, and Scrap
5550	Budgeting, Segment Reporting, and Pricing Products and Services
5560	Cost-Volume-Profit Analysis and Special Analyses for Management Decision Making
5570	Capital Budgeting
5580	Other Quantitative Methods—Inventory Quality, Planning, and Control; JIT Purchasing; Balanced Scorecard; and Benchmarking

5510 Manufacturing Accounting, Cost Estimation, Determination, and Drivers

5511 Terminology

5511.01 **Conversion costs:** Manufacturing costs required to convert raw materials into a finished product. These include direct labor and overhead costs.

5511.02 **Cost driver:** A measure of activity. Total cost should increase in direct proportion to the level of activity. The cost driver represents a cause and effect relationship between the activity and the set of costs, typically manufacturing overhead costs. Generally, there is a linear relationship between the activity and the amount of cost incurred.

5511.03 **Direct labor:** Labor that can economically be traced to units of finished product.

5511.04 **Direct material:** Material that can economically be traced to units of finished product.

5511.05 **Overhead:** All manufacturing costs other than direct material and direct labor. Other commonly used terms include manufacturing overhead, factory overhead, factory burden, and indirect manufacturing costs.

5511.06 **Overhead rate:** A rate used to charge overhead costs to work-in-process. It is based on estimated total overhead costs relative to some measure of volume. Common measures of volume or cost drivers include units produced, direct labor hours, direct labor dollars, and machine hours.

5511.07 **Period costs:** Costs not associated with the manufacturing process that are expensed in the period incurred. Period costs are referred to as "expenses" on the income statement.

5511.08 **Prime costs:** Costs directly traceable to specific units of finished product. These include direct material and direct labor.

5511.09 **Product costs:** Costs that are associated with the manufacturing process. Generally, they add value to units produced and are accounted for as if they "attach" to the units and follow them through work-in-process, finished goods inventory, and into cost of goods sold when the units are sold.

5512 Introduction—Manufacturing Accounting

5512.01 Manufacturing accounting (cost accounting) is primarily involved with determining the cost of the products manufactured. The cost is then used to:

a. value ending inventory for goods on hand at the end of an accounting period and

b. value cost of goods sold for products sold during the accounting period.

5512.02 It is important for a manufacturing firm to distinguish between *product costs* and *period costs*. Product costs include all costs associated with the manufacturing process. These costs generally add value to the goods produced and, for public reporting purposes, are accounted for as if they attach to the units produced. They flow through work-in-process and finished goods inventory and are finally expensed through cost of goods sold. Period costs are not associated with the manufacturing process and are expensed in the period incurred as selling, general, or administrative expenses.

Example:

Product Costs	**Period Costs**
Direct labor	Selling expenses
Direct material	General administration
Manufacturing overhead	Interest expense

The following chart illustrates the accounting for common expenditures of a manufacturing firm. Capital expenditures and product costs are carried in the balance sheet until their usefulness or benefit has expired. At that time, they are expensed in the income statement. Period costs are expensed in the period in which they are incurred.

Period and Product Costs for a Manufacturing Firm

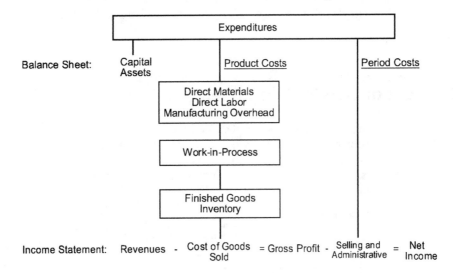

5512.03　The focus of manufacturing accounting is on product costs. Product costs are broadly classified into three groups:

1. Direct materials

2. Direct labor

3. Manufacturing overhead

The manufacturing process combines material, labor, and elements of manufacturing overhead to produce a finished product.

Manufacturing enterprises typically have three inventories to support this process:

1. Raw materials inventory

2. Work-in-process inventory

3. Finished goods inventory

The flow of costs through these accounts is illustrated in T-account form on the following page.

Flow of Costs through Manufacturing Accounts

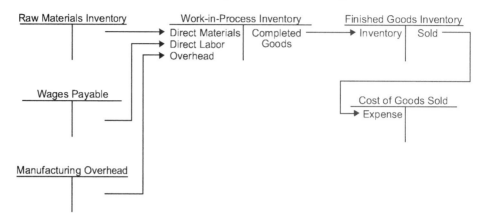

5513 Cost of Goods Sold Statement

5513.01 The cost of goods sold statement for a manufacturing enterprise is similar to that of a retail firm, except for purchases. Rather than purchasing goods for resale, a manufacturer produces goods for sale. Cost of goods manufactured is substituted for purchases. The beginning and ending inventory are labeled finished goods to distinguish them from raw materials and work-in-process inventories.

Example:

Cost of Goods Sold
Period _____

Beginning finished goods inventory	$ XX
Plus: Cost of goods manufactured	XX
Goods available for sale	XXX
Less: Ending finished goods inventory	XX
Cost of goods sold	$ XX

5514 Cost of Goods Manufactured Statement

5514.01 A cost of goods manufactured statement may be included as part of the cost of goods sold statement (section **5513.01**) or it may be shown as a separate statement. A cost of goods manufactured statement shows how the beginning inventory of work-in-process is increased by direct material, direct labor, and manufacturing overhead. Combined, these represent the total goods in process during the period. The difference between this amount and the ending work-in-process inventory is the cost of goods manufactured.

Example:

Cost of Goods Manufactured
Period _____

Beginning work-in-process inventory	$ XX
Plus:	
Direct material	XX
Direct labor	XX
Manufacturing overhead	XX
Total goods in process	XXX
Less: Ending work-in-process inventory	XX
Cost of goods manufactured	$XXX

5515 Material

5515.01 Direct materials are distinguished from indirect materials by the ability to identify them with a finished product. Direct materials can be physically identified with, or traced to, a finished product. Direct material is a *prime production cost*. Indirect material cannot be economically traced to the finished product and is included as an element of overhead (see section **5517**).

5515.02 Materials are initially recorded in *raw material inventory*. As they are used, the direct materials are transferred into *work-in-process,* while indirect materials go into *manufacturing overhead.*

5515.03 A just-in-time (JIT) manufacturing philosophy, which attempts to reduce substantially or eliminate raw materials inventory, is being adopted by many companies.

5516 Labor

5516.01 Direct labor is distinguished from indirect labor by the ability to identify it with a finished product. Direct labor can be physically identified with, or traced to, a finished product. Direct labor is a *prime production cost.* It is also a *conversion cost.* Indirect labor cannot be economically traced to the finished product and is included as an element of overhead (see section **5517**).

5516.02 Wages to manufacturing employees are split between direct and indirect labor. Direct labor is recorded directly into *work-in-process.* Indirect labor is recorded in *manufacturing overhead.*

5517 Overhead

5517.01 All manufacturing costs other than direct material and direct labor are included in overhead. Examples include indirect materials, indirect labor, utilities, depreciation, and taxes on manufacturing facilities. Overhead is classified as a *conversion cost.*

5517.02 Overhead is a necessary product cost, but it is not economically feasible to trace overhead to particular units of finished products. An allocation procedure is required to associate overhead cost with units produced for each unit to bear its full share of production costs. Generally accepted accounting principles require inventory to be valued at *absorption cost* of production. Absorption costing, however, is often misleading for decision making purposes. Variable costing is preferable for decision making purposes (see section **5563**).

5517.03 The amount of overhead charged to work-in-process is determined by multiplying an overhead rate by some measure of volume or what is sometimes called a cost driver. The rate has several names: burden rate, overhead rate, factory rate, or manufacturing overhead rate. The name is incidental.

5517.04 Of prime importance is the measure of volume or the cost driver on which the rate is based. A cost driver is a measure of activity, and total cost should increase in direct proportion to the increase in the level of activity. The cost driver represents a cause and effect relationship between the activity and the set of costs, typically manufacturing overhead costs. Generally, there is a linear relationship between the activity and the amount of cost incurred. Some common drivers include:

  a. Units produced

  b. Direct labor hours worked

c. Machine hours worked

d. Number of production runs for set-up costs

In practice, a measure or driver is selected because of a high correlation between changes in overhead cost and changes in the measure of volume. The cost driver or measure of volume for allocating overhead to work-in-process is generally given in practice problems of the CPA Examination.

Activity-based costing (ABC) is one approach to assigning overhead costs to units of production. Activity centers and cost drivers are central to this philosophy. (See section **5529** for a more detailed discussion of ABC.)

5517.05 The overhead rate is developed from estimates of the total overhead costs and total volume (driver) expected for the coming year. Total volume is projected at the *normal* or *expected volume.* Total overhead cost expected for the period is based on the flexible budget (see section **5518**).

Formula:

$$\text{Overhead rate} = \frac{\text{Estimated total overhead cost}}{\text{Estimated volume (driver)}}$$

5517.06 Overhead costs may be accounted for in one or two accounts. When a one-account system is used, the account is generally called "manufacturing overhead." The actual overhead costs are recorded as debits. Costs allocated to work-in-process are recorded as credits. A debit balance in this account represents *underapplied* overhead, and a credit balance indicates *overapplied* overhead.

5517.07 When two accounts are used for overhead, one is generally called "overhead control" and the other is "overhead applied." The control account accumulates the actual costs as debits, while the applied account accumulates allocations to work-in-process as credits. These two accounts are compared to determine whether overhead has been *over-* or *underapplied.* Both accounts are closed out at period end.

5518 Flexible Budgeting

5518.01 The purpose of a flexible budget is to adjust the total overhead cost expected for the period to the level of production achieved. In essence it says, "You tell me your level of operation, and I'll tell you what your overhead costs should be."

5518.02 Overhead consists of many different types of costs that react differently to changes in volume. The most common cost classifications are (a) fixed, (b) variable, (c) semivariable, and (d) step-variable.

These costs are combined into one formula called a flexible budget formula. Each cost will be defined (see section **5519.01**).

5518.03 A **fixed cost** remains constant in total over the relevant range of production (see section **5519.10**). The cost per unit, however, declines as volume increases. These relationships can be diagrammed as follows:

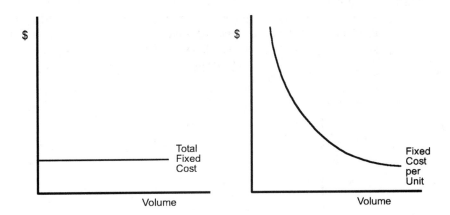

5518.04 **A variable cost** changes in total as volume changes. Assuming a linear relationship, total variable cost increases (decreases) proportionately with increases (decreases) in volume. The cost per unit, however, remains constant within the relevant range of production. These relationships can be diagrammed as follows:

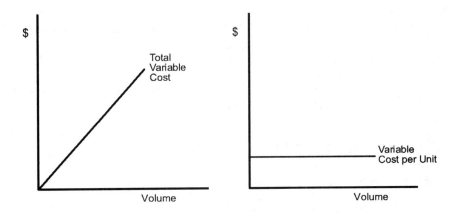

5518.05 **Semivariable costs** (sometimes called mixed costs) contain both a fixed portion and a variable portion. The fixed portion is the minimum cost required even if no output is produced. As output increases, assuming a linear relationship, the cost increases proportionally. This is diagrammed as follows:

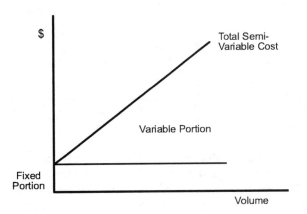

5518.06 **A step-variable cost** increases in "chunks." An amount of cost will sustain some increase in volume without increasing the cost. At some point, however, cost must be increased by a fixed amount to continue to increase volume. An example of this is factory supervisory salaries. As the number of direct laborers increases, eventually another supervisor position must be added. This causes total supervisory salaries to "jump" to a higher level. The following diagram illustrates these costs:

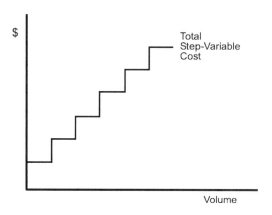

5518.07 **Total overhead** consists of all the listed types of costs. Since several of them change in total with changes in volume, total overhead cost will change with the volume of production. There is a need to combine these costs into one formula that can be used to estimate the amount of overhead cost at any specified volume of production. Accountants generally use a linear cost function on the assumption that it is accurate enough for its intended uses. The formula is called a *flexible budget formula.*

5519 Quantifying the Flexible Budget Formula

5519.01 A flexible budget formula is generally developed from historical cost data. Methods of quantifying the mathematical formula include the high point–low point method and least-squares regression analysis. Before each of these methods is reviewed, we will review the mathematical representation of an equation.

5519.02 An equation is a symbolic representation of the relationship between two or more variables. An equation with two variables is represented as:

$$Y = a + bX^c$$

where: Y = The dependent variable
X = The independent variable
a = A constant that represents the value of Y when b is zero
b = A constant (coefficient) that indicates the amount of change in Y when X changes
c = A constant (exponent) that indicates the power to which X is raised (the number of times X is multiplied by itself)

When the exponent c has a value of 1, the relationship between X and Y will be linear. Linear relationships are a straight line when graphed. Most of the applications tested on the CPA Examination assume a straight line or linear relationship.

5519.03 **Graphing a straight line:** When plotting a line on a graph, the vertical axis represents values of the dependent variable Y, and the horizontal axis represents values of the independent variable X. The constant *a* is called the Y intercept, or the amount of Y when X equals zero. The constant *b* is called the slope, or the amount of change in Y for each unit change in X. Any two points may be used to plot a straight line.

5519.04 **Curve fitting:** In developing a flexible budget formula, the accountant works with a set of data and develops a mathematical formula that accurately represents the data. The equation is then used to predict future costs under different operating conditions. The data set consists of n observations on two variables of interest, $(X_1, Y_1), (X_2, Y_2), \ldots (X_n, Y_n)$. The objective is to use the data set to determine the constants a and b in the straight-line equation.

Suppose the following data set is available from the historical accounting records to develop a flexible budget formula for factory overhead:

Month	Y Factory Overhead	X Units Produced
July	$3,100	10
August	3,800	14
September	5,000	20
October	3,000	11
November	3,800	15
December	2,600	8

5519.05 **High-low method:** The high-low method uses the high level of volume (independent variable) and the low level of volume to develop the equation. The equation is developed in two steps:

1. Compute variable cost per unit by dividing the change in total cost by the change in volume between the high and low volumes of activity.

2. Compute the fixed cost by subtracting the variable cost at one volume of activity from total cost at that same volume. This procedure is sometimes called the addition/subtraction method.

Solution:

Select the high volume and the low volume as shown:

	Low Volume	High Volume
Units produced	8	20
Factory overhead	$2,600	$5,000

Step 1: Compute variable cost:

$$\text{Variable costs} = (\$5,000 - \$2,600) \div (20 - 8)$$
$$= \$200 \text{ per unit}$$

Step 2: Compute fixed cost:

$$\text{Fixed costs} = \$5,000 - (20 \times \$200) = \$1,000$$
$$\text{or}$$
$$= \$2,600 - (8 \times \$200) = \$1,000$$
$$\text{Formula: } Y = \$1,000 + \$200X$$
$$\text{Factory overhead} = \$1,000 + \$200 \text{ per unit}$$

Simultaneous equations can also be used to solve for the fixed costs and variable costs (constants a and b, respectively). The following equations represent the high and low points, respectively.

$$\$5,000 = a + 20b$$
$$\$2,600 = a + 8b$$

One of the equations is solved (manipulated) for one of the unknown values and substituted in the second equation. The second equation is then solved and the value substituted in one of the equations to compute the other unknown.

Solution:

Step 1: Manipulate equation:
$$\$5,000 = a + 20b$$
$$a = \$5,000 - 20b$$

Step 2: Substitute into other equation and solve:
$$\$2,600 = a + 8b$$
$$\$2,600 = \$5,000 - 20b + 8b$$
$$b = \$200$$

Step 3: Substitute known value in one equation and solve:
$$\$5,000 = a + 20\,(\$200)$$
$$a = \$1,000$$
$$\text{Formula: } Y = \$1,000 + \$200X$$
$$\text{Factory overhead} = \$1,000 + \$200 \text{ per unit}$$

5519.06 **Least-squares regression analysis:** The least-squares method uses mathematical equations to fit the best line possible to the observed data set. It identifies the equation for a regression line that minimizes the sum of the squares of the lengths of the vertical-line segments drawn from the observed data points on the scattergraph to the regression line. The smaller the deviations of the observed values from this line (and, consequently, the smaller the sum of the squares of these deviations), the better is the fit of the line to the data points.

A least-squares regression analysis can be easily performed on a computer with a variety of software packages, including some spreadsheets. The calculations are rather complex and detailed and are not usually tested on the CPA Examination. (See a statistics or business analysis book for a detailed discussion of least-squares regression analysis.)

5519.07 When developing the flexible budget formula for factory overhead, a cost equation can be developed using several different measures of volume or cost drivers (e.g., units, direct labor hours, machine hours). The cost driver selected should be the one that has the best fit of the observed data points to the regression line. The use of a scattergraph can give some indication of how well the regression line fits the data set. If all costs plotted on the graph are very close to the line, there is said to be a high degree of correlation between changes in volume and changes in overhead cost, as illustrated in the next graph:

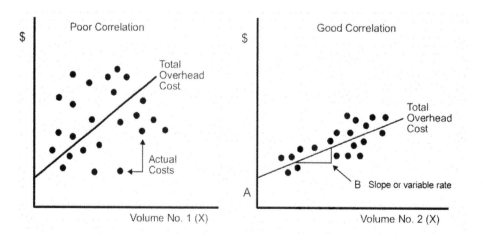

5519.08   **Correlation coefficient:** One of the desirable features of the least-squares regression analysis is that a correlation analysis can be performed to quantitatively measure how well the regression line fits the data points. A correlation coefficient *(r)* is computed to measure the association between two variables (in this case, factory overhead and an activity base). A high correlation coefficient indicates greater association between two variables. The activity base with the highest correlation coefficient should be selected.

Values of *r* range from -1 to +1. Whether *r* is positive or negative depends on the slope of the line. The association between *x* and *y* increases as the absolute value of *r* increases.

The value of *r* is often squared to compute a *coefficient of determination* that identifies the amount of variation in *y* that is explained by *x*. If *r* is 0.80 for example, when the activity base is expressed in units, then r^2 is 0.64 (0.80 × 0.80). This means that 64% of the variation in factory overhead can be explained by the number of units manufactured. A high r^2 value indicates an accurate overhead rate.

5519.09   **Use of the flexible budget formula:** Once the flexible budget formula has been developed, it is used in budgeting, developing an overhead rate, and variance analysis.

Illustration: The following examples show how the flexible budget formula is used to estimate total overhead and to compute the overhead rate.

Example 1: Volume is measured in direct labor hours and 40,000 direct labor hours are expected for the coming period. How much should total overhead be if fixed overhead is $10,000 and variable overhead is expected to be $.50 per direct labor hour?

Solution: $10,000 + ($0.50 × 40,000 direct labor hours) = $30,000

Example 2: What is the overhead rate in the example?

Solution: $30,000 ÷ 40,000 direct labor hours = $0.75/direct labor hour

5519.10   **Relevant range:** The flexible budget is applicable within a *relevant range* of production. The relevant range of production is a range of operating volume within which the cost relationships will be accurate. At extremely low levels of volume, some fixed costs can be avoided. To achieve extremely high levels of volume, costs will increase more than normal. The dotted line in the diagram shows how costs may actually change outside the relevant range.

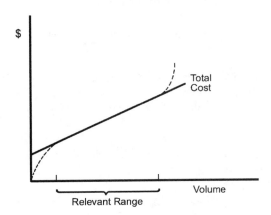

5520 Job Order Costing, Process Costing, and Activity-Based Costing (ABC)

5521 Terminology

5521.01 **Activity-based costing (ABC):** A system of allocating both manufacturing and nonmanufacturing costs to objects of interest to management, such as products, services, or customers.

5521.02 **Activity or activity center:** A repetitive task performed by a specialized group within a company as it executes business objectives.

5521.03 **Cost driver or activity measure:** A measure of activity selected for a cost center or activity because of the high correlation between the cost incurred by the cost center and the measure of activity.

5521.04 **Cost object:** Any item or activity for which management wants to determine the cost, such as products, services, or customers.

5521.05 **Cost pool:** A location for accumulating the costs associated with an activity or activity center.

5521.06 **Equivalent unit:** A measure used in process cost systems to compute the number of units that would have been completed had the same production effort been devoted to starting and completing a smaller number of units.

5521.07 **Job order cost system:** A system of accounting for a production process that produces products in batches or dissimilar units.

5521.08 **Process cost system:** A system of accounting for a production process that produces the same or similar products continuously.

5522 Job Order Versus Process Costing

5522.01 Job order and process costing are two systems that have been developed to account for two different manufacturing processes.

5522.02 Job order costing is used for manufacturing processes that produce products in batches where all units in the same batch are identical. The batches move from process to process, each batch being different from the others. A batch may also consist of a single unique product, such as a custom-built home.

5522.03 Common examples applicable to job order costing are printing, furniture manufacturing, and making custom draperies.

5522.04 Process costing is used for manufacturing processes that produce a single type of product continuously for an extended period of time. Changes in the product are not made or are made only infrequently.

5522.05 Manufacturing processes applicable to process costing include cement production, flour processing, and oil refining.

5522.06 The objective of both accounting systems is the same—determine the manufacturing cost per unit to be used primarily to value ending inventories and cost of goods sold. The unit cost has several other uses, such as cost control and pricing decisions. Our discussion in this section will focus on valuing ending inventories and cost of goods sold.

5523 Job Order Costing

5523.01 Each batch of identical units produced under a job order cost system is called a **job.** A *job order cost sheet,* or a computer file containing the same information, is used to accumulate the manufacturing costs, by type, for each job. In some cases, a job will consist of only a single unit. The form varies, but the following example illustrates the essential features:

Job Order Cost Sheet		
Name: _____	Job Order No: _____	
Product: _____	No. of Units _____	
Materials **Labor**	**Overhead**	
	Rate × Volume =	$
	Summary:	
	Materials	$
	Labor	$
	Overhead	$
	Total	$
	Cost/Unit	$

5523.02 Materials transferred from raw materials inventory into work-in-process are by requisition for a specific job. The requisition serves as a basis for recording the amount and price of the raw materials used on the job.

5523.03 Direct laborers account for their time by job. This serves as a basis for recording the amount and cost of direct labor for the job.

5523.04 Overhead is assigned to the job based on the overhead rate (see section **5517.05**) and the measure of volume. If, for example, the overhead rate is 150% of direct labor cost, the total direct labor cost accumulated on the job would be multiplied by 1.50 and that amount of overhead would be assigned to the job.

5523.05 The individual costs are accumulated in the summary portion of the job order cost sheet for the total cost of the job. The total cost is divided by the number of units produced for the cost per unit. This cost per unit is used to value the units in finished goods inventory and cost of goods sold.

5523.06 **Illustration:** Job order cost system and cost of goods manufactured statement (AICPA adapted).

Problem: The Helper Corporation manufactures one product and accounts for costs by a job order cost system. You have obtained the following information for the year ended December 31, 20X1, from the corporation's books and records:

— Total manufacturing cost added during 20X1 (sometimes called cost to manufacture) was $1 million, based on actual direct material, actual direct labor, and applied factory overhead based on actual direct labor dollars.

— Cost of goods manufactured was $970,000, also based on actual direct material, actual direct labor, and applied factory overhead.

— Factory overhead was applied to work-in-process at 75% of direct labor dollars. Applied factory overhead for the year was 27% of the total manufacturing cost.

— Beginning work-in-process inventory, January 1, was 80% of ending work-in-process inventory, December 31.

Required: Prepare a formal statement of cost of goods manufactured for the year ended December 31, 20X1, for Helper Corporation. Use actual direct material used, actual direct labor, and applied factory overhead. Show supporting computations in good form.

Solution: This problem requires a knowledge of the structure of a statement of cost of goods manufactured and the relationship of manufacturing costs, particularly the allocation of overhead into work-in-process.

Helper Corporation
Statement of Cost of Goods Manufactured
Year Ended December 31, 20X1

Beginning work-in-process inventory[d]		$ 120,000
Direct material used[c]	$370,000	
Direct labor[b]	360,000	
Factory overhead applied[a]	270,000	
Total manufacturing costs added		1,000,000
Manufacturing costs to account for		1,120,000
Less: Ending work-in-process inventory[d]		150,000
Cost of goods manufactured		$ 970,000

Supporting computations:

The breakdown of total manufacturing costs for 20X1:

(a) Factory overhead applied:
     27% × total manufacturing cost (0.27 × $1,000,000)

(b) Direct labor:
     75% of direct labor equals $270,000, so direct labor was $360,000 ($270,000 ÷ 0.75)

(c) Direct material used equals total manufacturing cost less direct labor and factory overhead applied ($1,000,000 - ($360,000 + $270,000)).

(d) The determination of beginning and ending work-in-process inventory:
     Let X = ending work-in-process inventory
     $$\$1,000,000 + 0.8X - X = \$970,000$$
     Solving for X:
     $$X = \$150,000$$
     $$0.8X = \$120,000$$

5524 Process Costing

5524.01 Process costing is used for manufacturing processes that produce a single type of product continuously. The objective is to compute a manufacturing cost per unit for valuing ending inventories of work-in-process, finished goods and cost of goods sold. Process costing is an averaging process:

$$\text{Cost per unit} = \frac{\text{Manufacturing costs}}{\text{Number of units produced}}$$

5524.02 The costing process is complicated by three factors:

1. The number of units produced may include partially processed units in beginning and ending inventory. This is resolved by computing equivalent units of production.

2. Manufacturing costs, consisting of direct material, direct labor, overhead, and costs transferred in from a prior production area, may not be added uniformly during the production process. This is resolved by computing a separate cost per unit for each element of manufacturing cost.

3. The assumed flow of costs through the manufacturing process may be a weighted average or a first-in, first-out (FIFO) flow. The computation of equivalent units and the accumulation of manufacturing costs differ, depending on the assumed flow.

5525 Equivalent Units of Production

5525.01 The equivalent units of production is the number of units that would have been completed had the same production effort been devoted to starting and finishing a smaller number of units.

Example: If 1,000 units are 3/4 complete (75%), there is said to be 750 equivalent units of production (1,000 × 75%).

5525.02 Where there are units-in-process at both the beginning and ending of a period, the equivalent units produced during the period are computed as follows:

Equivalent Units—Average Cost Method	
Units completed and transferred	XX
Plus: Eq. U. in-process at end of period	XX
Equivalent units for average cost method	XXX

Equivalent Units—FIFO Cost Method	
Method A	
Units completed and transferred	XX
Plus: Eq. U. in-process at end of period	XX
Less: Eq. U. in-process at beginning of period	(XX)
Equivalent units for FIFO cost method	XXX
Method B	
Eq. U. completed from beginning work-in-process	XX
Plus: Units started and completed during period	XX
Plus: Eq. U. in-process at end of period	XX
Equivalent units for FIFO cost method	XXX

Methods A and B of the Equivalent Units—FIFO Cost Method will provide the same answer if they are calculated properly.

5525.03 Note that the units completed and transferred consist of units that were in process at the beginning of the period as well as those units started and completed during the period. The unit data given in a CPA Examination question must often be manipulated to get it into a usable form.

5525.04 If units-in-process at the beginning or ending of the period are not equally complete as to material, labor, or overhead, a separate equivalent unit computation must be made for each.

5525.05 **Illustration:** Equivalent unit computation (AICPA adapted).

Problem: Material is added at the beginning of the process in Department A, and conversion costs are incurred uniformly throughout the process. Beginning work-in-process inventory on April 1 in Department A consisted of 50,000 units estimated to be 30% complete. During April, 150,000 units were started in Department A and 160,000 units were completed and transferred to Department B. Ending work-in-process inventory on April 30 in Department A was estimated to be 20% complete. What were the total equivalent units in Department A for both FIFO and average cost methods for April for materials and conversion costs, respectively?

Solution: If the FIFO method is being used:

Method A:

Equivalent Units	No. Units	% Complete for Materials	Equivalent No. Units Materials[a]	% Complete for Conversion	Equivalent No. Units Conversion[a]
Completed and transferred	160,000	100%	160,000	100%	160,000
Plus: In-process, ending	40,000	100%	40,000	20%	8,000
Less: In-process, beginning	50,000	100%	(50,000)	30%	(15,000)
Equivalent units			150,000		153,000

[a] *Equivalent No. Units = No. units × % completion*

Method B:

Equivalent Units	No. Units	% Complete for Materials	Equivalent No. Units Materials[a]	% Complete for Conversion	Equivalent No. Units Conversion[a]
Completed from beginning	50,000	0%	0	70%	35,000
Plus: Started and completed	110,000[b]	100%	110,000	100%	110,000
Plus: In-process, ending	40,000[c]	100%	40,000	20%	8,000
Equivalent units			150,000		153,000

[a] *Equivalent No. Units = No. units × % completion*
[b] *(160,000 - 50,000)*
[c] *(150,000 - (160,000 - 50,000))*

If the average cost method is being used:

Equivalent Units	No. Units	% Complete for Materials	Equivalent No. Units Materials[a]	% Complete for Conversion	Equivalent No. Units Conversion
Completed and transferred	160,000	100%	160,000	100%	160,000
Plus: In-process, ending	40,000	100%	40,000	20%	8,000
Equivalent units			200,000		168,000

[a] *Equivalent No. Units = No. units × % completion*

5525.06 Notice that the equivalent units are not the same for both the average and FIFO cost methods. Equivalent units-in-process at the beginning of the period are removed from equivalent units for the average cost method to compute equivalent units for FIFO costing. As a result, FIFO costing includes only work done in the current period. In contrast, the average cost method includes work done in the previous period on beginning work-in-process units.

5525.07 **Illustration:** Equivalent units for average versus FIFO cost methods (AICPA adapted).

Problem: On November 1, 20X1, Yankee Company had 20,000 units of work-in-process in Department 1 that were 100% complete as to material costs and 20% complete as to the conversion costs. During November, 160,000 units were started in Department 1 and 170,000 units were completed and transferred to Department 2. The work-in-process on November 30, 20X1, was 100% complete as to material costs and 40% complete as to conversion costs. By what amount would the equivalent units for conversion costs for the month of November differ if the FIFO method was used instead of the weighted-average method?

Solution: The beginning equivalent units-in-process for conversion cost is 4,000 (20% × 20,000) units. Equivalent units for FIFO will be 4,000 units less than for the weighted-average method.

5526 Manufacturing Cost Per Unit: Weighted-Average Method

5526.01 A separate cost per unit must be computed for material, labor, and overhead when they are applied to work-in-process at different rates. The computation depends on whether the weighted-average or FIFO method of cost flow is used. In effect, the weighted-average method "double counts" some units whereas the FIFO method does not.

5526.02 The weighted-average method adds the costs in beginning work-in-process to the current period costs to compute total manufacturing cost. This amount is divided by the equivalent units of production (see section **5525.02**) for an average cost per unit. The cost per unit is then multiplied by the units completed and transferred to compute the dollar amount to be transferred out of work-in-process. The amount remaining in work-in-process should equal the equivalent units of production in process times the cost per unit.

5526.03 The following form may be useful in structuring the computation of average cost per unit. The bottom portion shows how the cost per unit is applied to split total cost A between costs transferred to the next production process or into finished goods inventory and ending work-in-process.

	Beginning Work-in-Process	+	Current Cost	=	Total Cost	÷	Equivalent Units	=	Average Cost Per Unit
Material	$		$		$		U		$
Labor	$		$		$		U		$
Overhead	$		$		$		U		$
Total					$ A				$ B
Less: Amount transferred ($B × No. Units transferred)					$				
Equals: Ending work-in-process					$				

5526.04 **Illustration:** Weighted-average method of computing and applying manufacturing cost per unit (AICPA adapted).

Problem: On April 1, 20X1, the Collins Company had 6,000 units of work-in-process in Department B, the second and last stage of their production cycle. The costs attached to these 6,000 units were $12,000 of costs transferred in from Department A, $2,500 of material costs added in Department B, and $2,000 of conversion costs added in Department B. Materials are added in the beginning of the process in Department B. Conversion was 50% complete on April 1, 20X1. During April, 14,000 units were transferred in from Department A at a cost of $27,000 and material costs of $3,500 and conversion costs of $3,000 were added in Department B. On April 30, 20X1, Department B had 5,000 units of work-in-process 60% complete as to conversion costs.

Required:

a. Using the weighted-average method, what were the equivalent units for the month of April?

b. Using the weighted-average method, what was the cost per equivalent unit?

c. What amount of cost should be transferred into Department C, shipping, and what should be the value of ending work-in-process for Department B?

Solution:

Part a. Weighted-average equivalent units. Note that 15,000 units were completed and transferred (14,000 + 6,000 − 5,000).

Equivalent Units	Transferred In	Material Costs	Conversion Costs
Completed and transferred	15,000	15,000	15,000
Plus: In-process, ending	5,000	5,000	3,000[a]
Equivalent units	20,000	20,000	18,000

[a] $0.60 \times 5,000 = 3,000$

Part b. Weighted-average cost per unit.

	Beginning Work-in-Process	+ Current Cost	= Total Cost	÷ Equivalent Units	= Average Cost per Unit
Transferred in	$12,000	$27,000[a]	$39,000	20,000	$1.95
Material	2,500	3,500[b]	6,000	20,000	.30
Conversion	2,000	3,000[b]	5,000	18,000	.2778
Total			$50,000		$2.5278

[a] Costs transferred in

[b] Costs added during the period

Part c. Transferred to Department C.

Transferred to Dept. C (15,000 U at $2.5278)		$37,917
Ending work-in-process inventory Department B:		
Transferred in (5,000 × $1.95)	$9,750	
Materials (5,000 × $0.30)	1,500	
Conversion (3,000 × $0.2778)	833	
Total in-process		12,083
Total costs		$50,000

5527 Manufacturing Cost per Unit: First-In, First-Out (FIFO) Method

5527.01 When material, labor, and overhead are applied to the production process at different rates, a separate unit cost must be computed for each. The equivalent unit computation for FIFO was illustrated in section **5525.02**.

5527.02 The FIFO method assumes that the costs in beginning work-in-process are the first costs transferred to the next process or into finished goods inventory. None of these costs are included in the average manufacturing cost per unit during the period. The average cost per unit is based only on the current costs added to work-in-process for the period. This average cost per unit is used to value ending work-in-process. The rest of the costs are transferred to the next process or to finished goods inventory.

5527.03 The following form, which may be useful in structuring the computation of FIFO cost per unit, shows how total costs are split between ending work-in-process and costs transferred to the next production process or into finished goods inventory.

	Total Costs	Divided by Equivalent Units	Equals Cost Per Unit
Beginning work-in-process	$		
Current period costs:			
Material	$	U.	$
Labor	$	U.	$
Overhead	$	U.	$
Total costs	$	U.	$
Value ending work-in-process:			
Material (eq.u. × cost/u.)	$		
Labor (eq.u × cost/u.)	$		
Overhead (eq.u × cost/u.)	$		
Total work-in-process	$		
Transferred out	$		

5527.04 **Illustration:** FIFO method of computing and applying manufacturing cost per unit (AICPA adapted).

Problem: The Dexter Production Company manufactures a single product. Its operations are a continuing process performed in two departments—machining and finishing. In the production process, materials are added to the product in each department without increasing the number of units produced.

For the month of June 20X1, the company records indicated the following production statistics for the machining department:

Units-in-process, June 1, 20X1[a]	10,000
Units transferred from preceding department	0
Units started in production	80,000
Units completed and transferred out	70,000
Units-in-process, June 30, 20X1[a]	20,000
Units spoiled in production	0

[a] *Percentage of completion of units-in-process*

	June 1	June 30
Materials	100%	100%
Labor	80%	50%
Overhead	40%	25%

Cost records showed the following charges for the month of June:

Machining Department

Materials	$240,000
Labor	144,000
Overhead	71,000
Costs associated with units-in-process on June 1	51,200

Required:

Prepare in good form the following reports for the machining department for the month of June:

a. Quantity of production report, showing the total units to be accounted for and the disposition of the units. Show the equivalent unit computation for material, labor, and overhead.

b. Cost of production report, using the following columnar headings:

Machining Department

Total Cost	Per Unit Cost

Round all computations to the nearest cent.

Solution:

The Dexter Products Company
Quantity of Production Report
June 20X1

	Machining Department
Quantity to be accounted for:	
Work-in-process, June 1, 20X1	10,000
Put in process	80,000
To be accounted for	90,000
Quantity accounted for as follows:	
Transferred out	70,000
Work-in-process, June 30, 20X1	20,000
Total accounted for	90,000

Equivalent Units of Production	Material	Labor	Overhead
Completed and transferred	70,000	70,000	70,000
Plus: In-process, ending [a]	20,000	10,000	5,000
Less: In-process, beginning [a]	(10,000)	(8,000)	(4,000)
Equivalent units	80,000	72,000	71,000

[a] *No. of units × % completion*

Cost of Production Report
June 20X1

	Machining Department	
	Total Cost	Per Unit Cost
Beginning work-in-process	$ 51,200	
Current period costs:		
Material ($240,000 ÷ 80,000 u. = $3.00)	240,000	$ 3.00
Labor ($144,000 ÷ 72,000 u. = $2.00)	144,000	2.00
Overhead ($71,000 ÷ 71,000 u. = $1.00)	71,000	1.00
Total	$506,200	$ 6.00
Work-in-process, June 30, 20X1:		
Material ($3.00 × 20,000)	$ 60,000	
Labor ($2.00 × 10,000)	20,000	
Overhead ($1.00 × 5,000)	5,000	
Total in-process	85,000	
Transferred to finishing [a]	$421,200	

[a] *This consists of the following:*

Costs in beginning work-in-process		$ 51,200
Costs of current period associated with completed units:		
Materials ((70,000 - 10,000) × $3.00)	$180,000	
Labor ((70,000 - 8,000) × $2.00)	124,000	
Overhead ((70,000 - 4,000) × $1.00)	66,000	
Total		370,000
Total transferred to finishing		$421,200

5528   Complications to Job Order and Process Costing

5528.01   **Prior department process costs:** Some manufacturing processes have several departments or process steps. When partially processed items are transferred from one department to another, the prior process costs are also transferred. This consists of material, labor, and overhead incurred in prior departments, but it is all lumped together as *transferred-in costs*. Transferred-in costs are handled as material added at the beginning of the process. If other raw materials are added at the beginning of the process in the new department, the transferred-in costs may be combined with them. Otherwise, they are handled as a separate item with a separate equivalent unit and cost per unit computation. (See section **5525.05** for an example.)

5528.02   **Spoilage:** Job order and process cost problems occasionally have a spoilage factor included. There is a need to distinguish between normal spoilage and abnormal spoilage. Normal spoilage is spread across the good units produced. Abnormal spoilage is separated and written off as a loss in the period incurred. (See section **5545** for additional details.)

5529   Activity-Based Costing (ABC)

5529.01   Overhead costing is an important step in costing individual products. Traditionally, companies have used plant-wide or departmental overhead rates to assign overhead to units produced. Direct labor hours or dollars have frequently been used as the bases for overhead allocation. Over time, the relative amount of direct labor used to produce individual products has decreased substantially, making it a poor activity measure. Product diversity has caused significant differences in lot size and design complexity. Activity-based costing has been developed to address these problems.

5529.02   The objective of activity-based costing (ABC) is to more accurately measure the cost of a particular object, such as a product, a customer, or a manufacturing facility. These items are called cost objects. A *cost object* is any item for which management wants to determine the cost.

5529.03   ABC accounts for both manufacturing and nonmanufacturing costs by assigning them directly to the cost object if there is a direct traceability to the cost object, or to an intermediate activity when there is no direct traceability to the cost object. An *activity* represents a repetitive task performed by a specialized group within the company as it executes business objectives. An activity center may be any business process that management wants to plan for, control, and evaluate. Re-engineering is frequently applied at this point to eliminate nonvalue-adding activities. Examples of activity centers include materials handling, engineering, receiving, power, distribution, order processing, set-up, and machining.

5529.04   In setting up an ABC system, significant activities associated with providing goods and services to customers are first identified and a *cost pool* is created for each of these activities. An *activity measure* or a *cost driver* is identified for each activity cost pool. The activity measure selected for each cost pool should be based on the correlation between the activity measure and the amount of cost incurred by the activity. Costs accumulated in the activity cost pools are allocated to the cost objects by the selected activity measure.

5529.05   The specific steps involved in preparing a management report using ABC are as follows:

1.   Identify the cost objects most relevant to the business organization.

2.   Identify meaningful activities, create an activity cost pool for each activity, and identify an activity measure for each cost pool.

3. Assign costs to cost objects where the cost is directly traceable to the object or to an activity. When a cost relates to more than one activity, first-stage cost drivers are used to allocate the cost to the activities benefited by the cost.

4. Calculate an activity rate for each cost pool using the cost pool's activity measure.

5. Use the activity rate to allocate the costs in the activity cost pools to cost objects.

5529.06 Greater accuracy is achieved in ABC by identifying five levels of activity and identifying activity centers within each level as appropriate:

1. **Unit level**—Performed once for each unit produced (e.g., machining to drill a hole in each unit). These require unit-level cost drivers.

2. **Batch level**—Performed once for each batch produced (e.g., machine set-up). These require batch-level cost drivers.

3. **Product level**—Support the production of a product type or model (e.g., engineering). These require product-level cost drivers.

4. **Process level**—Support individual processes (e.g., maintenance of equipment). These require process-level cost drivers.

5. **Plant level**—Sustain overall plant operations (e.g., plant security and property taxes). These require plant-level cost drivers.

5529.07 **Example:** Book Co. uses the activity-based costing approach for cost allocation and product costing purposes. Printing, cutting, and binding functions make up the manufacturing process. Machinery and equipment are arranged in operating cells that produce a complete product starting with raw materials. Which of the following are characteristic of Book's activity-based costing approaches? (AICPA adapted)

I. Cost drivers are used as a basis for cost allocation.

II. Costs are accumulated by department or function for purposes of product costing.

III. Activities that do not add value to the product are identified and reduced to the extent possible.

a. I only.

b. I and II.

c. I and III.

d. II and III.

Answer: The correct answer is c. Costs are accumulated by activity center rather than by department or function. An activity-based costing (ABC) system has activities as the basic cost objects, and an ABC system does not accumulate cost drivers (or activity measures) as a means for cost allocation. An activity measure or cost driver is a factor that has a direct cause-effect relationship to a cost. Under ABC, activities that do not add to the value of the product are identified and reduced to the extent possible.

5529.08 Resources are consumed by activities. Manufacturing processes require activities to design, engineer, manufacture, sell, and deliver products. In ABC, a cost is first associated with the activities that cause it. First-stage cost drivers are used to assign costs to activity centers. Second-stage cost drivers are used to assign costs from activity centers to the individual products produced.

5529.09   **Example:** The following example compares the traditional approach to ABC. This company produces two products—Product X and Product Y. Some direct material and labor costs can be traced to each product. In addition, each product requires a machining operation with a set-up procedure in preparation for the machining operation. Calculate the cost per unit using the traditional approach and the activity-based costing approach.

The traditional approach uses direct labor hours to allocate overhead (both set-up and machining) to units produced. ABC identifies two activity centers—set-up and machining.

Basic cost and production data are as follows:

	Product X	Product Y	Total
Production and sales (units)	10,000	20,000	
Direct labor hours per unit	1	2	50,000
Machine hours per unit	5	1	70,000
Direct material cost per unit	$ 5	$ 6	$ 170,000
Direct labor cost per unit	$ 8	$16	$ 400,000
Number of production runs	20	2	22
Overhead Costs:			
Setup	$ 220,000		
Machining	280,000		
Total	$ 500,000		

Solution: The overhead rate under the traditional approach is $10 per direct labor hour ($500,000 ÷ 50,000 hours). The cost per unit is:

Traditional Approach	Product X	Product Y
Direct material cost	$ 5	$ 6
Direct labor cost	8	16
Factory overhead	10	20
Total	$23	$42

Under ABC, there are two activities—set-up and machining. Set-up costs are associated with that activity and assigned to products using *number of production runs* and finally to units produced based on the number of units of product produced. Likewise, machining costs are associated with that activity, assigned to products based on *number of machine hours,* and finally to units produced based on the number of units produced.

Activity-Based Costing	Product X	Product Y
Setup ($220,000 ÷ 22 sets) = $10,000/set	$200,000	$20,000
Machining ($280,000 ÷ 70,000) = $4/mh	200,000	80,000
Per unit cost:		
Direct material cost	$ 5	$ 6
Direct labor cost	8	16
Setup ($200,000 ÷ 10,000u); ($20,000 ÷ 20,000u)	20	1
Machining ($200,000 ÷ 10,000u); ($80,000 ÷ 20,000u)	20	4
Total	$ 53	$ 27

Notice the significant difference that can occur in the cost per unit. Under the traditional approach, high-volume products may be allocated excessive amounts of overhead cost when compared with the actual activities required to produce them. Low-volume products frequently create more transactions like set-up or machine time. These differences are more accurately reflected using activity-based costing.

5529.10 Under traditional methods of costing, only product costs are assigned to units produced. This may give an unreliable estimate of what a product really costs, because it omits such costs as research and development, engineering, marketing, and distribution. ABC considers all of these items in determining the cost of an object such as a product.

5529.11 Activity-based costing will be used more extensively as management comes to understand it better, computer technology reduces its cost, and the benefits from improved information exceed the cost. Benefits result only when ABC shifts a significant amount of cost from one product to another, as illustrated in the previous example. As long as both methods produce the same product cost, the less costly method will be preferred.

5529.12 Some of the more significant differences that may occur when ABC replaces traditional costing include the following:

1. Both nonmanufacturing and manufacturing costs many be assigned to products.

2. Some manufacturing costs may be excluded from a product cost.

3. Rather than only one plant-wide cost pool or several departmental cost pools for overhead, there can be many activity cost pools and each may have its own activity measure and allocation rate.

5529.13 The use of ABC-generated data for managerial performance evaluation and decision-making is called Activity-Based Management.

5530 Standard Costs and Variance Analysis

5531 Terminology

5531.01 **Standard:** The amount and cost of direct material, direct labor, and overhead required to produce one unit of finished product.

5531.02 **Standard cost system:** An accounting system that uses standard costs rather than actual costs to account for units as they flow through the manufacturing process. Variances are recorded when actual costs differ from standard costs.

5532 Introduction—Standard Costing

5532.01 The objective of a standard cost system is to help a business operate more effectively and more efficiently. It helps accomplish organizational goals by obtaining the optimum output from the inputs used.

5532.02 Standards and budgets are related. When the budget is broken down on a unit basis, it is called a **standard.** Standard costs are budgeted manufacturing costs on a unit basis.

5532.03 Standard costs have several benefits. They save on bookkeeping costs, provide a basis for performance measurements, provide useful data in product costing, and are used in the budgetary process.

5532.04 There are three basic types of standards that may be employed: (1) fixed or unchanging, (2) ideal or theoretical, and (3) currently attainable. Each type of standard has some advantages, but currently attainable standards are most commonly used.

5532.05 Fixed or basic standards, once established, are not changed. Initially, a fixed standard may be ideal and/or attainable, but because it is never changed, it is of limited use to management.

5532.06 Ideal or theoretical standards are based on utopian conditions for a given manufacturing process. Ideal standards presume that manufacturing costs will always be purchased at minimum prices, used at optimum efficiency, and produced at 100% manufacturing capacity. Ideal standards cannot be met and will consistently result in unfavorable variances. For this reason, they have undesirable behavioral consequences.

5532.07 Attainable standards are based on a high degree of efficiency. They can be met or even surpassed by employing excellent managers and employees. Attainable standards consider that manufacturing components can be purchased at good overall prices. Attainable standards also consider that (a) labor is not 100% efficient, (b) material usage will have some normal spoilage, and (c) manufacturing capacity cannot produce at 100% of theoretical capacity. Attainable standards are set above average levels of efficiency but may be met or surpassed by efficient production.

5532.08 Many people are generally involved in developing the standard costs. Those commonly involved include line personnel directly responsible for meeting the standard, engineers, accountants, and time and motion analysts. Accountants provide valuable cost data and variance analyses on existing standards that are very helpful in developing good standards.

5532.09 The approach generally followed in developing standards is to estimate the amount and cost of material, labor, and overhead required to efficiently produce one unit of product in the current period. The standards are used by accountants to value inventories of raw materials, work-in-process, and finished goods, and to value the cost of goods sold.

5532.10 When actual amounts differ from standard amounts, a variance is recorded. The variance should be assigned to the department or division that has the ability to control the activity that causes the variance. As a general rule, all variances should be recorded as soon as possible so corrective action may be taken. By doing so, variance analysis is useful to management because it points to the areas of operations most in need of management's attention.

5533   Flow of Standard Costs Through the Accounts

5533.01 Manufacturing accounts used in a standard cost system are similar to the accounts used for an actual cost system. Several variance accounts are added. Direct material has two variance accounts—*material price variance* and *material usage variance.* Direct labor also has two variance accounts—*labor price (rate) variance* and *labor usage (efficiency) variance.* Over- or underapplied overhead is analyzed to determine the cause. Separate overhead variance accounts may also be added.

5533.02 Exhibit A illustrates the flow of costs through the accounts. Lines and arrows connect the parts of each journal entry. Where the amounts at the ends of the lines are not equal, it is because a variance is being recorded. The letters and numbers in parentheses identify the variance account.

Exhibit A
Flow of Standard Costs through Accounts

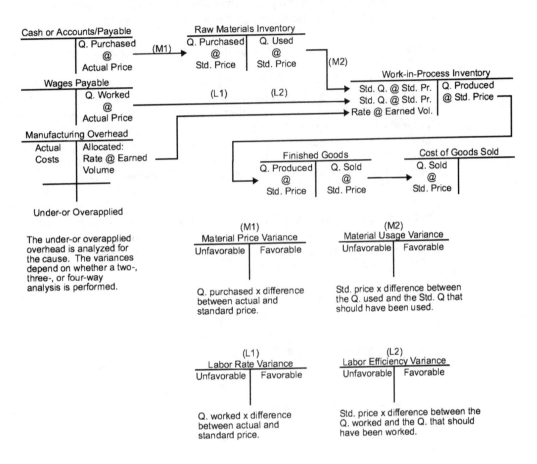

5534 Direct Material Variances

5534.01 Direct materials are usually recorded in a raw material inventory account at the standard cost. The difference between the actual cost and the standard cost for the direct materials purchased is a **price variance.** Its computation is:

Direct material price variance = Quantity purchased × (Standard price – Actual price)

5534.02 If the actual price exceeds the standard price, it is an unfavorable variance. By subtracting the actual price from the standard price, a negative amount will indicate that it is unfavorable:

Standard price – Actual price

$10.00 – $10.20 = – $0.20

5534.03 Some people have proposed that both price and usage variances be recorded at the time the material is transferred into work-in-process. However, during a given accounting period, the quantity purchased may not be the same as the quantity used, and the price variance would be reported in the wrong period. The variance is best associated with the activity when the price variance is recorded at the time of purchase and the usage variance is recorded at the time of use.

5534.04   Under manufacturing processes where a specified number of units are being produced, the standard quantity of raw materials needed for production is known and the usage variance can be recorded at the beginning of the production process. The standard quantity is recorded in work-in-process at the standard price. Any difference between the standard quantity needed and the amount requisitioned is a **usage variance**. The computation is:

Direct material usage variance = Standard price × (Standard quantity - Actual quantity)

5534.05   Under a manufacturing process where a given amount of raw material is processed to obtain as much finished product as possible, the usage variance is recorded at the completion of the production process. The actual raw materials used in production are transferred into work-in-process at the standard price. When production is complete and the number of units actually produced is known, the usage variance is computed as the difference between the raw materials that should have been used (standard quantity) and the amount actually used (actual quantity) to produce the units of finished product. The formula is the same, but the time of recording is different.

5534.06   The following summarizes the direct material variances when there is no change in the raw material inventory balance. This assumes that the quantity purchased is used immediately in work-in-process as would occur in a just-in-time (JIT) manufacturing process.

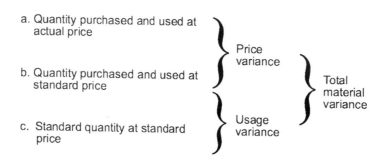

5535   Direct Labor Variances

5535.01   Workers classified as direct labor are paid for the time worked at the actual or agreed price. The objective, however, is to record in work-in-process the standard quantity of labor needed to produce the units at the standard labor rate. The difference between the amount paid and the amount recorded in work-in-process can be separated into a price (rate) and a usage (efficiency) variance as follows:

Direct labor rate variance = Hours worked × (Standard price - Actual price)

Direct labor efficiency variance = Standard price × (Standard hours - Actual hours)

The total labor variance is summarized as follows:

a. Quantity worked at actual price } Rate variance

b. Quantity worked at standard price }

Efficiency variance

c. Standard quantity at standard price }

Total labor variance

5535.02   In some process cost systems, the standard quantity of labor cannot be determined until the end of the period when the number of units actually produced is known. Under these systems, the actual direct labor used is recorded in work-in-process, and any usage variance is recognized when the units are completed and transferred to the next process or into finished goods inventory.

5536   Overhead Variance Analysis

5536.01   Manufacturing overhead costs are accumulated in a Manufacturing Overhead account as debit entries. Credit entries to this account record amounts allocated to work-in-process. The amount allocated to work-in-process under a standard cost system is based on an overhead rate (see section **5517.05**) and the earned or standard volume of activity. When volume is measured in units, **earned volume** is the number of units produced. Whenever volume is measured by some other input (e.g., direct labor hours, machine hours, or direct labor cost), earned or standard volume is the amount of the input that should have been used to produce the actual units of output.

5536.02   The over- or underapplied overhead can be analyzed in a variety of ways. The most common are called *two-way, three-way,* or *four-way* analysis. The following example will be used to illustrate each of these:

5536.03   **Example:** Standard cost data per unit includes the following:

Direct labor:	3 hours at $5.00 per hour
Direct material:	4 pounds at $4.15 per pound
Overhead:	$1.10 per direct labor hour × 3 hours = $3.30 per unit

The flexible budget formula is based on fixed costs of $18,000 and variable costs of $0.50 per direct labor hour. A normal volume of 30,000 direct labor hours is projected for the period.

The overhead rate is $1.10, computed as follows:

$$\$1.10 = \frac{\$18,000 + (\$0.50 \times 30,000 \text{ hours})}{30,000 \text{ hours}}$$

Actual cost data for the period:

Overhead costs

Fixed	$18,500
Variable	16,000
Total	$34,500

Units produced: 9,000 units
Direct labor hours worked: 28,000 hours

Summary of over- or underapplied overhead:

a. Actual cost $34,500

b. Allocated to work-in-process $4,800 Underapplied overhead
($1.10 x 27,000 D.L. hours) [a] $29,700

[a] *The earned or standard volume was 27,000 direct labor hours. This is the number of hours that should have been worked to produce 9,000 units (9,000 U. x 3 hours per U. = 27,000 D.L. hours)*

5536.04 A two-way analysis separates over- or underapplied overhead into two variances—controllable and uncontrollable or volume. The difference between the actual overhead cost and the amount of cost that should be incurred at the earned or standard volume is the **controllable or budget variance.** The difference between the cost that should have been incurred at the earned volume and the cost allocated to work-in-process is **uncontrollable** because it results from a difference between the normal volume and the earned or standard volume. This uncontrollable variance is often called a **volume variance**. The over- or underapplied overhead is split into these two variances by computing the overhead cost that should have been incurred at the earned or standard volume. The flexible budget formula is used. Based on the data shown in the example, the following variances are computed under a two-way analysis:

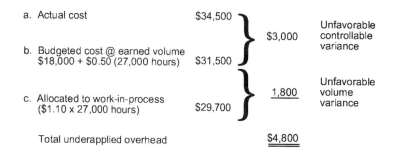

a. Actual cost $34,500 $3,000 Unfavorable controllable variance

b. Budgeted cost @ earned volume
$18,000 + $0.50 (27,000 hours) $31,500

c. Allocated to work-in-process   1,800 Unfavorable volume variance
($1.10 x 27,000 hours) $29,700

Total underapplied overhead $4,800

Notice that the total of the two variances equals the underapplied overhead. Notice also that the volume variance results from inefficient utilization of fixed overhead. At the normal volume of 30,000 direct labor hours, fixed costs are $0.60 per direct labor hour. Earned volume was 3,000 direct labor hours (30,000 - 27,000) below normal, which accounts for the $1,800 ($0.60 × 3,000) unfavorable volume variance.

5536.05 A three-way analysis separates over- or underapplied overhead into three variances: (1) spending, (2) efficiency, and (3) volume. The **volume variance** is the same as computed in the two-way analysis. However, what was a controllable variance in a two-way analysis is split into two parts. The difference between the actual costs and the overhead costs that should have been incurred at the actual volume of production is a **spending variance.** This results from prices that are different from those expected at the time the flexible budget formula was developed. The difference between the overhead costs that should have been incurred at the actual volume and the costs that should have been incurred at the earned volume is an **efficiency variance.** Based on the data shown in the example, the following variances are computed under a three-way analysis:

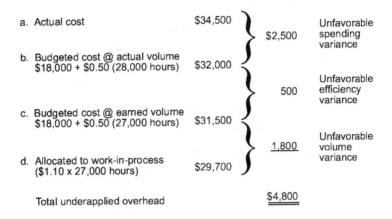

a. Actual cost $34,500

} $2,500   Unfavorable spending variance

b. Budgeted cost @ actual volume
$18,000 + $0.50 (28,000 hours) $32,000

} 500   Unfavorable efficiency variance

c. Budgeted cost @ earned volume
$18,000 + $0.50 (27,000 hours) $31,500

} 1,800   Unfavorable volume variance

d. Allocated to work-in-process
($1.10 x 27,000 hours) $29,700

Total underapplied overhead $4,800

Notice that the efficiency variance results from the direct laborers spending 28,000 hours to do what they should have been able to do in 27,000 hours. Since variable overhead costs increase $0.50 with each direct labor hour worked, $500 ($0.50 × 1,000 hours) of additional overhead cost resulted from this inefficiency.

5536.06   A four-way analysis of variance separates over- or underapplied overhead into four variances: (1) fixed spending, (2) variable spending, (3) efficiency, and (4) volume. The **efficiency** and **volume variances** are the same as computed in a three-way analysis. The **spending variance** is split between the fixed and variable expenses. Actual costs are compared with budgeted costs at actual volume for both fixed and variable expenses to compute the variances. Based on the data shown in the example, the following variances are computed under a four-way analysis:

	Fixed Spending Variance	Variable Spending Variance	Total		
a. Actual cost	$18,500 +	$16,000	= $34,500	} $2,500	Unfavorable spending variance
Spending variance ($18,500 - $18,000 = $500) ($16,000 - $14,000 = $2,000)	(500) +	(2,000)	=		
b. Budgeted @ actual volume $18,000 + $0.50 (28,000 hrs)	$18,000 +	$14,000	= $32,000	} 500	Unfavorable efficiency variance
c. Budgeted @ earned volume $18,000 + $0.50 (27,000 hrs)			$31,500	} 1,800	Unfavorable volume variance
d. Allocated to work-in-process ($1.10 x 27,000 hrs)			$29,700		
Total			$4,800		

Notice that both the $500 fixed spending variance ($18,000 - $18,500) and the $2,000 variable spending variance ($14,000 - $16,000) are unfavorable and that their combined total is equal to the total spending variance computed under the three-way approach.

5537 Disposition of Variance Amounts

5537.01 A decision must be made as to the disposition of the balance in the variance accounts. The account balances in question include the material price variance, material usage variance, labor price (rate) variance, labor usage (efficiency) variance, and manufacturing overhead variances.

5537.02 The following procedures are usually followed.

a. For interim period statements:

(1) If the variance results from a planned fluctuation within the annual period, the variance balance may be carried forward in the variance account. It is reported as a balance sheet item on the interim statement.

(2) If the variance does *not* result from a planned fluctuation within the annual period and if it is material, the variance must be allocated to the relevant inventory balances and to cost of goods sold based on the relative amounts of each. The relevant inventory balances will differ depending on the variance to be allocated. To determine which inventory items need to be adjusted, consider whether or not the amount of the inventory balance would be different if a more accurate standard had been applied during the period.

Example: An unfavorable overhead variance, resulting from unanticipated price increases, caused the overhead rate to be too low. Therefore, work-in-process, finished goods inventory, and cost of goods sold will be understated. These are corrected by allocating the overhead variance among them based on the relative amounts of overhead in each account.

(3) If the variance does not result from a planned fluctuation within the annual period and if it is immaterial, it is closed directly into cost of goods sold.

b. For year-end statements: At year end, a decision is made as to the materiality of the variances.

(1) If material, they are allocated to the relevant inventory balances and to cost of goods sold based on the relative amounts of each account.

(2) If not material, they are closed directly into the cost of goods sold.

5538 Production Mix and Yield Variances

5538.01 Some production processes require a mix of materials and labor to produce a quality finished product. The process is complicated by the ability to substitute one type of material or one type of labor for another type of material or labor. However, the substitute material or labor is often more expensive and the substitution can increase the production cost. Evaluating the impact on production cost for altering the mix of materials and labor is called "mix and yield variance analysis."

5538.02 Mix refers to the relative proportion of components in a mixture. Production mix refers to the relative proportion of different types of direct materials or direct labor used to manufacture a given product. Mix is measured relative to a standard proportion of inputs and has two components—materials mix, which is analyzed by calculating a materials mix variance, and labor mix, which is analyzed by calculating a labor mix variance.

5538.03 Yield refers to the quantity of finished output obtained from a given amount of input. Yield is measured relative to a standard amount of good output for a given amount of input. Yield also has two components—materials yield, which is analyzed by calculating a materials yield variance, and labor yield, which is analyzed by calculating a labor yield variance.

5538.04 In calculating mix and yield variances, materials and labor should be analyzed separately.

The materials usage variance (see section **5534.04**) is divided into two variances—materials mix variance and materials yield variance. The sum of the materials mix variance and the materials yield variance should equal the material usage variance.

The labor efficiency variance (see section **5535.01**) is divided into two variances—labor mix variance and labor yield variance. The sum of the labor mix variance and the labor yield variance should equal the labor efficiency variance.

The usage (efficiency) variance when several inputs are involved is equal to the difference between (a) Standard price × Actual mix × Actual total quantity, and (b) Standard price × Standard mix × Standard total quantity. The mix and yield portions are identified with an intermediate calculation—Standard price × Standard mix × Actual total quantity. This is illustrated as follows:

Standard price x Actual mix x Actual total quantity } Mix variance

Standard price x Standard mix x Actual total quantity

Standard price x Standard mix x Standard total quantity } Yield variance

5540 Joint Costs, Byproducts, Spoilage, Waste, and Scrap

5541 Terminology

5541.01 **Byproduct:** An output of a production process that is not a main product but which has a sales value and is often subject to additional processing beyond the split-off point.

5541.02 **Defective units:** Units of product that do not meet quality standards that are subsequently reworked.

5541.03 **Joint products:** Output of a production process that simultaneously produces more than one product with significant sales value.

5541.04 **Joint product costs:** All production costs incurred prior to the split-off point.

5541.05 **Scrap:** Residue material from a production process that has a measurable, but relatively minor, recovery value.

5541.06 **Split-off point:** A point in the production process where joint products are individually identifiable.

5541.07 **Spoilage:** Defective units that do not meet quality standards and are junked or sold for a disposal value.

5541.08 **Waste:** Material that is either lost through evaporation or shrinkage during the manufacturing process or remains but has no measurable recovery value.

5542 Joint Products and Joint Cost Allocation

5542.01 Many production processes yield more than one product. These products are called main products, byproducts, or scrap. The products that are the primary objective of the production process are called main products. Other products are called byproducts or scrap. Both byproducts and scrap have a residual value, but a byproduct is usually worth more than scrap and is often subject to additional processing beyond the split-off point.

5542.02 Generally accepted accounting principles require that each unit of main product bear its relative portion of all production costs. A procedure is required to allocate the joint costs incurred prior to the point at which the main products become individually identifiable. This is called the split-off point. The production process may be diagrammed as follows:

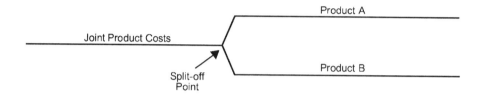

5542.03 There are several ways to allocate the joint product costs to the various products. The two most common procedures are based on a physical measure (e.g., pounds or units) or the relative sales value of the products at the split-off point.

5542.04 Keep in mind that all allocation procedures are arbitrary. They should not be considered in cost planning, control, additional processing, or pricing decisions. The objective of cost allocation is merely to spread the joint costs over the main products in some fair and equitable manner. The allocated amounts may be used in financial reporting or for income tax reporting.

5542.05 A physical measure like pounds or units produced may be used to allocate joint costs. This may result in a fair and equitable allocation if the amount of joint costs incurred is highly correlated with the physical measure used. However, physical measures often bear no relationship to the sales value or revenue producing capacity of the product. Allocation procedures based on physical measures often result in distorted profit margins between the products. Also, the physical measures method can only be used when all of the joint products are measurable in the same quantity base, such as units or pounds.

5542.06 **Example:** Allocation based on physical measures.

Val, Inc. manufactures products W, X, Y, and Z from a joint process. Additional information:

Product	Units Produced	Sales Value at Split-off
W	6,000	$ 80,000
X	5,000	60,000
Y	4,000	40,000
Z	5,000	20,000
	20,000	$200,000

Assuming that total joint costs of $160,000 were allocated using the units produced, the joint costs allocated to each product are:

Product		Joint Cost Allocation
W	(6,000 ÷ 20,000) × $160,000	$ 48,000
X	(5,000 ÷ 20,000) × $160,000	40,000
Y	(4,000 ÷ 20,000) × $160,000	32,000
Z	(5,000 ÷ 20,000) × $160,000	40,000
	Total	$160,000

5542.07 Allocation of joint costs by the relative sales value of products at the split-off point is probably the best and most widely used procedure. It allocates costs based on the ability of each product to bear those costs. More valuable products have a greater ability to bear the cost and more of the joint cost is allocated to them. All main products should show some gross profit margin under typical market conditions.

5542.08 A potential problem in using the relative sales value method is that there may not be a sales value at the split-off point. An appropriate sales value can generally be developed by subtracting the processing costs after the split-off point from the final sales price.

5542.09 **Example:** Allocation based on relative sales value.

Assuming the same facts for Val, Inc. as outlined in section **5542.06**, how much of the $160,000 joint product cost should be allocated to each product using the sales value at the split-off point?

Product		Joint Cost Allocation
W	(80,000 ÷ 200,000) × $160,000	$ 64,000
X	(60,000 ÷ 200,000) × $160,000	48,000
Y	(40,000 ÷ 200,000) × $160,000	32,000
Z	(20,000 ÷ 200,000) × $160,000	16,000
	Total	$160,000

5543 Byproducts

5543.01 **Byproducts** are an output of the production process with a relatively minor sales value when compared to the other joint products. Byproducts are distinguished from scrap and waste in that byproducts have a significant sales value and are often subject to additional processing. Scrap has a minor sales value and may be subject to additional processing; waste has no sales value and is not subject to additional processing.

5543.02 Methods to account for byproducts include the following:

a. Assign a cost at the time of production. The cost assigned to the byproduct is its net realizable value (expected market value less separable processing costs and any selling and administrative expenses necessary to sell the units). Byproduct inventory is debited, and work-in-process is credited. This reduces the production cost of the main products and recognizes any profit on the byproduct at the time of production.

b. Assign no cost to the byproduct and recognize revenue at the time of sale. Memorandum records of the physical quantity of byproduct are maintained for control purposes between the split-off point and point of sale, but no value is assigned to the items. Revenue from the sale is recognized as one of the following: (1) additional sales revenue, (2) a reduction in the cost of production, (3) a reduction in the cost of sales, or (4) other income. This method recognizes profit from the byproduct at the time of sale.

5544　Scrap

5544.01　**Scrap** is the material residue from a manufacturing operation and has minor recovery value.

5544.02　Accounting methods for scrap are similar to those for byproducts discussed in section **5543**:

    a.　assign a value to the scrap at production or

    b.　assign no value until the scrap is sold.

5544.03　If scrap can be identified with a particular job or product, the scrap value or revenue can be subtracted from the direct material cost of that job or product. If the scrap is part of general manufacturing, the scrap value or revenue may be subtracted from factory overhead. Yet another alternative is to record the scrap value or revenue as other income and report it separately on the income statement.

5545　Spoilage: Normal and Abnormal

5545.01　**Normal spoilage** arises under efficient operating conditions. It is a natural part of the production process and is uncontrollable in the short run. Normal spoilage is a necessary cost of the good units produced and should be borne by them.

5545.02　**Abnormal spoilage** is not expected to arise under efficient operations. It is not a natural part of the production process and should not be considered as a necessary cost of the good units produced. Abnormal spoilage should be written off as a loss for the period.

5545.03　Under a job order cost system, spoilage should be charged as follows:

    a.　**Normal** spoilage should be included as an element of factory overhead. The overhead rate should include an allowance for normal spoilage; therefore, any losses on spoiled units should be charged to factory overhead.

    b.　**Unusual** spoilage due to the exacting specifications of a particular job should be charged to that job. This is accomplished by subtracting any recovery value for the spoiled units from the production costs of the job. The good units are assigned the remaining production costs by dividing the net cost by the good units produced.

    c.　**Abnormal** spoilage should be charged directly to a separate loss account.

5545.04　Under a process cost system, the following procedures apply:

    a.　**Normal** spoilage should be assigned to the good units produced during the period. The equivalent units section needs a separate calculation for lost units. The amount of normal spoilage is calculated by multiplying the equivalent lost units by the cost per unit. This amount is assigned or allocated to the good units produced during the period whether they are still in process, transferred to the next department, or transferred to finished goods inventory.

    b.　**Abnormal** losses must have a separate equivalent unit calculation. The abnormal spoilage is computed by multiplying the equivalent lost units by the cost per unit. This amount is charged as a loss for the period.

5546 Defective Units

5546.01 **Defective units** are the output of a production process that does not meet quality control standards. They require some rework before being sold through normal market channels as *firsts* or *seconds*.

5546.02 The most common accounting question is where to record the cost of reworking the units. The following procedures should be followed:

   a. If it is *normal* and *common* to all jobs or units produced, charge to manufacturing overhead.

   b. If it is *normal* and *peculiar* to a specific job, charge it to work-in-process and identify it with that job.

   c. If it is *abnormal,* charge it to a special loss account.

5550 Budgeting, Segment Reporting, and Pricing Products and Services

5551 Terminology

5551.01 **Budget:** A formal quantitative expression of an enterprise's plans.

5551.02 **Cost center:** Segment of a business responsible for the incurrence and proper utilization of cost.

5551.03 **Economic value added:** A financial performance measure, which focuses on maximizing shareholder value.

5551.04 **Flexible budget:** A formula to adjust the expected overhead costs to the level of production achieved.

5551.05 **Gross margin analysis:** A technique for analyzing the changes in gross margin between budgeted and actual results or between current results and results of the preceding year.

5551.06 **Investment center:** Segment of a business responsible for costs, revenues, and profitable utilization of invested capital.

5551.07 **Product pricing:** Assigning monetary values to goods and services exchanged with external entities.

5551.08 **Profit center:** Segment of a business responsible for both costs and revenues.

5551.09 **Residual income:** Income remaining after subtracting a minimum desired rate of return on invested capital.

5551.10 **Responsibility accounting:** The process of dividing the company by segments according to the ability of individuals to control various activities. Accounting reports are developed for each segment consistent with the assignment of responsibility.

5551.11 **Return on investment:** A rate of return computed by dividing net income by invested capital.

5551.12 **Segment contribution margin:** Contribution margin provided by the segment less direct fixed costs associated with the segment.

5551.13 **Segment reporting:** The process of dividing an enterprise into reportable segments and preparing financial information on these segments.

5551.14 **Service department:** A department that generates no revenue but services the revenue-producing departments.

5552 Budgeting

5552.01 A **budget** is a formal quantitative expression of an enterprise's plans. The budget is prepared for the entire business or a major segment of the business. When the budget is broken down on a unit basis, it is called a **standard.**

The traditional or incremental approach to budgeting starts with the activities and costs of the prior year and adds an incremental layer for growth and/or inflation. **Zero base budgeting** is intended to challenge the incremental approach by considering nothing sacrosanct about the current year as a base for next year's estimates. Each year you must start at zero and justify the appropriateness of the item and its cost.

5552.02 The purpose of a budget is to help plan, coordinate, implement, and control enterprise activities. The budget should be set at an efficient level of operations, but it should not be viewed as a cost reduction tool. Cost reductions, however, are often achieved when a budgeting system is adopted because of the inefficiencies due to poor planning, coordination, and control prior to its adoption.

5552.03 Problems commonly associated with budgeting include inaccurate estimates and adverse reactions from employees. The budget is an estimate of what should be considered efficient operations in the future period. Estimates may be inaccurate and events may transpire that reduce the usefulness of the budget. Employees may react negatively to budgeting procedures. There is a tremendous amount of work involved in developing a good budget. Once it is developed, it tends to limit flexibility.

5552.04 Budgets may be classified in length as follows:

a. Long-term budget: 5–6 years

b. Intermediate budget: 2–4 years

c. Short-term budget: 1 year (annual budget)

These budgets are coordinated. The long-term budget provides general direction for the firm. An intermediate budget identifies specific steps to be accomplished in achieving the long-term goals. The annual budget is a detailed plan of operation for the coming year.

5552.05 A complete budget for a company is called a **master budget.** A master budget may be divided into several sub-parts as follows:

Master Budget

A. Operating Budget	B. Financial Budget	C. Special Budgets
1. Sales forecast	1. Cash forecast	1. Performance budget
2. Production budget	Cash receipts	2. Capital budgets
Material purchases	Cash disbursements	
Labor costs	2. Budgeted balance sheet	
Overhead costs	3. Budgeted cash flows statement	
Inventory levels		
3. Cost of goods sold budget		
4. Selling and administrative expense budget		

5552.06 The form of each budget is similar to the form used in developing normal financial statements. They are called *pro forma statements* rather than actual statements of results because they are statements that would be prepared if certain conditions and assumed events occurred.

5552.07 The following steps summarize the preparation of a master budget:

a. Develop a sales forecast. A sales forecast is the starting point for most companies because sales is the limiting factor. Expected sales are based on sales of prior years and the firm's percentage of the market adjusted for expected changes in economic conditions.

b. Determine the desired level of finished goods inventory.

c. Determine the amount of finished goods that must be produced or purchased. This is done by adjusting sales for a net increase (decrease) in the finished goods inventory (Production = Sales - Beginning inventory + Ending inventory).

d. Prepare a purchases or production budget. If the units are produced, the manufacturing costs (including direct material, direct labor, and overhead) required to produce the desired number of units are summarized in a statement of cost of goods manufactured. When a standard cost system is used, the standard costs per unit are used.

e. Estimate selling, administrative, and other general expenses.

f. Organize the preceding information into an income statement.

g. Prepare a cash forecast. This is usually done on a month-to-month or quarter-by-quarter basis to highlight cash flows and pinpoint times during the year when additional financing is required. For each month or quarter, a forecast is developed showing the beginning balance, plus the expected cash receipts, less expected cash disbursements for an ending balance. Critical in developing an accurate cash forecast is the experience of the company in collecting cash from sales and payments on accounts receivable, and the company policy on paying expenses and accounts payable. The CPA candidate must be able to work with different collection and payment schedules.

h. Organize the preceding information into a balance sheet and statement of cash flows.

5552.08 Problems on the CPA Examination focus on one or more sub-parts of the master budget. The most common areas are production or purchases budgets and cash forecasts. Capital budgeting is covered in a separate section (see section **5570**).

5553 Segment Reporting and Responsibility Accounting

5553.01 **Segment reporting** is a process of dividing an enterprise into reportable segments and preparing financial information by segment. We are concerned in this section only with segmented reporting for internal management use, not for external reporting.

5553.02 **Responsibility accounting:** Segmented reporting is useful in the management and control of an enterprise. It is consistent with the concept of responsibility accounting. Responsibility accounting breaks the company into *responsibility centers* according to the ability of individuals to control various activities. Accounting reports are then prepared for each responsibility center consistent with the assignment of responsibility. There are three types of responsibility centers:

1. **Cost centers:** Subdivisions of a business that are assigned responsibility for the incurrence and proper utilization of costs.

2. **Profit centers:** Subdivisions responsible for both costs and revenues.

3. **Investment centers:** Subdivisions responsible for costs, revenues, and profitable utilization of invested capital.

5553.03 The development of internal reports must be consistent with the type of responsibility center. Cost center reports should list controllable costs and may also list allocated portions of fixed costs. There are two general approaches to profit and investment center reporting—the contribution margin approach and the net income approach.

5553.04 The *contribution margin approach* subtracts variable costs and fixed costs that can be identified to a specific segment from segment revenue to give an amount called **segment contribution margin.** It is the amount provided by the segment to help cover unallocated fixed costs and yield an income. The contribution margin approach is most useful when making a decision to add or delete a segment of the business. The following form illustrates this approach:

		Division	
	Total	A	B
Sales	$	$	$
Less: Variable costs	$	$	$
Contribution margin	$	$	$
Less: Separable fixed costs	$	$	$
Segment contribution margin	$	$	$
Less: Unallocated costs	$		
Net income	$		

5553.05 The *net income approach* computes a net income for the revenue generating segments of the business. In computing net income for these segments, cost allocation is required for fixed costs that are used jointly by two segments and service department costs that generate no revenue but provide services to the revenue-producing segments.

5553.06 The procedures involved in allocating these costs are as follows:

a. Determine the cost object. Identify the segments that use the facility or the products that receive the benefit of the services.

b. Determine the costs to be allocated. This is the cost for the jointly used facility or the service department.

    c.   Select an appropriate activity base or allocation method. A base must be selected to allocate the costs. Some common bases include square footage, number of employees, sales, labor hours, and machine hours.

    d.   Allocate the costs based on the relative portion of the activity base used by each segment or product.

5553.07   When service departments render services to other service departments as well as production departments, you may be required to use direct allocation or step allocation.

    a.   **Direct allocation:** No costs of one service department are allocated to another service department. Costs are allocated directly to producing departments.

    b.   **Step allocation:** One service department's cost may be allocated to another service department, beginning with the service department that renders the most services to other departments.

5554 Performance Analysis

5554.01   Different methods are needed to evaluate the performance of the different types of responsibility centers.

    a.   **Cost centers:** Evaluated on costs incurred relative to budgeted and standard costs.

    b.   **Profit centers:** Evaluated on sales and costs relative to budgeted amounts. Contribution margin and vertical ratio analysis can also be applied.

    c.   **Investment centers:** Evaluated on the relationship of profits to invested capital. Alternative methods of evaluation are return on investment, residual income, and segment margin analysis.

5554.02   **Return on investment (ROI)** focuses on optimal use of invested capital. Net income from the income statement is divided by invested capital from the balance sheet as follows:

$$\text{ROI} = \frac{\text{Net income}}{\text{Invested capital}}$$

    a.   Return on investment can be divided into two elements:

$$\text{Profit margin} = \frac{\text{Net income}}{\text{Sales}}$$

$$\text{Capital employed turnover rate} = \frac{\text{Sales}}{\text{Invested capital}}$$

    b.   Profit margin multiplied by capital employed turnover rate equals the return on investment. CPA Examinations frequently have questions dealing with the impact on the return on investment when profit margin, capital employed turnover rate, or one of their elements changes.

    Example: A company's return on investment is affected by a change in (a) capital turnover, (b) profit margin, (c) both a and b, or (d) neither a nor b.

    Answer: (c) both a and b.

5554.03   **Residual income** is the amount of net income in excess of a minimum desired rate of return on invested capital. The minimum desired net income is first computed by multiplying the desired rate of return by invested capital. This amount is then subtracted from reported net income. A positive residual income is viewed favorably because it indicates earnings in excess of the required minimum.

Example:

Net income	$150
Return on Investment at minimum Rate of Return ($1,000 at 0.12)	120
Residual income	$ 30

5554.04 **Economic value added (EVA)** measures surplus or excess value created by an enterprise's investments. EVA is calculated as the excess of return on capital over cost of capital multiplied by invested capital. It is similar to net present value and specifically, to residual income calculation. Shortcomings of EVA include the focus on past, rather than future performance, and its complexity restricts its use to larger businesses. EVA can be depicted in an equation as follows: EVA = (Return on Capital – Cost of Capital) × (Capital Investment in Project).

5554.05 **Segment margin analysis:** Segment margin is the contribution margin of a segment less fixed costs that can be traced to the segment. Segment fixed costs are those that would be avoided if the segment is discontinued. The structure of this report is illustrated in section **5553.04**. Segment margin represents the amount the segment contributes toward covering common fixed costs and toward net income.

5555 Gross Margin Analysis

5555.01 Gross margin analysis (or gross profit analysis) is a way of analyzing unexpected changes in gross margin. It is a technique to isolate changes in each of the sales and cost elements that comprise the total change in gross margin.

5555.02 The first step in gross margin analysis is to compute the difference between actual gross margin and budgeted gross margin. This difference is called the **gross margin variance.** The gross margin variance is then divided into component parts.

a. **Sales price variance:** The effect on gross margin resulting from differences in sales price between planned and actual results.

b. **Sales mix variance:** The effect on gross margin resulting from differences in sales mix between planned and actual results.

c. **Sales volume variance:** The effect on gross margin resulting from differences in the quantity sold between planned and actual results.

d. **Cost price variance:** The effect on gross margin resulting from differences in manufacturing costs between planned and actual results.

5555.03 The following example illustrates the computations required in gross margin analysis (AICPA adapted).

Problem: Garfield Company, which sells a single product, provided the following data from its income statements for the calendar years 20X2 and 20X1:

	20X2
Sales (150,000 units)	$750,000
Cost of goods sold	525,000
Gross profit	$225,000

	20X1
	(Base Year)
Sales (180,000 units)	$720,000
Cost of goods sold	575,000
Gross profits	$145,000

In an analysis of variation in gross profit between the two years, what would be the effects of changes in sales price, sales volume, and cost?

Solution:

The change in gross profit to be accounted for is computed as follows:

Gross profit:	20X2	$225,000	
	20X1	145,000	
Total increase		$ 80,000	Favorable
Cost price variance:			
($575,000 - $525,000)		$ 50,000	Favorable
Sales price variance:			
20X1 sales price			
($720,000 ÷ 180,000 units)	$ 4.00		
20X2 sales price			
($750,000 ÷ 150,000 units)	$ 5.00		
Increase	$ 1.00		
Times units sold	150,000	$150,000	Favorable
Sales volume variance:			
Decrease in unit sales			
(180,000 - 150,000)	30,000		
Original sales price	4.00	$120,000	Unfavorable
Total variances		$ 80,000	Favorable

5556 Product and Service Pricing

5556.01 **Product pricing:** Product and service pricing refers to assigning monetary values to goods and services exchanged with external entities. Transfer pricing relates to intra-company sales. This section covers product pricing. Section **5557** covers transfer pricing.

5556.02 Pricing decisions differ substantially depending on the market structure within which a company operates. Market structure is determined by the number of firms in the market, barriers to entry, and communication among firms. Pure competition and monopoly are at the two extremes of market structure, with monopolistic competition and oligopoly in between. Very few markets are classified as purely competitive or purely monopolistic; most markets are monopolistic competition or oligopoly. Pricing strategies will differ depending on the type of market within which a company operates. Generally, a company will maximize profits when it prices its products and operates at a volume where marginal revenues equal marginal costs. These economic concepts are conceptually sound but difficult to implement because they are based on demand curves, cost functions, and competitor strategies that are difficult to measure and quantify. Therefore, most companies use a cost-based pricing strategy, but monitor and adjust the price based on competitor's prices, alternative products, customer's attitude, and the actual profit a given price provides.

5556.03 A long-term pricing policy requires the product's price to be high enough to cover all costs and provide an adequate return on invested capital. Methods for computing the product's price include the following:

    a. **Rate of markup:** A markup is added to the cost of the product to cover other operating costs and provide net income:

        Selling price = Product cost + (Product cost × Markup percentage)

The markup percentage is based on a desired return on assets employed, the expected amount of other costs, anticipated sales volume, and the unit's cost. If product cost is based on total manufacturing costs (using absorption costing), the following formula would be used to calculate the markup percentage:

$$\text{Markup \%} = \frac{(\text{Desired R of R} \times \text{Assets employed}) + \text{S \& A expenses}}{\text{Unit volume} \times \text{Unit manufacturing costs}}$$

b. **Rate of return on assets employed:** A desired return on assets employed is added to total operating costs and divided by the expected volume of sales.

$$\text{Selling price} = \frac{\text{Total cost} + (\text{Desired R of R} \times \text{Assets employed})}{\text{Unit sales volume}}$$

5556.04 Special product pricing decisions are covered in section **5564.10**.

5556.05 **Service pricing:** Many organizations (like repair shops, doctor offices, consulting organizations, and CPA firms) have labor as a major portion of the cost of the service they provide to their customers. Organizations like these typically use a time and materials pricing strategy. Two rates are used—one for time and a second for materials.

1. *Time*: A rate for time can be developed by estimating all the costs associated with the time component of the business, adding a desired amount for profit, and dividing by the estimated number of hours expected to be worked during the time period. An alternative to this (used by most CPA and consulting firms) is to calculate the desired gross pay per hour for each employee and multiply it by a standard multiple. When the employee works on a particular job, the amount charged to the client is equal to the number of hours worked times the rate per hour.

   Example: If a new accountant is to be paid $50,000 per year and is expected to work 2,000 hours for the year, the gross pay per hour is $25 ($50,000 ÷ 2,000 hours). Using a standard multiple of four, the new accountant's billing rate would be $100 per hour. Supposing the new accountant spends 20 hours on a particular job, the client would be charged $2,000 ($100 × 20 hours).

2. *Material loading charge*: A material loading charge is developed by estimating the costs associated with purchasing, handling, and storing the materials for the time period, adding a desired profit on the materials provided, and dividing by the total cost of the materials for the time period. When materials are used on a particular job, the amount charged to the customer is equal to the actual cost of the materials plus the materials loading charge.

   Example: Assume that a company expects to use $100,000 of materials during the year, and they expect to spend $40,000 on purchasing and handling the materials, plus they would like to earn $20,000 on the materials handled. Their materials loading rate would be 60% (($40,000 + $20,000) ÷ $100,000). If they actually used $5,000 of materials on a particular job, they would charge the client $8,000 ($5,000 + ($5,000 × .60)).

5557 Transfer Pricing

5557.01 **Transfer price** is the internal price charged by a selling department, division, or subsidiary of a company for a raw material, component, finished good, or service to a buying department, division, or subsidiary of the same company.

5557.02 **Transfer pricing methods:** There are three basic methods for establishing a transfer price:

   a. **Market-based price:** The transferring entity prices the goods or services to the buying entity at a price equal to that prevailing for those goods or services on the open market. Theoretically, this should be the same price at which the selling entity would sell the same goods or services to an external entity.

   Advantages of this method include the following:

   — Business units can operate as independent profit centers, with the manager being held responsible for the center's performance. This increases motivation for managers and aids performance evaluation by top management.

   — It fairly distributes profits among the various internal entities. This results in fair taxation by various countries for multinational organizations.

   Disadvantages of this method include the following:

   — A market price may not be available for intermediate products because no external market exists.

   — Using a market price and allowing a subdivision of a company to purchase intermediate parts from outside organizations may suboptimize net income for the company as a whole when idle capacity exists within the providing subdivision of the company.

   b. **Cost-based prices:** The transferring entity prices the goods or services to the buying entity at its cost of providing the good or service. The cost may be full cost, full standard cost, actual variable cost, or marginal cost. A decision must also be made about charging part of research and development to the cost of the product.

   Advantages for using cost include the following:

   — Cost data is generally available within the company.

   — This method is generally accepted by taxing authorities in a multinational environment.

   Disadvantages associated with this method include the following:

   — Identifying the cost of the good or service may be manipulated by the costs included in the calculation.

   — There is a loss of motivation to control costs within the providing division of the organization because all costs are passed on to the purchasing division. This erodes the competitiveness of the firm.

   — It does not provide any meaningful measure to evaluate the performance of the selling division of the company.

    c. **Negotiated price:** The transferring entity prices the goods or services to the buying entity at a price that is mutually acceptable to both the selling and buying divisions.

    Advantages with a negotiated price include the following:

    — A negotiated price can always be developed.

    — It makes managers responsible for their performance, provides reasonable measures to evaluate performance, and encourages cost minimization.

    Disadvantages with using this method include the following:

    — There may be significant time associated with negotiating a fair price.

    — It can result in suboptimization of enterprise net income.

5557.03 There is a range within which the transfer price should be established to optimize net income for the enterprise as a whole. The minimum transfer price should be equal to the variable costs of the selling division plus any lost contribution margin per unit on sales it could have made to outside entities that are lost by providing the goods or services to the internal division. The maximum transfer price should be equal to the price at which the buying division could purchase the good or service from an external entity.

5557.04 **Objectives in transfer pricing:** There are several objectives that must be balanced in selecting a transfer price, especially when the company operates in several different countries.

    a. Evaluate performance—One key objective of a transfer price is to fairly and accurately measure the performance of a segment and its management.

    b. Minimize taxation—Global taxes can be minimized by using transfer prices to move products at cost out of countries with high corporate taxes and generate profits in countries with low corporate taxes.

    c. Minimize tariffs—Tariffs can be minimized by using transfer prices to move products at cost to or from countries with high duties or customs and at market value for countries with low tariffs.

    d. Hedge exchange rates—Transfer prices can be used to reduce exposure to exchange rate risks by moving funds out of weak currencies into strong currencies.

    e. Move cash—Transfer prices can be used to move cash from countries with exchange controls that restrict the repatriation of dividends and capital.

    f. Improve competitive position—Lowering the transfer price to a subsidiary can enable it to lower its prices to match or undercut local competition.

5560 Cost-Volume-Profit Analysis and Special Analyses for Management Decision Making

5561 Terminology

5561.01 **Absorption costing (full costing):** A type of product costing that assigns fixed overhead to units produced as a product cost.

5561.02 **Breakeven:** The point at which an enterprise's revenues equal costs so that no profit or loss is incurred. It may be stated in units or sales dollars.

5561.03 **Contribution margin ratio:** A ratio of contribution margin to price computed as $(P - VC) \div P$, where P is price and VC is variable cost.

5561.04 **Margin of safety:** The excess of actual or budgeted sales over sales at the breakeven point. It is the amount by which sales could decrease before losses occur.

5561.05 **Relevant range:** Limits within which the volume of activity can vary and sales and cost relationships remain valid.

5561.06 **Sales mix:** The relative combination of products that compose a company's total sales.

5561.07 **Sunk cost:** A past cost that has been incurred and cannot be reversed.

5561.08 **Variable costing (direct or marginal costing):** A type of product costing that expenses fixed manufacturing overhead as a period cost.

5562 Cost-Volume-Profit Analysis

5562.01 Cost-volume-profit analysis is sometimes called breakeven analysis. It is a technique to evaluate the relationship between costs, volume of activity, and profit. It is useful in providing answers to the following types of questions:

    a. At what sales volume will we break even?

    b. What must the sales volume be to earn $X profit?

    c. How will profits be affected if the sales price is changed by $Y per unit?

    d. What is the effect on the breakeven point if variable costs are converted to fixed costs by increased mechanization?

5562.02 The key factors in cost-volume-profit analysis are revenues, fixed costs, and variable costs. Accountants generally assume that both revenues and costs are linear. As long as revenue per unit exceeds variable cost per unit, there will be a point at which the firm will break even. The breakeven point is where total revenues equal total costs. Above (below) this point there will be a profit (loss). The following diagram illustrates these relationships:

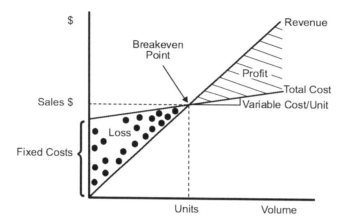

5562.03 Contribution margin per unit is the sales price less variable cost per unit. If the sales price exceeds the variable cost, the contribution margin is positive and each unit is providing something to cover fixed cost and generate a profit. A breakeven point is reached as soon as the cumulative contribution margin from all units equals the fixed cost. Expressed in equation form:

$$\text{Breakeven units} = \frac{FC}{(P - VC)}$$

where: FC =   Total fixed costs

P =   Price per unit

VC =   Variable cost per unit

5562.04 Questions on the CPA Examination often ask for breakeven stated in sales dollars. This can be obtained by computing breakeven in units and multiplying it by the sales price, or it can be computed directly as follows:

$$\text{Breakeven sales dollars} = \frac{FC}{\left(\dfrac{P - VC}{P}\right)}$$

The computation $(P - VC) \div P$ is called the contribution margin ratio.

5562.05 If the problem is to determine the number of units or sales volume required to generate a profit, the amount of desired profit is added to the fixed cost in the equations shown. Additional units must be sold to accumulate enough contribution margin to cover both the fixed cost and the desired profit. Note that this is profit before income tax. Variable cost per unit does not include any income tax.

$$\text{Units} = \frac{FC + NI}{(P - VC)} \qquad \text{Sales dollars} = \frac{FC + NI}{(P - VC) \div P}$$

Where: NI = Net income before income taxes

5562.06 If the desired profit is specified as an after-tax amount, the after-tax amount must be adjusted to a before-tax amount for inclusion in the equations. To get before-tax profit, divide the after-tax profit by one minus the tax rate:

$$\text{Before-tax NI} = \frac{\text{After-tax NI}}{1 - \text{tax rate}}$$

5562.07 Cost-volume-profit analysis as described has several assumptions built into it. If these are not valid, the results will be inaccurate. Assumptions that underlie cost-volume-profit analysis include the following:

a. Costs can be classified as either fixed or variable.

b. Total variable costs change at a linear rate. (Variable costs per unit remain unchanged.)

c. Total fixed costs remain unchanged over the relevant range of the breakeven chart. (Fixed costs per unit change.)

d. Sales price does not change with changes in volume.

e. There is only one product, and, if there are multiple products, the sales mix remains constant.

f. Productive efficiency does not change.

g. Inventories are kept constant or at zero.

h. Volume is the only relevant factor affecting costs.

5562.08 The results of cost-volume-profit analysis are frequently illustrated in a profit-volume graph. As the name implies, a profit-volume (P/V) graph focuses entirely on the relationship between volume and profit. It shows profit directly rather than as the difference between the revenue and cost curves as on a breakeven chart (see section **5562.02**).

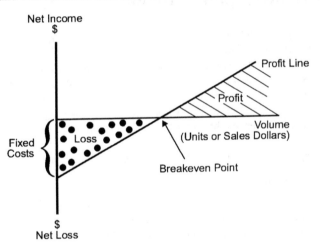

The vertical axis represents net income (net loss), and the horizontal axis represents volume. The vertical axis is extended below the origin to show a net loss. The measure of volume can be either units of production or sales dollars. The profit (loss) line is plotted by computing the profit (loss) at two levels of output. The two points most commonly used are zero production level and breakeven point. At an output of zero, the loss will be the fixed costs. The slope of the profit line is equal to the contribution margin. It slopes upward to the right and crosses the horizontal axis at the breakeven point.

5562.09 **Illustration:** Two examples follow to illustrate the computations involved in breakeven analysis (AICPA adapted).

Example: The Oliver Company plans to market a new product. Based on its market studies, Oliver estimates that it can sell 5,500 units in 20X1. The selling price will be $2.00 per unit. Variable costs are estimated to be 40% of the selling price. Fixed costs are estimated to be $6,000. What is the breakeven point?

Solution:

Variable cost per unit = $40\% \times \$2.00 = \$0.80$

Breakeven units = $\dfrac{\$6,000}{\$2.00 - \$0.80} = 5,000$ units

Breakeven sales dollars = $\dfrac{\$6,000}{(\$2.00 - \$0.80) \div \$2.00} = \$10,000$

Example: The Brieden Company sells rodaks for $6.00 per unit. Variable costs are $2.00 per unit. Fixed costs are $37,500. How many rodaks must be sold to realize a profit before income taxes of 15% of sales?

Solution:

Breakeven in sales ($) dollars:

$$S = \dfrac{\$37,500 + \$0.15(S)}{(\$6.00 - \$2.00) \div \$6.00} = \$72,580$$

Breakeven in units: $\dfrac{\$72,580}{\$6} = 12,097$ units

5563 Variable Versus Absorption Costing

5563.01 Variable costing is sometimes called direct or marginal costing. Absorption costing is sometimes referred to as full product costing. The difference between variable and absorption costing is the way fixed overhead costs are handled. Under variable costing, they are charged to expense as a period cost in the period incurred. No fixed overhead costs are allocated to the units produced. Absorption costing treats fixed costs as a product cost and allocates them to the units produced. Fixed costs follow the units through work-in-process and finished goods inventory, and are expensed through cost of goods sold when the units are sold.

5563.02 The following summarizes the major arguments in favor of each method.

a. Variable costing:

(1) Variable costing is felt to be more useful for management decision making because it separates fixed costs that do not change with volume. The impact of management decisions that change volume is more evident.

(2) Fixed factory overhead is more closely related to the capacity to produce than to the production of specific units. Since fixed costs would be incurred regardless of production and, since they relate to the capacity to produce for a period of time, they should be reported as a period cost.

b. Absorption costing:

(1) Fixed factory overhead is a necessary cost of production and units produced should bear all such costs. It is consistent with the concept that the cost of an asset should include all necessary costs to get it into proper form, location, and working condition.

(2) Absorption costing is required by both generally accepted accounting principles and the Internal Revenue Service.

5563.03 Problems on the CPA Examination are generally one of the following two types:

1. Analyzing the impact on absorption costing profit and variable costing profit for different levels of production and sales

2. Computing the product cost and net income for variable costing and absorption costing

5563.04 Over the long run, the difference between variable costing profit and absorption costing profit will be zero. The difference is not in the amount of expense but the timing of expense. In the short run, profit will be different when production and sales are not the same. Some fixed overhead will be inventoried or taken from inventory under absorption costing, which would not be done under variable costing.

5563.05 Fixed overhead must be accounted for differently when computing product costs, cost of goods sold, or net income under the two methods. Fixed overhead is a product cost for absorption costing and a period cost for variable costing.

5563.06 **Illustration:** Variable and absorption costing (AICPA adapted).

Problem: JV Company began its operations on January 1, 20X1, and produces a single product that sells for $7.00 per unit. Standard capacity is 100,000 units per year, and 100,000 units were produced and 80,000 units were sold in 20X1.

Manufacturing costs and selling and administrative expenses were as follows:

	Fixed Costs	**Variable Costs**
Raw materials	—	$1.50 per unit produced
Direct labor	—	1.00 per unit produced
Factory overhead	$150,000	0.50 per unit produced
Selling and administrative	80,000	0.50 per unit sold

There were no variances from the standard variable costs. Any over- or underapplied overhead is written off directly at year end as an adjustment to cost of goods sold.

Required:

a. Compute the unit cost under absorption costing for presenting inventory on the balance sheet at December 31, 20X1.

b. Compute the net income for 20X1 under variable costing.

Solution:

Part a. Absorption costing values units in ending inventory at full cost of production, including fixed factory overhead.

Production cost/unit:	
Raw materials	$ 1.50
Direct labor	1.00
Overhead: Variable	0.50
Fixed	1.50[a]
Total	$ 4.50

[a] *Cost per unit at standard capacity ($150,000 ÷ 100,000 units)*

Part b. Variable costing charges fixed factory overhead to expense as incurred. Income is computed as follows:

Sales (80,000 × $7.00)		$560,000
Less variable costs:		
Raw materials (80,000 × $1.50)	$120,000	
Direct labor (80,000 × $1.00)	80,000	
Overhead (80,000 × $0.50)	40,000	
Selling (80,000 × $0.50)	40,000	280,000
Contribution margin		$280,000
Less fixed costs:		
Overhead	$150,000	
Selling	80,000	230,000
Net income		$ 50,000

5564 Relevant Costs for Management Decisions

5564.01 Management is always faced with decisions on how to act now to achieve maximum profit in the future. Management-type decisions on the CPA Examination generally involve the manipulation of revenue and cost data to focus on the heart of the decision. There are some areas commonly tested and some basic concepts that are applicable. Each of the following will be reviewed:

    a. Identifying relevant costs

    b. Deciding to sell or further process joint or byproducts

    c. Deciding to produce internally or buy component parts

    d. Eliminating or modifying a business segment

    e. Pricing of special orders

    f. Utilizing limited capacity

The analysis can be based on an individual project approach or an incremental cost or revenue approach. Under the individual project approach, the total costs or revenues of each project are first computed, and the project with the lowest cost or highest revenue is selected. When the incremental approach is used, the incremental or added costs to move to the alternative proposal are subtracted from the incremental revenue provided by it. If the result is positive, it is considered a desirable alternative.

5564.02 **Relevant costs:** Critical in management decision making is the recognition that past (sunk) costs are irrelevant. Relevant costs for decision making are expected future costs that will differ among alternatives. Historical costs are useful only if they help predict the future.

5564.03 **Illustration:** The following example illustrates the irrelevance of past costs.

Example: An uninsured machine costing $50,000 is wrecked the first day. There are two alternatives—dispose of it for $5,000 cash and replace it with another machine at $51,000 or (b) rebuild it for $45,000 to be brand new as far as operating characteristics are concerned. Which alternative should be selected?

Solution: Rebuild, based on the following analysis. The $50,000 original cost is a sunk cost and irrelevant.

a.	New	$51,000	b.	Rebuild	$45,000
	Less salvage	5,000			
	Net cost	$46,000			

5564.04 **Sell or process further decision:** Joint product costs are the costs of a single process or series of processes that simultaneously produce two or more products of significant value. (See section **5542** for additional discussion of joint products and joint cost allocation.) Joint costs can be allocated to the products in a variety of ways, but all joint cost allocations are irrelevant in a decision to sell the product at the split-off point or process it further. This type of decision should be based on incremental revenues and incremental costs after the split-off point. If incremental revenue exceeds incremental cost, the additional processing is profitable.

5564.05 **Illustration:** The following example illustrates the relevant costs in a sell or process further decision.

Example: The Rancid City Meat Packing Company sells 5,000 pounds of low-grade beef scraps a week at a price of 9 cents per pound. By the company's method of allocating joint costs, the cost of these meat scraps has been calculated to be 12 cents per pound.

Rancid City's marketing vice president has just made a proposal to mix the beef scraps with grain, cook them, and pack the resulting mixture in cans under the private brand of a large regional chain of supermarkets. The mixture would be sold as dog food. One pound of beef scraps would provide the basic raw materials for two cans of dog food, which would be sold to the chain for 14 cents a can. Additional processing costs, including the costs of grain and other processing materials, would amount to $0.10 per can. Should the company accept or reject the proposal?

Solution: Reject the proposal and sell as is.

Incremental revenue to process further:

Processed (5,000 lbs. × 2 × $0.14/can)	$1,400
Sell as is (5,000 lbs. × $0.09/lb)	450
Incremental revenue	950
Incremental cost ($0.10 × 10,000 cans)	1,000
Net loss by additional processing	$ (50)

The allocated joint cost of twelve cents per pound is irrelevant.

5564.06 **Make or buy decision:** Management may be faced with a situation where they have idle facilities that may be used to produce a component that has been purchased externally. The costs that confuse the decision are the fixed overhead costs that are allocated to units produced internally but which would continue to be incurred if the product is purchased. These costs should be excluded from the decision. The product should be produced if there are idle facilities and the incremental cost to produce the product, including any opportunity cost of idle facilities, is less than the purchase price.

5564.07 **Illustration:** The following example illustrates a make or buy decision.

Problem: A company has 10,000 machine hours of idle capacity. It needs 7,000 units of component X for one of its product lines. It is estimated that each unit will take one machine hour for production. Currently, the company purchases it for $15 per part. Costs to produce component X are as follows:

	Per Unit	Total for 7,000 Units
Direct materials	$ 1	$ 7,000
Direct labor	8	56,000
Variable overhead	4	28,000
Fixed overhead*	5	35,000
Total	$18	$126,000

Assume that this is the cost for such things as depreciation on machinery and property tax on the plant and the equipment that will be incurred regardless of this decision.

Required: Should the parts be produced internally or purchased?

Solution: Produce internally. (Costs incurred regardless of the decision (i.e., the allocated fixed overhead) are not relevant to this decision.)

Purchase price/unit		$15
Incremental cost/unit:		
Direct material	$1	
Direct labor	8	
Variable overhead	4	
Total		13
Savings/unit		$ 2

5564.08 **Elimination of a business segment:** Some segments may report a loss when reports are prepared showing net income by segment. Based on this type of analysis, some managers will suggest that the segment be discontinued to increase overall enterprise profit. This overlooks the fact that all costs have been allocated to a segment, and some common costs will not be avoided by eliminating the segment. In this type of decision, the segment should not be discontinued as long as the segment contribution margin is positive (see section **5553** for computing segment contribution margin).

5564.09 **Illustration:** Evaluating elimination of business division (AICPA adapted).

Rice Corporation currently operates two divisions that had operating results for the year ended December 31, 20X2, as follows:

	West Division	Troy Division
Sales	$600,000	$300,000
Variable costs	310,000	200,000
Contribution margin	290,000	100,000
Fixed costs for the division	110,000	70,000
Margin over direct costs	180,000	30,000
Allocated corporate costs	90,000	45,000
Operating income (loss)	$ 90,000	$ (15,000)

Since the Troy Division sustained an operating loss during 20X1, Rice's president is considering the elimination of this division. Assume that the Troy Division fixed costs could be avoided if the division were eliminated. If the Troy Division had been eliminated on January 1, 20X2, Rice Corporation's 20X2 operating income would have been:

a. $15,000 higher

b. $30,000 lower

c. $45,000 lower

d. $60,000 higher

Solution: The correct answer is b. If the Troy Division had been eliminated on January 1, 20X2, the $300,000 sales, $200,000 variable cost, and $70,000 fixed costs would have been eliminated. The $45,000 allocation would not be eliminated but would be allocated to the remaining division. Therefore, the company would have reported $30,000 ($300,000 - $200,000 - $70,000) less operating income without the Troy Division. The $30,000 is the amount Troy Division contributes to cover common costs and generate net income.

5564.10 **Pricing of special orders:** Occasionally, a request is received to manufacture a product and sell it below the normal sales price. It is generally assumed that the special order will not encroach on existing sales. If it does, the order is generally rejected because the regular price is established to provide long-run profitability based on normal demand for the product. If the assumption is valid, profitability can be increased by accepting the special order if the price per unit exceeds the variable costs. Fixed costs normally allocated to all units produced should be excluded from the decision because they will be covered by normal sales at the normal price.

5564.11 **Illustration:** Special order pricing.

Problem: Gyro Gear Company produces a special gear used in automatic transmissions. Each gear sells for $28, and the company sells approximately 500,000 gears each year. Unit cost data for 20X1 is presented as follows:

	Variable	Fixed
Direct material	$6.00	
Direct labor	5.00	
Other costs:		
Manufacturing	$2.00	$7.00
Distribution	4.00	3.00

Gyro has received an offer from a foreign manufacturer to purchase 25,000 gears. Domestic sales would be unaffected by this transaction. If the offer is accepted, variable distribution costs will increase $1.50 per gear for insurance, shipping, and import duties. What is the relevant unit cost to a pricing decision on this offer?

Solution:

Variable costs of production		
Direct materials	$6.00	
Direct labor	5.00	
Other	2.00	$13.00
Variable costs of sale		
Normal	4.00	
Special	1.50	5.50
Total		$18.50

This special order will increase total firm profitability if the price exceeds $18.50.

5570 Capital Budgeting

5571 Terminology

5571.01 **Annuity:** Receipt or payment of a constant amount of money at equal intervals of time.

5571.02 **Capital budgeting:** Analysis of investment decisions, usually in plant or equipment, which have a useful life greater than one year.

5571.03 **Net present value:** The present value of the net cash inflows (outflows) discounted at a specified interest rate.

5571.04 **Opportunity cost:** The return from alternative choices that are rejected. The maximum contribution that is foregone by using limited resources in a particular way.

5571.05 **Payback period:** Period of time required to recover the initial investment without considering the time value of money.

5571.06 **Time-adjusted rate of return:** The interest rate that equates the present value of the net cash inflows and outflows.

5572 Introduction to Capital Budgeting

5572.01 **Capital budgeting** is the analysis of investment decisions that have a useful life longer than one year. Management uses capital budgeting to allocate resources to investment opportunities in an attempt to obtain the maximum return to the firm. The investment decisions are project oriented. The following questions are common:

　　a. Is this machine profitable?

　　b. Which of these machines is most profitable?

　　c. Is it profitable to add a product, segment, or new market?

　　d. Should a research and development project or an advertising program be implemented?

　　e. Should existing debt be extinguished?

5572.02 The relevant data in capital budgeting is cash-flow oriented. Regardless of the approach used, the following are essential:

　　a. Initial investment

　　b. Future net cash inflows or net savings in cash outflows

5572.03 Data for capital budgeting is relevant only if it affects the cash flows. Some data accumulated for financial reporting is either not useful or must be adjusted to be useful for capital budgeting. Financial accounting is primarily concerned with computing periodic earnings (using the accrual basis of accounting) for the firm or a reportable segment of the firm. Accrual accounting is not relevant in capital budgeting. The decision is project oriented, and the relevant data is the cash flow associated with that project.

5572.04 Because capital budgeting is long-term oriented, the time value of money is very important. Some approaches to capital budgeting account for the time value of money and some do not. Those that account for it are considered preferable because of the inequity of comparing a $1 investment today with a $1 return sometime in the future. Inflation that persists and the opportunity cost of having money sit idle make them unequal. Present-value techniques are useful in adjusting dollar amounts received or paid at different points in time to a common point in time. A brief review of the time value of money is provided in section **5573**.

5572.05 There are several approaches to capital budgeting. Those commonly used and tested on the CPA Examination are listed as follows (each of these will be explained and illustrated):

　　a. Net present value

　　b. Time-adjusted rate of return

　　c. Payback period

　　d. Accounting rate of return

5573   Time Value of Money

5573.01   Money at different points in time is not comparable because of the time value of money. Inflation and the opportunity cost associated with idle cash make comparisons inaccurate, thus complicating capital budgeting decisions because of their long life. Present value or future value computations are made to adjust for time and interest so that all cash flows are at a common point in time.

5573.02   **Future value of $1 sum:** A sum of money *(P)* invested today at a given interest rate *(i)* will increase in value over time *(n)*. The future value *(F)* can be computed as:

$$F = P \times (1 + i)^n$$

Factors have been computed for various combinations of i and n [$f_{in} = (1 + i)^n$] and are shown in future value tables. A portion of a future value table is shown next. The following equation is relevant when factors are used from the table:

$$F = P\,(f_{in})$$

The future amount of $1: $f_{in} = (1 + i)^n$

Period	8%	10%	12%
1	1.0800	1.1000	1.1200
2	1.1664	1.2100	1.2544
3	1.2597	1.3310	1.4049
4	1.3605	1.4641	1.5735
5	1.4693	1.6105	1.7623

Example: How much will $10,000 be worth in four years if the interest rate is 10%?

Formula solution: F $= \$10,000 \times (1 + .10)^4$
$= \$10,000 \times 1.4641$
$= \$14,641$

Table solution: F $= \$10,000 \times 1.4641$
$= \$14,641$

You should be familiar with the equations and be able to use the table factors to compute the future value of a sum of money when *n* and *i* are given. You should be able to work backward to compute any missing value (e.g., *n* or *i*) when the other values are given.

5573.03   **Present value of $1 sum:** The present value or discounted value of a $1 sum is just the opposite of future value. The question is, what amount *(P)* must be invested today at a given interest rate *(i)* to be worth a specified amount *(F)* in a given number of years *(n)*? The future value equation can be solved for *P* to obtain the following:

$$P = F\left(\frac{1}{(1+i)^n}\right)$$

The interest factor can be specified as follows:

$$P_{in} = \frac{1}{(1+i)^n}$$

Various combinations of *i* and *n* have been computed and included in a present-value table.

The present amount of $1:

$$P^{in} = \frac{1}{(1+i)^n}$$

Period	8%	10%	12%
1	0.9259	0.9091	0.8929
2	0.8573	0.8264	0.7972
3	0.7938	0.7513	0.7118
4	0.7350	0.6830	0.6355
5	0.6806	0.6209	0.5674

Notice that P_{in} is the reciprocal of f_{in}.

Example: An investment will pay $14,641 in four years. What is the present value of the payout if the interest rate is 10%?

$$\text{Table solution: } P = \$14,641 \times 0.6830$$
$$= \$10,000$$

5573.04 **Annuity:** An *ordinary annuity* is a series of equal cash flows at the *end* of equal intervals of time. An *annuity due* is a series of equal cash flows at the *beginning* of equal intervals of time.

Example of a 3-year ordinary annuity of $100:

	$100	$100	$100	
0	1	2	3	Time in years

Example of a 3-year ordinary annuity due of $100:

$100	$100	$100		
0	1	2	3	Time in years

5573.05 **Future value of an annuity:** The future value of an annuity can be computed by moving each of the annuity amounts to the end of the annuity's life using the factors from the table of future amount of $1 (section **5573.02**).

Example: What is the future value of a $100 ordinary annuity for three years when the interest rate is 10%?

$$F = (\$100 \times 1.2100) + (\$100 \times 1.1000) + (\$100 \times 1.0000)$$
$$= \$100 \times (1.2100 + 1.1000 + 1.0000)$$
$$= \$100 \times 3.3100$$
$$= \$331$$

The direct formula for computing the future value of an ordinary annuity is:

$$F = A\left(\frac{(1+i)^n - 1}{i}\right)$$

Factor values have been computed and are shown in the table that follows:

Period	8%	10%	12%
1	1.0000	1.0000	1.0000
2	2.0800	2.1000	2.1200
3	3.2464	3.3100	3.3744
4	4.5061	4.6410	4.7793
5	5.8666	6.1051	6.3528

Notice that the factor for 10% and three periods is 3.3100, which is the same as the factor computed in the prior example when the annual factors were totaled. Ordinary annuity factors in the table can be converted to annuity due factors by adding 1 to the number of periods and subtracting 1.000 from the value of the factor.

Example: What is the future value of a $100 annuity due for three years when money is worth 10%?

$$F = \$100 \times 3.641$$
$$= \$364.10$$

The factor 3.641 is the factor for four (3 + 1) periods at 10% (4.6410) minus 1.0000 from the value of the factor.

5573.06 **Present value of an annuity:** The present value of an annuity can be computed by moving each of the annuity amounts to the present time period using the factors from the table of present values of $1, by the present value of an annuity formula, or by the factor from a table of present values of an annuity of $1.

Formula for present value of an ordinary annuity:

$$P = A\left(\frac{1-(1+i)^{-n}}{i}\right)$$

Factor values have been computed and are shown in the table that follows:

Period	8%	10%	12%
1	0.9259	0.9091	0.8929
2	1.7833	1.7355	1.6901
3	2.5771	2.4869	2.4018
4	3.3121	3.1699	3.0373
5	3.9927	3.7908	3.6048

Example: What is the present value of an ordinary annuity of $100 for three years when interest is 10%?

$$P = \$100 \times 2.4869$$
$$= \$248.69$$

The ordinary annuity factors in the table can be changed to annuity due factors by subtracting 1 from the number of periods and adding 1.0000 to that factor.

Example: What is the present value of a $100 annuity due for three years and a 10% interest rate?

$$P = \$100 \times 2.7355$$
$$= \$273.55$$

The factor for two periods is obtained (1.7355) and 1.0000 is added to it.

5573.07 **Compound interest:** Unless stated otherwise, assume that interest is compounded annually. Frequently, however, interest will be stated as an annual amount but compounded semi-annually, quarterly, or even monthly. In these cases, you must adjust the interest rate and number of periods.

a. Adjust the interest rate according to the compounding period (16% interest compounded semi-annually is 8% per period).

b. Adjust n from the number of years to the number of compounding periods (five years compounded semi-annually is 10 periods).

The revised interest rate and number of periods can be used in any of the formulas or tables.

5574　Net Present Value

5574.01　The **net present value method** adjusts for the time value of money. It seeks to determine whether the present value of estimated future cash inflows at a desired rate of return will be greater or less than the cost of the proposed investment. The cash inflows, initial investment, and desired rate of return are givens. The present value of the cash inflows is calculated and compared to the initial investment. An investment proposal is desirable if its net present value is positive (i.e., if the present value of the cash inflows exceeds the investment).

5574.02　When several investment proposals with equal investments are being considered, they are ranked by net present values. The proposals with the highest net present values should be chosen. An implicit assumption of this method is that all net cash inflows can be reinvested at the rate used in computing net present value. If the proposals have unequal investments, they should be ranked according to their profitability index. The profitability index is computed by dividing the present value of the cash flows by the initial investment.

5574.03　**Illustration:** Net present value.

Problem: The company is considering the acquisition of a new machine that costs $20,000. It will be a labor-saving investment that will reduce payroll $5,000 per year. Its useful life is eight years and it will have zero salvage value. A minimum desired rate of return of 12% is used for capital budgeting decisions. Should the machine be acquired?

Solution: The relevant data is charted as follows:

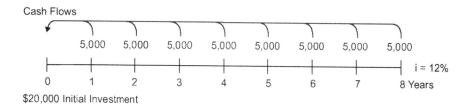

The present value of an ordinary annuity of $1 for eight periods at 12% is 4.9676.

Net present value:

Cash flows ($5,000 × 4.9676)	$24,838
Initial investment	20,000
Net present value—positive	$ 4,838

Because the net present value is positive, it is a desirable investment at a 12% interest rate.

5574.04　The net present value method is easily applied when the cash flows are not equal amounts.

Example: An investment alternative costs $10,000 and results in cash flows of $5,000, $4,000, and $3,000, respectively, for three years. The desired minimum rate of return is 14%.

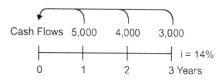

The present value of a lump sum of $1 received at the end of a year assuming 14% annual interest is 0.8772 (Year 1), 0.7695 (Year 2), and 0.6750 (Year 3).

Net present value:
Cash flow:

$5,000 × .8772 =	$ 4,386	
4,000 × .7695 =	3,078	
3,000 × .6750 =	2,025	$ 9,489
Initial investment		10,000
Net present value		$ (511)

Since this is a negative amount, the proposal would be rejected.

5575 Time-Adjusted Rate of Return

5575.01 A time-adjusted rate of return is also called an internal rate of return. It is a method used when the cost of the investment and annual cash flows are known and the rate of return is to be determined. The time-adjusted rate of return is the rate that equates the present value of the projected future net cash flows with the cost of the investment. Investments with a rate of return greater than the firm's desired rate of return are desirable. Those with a return less than the desired rate of return should be rejected.

5575.02 When more than one project is being considered, they are ranked according to their projected rate of return. Those with the highest rate of return are most desirable. An implicit assumption of this method is that all net cash inflows from the project under consideration can be reinvested at the computed rate of return.

5575.03 **Illustration:** Time-adjusted rate of return.

Problem: The company is considering the acquisition of a new machine that costs $20,000. It will provide a savings of $5,000 per year over its useful life of eight years. The salvage value is expected to be zero. What is the time-adjusted rate of return and should the machine be acquired?

Solution: The cash flows are charted as follows:

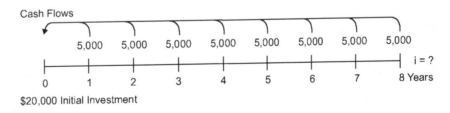

When the cash flows are an annuity, the present-value factor can be determined by dividing the initial investment by the annuity:

$$\frac{\$20,000}{\$5,000} = 4.000 \text{ present-value factor}$$

The time-adjusted rate of return can be obtained from the present-value table for an annuity by finding the rate for the number of periods (8) that has a factor closest to 4.000. In this case, the rate is slightly over 20%.

This project would be desirable if the minimum rate of return is 20% or lower.

5575.04 The time-adjusted rate of return is not easily applied when the cash flows are not equal annuity payments. A trial-and-error method must be used to obtain the rate of return.

Example: An investment opportunity costs $10,000 and returns $5,000, $4,000, and $3,000, respectively, the first three years. What is the time-adjusted rate of return?

Solution:

Part a. Using an interest rate of 10%, the net present value is $105, computed as follows.

Cash flow

$5,000 × .9091 =	$4,545.50	
4,000 × .8264 =	3,305.60	
3,000 × .7513 =	2,253.90	$10,105
Cash investment		10,000
Net present value		$ 105

Since this is a positive amount, a higher rate is selected.

Part b. At a 12% interest rate, there is a negative net present value of $211.30, computed as follows:

Cash flow

$5,000 × .8929 =	$4,464.50	
4,000 × .7972 =	3,188.80	
3,000 × .7118 =	2,135.40	$ 9,7898.70
Cash investment		10,000.00
Net present value		$ (211.30)

Since this is a negative amount, the interest rate is something less than 12%. By extrapolation, a rate of 10.67% is obtained:

$$0.10 + \frac{211 \div (211 + 105)}{100} = 0.1067$$

If the desired minimum rate of return is greater than 10.67%, this project should be rejected.

Computer software is available to compute the time-adjusted rate of return. Most programs use a trial-and-error method. Required inputs to the program are cash flows (both inflows and outflows) by period and a seed internal rate of return. The computer program uses the seed internal rate of return on the initial calculation and refines the rate on subsequent calculations until it has a rate that produces a net present value of zero (or very close to zero). Some financial calculators are also capable of producing these results.

5576 Payback Period

5576.01 The payback period does not adjust for the time value of money. It computes the length of time required to recover the initial cash investment. When the annual cash flows are equal, the payback period is computed by dividing the initial investment by the annual cash flow.

$$\text{Payback period} = \frac{\text{Initial investment}}{\text{Annual cash flow}}$$

If annual cash flows are not equal, they are accumulated until the cumulative amount equals the initial investment. The payback period is the length of time required to accumulate the amount of the initial investment.

5576.02 When several investment alternatives are being considered, they are ranked according to the payback period. The investment alternatives with the shortest period are considered most desirable.

5576.03 The advantage of this method is that it is simple and easily understood. The chief limitation is that it emphasizes liquidity and disregards profitability. It is most appropriate when precise estimates of profitability are not crucial, a weak cash and credit position has a heavy bearing on the selection of investment possibilities, or considerable risk is involved in the proposed project.

5576.04 **Illustration:** Payback period.

Problem: Compute the payback period for an investment opportunity that costs $20,000 and provides equal annual cash flows of $4,000 per year for eight years.

Solution:

$$\frac{\$20,000}{\$4,000} = \text{5-year payback period}$$

Notice how the payback method does not even consider the cash flows between the end of the payback period and the end of the investment's useful life—in this case, between Year 5 and Year 8.

5577 Accounting Rate of Return

5577.01 The accounting rate of return does not consider the time value of money. The annual net cash inflow is adjusted for depreciation and divided by the investment.

$$\frac{\text{Net cash inflow - Depreciation}}{\text{Investment}} = \text{Rate of return}$$

5577.02 Disagreement exists as to what the investment should be. Some alternatives include (a) initial cost, (b) average book value, or (c) annual book value. Either (a) or (b) is preferable to (c). Annual book value results in an increasing rate of return over the life of the investment. Initial cost or the initial investment is most commonly used on the CPA Examination.

5578 Expected Value and Cost of Capital in Capital Budgeting

5578.01 The statistical term **expected value** describes the numerical average of a probability distribution. It can be used to estimate future cash receipts from a capital budgeting project. This method is employed to estimate the most likely amount of future cash receipts by (a) estimating the various amounts of cash receipts from the project each year under different assumptions or operating conditions, (b) assigning probabilities to the various amounts estimated for each year, and (c) determining the mean value of the estimated receipts for each year. (For more detail, see section **5582**.)

5578.02 **Cost of capital** refers to an overall cost of obtaining investment funds. While different techniques may be used in computing cost of capital, it is generally agreed that a cost factor should be assigned to both debt and all stockholders' equity (including retained earnings). Some authorities suggest using a weighted-average cost of capital for capital budgeting purposes. Cost of capital is the desired or target rate of return used in the net present value method of discounted cash flow computations. It is also the minimum acceptable (cutoff) rate used in choosing among projects employing the time-adjusted rate of return method, described in section **5575**.

5579 The Implications of Tax on Capital Budgeting Decisions

5579.01 Income tax laws are broad and comprehensive. Almost every item in capital budgeting has a related tax effect. Some items that are excluded when income tax is not relevant must be included when income tax is relevant. These items include depreciation and gains and losses on asset dispositions that do not affect cash flows except as they relate to the payment of income taxes.

5579.02 The following examples summarize the implications of income tax on capital budgeting decisions:

  a. Gain or loss on the disposition of an existing facility is a taxable gain or a deductible loss for computing income tax.

  b. Cash flows in the form of revenue are taxable. Revenues must be computed net of tax.

  c. Cash outflows in the form of expenses are deductible in computing taxes payable. These cash outflows must be computed net of tax.

  d. Depreciation is not a cash flow, but it affects the amount of taxes payable. The reduction in taxes payable due to depreciation is a cash flow item that must be included in the analysis.

  e. Salvage value equal to book value results in no gain (loss) and has no tax considerations.

5579.03 The general approach is to compute all items net of tax and apply one of the capital budgeting approaches described.

5579.04 **Illustration:** Tax considerations in applying net present value.

Problem: ABC Company is considering the replacement of machine X with machine Y. Machine X has a book value of $0 and a salvage value of $8,000. Machine Y will cost $30,000 and will result in an annual savings of $10,000 per year because of increased operating efficiency. It has a useful life of six years and an expected salvage value of $6,000. Straight-line depreciation is used, and the company has an average tax rate of 40%. The desired minimum rate of return is 20%.

Solution:

After-tax cash flow from selling machine X:	
Sale price	$ 8,000
Book value	0
Gain	8,000
Less tax (40%)	3,200
Net cash inflow	$ 4,800

Net cash outflow to replace machine X:	
Cost of machine Y	$30,000
Cash available—machine X	4,800
Net initial investment	$25,200

Annual cash inflows or cash savings:

a. Operating savings $10,000
   Less tax (40%) 4,000
   Net $ 6,000

b. Depreciation:
$$\frac{\text{Cost - Salvage Value}}{\text{Life}} = \frac{\$30,000 - \$6,000}{6 \text{ years}} = \$4,000/\text{yr}$$

Cash flow from tax savings on depreciation: $4,000 × .40   = $1,600

c. Total annual cash flows:
   Operating savings $6,000
   Tax savings on depreciation 1,600
   Total $7,600

d. Salvage value of machinery in Year 6 has no tax consequences. The cash flow from the salvage value at the end of Year 6 is $6,000.

The cash flows are charted as follows:

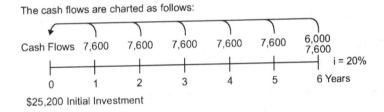

Net present value at 20% for six years:

Cash savings
   Annual: $7,600 × 3.3255 = $25,273.80
   Salvage, Year 6:   6,000 × 0.3349 =   2,009.40 $27,283.20
   Less: Initial investment   25,200.00
   Net present value $ 2,083.20

At a 20% interest rate, replacement of machine X with machine Y is a desirable investment.

5580 Other Quantitative Methods—Inventory Quality, Planning, and Control; JIT Purchasing; Balanced Scorecard; and Benchmarking

5580.01 Other quantitative methods frequently tested on the CPA Examination include probability analysis using expected values and inventory planning and control. Both economic order quantity (EOQ) and just-in-time (JIT) inventory are included under inventory planning and control. Balanced scorecard and benchmarking will also be addressed on the CPA examination. Each of these methods is covered in this section.

5580.02 Quantitative methods for curve fitting, including the high-low method and least-squares regression analysis, were covered under flexible budgeting (see section **5519**).

5581 Terminology

5581.01 Balanced Scorecard: Builds on total quality management by adding a feedback loop to monitor performance of strategic goals.

5581.02 Benchmarking: A tool for improving business processes by comparison with performance leaders.

5581.03 Cost of quality: Cost analysis that measures and monitors the cost of quality in four areas: prevention, appraisal, internal failure, and external failure.

5581.04 Economic order quantity (EOQ) model: A mathematical formula to compute the order quantity that minimizes the total cost of carrying inventory and set-up or ordering cost.

5581.05 Expected value: The mean or average value of a random variable over an infinite number of outcomes. It is calculated by weighting the value of each possible outcome by its probability and summing over all values.

5581.06 Just-in-time (JIT): A manufacturing philosophy that reduces or eliminates inventory—raw materials are received as they are needed for production and finished units are produced to meet customer demand.

5581.07 Nonvalue-adding activity: Any activity that could be eliminated without detracting from customer satisfaction with the final product.

5581.08 Order lead time: Time interval between placing an order and receiving the item in an inventory decision model.

5581.09 Payoff table: A matrix where the rows represent decision alternatives and the columns represent states of nature and the probability associated with each state. Each square within the matrix shows the payoff associated with that decision alternative and state of nature.

5581.10 Probability: A number between 0 and 1 that represents the odds that a particular event will occur. The sum of the probabilities of a set of events that are mutually exclusive (nonoverlapping) and collectively exhaustive (enumerate all possibilities) must add up to 1.

5581.11 Safety stock: Amount of additional inventory that is held to cover periods in which demand is greater than normal.

5581.12 Total quality control: Striving for a defect-free manufacturing process by involving all employees in a quality control effort.

5581.13 Total quality management: The application of quality principles to all aspects of the organization in an attempt to meet or exceed customers' expectations of quality.

5581.14 Value-adding activity: Activities that enhance customer satisfaction.

5582 Probability Analysis Using Expected Values

5582.01 **Probability analysis:** Most management decisions involve uncertainty. Uncertainty means that decisions must be made before knowing which of a set of possible future events will occur. Possible events are called states of nature. In decision making under uncertainty, the decision maker must choose a course of action before knowing which state of nature will occur. A prerequisite to making rational decisions under uncertainty is having some measure of the likelihood of occurrence of each possible state of nature. Such a measure is called **probability** and the development and use of probabilities is called **probability analysis.**

5582.02 **Developing probabilities:** The probability of an event $P(m)$ is computed by dividing the number of elements in the subset $n(m)$ by the number of elements in the universal set $n(u)$.

$$P(m) = \frac{n(m)}{n(u)}$$

Example: Historical data shows that the last 10 units sold consisted of eight units of model t and two units of model s. What is the probability that model t will be the next unit sold?

$$P(t) = \frac{8}{10} = 80\%$$

The development of probabilities is complicated when dealing with joint events (events that occur together), additive events (a collection of events such that any or all events can occur concurrently), and conditional probability (the probability of a particular event being contingent on another event). Most CPA Examination problems, however, deal with unconditional probability (the probability of an event occurring not being contingent on another event). Estimates of probability of individual events occurring are generally given and the problem requires the use of the probability estimates in some aspect of decision making.

5582.03 **Expected value:** Expected value of a random variable (x) is the average value that would occur if we were to average an infinite number of outcomes. Stated another way, it is the mean or average value of a random variable in the long run. The expected value of $x[E(x)]$ is calculated by weighting each value of x by its probability and summing over all values:

$$E(x) = \sum_{i=1}^{n} X_i P(X_i)$$

where: X_i is the ith value X can take on from 1 to n.
$P(X_i)$ is the probability associated with the X_i event.
n is the number of possible events.

Example: Suppose we are considering a capital budgeting decision to buy new equipment, but we need to know the expected payoff to the company if it is purchased. Our random variable is the expected cash flow, and the probability associated with each outcome is shown in the following probability distribution:

Expected Cash Flow	Probability Distribution
$10,000	.10
15,000	.20
20,000	.50
30,000	.20

What is the expected value?

Solution:

$E(x) = (\$10,000 \times 0.10) + (\$15,000 \times 0.20) + (\$20,000 \times 0.50) + (\$30,000 \times 0.20)$
$= \$20,000$

Keep in mind that, if the machine is acquired, the actual cash flow will probably not be $20,000. However, if this decision is repeated many times and if the probability distribution is accurate, on the average, the payoff will be $20,000 per year for each machine.

5582.04 **Variance:** The variance of a random variable *(x)* shows the dispersion of the observations. It is defined as the sum of the squared deviations of *x* from the expected value, weighted by their probability.

$$\sigma_x^2 = \sum_{i=1}^{n} \left(x_i - E(x) \right)^2 * P(x_i)$$

$$= \left[x_1 - E(x) \right]^2 * P(x_1) + \left[x_2 - E(x) \right]^2 * P(x_2) + \ldots + \left[x_n - E(x) \right]^2 * P(x_n)$$

Example: Using the machine data shown, compute the variance.

$$\sigma_x^2 = (10,000 - 20,000)^2 (.10) + (15,000 - 20,000)^2 (.20) + (20,000 - 20,000)^2 (.50) +$$
$$(30,000 - 20,000)^2 (.20)$$
$$= 35,000,000$$

A small variance indicates that the outcomes are closely clustered about the expected value.

5582.05 **Standard deviation:** The standard deviation is frequently reported in place of the variance. The standard deviation of *x* is the square root of the variance of *x*.

$$\sigma_x = \sqrt{\sigma_x^2}$$

Example: Using the machine data, compute the standard deviation.

$$\sigma_x = \sqrt{\$35,000,000} = \$5,916$$

5582.06 **Payoff table:** A decision maker is frequently faced with several decision alternatives and several possible states of nature. A state of nature is an uncontrollable event that will impact a decision. Each state of nature has a probability associated with its occurrence. The probabilities associated with the various states of nature must total 1.0.

A **payoff table** is developed by showing the states of nature in the column headings along with the probability associated with each. The decision alternatives are shown as row headings. Within each square of the matrix, the payoff associated with that decision alternative and state of nature is inserted.

Example: Management is deciding whether or not to build a new wing on the factory. The decision alternatives are "build" and "not build." There are three possible states of nature: improvement in the economy, economy stays the same, and economy deteriorates. The probability of each state is 0.20, 0.50, and 0.30, respectively. The various payoffs are shown in the matrix. If, for example, the wing is built and the economy improves, the payoff will be a $10,000 increase in profits per month. If it is built and the economy gets worse, profits will decrease by $5,000 per month.

State of Nature	Economy Improves	Economy Same	Economy Deteriorates	Expected Value
Probability / Decision Alternative	.20	.50	.30	
Build	10,000	2,000	(5,000)	1,500
Not Build	2,000	0	1,000	700

There are several decision rules that can be used, but the one most commonly tested on the CPA Examination is expected value. The expected value for each decision alternative is computed (by multiplying the probability of each state of nature by the payoff for that state of nature and summing for each decision alternative), and the alternative with the highest expected value is selected.

5583 Inventory Planning and Control (EOQ)

5583.01 **Inventory decision models** are designed to answer two basic questions.

1. What quantity of an item should be ordered or produced?

2. How often should an item be ordered or produced?

Information on demand, cost, lead times, and variability are required by the models.

5583.02 **Demand:** Most inventory models assume that there is a stable and uniform demand over the period. Demand in the economic order quantity (EOQ) model is specified in number of units per year.

5583.03 **Costs:** The relevant costs in the EOQ model are (a) annual costs of carrying one unit in stock, (b) ordering or set-up cost to purchase or produce the item, and (c) shortage costs. The purchase or production cost is not relevant because it will not change with the quantity ordered or produced. The annual carrying cost includes imputed interest on the investment in inventory, storage, insurance, obsolescence, spoilage, and theft. Ordering or set-up costs include preparing for a production run, preparing an order, evaluating bids, and receiving and paying vendor's invoices. Shortage costs include cost of lost sales, customer dissatisfaction, and lost customers.

5583.04 **Order lead time:** The time interval between placing an order and receiving the items.

5583.05 **Safety stock:** An additional quantity of inventory that is held to cover periods in which demand is greater than normal. The size of the safety stock is based on the degree of variability in demand (or standard deviation) and the acceptable risk of being out of stock.

5583.06 **Cost relationships:** Inventory decision models work with opposing costs. Carrying costs increase as the size of the order increases. Set-up or ordering costs, however, decrease as the size of the production run or order increases. The EOQ model seeks to minimize the combined total of these two costs as illustrated in the following graph:

438

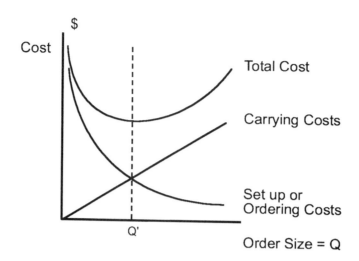

5583.07 **Fixed quantity system:** Most questions on the CPA Examination test your knowledge of a **fixed quantity system.** The fixed quantity system calculates a fixed order quantity *(Q)* that is used whenever an order is placed. The order is placed at the reorder point *(RP)*, which is dependent on the lead time *(LT)* and safety stock *(SS)*. The amount of the order is fixed, but the time of order placement varies from period to period, depending on demand. This system has two fixed parameters—order quantity and reorder point. Whenever the inventory level drops below the reorder point, an order is placed for the order quantity *(Q)*. These relationships are illustrated as follows:

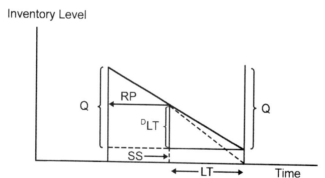

5583.08 **Order quantity computation:** The formula for computing the economic order quantity *(Q)* is:

$$Q = \sqrt{\frac{2DS}{Ci}}$$

where: D = Demand per year in units
S = Setup or ordering cost per order
C = Cost per unit
i = Carrying cost, expressed as a percentage of inventory cost
(C times i is the carrying cost per unit)

5583.09 **Reorder point computation:** Assuming that there is constant demand and lead time, the reorder point is the expected units of demand during lead time plus any required safety stock. This relationship can be illustrated as follows:

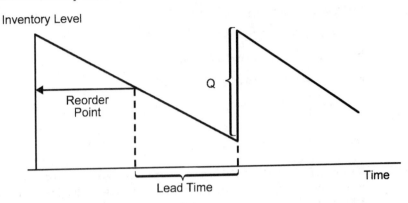

The formula for the reorder point (RP) is:

$$RP = D_{LT} + SS$$

where: D_{LT} = Average demand during lead-time period
SS = Safety stock

5583.10 **Example:** The following data will be used to illustrate the computation of order quantity and order point.

Demand (D)	= 40,000 units per year
Unit cost (C)	= $50
Carrying cost rate (i)	= 20% per year
Order cost (S)	= $115 per order
Lead time (LT)	= 3 days (assume 300 business days per year)
Safety stock (SS)	= 500 units

Solution:

$$Q = \sqrt{\frac{(2)(40,000)(115)}{(50)(.20)}}$$

$$= 959.2 \text{ or } 960$$

Reorder point:

$$RP = ((3 \div 300) \times 40,000) + 500$$
$$= 900 \text{ units}$$

In this example, when the stock of inventory is reduced to 900 units, an order will be placed for 960 units.

5584 Just-In-Time (JIT) Purchasing

5584.01 **Just-in-time (JIT)** is a manufacturing philosophy that promotes the simplest, least costly means of production. Under ideal conditions, the company would receive raw materials just in time to go into production, manufacture parts just in time to be assembled into products, and complete products just in time to be shipped to customers. JIT shifts the production philosophy from a *push* approach to a *pull* approach.

    a. The *push* begins with the acquisition of raw materials, which are pushed into production, through the various stages of production, and finally into finished goods inventory. It is hoped that finished goods can ultimately be sold to customers.

b. The *pull* approach starts with the demand for finished products from a customer. The customer order triggers the production of the goods. Inventories are acquired only to meet production needs.

Under ideal conditions, the company would produce:

a. only what customers want,

b. at the rate of customer demand,

c. with no unnecessary lead times, and

d. with zero idle inventory.

Goods are produced to meet demand and are delivered as they are produced. This eliminates finished goods inventory.

5584.02 Raw materials are delivered just in time to meet production needs, with a guaranteed high level of product quality so they can bypass inspection and go directly to production. This requires long-term purchase agreements with suppliers and coordination between purchasing and production. The result is a virtual elimination of raw material inventory.

5584.03 The rate of production for individual departments is determined by the needs of each succeeding department. Inventory buffers with predetermined maximum sizes are used to signal when a department should be working. The department works as long as the buffer is less than the maximum. This eliminates most work-in-process inventory.

5584.04 Changes are required in several areas of a manufacturing process to make JIT successful.

a. **Eliminate activities that do not add value to a product or a service.** Activities are identified as value-adding activities and nonvalue-adding activities. A **nonvalue-adding activity** is any activity that could be eliminated without detracting in any way from customers' satisfaction with the final product. Business process re-engineering is often used to identify and eliminate nonvalue-adding activities. Machining, milling, and polishing of products are all *value-adding activities,* as customer satisfaction would be reduced without them. Moving time, inspection time, and time in queues are all nonvalue-adding activities and should be eliminated as much as possible.

b. **Obtain agreements with suppliers.** Without a supply of raw materials in inventory, the company becomes very dependent on its suppliers. To minimize this problem, the number of suppliers is limited to a select few who guarantee both the quality and timeliness of raw materials. Raw materials are usually delivered in small quantities as needed for production. Responsibility for raw material quality is also shifted to the supplier.

c. **Develop manufacturing cells.** Traditional departments and processes are replaced with manufacturing cells that contain families of machines typically spread through several departments. A component or a complete product can be produced within one cell rather than being transferred between several departments.

d. **Obtain a flexible, highly trained workforce.** The cellular manufacturing environment requires a labor force that is capable of operating several different machines. The workforce must be capable of servicing the machines and performing inspections on finished products.

e. **Implement total quality control.** The streamlined flow of raw materials and components through the production process does not allow for product defects. No defects can be allowed in parts or raw materials received from suppliers, in work-in-process, or in finished goods. Emphasis is placed on doing things right the first time and avoiding rework or waste of any type. Products are inspected for quality at each stage of the process. Any defect halts the process until it is corrected. Responsibility for inspecting products is shifted from inspectors to production workers. There is a commitment for continuous improvement in all aspects of the company.

f. **Reduced set-up time.** Set-up time is the time required to change equipment, move materials, and obtain forms needed to shift production from one product to another. Meeting customer demand on short notice without any finished goods inventory requires the ability to shift production from one product to another with a short set-up time.

5584.05 **Example:** Nile Co.'s cost allocation and product costing procedures follow activity-based principles. Activities have been identified and classified as being either value-adding or nonvalue-adding as to each product. Which of the following activities, used in Nile's production process, is nonvalue-adding? (AICPA adapted)

a. Design engineering activity

b. Heat treatment activity

c. Drill press activity

d. Raw material storage activity

Answer: The correct answer is d. Customer satisfaction would be reduced if the activities under a, b, or c were eliminated. However, the storage of raw materials could be eliminated without reducing customer satisfaction.

5585 Improving Product Quality and Reducing Cost

5585.01 **Total quality control (TQC)** involves all employees in the quality control effort. It is the unending quest for perfect quality—the striving for a defect-free manufacturing process. Emphasis shifts from an acceptable level of quality to total quality control with zero defects as the objective.

5585.02 TQC and JIT are often combined so that the production process is stopped whenever something goes wrong. Because production schedules are so tightly synchronized, all employees must be involved to identify when a quality control problem occurs. Production is halted until the problem is identified and corrected.

5585.03 **Total quality management (TQM)** is the application of quality principles to all of the organization's endeavors to satisfy customers. It is a method of managing the organization to excel on all dimensions. The customer defines quality. Therefore, product quality performance measures are likely to include product reliability and service delivery in addition to product cost.

5585.04 By integrating TQC, TQM, and JIT, several benefits are achieved: (a) fewer defective units are produced before the problem is identified, (b) the process causing the problem can be fixed before more bad units are produced, (c) immediate attention gives rise to easier problem identification and solution, and (d) higher-quality products improve customer satisfaction.

5585.05 **Example:** Nonfinancial performance measures are important to engineering and operations managers in assessing the quality levels of their products. Which of the following indicators can be used to measure product quality? (AICPA adapted)

    I. Returns and allowances

    II. Number and types of customer complaints

    III. Production cycle time

    a. I and II only.

    b. I and III only.

    c. II and III only.

    d. I, II, and III.

Answer: The correct answer is a. Both of these items provide feedback from customers. Production cycle time—the length of time required to convert raw materials into finished products—does not necessarily relate to quality.

5585.06 Every effort should be made to produce a quality product and to produce it right the first time. Cost of quality (COQ) is an area of cost analysis that measures and monitors quality costs in four areas:

    1. **Prevention:** Costs of preventing bad quality (such as worker training and quality circles)

    2. **Appraisal:** Costs of monitoring the level of bad quality (such as product testing and scrap reporting systems)

    3. **Internal failure:** Costs of fixing bad quality (such as rework labor)

    4. **External failure:** Costs of bad quality that are not discovered before shipment (such as warranty claims or customer ill-will)

The objective is to minimize the total cost of quality. Total cost of quality is the sum of prevention and appraisal costs, which increase with quality level, and internal and external failure costs, which decrease with quality level. This is illustrated as follows:

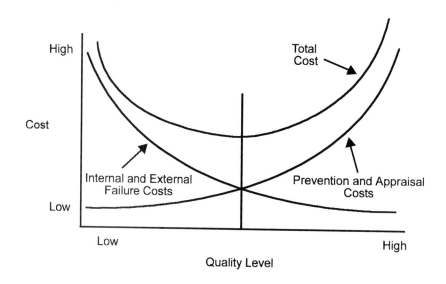

5585.07 **Continuous improvement** (sometimes called **target-based costing**) is a concept that seeks to reduce costs while maintaining quality. Cost control using traditional engineering standards maintains the status quo. Continuous improvement seeks to reduce costs that frequently disturb the established order. One way to achieve this is by using market-driven standards rather than engineering-driven standards. Engineering-driven standards are based on existing technology. The engineering-driven standard plus a desired markup equals the desired market price. Market-driven standards work in reverse order. A competitive market price that yields the desired market share less the desired markup equals allowable cost. The allowable cost becomes the target standard. Continuous improvement is sought until the target standard is achieved. This changes the focus from optimizing within existing technology to modifying technology until the desired standard is achieved. Thus, actual cost from a prior period becomes a starting point for further tightening.

5586 Life Cycle Costing

5586.01 **Life cycle costing** generally refers to the summation of a purchaser's costs from the point of initial purchase to the point of ultimate disposition of the product by the purchaser several years in the future. This concept deals explicitly with the relationship between what the customer pays for a product and the total cost the customer incurs over the product's entire life. This type of information can be very valuable in the following areas:

a. Better product design to reduce post-purchase costs to the customer

b. Improved market segmentation and product positioning

5587 Business Process Re-engineering (BPR)

5587.01 **Business process re-engineering (BPR)** is the search for, and implementation of, radical change in business processes to achieve breakthrough results. It reexamines how a company performs basic business processes in fundamentally different ways to radically improve efficiency. Most change efforts start with what exists and fixes it. Re-engineering starts with the future and works backwards, unconstrained by existing methods, people, or departments.

5587.02 A combination of factors induces companies to pursue BPR, including (a) reducing costs and increasing profits, (b) keeping up with the competition, or (c) achieving breakthrough results that will set the company apart from the competition.

5587.03 Manufacturing enterprises have been among the first to embrace BPR because of the need to be more competitive internationally and reduce product cycle time (the time required to convert raw materials into finished products).

5587.04 Three tests can be used to determine if a company is doing BPR.

1. Is the effort focused on critical business processes that, if they are changed, can have a major impact on performance? A company's processes can be classified into critical processes (those that are central to providing goods and services to customers) and support processes (those that support critical business processes). BPR focuses on critical business processes.

2. How ambitious is the desired improvement? A company looking for a 10–20% improvement would not be considered to be using BPR, which generally looks to improve the process by 100–150%.

3. How receptive is senior management to change? Because BPR requires fundamental changes in critical business processes, senior management must be committed to change.

5587.05 **Information technology (IT)** is usually at the heart of BPR. IT is the engine that allows BPR to take place. Intelligent workstations allow the company to decentralize control throughout the organization. Groupware software helps coordinate a variety of activities performed by many individuals, and all of this is tied together with communication networks in a client-server environment.

5588 Balanced Scorecard

5588.01 Balanced scorecard is a strategic management approach, which uses a future diversified view to balance the traditional reliance on historical financial performance measures.

5588.02 Feedback relating to internal business processes has utilized TQM methodology for several decades. Balanced scorecard extends this to include evaluation of external outcomes relating to four perspectives:

    a. Customer

    b. Learning and growth

    c. Internal business process

    d. Financial

The focus on outcomes of these business strategies, in addition to internal process results, creates a double-loop feedback system.

5589 Benchmarking

5589.01 Benchmarking entails comparison of process performance with other process performers, usually best-in-class performers. These performers may be internal or external, and they are not limited to the benchmarking entity's industry or area.

5589.02 Resources needed to engage in benchmarking are widely available through cooperative organizations, service firms, and the Internet.

Index